Philosophy, Public Policy, and Transnational Law

Series editor
John Martin Gillroy
Lehigh University
Bethlehem, PA, USA

Philosophy, Public Policy, and Transnational Law seeks, uniquely, to publish new and innovative arguments about global law and policy that transcend realist/positivist assumptions and the conventions of current legal/policy discourse. This series means to encourage the application of systematic philosophical and theoretical arguments to practical policy and legal issues that combine domestic, comparative or international law. We will pursue scholarship that integrates the superstructure of the positive law with its philosophical and public policy substructure, and which, in this way, produces a more three dimensional understanding of transnational law and its evolution, meaning, imperatives and future. We seek dissertations, solo and edited volumes, as well as innovative reports that integrate new methods, epistemologies and interdisciplinary perspectives with practical issues on the full range of policy and legal dilemmas challenging transnational relations.

More information about this series at
http://www.springer.com/series/14550

Michael Burkard

Conflicting Philosophies and International Trade Law

Worldviews and the WTO

palgrave
macmillan

Michael Burkard
Institute of European
and International Economic Law
University of Bern
Bern, Switzerland

Philosophy, Public Policy, and Transnational Law
ISBN 978-3-319-61066-5 ISBN 978-3-319-61067-2 (eBook)
https://doi.org/10.1007/978-3-319-61067-2

Library of Congress Control Number: 2017947712

Cover credit: imageBROKER/Alamy Stock Photo

Printed on acid-free paper

This Palgrave Macmillan imprint is published by Springer Nature
The registered company is Springer International Publishing AG
The registered company address is: Gewerbestrasse 11, 6330 Cham, Switzerland

Foreword

Assessing and managing risks relating to the production and consumption of food stuffs for humans and to the environment has been one of the most complex legal issues in WTO law, ever since the Agreement on Sanitary and Phytosanitary Measures was adopted at the end of the Uruguay Round and entered into force in 1995. The problem was expounded in a number of cases. Panels and the Appellate Body adopted different philosophies in interpreting the agreement and the basic concept of risk assessment. The latter entails fundamental question of law and science. Different interpretations reflect different underlying perceptions of science and its relationship to the law.

This book, based upon a doctoral thesis adopted by the Faculty of Law of the University of Bern, Switzerland, and which at the time was supported by the Swiss National Research Foundation and undertaken in the context of NCCR International Trade Regulation which I had the pleasure to direct, undertakes an updated in-depth analysis of these underlying perceptions. Michael Burkard expounds the essence and differences of positivism and relativism in philosophy and natural sciences. He clarifies the relationship of fundamental concepts such as risk, hazards and probability. This investigation is a remarkable effort on the part of a lawyer keen to learn more about the fundamentals based upon which the law—often unconsciously—is operated by the legal profession and the trade community. Based on these insights, Michael turns to a critical assessment of jurisprudence both of panels and the Appellate Body. Extensively referring and discussing the literature, he deconstructs findings and decisions in light of implied and assumed underlying philosophies and perceptions as to the relationship of law and science, in particular in the field of food standards. Finding that both positivism and relativism does not provide adequate answers, he turns to critical rationalism and applies the methodologies of falsification developed by Karl R. Popper. Critical rationalism allows combining discourse in science and law and helps preparing the ground for a new approach to risk assessment and risk management. Linking the problem to the doctrine of multilevel governance the author develops a theory allocating risk assessment to international for a while leaving the matter of risk management to national and democratically accountable government. While the author throughout the thesis questions the possibility of separating risk assessment and risk management, the thesis offers new avenues which may assist in structuring a complex and difficult problem.

The book is of considerable interest to scientists dealing with risk assessment and policy makers responsible for risk management. It is of interest to legal theory and the interface of law and beyond food safety, and finally to the trade lawyer confronted with complex scientific issues in transnational commerce. It proves the point that in the end nothing is more practical than theory. The wider dissemination of this work made possible by Palgrave therefore is most welcome. It completes a long-standing research effort of the author who today is a practising lawyer. It was a pleasure to work with Michael during his Ph.D. years at the World Trade Institute and to learn from his insights.

Bern, Switzerland
May 2017

Thomas Cottier

Series Editor Preface

Where once a scholar interested in studying either the human or natural world began from the standpoint of philosophical analysis, this trend has been reversed since the rise of social science and its imperative to replace philosophy with 'theory', that began in the mid-nineteenth century. A critical reason for the existence of this book series is to reintroduce philosophical study into the investigation of transnational policy and law. While there are many ways to do this, what characterises a philosophical, as opposed to a theoretical, point of view is that the former values comprehensive scope over narrow focus and the illumination of the essence of the law's inherent logic of concepts over an exclusive concentration on the parameters of its superficial structure.

Specifically, the comprehensive search for the essence of society and the natural world has been replaced by the compartmentalised and highly focused effort to find a specific theory for each independent corner or contextual problem of the human experience, taken in isolation. Here, the only use found for the comprehensive philosophy of the past is as disconnected conceptual bits and pieces within these new theoretical structures. Part of the contemporary imperative for reintegrating philosophical study into transnational policy and law is to both illuminate the wider context of these theoretical corners and demonstrate how a fuller philosophical understanding of the conceptual essence of the law renders a higher degree of clarity in the analysis of the specific problems of contemporary legal practice. Michael Burkard's book does both these things very well.

There are two areas of transnational law and policy that have infrequently been treated together: the WTO and Environmental Risk. With calls for making the dispute settlement system of the WTO the foundation for international constitutional law and as environmental risk persists as one of the most ubiquitous problems of our age, Michael Burkard's book is an especially timely and unique treatment of the epistemological and methodological dilemmas associated with this legal nexus.

A unique dimension of this book is the meticulous consideration of the similarities and distinctions between positivism and relativism. These distinctions are commonly considered to be independent contradictory points of departure for scientific consideration of risk in transnational law and the foundational points of departure for modern 'theoretical' analysis, requiring no more fundamental consideration of their conceptual essence. Burkard's argument deconstructs these positions to a much more essential level, exposing their epistemological and methodological dynamics, while also more adequately illuminating the distinct advantages and disadvantages of each. Burkard's comparative study of the philosophical substructure that underlies the 'science' of the policy involved is singular in the literature and should invigorate the practice of transnational risk law.

In addition to working within the positivist—relativist framework of modern theory and exposing the inherent philosophical logics that underpin current policy, he also, on the basis of this deeper epistemological analysis of method, synthesises a more balanced 'critical' approach to make the policy and law of transnational environmental risk regulation more effective. By first submitting existing positive law to more comprehensive philosophical analysis, both his critical and constructive arguments expertly highlight the problems involved in current WTO risk law. From the roots of conceptual conflicts between the panel and appellate structures of WTO dispute settlement system that have retarded policy in this critical area of the law to his more comprehensive and essential analysis of international legal practice, Burkard's findings make his recommendation of a methodological change in the fundamental analysis of WTO law more persuasive and more powerful than previous work in this area. His conclusions merit our very serious attention.

By first distinguishing risk as a particular class of cases pertaining to the regulation of the environment and then by unpacking the full methodological and epistemological essence of relativism and positivism, this book transforms the consideration of both the adequacy of the WTO dispute settlement system and the ability of current theoretical constructs to effectively incorporate the unique characteristics of environmental risk into international public law. Utilising WTO case law, it is his comprehensive philosophical analysis of the essence of practice in transnational risk law and policy that makes Michael Burkard's book a perfect addition to our series on PHILOSOPHY, PUBLIC POLICY AND TRANSNATIONAL LAW.

This book sheds new light on a number of questions concerning the role of the WTO in the contemporary evolution of transnational law. The philosophical illumination of conventional theory and practice present in this book, especially in terms of policy questions dealing with those areas of law that must transcend sovereignty for authority beyond the state, make this monograph a welcome addition to our series.

Bethlehem, USA John Martin Gillroy

Contents

Part II The Science-Based Approach of the SPS Agreement in Particular

Part III Future Prospects for Regulation

Abbreviations

AB	Appellate Body
ADI	Acceptable Daily Intake
AKST	Agricultural Knowledge, Science and Technology
ALOP	Appropriate Level of [sanitary or phytosanitary] Protection
ATTAC	Association pour une taxation des transactions financières pour l'aide aux citoyens/Association for the Taxation of Financial Transactions for the Aid of Citizens
BMJ	British Medical Journal
BSCC	Biotechnology Science Coordinating Committee
BSE	Bovine Spongiform Encephalopathy
Bt	Bacillus Thuringiensis
CAC	Codex Alimentarius Commission
CCCF	Codex Committee on Contaminants in Foods
CCFA	Codex Committee on Food Additives
CCPR	Codex Committee on Pesticide Residues
CITES	Convention on International Trade in Endangered Species of Wild Fauna and Flora
COP	Conference of the Parties
DC	Developing Country
DG	Directorate-General
DG SANCO	Directorate General for Health and Consumer Protection (European Commission)
DSB	Dispute Settlement Body
DSU	Understanding on Rules and Procedures Governing the Settlements of Disputes
EBDC	Ethylene bisdithiocarbamate
EC	European Communities

ECJ	European Court of Justice
EFSA	European Food Safety Authority
EPA	Environmental Protection Agency
ETU	Ethylene Thiourea
EU	European Union
FAO	Food and Agriculture Organization of the United Nations
FDA	Food and Drug Administration
FOEN	Swiss Federal Office for the Environment
FOPH	Swiss Federal Office of Public Health
GAP	Good Agricultural Practices
GATT	General Agreement on Tariffs and Trade
GE	Genetic Engineering
GM	Genetic Modification/Genetically Modified
GMO	Genetically Modified Organism
HACCP	Hazard Analysis Critical Control Point
IAASTD	International Assessment of Agricultural Knowledge, Science and Technology for Development
ICMSF	International Commission on Microbiological Specifications for Foods
ID	Intelligent Design
IHR	International Health Regulation
IPCC	Intergovernmental Panel on Climate Change
IPPC	International Plant Protection Convention
ISO	International Organization for Standardization
IUCN	International Union for Conservation of Nature
JECFA	Joint FAO/WHO Expert Committee on Food Additives
JEMRA	Joint FAO/WHO Expert Meetings on Microbiological Risk Assessment
JMPR	Joint FAO/WHO Expert Meetings on Pesticide Residues
LGBTQ	Lesbian, Gay, Bisexual, Transgender, Queer
LDC	Least Developed Country
LMO	Living Modified Organism
MEA	Multilateral Environmental Agreement
ML	Maximum Level
MRL	Maximum Residue Limit
NBIC	Nanotechnology, Biotechnology, Information Technology and Cognitive Science
NGO	Non-Governmental organisation
NOEL	No Observed Effect Level
NRC	National Research Council
NRP	Swiss National Research Programme
OECD	Organisation for Economic Co-operation and Development

OIE	Office International des Epizooties/World Organisation for Animal Health
OSTP	Office of Science and Technology Policy
Ppb	Parts per billion
PPP	Public Private Partnership
R&D	Research and Development
SCVPH	Scientific Committee on Veterinary Measures relating to Public Health
SPS	Sanitary and Phytosanitary
SPS Agreement	WTO Agreement on the Application of Sanitary and Phytosanitary Measures
STS	Science, Technology, and Society Studies
TBT Agreement	WTO Agreement on Technical Barriers to Trade
UNECE	United Nations Economic Commission for Europe
UNEP	United Nations Environment Programme
UNFCCC	United Nations Framework Convention on Climate Change
US	United States
USDA	United States Department of Agriculture
WHO	World Health Organisation
WMO	World Meteorological Organization
WTO	World Trade Organisation

List of Tables

CHAPTER 1

Introduction

The Agreement on the Application of Sanitary and Phytosanitary Measures (SPS Agreement) came along with the promise of resolving existing and mitigating prospective trade disputes. When the SPS Agreement came into effect in 1995, a burning issue was the transatlantic trade dispute over hormone-treated beef. The background of the *beef—hormones* dispute was the fact that the European Communities (EC) blocked the importation of hormone-treated beef, a move which particularly affected beef exporters from the USA. Whereas US exporters averred that their beef is safe, the EC unceasingly claimed that hormone-treated beef may pose a risk to consumers. In addition to the *beef—hormones* dispute, another trade conflict already loomed on the horizon, spurred by controversies over GMOs. In either case, the USA and other highly efficient agricultural producers pointed at the weak scientific basis of the EC's position, thus implying disguised protectionisms. The EC, on the other hand, were driven by a critical general public mounting a broad array of arguments such as health concerns, environmental and socio-economic considerations and precaution.

Confronted with rising transatlantic tensions, the SPS Agreement was introduced as a novel approach for neutral and objective arbitration in international trade disputes. The novelty of the SPS Agreement consists in its deference to science. Unlike the juristic weighing and balancing required by Article XX of the General Agreement on Tariffs and Trade (GATT 1947), the SPS Agreement was expected to deliver judgements upon the legitimacy of SPS measure to science. That paradigm shift from

M. Burkard, *Conflicting Philosophies and International Trade Law*, Philosophy, Public Policy, and Transnational Law,
https://doi.org/10.1007/978-3-319-61067-2_1

juridical argument to scientific rigour was operationalised by the legal requirement to base any SPS measure on a risk assessment.

In reality, however, the promise of the SPS Agreement to resolve trade disputes by deference to science did not materialise. Instead of the expected objectification and scientification of trade policies, Panels and the Appellate Body witnessed a politicisation of science. Fundamentally, Panels and the Appellate Body were challenged by two conflicting conceptions of science. Is science absolute and universal, yet to the price of a limited scope of applicability, restricted to laboratory containment? Or, at the other hand, is science relative, contingent upon the conditions within which it operates, which means to scarify commensurability?

In the *beef—hormones* dispute, the USA relied on scientific evidence demonstrating that the hormones in question, if applied according to good veterinary practices, do not pose a risk to human health. The EC, to the contrary, pointed at the fact that in some instances, compliance with good veterinary practices cannot be ensured. Therefore, the EC argued that in cases of misuse or abuse, the hormones in question may pose a risk to consumers. The Panel in the *EC—Hormones* dispute basically followed the argument of the USA and scientific evidence validating its claim, stating that the hormones in question, if applied according to good veterinary practices, are safe. The Appellate Body, in contrast, adopted a more nuanced position. In particular, the Appellate Body considered the EC's argument for taking into account potential malpractices in the application of the hormones in question. The Appellate Body found that the Panel erred by restricting the scope of scientific analysis to the extent that it excluded 'all matters not susceptible of quantitative analysis by the empirical or experimental laboratory methods commonly associated with the physical sciences' (*EC—Hormones*, Appellate Body report, para. 187). In light of the conflict between two antagonistic conceptions of science, the following famous quote of the Appellate Body in the *beef—hormones* dispute gets its deeper meaning:

> It is essential to bear in mind that the risk that is to be evaluated in a risk assessment under Article 5.1 is not only risk ascertainable in a science laboratory operating under strictly controlled conditions, but also risk in human societies as they actually exist, in other words, the actual potential for adverse effects on human health in the real world where people live and work and die (*EC—Hormones*, Appellate Body report, para. 187).

Notably, the conflict between absolute concepts of laboratory ascertainability versus relative conceptions of 'real world'—science re-emerged in following WTO disputes, dividing Panels and the Appellate Body. Prominent in this respect is the *Continued Suspension* case, launched by the EC in 2005. In rather similar ways as was the case in *EC—Hormones*, the Panel in the *Continued Suspension* case tried to exclude real-world problems, such as compliance with good veterinary practices, from scientific analysis. The formal tool for making a distinction between 'pure science' and the 'real world' was the separation of different risk analysis phases. According to the Panel, the phase of risk assessment has to focus on scientific evidence only, whereas in the subsequent risk management phase 'real world'—issues might be taken into account. The Appellate Body, however, confirmed its earlier broad, that is, relative conception of science taking into account risks as they actually exist in the real world:

> Therefore, in our view, the Panel's interpretation of 'risk assessment' resulted in the same 'restrictive notion of risk assessment' that the Appellate Body found to be erroneous in *EC—Hormones*. The Panel sought in this case to rewrite the Appellate Body Report in *EC—Hormones* and to re-establish the rigid distinction between 'risk assessment' and 'risk management' that the Appellate Body had rejected in that case (*US—Continued Suspension*, Appellate Body Report, para. 542).

Various attempts can be found for explaining gaps between the US and EU trade policies related to agriculture and food safety, ranging from protectionism charges to cultural differences. It seems, however, to be eye-opening considering gaps in trade policy approaches together with corresponding Panel and Appellate Body findings. Doing so, one comes to realise that trade policy gaps may be reflected in controversial reasoning provided by Panels and the Appellate Body respectively. Such a comprehensive approach leads to the preliminary finding that varying trade policies as well as contradictory verdicts by Panels and the Appellate Body may have deeper rooted causes. The preliminary assumption that there are deeper rooted causes for persistent trade disputes over SPS issues and corresponding divisions between Panel and Appellate Body interpretations serves as working hypothesis for the book at hand. Building upon the working hypothesis, deeper rooted causes for antagonistic concepts of science and their inconsistent reading by Panels and the Appellate Body are examined. Tracing underlying causes for persisting SPS disputes and inconsistent Panel and Appellate Body rulings back to antithetic philosophical world conceptions enables a rational understanding of respective worldviews. If the assumption holds that antithetic philosophical world conceptions are at the root of many actual SPS disputes, a rational understanding of these philosophical concepts is a precondition for the resolution of the disputes in question. The key applied for opening the door towards a rational analysis and understanding of antithetic world conceptions underlying actual food safety controversies and trade disputes is critical epistemology, as developed by Karl R. Popper in particular. The purpose of the research endeavour presented in the book at hand may hence be summarised as an attempt to transcend the narrow scope of most discussions over SPS problems. Ordinarily, SPS disputes are perceived as particular expressions of the conflict between trade liberalisation and protectionism. To pursue the SPS discussion beyond the juxtaposition of liberalisation and protectionisms shall enable deeper insights as a comprehensive basis for new approaches towards a reform of the SPS Agreement.

In Part One, entitled *Being Determines Consciousness*, the controversial debate about risks and SPS risks, in particular, is related to antagonistic philosophical concepts.

In Chap. 1, diverging concepts of risk are located on a spectrum introduced by Shrader-Frechette in her seminal work on *Risk and Rationality. Philosophical Foundations for Populist Reforms* (1991). According to Shrader-Frechette, exponents in risk debates 'are arrayed on a spectrum extending from the relativists to the naive positivists'.

In Chap. 2, the antithetical philosophical world conceptions are outlined. On the one hand, there is positivism. From a positivist perspective, risk analysis is a scientific concept, and scientific concepts are considered appropriate for establishing 'the truth'. Following positivism, science is able to provide answers to all questions sooner or later, e.g. whether something is safe or not or whether something is true or not, with absolute precision and universal validity. Relativism, on the other hand, considers science as part and parcel of the environment within which it operates. Albeit considered an indispensable tool, science is regarded just as one possible way for approaching burning issues of society. Given its contingency upon real world conditions, scientific findings are not considered universally valid, but relative to the circumstances, the time and the place of their making.

In Chap. 3, the origins of the risk concept are examined. It is shown that the concept of risk once was developed as a business tool for entrepreneurs, designed for expanding the scope of rational economic action. For rational entrepreneurs, the concept of risk is a tool for prospecting possible profits and losses. The entrepreneurial concept of risk alludes to the positivist world conception. It was not until the Industrial Age and corresponding threats such as large-scale food contamination, chemical spills and nuclear accidents when risk transcended the economic sphere and immersed broader society, bringing about *Risk societies*. For the general public potentially affected in the event of loss, risk is not a tool for prospective analysis but a *topos* for manifest harm. Considering its societal implications, risk perceived in *Risk societies* comes close to relativism. Thus, depending on perspective and interest, risk may be perceived differently.

In Chap. 4, the two distinct expressions of the risk concept are applied to food and agriculture. On the one hand, there are agricultural producers applying methods of risk management as tools for enlarging production and maximising profits. On the other hand, there is society, implementing food safety laws and environmental regulation, thus restricting producers and processors along the food chain.

In Chap. 5, frontlines between the two antithetic approaches towards food and agriculture are further examined. A stringent line is established between farming practices, philosophical concepts and actual SPS disputes. Following Justus von Liebig, empirical farming relates to positivism, whereas rational farming refers to relativism. Empirical farming focuses on production increase and profit maximisation, whereas rational farming tries to maintain nutrient cycles and equilibria between farm inputs and outputs. The controversy about the application of GMOs in agriculture, so-called green biotechnology, is presented as a last frontier between empirical and rational agriculture.

Part Two, entitled *The Science-Based Approach of the SPS Agreement in Particular*, now turns to the substance of the SPS Agreement.

In Chap. 6, the promise for objectivity, as implied in the science-based approach of the Agreement, is outlined.

In Chaps. 7–9, inconsistent interpretations of Panels and the Appellate Body are related to distinct risk concepts and corresponding antagonistic philosophical concepts. In Chap. 7, the Panel's interpretation of risk and science is associated with the positivist tradition. In contrast, the Appellate Body's quest for middle ground is found to be closer to relativist positions (Chap. 8). In Chap. 9, selected problems resulting from diverging interpretations of risk and science by Panels and the Appellate Body are scrutinised. It is looked at the tendency to expand the scope of the SPS

Agreement to environmental issues and the problem of inconsistent interpretations of the precautionary principle in international law, in particular regarding the SPS Agreement and the Cartagena Protocol on Biosafety, respectively.

The final Part Three on *Future Prospects for Regulation* embarks on exploring an alternative proposal for SPS regulation. To this purpose, positivist and relativist approaches are conceived in respective pure forms and juxtaposed (Chaps. 10 and 11). From a positivist perspective, the jurisdiction of the Appellate Body was a misconception of the science-based approach of the SPS Agreement. From a positivist point of view, science should be the one and only arbiter in international trade disputes over food safety questions and animal and plant health issues. Therefore, a positivist attempt would accomplish the promise for *objectivity* implied in the science-based approach of the SPS Agreement by making international standards really mandatory. From a positivist perspective, there is no need for higher levels of protection than those established by 'science'.

From a relativist perspective, the problem is not primarily the jurisdiction of the Appellate Body. From a relativist point of view, the main problem is the science-based approach of the SPS Agreement as such. From a relativist perspective, science is neither objective nor value-free. Hence, science is an inappropriate arbiter in international trade disputes. In contrast, a relativist proposal essentially consists in the claim for abandoning science as primary yardstick for deciding upon the legitimacy of SPS measures and appropriate levels of protection (ALOP). Hence, instead of the science-based approach of the SPS Agreement, relativist proposals are calling for more room for manoeuvre for national sovereigns in deciding upon levels of protection deemed appropriate. However, relativist proposals might bring back the epistemological problem of *subjectivity* in risk assessment and foster protectionism.

Based on a rational analysis of the two antipodes, an alternative approach is finally elaborated (Chap. 12). A rational analysis of positivist and relativist attempts enables to build upon strengths and avoid weaknesses of the two antithetic approaches. For doing so, reference is made to the theory of multilayered governance and critical epistemology. The proposal put forward, termed critical approach, differs from both the positivist and the relativist proposal. On the one hand, the critical approach recognises science as an indispensable source of knowledge. On the other hand, the critical approach abandons the ideal of objective, yet 'pure' science. Following critical rationalism, the critical approach aims at re-contextualise science, exposing it to permanent criticism by peers and society at large. Once implemented, the proposed critical approach would refocus the objective of the SPS Agreement. Instead of only safeguarding fair competition in agricultural trade, a reformed SPS Agreement would assume the additional role of a guardian for open competition of scientific opinions at the international level. Through new meaning, a reformed SPS Agreement would recall the sometimes forgotten 'idealistic' objective of the GATT/WTO framework: the advancement of the 'Open Society' through trade.

PART I

Being Determines Consciousness

Introduction

The Agreement on the Application of Sanitary and Phytosanitary Measures (SPS Agreement) came along with the promise of resolving existing and mitigating prospective trade disputes. When the SPS Agreement came into effect in 1995, a burning issue was the transatlantic trade dispute over hormone-treated beef. The background of the *beef—hormones* dispute was the fact that the European Communities (EC) blocked the importation of hormone-treated beef, a move which particularly affected beef exporters from the USA.

Whereas US exporters averred that their beef is safe, the EC unceasingly claimed that hormone-treated beef may pose a risk to consumers. In addition to the *beef—hormones* dispute, another trade conflict already loomed on the horizon, spurred by controversies over GMOs. In either case, the USA and other highly efficient agricultural producers pointed at the weak scientific basis of the EC's position, thus implying disguised protectionisms. The EC, on the other hand, were driven by a critical general public mounting a broad array of arguments such as health concerns, environmental and socio-economic considerations and precaution.

Confronted with rising transatlantic tensions, the SPS Agreement was introduced as a novel approach for neutral and objective arbitration in international trade disputes. The novelty of the SPS Agreement consists in its deference to science. Unlike the juristic weighing and balancing required by Article XX of the General Agreement on Tariffs and Trade (GATT 1947), the SPS Agreement was expected to deliver judgements upon the legitimacy of SPS measure to science. That paradigm shift from juridical argument to scientific rigour was operationalised by the legal requirement to base any SPS measure on a risk assessment.

In reality, however, the promise of the SPS Agreement to resolve trade disputes by deference to science did not materialise. Instead of the expected objectification and scientification of trade policies, Panels and the Appellate Body witnessed a politicisation of science. Fundamentally, Panels and the Appellate Body were challenged by two conflicting conceptions of science. Is science absolute and universal, yet to the price of a limited scope of applicability, restricted to laboratory containment? Or, at the other hand, is science relative, contingent upon the conditions within which it operates, which means to scarify commensurability?

In the *beef—hormones* dispute, the USA relied on scientific evidence demonstrating that the hormones in question, if applied according to good veterinary practices, do not pose a risk to human health. The EC, to the contrary, pointed at the fact that in some instances, compliance with good veterinary practices cannot be ensured. Therefore, the EC argued that in cases of misuse or abuse, the hormones in question may pose a risk to consumers. The Panel in the *EC—Hormones* dispute basically followed the argument of the USA and scientific evidence validating its claim, stating that the hormones in question, if applied according to good veterinary practices, are safe. The Appellate Body, in contrast, adopted a more nuanced position. In particular, the Appellate Body considered the EC's argument for taking into account potential malpractices in the application of the hormones in question. The Appellate Body found that the Panel erred by restricting the scope of scientific analysis to the extent that it excluded 'all matters not susceptible of quantitative analysis by the empirical or experimental laboratory methods commonly associated with the physical sciences' (*EC—Hormones*, Appellate Body report, para. 187). In light of the conflict between two antagonistic conceptions of science, the following famous quote of the Appellate Body in the *beef—hormones* dispute gets its deeper meaning:

It is essential to bear in mind that the risk that is to be evaluated in a risk assessment under Article 5.1 is not only risk ascertainable in a science laboratory operating under strictly controlled conditions, but also risk in human societies as they actually exist, in other words, the actual potential for adverse effects on human health in the real world where people live and work and die (*EC—Hormones*, Appellate Body report, para. 187).

Notably, the conflict between absolute concepts of laboratory ascertainability versus relative conceptions of 'real world'—science re-emerged in following WTO disputes, dividing Panels and the Appellate Body. Prominent in this respect is the *Continued Suspension* case, launched by the EC in 2005. In rather similar ways as was the case in EC—Hormones, the Panel in the *Continued Suspension* case tried to exclude real-world problems, such as compliance with good veterinary practices, from scientific analysis. The formal tool for making a distinction between 'pure science' and the 'real world' was the separation of different risk analysis phases. According to the Panel, the phase of risk assessment has to focus on scientific evidence only, whereas in the subsequent risk management phase 'real world'—issues might be taken into account. The Appellate Body, however, confirmed its earlier broad, that is, relative conception of science taking into account risks as they actually exist in the real world:

Therefore, in our view, the Panel's interpretation of 'risk assessment' resulted in the same 'restrictive notion of risk assessment' that the Appellate Body found to be erroneous in *EC—Hormones.* The Panel sought in this case to rewrite the Appellate Body Report in *EC—Hormones* and to re-establish the rigid distinction between 'risk assessment' and 'risk management' that the Appellate Body had rejected in that case (*US—Continued Suspension*, Appellate Body Report, para. 542).

Various attempts can be found for explaining gaps between the US and EU trade policies related to agriculture and food safety, ranging from protectionism charges to cultural differences. It seems, however, to be eye-opening considering gaps in trade policy approaches together with corresponding Panel and Appellate Body findings. Doing so, one comes to realise that trade policy gaps may be reflected in controversial reasoning provided by Panels and the Appellate Body respectively. Such a comprehensive approach leads to the preliminary finding that varying trade policies as well as contradictory verdicts by Panels and the Appellate Body may have deeper rooted causes. The preliminary assumption that there are deeper rooted causes for persistent trade disputes over SPS issues and corresponding divisions between Panel and Appellate Body interpretations serves as working hypothesis for the book at hand. Building upon the working hypothesis, deeper rooted causes for antagonistic concepts of science and their inconsistent reading by Panels and the Appellate Body are examined. Tracing underlying causes for persisting SPS disputes and inconsistent Panel and Appellate Body rulings back to antithetic philosophical world conceptions enables a rational understanding of respective worldviews. If the assumption holds that antithetic philosophical world conceptions are at the root of many actual SPS disputes, a rational understanding of these philosophical concepts is a precondition for the resolution of the disputes in question. The key applied for opening the door towards a rational analysis and understanding of antithetic world conceptions underlying actual food safety controversies and trade disputes is critical epistemology, as developed by Karl R. Popper in particular. The purpose of the research endeavour presented in the book at hand may hence be summarised as an attempt to transcend the narrow scope of most discussions over SPS problems. Ordinarily, SPS disputes are perceived as particular expressions of the conflict between trade liberalisation and protectionism. To pursue the SPS discussion beyond the juxtaposition of liberalisation and protectionisms shall enable deeper insights as a comprehensive basis for new approaches towards a reform of the SPS Agreement.

In Part I, entitled *Being Determines Consciousness*, the controversial debate about risks and SPS risks, in particular, is related to antagonistic philosophical concepts.

In Chap. 1, diverging concepts of risk are located on a spectrum introduced by Shrader-Frechette in her seminal work on Risk and Rationality. Philosophical Foundations for Populist Reforms (1991). According to Shrader-Frechette, exponents in risk debates 'are arrayed on a spectrum extending from the relativists to the naive positivists'.

In Chap. 2, the antithetical philosophical world conceptions are outlined. On the one hand, there is positivism. From a positivist perspective, risk analysis is a scientific concept, and scientific concepts are considered appropriate for establishing 'the truth'. Following positivism, science is able to provide answers to all questions sooner or later, e.g. whether something is safe or not or whether something is true or not, with absolute precision and universal validity. Relativism, on the other hand, considers science as part and parcel of the environment within which it operates. Albeit considered an indispensable tool, science is regarded just as one possible way for approaching burning issues of society. Given its contingency upon real world conditions, scientific findings are not considered universally valid, but relative to the circumstances, the time and the place of their making.

In Chap. 3, the origins of the risk concept are examined. It is shown that the concept of risk once was developed as a business tool for entrepreneurs, designed for expanding the scope of rational economic action. For rational entrepreneurs, the concept of risk is a tool for prospecting possible profits and losses. The entrepreneurial concept of risk alludes to the positivist world conception. It was not until the Industrial Age and corresponding threats such as large-scale food contamination, chemical spills and nuclear accidents when risk transcended the economic sphere and immersed broader society, bringing about *Risk societies.* For the general public potentially affected in the event of loss, risk is not a tool for prospective analysis but a *topos* for manifest harm. Considering its societal implications, risk perceived in *Risk societies* comes close to relativism. Thus, depending on perspective and interest, risk may be perceived differently.

In Chap. 4, the two distinct expressions of the risk concept are applied to food and agriculture. On the one hand, there are agricultural producers applying methods of risk management as tools for enlarging production and maximising profits. On the other hand, there is society, implementing food safety laws and environmental regulation, thus restricting producers and processors along the food chain.

In Chap. 5, frontlines between the two antithetic approaches towards food and agriculture are further examined. A stringent line is established between farming practices, philosophical concepts and actual SPS disputes. Following Justus von Liebig, empirical farming relates to positivism, whereas rational farming refers to relativism. Empirical farming focuses on production increase and profit maximisation, whereas rational farming tries to maintain nutrient cycles and equilibria between farm inputs and outputs. The controversy about the application of GMOs in agriculture, so-called green biotechnology, is presented as a last frontier between empirical and rational agriculture.

Part II, entitled *The Science-Based Approach of the SPS Agreement in Particular*, now turns to the substance of the SPS Agreement.

In Chaps. 6, the promise for objectivity, as implied in the science-based approach of the Agreement, is outlined.

In Chaps. 7–9, inconsistent interpretations of Panels and the Appellate Body are related to distinct risk concepts and corresponding antagonistic philosophical concepts. In Chap. 7, the Panel's interpretation of risk and science is associated with the positivist tradition. In contrast, the Appellate Body's quest for middle ground is found to be closer to relativist positions (Chap. 8). In Chap. 9, selected problems resulting from diverging interpretations of risk and science by Panels and the Appellate Body are scrutinised. It is looked at the tendency to expand the scope of the SPS Agreement to environmental issues and the problem of inconsistent interpretations of the precautionary principle in international law, in particular regarding the SPS Agreement and the Cartagena Protocol on Biosafety, respectively.

The final Part III on *Future Prospects for Regulation* embarks on exploring an alternative proposal for SPS regulatio1n. To this purpose, positivist and relativist approaches are conceived in respective pure forms and juxtaposed (Chapter 10 and 11). From a positivist perspective, the jurisdiction of the Appellate Body was a misconception of the science-based approach of the SPS Agreement. From a positivist point of view, science should be the one and only arbiter in international trade disputes over food safety questions and animal and plant health issues. Therefore, a positivist attempt would accomplish the promise for *objectivity* implied in the science-based approach of the SPS Agreement by making international standards really mandatory. From a positivist perspective, there is no need for higher levels of protection than those established by 'science'.

From a relativist perspective, the problem is not primarily the jurisdiction of the Appellate Body. From a relativist point of view, the main problem is the science-based approach of the SPS Agreement as such. From a relativist perspective, science is neither objective nor value-free. Hence, science is an inappropriate arbiter in international trade disputes. In contrast, a relativist proposal essentially consists in the claim for abandoning science as primary yardstick for deciding upon the legitimacy of SPS measures and appropriate levels of protection (ALOP). Hence, instead of the science-based approach of the SPS Agreement, relativist proposals are calling for more room for manoeuvre for national sovereigns in deciding upon levels of protection deemed appropriate. However, relativist proposals might bring back the epistemological problem of *subjectivity* in risk assessment and foster protectionism.

Based on a rational analysis of the two antipodes, an alternative approach is finally elaborated (Chap. 12). A rational analysis of positivist and relativist attempts enables to build upon strengths and avoid weaknesses of the two antithetic approaches. For doing so, reference is made to the theory of multilayered governance and critical epistemology. The proposal put forward, termed critical approach, differs from both the positivist and the relativist proposal. On the one hand, the critical approach recognises science as an indispensable source of knowledge. On the other hand, the critical approach abandons the ideal of objective, yet 'pure' science. Following critical rationalism, the critical approach aims at re-contextualise science, exposing it to permanent criticism by peers and society at large. Once implemented, the proposed critical approach would refocus the objective of the SPS Agreement. Instead of only safeguarding fair competition in agricultural trade, a reformed SPS Agreement would assume the additional role of a guardian for open competition of scientific opinions at the international level. Through new meaning, a reformed SPS Agreement would recall the sometimes forgotten 'idealistic' objective of the GATT/WTO framework: the advancement of the 'Open Society' through trade.

CHAPTER 2

Between Positivism and Relativism

In her seminal work *Risk and Rationality* (1991), Shrader-Frechette introduced the terms *naïve positivism* and *cultural relativism*[1] for setting the scene for the risk debate: 'In the debate over what methodological norms, if any, guarantee the rationality of risk evaluation, analysts are arrayed on a spectrum extending from the relativists to the naive positivists (Shrader-Frechette 1991, p. 8)'. Shrader-Frechette described the two antithetic poles as follows:

> At the left end of the spectrum are the cultural relativists, such as anthropologist Mary Douglas and political scientist Aaron Wildavsky. They believe that 'risks are social constructs,' that 'any form of life can be justified.... no one is to say that any one is better or worse,' that there is 'no correct description of the right behavior [regarding risk],' and therefore that the third stage of risk assessment, risk evaluation, is wholly relative. At the other, naïve-positivists, end of the spectrum are engineers such as Chauncey Starr and Christopher Whipple. They maintain that risk evaluation is objective in the sense that *different* risks may be evaluated according to the *same* rule – for example, a rule stipulating that risks below a certain level of probability are insignificant. They also claim that risk assessment, at least at the stage of calculating probabilities associated with harms and estimating their effects, is completely objective, neutral, and value free. (Shrader-Frechette 1991, p. 8)

Naïve positivist, Shrader-Frechette explained, only trust in facts and empirical confirmability. They believe that facts, and only facts, are neutral and objective. The trust in facts, in turn, makes naïve positivist believe that

M. Burkard, *Conflicting Philosophies and International Trade Law*,
Philosophy, Public Policy, and Transnational Law,
https://doi.org/10.1007/978-3-319-61067-2_2

the factual stages of risk assessment, i.e. hazard identification and risk estimation, 'can be wholly objective and value free'. The overemphasis of facts over value judgements makes naïve positivists believe 'that risk estimates can completely exclude normative (ethical and methodological) components' (Shrader-Frechette 1991, p. 39). Shrader-Frechette termed the naïve positivists' belief in objective and allegedly 'neutral' facts as the 'principle of complete neutrality' (Shrader-Frechette 1991, p. 39). As the root of naïve positivists' obsession with facts and neutrality, Shrader-Frechette identified the fact–value dichotomy:

> Perhaps many risk assessors and scientists have erroneously believed that it is possible to make value-free, confirmed judgments, about either risks or science, because they subscribe to an extreme form of the fact-value dichotomy, a famous tenet of naïve positivism. This is the belief that facts and values are completely separable, and that there are facts that include no value judgments. Applied to hazard assessment, this claim is that risk analysis ought to consist of *factual* and neutral risk estimates, although the policy decision made as a consequence of them may be *evaluative*. (Shrader-Frechette 1991, p. 43)

Albeit questioning whether complete objectivity is achievable, Shrader-Frechette admitted that 'the traditional positivist motivation behind belief in the fact–value dichotomy is a noble and important one' (Shrader-Frechette 1991, p. 43). Shrader-Frechette acknowledged that value-free observations, 'if they exited, would guarantee the objectivity of one's research (Shrader-Frechette 1991, p. 44)'.[2] The problem of the naïve positivists' approach, however, is that risk assessments are typically applied in situations where factual information is either incomplete or under conditions of scientific uncertainty: in cases where all possible outcomes of an activity, as well as the probability of each outcome would be known, obviously there would be no need for risk estimates. With a view on the problem of insufficient scientific information and 'probabilistic uncertainty', Shrader-Frechette noted:

> As witness of this uncertainty, the current technological landscape is littered with the bodies of victims of various hazards. From Chernobyl to Bhopal, there are victims of risks that experts allegedly measured objectively, catastrophes that were not supposed to happen. (Shrader-Frechette 1991, p. 30)[3]

Turning to the other end of the epistemological spectrum, Shrader-Frechette observed that cultural relativism, in contrast to naïve positivism, tends to overemphasise value judgements.[4] With regard to risk assessment, these observations translated into the finding that positivists overemphasise the 'objective' first two steps of risk assessment, i.e. hazard identification and hazard estimation, whereas relativists overemphasise the following, 'subjective' step of risk assessment, i.e. risk evaluation.[5]

The starting point of the critique of cultural relativists is what Shrader-Frechette called 'an astute (although not original) insight (Shrader-Frechette 1991, p. 31)'. The relativists' insight consisted of recognising the impossibility to achieve wholly objective, i.e. value-free risk evaluations. As a consequence, relativists criticised '[risk] assessors for their repeated error in assuming that lay estimates of risk are mere "perceptions" whereas expert analyses are "objective" (Shrader-Frechette 1991, p. 31)'. And Shrader-Frechette conceded that 'the cultural relativists are correct in affirming that engineers and housewives both employ value judgments, especially in evaluating risk acceptability' (Shrader-Frechette 1991, p. 31).[6] From that insight, cultural relativists conclude that 'any judgement of risk evaluation is merely a social construct (Shrader-Frechette 1991, p. 31)'.

Shrader-Frechette's review[7] of considerations developed and employed by various risk relativists provided a set of five main relativist arguments. Following Shrader-Frechette, these five main arguments put forward by risk relativist are the following [Shrader-Frechette 1991, pp. 31–32, start citation]:

1. Increased knowledge and additional reasoning about risks do not make people more rational about hazards.
2. Risk assessments are like judgments in aesthetics.
3. "Any form of life," including risk behavior and attitudes, "can be justified," since all people—including experts who disagree about hazard analysis—are biased in their perceptions of danger.
4. Modern persons are no different from "primitives" (Douglas and Wildavsky's term) in that social structures dictate their views on, and responses to, alleged hazards.
5. More specifically, environmentalists' views on risk are a result of their "sectarian problems" [citation end].

Albeit environmental issues, as addressed in Point 5 above, were a major point in Shrader-Frechette's *Risk and Rationality*,[8] they are factored out in the following, thus providing room for an analysis of relativist arguments in general. Bare from contemporary political context, the four remaining arguments of relativists are considered as general expressions of relativism and not only targeted on laypersons in the USA. For generalising the four remaining relativist arguments properly, they are rewritten and commented as follows:

1. Increased knowledge and additional reasoning about risks do not make people more rational about hazards.
   - In other words, people are unreceptive to scientific explanation. This means that relativists consider the knowledge gap between scientific experts and the public as unbridgeable (public–expert divide).
2. Risk assessments are like judgments in aesthetics.
   - In other words, risk assessment is rather an art than science. Argument (2) is an expression of epistemological subjectivity.
3. 'Any form of life', including risk behaviour and attitudes, 'can be justified', since all people—including experts who disagree with hazard analysis—are biased in their perceptions of danger.
   - In other words, there is neither right or wrong, nor correct or incorrect, in risk assessment. Argument (3) expresses the notion of epistemological relativism.
4. Modern persons are no different from 'primitives' (Douglas and Wildavsky's term) in that social structures dictate their views on, and responses to, alleged hazards.
   - Douglas and Wildavsky argue that the views on hazards of 'modern persons' and 'primitives' alike are shaped by respective social structures. It has to be noted that Douglas and Wildavsky have equated 'modern persons' with 'primitives' only in the way their views on hazards are shaped. Because the observation of Douglas and Wildavsky only makes sense under the assumption that these social structures are different, i.e. not equal, argument (4) can be termed culturalist. Furthermore, because social structures are embedded in particular contexts, e.g. linguistic and geographic contexts, argument (4) is also an expression of contextualism.

Hence, the relativist approach to risk and risk assessment, as observed by Shrader-Frechette, can be summarised as follows: consent over risk and risk assessment is impossible because knowledge gaps between experts and the public are unbridgeable (argument 1) and the assessment of risk is inevitably subjective and relative to the assessor and contingent upon social and cultural context (arguments 2–4).

In today's post-ideological times, the antagonism between positivism and relativism is barely made explicit. More likely, the gap between the two world views is expressed as an inclination or affiliation to a more 'realist' or 'rationalist' approach, on the one hand, or to a more 'sociologist' or 'historical' approach, on the other hand. Before proceeding to the specific questions about epistemological problems with respect to risk, it may be helpful to shed some light on expressions of the positivism–relativism distinction commonly used today.

In this perspective, Philip Kitcher discerned between a 'realist-rationalist cluster', on the one hand, and a 'socio-historical cluster', on the other hand. According to Kitcher, the 'realist-rationalist cluster' is characterised by the following features (Kitcher 1998, pp. 34–35, start citation):

1. In the most prominent areas of science, the research is progressive, and this progressive character is manifest in increased powers of prediction and intervention.
2. Those increased powers of prediction and intervention give it the right to claim that the kinds of entities described in scientific research exist independently of our theorizing about them and that many of our descriptions are approximately correct.
3. Nonetheless, our claims are vulnerable to future refutation. We have the right to claim that tour representations of nature are roughly correct while acknowledging that we may have to revise them tomorrow.
4. Typically our views in the most prominent areas of science rest upon evidence, and disputes are settled by appeal to canons of reason and evidence.
5. Those canons of reason and evidence also progress with time as we discover not only more about the world but also more about how to learn about the world [citation end].

On the other hand, the 'socio-historical cluster' was characterised by Kitcher by outlining the following points (Kitcher 1998, p. 36, start citation):

1. Science is done by human beings, that is, by cognitively limited beings who live in social groups with complicated structures and long histories.
2. No scientist ever comes to a laboratory or the field without categories and preconceptions that have been shaped by the prior history of the group to which he or she belongs.
3. The social structures present within science affect the way in which research is transmitted and received, and this can have an impact on intratheoretical debates.
4. The social structures in which science is embedded affect the kinds of questions that are taken to be most significant and, sometimes, the answers that are proposed and accepted [citation end].

However, regardless of respective labels, divisions between 'realist' and 'rationalist' approaches, on the one hand, and 'sociologist' or 'historical' approaches, on the other hand, are the result of a more fundamental schism. In essence, the conflict revolved around the question what should follow in the footsteps of religious explanations of human life; science or philosophy, positivism or historicism? As long as religious, *i.e.* metaphysical explanations prevailed, inconsistencies between scientific evidence and religious beliefs could be bridged.[9] However, as soon as science began to emancipate from religion, new approaches to the old question about the meaning of life were required. Muhsin Mahdi described the challenged represented by new scientific disciplines as 'the difficulty that emerged in the study of man and society as a result of the emancipation of philosophically neutral physics and chemistry (Mahdi 1996, p. 1038)'.

Challenged by the emancipation of science, one approach consisted in refraining from explanation and interpretation. Hence, that approach resulted in a separation of scientific activities from corresponding interpretation and valuation. Such attempts are usually subsumed under the generic term of 'positivism.' Muhsin Mahdi explained:

> Positivism resolves this difficulty [i.e. the emancipation of science] by means of a science of man and society that is philosophically neutral regarding values or judgements of value, the things about which people have disagreed and will continue to disagree. Facts, on the other hand, are thought to be things about which people could agree regardless of their judgments of value. (Mahdi 1996, p. 1038)

The other approach for answering fundamental question was to integrate new scientific discoveries into respective actual context. The generic term for such attempts is historicism, contextualism, or relativism. Muhsin Mahdi described historicism as an approach realising that 'the hope for agreement regarding facts is illusory: one needs a science that recognizes the fact of unresolvable disagreement regarding facts as well (Mahdi 1996, p. 1039)'. As its name indicates, the scientific method selected by historicism is the science of history. With regard to the historical scientific method, Muhsin Mahdi noted the following:

> As regards judgements of value, this science [i.e. history] will overcome disagreements regarding them not by asserting that they cannot be understood as judgments of value but by a peculiar understanding of these judgments of value: by understanding them as relative to comprehensive views and by understanding that these comprehensive views change and differ from one period to another or one culture to another. (Mahdi 1996, p. 1039)

With a view on the focus of the study at hand, the crucial difference between positivism and historicism is the respective approach towards facts and values: whereas the hallmark of positivism is the distinction between facts and values, historicism rejects that distinction:

> … [H]istoricism rejects the distinction between facts and values because it believes that both depend on a comprehensive view or a world view (a *Weltanschauung*) that changes from one society to another and from one period to another. By limiting itself to the study of facts and relations between facts, positivism sticks to part of the surface, as it were, and is not able to penetrate to the origin of these manifestations, which can be properly understood only as manifestations of the comprehensive view that underlies them. These manifestations include values, what people think or believe to be good or true or beautiful, and the articulation of these thoughts in science and art. (Mahdi 1996, p. 1038)[10]

Turning to risk as an epistemological phenomenon specifically, the antagonism between positivist and relativist concepts may take various forms, terms and expressions. Although applying different terms, several authors have depicted the phenomenon of risk from an antithetic perspective. Ulrich Beck, for example, used the terms *realism* and *constructivism* for referring to the epistemological debate (Beck 2005, pp. 23–26).

Ulrich Beck traced the epistemological realism–constructivism dichotomy back to two distinguished types of science. Beck observed:

> In this context it is useful to distinguish two types of science which are beginning to diverge in the civilization of threat. On the one hand, there is the old, flourishing laboratory science, which penetrates and opens up the world mathematically and technically but devoid of experience and encapsulated in a myth of precision; on the other, there is a public discursivity of experience which brings objectives and means, constraints and methods, controversially into view. Both types have their particular perspective, shortcomings, constraints and methods. Laboratory science is systematically more or less blind to the consequences which accompany and threaten its successes. The public discussion – and illustration – of threats, on the other hand, is related to everyday life, drenched with experience and plays with cultural symbols. It is also media-dependent, manipulable, sometimes hysterical and in any case devoid of a laboratory, dependent in that sense upon research and argumentation, so that it needs an accompanying science (classical task of the universities). It is thus based more on a kind of science of questions than on one of answers. It can also subject objectives and norms to a public test in the purgatory of oppositional opinion, and in just this way it can stir up repressed doubts, which are chronically excluded in standard science, with its blindness to threats and consequences. (Beck 1994, pp. 30–31)

On these grounds, Beck doubted whether experts—torn between the positivism of their professional background and the relativism of societies' expectations—are able to deliver unbiased outcomes. Beck explained, taking into account societal interdependencies: 'In risk issues, no one is an expert, or everyone is an expert, because the experts presume what they are supposed to make possible and produce: cultural acceptance [of risk] (Beck 1994, p. 9)'.

The perception of two types of science goes back to the Greek distinction between *techne* or *episteme*, on the one hand, and *phronesis*, on the other hand. Whereas the former is said to be 'represented by the laboratory science', the latter is said to be 'based on common sense-based science befitting the "real world where people live and work and die" (Cho 2010)'.[11] Hence, the distinction between abstract laboratory sciences and contextualised common-sense approaches has a long tradition. In this respect, Sungjoon Cho observed:

> In everyday lives, scientific inquiries, particularly those related to health risks, tend to connote a certain "truth" claim: for example, "hormone-treated beef

> is unsafe to consume," or in a more radicalized form "we may get cancer if we eat a hormone-treated beef." As discussed above, the conventional (mainstream) science tackles these inquiries through a sophisticated set of "methodologies" which positivistic scientific knowledge produces after rigorous scientific investigation. Therefore, according to this conventional standpoint being scientific means being "objective" and "universal." Under this rubric, what science means in the United States should be the same as in Europe. (Cho 2010)

Having related positivist scientific approaches to *techne* or *episteme*, Sungjoon Cho associated contextualising and historicizing approaches such as Gadamer's hermeneutics with *phronesis*:

> However, philosophers have long challenged this positivistic lab scientism. Edmund Husserl famously criticized this version of modern science as a "mathematization of nature" which is arguably detached from our real life, that is to say, "lifeworld" (*Lebenswelt*). Following Husserl's tradition, Hans-Georg Gadamer objected to the conventional premise that an exhaustible scientific "method" is an exclusive avenue to a truth claim. According to Gadamer, this version of science is nothing more than the "paradigmatic expression of the condition that gave rise to epistemology" or even the "naiveté of an ontology of the world based on the objectivism of mathematical natural science." According to Gadamer, the lifeworld is an "intuitively given world" amid ever streaming horizons and has a "finite, structure-relative" arrangement yet with "indeterminate open horizons." In contrast, the world of science holds the "symbolic givenness of a logical substruction that can no more be given by itself than infinite series of numbers." While "objective science may be a factor in our own lifeworld," it can only be understood by "historical exploration of its origin and its limits of validity". (Cho 2010)

The concept of 'lifeworld' (*Lebenswelt*) and Gadamer's hermeneutics may help to shed light on a crucial divide within risk assessment concepts. On the one hand, there are approaches aiming at separating facts from values in risk assessment, basing on the premise that science can be neutral, context-free and carried out without any prejudice. On the other hand, opposing voices argue that any kind of human knowledge is inevitably embedded in the human 'lifeworld':

> In sum, Gadamer's hermeneutics accuse scientific positivism, the pedigree of which might be traced back to August Comte, of a self-fulfilling prophesy

> gravely detached from the lifeworld. According to Gadamer, those presuppositions or prejudices, which constitute our lifeworld or tradition (history), are in fact necessary for us to unearth the truth, including the scientific truth, from those texts or phenomena before us. They never distract or prevent us from getting to the truth. (Cho 2010)

From a legal perspective, antagonistic world views can be found, for instance, in different theories of administrative constitutionalism. In this respect, Elizabeth Fisher contrasted a rational-instrumental with a deliberative-constitutive paradigm of administrative constitutionalism. The rational-instrumental paradigm of administrative constitutionalism, on the one hand, is based on a rather instrumental or functional understanding of public administration. In particular, Fisher observed that the rational-instrumental paradigm of administrative constitutionalism

> … construes public administration to be an 'instrument' of the legislature – a 'robot' or 'transmission belt' whose task is strictly to obey the preordained democratic will (as expressed in legislation) and to act effectively and efficiently. Its discretion is to be constrained as much as possible, and ideally by an analytical methodology (such as risk assessment or cost/benefit analysis) which ensures that administration applies the facts to the legislative mandate in as accurate a way as possible. (Fisher 2006, p. 335)

Hence, the rational-instrumental paradigm of administrative constitutionalism addresses risk as 'objective and quantifiable and the problems of complexity, uncertainty and socio-political ambiguity as largely manageable (Fisher 2006, p. 337)'.

On the other hand, the deliberative-constitute paradigm of administrative constitutionalism promotes

> … a model of public administration that is designed to address the complexities of risk problems by understanding public administration as being constituted by the legislature so as to wield substantial and continuing problem-solving discretion in relation to particular issues. This exercise of discretion is wide ranging and the nature and exercise of this discretion will vary depending on the specific problem. Tools such as risk assessment may have a role to play, but their legitimacy is not guaranteed, and, in every circumstance, the quality and veracity of scientific knowledge must be assessed. Likewise, a significant role is recognised for deliberation, in that the process of considering the different factors involved in a decision will

> produce a result which is greater than the sum of these factors. (Fisher 2006, pp. 335–336)

Thus, the deliberative-constitutive paradigm of administrative constitutionalism considers risks as inherently 'complex socio-political disputes in which complexity, uncertainty and socio-political ambiguity dominate' (Fisher 2006, p. 337).

Tomas Hellström applied the terms *objectivism* and *constructivism/contextualism* for describing antagonistic approaches towards risk (Hellström 1998, pp. 4–6). In the scope of the study at hand, the terms objectivism and constructivism/contextualism are used tantamount to the terms introduced by Shrader-Frechette, i.e. positivism and relativism.

A basic distinction between the two concepts of risks relates to the dimensions against which risks are assessed. Objectivist concepts of risk, which encompass technical risk analysis in general and food safety risk analysis in particular, are typically assessing risks against only one dimension. Hellström pointed at the following examples of risk dimensions: (i) risk may be presented as the probability of harm ('risk of exposure'); or (ii) risk may be presented as a consequence ('the risk from smoking'); or (iii) risk may be presented as describing a dangerous situation ('a hazardous waste plant creates a risk'). Hellström noted that '[a] statement of risk based on only one of these aspects (e.g. probability of occurrence) has been referred to as a one-dimensional concept of risk'. Hellström contrasted such one-dimensional concepts of risk to multidimensional approaches which are typically found in environmental risk assessment (Hellström 1998, p. 7). Whereas one-dimensional risk concepts were related to objectivist approaches, including technical and toxicological risk analysis, Hellström seemed to connoted multidimensional concepts of risk to constructivist and contextualist approaches.

Objectivists presume that there is a 'true and real risk' which can be expressed in one single number and to which, finally, everybody must agree by virtue of rational arguments.[12] The perception of scientifically ascertainable risks as generally acknowledged facts introduces a notion of universalism into the objectivist risk concept. A proponent of scientific universalism and the belief in the universal validity of scientific principles was Robert Merton. Merton's emphasis on universalism as a determining 'norm' of science is based on a distinction between internal and external factors. Whereas internal factors have to follow certain methodological standards, external factors should be kept out of the realm of scientific activity.[13] Particularly scholars with an interest in the history and philosophy of science, such as Toulmin, Duhem and von Helmholtz, have criticised Merton's distinction between internal and external factors.[14] From a broader perspective, Tracey Epps summarised criticism on Merton's concept as follows:

> Merton's ideas are useful in summarizing familiar characteristics of science. Nevertheless, they have been subject to much criticism and the perception of science as objective and neutral is far from being universally accepted. Instead, it is subject to challenge both in academia, and in the wider world. The academic challenge focuses on whether objective knowledge is possible and the extent to which science is socially constructed. In the wider world, the challenge focuses more on the actual use of science in different contexts, including in regulatory decision-making. (Epps 2008, p. 148)

Volker Böhnigk (1999) explained that Merton's insistence of science as an 'aseptic' endeavour is based on an understanding of science as a purely rational endeavour and scientists as *rationalistic* machines. In a rationalistic mindset, Böhnigk argued, science is perceived as an authoritative set of norms and criteria, such as universal validity, neutrality and the idea of the unity of all sciences. For a perception of science as a discipline based on an authoritative canon of abstract norms, Böhnigk (1999, p. 16) used the term *objectivism*.[15]

With regard to risk theory, in particular, Hellström referred to the 'objectivist orientation' as 'those practices within risk research that treat risk as a measurable physical attribute (Hellström 1998, p. 11)'. Hellström further discerned between approaches focusing on one measurable attribute and others taking into account varieties of factors. Examples for the former are financial, actuarial and health risk analyses, focusing on the probability of occurrence of a loss or a health risk. Objectivist approaches focusing on one single aspect (e.g. probability of occurrence) are called *one-dimensional* risk concepts (Hellström 1998, p. 7). On the other hand, there are *multidimensional* concepts of risk, in particular, environmental risk assessments. Albeit multidimensional risk concepts are integrating a variety of factors, objectivist approaches to environmental risk assessments are inclined to physical attributes amenable to probability calculations.

The objectivist approach towards risk was deconstructed by the school of the constructivists, or contextualists. The constructivists pointed at the fact that risk, by definition of the objectivists themselves, is not real, but the product of a probability prediction in relation to the severity of the issue at stake.[16] However, predictions of future events and the idea of probability itself are, by definition, not a matter of universal truth or 'reality', but the product of human presumptions. Instead, the constructivists perceived risk as a social construct, emphasising its social context.[17] The constructivists observe that risk, as a function of probability considerations, is contingent upon the perspective of the person and its social context; risk is never an absolute number, but relative to the circumstances and the people involved.[18]

Hellström also noted some common features with approaches putting forward a so-called objective–perceived risk dichotomy. Particularly popular among technocrats criticising 'subjective biases of laypersons', the objective–perceived risk dichotomy is based on the assumption that 'irrational emotional factors enormously multiply public judgments of the scale of some objective risks, such as nuclear power, while reducing the scale of others, such as car accidents'.[19]

Hellström pointed out three categories of objectivist approaches to risk: (a) technical approaches, (b) economic approaches and (c) psychometric approaches. Technical approaches towards risk are intended to measure and forecast probabilities of system failure and accidents. Under the term technical approaches, Hellström subsumed (i) actuarial analysis, (ii) toxicological/epidemiological analysis and (iii) probabilistic risk assessments (Hellström 1998, p. 12). Hence, toxicological and food safety risk analysis belongs to the cluster of technical approaches.

The focus of toxicological and epidemiological risk analysis is on the causality between hazards and risks. Hellström explained: 'Through toxicological (e.g. animal experimentation) and epidemiological (e.g. quasi-experimental comparison between exposed and non-exposed populations) causal agents are isolated from intervening variables to produce a risk characterization (Hellström 1998, p. 12)'.

Hellström (1998, p. 10) provided the following overview over the objectivist/constructivist divide (Table 1):

Shrader-Frechette (1991, pp. 8 and 9) herself adopted some sort of 'middle position' between the cultural relativists and the naïve positivists which she called 'scientific proceduralism'.[20] Her aim was to show 'how risk evaluation (the third stage of [risk] assessment) can be rational and objective, even though there are not completely value-free rules applicable to every risk-evaluation situation'. To this purpose, Shrader-Frechette

Table 1 Objectivism-Constructivism

	Objectivism	*Constructivism-contextualism*
View of science	Instrumentalist, essentially truthseeking, natural science oriented, experimental, demarcationist, analytical reduction in defining the research object	Critical function, socially contingent, socially responsible, anti-reductionist in its attempt to expand a research problem outwards and upwards rather than narrowing them down
View of reality	Realist, essentialist, focus on the explanatory properties of representation of the causal structure of the world. Causalist, mechanistic	Images of reality are viewed as essentially contingent on social and cultural factors. Organismic types of explanatory factors are sought in human actions as derived from imageries and social perceptions
Ethos	Strives to emancipate humans from nature. Ethos is procedural scientific and instrumentalist	Strives to emancipate humans from social and political control, in some cases predicated on the assumption that the human condition is essentially one divorced from nature

articulated in 'why and how both the cultural relativists and the naive positivists err in their general accounts of risk evaluation'.[21]

Notes

1. It has to be noted that terms may vary. Ian Holland and Aynsley Kellow, for instance, are using the terms 'Reductionism' and 'Constructivism' for describing similar epistemological variances (see Ian Holland and Aynsley Kellow, 'Trade and risk management: exploring the issues', in David Robertson and Aynsley Kellow, *Globalization and the Environment. Risk Assessment and the WTO* (Edward Elgar 2001), pp. 235–239).
2. In contrast to naïve positivists, however, Shrader-Frechette was of the view that both facts and values are forming human perception of reality. In particular, Shrader-Frechette considered that values are indispensable components for the development of scientific theory: 'A great many philosophers of science (myself included) maintain that both our values and the action of the external world on our senses are responsible for our perceptions, observations, and facts. Even though facts are value laden, we still may have a sufficient reason for accepting one theory over another. Conceptual and logical reasons also ground theory choice and hence objectivity. One theory may have more explanatory or predictive power, or unify more facts, for example (Shrader-Frechette 1991, p. 44)'.

3. Shrader-Frechette discerned between *risk* and (*probabilistic*) *uncertainty*. In situations of risk, probabilities of given outcomes are known, whereas in situations of uncertainty, probabilities of given outcomes are unknown.
4. Considering arguments of cultural relativists, Shrader-Frechette extensively referred to the groundbreaking work of Mary Douglas and Aaron Wildavsky, *Risk and Culture* (University of California Press, 1982).
5. Shrader-Frechette applied a three-step model of risk assessment, consisting of the three steps: (1) hazard identification, (2) risk estimation and (3) risk evaluation (Shrader-Frechette 1991, p. 5).
6. However, Shrader-Frechette observed that '[s]ome of these relativists reserve their harshest criticism for the U.S. public', i.e. the mentioned 'housewives', while sparing the "engineers". Thus, Shrader-Frechette pointed at an obvious inconsistency in the line of arguments of 'some of these relativists'. On the one hand, cultural relativists base their major argument, namely that risk evaluation is wholly relative and a social construct, on the observation that risk evaluation unavoidably comes along with value judgements. On the other hand, however, the same relativists 'single out U.S. environmentalist or sectarian laypersons (as opposed to technical experts) as having particularly biased constructs'. Therefore, Shrader-Frechette concluded that 'cultural relativism contributes to a *proindustry bias* towards risk, a bias that disenfranchises the lay public and supports the status quo' (Shrader-Frechette 1991, p. 31, emphasis added). Such findings may have motivated Shrader-Frechette to focus particularly on cultural relativism. Her attempt for rehabilitating environmental concerns and laypersons' judgement, as expressed in *Risk and Rationality* (1991), may be better understood in context. In context of the USA of the 1980s, *Risk and Rationality* may also be read as a defence of environmental movements concerned with, and federal agencies in charge of environmental protection and public health. In the wake of the Presidency of Ronald Reagan, environmental and public health concerns came under pressure:

   > The Reagan administration in the early 1980s was hostile towards the environmental movement, attempting a strategy of active exclusion. Attempts were made to demonise and exclude environmentalists from government. The regulatory basis of environmental administration was wound back, in keeping with market liberalism and individualist values. (…) In keeping with its ideological commitment to reducing the burden of regulation on business, the Reagan administration immediately began to dismantle the institutional capacity of the state to manage and regulate environmental affairs (John S. Dryzek, David Downes, Hans-Kristian Hernes,

> Christian Hunold, David Schlosberg, *Green States and Social Movements. Environmentalism in the United States, United Kingdom, Germany, and Norway.* (Oxford University Press, 2003), pp. 34 and 136)

Political headwinds against environmental concerns did not leave academia unaffected. As Shrader-Frechette observed, relativists such as Douglas and Wildavsky questioned the ability of laypersons for making rational risk decisions. On the other hand, segments of Congress, unhappy with regulatory activities in the field of environment and public health, initiated evaluations of risk assessment procedures applied by federal agencies, in particular the EPA and the Food and Drug Administration (FDA). One of these evaluations was the famous report *Risk Assessment in the Federal Government: Managing the Process*, published in 1983 by the National Research Council (NRC) and known as the *Red Book)*. With its emphasis on a conceptual separation between science and policy, *i.e.* risk assessment and risk management, the *Red Book* may be considered as a positivist attempt to contain regulatory activities of federal agencies in the USA.

7. Shrader-Frechette's review comprised, among many others, relativists such as Mary Douglas and Aaron Wildavsky (*Risk and Culture*), Melville Herskovits (*Cultural Anthropology*) and William Graham Sumner (*Folkways*).
8. A major point of Shrader-Frechette in *Risk and Rationality* was her refutation of claims that laypeople are irrational environmentalists and sectarians. In particular, Shrader-Frechette disproved arguments of a vocal segment of 'antipopulist' social scientists asserting that laypersons 'are dominated by "superstitions" about environmental risks and by fundamentalist desires for unrealistic environmental "purity" (Shrader-Frechette 1991, pp. 15–17)'.
9. A contemporary example for attempts to reconcile scientific evidence with religious faith is creationism. In short, creationism rejects the scientific theory of evolution and explains life on earth by referring to a metaphysical 'creator'.
10. However, besides these obvious differences, Mahdi pointed at important—and frequently overlooked—similarities between positivism and historicism: 'Positivism and historicism have many things in common. Both are essentially modern, the stepchildren of the distinction between philosophy and the peculiarly modern view of science, and the offspring of the belief in progress and the absolute superiority of modern science and scientific history over all earlier thought' (Mahdi 1996, p. 1041). Mahdi's observation highlights the fact that both approaches, i.e. positivism as well as historicism, were similarly ambitious endeavours initially. Original positivism, as conceived by Auguste Comte, was inspired by the vision that

agreements regarding scientifically established facts are attainable and thus universally valid. Historicism, in turn, was carried by the belief 'that values and philosophies and comprehensive views can be known, and can be known scientifically' (Mahdi 1996, pp. 1038–1039). Hence, whereas positivism was based on the presumption that natural sciences provide value-free outcomes, historicism basically claimed similar philosophically neutrality for its historical method.

11. The initial Greek distinction established by Aristotle in the Nicomachean Ethics was, however, that between *phronesis*, on the one hand, and *sophia* on the other hand. In an earlier draft version of the paper, dated July 31, 2009 and entitled 'Science, Hermeneutics and International Law: Rethinking the *Hormones* Dispute' presented at the ESIL-ASIL research forum in Helsinki, October 2–3, 2009, Cho himself suggested the opposite *episteme—phronesis* for discerning between opposite approaches towards science, i.e. positivist and constructivist approaches respectively.
12. The notion that risk can be quantified in a number which then reflects a universal 'reality' shows the vicinity of the objectivist approach to the philosophical school of Positivism and the interchangeability of both terms.
13. Böhnigk 1999, p. 44.
14. Böhnigk 1999, pp. 44–45, referring to Stephen E. Toulmin, Pierre Duhem and Hermann v. Helmholtz.
15. The term *objectivism* is used in various contexts. For instance, Gottlob Frege used the term *objectivism* as an opposing philosophical concept to Immanuel Kant's *rationalism*; and a particular notion of *objectivism* was developed by Ayn Rand and her *objectivist movement*.
16. Technically, risk (R) is commonly defined as the product of the magnitude of negative consequences (C) as a result of a certain event, and the probability (P) of occurrence of that event, providing the formula $R = P \times C$.
17. Hence, the synonymous term *contextualists*.
18. The fact that risk is relative to its observer was illustrated by Kaplan and Garrick (1981) and the example of the rattlesnake in the mailbox. Kaplan and Garrick recalled: 'We had a case in Los Angeles recently that illustrates this idea. Some people put a rattlesnake in a man's mailbox. Now if you had asked that man: "Is it a risk to put your hand in your mailbox?" He would have said, "Of course not." We, however, knowing about the snake, would say it is very risky indeed'. For Kaplan and Garrick, the allegory of the rattlesnake in the mailbox demonstrates that risk 'is a subjective thing—it depends who is looking'. As Kaplan and Garrick noted, some scholars refer to the fact that risk is relative by using the phrase 'perceived risk'. However, Kaplan and Garrick worried that the phrase 'perceived risk' suggests the existence of another kind of risk which is not only perceived, that is to say, the existence of an 'absolute risk'. The problem of Kaplan and Garrick was

that notions of absolute and perceived risk 'brings us in touch with some fairly deep philosophical matters, which incidentally are reminiscent of those raised in Einstein's theory of the relativity of space and time'.

19. See, for example, Brian Wynne, "Risk Perception, Decision Analysis, and the Public Acceptance Problem". Published in Brian Wynne (ed.), *Risk Management and Hazardous Waste. Implementation and the Dialectics of Credibility* (Berlin: Springer-Verlag, 1987), 357.
20. Shrader-Frechette defended her 'middle position', that is, *scientific proceduralism*, 'by means of arguments drawn from analogous debates over *naturalism* in contemporary philosophy of science'. Following the analogy drew by Shrader-Frechette, for philosophers of science as well as for risk evaluators holding some sort of middle position, the challenges are rather similar. Naturalistic philosophers such as Dudley Shapere, Larry Laudan and Roland Giere, holding a middle position between the relativists and the logical empiricists, are challenged 'to show precisely how theory choice or theory evaluation can be rational, even thought there are no universal, absolute rules of scientific method that apply to every situation'. Risk evaluators in pursuit of some middle position between the cultural relativists and the naïve positivists are challenged 'to show how risk evaluation (the third stage of [risk] assessment) can be rational and objective, even though there are no completely value-free rules applicable to every risk-evaluation situation'.
21. Shrader-Frechette summarised her attempt as follows: 'My purpose in this volume [i.e., *Risk and Rationality*] is (1) to articulate why and how both the cultural relativists and the naïve positivists err in their general accounts of risk evaluation; (2) to explain the misconceptions in a number of specific risk-evaluation strategies allegedly deemed "rational"; and (3) to argue for a "middle position" on the methodological spectrum of views about how to guarantee the rationality of risk evaluation'.

References

Beck, Ulrich. "World Risk Society". *Polity Press in association with Blackwell Publishers*, 2005 (first published 1999).

Beck, Ulrich. "The Reinvention of Politics: Towards a Theory of Reflexive Modernization". Published in Ulrich Beck, Anthony Giddens and Scott Lash, *Reflexive Modernization. Politics, Tradition and Aesthetics in the Modern Social Order*. Polity Press, 1994.

Volker Böhnigk, *Weltversionen. Wissenschaft zwischen Relativismus und Pluralismus* (Passagen Verlag, 1999), Wien.

Cho, Sungjoon. "From Control to Communication: Science, Philosophy and World Trade Law". *Cornell International Law Journal*, forthcoming. Available at SSRN. Accessed December 5, 2010. http://ssrn.com/abstract=1583023.

Epps, Tracey. "International Trade and Health Protection. A Critical Assessment of the WTO's SPS Agreement". Edward Elgar, 2008.

Fisher, Elizabeth. "Beyond the Science/Democracy Dichotomy: The World Trade Organisation Sanitary and Phytosanitary Agreement and Administrative Constitutionalism". Published in Christian Joerges and Ernst-Ulrich Petersmann (eds.), *Constitutionalism, Multilevel Trade Governance and Social Regulation*. Hart Publishing, 2006, 327–349.

Hellström, Tomas. "Risk-Based Planning. Institutional Uncertainty in the Science-Policy Interface". Doctoral Dissertation at Göteborg University, Department of Theory of Science and Research. *Göteborg University*, 1998.

Holland, Ian and Kellow, Aynsley. "Trade and risk management: exploring the issues". Published in David Robertson and Aynsley Kellow, *Globalization and the Environment. Risk Assessment and the WTO*. Edward Elgar, 2001, 229–248.

Kaplan, Stanley and Garrick, B. John. "On The Quantitative Definition of Risk". 1 (1) *Risk Analysis*, 1981, 11–27.

Kitcher, Philip. "A Plea for Science Studies". Published in Noretta Koertge (ed.), *A House Built on Sand. Exposing Postmodernist Myths about Science*. Oxford University Press, 1998, 32–56.

Mahdi, Muhsin. "Approaches to the history of Arabic science". Postface to Roshdi Rashed (ed.), *Encyclopedia of the History of Arabic Science* (vol. 3), *Technology, Alchemy and Life Sciences*. Routledge, 1996, 1026–1044.

Shrader-Frechette, Kristin S. "Risk and Rationality. Philosophical Foundations for Populist Reforms". *University of California Press*, 1991.

Wynne, Brian. "Risk Perception, Decision Analysis, and the Public Acceptance Problem". Published in Brian Wynne (ed.), *Risk Management and Hazardous Waste. Implementation and the Dialectics of Credibility*. Springer-Verlag, 1987, 356–396.

CHAPTER 3

Two Concepts of Reality

In *Risk and Rationality (1991)*, Shrader-Frechette based her account of opposing approaches to risk, i.e. positivism and relativism, on two conflicting philosophical positions. The starting point of Shrader-Frechette's account was her observation that the terms rationality and rational are normative. On these grounds, Shrader-Frechette noted:

> Controversies about the 'rationality' of various evaluations of risk are no easier to settle than analogous debates in science. Conflicts among philosophers of science (about what methodological rules, if any, guarantee the rationality of science) generate *alternative accounts* of scientific explanation, as well as disputes over which scientific theory is correct. Likewise, conflicts among risk assessors (about what methodological rules, if any, guarantee the rationality of responses to hazards) generate both *alternative accounts* of acceptable harm and disputes over whose risk-evaluation theory is correct.[1]

In the following, some light shall be shed on alternative accounts of the philosophy of science and scientific theory which, in turn, are forming the bases for alternative accounts of risk-evaluation theories.[2] Shrader-Frechette tracked the alternative accounts of the philosophy of science back to two opposing positions. On one side, Shrader-Frechette observed pluralist or relativist views, whereas, on the other side, she found logical-empiricist positions. Shrader-Frechette noticed:

> In the debate over the rationality of science, philosophers and scientists are arrayed on a spectrum extending from pluralist or relativist views to

M. Burkard, *Conflicting Philosophies and International Trade Law*, Philosophy, Public Policy, and Transnational Law,
https://doi.org/10.1007/978-3-319-61067-2_3

> logical-empiricist positions. At the left end of the spectrum, the pluralist end, are epistemological anarchist Paul Feyerabend and others who believe that there is no scientific method, that 'anything goes', and that 'no system of [scientific] rules and standards is ever safe'. At the other end of the spectrum are logical empiricists, such as Israel Scheffler and Rudolf Carnap, who believe that there are at least some universal and fixed criteria for theory choice and that these criteria guarantee the rationality of science.[3]

Scott Lash used slightly different terms for describing the same dichotomy between *scientism* and *culturalism*.[4] Lash discerned between antagonistic approaches which he called 'rationalistic (cognitivist) or *scientistic* understandings', on the one hand, and 'culturalist or hermeneutic views', on the other hand.[5] According to Lash, scientism and culturalism should be viewed as part of a 'continuum in contemporary theory'.[6] For Lash, the division between scientism and culturalism 'represents the distinction between in the broadest sense scientific sociology on the one side and cultural theory on the other'.[7] Lash depicted respective ends of the 'continuum in contemporary theory' as follows:

> At the science end of continuum there is the hard realism of an Althusserian Marxist such as David Harvey. Harvey pits his Marxist historical materialism against the 'soft' dialectical materialism of hermeneutic Marxism. For him culture, postmodern or other, is more or less reduced to a causal effect of transnational capital. For Harvey it makes sense only to understand nature instrumentally, and environmental matters as matters almost exclusively for experts. A concerns with other sorts of cultural and emotional involvements and responses of laypeople with the natural would be dismissed by analysts such as Harvey as the concerns of back-to-nature communal Romantic dreamers.
>
> At the 'culturalist' end of the spectrum stand such unlikely bedfellows such as Mary Douglas and Jacques Derrida, who reduce the social to the cultural and deconstruct the distinction between tradition and modernity.[8]

Obviously, however, the respective thinkers mentioned by Kristin Shrader-Frechette and Scott Lash did not operate in an intellectual vacuum; they stood in much older philosophical and epistemological traditions.

John Rawls, for instance, discerned between two traditions in political philosophy. On the one hand, Rawls identified the Platonic conception according to which political philosophy is assigned to establish truth and justice authoritatively.[9] Rawls explained that the Platonic conception of political philosophy not only comes along with a truth-claim, but also implies the implementation of the established truth by any means necessary. As examples, Rawls referred to Plato's philosopher kings and Lenin's revolutionary avant-garde.[10] On the other hand, Rawls identified a conception which he called 'democratic'. According to the democratic conception, political philosophy forms part of the stock of ideas and beliefs inherent to society. In this latter conception, political philosophy may influence political decision-making to a certain extent, but not in authoritative manners.[11]

Steve Fuller summarised the underlying epistemological dichotomy by the following stark contrast:

> Is whether a sentence is true or false, or whether a state of affairs obtains or not, relative to our state of knowledge? 'No,' says the *realist*. 'Yes,' says the *antirealist*.[12]

From a broader perspective, Steve Fuller found correlations between religious concepts and risk concepts. In lucid words, Fuller related scientific traditions to cornerstones of the European mindset:

> One of the most vivid metaphors that Jesus used to address his Apostles was of the lamp hidden beneath a bushel basket, a situation that of course only served to subvert the lamp's illumination. By this metaphor, Jesus meant to decry the reluctance of Christian converts to spread the Gospel, for fear of persecution as they inevitably upset the social order. (…) The episode's exemplariness comes from revealing the dual-tracked character of Western conception of Reason. The first track extends from Socratic questioning in the Athenian forum through the Enlightenment to Ernst Mach and Karl Popper. It is critical, libertarian, and risk seeking – and it also seems to be the track that Jesus himself espoused. The second track extends from the cloistered setting of Plato's Academy through positivism (probably in all of its incarnations but certainly in Auguste Comte's) to Max Planck and Thomas Kuhn. It is foundational, authoritarian, and risk averse – and it also characterizes the track with which institutional Christianity, especially the Roman Catholic Church, has often identified.[13]

Focusing on epistemological differences, certain aspects of these distinct philosophical traditions shall be outlined. Starting from the right end of the spectrum opened by Shrader-Frechette, one has to consider Rudolf Carnap and the school of neopositivism.

1 Positivist Traditions

1.1 The Vienna Circle

Rudolf Carnap (1891–1970) was an eminent Member of the *Vienna Circle* which, in turn, was part of a broader school of thought called *logical positivism*, *logical empiricism* or *neo-positivism*.[14] The *Vienna Circle* was operational in Vienna since around 1929.[15] Due to the rise of the Nazi regime in Germany and Austria, many Members of the *Vienna Circle* emigrated disseminating the ideas of the *Vienna Circle* particularly in Britain and the USA.[16] Parameters of the *Vienna Circle* were a centring on logical explanation and verification and a denegation of metaphysics.[17] For example, the *Vienna Circle* criticised metaphysics on the ground that the latter was not *intersubjective*. With intersubjectivity, the *Vienna Circle* understood that verification and evidentiary value requires that at least two persons, if not everybody, must be able to comprehend a certain statement.[18] Though, for expressing intersubjectivity today, *objectivity* and *objectivism* as its ideological expression seem to be more common terms. Because metaphysics are lacking such clarity, it was rejected. The rejection of metaphysics, however, was tantamount of rejecting philosophic traditions and philosophers basing on, or at least not rejecting, metaphysics, such as the so-called Neo-Hegelians and Martin Heidegger.[19] An excerpt of the Vienna Circle's manifesto *The Scientific Conception of the World* (1929) may shed some light on the positivist approach:

> We have characterised the *scientific world-conception* essentially by *two features. First* it is *empiricist and positivist*: there is knowledge only from experience, which rests on what is immediately given. This sets the limits for the content of legitimate science. *Second*, the scientific world-conception is marked by application of a certain method, namely *logical analysis*. The aim of scientific effort is to reach the goal, unified science, by applying logical analysis to the empirical material.[20]

Thus, positivist, i.e. empiricist science and a positivist method, i.e. logical analysis, are the two pillars of the *Vienna Circle's* world-conception. The goal of Neopositivists was to bridge the two pillars, the pillar of empirical science on the one hand, and its understanding by logical analysis, on the other hand. The bridge between 'the given' and its analytical perception would be unified science. In other words, the scientific world-conception was based on the assumption that there were two kinds of realities requiring bridging operations. The scientific world-conception presupposed a division between 'the given', on the one hand, and human perception, on the other hand. Harold Kincaid explained the assumption underlying Neopositivism as follows:

> The [neo-]positivists believed that there are two kinds of truths: empirical, factual truths of observations and truths based on the meaning of words. Good science was the paradigm of the former; mathematics and logic, the paradigm of the latter. Like Hume before them, the [neo-]positivists used this division to draw some striking conclusions. Traditional philosophy clearly was not based on facts of experience; yet, its metaphysical claims about substance, soul, and the like were not true simply by definition, and the [neo-]positivists thus recommended – in Humes's words – that such doctrines should be 'committed to the flames'.[21]

Neopositivists, Kincaid observed, were on the one hand 'philosophical radicals' in many respects. However, 'they were nonetheless quite traditional in others'.[22] The radicalism of the Neopositivists seemed of having centred on the second of the two pillars of the scientific world-conception, i.e. logical analysis, and bridging operations between the two pillars, namely 'the given' and its perception. On the other hand, however, Neopositivists seemed of having adhered to rather traditional approaches. The observation of persisting traditionalism seems particularly true with respect to the underlying assumption of a division between 'the given' and its perception, and the empirical approach to 'the given'. With regard to the latter, it is remarkable that most Neopositivists remained committed to traditional epistemology. Harold Kincaid observed:

> "For example, some [neo-]positivists were committed to 'the given,' the doctrine that sensory experience directly confronts us with information that is self-evident, relying upon no further inferences or theory. That idea had a long philosophical history and was far from radical. In the [neo-]positivist's philosophy of science, the given appeared as 'protocol sentences' or 'observation reports' – the empirical bedrock of experience which is certain and from which all theories are derived and confirmed. Quoting Carnap (1934, p. 45) again, protocol sentences 'refer to the given, and describe directly given experience'; they are 'statements needing no justification and serving as the foundation for the remaining statements of science'."[23]

The neopositivist traditionalism with regard to scientific empiricism on the one hand, and their radicalism with respect to logical analysis on the other hand are at the heart of the scientific world-conception. It provided the epistemological basis for the rigorous separation of the two realms, i.e. empirical truths and conceptual truths. Kincaid summarised the core notions of Neopositivism as follows:

> But these core notions – that there is a clear distinction between empirical truths and conceptual ones, that science provides the former by beginning with the certainty of direct experience, that philosophy can, via conceptual analysis, tell us what explanation, evidence, and other scientific concepts require – formed a lasting legacy. That legacy has influenced how philosophers and scientists view the scientific enterprise and that legacy continues.[24]

In terms of a conclusion, core notions of Neopositivism can be summarised as follows:

(1) There is a division between the real world, 'the given', and its perception and expression by humans.
(2) The real world, 'the given', can be grasped by empirical sciences.
(3) The truth, established by empirical sciences, can be expressed in protocol sentences and observation reports.
(4) Protocol sentences and observation reports can be understood, described and conceptualised by logical analysis, thereby bridging the division between the world and words, 'the given' and concepts, facts and theory: *Unified science*.

With regard to the focus of the study at hand on the separation of facts and values in risk assessment, it is noteworthy that the neopositivist approach put emphasis on the second pillar of knowledge, i.e. logical analysis. As mentioned above, Neopositivists rather traditionally presumed that 'the given' can, and shall be approached by empirical sciences. The rigour of Neopositivists centred on the methodology for logically analysing 'given facts' provided by empirical sciences. The application of logical and mathematical methods for conceptualising empirical facts was an attempt to bridge the division between 'the given' and its perception. The application of logic, i.e. scientific analysis was conceived as an appropriate tool for bridging the division between the factual and the perceived world. However, the application of logical analysis was intended as means, not as end. The goal of Neopositivism was to bridge the gap between the two worlds and to achieve *unified science*. In other words, the division between the real world and human perception was conceived a major obstacle for human knowledge, a gap to be overcome.

David Stump noted that the *scientific world conception* was not genuine to Neopositivism or scientific philosophy in general, but part of a broader movement extending to art, literature and social movements.[25] In particular, Stump pointed at connections between the *Vienna Circle* and the *Bauhaus*, and observed:

> The two institutions [i.e. the *Vienna Circle* and the *Bauhaus*] supported each other by expressing a modern, scientific world view and more broadly by developing a modern, scientific way of life (…). While striving for a new kind of objectivity, they developed, respectively, an anti-traditional philosophy, and an anti-traditional aesthetic that shared scientism and the use of machine images, and that built from simple elements according to explicit rules in order to avoid intuition and general concepts.[26]

Along with objectivism, empiricism, logicism and the verification principle, another important feature of the *Vienna Circle* was its quest for *unified science*.[27] Starting from the observation that no scientific discipline, neither natural sciences nor social sciences, could operate in isolation, but are using terms and methods from each other, the *Vienna Circle* was searching for unifying principles.[28] Because of the belief that only material things are accessible for intersubjective statements,[29] the *Vienna Circle* based its search for a language virtually unifying all sciences on physics and physical principles.[30] Therefore, the quest of the *Vienna Circle* for unified science was also termed *physicalism*.[31] The *Vienna Circle* provided the following insight into its project for unifying science:

> The scientific world conception is characterised not so much by theses of its own, but rather by its basic attitude, its points of view and direction of research. The goal ahead is *unified science*. The endeavour is to link and harmonise the achievements of individual investigators in their various fields of science. From this aim follows the emphasis on *collective efforts*, and also the emphasis on what can be grasped intersubjectively; from this springs the search for a neutral system offormulae, for a symbolism freed from the slag of historical languages; and also the search for a total system of concepts. Neatness and clarity are striven for, and dark distances and unfathomable depths rejected. In science there are no 'depths'; there is surface everywhere: all experience forms a complex network, which cannot always be surveyed

> and can often be grasped only in parts. Everything is accessible to man; and man is the measure of all things. Here is an affinity with the Sophists, not with the Platonists; with the Epicureans, not with the Pythagoreans; with all those who stand for earthly being and the here and now. The scientific world-conception knows *no unsolvable riddle*.[32]

An additional characterising feature of logical positivism was *internationalism*. David Stump observed 'that the two waves of international [scientific] cooperation—before and after WWI—coincide with the rise of scientific philosophy and with the rise of Logical Positivism, respectively'.[33]

Carnap's mindset was influenced by, *inter alia*, the philosopher Bertrand Russell (1872–1970).[34] Russell's legacy as a political thinker and pacifist is still vivid.[35] At the beginning of the twentieth century, however, Russell became famous as an outstanding philosopher and mathematician.[36] Together with Alfred North Whitehead, Russell authored the groundbreaking work *Principia Mathematica (1910–1913)*. With his essay *On Denoting* (1905), Russell contributed to the development of a formalised, objective language, an issue which became an ideal of logical positivism and analytical philosophy.[37]

Preparatory work for Russell's *Principia Mathematica* and the formalism of logical positivism was provided by the mathematician Gottlob Frege (1848–1925).[38] Frege pioneered the modernising of traditional forms of logic, dating back to Aristotle, into a new logical system. His works, among others the seminal *Begriffsschrift*; the *Foundations of Arithmetic*, and the *Basic Laws of Arithmetic*[39] laid the foundations for various attempts of philosophers and scientists for establishing clear, i.e. intersubjective forms of objective scientific communication. Attempts to create a *formula language* (in German: Formelsprache) inspired further attempts to bridge communication gaps between two and more persons by new systems of procedural methods ('protocols', 'basic sentences', 'protocol sentences'). As Steve Fuller noted, 'Frege is, of course, famous for maintaining that language was necessary for the expression of truth, which occurred whenever the truth conditions of a sentence were "satisfied" by a state of affairs'.[40]

1.2 From Comte's Positivism to Empiriocriticism

As already indicated by the prefix *neo-* before positivism, the school called *neo-positivism, logical positivism* or *logical empiricism* stood, in turn, in a much older tradition, namely *positivism*[41] itself.[42] Positivism is usually depicted as being more some sort of mindset rather than a monolithic philosophical system.[43] As indicative for a positivist mindset, the following common features can be observed:

- The belief in perceptible, accessible and ascertainable, hence 'given' or 'positive' facts.[44] A neat example for the concept of positivism is its application in law: legal positivism basically stipulates that the law has not to be interpreted but to be understood and applied as it is written.[45]
- The disbelief in any form of reality behind comprehensible facts. Accordingly, positivism rejects any notion of entities, beings, forces or laws operating behind the scenes of the perceptible world. As a consequence, positivism runs counter to all philosophical tendencies descending from Platonic ideas. In other words, a significant feature of positivism is its fierce disaffirmation of any kind of 'metaphysics'. By the same token, strict positivists are also rejecting concepts of Materialism and Idealism alike, because both concepts are making statements beyond what is immediately verifiable; Materialism declares that basically *everything* is physical, whereas Idealism holds that essentially *everything* is ideational.[46] In view of positivism, both statements are beyond practical verification.[47]

Founding father of the term positivism was Auguste Comte (1798–1857).[48] In his fundamental work, *The Course in Positivists Philosophy* (in French: *Cours de philosophie positive)*, a series of texts published between 1830 and 1842, Comte developed the *law of three stages.*[49] According to the law of three stages, human development undergoes the following three stages: (i) the theological or fictitious stage, (ii) the metaphysical or abstract stage and (iii) the positive or scientific stage.[50]

In the theological or fictitious stage, man is affected by superstitious beliefs, expressed by fetishism, polytheism and monotheism.[51] In the metaphysical or abstract stage, philosophical concepts are replacing fictitious beliefs.[52] Superstitious ideas of divine powers are replaced by philosophical concepts about abstract laws of nature. In the positive stage, finally, human thinking abstains from trying to comprehend ultimate causes behind tangible reality, such as the genesis, the universe or the meaning of life. Instead, scientific thinking starts centring on factual issues ascertainable by sense and reason.[53] According to Comte, society in the positive stage is governed by scientific experts: a council of positivist philosophers and sociologists shall be the supreme intellectual institution and oversee, in particular, education.[54] Executive government, however, shall be in the hands of business-oriented practitioners, *e.g.* economists, bankers, merchants, manufacturers and farmers.[55] Thus, science and economy are the drivers of Comte's positivist society of the future.[56]

It is the particular role attributed to science distinguishing positivism from later and antagonistic philosophical approaches, in particular, historicism. According to Muhsin Mahdi, positivism conceived science as an instrument for improving humanity. Mahdi observed that for positivism

> [t]he aim of science is to describe and predict so as to ameliorate the human condition: 'Science whence comes prediction; prediction whence comes action', said Auguste Comte. This science is seen as the last stage in a general progress of mankind whose history has been dominated by a progressive evolution that has been universal, unilinear, continuous and necessary.[57]

The confidence in science and scientific expertise expressed by Comte's *law of three stages* has to be understood in light of the tradition of scientific world-conceptions dating back to the Renaissance and the Enlightenment in Europe. René Descartes (1596–1650) and other philosophers of the seventeenth century, in particular, Francis Bacon (1561–1626), Blaise Pascal (1623–1662), Gottfried Wilhelm Leibniz (1646–1716) and Christian Wolff (1679–1754), established mathematics—and sciences based thereupon—as the universally valid pathway to human knowledge.[58] The inventive step taken by Descartes was to approach old philosophical questions by new means.[59] Mediaeval philosophers such as Aurelius Augustinus (354–430) had approached fundamental questions, for instance, questions about the relationship between man and God or between body and soul, with metaphysics, i.e. religion. In contrast, Descartes introduced criteria of logic and of universal validity for evaluating the appropriateness of philosophical approaches to these fundamental questions.[60] Thereby, only logical and universal valid disciplines such as mathematics, geometry and sciences based thereupon stood the proof. As a consequence of further analysis pursued over following decades, the fundamental question about the relationship between man and God transformed in light of new approaches applied by analytical sciences.[61] In particular, the focus on the man–God relationship was broken up into sub-questions accessible by the new sciences. Thus, the question about the relationship between man and God reappeared as questions about the relationship between man and 'the given', that is, pre-existing nature. However, the transformation of religious questions into scientific ones not only bore tremendous scientific achievements, but also philosophical upheavals. Mediaeval philosophers such as Augustinus had conceived the world as a holy entity governed by a metaphysical power, that was, the kingdom of God (Civitas Dei).[62] In contrast, Descartes and his followers reconceived the man–God dichotomy as a dualism between mind and matter, man and nature. The Cartesian world-conception presumes a dualism between mathematical, logical, analytical and hence 'rational' concepts, on the one hand, and corporal matter unable to rational reasoning, on the other hand. A consequence of this dualism was the perception of animals as machines. Störig observed that from a Cartesian point of view, an animal crying because it's being beaten is no different than a pipe organ sounding because its keys are touched.[63] Störig further noted that the mechanical world-conception of the Cartesian school of thought paved the way for later Materialists to extend the 'rational' approach from animals to humans; humans are conceived as machines, albeit rather complicated ones.[64] And Eduard Kaeser observed that the Cartesian equation of animals with machines provided the following dangerous syllogism: animals are machines; men are animals; hence men are machines.[65]

The Cartesian dualism between man and 'the given', i.e. nature, thus implied a separation between the two. The separation between man and nature, in turn, is a precondition for the revalidation of man and nature, respectively. Whereas mediaeval scholasticism implied the supremacy of metaphysics, i.e. God, the 'rational' Cartesian world-conception subdued 'given' natural matters to the power of scientific analysis. The Cartesian approach 'objectified' natural matters, virtually making objects out of living beings. The example of animals shows how the devalorisation of 'the given', i.e. nature, worked: by equating animals with machines, the former were devalorised to mechanisms without any faculty of reason, hence subhuman structures. In other words, the Cartesian approach of objectifying 'given' matters of nature was the philosophical matrix underlying human domination and exploitation of nature.[66] The scientific approach of Cartesian objectivism transformed animals into *res extensa*, meaning 'extended objects'.[67] It is this particular function of the Cartesian subject–object dichotomy arousing many-voiced criticism, most notably from animal rights proponents and holistic approaches in ecology, such as *deep ecology*.

The meaning of positivism, however, seems of having narrowed over time. Whereas Comte started with a holistic concept for effectively unifying science and to virtually erect an alternative, science-based religion,[68] Neopositivists contented themselves with developing a unifying language for all sciences. Nowadays and in particular in the aftermath of the so-called positivism dispute (in German: Positivismusstreit), the term positivism comes along with a rather negative connotation. In this context, Alfred Schmidt, a collaborator of Adorno and Horkheimer, provided a stringent description of a present-day notion of positivism: 'Schmidt characterizes positivism as a tendency of thought in which 'the method of the various single sciences is taken absolutely as the only valid method of knowledge' (*die einzelwissenschaftlichen Verfahren als einzig gültige Erkenntnis verabsolutierende Denken*), and he identifies it, correctly, with an over-emphasis on "sensually ascertainable facts"'.[69] Although Schmidt's depiction of positivism was an intended allegation against Popper, Popper fully agreed in substance and added, slightly amused:

> He [i.e. Alfred Schmidt] is clearly unaware of the fact that my alleged positivism, which was used to give the book *Der Positivismusstreit* its name, consisted of a fight against all this, which he describes (fairly correct) as 'positivism'. I have always fought for the right to operate freely with speculative theories against the narrowness of the '*scientistic*' theories of knowledge and, especially, against all forms of *sensualistic empiricism*. I have fought against the *aping* of the natural sciences by the social sciences, and I have fought for the doctrine that positivistic epistemology is *inadequate* even in its analysis of the natural sciences which, in fact, are not 'careful generalizations from observation', as is usually believed, but are essentially speculative and daring.[70]

Hence, from this statement of Popper, the following common features of today's perception of positivism may be distilled: (i) narrow 'scientistic' theories of knowledge, i.e. *scienticism* in the form of 'sensualistic empiricism', (ii) 'the aping of the natural sciences by the social sciences', and (iii) the belief that positivistic epistemology is *adequate* in its analysis of the natural sciences.

From these statements and positions, a fourth criterion emerges as a philosophical essence of positivism, namely its refutation of dialectics. Nicholas Georgescu-Roegen even observed an antagonistic relationship between dialectical concepts of science, often ascribed to Hegelian origins, and positivistic concepts of science.[71] Georgescu-Roegen noted that from a positivistic point of view, dialectic concepts of science 'are antagonistic to science: knowledge proper exists only to the extent to which it is expressed in *arithmomorphic* concepts. The position recalls that of the Catholic Church: holy thought can be expressed only in Latin'.[72]

Following the rather authoritative fourth criterion, a fifth criterion may be added. The fifth criterion consists of a somewhat 'elitist' understanding of science. The elitist attitude of certain positivist scientists was best described by Popper who noted that "these physicists, and other positivists, try to tell us [today]: that we cannot, in principle, hope ever to understand anything about the structure of matter: that the theory of matter must forever remain the private affair of the expert, the specialist—a mystery shrouded in technicalities, in mathematical techniques, and in "semantics"'.[73]

A sixth criterion of Neopositivism, in particular, its specific development in the USA, is the alleged 'neutrality' of Neopositivism in political and religious matters. In this respect, Popper observed that positivists do not wish to address questions outside the range of problems ascertainable by 'positive' empirical sciences.[74] Hence, positivists disregard philosophical problems as 'meaningless pseudo problems'.[75] Popper noted that the disregard of philosophical problems as 'meaningless pseudo problems' is a very easy way to go: one only needs to define the term 'meaning' narrowly enough.[76] A narrow definition of the term 'meaning', confining it to questions ascertainable by empirical sciences, renders any debate about the term 'meaning' meaningless.[77] Citing Wittgenstein, Popper concluded that, once 'enthroned', the 'dogma of meaning' is beyond criticism, but 'sacrosanct and definitive'.[78]

Fred Eidlin worked out differences within the positivist school of thought with regard to meaning and values. Eidlin discerned positivists who are value-naturalists, on the one hand, from positivists who are value-non-cognitivists, on the other hand.[79] Most positivists, Eidlin noted, are value-non-cognitivists.[80] Value-non-cognitivists are of the view that facts are logically independent from implied values and that statements about values, compared to factual statements, are non-scientific.[81] Value-naturalists, in contrast, go farther. Value-naturalists do not only treat values in the same way as they are treating facts, that is, empirically; such an approach could also be tried by value-non-cognitivists and is not, per se, value-naturalistic. But value-naturalists go farther insofar they try to deduce ethical principles from factual premises.[82] Eidlin provided the example of survival and the ban on killing. A 'naïve positivist-oriented social scientists', as Eidlin also called value-naturalists, may deduce from the fact that humans want to survive that survival is a natural value. Or, a naïve positivist-oriented social scientist may deduce from the fact that murder is proscribed in most societies that the ban on killing is a value or norm deducible from facts.[83] Subsequently, such facts-to-value deductions are frivolously generalised by value-naturalists.[84] Eidlin argued that the reason why value-naturalism is such an easy position is its congruence with common sense.[85] In Eidlin's view, the congruence of value-naturalism with common sense is the cause that positivist-oriented research in social sciences is dispersed with implicit, if not explicit value-naturalist elements.[86]

However, the standpoint of value-non-cognitivists, that is, considering facts as independent from values and statements about values as non-scientific, did also attract criticism. Criticism may arise, first of all, in cases value-non-cognitivism translates into silence and alleged 'neutrality' vis-à-vis political and ethical questions and religious metaphysics.

David Stump reflected on the question 'whether there can be any connection between epistemologies and values and consider the philosophy of science as a possible political force'.[87] By pursuing his reflections, Stump discovered 'at least four possible ways to recover a modicum of value orientation within the philosophy of science'.[88] As one of these possible ways to recover minimal value orientations, Stump suggested to look at epistemological approaches of respective philosophical schools of thought. Stump explained:

> (…) even if there is no direct connection between a particular epistemology and political values, certain epistemologies may limit the range of possible values. This is shown in the philosophy of science itself, to some extent, by those who accept the fact/value distinction, thus eliminating value judgments from science.[89]

Though, the disregard of values as 'metaphysics' and the attempt to eliminate value-judgements from science are characterising features of positivism and of Logical positivism in particular. Positivism and Logical positivism are applying an especially rigorous form of epistemology aiming at 'eliminating value judgments from science'. Therefore, considered from the perspective of epistemology, positivism and Logical positivism can be added to those epistemologies which 'limit the range of possible values'. Giving its aim at separating facts from values and science from judgement, the objective of the epistemological approach developed by positivism and logical positivism is, in fact, the counter piece to the connection of epistemology and values. Thus, from an epistemological point of view, positivism and logical positivism can be considered as the antithesis to Stumps' notion of 'the philosophy of science as a possible political force': by virtue of the fact–value dichotomy, positivist epistemology is intrinsically apolitical.[90]

Bringing the two observations made above together, i.e. the depoliticisation of logical positivists immigrated to the USA, and the recognition of positivist epistemology as apolitical, a new feature of Neopositivism can be observed. Void of political ideas and ideals, only the epistemological method of separating facts and values remained, giving Neopositivism a new meaning. Whereas logical positivism in Europe had combined Enlightenment values with the idea of modernity in general and with modern science in particular, Neopositivism in the USA confined itself to the latter. Hence, the philosophy of logical positivism shrank to the application of positivist epistemology in scientific environments; the philosophy of positivism was reduced to a mere epistemological method which may be called a positivist method, positivist approach, or *empiriocriticism*.

1.3 Pensée Unique

In the wake of the victory of conservative forces against Napoleonic France, sealed at the Vienna Congress (1814/1815), times were rather unreceptive for Comte's ideas on the continent.[91]

In Britain, in contrast, Comte's ideas fell on fertile ground. British philosophers such as Francis Bacon (1561–1626), Jeremy Bentham (1748–1832) and John Stuart Mill (1806–1873) had prepared the ground for empirical, utilitarian and positivist approaches. Empiricism, utilitarianism and positivism, in turn, were well received by ascending middle classes, thriving overseas trade and accelerating industrialisation.[92] Britain is, thus, a good example for interdependencies between politics, economy and philosophical ideas. Margaret C. Jacob, for instance, put forward the thesis that Empiricism in England was a tool for the emerging middle classes against absolutism. Jacob observed:

> Experimentalism was intended to channel the aggressions and ambitions of the great as well as the lowly. Boyle, Newton, and the next generations of interpreters – Bentley, Clarke, and their followers – were just as afraid of absolute sovereigns and their henchmen as they were afraid of republicans. The vision of science and religion that the Newtonians inherited and expanded gave birth to the *physicotheology* so beloved by eighteen-century

> liberal Protestants in Europe and the American colonies. This middle way worked for a time to prevent the return of absolutism. For its believers, it justified resistance to any pressure for reform.
>
> However imperfectly from our perspective, Erastian[93] churchmen and experimental scientists grappled effectively with their historical moment because they were neither absolutists nor cynical relativists.[94]

It is this particular merger of science and Protestantism, termed physicotheology by Jacob, which bridged the role and the understanding of science in Britain and in the USA.

Positivism entered the USA in two waves. As mentioned above, the first wave of positivist thinking—instigated by Comte—fell on fertile grounds in Britain. Conveyed through the works of Francis Bacon, John Stuart Mill and Jeremy Bentham, positivist philosophy became accessible in the USA, too.

The second wave of logical empiricist or neopositivist thinking arrived in the USA in the aftermath of the rise to power of the Nazi regime in Germany. Interestingly, though, the political impetus of the Vienna Circle seems of having faded away during the transatlantic crossing.[95] A. W. Carus put it that analytical philosophy, after having crossed the Atlantic, 'has lost (…) the desire to change the world'.[96] Carus observed:

> [Analytical philosophy] has lost its continuity with the eighteen-century Enlightenment; it has lost contact with the wellspring of philosophy since Socrates, the urge to criticize complacent, unreflective, and fashionable modes of thought. Analytical philosophy has reverted to the task philosophy professors have excelled at through the ages, which is to justify by detailed, abstruse arguments the unreflective common sense that everyone else already takes for granted. In short, analytical philosophy has become precisely the sort of thing that the Vienna Circle attacked so merciless during its vitriolic phase.[97]

With reference to recent research, David Stump gave an account of some of the reasons for the depoliticisation of remnants of the Vienna Circle after emigration from Nazi Germany to the USA. Stump noted:

> Recent works explore why the Members of the Vienna Circle became less political when they came to the United States (e.g. Giere, 1996) and the general chilling effect of McCarthyism on philosophy (McCumber, 2000). Members of the Vienna Circle may have been hiding their past connections to left-wing groups because of the anti-Communist climate in the United

> States, or thy may have felt the need to become respectable academic or (...) perhaps the political values expressed by the Vienna Circle, with the exception of Neurath, have been rather overstated.[98]

Be that as it may, the depoliticised version of Neopositivism was welcomed in the USA with open arms. First of all, scientists and physicists, in particular, were welcomed for fostering US war efforts, in particular, the Manhattan Project. Additionally, though, a genuine US American philosophical tradition may have prepared receptive grounds for positivist approaches. That philosophical school of thought is known as *Pragmatism* and related to, *inter alia*, Charles Sanders Peirce (1839–1914), William James (1842–1910) and John Dewey (1859–1952).[99] Noteworthy features of Pragmatism are its refutation of idealistic speculation, as was the case in German Idealism, and the reduction of utility to tangible factors such as 'cash-value', 'profit' and 'results'.[100] By the same token, the notion of truth changed from a substantive question to a procedural issue. Peirce, for instance, relied on a procedural attempt for approaching *truth*: 'The opinion which is fated to be ultimately agreed to by all who investigate, is what we mean by the truth, and the object represented in this opinion is the real'.[101] Following Peirce, the 'Community of (rational) Investigators' would form some kind of 'Supreme Court of Rationality', approaching truth by iterative procedures.[102] By rendering truth contingent upon utility and reducing utility to cash-value, Pragmatism virtually boiled down the notion of truth to a measurable and quantifiable cash-equivalent.[103]

The spin of Pragmatism towards utilitarianism was furthered by William James, in particular. According to Luc Ferry, US American expressions of utilitarianism consider 'utility' in light of the satisfaction a product or merchandise brings to the consumer: 'It is this consumerist vision that critical intellectuals denounce, justifiably in part, as the sign of a "global Americanization"'.[104] Considering legal theory, in particular, it was Ronald Dworkin relating legal positivism to utilitarianism. In *Rights, Killing, and Suffering* (1983), Raymond Frey observed:

> In *Taking Rights Seriously*, Ronald Dworkin opposes what he sees as the prevalent theory of law, which is the legal positivism that derives from the work of John Austin and Jeremy Bentham. One significant aspect to Dworkin's discontent with positivism is his disenchantment with utilitarianism (or what he calls 'economic' utilitarianism), which he describe in his Introduction as the normative underpinning of positivism.[105]

An example of the absorption of neopositivist approaches in the USA was *Behaviourism.* In a nutshell, Behaviourism can be defined as a theory explaining human and animal behaviour without reliance on psychological or mental processes.[106] The influence of Neopositivism on Behaviourism can well be demonstrated by invoking the example of Skinner. Burrhus Frederic Skinner (1904–1990), a US American psychologist and philosopher, pioneered a specific form of Behaviourism also known as *Radical Behaviourism.*[107] Gerald Holton noted that Skinner got inspiration particularly from the lecture of the works of Ernst Mach (1838–1916), an Austrian physicist and philosopher.[108] In the field of philosophy, Mach established the philosophy of science as a discrete philosophical branch which turned out as a building block for Neopositivism. Working out elements of Neopositivism in Skinner's work, Holton observed:

> In writing his doctoral thesis, young Skinner saw a way of applying the Machian point of view [i.e. the point of view of neopositivist Ernst Mach] to the clarification of such concepts as the 'reflex' of intact organisms, something he considered to be as basic in psychology as, say, mass is in physics. As Skinner recollected, he was 'following a strictly Machian line, in which behavior was analyzed as a subject matter in its own right as a function of environmental variables without reference to either mind or the nervous system' (…). In this radically empiricist mode, the study of behavior reduced itself for Skinner, to start with, to the observation of the motion of the foot of a food-deprived rat, pressing down a small lever in an experimental box of standard size. Explanation was reduced to description, causation to the notion of function, and the chief goal was the correlation between observed events.[109]

As exemplified by James' pragmatism, Dewey's instrumentalism and Skinner's behaviourism, rigorous but practical applications of positivist approaches were characteristic features of positivism in the USA. Applied on economics, however, positivist approaches showed lasting impact. A particular strand of economics adopting scientific methodology was the Austrian School. Representatives of the Austrian School such as Carl Menger (1840–1921) conceived economics as hard science and economic 'laws' as something which has to be discovered scientifically. Cognitions of the Austrian School and other economic approaches applying scientific methodology in economics fell on fertile soil in the Anglo-Saxon world and in the USA in particular, showing a lasting impact. Nicholas Georgescu-Roegen, for instance, wondered about the 'stubborn attachment' to models of thought developed by hard sciences:

> It is curious, therefore, that economists have over the last hundred years remained stubbornly attached to one particular idea, the mechanistic epistemology which dominated the orientation of the founders of the Neoclassical School. By their own proud admission, the greatest ambition of these pioneers was to build an economic science after the model of mechanics. (...) The latter-day economists, without a single second thought, have apparently been happy to develop their discipline on the mechanistic tracks laid out by their forefathers, fiercely fighting any suggestion that economics may be conceived otherwise than as a sister science of mechanics.[110]

As Georgescu-Roegen explained, the application of models developed by hard sciences resulted in a scientification of economics:

> The consequence of this indiscriminate attachment to the mechanistic dogma, whether in an explicit or a tacit manner, is the viewing of the economic process as a mechanical analogue consisting – as all mechanical analogues do – of a principle of conservation (transformation) and a maximization rule. The economic science is thus reduced to a *timeless* kinematics. (...) The pillar of equilibrium theory is that, if events alter the demand and supply propensities, the economic world always returns to its previous conditions as soon as these events fade out. An inflation, a catastrophic drought, or a stock-exchange crash leaves absolutely no mark on the economy. Complete reversibility is the general rule, just as in mechanics.[111]

Albeit recognising influences from history, culture and other 'soft factors', the vision of a scientific approach in economics still lives on today. In the introduction to their book Economics, Paul Samuelson and William Nordhaus outlined 'the logic of economics' as follows:

> Economists use the *scientific approach* to understand economic life. This involves observing economic affairs and drawing upon statistics and the historical record. For complex phenomena like the impacts of budget deficits of the causes of inflation, historical research has provided a rich mine of insights. Often, economics relies upon analysis and theories. Theoretical approaches allow economists to make broad generalizations, such as those concerning the advantages of international trade and specialization or the disadvantages of tariffs and quotas.[112]

As already mentioned, scientific methodology in economics found a receptive environment in the USA already accustomed to pragmatism and instrumentalism. In the scope of the study at hand, reflections of positivism in economics applied in international trade and the GATT/WTO system are of particular interest. In the following, certain characterising features of positivism, as worked out above, shall be reconsidered as reflections of positivism in the GATT/WTO approach to international trade. Two particular features characterising notions of positivism, i.e. scientism and the aping of hard sciences, have already been mentioned. Another feature indicative for positivism are expressions of (scientific/epistemological) elitism. In this respect, the initial period of the GATT is a telling example, as Robert Howse observed:

> As the high politics of international relations increasingly focused, with the Cold War, on matters of international security and the East-West conflict, the administration and incremental development of the trade system was increasingly entrusted to a specialized policy elite insulated from, and not particularly interested in, the larger political and social conflicts of the age. (…) This new *trade policy elite* developed professional working procedures and norms within the GATT, organized the agenda for negotiations, and – with very little to go on from the treaty text itself – created and sustained an effective arbitral mechanism for dispute settlement. As persons with the bent of managers and technical specialists, they tended to understand the trade system in terms of the policy science of economics, not a grand normative political vision. A sense of pride developed that an international regime was being evolved that stood above the "madhouse" of politics (if one can borrow Pascal's image), a regime grounded in the insights of *economic "science,"* and not vulnerable to the open-ended normative controversies and conflicts that plagued most international institutions and regimes, most notably, for instance, the United Nations.[113]

Joseph Weiler explained that the early GATT system was a self-referential system, made out of a network of selected professionals sharing a common agenda and operating in a shielded environment:

> GATT successfully managed relative insulation from the "outside" world of international relations, and it established among its practitioners a closely knit environment revolving around shared normative values (of free trade) and shared institutional ambitions. GATT operatives became a classical "net-work" of first-name contacts and friendly relationships. (…) Within this ethos there was an institutional goal – preventing trade disputes from spilling into the wider circles of international relations. A trade dispute was an "internal" affair that needed to be resolved as quickly and smoothly as possible within the organization.[114]

Additional elements of positivism, as shown above, were the belief in positivist epistemology, the rejection of dialectics, and the abstention from value-judgements and from political implications. In tandem with scientism, pursuing such a positivist economic agenda may result in an axiomatic and determinist economic doctrine. Terms associated with positivist economics, in particular, are usually known as Economism and economical Determinism; in the field of international trade, in particular, the terms *globalism* and *pensée unique* became common. As Eva Maria Belser noticed, positivist economics applied on international trade came along with abstract claims for distributive justice based on economic theory.[115] As Eva Maria Belser observed, arguments for trade regulation vaporised in light of positivist economics: proponents for trade regulation were either criticised for not comprehending economic 'laws', or for being rent-seekers.[116] Because the economic theory of comparative advantage comes along with the promise of rising general welfare in the abstract, Belser introduced the term 'atavistic justice'.[117] Other authors introduced different terms for referring to what Belser called 'atavistic justice'.

Ulrich Beck, for instance, used the term *globalism* for referring to the application of reductionist economic principles to world trade.[118] Beck understood *globalism* as 'the rule of a world market permeating and altering everything'.[119] Therefore, Beck aimed at revealing 'the primacy and the dictates of the world market implied in neoliberal ideology'.[120] According to Beck, the essence of *globalism* is 'an antiquated economism, a restoration of historical metaphysics, an allegedly apolitical revolution from above'.[121] Beck revealed that the nature of *globalism* essentially consists of a reduction of complexity. According to Beck, *globalism* reduces the new complexity of global interdependencies to respective economic expressions.[122] By doing so, all other non-economic dimensions of globalisation such as cultural, ecological and political expressions of new transnationalities are neglected. Hence, world society is reduced to a world market. On these grounds, Beck found that neoliberal *globalism* is a manifestation of linear, one-dimensional and mono-causal thinking expressed by Economism. However, Beck explained that the origins and causes of Economism in its contemporary form of world-market metaphysic is nothing new. As with all sorts of metaphysics, Beck observed, also world-market metaphysics, i.e. *globalism*, are expressions of the quest for simplicity in an increasingly complex world.[123] Summing up and following Beck's considerations, *globalism* essentially consists in the application of reductionist, i.e. positivist economics on a global scale.

The essentially metaphysical, i.e. ideological character of *globalism* was further analysed by Ankie Hoogvelt. Working out the difference between *globalism* and globalisation, Hoogvelt noted:

> The distinction between globalization and globalism is all-important. Whereas globalization is an objective, real historical process which marks, in a sentence, the ascendancy of real-time, trans-border economic activity over clock-time economic activity (whether domestic or trans-border), globalism is the reification of this process of globalization as some meta-historical force that develops outside the human agency, conditioning and limiting the scope for action of individuals and collectivities alike, be they nation-states or local groups. Globalism as an ideology adds a belief in the *inescapability* of the transnationalization of economic and financial flows to the existing credos of neo-liberalism, namely the belief in the efficiency of free competitive markets and the belief that this efficiency will maximize benefits for the greatest number of people in the long run.[124]

Ignacio Ramonet, director of the French newspaper *Le Monde diplomatique* from 1990 to 2008, encapsulated the ideological characteristics of *globalism* into the French term *pensée unique*.[125] *Pensée unique*, Ramonet explained, is based on the doctrine of the prevalence of economics over politics. The doctrine of the primacy of economics, in turn, is an expression of a reductionist understanding of economics. *Pensée unique*, Ramonet noted, justifies the primacy of economics by the allegedly 'natural' and hence unalterable character of 'market forces'. In fact, *pensée unique* declared, asserting a 'realist' or 'pragmatic' point of view, that capitalism and 'the market' are the natural state of things.[126] However, the reliance on 'market mechanisms' such as the 'invisible hand' showed the mechanistic, yet atavistic and finally metaphysical character of the *pensée unique* approach. Because of its power to enforce conform thinking, Ramonet compared *pensée unique* with new forms of dogmatism and even catechism and criticised the resulting 'new obscurantism'.[127]

A summary of the story of positivism reads as a narrowing down of (a) holistic beginnings, initiated by Comte and encompassing both scientific and societal issues, to (b) a philosophy of science in the neopositivist era of the Vienna Circle, and finally to (c) the contemporary notion of positivism as a mere method, or instrument, in the hands of scientists and economists.

The contemporary instrumental or functional notion of positivism can be characterised by the five features worked out above. In terms of a recall, these features are (i) scienticism (ii) the imitation of natural sciences by the social sciences, (iii) the belief in positivistic epistemology, (iv) anti-dialectics, (v) scientific/epistemological elitism, (vi) political 'neutrality' and the reduction of positivism to an epistemological method, i.e. the 'positivist method' or 'positivist approach', or *empiriocriticism*. Finally, the positivist approach or method got (vii) a particular spin through US American pragmatism. The resulting positivist method was an effective and allegedly value-neutral tool particularly suitable for combining scientific rigour[128] with economic purposes.

2 Relativist Records

As mentioned above, 'classical' Neopositivists have tried to improve human judgement by logical analysis. Thereby, scientific facts would have been made accessible through scientific methods, i.e. analytical considerations based on logic and mathematics. Contemporary Positivists, in contrast, are emphasising the requirement of improving the scientific pillar of knowledge, i.e. empirical fact-finding. Contemporary positivists seemingly have abandoned the enthusiasm for 'rationalising' human perception through *unified science.*[129] Instead, their calls have shrunken to a request for a strict separation of scientific fact-finding and human judgement, thus forsaking the goal of bridging facts and perception through a bridging and unifying exercise.

The 'pragmatic' turn of contemporary positivists to limit their claims to a call for separating fact-finding and judgement-making operations may be seen as an answer to the critique of epistemologists of Neopositivism. Critics of the neopositivist approach, such as Willard Quine,[130] rose the fundamental question whether findings from the empirical sciences do, in fact, depict the 'real world'. Or are methods applied by empirical sciences themselves inevitably based on prior knowledge of scientists applying them? Harold Kincaid noted:

> Quine, however, denied that we could sharply divide evidence this way, because testing is a holistic affair. Following Duhem (1954), Quine argued that hypotheses do not confront experience or evidence one by one. Rather, testing a single hypothesis requires a host of background theory about the experimental apparatus, measurement theory, what data are relevant, what must be controlled, and so on. So, when experiments fail, they only tell us something is wrong somewhere. We can save any hypothesis from doubt by changing our background assumptions. Theories face the test of evidence as wholes.[131]

On these ground, one might well assume that knowledge is not only based on empirical science, but rather on a 'web of belief'.[132] Scientific activity and conceptual analysis are inevitably surrounded by this 'web of belief'. Again Kincaid:

> All parts of the web are indirectly relevant to all others. There is no absolute way to isolate the analytic, necessary truths from the merely empirical. In the end there are no *a priori* truths. By denying a sharp conceptual – empirical distinction and pointing out the holistic nature of testing, Quine provided the intellectual foundations for a broad change in the philosophy of science.[133]

In the following, epistemological approaches questioning a priori truths are aggregated under the term 'relativism'.[134]

Addressing notions of relativism, Shrader-Frechette referred to different schools of thought. On the one hand, Shrader-Frechette invoked *epistemological anarchism*, as expressed by Paul Feyerabend.[135] On the other hand, Shrader-Frechette extensively quoted from Mary Douglas' and Aaron Wildavsky's work *Risk and Culture*.[136] In the following, the focus is on the latter aspect, i.e. *cultural relativism*.

2.1 Cultural Relativism

Summarising the credo of cultural relativism that 'anything can be justified, given a particular culture', Shrader-Frechette referred, for instance, to Melville Herskovits (1895–1963).[137] Herskovits, though, was not working in isolation but was part of a school of cultural anthropologists and historians with a tradition of similar historical dimension as the school of the positivists. Herskovits himself, for example, did his Ph.D. under the guidance of Franz Boas (1858–1942). Boas, who grew up and studied in Germany before moving to the USA, was a pioneer of modern anthropology. Another proponent of the French tradition of anthropology and epistemological relativisms is Bruno Latour (* 1947).[138]

Contemporary expressions of cultural relativism may appear as multiculturalism and interculturalism. Multiculturalism and interculturalism are both rather well-established approaches, coming along with notions of cultural pluralism and liberal tolerance. Interestingly, though, recent developments started to question these approaches from the perspective of *deconstruction*. Introducing a project examining tango dance as a trans-cultural practice in times of globalisation, Gabriele Klein observed that latest fields of study, such as translation studies and postcolonial studies, are undermining the positions of multiculturalism and interculturalism by questioning the notion of 'cultural identity' itself.[139] Criticism in particular from the perspective of postcolonial studies centres on the fact that both multiculturalism and interculturalism adhere to essentialist concepts of cultural identity. According to multiculturalism and interculturalism, each 'culture' is related to specific essentials, such as ethnicity, religion, skin colour, gender and so forth, which are perceived as predetermined and invariable. Hence, by pretending cultural pluralism, multiculturalism and interculturalism, in fact, are amplifying cultural differences presumed as being set in stone. Following this line of thought, a deconstructivist analysis finds that multiculturalism and interculturalism are implicit bases for liberal states. By enabling the majority to define 'other cultures' and to protect their 'own culture', multiculturalism and interculturalism are understood as expressions of a state defining itself as a 'nation': hence, multiculturalism and interculturalism are perceived as instruments of liberal nation states for maintaining civil stability through the organisation of intercultural exchange.[140]

Deconstruction, in contrast, undermines essentialist presuppositions of multiculturalism and interculturalism by decoding 'culture' as a system of signals. And those inter-related signals, through interaction and communication, are forming people. Klein, following the deconstructivist theory, noted that 'being German, being black or being gay is hence just the product of a cultural activity (…)'.[141]

The deconstruction of multiculturalism and interculturalism corresponds with a transitional phase in the formation of anthropological studies, namely the turn from a functionalist approach to the quest for 'global conversation'. According to Anthony Giddens, anthropology passed through three phases; the first phase of taxonomy, the second phase of functionalism, and the third phase of cosmopolitan conversation.[142] In the first phase of taxonomy, anthropologist and ethnographers, in particular, sought to classify and categorise 'the other' and 'the alien'. Giddens noted that in the phase of taxonomy, '[t]he alien character of other traditions was a persistent source of compelling interest, puzzlement and generalized anxiety (…) the alienness of non-Western traditions was a real counterpart to the "given" form of nature, an external environment of Western expansionism to be "understood" and probably trampled over in much the same way'.[143]

In the second phase of functionalism, anthropologists discovered that 'the other' is essentially as intelligent as they were themselves. However, the acknowledgement of intelligence and hence, equality of 'the other' was contained by functionalism. Giddens observed:

> Functionalism recognizes the authenticity of other traditions, but relates that authenticity only to their inner cohesion, as situated cultural wholes. The integrity of ['other'] traditions thus becomes acknowledged, but the 'dialogic' relation established is one that presumes the separateness of the alien. 'Intelligence' is entirely *contextual*; each culture is adapted to the milieu in which it is 'discovered'.[144]

Referring to the anthropologist Nigel Barley, Giddens described the third phase of anthropological research as 'the recovery of a narrative style', bringing back the author into the plot. Comparing Barley's approach with earlier anthropological attempts, Giddens remarked that '[t]he "absence of the author" in most pre-existing anthropological studies is not a reflection of the fact that the texts speak for themselves; rather, the author is absent because such studies are not full dialogic engagements with "other cultures"'.[145] Full dialogic engagement, in contrast, may provide the possibility 'of a cosmopolitan conversation of humankind'.[146] According to Giddens, self-involvement of anthropologists, following the example of Nigel Barley, might open possibilities for global dialogue, but may come along with a price. Giddens noted:

> Embarrassment and a certain diffuse anxiety, occasionally laced with an awareness of danger, emerge as the prime negative aspects of the anthropological encounter; on the positive side, along with self-illumination, there is humour and the pleasures of discovering a common humanity.[147]

2.2 *Historical Relativism*

Cultural relativism, as expressed by Boas and fellow anthropologists and historians of these times, has common traits with *historicism*, a school of thought particularly connoted to Germany philosophers and historians in the nineteenth century.[148]

A representative of historicism is Wilhelm Dilthey (1833–1911). Dilthey rejected the notion that reality in general and human life, in particular, can be fully apprehended by rational means alone.[149] As a consequence, natural sciences are not appropriate for understanding all aspects of life. Therefore, *human sciences*[150] have to be developed and acknowledged as independent and distinct from natural sciences.[151] Störig observed that Dilthey's thinking, in particular, his view that history shall be the pre-eminent scientific discipline able to understand 'irrational' aspects of human existence, led him on the path towards *relativism*.[152] The focus on 'irrationalism' of nineteenth century historians in Germany may have stemmed from overlaps between the 'historical method' and romanticism. Gadamer explained that it was Dilthey 'who consciously [took] up *romantic hermeneutics* and expand[ed] it into a historical method, indeed, into an epistemology of the human sciences'.[153] And Gadamer also provided some insight into the 'historical method', as applied by Dilthey:

> Dilthey's logical analysis of the concept of continuity in history is, in fact, the application to history of the [romantic] hermeneutical principle that we can understand a detail only in terms of the whole text, and the whole only in terms of the detail.[154]

Dilthey, however, was not alone in considering natural sciences differently from human sciences. Wilhelm Windelband (1848–1915) conceived a dichotomy between nomothetic and idiographic sciences: whereas nomothetic sciences are appropriate for recognising general laws, particularly laws of nature (natural sciences), idiographic sciences are those appropriate for conceiving specific cultural traits (cultural sciences).[155] In focusing on cultural peculiarities in particular in history, Windelband's approach implied a precept for discerning and weighing among the unique and individual. Such a precept was the linkage of cultural characteristics and historical specificities to values.[156] By centring cultural sciences on transcendent values, Windelband marked a counterpoint to empiricism and positivism.[157]

The attempt for individualising the history of specific peoples—above all, Germans—was an intention widespread among historians and philosophers in Germany during the nineteenth century, in particular among conservatives and romantics.[158] An example of a conservative historian was Leopold von Ranke (1795–1886). Ranke dissented with the then hegemonic Hegelian worldview that history is unfolding according to an abstract dialectical process (Hegel's *Weltgeist*).[159] In contrast, Ranke hold that 'every epoch in history is similarly proximate to God'.[160]

It shall be noted that expressions of historical relativism persisted over time. One might even say that the defeat of Germany in World War II and the rise of 'Anglo-Saxon scientific theories' induced some kind of recollection of (German) romanticism. An example of a neo-romanticist philosopher was Hans-Georg Gadamer (1990–2002) and his concept of philosophical *hermeneutics*.[161] In 1959, Gadamer worried whether his book *Truth and Method* might come too late, observing that 'the signs of a new wave of technologic history-aversion were on the rise'.[162] As the cause for the new wave of 'technologic history-aversion', Gadamer identified 'a new positivist self-conception [of the historical sciences], fostered by the reception of American and English methods and problems, pushed forwards'.[163] Essentially, Gadamer contrasted (implicitly German) romantic humanities on the one hand with Anglo-Saxon scientific research, applying new methods such as statistics, formalisation, scientific planning and technical organisation, on the other hand.[164] In contrast to formalised and engineered Anglo-Saxon research methods, Gadamer conceived 'historic human sciences', as he called historical sciences, as rooted in German romanticism. Therefore, Gadamer was of the opinion that historical sciences 'maintained a humanistic heritage which distinguishes them from all other kinds of modern research and brings them close to other, quite different, extra-scientific experiences, and especially those proper to art'.[165]

Instead of a positivist approach, Gadamer established a hermeneutical method towards truth. Considering the hermeneutical method, Sungjoon Cho observed:

> Gadamer was of the view that truth, including scientific truth, may be obtained only through "understanding" or "interpretation" ("hermeneutics") which is a "dialogical-dialectical interchange between interpreter and *interpretandum*". Importantly, understanding cannot be driven from a vacuum. Our attitude toward "interpretandum" (what is interpreted), such as a text, event or other's behavior is pre-determined by pre-understandings of past interpreters to which we are inevitably inherited (linked) through a chain of interpretations ("interpretational lineage"). Interpretation is not "presuppositionless" because an interpreter cannot escape from his or her ontological premise, i.e., a "finite temporal situation as the horizon within which the beings he understands have their initial meaning for him.[166]

It is Gadamer's emphasis of 'belongingness' (in German: *Zugehörigkeit*) and the 'fusion of horizons' as preconditions for 'true understandings' which put him into opposition to positivist claims for universalism. Sungjoon Cho noted that Gadamer's emphasis of presupposition is intentional:

> Note that this pre-understanding is not a mere bias which, in association with enlightenment, is purged by the power of reason, but rather a "belongingness" (*Zugehörigkeit*) to the tradition. This innate historical distance ("alienation") between the interpretandum and the interpreter can be overcome only by the "consciousness of effective history." Only then, the interpretandum's horizon and the interpreter's own horizon are fused ("fusion of horizons"), and an authentic understanding of the interpretandum is achieved. The "universal praxis" of human reason or rationality can no longer monopolize the language of science.[167]

Historical relativism was, however, not unique to Germany. In the Anglo-Saxon hemisphere, historical relativism reappeared in the form of *historical constructivism*. A mentor of historical constructivism in the USA was Thomas Samuel Kuhn (1922–1996). In his momentous work *The Structure of Scientific Revolutions* (1996), Kuhn 'argued that the history of science exhibits certain ruptures of development, so-called scientific revolutions, such that between successor theories there obtain conceptual incommensurabilities which render an algorithmic choice and claims to straightforward continuity between them impossible'.[168] In contrast, Kuhn was of the view that 'much of normal, non-revolutionary science proceeds by puzzle-solving within a so-called paradigm (a disciplinary matrix of conceptual frame, experimental procedures and exemplary solutions) whose basic assumptions remain unquestioned except in periods of crisis'.[169] For such views, Kuhn became 'the historian of science most closely associated with the rejection of positivist philosophy of science and the turn to a socio-historical approach in its place'.[170]

2.3 Romanticism

Emphasising singular periods and peoples in history is a rather common trait in German historiography, dating back to the philosopher, Johann Gottfried von Herder (1744–1803). Herder, a historian and philologist, amongst other things, was particularly interested in individual expressions of cultures and peoples, calling it *Volksgeist*.[171] The novelty of Herder's thinking was, according to Störig, that every age and every people embody a unique purpose on its own, not adjacent to another age and other peoples living before or afterwards.[172] In other words, Herders' perception of history is not one of evolutionary development from one stage to another, but that of a multiplicity of cultural expressions stemming from one single transcendent origin.[173] Thereby, Herder's metaphysics run counter to Kantian philosophy.[174] As Störig observed, a predominant aspect of the philosophy of Immanuel Kant (1724–1804) is the dualistic differentiation between the world of sensations and the world of reason, a dichotomy which Herder rejected.[175]

However, Herder's opposition to Kant and the reference to Kantian philosophy provide insight into basic features of both relativism and positivism. According to Störig, the dualistic philosophy of Kant subsequently transposed into two contrarian philosophical strands, namely idealism, on the one hand, and positivism and materialism on the other hand.[176] It has to be noted that, although contrarian in their worldviews, both philosophical strands, i.e. idealism and positivism/materialism, were stemming from the Kantian source. But were to put relativism and historicism? Störig explained that, as a reaction against Kantian rationalism, a protest movement emerged, called *romanticism*.[177] Störig found that relativism and historicism are expressions of the romantic protest movement against Kantian rationalism.[178]

Scott Lash, analysing features of modernity and reflections about modernity, came to similar conclusions. Lash observed that romanticism was basically a reflection of the tradition of scientism:

> In this sense there are paradigmatically not one but two modernities, the first with scientific assumptions traversing a genealogy including Galileo, Hobbes, Descartes, Locke, the Enlightenment, (the mature) Marx, Corbusier, sociological positivism, analytic philosophy and Habermas. The other modernity is aesthetic. Apart from brief surfacings in the baroque, in some Dutch landscapes, it appears with vigour as a critique of the first modernity in nineteenth-century Romanticism and aesthetic modernism. If we are to understand reflexivity in the sense of the sociologists of science as the self-reflection of a paradigm, then late nineteen-century literary and artistic modernism was the first time that modernity became properly reflexive. The lineage of this second modernity, which grew through reflection on and as a reflex in regard to the first is Romanticism, the young Hegel, Baudelaire, Nietzsche, Simmel, surrealism, Benjamin, Adorno, Heidegger, Schultz, Gadamer, Foucault, Derrida, and (in contemporary sociology) Baumann.[179]

From the observations of Lash, one is able to identify the first characterstic of Romanticism, that is, a rejection, yet a veritable rebellion, against the impositions of that first modernity coming along with scientific rigour and the corresponding demystification of man and nature. Instead, a longing for embeddedness in nature displays a deeply rooted scepticism against the materialistic promises of modern science and technology. In this perspective, Romanticism can be characterised as being 'anti-science'.

A second observation of Lash sheds light on the essence of the romantic revolt: as intrinsically 'non-rational', Romanticism expresses itself rather artistically than by abstract thinking. Thus, romantics emphasise the importance of the (German) language as an expression of the spirit of the (German) people (*Volksgeist*), and artists such as the lyric Friedrlich Hölderin (1770–1843) and the illustrious composer Richard Wagner (1813–1883) found fertile grounds.[180] Hence, Romantic expression works with lyrics rather than scientific treatises, targeting on sensation rather than intellectual processing.

As third observation reads that precisely because of their often euphuistic diction, romantic thinkers barely attracted the attention of their academic peers usually deeply involved in the 'scientific modernity' (to use Lash's label). Nevertheless, it has to be pointed out that a line of thinking, or, to put it more specific, a sense of spiritual belonging can be retraced from Herder's "national character' (*Volksgeist*) and Dilthey's 'philosophy of life' (*Lebensphilosophie*) to Dilthey to Houston Stewart Chamberlain's 'Foundations of the Nineteenth Century' (1899), Owald Spengler's 'Decline of the West' (1918/1922) and Martin Heidegger's fundamental ontology, his critique of technology, calling technology an 'enframing' (*Gestell*), and his affiliation with Nazism. Therefore, a specific aspect of this variation of relativism is barely addressed from a scientific point of view, that is, the potential of popular movements rooted in historical relativism—in its romantic expression—for annihilating 'the other'. In sharp contrast to postmodernism, as it is shown below, romanticism stemming from historical relativism is far from being tolerant. Patrick J.J. Phillips, with the aim to combat the misapprehension that relativism is per se tolerant, provided the example of Carl Schmitt (1888–1985) for demonstrating the tendency towards nihilism inherent to neoromantic relativism. Phillips observed:

> In the absence, indeed the impossibility, of an overarching set of moral and political principles or imperatives, and in his denial of the possibility of objective deliberation between differing political or moral viewpoints, Schmitt is identified as sharing the relativis camp. But surprisingly his conclusions are not those one might intuitively expect of a relativist. For Schmitt does not conclude on the basis of his account of the subjectivity of all moral

> and political principles that all beliefs regarding such matters *ought* to or *must* be respected and tolerated. But rather, that the process of politics is a battleground between on the one hand self-defined friends and on the other hand enemies who wish to subvert, or have the potential to subvert, their goals. (…) Starkly, Schmitt believed that that the realization of relativism leads, inexorably, to a dismissal of the rational element in politics and ethics and demanded the necessity for the dominance of the powerful over the weak, even to the point of the annihilation of those who disagreed or dissented from the party line. For Schmitt, might makes right and this in turn renders life nasty, brutish and short for his political opponents.[181]

This characterising feature, i.e. the tendency to debase those identified as 'others', discerns today's successors of historical relativism from their counterparts rooting in cultural relativism.[182] A second characterising feature of today's expressions of historical relativism is its scorn against reason and comprehensible argument. Two examples may help to explain these two features distinguishing the two modern expressions of relativism:

> Whereas modern representatives of cultural relativism, for example, Peter Singer, are eager to gather and to provide scientific evidence for demonstrating the familiarity between human beings and primates, this is not the case with today's representatives of historical relativism; white supremacist Richard B. Spencer, for example, gives little attention to scientific evidence supporting—or disputing—his racial ideology.

Based on the findings that modern expressions of cultural relativism are, firstly, upholding the ideal of reasonable, that is, refutable, argumentation and are, secondly, on an instrincically emancipatory mission for universal equality, their rooting in romanticism is not easy to notice. The very essence of their romanticism is, in fact, their adherence to a presupposed and postmodern utopia which shall come after the fall of the rational, but unjust capitalist system and bringing along universal freedom, equality and justice, whereas the way to materialise this utopia is reasonable and rational. For this reason, modern expressions of cultural relativism are identified as universalistic and emancipatory and summarised under the term postmodernism.

Ramifications of historical relativism, on the other hand, are identified as putting sentiment over reason, and to array along identitarian, i.e. folkish (*völkisch* in German) lines. For this reason, modern expressions of historical relativism are identified as nationalistic and reactionary and summarised under the term neo-romanticism.

2.4 From Scientific Relativity to Relativism

Interestingly, certain theories developed by natural sciences themselves turned out as gateways for modern expressions of relativism. Most important in this regard were Albert Einstein's theory of relativity published in 1905,[183] the formulation of the uncertainty principle by Werner Heisenberg in 1926, and the establishment of quantum theories by Heisenberg, Erwin Schrödinger and Paul Dirac in the 1920s.[184]

The reception of these modern theories of science showed some paradoxical effects. On the one hand, modern scientific theories virtually annihilated Laplace's doctrine of scientific determinism.[185] Stephen Hawking noted:

> The uncertainty principle had profound implications for the way in which we view the world. Even after more than fifty years they have not been fully appreciated by many philosophers, and are still the object of much controversy. The uncertainty principle signaled an end to Laplace's dream of a theory of science, a model of the universe that would be completely deterministic: one certainly cannot predict future events exactly if one cannot even measure the present state of the universe precisely![186]

Albeit the end of scientific determinism destroyed the illusion of scientific predictability and positiveness, it paradoxically (re-)opened a gateway for new kinds of metaphysics. Hawking observed:

> In general, quantum mechanics does not predict a single definite result for an observation. Instead, it predicts a number of different possible outcomes and tells us how likely each of these is. (…) Quantum mechanics therefore introduces an unavoidable element of unpredictability or randomness into science. Einstein objected to this very strongly, despite the important role he had played in the development of these ideas. (…) Einstein never accepted that the universe was governed by chance; his feelings were summed up in his famous statement 'God does not play dice'. Most other scientists, however, were willing to accept quantum mechanics because it agreed perfectly with experiment.[187]

Using the example of the theory of relativity, John Desmond Bernal showed how scientific theories may become instrumental for the (re-) establishment of 'mystical subjectivism'.[188] In this regard, Bernal emphasised the key role scientists, in particular physicists and mathematicians, are playing in popularising science. Bernal observed that for popularising scientific findings, 'eminent scientists who from time to time write about their own science in relation to wider problems', such as philosophical, political or religious issues, are taking centre stage.[189] Bernal noted:

> More particularly, one of the most notable factors is the preponderance of physicists and mathematicians among those who speak for general science. (…) Now the theoretical physicists, from their primary concern with mathematical formulae, are apt to pass over very easily into metaphysics, and cone that boundary is passed it is very difficult to put a stop to loose thinking. The mathematician is not critical of the actuality of things: the most absurd statement can be readily accepted as long as they make a formal logical whole. Nature itself is for the physicist simply a set of observations to be reduced to mathematical formulae – to reduce the most extravagant theologies to other formulae gives them equal satisfaction – witness the great Hindu mathematicians and even Newton, one of the most concrete-minded of great physicists. This lack of a sense of reality, coupled almost invariably with an absence of psychological criticism, leads to an almost *mystical subjectivism* once the boundaries of strict science are crossed.[190]

Turning to the theory of relativity, in particular, Bernal observed that this theory was welcomed for, at first glance, astounding reasons:

> The idea of the theory of relativity as a destruction of absolutes was (…) successful because it formed a bridge between the tendencies of science and philosophico-religious speculation. The religious-minded thinker, finding that an absolute religious dogmatism was impossible to maintain in face of science and that is was equally impossible for him to accept a dogmatic science, seized on such ideas as the dependence of the truth of the observer's point of view and the formal subjective explanation of the "force" of gravitation as ways of reconciling himself without inconsistency to both worlds.[191]

Bernal, however, went further and suggested a Marxist framework for understanding the remarkable re-mystification of science in the early twentieth century. Bernal's analysis is displayed not only because of its explanatory value, but also for reiterating the point that scientific theories, for example, concepts of risk, are based upon philosophical foundations, such as positivism and relativism respectively, which in turn are influenced by political considerations. Bernal explained:

> The temporary stabilisation of capitalism between 1921 and 1929 was an opportunity for reviewing the relations of science and religion in the light of the new discoveries, and of the recent political events. The need for a reconciliation between science and religion was greater than ever, because for the first time in history there existed not only a body of men but a powerful and growing state in which religion had been openly proclaimed unnecessary and harmful, while science was to be the basis of the reconstruction of material and social life. The fear and the portent of the Russian Revolution overshadows all popular scientific writing of the time. It was not difficult to find opportunities for a new reconciliation in the recent advances of science. The first great opportunity was Einstein's relativity theory which has given rise to as much popular nonsense as it has to intricate mathematics. Because, owing to the presence of matter, we cannot see quite straight, or as scientists prefer to put it, space is curved, philosophers argue that nobody really knows anything about anything, and that it all depends on your point of view. Even the much more important quantum theory, which has given us an immensely extended understanding and control over chemical and electrical processes, is made in the hands of [James] Jeans[192] an opportunity for similar mysticism.[193]

Interestingly, some of these scientists who are sharing their views with the public, as mentioned by Bernal, are seemingly merging features of positivism, i.e. the quest for a unified scientific theory, with characteristics of relativist metaphysics, namely the regress to some supernatural entity.[194] Stephen Hawking, probably the most prominent of today's physicists, observed that the search for a unified scientific theory has a long tradition of followers, among others and most prominent, Albert Einstein.[195] And Hawking himself endorsed the objective of 'unified science', noting that '[t]he eventual goal of science is to provide a single theory that describes the whole universe'.[196] Hawking himself, by drawing the following parameters for a unified theory of science, provided an example of merging the positivist objective of 'unified science' with metaphysical religious ideas:

> When we combine quantum mechanics with general relativity, there seems to be a new possibility that did not arise before: that space and time together might form a finite, four-dimensional space without singularities or boundaries, like the surface of the earth but with more dimensions. (…) But if the universe is completely self-contained, with no singularities or boundaries, and completely described by a unified theory, that has profound implications of the role of God as Creator.[197]

The merging of features of positivism, in particular, its quest for a holistic scientific theory, with characteristics of relativist metaphysics became particularly popular among the *New Age* movement. New Age thinkers tried to link up modern physics with various elements of mysticism, religion and other forms of metaphysics. New Age representative Fritjof Capra, for example, drew analogies between Heisenberg's wave-particle duality and Chinese Taoism (Yin-Yang complementarity).[198] Interestingly, though, Capra also included economics into his analysis and called for its renewal in line with a new and holistic awareness. In particular, Capra argued that a post-mechanistic economic theory must take into account not only ecological, sociologic, political and psychological data, but should 'clearly bear a relation to cultural phenomena'.[199] On the whole, Capra's and other New Age philosophers' work can be considered as attempts to overcome the dualistic worldview established by Descartes, namely the mind–body dichotomy (*res cogitans/res extensa*).[200]

Certain scientific disciplines seem to be particularly prone to religious allusions. Beside astrophysics and environmental sciences, religious arguments have been aired clearly audible by evolutionary biologists and genetic engineers. In evolutionary biology, an increasing trend can be observed ascribing evolution to metaphysical forces by purporting the theory of 'intelligent design (ID)'. A proponent of 'intelligent design' is, for example, biochemist Michael Behe, author of the book *Darwin's Black Box* (1996).[201] In genetics, Dr. Richard Seed is an example of a physicist and genetic engineer justifying his call for human cloning with religious arguments.[202] Particular novel technologies such as space sciences, robotics, computer sciences, genetic engineering and nanotechnology are often laden with a certain promise for transcendency.[203]

2.5 Postmodernism and Populism

In *A House Built on Sand* (1998), Noretta Koertge addressed what she called 'Postmodernists', i.e. Relativists, as proponents of 'interdisciplinary endeavors called Science, Technology, and Society Studies (STS) or Science and Culture Studies'.[204] Under the term STS or Science and Culture Studies, Koertge subsumed a wide array of disciplines and approaches: 'Within their veritable carnival of approaches and methodologies we find feminists and Marxists of every stripe, ethnomethodologists, deconstructionists, sociologists of knowledge and critical theorists—those who find significance in rhetoric and others who emphasize the role of patronage and the power of empire'.[205] Koertge went on to summarise precepts she considered 'to be widely shared' by proponents of STS or Science and Culture Studies, i.e. Relativists, in the following, rather polemic, language:

- Every aspect of that complex set of enterprises that we call science, including, above all, its content and results, is shaped by and can be understood only in its local historical and cultural context.
- In particular, the products of scientific inquiry, the so-called laws of nature, must always be viewed as social constructs. Their validity depends on the consensus of "experts" in just the same way as the legitimacy of a pope depends on a council of cardinals.
- Although scientists typically succeed in arrogating special epistemic authority to themselves, scientific knowledge is just "one story among many". The more epistemological authority that science has in a given society, the more important it is to unmask its pretensions to be an enterprise dedicated to the pursuit of objective knowledge. Science must be "humbled".
- Since the quest for objective knowledge is a quixotic one, the best way to appraise scientific claims is through a process of political evaluation. Since the "evidence" for a scientific claim is never conclusive and is always open to negotiation, the best way to evaluate scientific results is to ask who stands to benefit if the claim is taken to be true. Thus, for the citizen the key question about scientific result should not be how well tested the claim is but, rather, Cui bono?
- "Science is politics by other means": the results of scientific inquiry are profoundly and importantly shaped by the ideological agendas of powerful elites.
- There is no univocal sense in which the science of one society is better than that of another. In particular, Euroscience is not objectively superior to the various ethnosciences and shamanisms described by anthropologists or invented by Afrocentrists.
- Neither is there any clear sense in which we can talk about scientific progress within the European tradition. On the contrary, science is characterized chiefly by its complicity in all the most negative and oppressive aspects of modern history: increasingly destructive warfare, environmental disaster, racism, sexism, eugenics, exploitation, alienation and imperialism.

- Given the impossibility of scientific objectivity, it is futile to exhort scientists and policymakers to try harder to remove ideological bias from the practice of science. Instead, what we need to do is deliberately introduce "corrective biases" and "progressive political values" into science. There is a call for "emancipatory science" and "advocacy research".[206]

Leading over to the focus on trade disputes, certain particular expressions of relativism shall be introduced at this point, namely relativism with respect to gender, animal rights and the environment. These topics are exemplifying problems of separating facts and values.

From a theoretical perspective, feminism, gender studies and the LGBTQ[207] movement may also be seen in the tradition of deconstruction. In this respect, feminism may be perceived as a particular form of relativism because it deconstructed, *inter alia*, alleged universalism implied in words such as 'man', 'human' and 'mankind'. Focusing on economic aspects and gender studies in particular, Kathi von Daeniken and Brigitte Schnegg defined the use of gender as an analytical category to challenge 'the assumption that markets, trade policies and trade agreements are gender neutral'.[208] Well to the contrary, Alessandro Nicita and Simonetta Zarrilli observed that trade effects are different across gender:

> Due to cultural, economic and social factors, the effects of trade policies on economic and social activities tend to be different across gender. Women and men may have different skills, different economic and social roles, and different access to resources. The main issue relating trade and gender is that to reap the full benefit from trade integration, economies and workers have to adapt. This adaptation problem is more relevant for countries with rigid labour and capital markets, and for women, who in general are, in an economic sense, less able to adjust. This handicap originates because of women relative disadvantages in term of education, command over resources and in gaining access to credit, new technologies, training, and marketing networks.[209]

As an analytical category, gender may also provide useful insights with regard to epistemology. In *Coming to Understand. Orgasm and the Epistemology of Ignorance (2008)*, Nancy Tuana came to the following interesting conclusions, *inter alia*:

- Any complete epistemology must include a study of ignorance, not just knowledge.
- Ignorance—far from being a simple, innocent lack of knowledge—is a complex phenomenon, which, like knowledge, is interrelated with power. For example, ignorance is frequently constructed, and it is linked to issues of cognitive authority, trust, doubt, silencing, and so forth.
- While many feminist science studies theorists have embraced the interrelationship of knowledge and values, we must also see the ways in which ignorance, too, is so interrelated. (…)[210]

Furthermore, feminism seems to be a good example for showing the persistence of philosophical traditions in modern schools of thought. In his book *The new ecological order* (1995), Luc Ferry discerned between an 'existentialist' or 'republican' feminism of a Simone de Beauvoir in *The Second Sex* (1949),[211] and a distinct expression of feminism called *ecofeminism*. Luc Ferry summarised characterising features of the early existentialist or republican feminism as follows: 'The result is a feminism that is humanist (refusing to confuse humanity and animality), egalitarian (women are no more bound than men to the determinations of nature), and republican (it is by breaking away from the sphere of the particular determinations of nature in general that one rises to the universality of culture and ethics)'.[212] Ecofeminism, in contrast, relates the oppression of women to the oppression of nature, both enforced by men. From an ecofeminist perspective, 'the only truly relevant question [is]: How can the ties uniting the domination of women and that of nature *by males* be described? The deconstruction of the humanist tradition, which is, of course, called for in both cases, cannot be fully accomplished if one fails to perceive that the critique of anthropocentrism must be replaced by that of *androcentrism*'.[213] As a result, ecofeminism takes a rather different stance compared to early existentialist feminism 'by affirming her *difference* from "males," by insisting instead on her *specific* proximity to nature, that the women, like the proletariat in day past, incarnates the redemptive portion of humanity'.[214] Looking at the root of the emphasis on difference by ecofeminism and its ecological component, Luc Ferry observed:

> … [T]he origin of and link between the exploitation of women and that of nature can be explained by three at times divergent philosophical positions. The first traces this double oppression to the appearance of *dualism*, the second

> to that of *mechanistic science*, while the third bases it directly on *difference*, on sexually differentiated personality formation or consciousness.[215]

Vandana Shiva, for example, observed a dualism in economic approaches. Whereas she related growth-oriented economics to patriarchy, Shiva conceived a *sustenance economy* based on women:

> In the sustenance economy, people work to directly provide the conditions necessary to maintain their lives. This is the economy through which human production and reproduction is primarily possible. It is the women's economy where, because of the patriarchal division of labor, societal reproduction takes place. Women's work provides sustenance and support to all human activities – including the visible activities of the marked dominated economy. The sustenance economy is the economy of the two-thirds of humanity engaged in craft production, peasant agriculture, artisanal fishing, and indigenous forest economies. The sustenance economy includes all spheres in which humans produce in balance with nature and reproduce society through partnerships, mutuality, and reciprocity.[216]

Based on such findings, Luc Ferry located ecofeminism close to the *deep ecology* movement.[217] Considering the human–nature relationship, Luc Ferry distinguished between three different approaches; the first is anthropocentric, the second is 'utilitarian', and the third is *ecocentric* or *deep ecology*. Ferry explained:

> The first is no doubt the most ordinary, but it is also the least doctrinaire and, therefore, the least dogmatic; it is based on the idea that, by protecting nature, man is still first and foremost protecting himself, even if it is from himself in his capacity as mad scientist. The environment is endowed with no intrinsic value here. Rather this scenario stems from an awareness that by destroying the milieu that surrounds him, man may be endangering his own existence or, at the very least, depriving himself of the conditions for a good life on this earth. Thus nature is taken only *indirectly* into consideration, based on a position that may be classified as 'humanist,' even *anthropocentrist*; it is considered merely to be the human environment, literally that which surrounds him – the periphery, then, and not the center. As such, it cannot be considered a legal subject, an entity possessing absolute value in and of itself.
>
> The second current takes a step in the direction of attributing moral significance to certain nonhuman beings. It consists in giving serious consideration

> to the 'utilitarian' principle according to which one must not only look out for man's best interests, but, more generally, try to both diminish the total suffering in the world as much as possible and increase the quantity of well-being. From this perspective, which is quite common in the Anglo-Saxon world, where it is the basis for the enormous animal liberation movement, all beings capable of feeling pleasure and pain must be considered legal subjects and treated as such. (...)
>
> The third tendency is the one we have seen at work in the call for the rights of trees, which is to say of nature in and of itself, including in its vegetable and mineral forms. (...) For this is the primary issue in this third version of ecology – that the old 'social contract' devised by political thinkers must give way to a 'natural contract,' in which the entire universe becomes a subject of law: it is no longer a matter of defending man, considered as the center of the world, from himself, but rather of defending the *cosmos* from him. The ecosystem or 'biosphere' is endowed with an intrinsic value far superior to that of this species – this generally quite destructive species that is the human race.[218]

With respect to the third tendency observed by Luc Ferry, i.e. ecocentrism, attention has to be drawn to Arne Naess (1912–2009). Naess, the founder of the *deep ecology* movement, argued in favour of a value-oriented approach and normative evaluations of environmental risks. With a view on environmental questions, Naess held that '[o]bjective science cannot provide principles for action'.[219] Naess observed:

> In the early days of the growth of ecological consciousness, ecologists sometimes said things like 'knowledge about what should not be done ... is derived from the sciences and particularly from ecology.' (K. Cadwell, quoted in Darling [1965]). Statements like this encourage the untenable belief that, if only the grants to ecological and other scientific studies were large enough, the experts could *derive* a conclusion about what we can do. *But we cannot act without norms*! If, because of waterway pollution, we decide that a factory must be shut down or moved, we accept, in addition to the more or less scientific hypotheses about the effects of waterway pollution, a long string of evaluations which are not part of any science: 'waterways *ought* not be poisoned!', 'the employees of the factory *ought* not to go without work'.[220]

Based on his relativist point of view, Naess consistently rejected any generalisation of environmental studies. By so doing, Naess also refuted attempts for enhancing ecology to some kind of paramount, yet universal science as *Ecologism:*

> Many of those who emphasise the tremendous breadth of ecology tend, simultaneously, to limit it somewhat. They conceive of it as a natural science or use primarily examples characteristic of natural science. (...) Ecology may comprise a great deal, but is should never be considered a *universal science*. When concentrating on the relations between things, of course many aspects of their limited separateness are ignored. Ecologism is excessive universalisation or generalisation of ecological concepts and theories. The attempt to fully replace the theory of knowledge with certain ecological theories about behaviour and survival leads to very great difficulties ('labyrinthine epistemology') or, more correctly, one encounters great inconsistency and paradox. (Naess, 1939)[221]

Turning to the relationship between science and policy, Naess pointed at the fact that objectivistic scientific approaches are often used as pretexts for political procrastination: 'The general attitude among politicians has been that if a major type of interference in the ecosystem cannot be *proven* to be bad then it is justifiable to continue with business as usual'.[222] In other words, positivist, i.e. value-free approaches in science may translate into similarly value-neutral political positions, which, however, may often be used as disguised dilatory tactics.

In contrast, Naess put forward a concept called *Ecosophy*. As Naess explained, the term *Ecosophy* is partially drawn from the world *philosophy* which can mean either a particular field of study or 'one's own personal code of values and a view of the world which guides one's own decisions (insofar as one does fullheartedly fell and think they are the right decisions)'.[223] Using philosophy in that latter sense, Naess described the relativist component of *Ecosophy* as follows:

> We study ecophilosophy, but to approach practical situations involving ourselves, we aim to develop our own ecosophies. In this book, I introduce one ecosophy (...) You are not expected to agree with all of its values and paths of derivation, but to learn the means for developing your own systems or guides (...) Saying 'your own' does not imply that the ecosophy is in any way an original creation by yourself. It is enough that it is a kind of total view which you feel at home with, 'where you philosophically belong'. Along with one's own life, it is always changing.[224]

The brief survey on the three ecological approaches showed an increasing degree of relativism: The first approach was associated with the philosophical concept of *Rationalism*, as developed by philosopher René Descartes, denying any claim for rights for non-human beings. The second approach was related to *utilitarianism*, attributing some sorts of rights at least to animals. Whereas the first and second approach is sticking to *anthropocentrism*, the third approach, i.e. deep ecology, virtually transcends to new forms of *ecocentrism* or *biocentrism*. Thereby, deep ecology challenges dominant worldviews of Cartesianism and utilitarianism. With respect to the antagonism between anthropocentric and ecocentric worldviews, Luc Ferry observed that 'the theses at war in *the conflict between ecocentrism and anthropocentrism ultimately never manage to define the basic facts of the problem. One accords too much to nature, the other too little, each side finding solace, as in any opposition, in the adversary's weaknesses*'.[225] In search of philosophical roots of anthropocentrism and ecocentrism respectively, it is easy to associate Cartesian and utilitarian approaches to 'rational' schools of thought rooted in the Enlightenment, Humanism and the French Revolution. Again Luc Ferry:

> [B]eginning with Cartesianism and its struggle against medieval animism, the idea took form that true nature is not the nature we perceive directly through our senses but the nature we grasp through an effort of the *intellect*. According to Descartes, it is through reason that we apprehend the essence of things. And what the French classics would call 'nature' is precisely this essential reality, which is opposed to the appearances that are readily able to be perceived.[226]

If Cartesianism is at the origin of anthropocentric concepts of nature, what then are the philosophical roots of ecocentrism? Luc Ferry identified sentimentalism and romanticism as the bases for ecocentric concepts. Luc Ferry observed:

> It was against this classical vision of beauty that the aesthetics of sentiment revolted. Far from being mathematical, crafted, and human, here true nature is associated with *original authenticity*, the feeling for which we have lost, as Rousseau would have it, due to the culture of sciences and the arts. Thus what is natural is not at issue here, as it was among the classics, but rather what *is not yet denatured*, what is in its 'primitive state'. Forests, mountains, and oceans reassert their place against the artifice of geometry.[227]

In contrast to Cartesianism, sentimentalism recognised the intrinsic value in nature and considered humans as part and parcel of it. However, it took romanticism to reverse the value balance in favour of nature and to the detriment of men. According to the romantic conception, '[n]ature is defined as "Life", as the "divine" union of body and soul, of sensibility and reason'.[228] Thereby, romanticism honoured 'nature' by associating it with the lost golden age, apprehensible only by sentiment, not by reason.[229] According to Luc Ferry, it was the veneration of 'authentic nature' and its apprehension through sentiment which made romantic conceptions of nature prone to Nazi ideology. Ferry wrote:

> It was essentially these two themes that Nazi ecology would retain, opposing French, rationalist, humanist classicism, full of artifice, and the '*German*' image of an original nature – primitive, pure, virgin, authentic, and irrational, because accessible *only thorough the paths of sentiment*.[230]

In his attempt to demonstrate links from Nazi ecology to contemporary expressions of environmentalism, in particular, deep ecology, Luc Ferry observed increasing intrinsic value attributed to 'nature' by National Socialists. The baseline was marked by attempts for Germanising (*verdeutschen*) the word 'nature' into *Urlandschaft*, 'earth' or 'original land'. But at the horizon emerged the contours of modern forms of animism. With particular reference to Walther Schoenichen[231] and Wilhelm Heinrich Riehl,[232] Ferry observed a 'deconstruction of the primacy of individual interests' and an early call for rights to non-human beings:

> With such a definition, Nazi ecology essentially preestablishes a link between the aesthetics of sentiment and what would later become the central theme of deep ecology: the idea that the natural world is *worthy of respect in and of itself*, independent of all human considerations. Thus Schoenichen particularly emphasizes the texts of Wilhelm Heinrich Riehl, which foreshadow the 'environmentalist' critique of utilitarian – hence *anthropocentric* – justifications for ecology: '(...) We must protect the forest, not only so that the stove will not go cold in winter, but to that the pulse of the people may continue to beat in joyous, vital warmth, so that Germany will remain German. ... For centuries, we have been bombarded with the ideas that it is progress to defend the rights of cultivated lands. But now we are saying that it is progress to demand the rights of the wild nature next to these lands. And not only the rights of the wooded lands, but also of the sand dunes, swamps, garigues, reefs, and glaciers!'[233]

With respect to the human–animal relationship, in particular, Hans-Peter Breβler identified several philosophical responses to the anthropocentrism of René Descartes. From a humanist perspective, Michel de Montaigne and David Hume called for benevolence and compassion also for animals.[234] Immanuel Kant considered animals as beings without consciousness. Therefore, Kant conceived the prohibition of animal abuse primarily as a protection against brutalising impacts on humans.[235] However, Breβler retraced effective beginnings of equalising humans and animals with works of Jean-Jacques Rousseau (1712–1778) and the utilitarian Jeremy Bentham (1748–1832).[236] Hermann Samuel Reimarus (1694–1768) and Georg Friedrich Meier (1718–1777) already developed an antithesis to Descartes' view of animals as machines, depicting the Creation as a unity to which all beings belong.[237] However, according to Breβler it was Henry Salt (1851–1993) who invented the term 'animal rights', relying on Charles Darwin's theory of evolution and the affinity of sensitive beings.[238] Finally, Breβler also mentioned Arthur Schopenhauer (1788–1860) and his advocacy for animal welfare.[239] The overview on the human–animal relationship provided by Breβler confirms observations made by Luc Ferry with regard to the evolving nature of philosophical approaches towards nature and animals in particular. Whereas first critics of the Cartesian view on animals as machines applied anthropocentric or utilitarian considerations, later and more fundamental anti-Cartesian criticism displayed a romanticist mindset.

Eduard Kaeser explained this duality as two traditions in biology, each applying a different ethos in scientific research. The first tradition is the one of René Descartes and Francis Bacon, establishing *dissecare naturam*, meaning to dissect nature, as scientific method. Kaeser termed this first approach to scientific research as the 'ethos of objectivity'. Based on the objectivism of such a 'philosophy of dissection', animals became virtually *res extensa*, i.e. extended objects.[240] The second tradition covers approaches which perceive living beings as fellow creatures, 'maybe even as fellow subjects', as Kaeser observed. Kaeser called this second approach to scientific research the 'ethos of solidarity'.[241]

Luc Ferry summarised the dualism between Cartesian and romanticist worldviews and their continuing ramifications till today in the following words:

> Our entire democratic culture, our entire economic, industrial, intellectual, and artistic history since the French Revolution has been marked, for basic philosophical reasons, by the glorification of *uprootedness*, or *innovation*,

> which amounts to the same thing – a glorification which romanticism, followed by fascism and Nazism, have continually denounced as ruinous to national identity, even to local particularities and customs. The antihumanism of these movements, which was explicit on a cultural level, was accompanied by a concern for rootedness that lent itself to the development of a great attraction to ecology.[242]

As a conclusion, one may observe that studies conducted by Luc Ferry and others established links between the philosophical tradition of romanticism and certain manifestations of modern environmentalism, in particular, the *deep ecology* movement. For doing so, it was inevitable pointing at interlinks between romanticism and *deep ecology*, in particular, Nazi ecology. In the scope of the thesis at hand, the objective was not to associate, or inculpate, *deep ecology* and other limbs of modern environmentalism with Nazism or other forms of totalitarianism.[243] The sole objective of making reference to historical and philosophical origins of nature conservancy, the animal rights movement, ecofeminism and environmentalism at large was to shed light on philosophical traditions extending to contemporary disputes. From the narrow perspective of the study at hand, the capacity to understand opposing philosophical and epistemological roots underpinning different positions in international trade disputes, such as disputes over livestock cloning, hormone treatment of cattle and the use of genetically modified organisms (GMOs) in agriculture, is considered to be a necessary condition for any agreement upon thorny issues.[244]

Thus, understanding opposing worldviews is considered a precondition for overcoming the rational—irrational dualism frivolously applied in risk disputes. Understanding philosophical roots of different risk concepts may foreclose the easy resort of accusing the opponent of being 'rationalist' or 'irrational'. Understanding the broader worldview within which the opponent is assessing risks may even challenge traditional understandings of 'rationality'. In fact, risk assessments may provide variable outcomes depending on the point of reference: whether I consider a risk from my individual perspective of profit maximisation, or whether I consider a risk from the perspective of my family, my kinship, my nation, my gender, my denomination, or from the perspective of the entire globe or even the whole cosmos, may provide different, but equally 'rational' outcomes.

To demonstrate effects on risk and risk assessment contingent upon whether a positivist or a relativist perspective is adopted, the example of agriculture is invoked in the following chapter. However, to conclude the chapter at hand, an overview over opposing worldviews, in particular, positivism and relativism, is provided.

3 Globalism vs. Alter-Globalisation

Summing up, one can arrange positivism and relativism into the following broader picture: From Kantian philosophy, two contrarian strands of philosophical thought evolved, namely idealism on the one hand and materialism/positivism, on the other hand. Additionally, as a reaction against Kantian rationalism, romanticism emerged as a protest movement, from which derived historicism and relativism. Another protest movement was anarchism, rebelling against capitalist exploitation in the emerging industrial society.[245] Although close to Marxism at first glance, anarchism is rooted in a different philosophical tradition, namely the libertarian tradition.[246] Libertarian traditions can be observed long before Pierre-Joseph Proudhon (1809–1865), in particular in the philosophical school of the Stoics, established by Zeno of Citium.[247] Marxism, in turn, is located between materialism and idealism. The reason for this is that, albeit claiming to be solely based on materialist considerations,[248] the dialectical component in Marxism refers back to Hegelian thinking.

Over time, the scientific world-conception narrowed down to a mere method, sometimes called empiriocriticism or positivist approach. Features characterising the positivist approach have been established as (i) scienticism (ii) the imitation of natural sciences by the social sciences, (iii) the belief in positivistic epistemology, (iv) anti-dialectics, (v) scientific/epistemological elitism, (vi) political 'neutrality' and the reduction of positivism to an epistemological method called 'positivist approach'. Finally, the positivist approach (vii) received a business-oriented spin through US American Pragmatism. As a result, contemporary expressions of the positivist approach are allegedly value-neutral but, in fact, effective tools for the pursuit of economic ends by scientific means. Unsurprisingly, though, positivist approaches in various disciplines, particularly in economics, have become influential tools advocating for market expansion and economic universalism, i.e. globalisation.

Positivist attempts, however, are challenged by expressions of relativism. With particular respect for the implications of the globalisation debate on prospects for WTO law, the following expressions of relativism are emphasised:

First, there are the descendants of romanticism, i.e. contemporary expressions of historicism and postmodernism. With a view on the globalisation debate, the following specific strains of Postmodernism deserve closer attention: environmentalism, 'third-world approaches', feminism and animal rights groups. However, whereas most of these groups are advocating for 'diversity', calling for equal rights and tolerance for specific segments of society (in the broadest sense of the word), the other, historical or, to put in in political terms, reactionary strain of relativism shall not be forgotten. Whereas the former, emancipatory groups have been predominant in the 1970s, 1980s and early 1990s and usually part of the New Left movement, the latter have gained significant ground since. In the perspective of the present book, it is no coincidence that the neo-historical strain of relativism is on the rise particularly since the Uruguay Round of the WTO resulted in an unprecedented globalisation of economic competition. As a consequence of this, those disadvantaged by adverse effects of globalisation turned to so-called populist movements. And again, it comes as little surprise that all of these populist movements, be it in the USA or in the EU, are showing elements of Romanticism, that is, scepticism towards scientific facts, preference for sentimental or intuitive comprehension to the detriment of intellectual understanding, and the rejection of everything presumed to be 'alien'. Therefore, that right-wing strain of philosophical thought, or sentiment, respectively, is also described as neo-romantic, reactionary or populist.

Secondly, there are the remnants of anarchism. Third, there are successors of Marxism/dialectical materialism.[249]

These various strains of relativism are constitutive elements of alter-globalisation movements such as ATTAC, the Word Social Forum (WSF), and *Altermondialisme*[250] in general, one the one hand, and of the populist challenge to globalisation, on the other hand.

In terms of a summary, the philosophical schools of thought aforementioned, their respective origins and the zone of contemporary conflict are visualised in the following chart on philosophical world-conceptions (Table 1).

Table 1 Conflicting world-conceptions

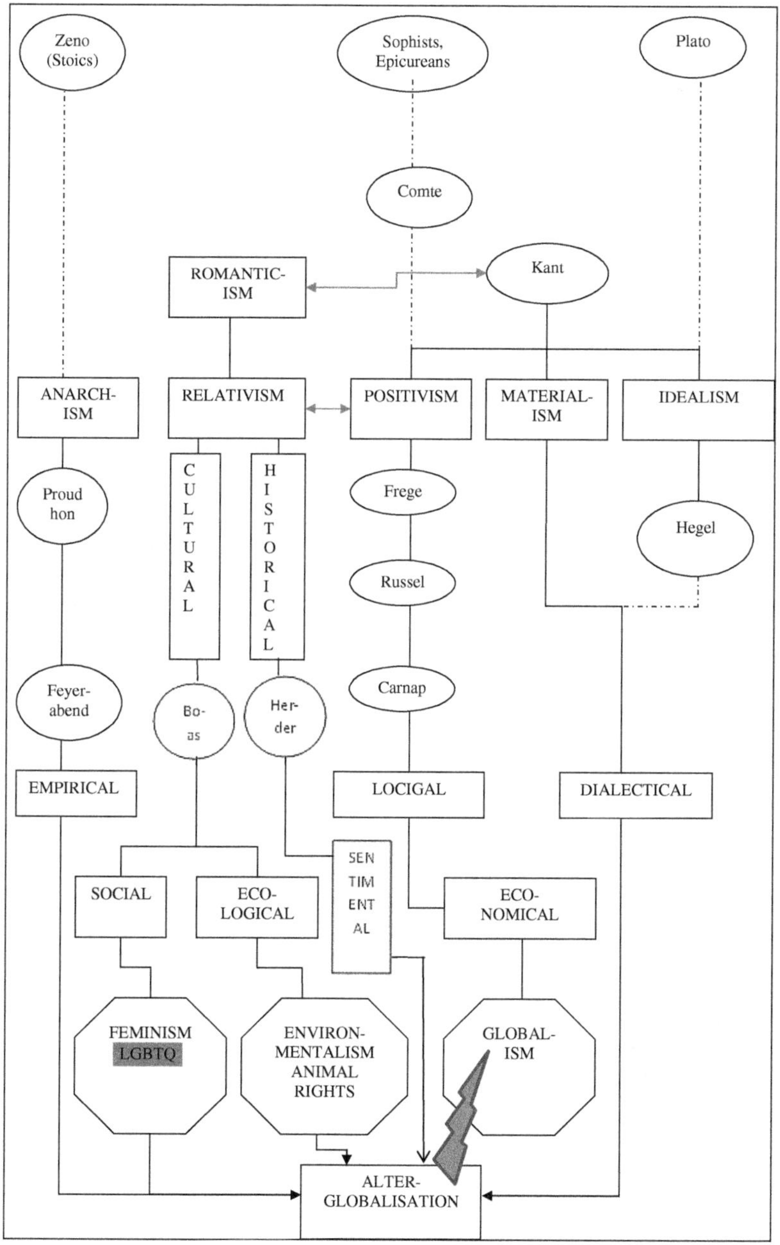

Notes

1. Kristin S. Shrader-Frechette, *Risk and Rationality. Philosophical Foundations for Populist Reforms* (University of California Press, 1991), p. 7 (emphasis added).
2. The author is well aware that the philosophical traditions mentioned in this book are all Western concepts. In no way the focus on Western concepts shall imply a disregard of non-Western philosophical concepts. But due to limited knowledge about non-Western philosophical concepts, the author relies on the assumption that people challenged by risk and risk theory are always and everywhere influenced by some kind of philosophical ideas. Nevertheless, an example of a 'heterodox' non-Western school of thought may be provided in short: the Carvaka philosophy, also known as Lokayata, was an Indian school of thought critical to orthodox strands of Hindu philosophy. In fundamental criticism to predominant philosophical strands of Hinduism, Carvaka philosophers developed a thorough form of materialism, arguing that mental activities basically are excited by material causes (Störig 1980, p. 43). Basnagoda Rahula, in turn, provided evidence that Greek philosophy, in particular the Sophist school of thought, was heavily influenced by Indian philosophy. Rahula provided evidence that 'the possible availability of Buddhist and other Indian rationalist concepts in Greece and the certain search of by some Greeks for such concepts in India, Persia and Babylon (…) strongly support the argument that sophist rhetoric was nourished by Indian rationalism' (Rahula 2000, p. 350). However, the findings of Rahula went further. Rahula provided arguments that atomic theory, usually accredited to Greek philosophers Leucippus (Greek: Leukippos) and Democritus (Greek: Demokritos) as originally developed theory, was actually inspired by Indian thinking. Moreover, Rahula explained that there existed two distinct strands of atomic theory, or atomism, in India. At the one hand, Rahula observed, there was '[t]he concept of Brahma, the earliest *idealistic* myth in India and the absolute truth behind the sensory world, attained maturity, holding within itself the origin of atomic development' (Rahula 2000, p. 207, emphasis added). On the other hand, however, the idealistic concept of Brahma faced challenge by 'sceptics, materialists, and some schools within the Brahmin tradition itself'. In particular, Rahula noted that 'dissenters of the Brahmin tradition used the same theory of atoms to deny any permanent entity in the individual and beyond-sensory phenomenon' (Rahula 2000, p. 208). Rahula summarised the two conflicting concepts of atomism developed in India as follows:

As far as the available evidence indicates, the Brahmin tradition [*i.e.*, the idealistic conception] emphasized a single essence or *anu* behind human body and sensual objects while materialists and Ajivikas recognised the elements as immutable atomic units. (Rahula 2000, p. 209)

In the scope of the study at hand, Rahula's findings are of particular interest in two respects. First, it is recalled that the Vienna Circle itself diagnosed 'an affinity with the Sophists, not with the Platonists; with the Epicureans, not with the Pythagoreans' (Neurath 1973, p. 306). Second, the schism between *idealistic* Brahmin philosophy and *materialistic* critique, as expressed by Ajivikas and Carvakas, among others, may be considered as the real foundation of the materialism–idealism dichotomy in Western philosophy. With similar conclusions, but from a critical perspective on scientific theories in general, Bernal noted:

[A] historical continuity links the theory as held in the ancient world with the modern one; and even, in a great number of cases, it is the ancient theory that has led to the propounding of the modern one rather than any evidence drawn from observation. As a concrete example we may take the case of the atomic theory: its origin is obscure, but there are hints of it both in Babylonian and Indian philosophies. Even if we give the credit of its first statement to Democritus we cannot imagine that it was arrived at otherwise than by that analogical type of reasoning that gave rise to the four elements and the four humours. There is no logical support for atomism, no reason, possibly within the reach of the Greeks, to put a stop arbitrarily to the concept of repeatedly dividing bodies; but once the analogy of a universe built out of sand or bricks is grasped, it associates itself with an aesthetic and moral attraction for certain types of mind. A universe of particles – how fascinating to build for oneself such a universe. The particles being inert, the gods retire into an indefinite background, and man is left the *master of the universe* if he can understand how this building takes place (Bernal 1949, pp. 95–96, emphasis added).

3. Kristin S. Shrader-Frechette, *ibid.* p. 7 (footnotes omitted). Shrader-Frechette further pointed at some sort of middle position between the relativist and the logical empiricists, where she located the so-called *naturalists*, such as Dudley Shapere, Larry Laudan and Roland Giere. According to Shrader-Frechette, naturalists 'maintain that theory evaluation can be rational even though there are no absolute rules for science, applicable in every situation' (Kristin S. Shrader-Frechette, *ibid.*, pp. 7–8).
4. Scott Lash, 'Expert-Systems or Situated Interpretation? Culture and Institutions in Disorganized Capitalism', in Ulrich Beck, Anthony Giddens and Scott Lash, *Reflexive Modernization. Politics, Tradition and Aesthetics in the Modern Social Order* (Polity Press, 1994), p. 199.
5. Scott Lash, *ibid.*

6. Scott Lash, *ibid.*
7. Scott Lash, *ibid.*
8. Scott Lash, *ibid.*
9. In the scope of the study at hand, two issues are of particular interest with regard to the Platonic conception.
   First, Plato discerned between 'the upper-world', i.e. the world of ideas, and a 'lower-world', where things different from ideas may exist. According to Georgescu-Roegen, Plato perceived ideas as living 'in a world of their own, "the upper-world", where each retains "a permanent individuality" and, moreover, remains "the same and unchanging"' (Nicholas Georgescu-Roegen, *Analytical Economics. Issues and Problems* (Harvard University Press, 1967, Massachusetts), p. 25, with reference to Plato's *Dialogues*, *e.g. Phaedo*, and *Philebus*. In this regard, Georgescu-Roegen noted that 'Plato's doctrine of ideas being "fixed patterns" permeated all his Dialogues' (Georgescu-Roegen, *ibid.*, p. 25, footnote no. 27). Hence, the notion of an 'upper-world' and a 'lower-world' may indicate some sort of division between a 'world of ideas' and a 'world of things'.
   Second, Georgescu-Roegen noted that Plato's 'extreme idealism' … 'underlies many modern thoughts of "clear thinking"' (Nicholas Georgescu-Roegen, *ibid.* p. 25). In particular, Georgescu-Roegen pointed at the 'Platonic tenet that only a privileged few are acquainted with ideas but cannot describe them publicly' (Nicholas Georgescu-Roegen, *ibid.* p. 25). The notion of the chosen few who are more clear-sighted than the many is reflected in the increasing demand for expert advice and tendencies, as critiques claim, towards technocratic rule.
10. John Rawls, *Geschichte der politischen Philosophie* (Suhrkamp 2008), p. 27. It has to be noted that John Rawls, by pointing to the examples of Plato's philosopher kings and Lenin's revolutionary avant-garde, did not rely on ideological categories, but on political implementation. From the viewpoint of ideological categories, Platonism and Leninism are rather opposing worldviews. Rawls, however, pointed at similarities of Platonism and Leninism when it comes to the implementation of respective ideologies by political means.
11. John Rawls, *ibid.* pp. 27–28.
12. Steve Fuller, *Social Epistemology*. 2nd Edition (Indiana University Press, 2002), p. 65 (original emphases).
13. Steve Fuller, *Thomas Kuhn. A Philosophical History of Our Times* (The University of Chicago Press, 2000), pp. 38–39.
14. However, neither Neopositivism as a philosophical concept nor the term Neopositivism itself was entirely new. Along with Henri Poincaré, Pierre Duhem and the concept of conventionalism, Anastasios Brenner particularly pointed at the French philosopher Édouard Le Roy as inventor of the term 'new positivism':

[A] historical examination of the philosophical context of the turn of the 19th and 20th centuries reveals that the endeavor to reformulate positivism preceded the Vienna Circle considerably. Before taking root in Austria, neo-positivism was a French current of thought. Indeed, as early as 1901, Édouard Le Roy published an article entitled 'Un positivisme nouveau'. He claimed in this article to perceive the beginning of an intellectual movement and drew up the program of reorienting positivism (Anastasios Brenner, 'The French Connection: Conventionalism and the Vienna Circle', in Michael Heidelberger, Friedrich Stadler (eds.), *History of Philosophy of Science. New Trends and Perspectives* (Kluwer Academic Publishers, 2002), p. 278).

15. In 1929, the *Vienna Circle* published its programmatic scripture *Wissenschaftliche Weltauffassung* (in English: *Scientific Conception of the World*).
16. Philosophical schools in Britain and the USA influenced by the *Vienna Circle* are usually referred to as *Analytical Philosophy.* Analytical philosophers were, for example, Charlie Dunbar Broad, Richard Mervyn Hare and Charles Leslie Stevenson (Hans Joachim Störig, *Kleine Weltgeschichte der Philosophie*, Vol. 2 1980), p. 332.
17. An early but fundamental work of Rudolf Carnap was entitled *Der logische Aufbau der Welt* (1928), which was later translated by Rolf A. George and published under the title *The Logical Structure of the World, and Pseudoproblems in Philosophy* (Routledge and Kegan Paul, London 1967).
18. Hans Joachim Störig, *Kleine Weltgeschichte der Philosophie*, Vol. 2 (Fischer, 1980), p. 323.
19. Hans Joachim Störig, *ibid.*, in particular pp. 320–333.
20. Excerpt from 'The Scientific Conception of the World: The Vienna Circle', known as the *Vienna Circle Manifesto* (in German: *Wissenschaftliche Weltauffassung*), published by the *Vienna Circle* in 1929, reprinted in Otto Neurath, *Empiricism and Sociology*, edited by Marie Neurath and Robert S. Cohen, volume 1 of the Vienna Circle Collection (D. Reidel Publishing, 1973), p. 309 (original emphases). The *Vienna Circle* did not provide the author's name(s). The pamphlet was produced in teamwork: Otto Neurath did the writing, Hans Hahn and Rudolf Carnap the editing of the text, and other Members of the *Vienna Circle* contributed as well, for example Herbert Feigl and Friedrich Waismann (see Otto Neurath, *Empiricism and Sociology*, edited by Marie Neurath and Robert S. Cohen, volume 1 of the Vienna Circle Collection (D. Reidel Publishing, 1973), p. 318, reference no. 2).
21. Harold Kincaid, *Philosophical Foundations of the Social Sciences. Analyzing Controversies in Social Research* (Cambridge University Press, 1996), p. 18.
22. Harold Kincaid, *ibid.*

23. Harold Kincaid, *ibid.* pp. 18–19.
24. Harold Kincaid, *ibid.* p. 19. Kincaid added that 'unnoticed positivist assumptions' may continue to influence epistemological debates.
25. David J., Stump, 'From the Values of Scientific Philosophy to the Value Neutrality of the Philosophy of Science', in Michael Heidelberger, Friedrich Stadler (eds.), *History of Philosophy of Science. New Trends and Perspectives* (Kluwer Academic Publishers, 2002), p. 151.
26. David J., Stump, *ibid.;* with references to Peter Galison (1990), 'Aufbau/Bauhaus: Logical Positivism and Architectural Modernism', in *Critical Inquiry* 16:709–52). With view on Neurath's work in particular, Stump found that the *scientific world conception* 'is connected to progressive, educated, Enlightenment values, and to the idea of modernity in general' (David J., Stump, *ibid.* p. 152).
27. Volker Böhnigk criticised positivists' attempts for establishing 'unified science'. Böhnigk noted that the 'unified science' programme of logical empiricists such as Rudolf Carnap, Otto Neurath and Ernest Nagel basically consisted of reducing the whole scientific apparatus to a last and fundamental (physical) theory (Volker Böhnigk, *Weltversionen. Wissenschaft zwischen Relativismus und Pluralismus* (Passagen Verlag, 1999), p. 48). The tool for achieving such a unified scientific formula was reduction and reductionism. However, as Böhnigk explained, it turned out that the reduction of scientific theories faced insurmountable methodological hurdles and logical limits (Volker Böhnigk, *ibid.* pp. 48–49). Even in the field of physics, various theories can be found whose relationships remain unclear. As an example from the field of quantum mechanics, Böhnigk pointed at the relationship between theories provided by Erwin Schrödinger's wave mechanics, on the one hand, and Werner Heisenberg's matrix mechanics, on the other hand. Although the theory goes that the two approaches are isomorphic in nature, that is, waves may transform into particles and vice versa, the theory is only heuristically proved. As Paul Dirac noted, it is still uncertain, therefore, whether the two approaches are *really* isomorphic or not (Volker Böhnigk, *ibid.* p. 50; with reference to Paul Dirac who worked together with Werner Heisenberg and Erwin Schrödinger on the theory of quantum mechanics in the 1920s (see also Stephen Hawking, *A Brief History of Time. From the Big Bang to Black Holes* (Bantam Books, 1989), p. 59). From this and other examples Böhnigk concluded that neither the natural sciences nor the social sciences have been able to develop a unified, coherent theory. On these grounds, Böhnigk refuted a philosophical stance pretending universal validity of scientific findings and convergence of scientific theories as 'hollow assumption' (Volker Böhnigk, *ibid.* p. 51). On the other hand, Böhnigk defended himself against criticism of

being a relativist, bewailing that some philosophers have developed an 'idiosyncratic idea of relativism, with a bizarre content' (*ibid.*, p. 113).

28. The attempt to apply methods and principles from the physical sciences to social sciences, in particular onto sociology, maintained its potential for controversy. An example is the so-called *Positivismusstreit* (debate about positivism) among scholars in the 1960s in Germany (at the same time, a similar debate took place in the USA, known as the *Behaviorism* controversy; see footnote no. 173 below). On one side stood Karl Raimund Popper, a critical rationalist, who was invited as a keynote speaker to a conference of the German Society of Sociology in Tübingen, Germany, in 1961. On the other side were representatives of the Frankfurt School of sociologists, in particular Theodor W. Adorno and Jürgen Habermas. At the conference, Popper developed 27 theses with which he argued that, first, the method applied—or should be applied—by social sciences is basically the same as in natural sciences, namely 'trial and error' (thesis no. 6). Second, Popper insisted on the existence and viability of a strictly objective approach also for social sciences. Calling it *situational logic* or *logic of the situation*, Popper asserted that a method relating individual action to the situation within which it is performed shall enable objective analyses also in social sciences (thesis no. 25) (see Karl R. Popper, 'Die Logik der Sozialwissenschaften', in Heinz Maus, Friedrich Fürstenberg (eds.) *Der Positivismusstreit in der deutschen Soziologie* (Luchterhand 1969), pp. 103–123, in particular pp. 105–106 and 120–121). In response, Adorno and Habermas argued that methodological rationality may bear different implications, depending on whether rational methods are applied in physical or in social sciences. In particular, Adorno and Habermas emphasised that rationality in end-and-means relationships is not tantamount to rational decisions on particular ends at issue. In other words, when it comes to interests and power in human societies, the application of rational methods for raising efficiency does not guarantee that the ultimate purpose, for instance productivity increase, is itself rational (see Theodor W. Adorno, Zur Logik der Sozialwissenschaften. Korreferat', in Heinz Maus, Friedrich Fürstenberg (eds.) *Der Positivismusstreit in der deutschen Soziologie* (Luchterhand 1969), pp. 135–143, in particular pp. 137–138; and Jürgen Habermas, 'Analytische Wissenschaftstheorie und Dialektik. Ein Nachtrag zur Kontroverse zwischen Popper und Adorno', in Heinz Maus, Friedrich Fürstenberg (eds.) *Der Positivismusstreit in der deutschen Soziologie* (Luchterhand, 1969), pp. 155–191, in particular pp. 187 and 190–191). In philosophical terms, the dispute can be seen as a controversy between Popper's approach of *critical rationalism* centring on scientific rigour, objectivity and the value freedom of rational scientific method, whereas

on the other side Adorno and Habermas argued in favour of a *dialectical approach*, able to apply the critical method (which both camps upheld) also against the power structure within which (social) science actually operates. Before this background, the term 'Positivismusstreit' (dispute about positivism) is a misnomer (in the same sense Hans Albert, 'Kleines verwundertes Nachwort zu einer großen Einleitung,' in Heinz Maus, Friedrich Fürstenberg (eds.) *Der Positivismusstreit in der deutschen Soziologie* (Luchterhand, 1969), p. 336). Popper himself wondered about the discretionary (mis-)use of the term positivism, noting that '[t]he suggestion that anybody interested in natural science is to be condemned as a positivist would make positivists not only of Marx and Engels, but also of Lenin—the man who introduced the equation of "positivism" and "reaction"' (see Karl R. Popper, 'Reason or Revolution?' in *The Myth of the Framework. In defence of science and rationality.* Edited by M.A. Notturno (Routledge, 1994), p. 76). The irreconcilable positions of diverging philosophical approaches in the so-called positivism debate may shed light on comparably opposing views in the risk assessment controversy. In the risk assessment controversy, positivist attempts for streamlining scientific risk assessment by isolating it from societal interference are standing in conflict with relativist suggestions for 'democratising' risk assessment by introducing public debate and deliberative procedures in risk assessment and risk polices.

29. In his doctoral thesis, *An Attempt at a Realistic Interpretation of Experience*, Paul Feyerabend related language to philosophical concepts. In short, Feyerabend contrasted two paradigms, *Positivism* on the one hand, with *Realism*, on the other hand. Feyerabend observed that the positivist focus on logical language renders the validity of (positivist) theory contingent upon intersubjective rapprochement. In this regard, Steve Fuller explained that 'a positivist theory of reference would group together observation sentences uttered by individuals in different languages that were triggered by sensations of the same type. It would thus depend crucially on the possibility of intersubjective agreement among language users'. In contrast, Fuller continued, 'a realist theory of reference would be identical with the latest physical theory, or at least the best available account of the causes of linguistic behavior, regardless of whether most actual language users know (the best theory of) what their observation sentences are true of' (Steve Fuller, *Social Epistemology.* 2nd Edition (Indiana University Press, 2002), p. 102).
30. Popper observed that the search of Positivists for *unified science* by means of a language covering all sciences came at the price of *decontextualisation.* Popper noted:

... [The Positivists] believed that their criterion of meaning could be applied to any *linguistic expression*, without reference to its *context*. (They thought that all that was needed was a knowledge of the rules of the language to which the expression belonged.). They believed that their criterion of meaning would enable them to *detect nonsense* wherever it might occur. Thus they sometimes described their aim as 'the elimination of metaphysics by way of language analysis'. And they believed that they had a method, a technique, which would allow them to eliminate metaphysical elements – that is to say nonsense – also from scientific theories (Karl R. Popper, *Realism and the Aim of Science. From the Postscript to the Logic of Scientific Discovery.* Edited by W.W. Bartley, III (Hutchinson & Co., 1983), p. 179; original emphases).

In a footnote, referring to the clause 'the elimination of metaphysics by way of language analysis', Popper noted that '[t]his was Carnap's research programme' (Karl R. Popper, *ibid).*

31. Hans Joachim Störig, *Kleine Weltgeschichte der Philosophie*, Vol. 2 (Fischer Taschenbuch Verlag, 1980, Frankfurt a.M.), p. 327.
32. Carnap, Rudolf; Hahn, Hans; and Neurath Otto, 'The Scientific Conception of the World: The Vienna Circle', known as the *Vienna Circle Manifesto*, in Otto Neurath, *Empiricism and Sociology*, edited by Marie Neurath and Robert S. Cohen, volume 1 of the Vienna Circle Collection (D. Reidel Publishing Company, Dordrecht-Holland, 1973), p. 306 (original emphases). Somehow surprisingly, the neopositivist pursuit of *unified science* experiences some sort of revival these days. Inspired by scientific discoveries at the nano scale, a new, yet rather *physicalistic* theory of converging (physical) sciences appeared. In a report on the convergence of nanotechnology, biotechnology, information technology and cognitive science (NBIC), proponents of the thesis of scientific convergence declared:

We stand at the threshold of a new renaissance in science and technology, based on a comprehensive understanding of the structure and behavior of matter from the nanoscale up to the most complex system yet discovered, the human brain. *Unification of science* based on unity in nature and its holistic investigation will lead to technological convergence and a more efficient societal structure for reaching human goals. In the early decades of the twenty-first century, concentrated effort can bring together nanotechnology, biotechnology, information technology, and new technologies based in cognitive science (Mihail C. Roco and William Sims Bainbridg (eds.), *Converging Technologies for Improving Human Performance. Nanotechnology, Biotechnology, Information Technology and Cognitive Science.* Joint report of the National Science Foundation (NSF) and the Department of Commerce (Kluwer Academic Publishers, 2003), p. 1 (emphasis added). For more on NBIC, see footnotes 193, 265 and 516 below.

33. David J., Stump, 'From the Values of Scientific Philosophy to the Value Neutrality of the Philosophy of Science', in Michael Heidelberger, Friedrich Stadler (eds.), *History of Philosophy of Science. New Trends and Perspectives* (Kluwer Academic Publishers, 2002), p. 151. With view on politics, Stump added that '[i]nternationalism was important to the Logical Positivists as a vehicle to express their opposition to rising German nationalism' (David J., Stump, *ibid.*). However, Stump cautioned against ostensible parallels between science and internationalism. Stump noted:

> One tends to think of science as intrinsically international, thus is would be natural to think of scientific philosophy as intrinsically international as well. However, the temporal parallels between the rise of scientific philosophies and of internationalism in general society require us to consider whether internationalism really is a necessary aspect of scientific philosophy. International cooperation in science went through a difficult period during WWI, with scientists participating in the war effort, especially in Germany, and again in WWII, but science as it is practiced today is surely an international institution. A close comparison of how philosophy has been organized over the last two centuries would be required to see the affect, if any that the rise and fall of international cooperation had on philosophical institutions (David J., Stump, *ibid.*).

34. See, for example, David J., Stump, *ibid.* p. 147. Stump observed that 'Russel's program influenced Carnap directly, though the idea of applying modern logic to philosophical problems became a defining feature of analytical philosophy and was applied to many areas of philosophy, not only to the philosophy of science' (David J., Stump, *ibid.*).
35. Albeit the focus of the study at hand is not on individual thinkers but on respective philosophical traditions, an exception has to be made in the case of Bertrand Russell. During his long life, Russell was dedicated to the pacifist cause. During World War I, in 1916, he was dismissed from college because of his pacifist activities and later even imprisoned. My grandmother told me about Bertrand when I was a child. In her younger days herself a Member of pacifist groups in Switzerland associated to the *Nie-wieder-Krieg!* (nevermore war!) movement in Germany, my grandmother honoured Russell as one of the few intellectuals of her times staying committed to pacifism and humanitarianism. That is the reason why I devote this study to my grandmother.
36. David Stump pointed at Russell's aim of combining philosophical thought with scientific advancement. For an example, Stump pointed at Russell's observation that 'the mathematical theory of the infinite is a triumph of scientific method in philosophy' and that 'the new mathematical theory of

the infinite surpasses at least two thousand years of philosophical thinking about the infinite' (David J., Stump, *ibid.* p. 149).

37. Hans Joachim Störig, *Kleine Weltgeschichte der Philosophie*, Vol. 2 (Fischer, 1980), pp. 318–319. Russell called his concept of an ideal language *logical atomism*, which might be understood as an attempt for directly linking intersubjective language to objective reality, that is, formalised terms to information received. By connecting sensual perception (sense-data) with a logical system, Russell's concept of logical atomism may be associated with stringent forms of empiricism.
38. Hans Joachim Störig, *ibid.* p. 321.
39. The German term *Begriffsschrift* may be translated as Concept Script. The *Begriffsschriftt* was published in 1879 under the full title *Begriffsschrift, eine der arithmetischen nachgebildete Formelsprache des reinen Denkens.* The *Foundations of Arithmetic* were published in 1884 under the German title *Die Grundlagen der Arithmetik. Eine logisch mathematische Untersuchung über den Begriff der Zahl.* Finally, *Basic Laws of Arithmetic* (German title: *Grundgesetze der Arithmetik: begriffsschriftlich abgeleitet)* was published in 1893 (Vol. 1) and 1903 (Vol. 2) in Jena/Germany.
40. Steve Fuller, *Social Epistemology.* 2nd Edition (Indiana University Press, 2002), p. 40.
41. Looking at etymological origins of the word 'Positivism', Walter Bröcker observed that originally there were two distinctions; one discerning the (originally Greek) words *positivus–naturalis*, the other distinguishing between *affirmatio–negatio.* Whereas the latter distinction was originally intended to describe judgements, it was later confused with the former distinction. On these grounds, Bröcker concluded, the term *positive* came into use also for indicating numbers (see Walter Bröcker, *Dialektik Positivismus Mythologie* (Vittorio Klostermann, 1958), p. 44).
42. Following Eric Hobsbawm, Positivism is understood as a mindset conceptualising the world build upon 'true' scientific theories and verifiable by 'positive', i.e. natural sciences. Considering lacunas of positive sciences discovered in the meantime, Neopositivism, in contrast, limited itself to a reconstruction of scientific purity by means of reduction, formalisation and axiomatisation. Following Henri Poincaré, the positivist criteria for scientific theories was no more the question whether they were right or wrong, but whether they were practical (see Eric J. Hobsbawm, *Das imperiale Zeitalter 1875–1914.* (Campus, 2008), pp. 322–323).
43. Hans Joachim Störig, *Kleine Weltgeschichte der Philosophie*, Vol. 2 (Fischer, 1980), pp. 308–309.
44. Nevertheless, positivism is not the same as *empiricism.* Störig pointed at the example of the philosopher Nicolai Hartmann. According to Störig, Hartmann could be called an empiricist, because his thinking derived from

scientifically ascertainable facts. On the other hand, however, Hartmann's critical realism and ontology considered the possibility that 'things' might actually exist in an objective reality without being accessible to human perception. Such considerations, though, are beyond the scope of positivism which rejects anything intangible as 'metaphysics' (see Hans Joachim Störig, *ibid.* p. 310).

45. Hans Joachim Störig, *ibid.* p. 309. In fact, the philosophy of Positivism 'provided the primary jurisprudential resource for the jurists of the late nineteenth century' (Antony Anghie, *Imperialism, Sovereignty and the Making of International Law* (Cambridge University Press, 2005), p. 41. The new focus on 'positive law' marked a shift away from 'natural law' which consisted of a set of 'transcendental principles' such as justice and morality and by which the sovereign was meant to be bound (Antony Anghie, *ibid.,* pp. 41–42). For legal positivist, in contrast,

> The sovereign is the foundation of positivist jurisprudence; and nineteenth-century positivist jurists essentially sought to reconstruct the entire system of international law based on their new version of sovereignty doctrine. (...) Thus for positivists, the rules of international law were to be discovered not by speculative inquiries into the nature of justice or teleology, but by a careful study of the actual behaviour of states and the institutions and laws which they created. (Antony Anghie, *ibid.*, pp. 41 and 43)

46. Hans Joachim Störig, *ibid.* pp. 309–310. Whereas the positivist rejection of Idealism seems obvious, the positivist rejection of Materialism is not self-explanatory. The following ostensive explanation is taken from Karl R. Popper. Popper observed that *Maxwell's equations* (modern field theory) emerged from a long sequence of scientific theories and respective refutations. In this regard, Popper noted that already Kant had refuted Leibnitz' theory of monads. According to Leibnitz' *monadology,* matter basically consists of individualised, point-shaped elements and is, therefore, not continuous. In contrast, Kant depicted the notion of matter as a continuous and dynamic phenomenon. Popper valuated Kant's proposal primarily on the basis of its novel idea of matter as a dynamic continuity. Popper explained that Kant's proposal was one of the philosophical basements upon which subsequent scientists and philosophers (Popper listed the names of Faraday, Maxwell, Einstein, De Broglie and Schrödinger) could build on theories such as modern field theory. By referring to the long tale of ideas about origins of matter and modern field theory, Popper argued that it is precisely the 'speculative character' of ideas developed by theoreticians advancing scientific knowledge. Owing to the predisposition of speculative or 'metaphysical' ideas to critical review, scientific knowledge

as a whole may progress. Turning to the stance of positivism towards 'speculation' in science, Popper noted that Positivism has always been contrary to scientific speculations. In particular, Popper observed that the physicist and philosopher Ernst Mach (1838–1916) was still of the view that there is no physical explanation for matter. According to Mach, Popper noted, matter was just a metaphysical 'substance', and thus redundant, if not meaningless. Notably, Mach advanced this view in a time when metaphysical theories about the structure of matter increasingly were transformed into testable physical theories. Ironically though, that Mach's theory had its biggest influence in times where modern atomic theory became widely accepted and continued to influence leading nuclear physicists such as Bohr, Heisenberg and Pauli. Looking at these scientific trends, Popper exclaimed:

Yet the wonderful theories of these great physicists are the result of attempts to understand the structure of the physical world, and to criticize the outcome of these attempts. Thus their own physical theories may well be contrasted with what these physicists, and other positivists, try to tell us today: that we cannot, in principle, hope ever to understand anything about the structure of matter: that the theory of matter must forever remain the private *affair of the expert, the specialist* – a mystery shrouded in technicalities, in mathematical techniques, and in 'semantics': that science is nothing but an *instrument*, void of any philosophical or theoretical interest, and only of 'technological' or 'pragmatic' or 'operational' significance. I do not believe a word of this *post-rationalist doctrine* (Karl R. Popper, *Quantum Theory and the Schism in Physics. From the Postscript to the Logic of Scientific Discovery.* Edited by W.W. Bartley, III (Hutchinson & Co., 1982), pp. 170–173, emphases added).

From this paragraph provided by Popper, one can educe additional features of Positivism: First, some sort of elitist understanding of scientific research which is considered 'the private affair of the expert, the specialist'; and second, an 'instrumentalist', 'technological', 'pragmatic' or 'operational' approach towards science which is depicted as 'void of any philosophical or theoretical interest'. Third, Popper termed such an approach 'a post-rationalist doctrine'.

47. Störig observed that already Vladimir Iilyich Lenin (1870–1924) was aware of increasing tensions between traditional perceptions of matter and the material world and new scientific knowledge. In his book *Materialism and Empiriocriticism: Critical Comments on a Reactionary Philosophy* (published 1909), Lenin rejected traditional and narrow notions of matter and the material world. In contrast, Lenin considered that matter is 'a philosophical category' for denominating 'objective reality' (Hans Joachim

Störig, *Kleine Weltgeschichte der Philosophie*, Vol. 2 (Fischer, 1980), p. 246). By so doing, Lenin also took up position against what he called *Empiriocriticists*, in particular Ernst Mach and Richard Avenarius and their quest for economical abstractions of scientific phenomena (see Hans Joachim Störig, *ibid.* pp. 246 and 312). Karl Popper, in turn, argued that materialism as a philosophical school of thought had virtually overcome itself, due to the successful inspiration of scientific research which, at the end of the day, transcended traditional materialism (Karl R. Popper and John C. Eccles, *Das Ich und sein Gehirn.* 11th edition (Serie Piper, 1994), pp. 24–28). John Desmond Bernal, however, warned that overcoming materialism by modern scientific theories, such as the theory of relativity, may pave the way for reintroducing relativism and metaphysics through the backdoor. Bernal wrote:

Modern physics is supposed to have destroyed the older materialism and this is supposed to be an excuse for holding any kind of opinion, mystical, philosophical, or religious. In fact materialism has grown so rapidly that it has temporarily lost its language and is rapidly in the process of finding a new one through the connecting of the biophysics of sensation with the ultimate wave-mechanics picture of the universe. But supposing materialism has lost its justification, there is still no excuse for returning to beliefs which will not tolerate historical or psychological criticism. If science is misunderstood at the present time, it is mostly for the lack of this criticism (John Desmond Bernal, *The Freedom of Necessity.* (Routledge & Kegan Paul, 1949), p. 100)

48. Hans Joachim Störig, *Kleine Weltgeschichte der Philosophie*, Vol. 2 (Fischer, 1980), p. 309. Störig noted that albeit the term Positivism was new at that time, it actually paraphrased old ideas. According to Störig, the term Positivism may be used for denominating those schools of thoughts adhering to the basic principles outlined above, i.e. the belief in given, apprehensible facts and the rejection of metaphysics.
49. Hans Joachim Störig, *ibid.* p. 137.
50. Hans Joachim Störig, *ibid.* p. 139.
51. Hans Joachim Störig, *ibid.*
52. Hans Joachim Störig, *ibid.*
53. Hans Joachim Störig, *ibid.* pp. 139–140. Störig noted that Comte's ultimate goal would be a stage at which virtually all phenomena could be deduced from one overarching fact, for example gravitation. Störig drew the analogy to Einstein's attempt for establishing a unified field theory (Hans Joachim Störig, *ibid.* p. 140). Hence, later attempts of neopositivists for unifying science by a formula language can be seen as pursuits of Comte's aspiration.

54. Hans Joachim Störig, *ibid.* p. 144.
55. Hans Joachim Störig, *ibid.*
56. Hans Joachim Störig, *ibid.*
57. Muhsin Mahdi, *Approaches to the history of Arabic science*, *Postface* to Roshdi Rashed (ed.), *Encyclopedia of the History of Arabic Science* (vol. 3), *Technology, Alchemy and Life Sciences* (Routledge, 1996), [pp. 1026–1044], p. 1036. The role attributed to science by Positivism is the distinct feature of the latter. The role of science distinguishes Positivism from antagonistic philosophical schools of thought, in particular Historicism. Whereas the role of science in Positivism is an absolute one, its role is relative in Historicism, namely contingent upon respective context.
58. Hans Joachim Störig, *Kleine Weltgeschichte der Philosophie*, Vol. 1 (Fischer, 1979), p. 317.
59. The scientific worldview, however, did not appear out of nowhere. René Descartes and likeminded European philosophers did not 'invent' enlightened thinking out of the blue but built upon a long tradition of scientific knowledge. In mediaeval Europe, that knowledge was overshadowed by Christian mysticism. However, and contrary to widespread belief, the reorientation towards scientific concepts was less an inventive step by European philosophers but a rediscovery of scientific traditions (hence: re-naissance). In contrast to Eurocentric hypotheses such as the modernist thesis (see below), it is well-researched today that science was not only brought back to mediaeval Europe by the Arabs, but also revolutionised by the latter. In this respect, Robert Briffault observed:

> The debt of our science to that of the Arabs does not consist in startling discoveries or revolutionary theories; science owes a great deal more to Arab culture, it owes its existence. The ancient world was, as we saw, pre-scientific. The astronomy and mathematics of the Greeks were a foreign importation never thoroughly acclimatized in Greek culture. The Greeks systematized, generalized and theorized, but the patient ways of investigation, the accumulation of *positive knowledge*, the minute methods of science, detailed and prolonged observation, experimental inquiry, were altogether alien to the Greek temperament. Only in Hellenistic Alexandria was any approach to scientific work conducted in the ancient classical world. What we call science arose in Europe as a result of a new spirit of inquiry, of new methods of investigation, of the method of experiment, observation, measurement, of the development of mathematics in a form unknown to the Greeks. That spirit and those methods were introduced into the European world by the Arabs (Robert Briffault, *The Making of Humanity* (George Allen & Unwin Ltd., first published in 1919) p. 191, emphasis added).

In 529, emperor Justinian of Byzantium had even ordered to close down the academy in Athens once founded by Plato himself. Therefore, as Rainer Traub noted, many of the most inventive minds of those days gathered in Alexandria (Rainer Traub, *Sturz in den Schatten*, in *SPIEGEL GESCHICHTE*, issue 5, 2010, p. 96). Alexandria, however, was taken over by the Arabs in 642, leading to a renewal and further development of scientific knowledge throughout the Arab Empire, extending from the Atlantic to the Hindu Kush (Rainer Traub, *ibid.*).

60. In fact, the honour of inventor of scientific methodology is owed to outstanding Arab scientist Ibn Al-Haytham (965–1039; full name: Abu 'Ali al-Hasan Ibn al-Haytham, also known in the West as Alhazen). In a nutshell, Ibn al-Haytham revolutionised Ptolemaic optics and invented the *camera obscura* (*qamara*; see Salim T S Al-Hassani (ed.), *1001 Inventions: Muslim Heritage in Our World.* 2nd edition published by Foundation of Science, Technology and Civilisation (FSTC Ltd., 2007), p. 318. By testing theories empirically, Ibn al-Haytham pioneered scientific methodology:

> Ibn al-Haitham revolutionised optics, taking the subject from one being discussed philosophically to a science based on experiments. He rejected the Greek idea that an invisible light emitting from the eye caused sight, and instead rightly stated that vision was caused by light reflecting off an object and entering the eye. (Salim T S Al-Hassani, *ibid.*)

Ibn al-Haytham's *Book of Optics* (Arabic: *Kitab al-Manazir*) was thus not only a critique of Ptolemy's work *Almagest*, but laid the foundations for experimental scientific methodology and influenced following European scholars such as Roger Bacon (1214–1292), Nicolaus Copernicus (1473–1543), Galileo Galilei (1564–1642), Johannes Kepler (1571–1630) and René Descartes himself (see Salim T S Al-Hassani, *ibid.*, pp. 322–323; Saleh Beshara Omar, *Ibn al-Haytham's Optics* (Bibliotheca Islamica, Minneapolis, 1977), §§ 151–152; Henri Hugonnard-Roche, *The influence of Arabic astronomy in the medieval West*, in Roshdi Rashed (ed.), *Encyclopedia of the History of Arabic Science,* (vol. 1), *Astronomy—Theoretical and Applied* (Routledge, 1996), pp. 284–305; Gül A. Russell, *The emergence of physiological optics*, in Roshdi Rashed (ed.), *Encyclopedia of the History of Arabic Science,* (vol. 2), *Mathematics and the Physical Sciences* (Routledge, 1996), pp. 672–715; David C. Lindberg, *The Western reception of Arabic optics*, in Roshdi Rashed (ed.), *Encyclopedia of the History of Arabic Science,* (vol. 2), *Mathematics and the Physical Sciences* (Routledge, 1996), pp. 716–729). It was the inventive combination of induction as a philosophical approach with experimental verification on the ground for which Ibn al-Haytham should be honoured as the founder of scientific methodology. The eminent role of Ibn al-Haytham for the advancement of modern science was summarised by Matthias Schramm as follows:

The problem of combining and harmonizing Aristotle's metaphysical approach to nature with the mathematical description of the phenomena introduced by Greek astronomers and opticians was discussed already in later Antiquity. (…) [T]he discussion remained limited to the domain of problematic reasoning and it was not before the Islamic period that a different approach was made, when the Arab astronomer and optician Ibn al-Haytham advanced the first consistent theory aiming at a mechanical foundation of Ptolemy's cinematics. (…) The experimental method, not yet fully developed in Ibn al-Haytham's mechanics, assumes increasing significance in his optical writings. By examining the question of the moon's capacity of emitting light without being a polished mirror Ibn al-Haytham was led to the discovery that all coloured bodies emit light, and that light and colour are virtually identical. By way of systematical experiment destined to prove these assertions he arrived at constructing the Camera obscura. On closer examination of Ibn al-Haytham's conception of mathematical models and of the rôle they play in his theory of sense-perception, it becomes evident that he was the true founder of physics in the modern sense of the word; in fact he anticipated by six centuries the fertile ideas that were to mark the outset of this new branch of science (Matthias Schramm, *Ibn al-Haythams Weg zur Physik* (Franz Steiner Verlag GmbH, 1963), p. XII (Summary).

According to some scholars, Ibn al-Haytham should not only be recognised as the founder of scientific methodology, but as the mastermind of the positivist school of thought. Roshdi Rashed, for example, noted the following:

In reforming optics he as it were adopted "positivism" (before the term was invented): we do not go beyond experience, and we cannot be content to use pure concepts in investigating natural phenomena. Understanding of these cannot be acquired without mathematics. Thus, once he has assumed light is a material substance, Ibn al-Haytham does not discuss its nature further, but confines himself to consider its propagation and diffusion. In his optics "the smallest parts of light", as he calls them, retain only properties that can be treated by geometry and verified by experiment; they lack all sensible quality except energy. That is to say we begin by insisting on making optics geometrical, or on reforming geometrical optics, leaving aside the "why" questions that have to do with teleological physics (…) (Roshdi Rashed, *The Celestial Kinematics of Ibn al-Haytham*, in Arabic Sciences and Philosophy, vol. 17 (2007) [pp. 7–55] p. 19).

61. Beside Arabic origins of rational, i.e. enlightened thinking, as mentioned above, another non-European philosophical tradition which influenced seventeenth-century philosophers in Europe shall be briefly mentioned, namely Chinese Confucianism. It is well documented that Gottfried Wilhelm Leibniz and Christian Wolff in particular were influenced by the thinking of Chinese philosophers Confucius and Mencius. With his famous speech at the University of Halle in 1721, entitled 'On the Practical Philosophy of the Chinese' (in German: 'Über die praktische Philosophie der Chinesen'), Wolff caused a scandal by arguing that a decent living within a working society can be based on rational thinking only, thus rendering Christian metaphysics obsolete (Henrik Jäger, 'Die anderen Quellen der Aufklärung – Wie die chinesische Tradition in das europäische Denken des 17. und 18. Jahrhunderts eingegangen ist', in *Neue Zürcher Zeitung*, Nr. 241, October 16, 2010, p. 65. For further references to non-European philosophy, see footnote no. 65 above).
62. Hans Joachim Störig, *Kleine Weltgeschichte der Philosophie*, Vol. 1 (Fischer, 1979), pp. 229–235.
63. Hans Joachim Störig, *ibid.* p. 322.
64. Hans Joachim Störig, *ibid.* p. 322.
65. Eduard Kaeser, *Pop Science. Essays zur Wissenschaftskultur* (Schwabe, 2009), p. 157. Kaeser added that 'the 'monstrosity is in the logic, not in the laboratory. And what happens with the animal in the laboratory may sooner or later happen with us too. We are its closest' (Eduard Kaeser, *ibid.*; in German: 'Das Ungeheuerliche liegt in der Logik, nicht im Labor. Und was mit dem Tier im Labor geschieht, kann über kurz oder lang auch mit uns passieren. Wir sind seine Nächsten').
66. It was not by hazard that René Descartes lived and worked most of his lifetime in the Netherlands. The seventeenth century was also called the Dutch Golden Age where riches from overseas trade spurred science, arts and civic liberties. Also termed 'the venturesome era' by Pradier, the Dutch Golden Age saw the rise of the Dutch East India Company, the first multinational corporation listed at the Amsterdam Stock Exchange. Seventeenth-century Amsterdam was also at the centre of the first well-recorded speculative bubble, the so-called Tulip mania: during the 1630s, prices for tulip bulbs rose to extraordinary high levels, but suddenly collapsed in 1637. In the focus of the study at hand, it is noteworthy that the tulip bubble of the 1630s already showed the ambiguity of financial risk control again observed during the food crisis of 2008: the inventive financial instruments applied, in particular futures contracts and short selling, were primarily used for speculative purposes increasing the bubble, rather than for hedging purposes containing the mania (see Hans Joachim Störig, *Kleine Weltgeschichte der Philosophie*, Vol. 1 (Fischer, 1979), p. 318;

Pierre-Charles Pradier, *La notion de risqué en économie*, (Éditions La Découverte, Paris, 2006), p. 14; André Kostolany, *Die Kunst über Geld nachzudenken* (Econ Ullstein List Verlag, 2000), pp. 146–149).

67. Eduard Kaeser, *Pop Science. Essays zur Wissenschaftskultur* (Schwabe Verlag Basel, 2009), p. 154.
68. Comte's thinking amounted to an alternative religion, to a secular *weltanschauung* virtually covering all aspects of life. In his work *The Catechism of Positive Religion*, Comte established an alternative, i.e. positivist philosophy of life, based on the device: *'Love as a principle and order as the basis; progress as the goal'* (in French: *'L'amour pour principe et l'ordre pour base; le progrès pour but'*). (Hans Joachim Störig, *Kleine Weltgeschichte der Philosophie*, Vol. 2 (Fischer, 1980), p. 144). A shortened version of the positivist motto can still be seen on the national flag of Brazil. In Portuguese, it reads: *'Ordem e Progresso'* (*"Order and Progress"*).
69. Karl R. Popper, 'Reason or Revolution?' in *The Myth of the Framework. In defence of science and rationality*. Edited by M.A. Notturno (Routledge, 1994), p. 75 and footnote no. 10; with reference to a letter written by Dr Alfred Schmidt to the German newspaper *Die Zeit*, 12 June 1970, p. 45.
70. Karl R. Popper, *The Myth of the Framework. In defence of science and rationality*. Edited by M.A. Notturno (Routledge, 1994), p. 75 (footnote omitted, emphasises added). In diametric opposition to positivist notions, Popper's *critical rationalism* even embraced metaphysics: 'Finally I have not only stressed the meaningfulness of metaphysical assertions and the fact that I am myself a metaphysical realist, but I have also analysed the important historical role played by metaphysics in the formation of scientific theories' (see Karl R. Popper, *The Myth of the Framework. In defence of science and rationality*. Edited by M.A. Notturno (Routledge, 1994), p. 75). For such reasons, Nassim Nicholas Taleb said 'I have to note that Popper is the antidote to positivism' (Nassim Nicholas Taleb, *Fooled by Randomness. The Hidden Role of Chance in Life and in the Markets*. 2nd Edition (Penguin Books, 2004), p. 128).
71. Nicholas Georgescu-Roegen, *Analytical Economics. Issues and Problems* (Harvard University Press, 1967), p. 27.
72. Nicholas Georgescu-Roegen, *ibid*. p. 27, italics added. Georgescu-Roegen introduced the term *arithmomorphic* concept to betoken scientific concepts expressing reality in real numbers. Georgescu-Roegen worked out the antinomy between arithmomorphic concepts and dialectical concepts of science; between concepts based on the idea that reality is scientifically ascertainable and reducible to one single number, on the one hand, and concepts emphasising the continuous flow of things requiring iterative approaches for grasping reality. The positivistic critique of dialectical concepts is encapsulated in the sentence of 'the muddled waters of Hegelian

dialectics', whereas dialectical approaches may be traced back to the sentence of Herakleitos considering that 'one cannot step twice into the same river' (see Georgescu-Roegen, *ibid.,* pp. 21–35). The saying of Herakleitos is understood as expressing 'the problem of the opposition between Being and Becoming', a viewpoint in which science, according to Georgescu-Roegen, does not partake anymore: 'Science, however, has long since [Herakleitos] decided to embrace the viewpoint of "vulgar philosophy", which viewpoint is that there is both Being and Becoming' (see Nicholas Georgescu-Roegen, *Energy and Economic Myths. Institutional and Analytical Economic Essays* (Pergamon Press, 1976), p. 79).

Georgescu-Roegen himself seemed of having taken some middle stance between positivistic and purely dialectic concepts. Georgescu-Roegen perceived theoretical science as 'a living organism'. He recognised the aliveness of science in the fact that it 'continuously creates new facts from old facts, but its growth is organic, not accretionary'. The organic growth of theoretical science is maintained by 'a continuous secretion of experimental suggestions which are tested and organically integrated into the science's anatomy' (Nicholas Georgescu-Roegen, *Analytical Economics. Issues and Problems* (Harvard University Press, 1967), pp. 14–15). The notion that (theoretical) science is a living and evolving organism seemed to have moved Georgescu-Roegen beyond the opposition of arithmomorphic, *e.g.* positivistic, and strictly dialectical, i.e. Hegelian, concepts of science. Georgescu-Roegen himself referred to 'vulgar philosophy' for denoting a viewpoint 'that there is both Being and Becoming', indicating that, as a matter of fact, both aspects are required to embrace an entire view of reality (Nicholas Georgescu-Roegen, *Energy and Economic Myths. Institutional and Analytical Economic Essays* (Pergamon Press, 1976), p. 79. On the other hand, Georgescu-Roegen noted that 'to abandon this dualism [*e.g.* the dualism between positivistic and dialectic concepts], is to renounce *analysis*; and to renounce analysis is to do away with *theoretical science.* However, we must not expect that analysis can remain entirely immune to the epistemological ills inherent in any dualism' (Nicholas Georgescu-Roegen, *ibid.*, p. 79).

73. Karl R. Popper, *Quantum Theory and the Schism in Physics. From the Postscript to the Logic of Scientific Discovery.* Edited by W.W. Bartley, III (Hutchinson & Co. Publishers Ltd., 1982), pp. 172–173).
74. Karl R. Popper, *Logik der Forschung (*English title: *The Logic of Scientific Discovery*) 6th edition, (J.C.B Mohr (Paul Siebeck), Tübingen 1976), p. 23.
75. Karl R. Popper, *ibid.* p. 23. Yet, positivists' disregard of philosophical problems as 'pseudo problems' is not expressed as requests or proposals, but as knowledge (Karl R. Popper, *ibid.* pp. 23–24.

76. Karl R. Popper, *ibid.* p. 24.
77. Karl R. Popper, *ibid.* p. 24.
78. Karl R. Popper, *ibid.* p. 24.
79. Fred Eidlin, 'Poppers ethischer und metaphysischer Kognitivismus (Warum Wörter manchmal wichtig sein können)'. In Kurt Salamun (ed.), *Karl R. Popper und die Philosophie des Kritischen Rationalismus. Zum 85. Geburtstag von Karl R. Popper* (Rodopi, 1989), p. 162.
80. Fred Eidlin, *ibid.* p. 163.
81. Fred Eidlin, *ibid.* p. 163.
82. Fred Eidlin, *ibid.* p. 165.
83. Fred Eidlin, *ibid.* p. 165.
84. Fred Eidlin, *ibid.* p. 165.
85. Fred Eidlin, *ibid.* pp. 165–166.
86. Fred Eidlin, *ibid.* p. 166.
87. David J., Stump, 'From the Values of Scientific Philosophy to the Value Neutrality of the Philosophy of Science', in Michael Heidelberger, Friedrich Stadler (eds.), *History of Philosophy of Science. New Trends and Perspectives* (Kluwer, 2002), p. 155.
88. David J., Stump, *ibid.* p. 156.
89. David J., Stump, *ibid.* p. 156.
90. However, positivist epistemology may be considered 'a-political' only insofar its methodological approach is concerned. On the other hand, mere abstention from value judgement is not unanimously considered as an 'apolitical' position. Lenin, for example, used the relationship of science and religion for demonstrating the political impact of allegedly 'apolitical' positions of scientists. In particular, Lenin observed that certain *Empiriocriticists*, as he called Positivists, shunned to apply their 'positive', i.e. intersubjective methodological approach to religious matters. On these ground, Lenin noted that the non-appliance of objective epistemological methods on religious matters is tantamount to subjectivity. In political context, though, Lenin held that the silence or even ambiguity of Positivists such as Ernst Mach and Josef Petzoldt was amounting to abet 'the bourgeois reaction', noting that "the neutrality of a philosopher in this [religious] matter is tantamount to sycophancy vis-à-vis of *Fideism* [that is, a subjectivistic epistemological approach basing on the pre-eminence of faith]" (V. I. Lenin, 'Materialismus und Empiriokritizismus. Kritische Bemerkungen über eine reaktionäre Philosophie', in *W. I. Lenin. Sämtliche Werke*. Vol. XIII. Translated into German from the 2nd revised Russian Edition, published in 1909 (Verlag für Literatur und Politik, Wien-Berlin, 1927), p. 352, translation from German into English by the author). Whether adopting a Marxian perspective or not, the example shows the intellectual dubiety of allegedly 'apolitical' or 'neutral' scientific positions.

On this note, it might be an interesting intellectual game to apply Lenin's litmus test to contemporary positivist scientists. Assuming it turns out that a significant segment of today's positivist scientists are still shunning to apply the requirement for scientific verification on religious matters (or the requirement for scientific falsification on atheism), then Positivism should, indeed, no longer be attributed to Materialism, but to Idealism.

91. Hans Joachim Störig, *Kleine Weltgeschichte der Philosophie*, Vol. 2 (Fischer, 1980), p. 145. Comte's income situation was so deplorable that he was compelled to hinge on the support of his friends over extended periods of his life. One of his friends and supporters was John Stuart Mill (Hans Joachim Störig, *ibid.*, p. 137).
92. Hans Joachim Störig, *ibid.* pp. 145–147.
93. A term derived from Thomas Erastus and *Erastianism*, indicating an understanding of the state prevailing in religious matters.
94. Margaret C. Jacob, 'Reflections on Bruno Latour's Version of the Seventeenth Century', in Noretta Koertge (ed.), *A House Built on Sand. Exposing Postmodernist Myths About Science* (Oxford University Press, 1998), p. 252 (emphasis added).
95. In its heydays, the perception and self-perception of Neopositivism as a politically progressive movement was a rather self-explaining feature, seemingly. In retrospect, however, the association of the Vienna Circle with political Liberalism may require some explanation, best given by the Vienna Circle itself:

> That Vienna was specially suitable ground for this development [i.e. a scientific world conception] is historically understandable. In the second half of the nineteenth century, liberalism was long the dominant political current. Its world of ideas stems from the enlightenment, from empiricism, utilitarianism and the free trade movement of England. In Vienna's liberal movement, scholars of world renown occupied leading positions. Here an anti-metaphysical spirit was cultivated, for instance, by men like Theodor Gomperz who translated the works of J. S. Mill, Suess, Jodl and others (Rudolf Carnap, Hans Hahn, Otto Neurath, 'The Scientific Conception of the World: The Vienna Circle', known as the *Vienna Circle Manifesto*, in Otto Neurath, *Empiricism and Sociology*, edited by Marie Neurath and Robert S. Cohen, volume 1 of the Vienna Circle Collection. (D. Reidel Publishing Company, 1973), p. 301)

With regard to later allegations that Neopositivism was coming along with an elitist understanding of science, as observed by Karl Popper, for example, it may be informative to shed light on a particular field of interest of the Vienna Circle, namely progressive education:

Thanks to this spirit of enlightenment, Vienna has been leading in a scientifically oriented people's education. With the collaboration of Victor Adler and Friedrich Jodl, the society of popular education was founded and carried forth; 'popular university courses' and the 'people's college' were set up by the well-known historian Ludo Hartmann whose anti-metaphysical attitude and materialist conception of history expressed itself in all his actions. The same spirit also inspired the movement of the 'Free School' which was the forerunner of today's school reform (Rudolf Carnap, Hans Hahn, Otto Neurath, 'The Scientific Conception of the World: The Vienna Circle', known as the *Vienna Circle Manifesto*, in Otto Neurath, *Empiricism and Sociology*, edited by Marie Neurath and Robert S. Cohen, volume 1 of the Vienna Circle Collection (D. Reidel Publishing Company, Dordrecht-Holland, 1973), p. 302).

The translation of Enlightenment values into concrete political action, in particular the call for popular education, marks a stark contrast between early Logical Empiricists of the Vienna Circle and later Neopositivists. As noted by Popper, for instance, later Neopositivism became more and more inclined to scientific elitism and punditocracy. The contrast between a political agenda presupposing the susceptibility of the public for scientific knowledge and an elitist concept of science should be treasured for the discussion about public involvement in risk assessment, following later in this paper. In terms of a preview, reference is made to Shrader-Frechette who observed that 'methodological errors (...) arise out of an expert-dominated conception of risk assessment as a wholly objective, purely scientific enterprise' (Kristin S. Shrader-Frechette, *Risk Analysis and Scientific Method. Methodological and Ethical Problems with Evaluating Societal Hazards* (D. Reidel Publishing Company, 1985), p. 202). With view on methodological solutions, Shrader-Frechette continued:

The methodological solutions needed to correct these errors arise out of a cooperative (citizen plus scientist) conception of risk assessment as a normative, policy-oriented enterprise with significant scientific elements. Unless the normative aspect of risk assessment is recognized, and unless the conception of the enterprise is changed accordingly, real negotiation over controversial technological policies will be impossible. This is because the first step in negotiation is mutual recognition of the complex sources of conflict. In this case, the controversy over technological and environmental risk is not merely over scientific methodology, but also over social values. Bit if this conflict is at least in part a controversy over societal values, and if Thomas Jefferson was correct that the only safe locus of societal power is in the people themselves, then the risk-assessment powers of society ought to be placed in part in the people themselves. If so, then analytic assessors must help both to *educate the public* and to amend, reformulate, and clarify risk-assessment methods (Kristin S. Shrader-Frechette, *ibid.* pp. 202–203, emphasis added).

96. A.W. Carus, 'The Philosopher without Qualities', in Michael Heidelberger, Friedrich Stadler (eds.), *History of Philosophy of Science. New Trends and Perspectives* (Kluwer Academic Publishers, 2002), p. 374.
97. A.W. Carus, *ibid.* pp. 374–375.
98. David J, Stump, 'From the Values of Scientific Philosophy to the Value Neutrality of the Philosophy of Science', in Michael Heidelberger, Friedrich Stadler (eds.), *History of Philosophy of Science. New Trends and Perspectives* (Kluwer, 2002), p. 155. It seems, however, that John McCumber has reached a different final conclusion with regard to the impact of Positivism in the USA. Whereas A.W. Carus and David Stump regarded the depolitisation of Positivism in the USA as a loss of meaning, McCumber seemed of having arrived at a more nuanced conclusion. Thomas Uebel noted: 'Rather than perpetuate the extremes of the Science Wars, McCumber employs the socio-political contextualization of analytical philosophy's rise to dominance in the post-World War II North America to ground a discussion that seeks to transcend an ongoing and unproductive divide in philosophy' (Thomas Uebel, 'The Poverty of 'Constructivist' History (and Policy Advice)', in Michael Heidelberger, Friedrich Stadler (eds.), *History of Philosophy of Science. New Trends and Perspectives* (Kluwer, 2002), p. 389; with reference to John McCumber, *Time in the Ditch. American Philosophy and the McCarthy Era* (Northwestern University Press, 2001).
99. Hans Joachim Störig, *Kleine Weltgeschichte der Philosophie*, Vol. 2 (Fischer, 1980), pp. 241–243.
100. Hans Joachim Störig, *ibid.* p. 241.
101. Charles Sanders Peirce, *Collected Papers*, Vol. V/VI (1934), p. 268, cited from Jürgen Habermas, *Kommunikatives Handeln und detranszendentalisierte Vernunft* (Reclam 2001), p. 20, footnote 13.
102. Jürgen Habermas, *Kommunikatives Handeln und detranszendentalisierte Vernunft* (Reclam 2001), pp. 20–21. Although Habermas questioned the 'epistemological' approach of Peirce as a model, he considered that to centring on *truth* as an angle might have a regulative function for evaluating (scientific) information. Furthermore, Peirce's proposal for a 'community of rational investigators' resembles Arthur Kantrowitz' model of a 'Science Court' (for more on the Science Court, see footnotes no. 166, 819 and 1418 below).
103. Hans Joachim Störig, *Kleine Weltgeschichte der Philosophie*, Vol. 2 (Fischer, 1980), p. 241.

104. Luc Ferry, *The new ecological order*. Original title: *Le nouvel ordre écologique: L'arbre, l'animal et l'homme* (Paris: Bernard Grasset, 1992), translated by Carol Volk (The University of Chicago Press, 1995), p. 149.
105. Raymond G. Frey, *Rights, Killing, and Suffering. Moral Vegetarianism and Applied Ethics* (Basil Blackwell Publisher Limited, 1983), p. 61.
106. See, for instance, Hans-Joachim Niemann, *Lexikon des Kritischen Rationalismus* (Mohr Siebeck, Tübingen 2004), p. 39.
107. Jürgen Falter, for example, argued that only radical and classical expressions of Behaviourism, as they have been developed by Burrhus Frederic Skinner and John Broadus Watson, should be subsumed under the 'Positivism' label (Jürgen W. Falter, 'Der ‚Positivismusstreit' in der amerikanischen Politikwissenschaft: Entstehung, Ablauf und Resultate der sogenannten Behavioralismus – Kontroverse in d. Vereinigten Staaten 1945–1975'. In *Beiträge zur sozialwissenschaftlichen Forschung, Band 37* (Westdeutscher Verlag, 1982), p. 199.
108. Gerald Holton, 'B.F. Skinner and P.W. Bridgman: The Frustration of a *Wahlverwandtschaft*' in Michael Heidelberger, Friedrich Stadler (eds.), *History of Philosophy of Science. New Trends and Perspectives* (Kluwer, 2002), pp. 335–337.
109. Gerald Holton, 'B.F. Skinner and P.W. Bridgman: The Frustration of a *Wahlverwandtschaft*' in Michael Heidelberger, Friedrich Stadler (eds.), *History of Philosophy of Science. New Trends and Perspectives* (Kluwer, 2002), p. 337. Similar to the *Positivismusstreit* (debate about Positivism) in Europe and particularly in Germany (see footnote no. 92 above), applications of neopositivist approaches to social sciences encountered opposition in the USA also. A major opponent of neopositivist attempts in social sciences was, for example, the 'Caucus for a New Political Science', established in 1967. The 'Caucus for a New Political Science' criticised expressions of Neopositivism in the USA, known as *Behaviorism*, in general and the neopositivist mainstream in the American Political Science Association (APSA) in particular. Accordingly, in the USA, the debate about Positivism became known as the *Behaviorism controversy* (Jürgen W. Falter, 'Der ‚Positivismusstreit' in der amerikanischen Politikwissenschaft: Entstehung, Ablauf und Resultate der sogenannten Behavioralismus – Kontroverse in den Vereinigten Staaten 1945–1975'. In *Beiträge zur sozialwissenschaftlichen Forschung, Band 37* (Westdeutscher Verlag, 1982), in particular pp. 53–62.
110. Nicholas Georgescu-Roegen, *Energy and Economic Myths. Institutional and Analytical Economic Essays* (Pergamon Press, 1976, New York), pp. 3–4.
111. Nicholas Georgescu-Roegen, *ibid.* p. 4 (original emphasis). Jacques Sapir, for instance, showed that positivist economists applied findings from

thermodynamic studies, such as the ergodic hypothesis, and developed econometrics based thereupon (Jacques Sapir, *Les trous noirs de la science économique. Essai sur l'impossibilité de penser le temps et l'argent* (Éditions Albin Michel, 2003), pp. 111–114). With respect to the alleged scientificity of economics, Sapir observed that econometric methods were applied for testing economic 'laws' which at the same time were foundational for these very same econometric methods [In French, the paragraph reads as follows: 'Les tests économétriques sont ainsi réputés établir notre connaissance des lois du système; mais pour que nous puissions interpréter leurs résultats en ce sens, il faut supposer a priori que de telles lois existent, sont générales, et que nous les connaissions. Cette fétichisation de l'usage des mathématiques et de la formalisation avait déjà été analysée et dénoncée par Keynes dans le *Traité des probabilités*' (Jacques Sapir, *ibid*., p. 114)]. Despite efforts to achieve scientificity, however, Sapir showed that positivist economics were unable to meet Popper's refutability criteria (Jacques Sapir, *ibid*., pp. 50–53. The title of the chapter reads, in French: 'Les économistes et l'extinction du poppérisme').

112. Paul A. Samuelson and William D. Nordhaus, *Economics*. 16th edition (Irwin/McGraw-Hill, 1998), p. 6 (original emphasis).
113. Robert Howse, 'From Politics to Technocracy – and Back Again: The Fate of the Multilateral Trading Regime' (2002), 96 *The American Journal of International Law*, 1 [94–117] 98 (footnote omitted, emphases added).
114. Joseph H.H. Weiler, 'The Rule of Lawyers and the Ethos of Diplomats: Reflections on WTO Dispute Settlement', in Roger B. Porter, Pierre Sauvé, Arvind Subramanian, and Americo Beviglia Zampetti (eds.), *Efficiency, Equity, and Legitimacy. The Multilateral Trading System at the Millennium* (Brookings Institution Press, 2001), pp. 334–350, pp. 336–337.
115. In particular, Eva Maria Belser referred to the economic concepts of the Pareto optimality and the Kaldor-Hicks efficiency (Eva Maria Belser, *The White Man's Burden. Arbeit und Menschenrechte in der globalisierten Welt* (Stämpfli Verlag AG Bern, 2007), pp. 302–305. Belser, however, noticed that the Kaldor-Hicks efficiency is based on the assumption that distributive justice will happen at respective national levels. In this respect, Belser referred to Robert Howse who added the following:

Thus, the notion that a more effective policy instrument than trade protection is always available to achieve any legitimate public end vastly oversimplifies the problem of politics. This notion tended to convert the *political* vision of embedded liberalism – dependent upon a *particular* value-laden idea of the liberal democratic, progressive, redistributive social welfare state – into an apparently timeless truth or dogma, valid across regimes, and more or less valid regardless of changed or changing economic and social circumstances, or changing public values. One simply *assumed* a certain toolbox of effective nontrade policy instruments, and the stability and viability of the social bargains within states as well, or at least the stability of institutions that construct and reconstruct such social bargains. Keynes had known better – for him, the prescription of free or freer trade was contingent and contextual, and might well have to yield to the demands of justice in given social and economic circumstances (Robert Howse, 'From Politics to Technocracy – and Back Again: The Fate of the Multilateral Trading Regime' (2002), 96 *The American Journal of International Law*, 1 [94–117] 100 (original emphases, footnotes omitted).

116. Eva Maria Belser, *The White Man's Burden. Arbeit und Menschenrechte in der globalisierten Welt* (Stämpfli, 2007), pp. 304–305.
117. Because positivist economics are factoring out concrete injustices at micro levels but are referring to abstract justice *qua* rising general welfare, Belser coined the term 'atavistic justice' (in German: *Gerechtigkeitsatavismen*; Eva Maria Belser, *ibid.*, p. 302).
118. Ulrich Beck, *Was ist Globalisierung?* (Suhrkamp, 1997), p. 195.
119. Ulrich Beck, *ibid.* The German original reads: 'Von dieser Komplexität der Globalität ist klar zu unterscheiden die *neue Einfachheit des Globalismus*, verstanden als alles durchdringende, alles verändernde Weltmarktherrschaft' (translation in English by the author).
120. Ulrich Beck, *ibid.*
121. Ulrich Beck, *ibid.* In the German original, the whole paragraph reads: 'Vielmehr soll das in der neoliberalen Ideologie des Globalismus verkündete Primat und Diktat des Weltmarktes für alle – für alle Dimensionen der Gesellschaft – als das aufgedeckt werden, was es ist: ein ins Gigantische projizierter, antiquierter Ökonomismus, eine Erneuerung der Geschichtsmetaphysik, eine sich unpolitisch gebende Gesellschaftsrevolution von oben' (translation in English by the author).
122. Ulrich Beck, *ibid.*, p. 196.
123. Ulrich Beck, *ibid.*, p. 196. In the German original, the whole paragraph reads as follows:

Globalismus reduziert die neue Komplexität von Globalität und Globalisierung auf *eine* – die wirtschaftliche – Dimension, *die auch noch linear* gedacht wird als ständige Ausdehnung der Abhängigkeiten vom Weltmarkt. Alle anderen Dimensionen – ökologische Globalisierung, kulturelle Globalisierung, polyzentrische Politik, die Entstehung transnationaler Räume und Identitäten – werden, wenn überhaupt, nur in der unterstellten Dominanz der wirtschaftlichen Globalisierung thematisiert. Weltgesellschaft wird so zur Welt*markt*gesellschaft verkürzt und verfälscht. In diesem Sinne ist der neoliberale Globalismus eine Erscheinungsform des *eindimensionalen* Denkens und Handelns, eine Spielart *monokausaler* Weltsicht, also des Ökonomismus. Reiz und Gefahr dieser keineswegs neuen Geschichtsmetaphysik des Weltmarktes entstammen derselben Quelle: der Suche, der Sucht nach Einfachheit, um sich in der undurchschaubarer gewordenen Welt zurechtzufinden (Ulrich Beck, *ibid.*, pp. 196–197; original emphases).

124. Ankie Hoogvelt, *Globalization and the Postcolonial World. The New Political Economy of Development.* 2nd Edition (Palgrave Macmillan, 2001), pp. 154–155, original emphasis. With particular view on the essentially ideological, i.e. non-scientific character of Globalism, Hoogvelt added that '[t]hese beliefs are based on what Pierre Bourdieu has described as *"doxa"*—"an evidence not debated and undebatable"' (Ankie Hoogvelt, *ibid.*).
125. The French term *pensée unique* could be translated as uniform, unitary or standardised thinking, or the one-way thought, approximately. Ramonet was a founding father of the non-governmental organisation ATTAC. Founded in France as an association in favour of the introduction of a Tobin tax against financial speculation, the Association for the Taxation of Financial Transactions for the Aid of Citizens (in French: Association pour une taxation des transactions financières pour l'aide aux citoyens) ATTAC has evolved into an NGO actively engaged in various issues related to the globalisation debate.
126. Ignacio Ramonet, 'La pensée unique', in *Le Monde diplomatique*, January 1995, p. 1. In his seminal article, Ramonet also drew attention to a number of concrete policies resulting from the adoption of *pensée unique*, such as, *inter alia*, international competition with unrestricted movement of goods and the division of labour on the global scale, hard currency policies, deregulation, privatisation, and the call for less government in general.
127. Ignacio Ramonet, *ibid.*
128. Starting with the establishment of the uncertainty principle by Werner Heisenberg in 1926, modern science increasingly turned to models of probability and randomness. In addition of being an effective analytical tool, certain scientists may have sought refuge in positivist Empiricism as a way to preserve a notion of certainty in an increasingly complex scientific enterprise.
129. From time to time however, scientific progress gives rise to renewed hopes for achieving *unified science* in the literal sense of the world, that is, on material basis. One particular revival of the pursuit of *unified science* was triggered by the dawn of nanosciences and the possibility of converging

promising technologies such as nanotechnology, biotechnology, information technology and cognitive (neuro-)science (NBIC). In a report on converging technologies, it was announced that '[t]he building blocks of matter that are fundamental to all sciences' have been detected:

Convergence of diverse technologies is based on *material unity at the nanoscale and on technology integration from that scale.* The building blocks of matter that are fundamental to all sciences originate at the nanoscale. Revolutionary advances at the interfaces between previously separate fields of science and technology are ready to create key *transforming tools* for NBIC technologies. Developments in systems approaches, mathematics, and computation in conjunction with NBIC allow us for the first time to understand the natural world, human society, and scientific research as *closely coupled complex, hierarchical systems* (Mihail C. Roco and William Sims Bainbridg (eds.), *Converging Technologies for Improving Human Performance. Nanotechnology, Biotechnology, Information Technology and Cognitive Science.* Joint report of the National Science Foundation (NSF) and the Department of Commerce (Kluwer Academic Publishers, 2003), p. ix (original emphasis). Web access: http://www.wtec.org/ConvergingTechnologies/Report/NBIC_report.pdf, visited December 22, 2010). For more on NBIC, see footnotes no. 96 above and no. 265 and 516 below.

130. Willard Van Orman Quine (1908–2000) was a logician in the tradition of the *Analytical Philosophy* who questioned, and transcended, positions of logical Positivism.
131. Harold Kincaid, *Philosophical Foundations of the Social Sciences. Analyzing Controversies in Social Research* (Cambridge University Press, 1996), p. 20.
132. Harold Kincaid, *Philosophical Foundations of the Social Sciences. Analyzing Controversies in Social Research* (Cambridge University Press, 1996), p. 20, citing William Quine and J. S. Ullian, *The Web of Belief* (Random House, New York, 1970).
133. Harold Kincaid, *Philosophical Foundations of the Social Sciences. Analyzing Controversies in Social Research* (Cambridge University Press, 1996), p. 20 (original italics).
134. Karl Popper defined—and criticised—Relativism as follows: 'One of the components of modern irrationalism is relativism (the doctrine that truth is relative to our intellectual background, which is supposed to determine somehow the framework within which we are able to think: that truth may change from one framework to another), and, in particular, the doctrine of the impossibility of mutual understanding between different cultures, generations, or historical periods—even within science, even within physics' (Karl R. Popper, *The Myth of the Framework. In defence of science and*

rationality. Edited by M.A. Notturno (Routledge, 1994), p. 33; in similar ways: Karl R. Popper, 'The Self, Rationality, and Freedom', in *Knowledge and the Body-Mind Problem. In defence of interaction*. Edited by M.A. Notturno (Routledge, 1994), p. 137.

135. Kristin S. Shrader-Frechette, *Risk and Rationality. Philosophical Foundations for Populist Reforms* (University of California Press, 1991), p. 7. Considering the focus of the study at hand on the separation of science and policy in risk assessment, it may be of interest that Feyerabend suggested—in analogy to the separation of religion and state—a separation of science and state. Such a thorough separation of science and the state would enable alternative forms of science to flourish, thus increasing the variety of answers to the problems of society (see Eduard Kaeser, *Pop Science. Essays zur Wissenschaftskultur* (Schwabe Verlag, Basel 2009), p. 46). Thinking Feyerabend's approach through to the end might open the floor for alternative forms of risk assessment as well.
136. Kristin S. Shrader-Frechette, *Risk and Rationality. Philosophical Foundations for Populist Reforms* (University of California Press, 1991), in particular pp. 8, 29, 31.
137. Kristin S. Shrader-Frechette, *ibid.* p. 31, footnote no. 30.
138. See Margaret C. Jacob, 'Reflections on Bruno Latour's Version of the Seventeenth Century', in Noretta Koertge (ed.), *A House Built on Sand. Exposing Postmodernist Myths About Science* (Oxford University Press, 1998), p. 240.
139. Gabriele Klein, 'Bodies in Translation. Tango als kulturelle Übersetzung'. In Gabriele Klein (ed.), *Tango in Translation. Tanz zwischen Medien, Kulturen, Kunst und Politik* (transcript Verlag, 2009), in particular the chapter on cultural theories ('Übersetzung als kulturtheoretisches Konzept'), pp. 24–28.
140. Gabriele Klein, *ibid.* pp. 24–25.
141. Gabriele Klein, *ibid.* pp. 24, translation from German into English by the author.
142. Anthony Giddens, 'Living in a Post-Traditional Society', in Ulrich Beck, Anthony Giddens and Scott Lash, *Reflexive Modernization. Politics, Tradition and Aesthetics in the Modern Social Order*. Polity Press, 1994), p. 97.
143. Anthony Giddens, 'Living in a Post-Traditional Society', in Ulrich Beck, Anthony Giddens and Scott Lash, *Reflexive Modernization. Politics, Tradition and Aesthetics in the Modern Social Order* (Polity Press, 1994), p. 97.
144. Anthony Giddens, 'Living in a Post-Traditional Society', in Ulrich Beck, Anthony Giddens and Scott Lash, *Reflexive Modernization. Politics, Tradition and Aesthetics in the Modern Social Order*. Polity Press, 1994), p. 97 (emphasis added).

145. Anthony Giddens, 'Living in a Post-Traditional Society', in Ulrich Beck, Anthony Giddens and Scott Lash, *Reflexive Modernization. Politics, Tradition and Aesthetics in the Modern Social Order*. Polity Press, 1994), p. 97.
146. Anthony Giddens, 'Living in a Post-Traditional Society', in Ulrich Beck, Anthony Giddens and Scott Lash, *Reflexive Modernization. Politics, Tradition and Aesthetics in the Modern Social Order*. Polity Press, 1994), p. 100, citing the philosopher Richard Rorty.
147. Anthony Giddens, 'Living in a Post-Traditional Society', in Ulrich Beck, Anthony Giddens and Scott Lash, *Reflexive Modernization. Politics, Tradition and Aesthetics in the Modern Social Order*. Polity Press, 1994), p. 98.
148. In a nutshell, Historicism argues that due to historical relativity, laws developed in natural sciences are not applicable in social sciences (Karl Popper, *Das Elend des Historizismus*, authorised translation from the 2nd English edition *The Poverty of Historicism*, London, Routledge&Kegan Paul, 1960, translated by Dr. Leonhard Walentik, (J.C.B. Mohr (Paul Siebeck) 1965), p. 5. It has to be noted that Popper distinguished between 'historicism' as a label for theories of history he deemed inappropriate, and 'historical relativism' which he referred to as 'historism' (see (Karl R. Popper, 'A Pluralist Approach to the Philosophy of History', in *The Myth of the Framework. In defence of science and rationality*. Edited by M.A. Notturno (Routledge, 1994), p. 131.
149. Hans Joachim Störig, *Kleine Weltgeschichte der Philosophie*, vol. 2 (Fischer, 1980), p. 240. With his focus on the 'living environment' (in German: *Lebenswelt*), Dilthey added a particular and rather holistic spin to hermeneutics (see Thomas Nipperdey, *Deutsche Geschichte 1866–1918*. Volume I. *Arbeitswelt und Bürgergeist* (Verlag C.H. Beck, 1994), pp. 684–686.
150. In English: humanities; in German: Human-/Geisteswissenschaften.
151. Hans Joachim Störig, *Kleine Weltgeschichte der Philosophie*, vol. 2 (Fischer, 1980), p. 240.
152. Hans Joachim Störig, *ibid*. p. 240. It may be added that the separation of natural sciences from human sciences, leading towards relativism, can be considered as an antipode to the positivist quest for unified science. Whereas Auguste Comte and the later Neopositivists tried to unify science thorough paramount disciplines, i.e. sociology and logic respectively, historicists like Dilthey established history as leading and unique branch of science (Hans Joachim Störig, *ibid*., pp. 142 and 240).
153. Hans-Georg Gadamer, *Truth and Method*, translated by William Glen-Doepel, edited by John Cumming and Garrett Barden, 2nd edition (Sheed and Ward Lt., 1979), p. 174 (emphasis added).

154. Hans-Georg Gadamer, *ibid.* p. 174. From Gadamer's observations, one may draw the conclusion that the 'historical method' consisted of a comprehensive approach towards text and context, apprehending both layers simultaneously. Looked at from this angle, one may well see the trend from the 'historical method' of nineteenth-century Germany to modern concepts of contextualism.
155. Hans Joachim Störig, *Kleine Weltgeschichte der Philosophie*, vol. 2 (Fischer, 1980), p. 217. The controversy over whether and how to discern between nomothetic and idiographic sciences is still open. In *Poverty of Historicism*, Karl Popper insisted on the thesis of unified scientific method against the historicist attempt to separate natural and cultural sciences and to put history into an exceptional position (Karl Popper, *Das Elend des Historizismus*, authorised translation from the 2nd English edition *The Poverty of Historicism*, London, Routledge & Kegan Paul, 1960, translated by Dr. Leonhard Walentik, (J.C.B. Mohr (Paul Siebeck), 1965), pp. 102–115; in similar ways, Karl R. Popper, 'A Pluralist Approach to the Philosophy of History', in *The Myth of the Framework. In defence of science and rationality.* Edited by M.A. Notturno (Routledge, 1994), pp. 137–153, in particular p. 139 where Popper reiterated his thesis that 'all those historians [some lines above, Popper had explicitly mentioned, among others, Windelband and Dilthey] and philosophers of history who insist on the gulf between history and the natural sciences have a radically mistaken idea of the natural sciences').
156. Hans Joachim Störig, *Kleine Weltgeschichte der Philosophie*, vol. 2 (Fischer Taschenbuch Verlag, 1980, Frankfurt a.M.), p. 217.
157. Hans Joachim Störig, *ibid.*
158. The observation that Historicism emerged from German Romanticism was expressed, for example, by Hans-Georg Gadamer. Gadamer noted: 'So we see that romantic hermeneutics and the background to it, the pantheistic metaphysics of individuality, was a decisive influence on the theory of historical research in the nineteenth century [in Germany]' (Hans-Georg Gadamer, *Truth and Method*, translated by William Glen-Doepel, edited by John Cumming and Garrett Barden, 2nd edition (Sheed and Ward Lt., 1979), p. 174.
159. Hans Joachim Störig, *Kleine Weltgeschichte der Philosophie*, vol. 2 (Fischer Taschenbuch Verlag, 1980), pp. 157–158. Georg Wilhelm Friedrich Hegel (1770–1831), in turn, was characterised by Karl Popper as 'both a relativists and an absolutist'. Popper configured Hegel at the top of 'a long chain of post-Kantian, that is, post-critical or post-rationalist philosophers —mainly German—who upheld the myth of the framework [i.e. the myth that frameworks of laws and customs cannot be rationally discussed]' (See Karl R. Popper, *The Myth of the Framework. In defence of science and*

rationality. Edited by M.A. Notturno (Routledge, 1994), p. 47. Poppers allegation that Hegel was an 'absolutist' sheds light on the distinction between philosophical approaches used either as ideology or as scientific method. With reference to the so-called positivism dispute (in German: *Positivismusstreit*), Popper explained: 'As it now stands, the main issue of the book [i.e., *Der Positivismusstreit in der deutschen Soziologie*] has become Adorno's and Habermas' accusation that a 'positivist' like Popper is bound by his methodology to defend the political *status quo*. It is an accusation which I myself raised in my *Open Society* against Hegel, whose identity philosophy (what is real is reasonable) I described as 'moral and legal positivism'. In my address I had said nothing about this issue, and I had no opportunity to reply. But I have often combated this form of 'positivism' along with other forms. And it is a fact that my *social theory* (which favours gradual and piecemeal reform, reform controlled by a critical comparison between expected and achieved results) contrasts with my *theory of method*, which happens to be a theory of scientific and intellectual revolution' (Karl R. Popper, 'Reason or Revolution?' in *The Myth of the Framework. In defence of science and rationality*. Edited by M.A. Notturno (Routledge, 1994), p. 68; original emphases).
It has to be noted, though, that Hegel's *dialectical method* and *absolute idealism* is usually associated with the idealistic strain of post-Kantian philosophy, rather than with romanticism (see Hans Joachim Störig, *Kleine Weltgeschichte der Philosophie*, vol. 2 (Fischer, 1980), pp. 127–129.

160. Hans Joachim Störig, *ibid*. p. 158 (German citation by Störig, translation by the author).
161. Philosophical hermeneutics raised objections against 'the ideal of objectivity' and the application of objectivistic methodological criteria in the human sciences. Osman Bilen explained: 'Understanding in the human sciences is accomplished not from a free and distanced position but arises from immediate life concerns, prejudices and traditions that shape both the interpreting subject and the object of the research. Moreover, not only is the interpretation guided by fore-understanding, but also the objectivity of the result cannot be measured by the yardstick of method according the model of the natural sciences' (Osman Bilen, *The Historicity of Understanding and The Problem of Relativism in Gadamer's Philosophical Hermeneutics* (The Council for Research in Values and Philosophy, 2000), p. 150).
162. Hans-Georg Gadamer, *Wahrheit und Methode*, 3rd Edition (J.C.B. Mohr (Paul Siebeck) 1972), p. 513. Because the epilogue of the 3rd German edition, published 1972, was not integrated in the 2nd English edition of 1979, the quotations are taken from the German version and translations by the author. Nevertheless and also because of its characteristic style, the respective paragraph shall be provided in German:

Als ich Ende 1959 das vorliegend Buch beendete, war ich mir darüber sehr unsicher, ob es nicht "zu spät"käme, d.h. ob die Bilanz traditionsgeschichtlichen Denkens, die in ihm gezogen wurde, nicht schon beinahe überflüssig sei. Zeichen einer neuen Welle technologischer Geschichtsfeindlichkeit mehrten sich. Ihr entsprach die steigende Rezeption der angelsächsischen Wissenschaftstheorie und analytischen Philosophie, und schließlich verhieß auch der neue Aufschwung, den die Sozialwissenschaften, darunter vor allem die Sozialpsychologie und die Soziolinguistik, nahmen, der humanistischen Tradition der *romantischen Geisteswissenschaften* keine Zukunft. Das aber war die Tradition, von der ich ausgegangen war. Sie stellte den Erfahrungsboden meiner theoretischen Arbeit dar – wenn auch keineswegs ihre Grenze oder gar ihr Ziel. Aber selbst innerhalb der klassischen geschichtlichen Geisteswissenschaften war ein Stilwandel in Richtung auf die neuen methodischen Mittel der *Statistik*, der *Formalisierung*, war der Drang zur *Wissenschaftsplanung* und *technischen Organisation* von Forschung unverkennbar. Ein neues "positivistisches" Selbstverständnis, das durch die Rezeption amerikanischer und englischer Methoden und Fragestellungen befördert wurde, drängte vorwärts.

(Hans-Georg Gadamer, *Wahrheit und Methode*, 3rd Edition (J.C.B. Mohr (Paul Siebeck), 1972), p. 513, emphases added.

163. Hans-Georg Gadamer, *ibid.*
164. Hans-Georg Gadamer, *ibid.*
165. Hans-Georg Gadamer, *Truth and Method*, translated by William Glen-Doepel, edited by John Cumming and Garrett Barden, 2nd edition (Sheed and Ward Lt., London 1979), p. xvii (foreword to the 2nd Edition).
166. Sungjoon Cho, 'From Control to Communication: Science, Philosophy and World Trade Law' (2010). Cornell International Law Journal, forthcoming. Available at SSRN: http://ssrn.com/abstract=1583023 (visited December 5, 2010).
167. Sungjoon Cho, *ibid.* (footnotes omitted).
168. Thomas Uebel, 'The Poverty of "Constructivist" History (and Policy Advice)', in Michael Heidelberger, Friedrich Stadler (eds.), *History of Philosophy of Science. New Trends and Perspectives* (Kluwer, 2002), p. 379.
169. Thomas Uebel, *ibid.* pp. 379–380.
170. Thomas Uebel, *ibid.* p. 379. By reviewing works of another constructivist author, Steve Fuller, who wrote about Kuhn (*Thomas Kuhn. A Philosophical History for Our Time*, and *The Governance of Science*), Uebel consented to the view expressed in Noretta Koertge (ed.), *A House Built on Sand. Exposing Postmodernist Myths About Science* (Oxford University Press, 1998) that 'some of the social constructivist literature on science tends to owe its revolutionary appeal to subtle elisions in argument

and not so subtle confusions of related concepts' (Thomas Uebel, *ibid.* p. 388).

171. *Volksgeist*, an intricate German term, may be translated as 'national character', although the Germanism 'Volk' and the English term 'nation' are not synonymic; the Germanism 'Volk' seems to be closer to the similarly ambiguous English term 'cultural nation'.
172. Hans Joachim Störig, *Kleine Weltgeschichte der Philosophie*, vol. 2 (Fischer, 1980), p. 110.
173. Hans Joachim Störig, *ibid.*
174. Hans Joachim Störig, *ibid.*
175. Hans Joachim Störig, *ibid.* pp. 110–111. A concise account of Kant's theory of knowledge was provided by Karl Popper. Using Kant's terminology, whereby 'knowledge a priori means knowledge that we possess *prior* to sense-observation; and knowledge a posteriori means knowledge we possess *posterior* to sense-observation', Popper explained Kant's reasoning as follows: [citation start]

(A) Most knowledge of detail, of the momentary state of our surroundings, is a posteriori.

(B) But such a posteriori knowledge is impossible without a priori knowledge that we somehow *must* possess before we can acquire observational or a posteriori knowledge: without it, *what our senses tell us can make no sense.* We must establish an overall frame of reference, or else there will be no context available to make sense of our sensations.

(C) This a priori knowledge contains, especially, knowledge of the structure of space and time (of space and time relations), and of causality (of causal relations). [citation end]

See Karl R. Popper, 'Towards an Evolutionary Theory of Knowledge', in Karl R. Popper, *A World of Propensities* (Thoemmes Antiquarian Books Ltd., 1990), pp. 45–46 (italics in original). In his epistemological theory, Popper goes even further than Kant, noting that 'all observations are theory-impregnated, and that their main function is to check and refute, rather than to prove, our theories' (see Karl R. Popper, 'Reason or Revolution?' in *The Myth of the Framework. In defence of science and rationality*. Edited by M.A. Notturno (Routledge, 1994), p. 75.

176. Hans Joachim Störig, *Kleine Weltgeschichte der Philosophie*. Vol. 2 (Fischer, 1980), p. 106. As mentioned above, Positivism is not tantamount to Materialism. Well to the contrary, positivists disapprove the materialist notion that virtually *everything* is physical as unverifiable metaphysics.
177. Hans Joachim Störig, *ibid.* p. 106. Hence, the term 'reactionary' is appropriate for conflating the essence of Romanticism.

178. Hans Joachim Störig, *ibid.* pp. 106–107. However, in terms of a caveat, it has to be noted that the traditional classification of philosophical schools of thought, as provided by Störig, for example, is not beyond question. In particular—and perhaps surprisingly—the attribution of Positivism to Materialism, although rather hegemonic these days, remained not always undisputed. In *Materialism and Empiriocriticism*, an intellectual controversy with the ideas of Ernst Mach, Vladimir Iilyich Lenin depicted a more dialectical view on philosophy, discerning only between two major schools of thought, namely Materialism and Idealism. With reference to Marx and Engels, Lenin denied philosophical attempts other than Materialism any intellectual autonomy, subsuming them under a broad notion of Idealism (see V.I. Lenin, 'Materialismus und Empiriokritizismus. Kritische Bemerkungen über eine reaktionäre Philosophie', in *W.I. Lenin. Sämtliche Werke.* Vol. XIII. Translated into German from the 2nd revised Russian Edition, published in 1909 (Verlag für Literatur und Politik, Wien-Berlin, 1927), in particular pp. 342–355). Interestingly, though, Lenin also recognised Positivism as a form of disguised Idealism. Lenin's respective arguments seem noteworthy. Lenin started with a definition of Positivism as a school of thought based on 'positive' knowledge, that is, 'empiricism' in the first instance. However, Lenin observed that Positivists were interpreting 'empiricism' not as an approach towards the material world independent from man, but as man's very perception. Lenin further observed that Positivists are leaving it open, at best, whether or not human perception is a reflection of a material world existing independently from that perception. Lenin found that the idealism of Positivists was most clearly expressed in the field of the social sciences. Positivists, Lenin noted, were making societal developments contingent upon the development of ideas and sciences, etc., instead of the other way round, i.e. instead of drawing ideas from developments in society (see V.I. Lenin, *ibid.*, p. 394, note one on Positivism).
179. Scott Lash, 'Expert-Systems or Situated Interpretation? Culture and Institutions in Disorganized Capitalism', in Ulrich Beck, Anthony Giddens and Scott Lash, *Reflexive Modernization. Politics, Tradition and Aesthetics in the Modern Social Order.* Polity Press, 1994), p. 212.
180. With regard to painting, one has to consider Caspar David Friedrich (1774–1840).
181. Patrick J.J. Phillips, "The Challenge of Relativism—Its Nature and Limits", Continuum International Publishing Group (2007): 132–133 (original emphases).
182. A modern example of the thinking in a '"we-against-the-others dichotomy' is Samuel P. Huntington's *The Clash of Civilizations* (1996).

183. Nicholas Georgescu-Roegen illustrated implications of the notion of relativity in physics on epistemology by putting forward the example of two voyagers in space observing the same incident as two different facts: '[O]ne observer may see "a flash of yellow light" while the other may only feel "a glow of heat on his finger". How can they be sure then that they have reported the same event since they cannot turn to simultaneity in the absence of absolute time?' asked Georgescu-Roegen (Nicholas Georgescu-Roegen, *Analytical Economics. Issues and Problems* (Harvard University Press, 1967, Massachusetts), p. 37, with reference to Percy Williams Bridgman (*The Nature of Physical Theory,* Princeton University Press, 1936) from whom Georgescu-Roegen took the example).
184. Stephen Hawking, *A Brief History of Time. From the Big Bang to Black Holes* (Bantam Books, 1989), pp. 20–21 and 58–59.
185. Stephen Hawking, *ibid.* p. 59. Pierre-Simon Marquis the Laplace (1749–1827) assumed that the universe was governed by universal laws—similar to mechanical laws—whose knowledge would enable accurate predictions. Hawking provided the following example: '[I]f we knew the positions and speeds of the sun and the planets at one time, then we could use Newton's laws to calculate the state of the Solar System at any other time. Determinism seems fairly obvious in this case, but Laplace went further to assume that there were similar laws governing everything else, including human behaviour' (Stephen Hawking, *ibid.*, p. 57).
186. Stephen Hawking, *ibid.* p. 59.
187. Stephen Hawking, *ibid.* p. 60.
188. John Desmond Bernal, *The Freedom of Necessity*, Routledge & Kegan Paul, 1949), p. 100.
189. John Desmond Bernal, *ibid.* p. 99.
190. John Desmond Bernal, *ibid.* pp. 99–100.
191. John Desmond Bernal, *ibid.* p. 98. Bernal explained that the popularity of the theory of relativity was heightened by the fact that particular segments of the scientific community also seized the opportunity to reconcile with metaphysic beliefs. Bernal noted: 'The scientists, on the other hand, were able to see that it was not necessary to attach themselves to a rigid framework of matter and ether in order to explain the data of observation, and that in fact it was better to abandon it, and that made them more inclined to include in their personal beliefs metaphysical elements which before they would have been ashamed to admit' (John Desmond Bernal, *ibid.*).
192. James Hopwood Jeans (1877–1946) was a physicist and cosmologist. Bernal summarised the 'mysticism' of scientists such as James Jeans as follows:

The changes in the appearances of the properties of things that we call chemistry are the results of movements which occur on a scale altogether too small for our senses to appreciate them directly. To handle them conveniently we have recourse to certain arguments which for convenience are put into mathematical symbols. The things with which these symbols deal are not the ordinary objects of our senses, though those objects are made out of them. But, argues [James] Jeans, if we cannot say what the things are, they cannot be ordinary things; they must be purely mathematical themselves, and since the universe is made out of them and God made the universe, God himself must be a mathematician. The argument is not a new one. Plato put it forward in ancient Greece, and it is probably three thousand ears older than that. But when it was first put forward it was an honest attempt of the people who had just evolved the basic trades – the smiths, the carpenters, the potters – to explain the making of the world in terms of the things they themselves were making for the first time. Now it is the last apologetic attempt to preserve a tottering social order (John Desmond Bernal, *The Freedom of Necessity*, Routledge & Kegan Paul, London 1949), p. 107).

193. John Desmond Bernal, *ibid.* p. 107.
194. Any convergency between Positivism and Idealism seems to be at odds with a traditional mindset depicting the two philosophical strands as antithetic on principle. However, from other perspectives, other interpretations may unfold. Hypothesising a Marxist perspective, for instance, implies the recognition of Positivism—as well as Realism—as a disguised form of Idealism (V.I. Lenin, 'Materialismus und Empiriokritizismus. Kritische Bemerkungen über eine reaktionäre Philosophie', in *W.I. Lenin. Sämtliche Werke.* Vol. XIII. Translated into German from the 2nd revised Russian Edition, published in 1909 (Verlag für Literatur und Politik, 1927), p. 348). From a Marxist perspective, Vladimir Iilyich Lenin observed that the majority of scientists were taking a clear stance for Materialism. However, Lenin noted that a minority of physicists, under the impression of collapsing theories and relativity, was sliding via Relativism into Idealism. On these grounds, Lenin concluded that 'the fashionable physical Idealism of our days is a similarly reactionary and ephemeral straw fire as it was the physiological Idealism in the recent past' (V. I. Lenin, *ibid.* pp. 366–367; translation from German into English by the author).
195. Stephen Hawking, *A Brief History of Time. From the Big Bang to Black Holes* (Bantam Books, 1989), pp. 11–14 and 163.
196. Stephen Hawking, *ibid.* p. 11. It seems, however, that Hawking related the objective of a unified scientific theory to a rather metaphysical reason. By determining the "ultimate triumph of human reason" as an understanding of "the mind of God", Hawking implicitly limited human reason by a metaphysical framework. Hawing wrote:

However, if we do discover a complete theory, (…) [t]hen we shall all, philosophers, scientists, and just ordinary people, be able to take part in the discussion of the question of why it is that we and the universe exist. If we find the answer to that, it would be the ultimate triumph of human reason – for then we would know the mind of God. (Stephen Hawking, *ibid.* p. 185)

197. Stephen Hawking, *ibid.* p. 184. In defence of (neo-)Positivism, it has to be noted that logical empiricists had found a way to address challenges posed by the theory of relativity by rational arguments rather than by relying on metaphysical ideas. The rational approach of logical empiricists to challenges posed by the theory of relativity consisted in 'a radically new conception of the [Kantian] a priori' (Michael Friedman, 'Kant, Kuhn, and the Rationality of Science'. In: Michael Heidelberger, Friedrich Stadler (eds.), *History of Philosophy of Science. New Trends and Perspectives* (Kluwer, 2002), p. 27. Friedman noted:

Perhaps the clearest articulation of the logical empiricists's new view was provided by Hans Reichenbach in his first book, *The Theory of Relativity and A Priori Knowledge*, published in 1920. Reichenbach distinguishes two meanings of the Kantian a priori: necessary and unrevisable, fixed for all time, on the one hand, and 'constitutive of the concept of the object of [scientific] knowledge', on the other. Reichenbach argues, on this basis, that the great lesson of the theory of relativity is that the former meaning must be dropped while the latter must be retained. Relativity theory involves a priori constitutive principles as necessary presuppositions of its properly empirical claims, just as much as did Newtonian physics, but these principles have essentially changed in the transition from the latter theory to the former: whereas Euclidean geometry is indeed constitutively a priori in the context of Newtonian physics, for example, only *infinitesimally* Euclidean geometry is constitutively a priori in the context of general relativity. What we end up with, in this tradition, is thus a relativized and dynamical conception of a priori mathematical-physical principles, which change and develop along with the development of the mathematical and physical sciences themselves, but which nevertheless retain the characteristically Kantian constitutive function of making the empirical natural knowledge thereby structured and framed by such principles first possible (Michael Friedman, *ibid.* p. 27; original emphasis, footnote omitted).

198. Fritjof Capra, *Wendezeit. Bausteine für ein neues Weltbild.* Original English title: *The Turning Point* (1982) (Ex Libris, 1984), p. 82.
199. Fritjof Capra, *ibid.* p. 256. An interesting example for new economic approaches provided Capra himself by pointing at the fact that, on a new

calculative basis of energy input per calorie produced, the US agroindustry is the least productive agricultural production system worldwide (Fritjof Capra, *ibid.* p. 252).

200. Fritjof Capra, *ibid.* pp. 58–59. René Descartes (1596–1650) was an eminent philosopher and mathematician pioneering analytical scientific thinking (see, for example, Hans Joachim Störig, *Kleine Weltgeschichte der Philosophie,* vol. 1 (Fischer, 1980), pp. 318–326. Before this philosophical background, attempts of contemporary Positivism for establishing a rigid separation of values and facts in risk assessment may be considered in the continuum of the Cartesian mind–body dichotomy—and attempts of contemporary Relativism for integrating value considerations into risk assessment in the tradition of holistic approaches.
201. Eduard Kaeser, *Pop Science. Essays zur Wissenschaftskultur* (Schwabe Verlag, 2009), p. 143.
202. Eduard Kaeser, *ibid.* pp. 109–110.
203. Eduard Kaeser, *ibid.* pp.114–115. On these ground, Kaeser called such novel technologies 'transcendence technologies' (in German: Transzendenztechnologien). The convergence of various 'transcendence technologies' such as nanotechnology, biotechnology, information technology and cognitive science (NBIC) has aroused a revival of promises for redeeming mankind with scientific means. In a report entitled *Converging Technologies for Improving Human Performance*, Mihail C. Roco and William Sims Bainbridg announced:

At this unique moment in the history of technical achievement, *improvement of human performance* becomes possible. Caught in the grip of social, political, and economic conflicts, the world hovers between optimism and pessimism. NBIC convergence can give us the means to deal successfully with these challenges by substantially enhancing human mental, physical, and social abilities. Better understanding of the human body and development of tools for direct human-machine interaction have opened completely new opportunities. Efforts must center on individual and collective human advancement, in terms of an enlightened conception of human benefit that embraces change while preserving fundamental values (Mihail C. Roco and William Sims Bainbridg (eds.), *Converging Technologies for Improving Human Performance. Nanotechnology, Biotechnology, Information Technology and Cognitive Science.* Joint report of the National Science Foundation (NSF) and the Department of Commerce (Kluwer Academic Publishers, 2003), p. 3 (original emphasis). See also Stefan L. Gammel, 'Visionen der Nano(bio)technologie', in Kristian Köchy, Martin Norwig, Georg Hofmeister (eds.), Nanobiotechnologien. Philosophische, anthropologische und ethische Fragen (Verlag Karl Alber, 2008), [pp. 203–228], in particular pp. 206–214). For more on NBIC, see footnotes no. 96 and 193 above, and no. 516 below.

The latest candidate for becoming a new 'transcendence technology' may be astrobiology, the study and prospection of life forms in the universe.

204. Noretta Koertge, 'Scrutinizing Science Studies', in Noretta Koertge (ed.), *A House Built on Sand. Exposing Postmodernist Myths about Science* (Oxford University Press, 1998), p. 3.
205. Noretta Koertge, *ibid.*
206. Cited from Noretta Koertge, 'Scrutinizing Science Studies', in Noretta Koertge (ed.), *A House Built on Sand. Exposing Postmodernist Myths about Science* (Oxford University Press, 1998), pp. 3–4.
207. Lesbian, gay, bisexual, transgender, queer.
208. Kathi von Daeniken and Brigitte Schnegg, 'Gender as a Horizontal Issue within NCCR Trade Regulation'. Handout to the presentation provided at the *Annual Conference 2010 of NCCR Trade Regulation*, on June 29, 2010, at the World Trade Institute in Bern, p. 2.
209. Alessandro Nicita and Simonetta Zarrilli, 'Trade Policy and Gender—Unfolding the Links' (2010), 44 *Journal of World Trade* [203–222], 205.
210. Nancy Tuana, 'Coming to Understand. Orgasm and the Epistemology of Ignorance,' in Robert N. Proctor and Londa Schiebinger (eds.), *Agnotology. The Making and Unmaking of Ignorance* (Stanford University Press, 2008), p. 140.
211. French original title: *Le Deuxième Sexe.*
212. Luc Ferry, *The new ecological order.* Original title: *Le nouvel ordre écologique: L'arbre, l'animal et l'homme* (Bernard Grasset, 1992), translated by Carol Volk (The University of Chicago Press, 1995), p. 116.
213. Luc Ferry, *ibid.* p. 117 (original emphases).
214. Luc Ferry, *ibid.* p. 125 (original emphases).
215. Luc Ferry, *ibid.* p. 118 (original emphases).
216. Vandana Shiva, *Earth Democracy. Justice, Sustainability, and Peace.* Zed Books, 2005), p. 17.
217. Luc Ferry, *The new ecological order* (The University of Chicago Press, 1995), in particular pp. 116–117. However, Ferry stressed the point that the focus of ecofeminist critique is on *androcentrism*, not on *anthropocentrism*.
218. Luc Ferry, *ibid.* pp. XXIII–XXIV (original emphases).
219. Arne Naess, *Ecology, Community and Lifestyle. Outline for an Ecosophy.* Translated and revised by David Rothenberg (Cambridge University Press, 1991), p. 40.
220. Arne Naess, *ibid.* p. 41 (original emphases).
221. Arne Naess, *ibid.* pp. 39–40 (emphases added). However, Naess extended his observation beyond ecology, noting that '[i]n debate, to label a

standpoint an 'ism' often means it generalises the concepts of science *too much*. For example, sociologism, historicism, etc.' (Arne Naess, *ibid.* p. 39). Thus, taken out of the specific context of Ecologism, Naess' critique of attempts for establishing a paramount scientific discipline by creating a new 'ism' might equally apply on, for instance, *economism*.

222. Arne Naess, *ibid.* p. 211 (original emphasis).
223. Arne Naess, *ibid.* p. 36.
224. Arne Naess, *ibid.* p. 37.
225. Luc Ferry, *The new ecological order* (The University of Chicago Press, 1995), p. 129 (original emphases).
226. Luc Ferry, *ibid.* p. 95 (original emphases). A famous expression of the 'rational' concept of nature is the French-style garden, 'which is based entirely on the idea that, to arrive at nature's true essence or, rather, at "nature's nature", it is necessary to employ artifice, to "geometrize" it. For it is through mathematics, by use of the most abstract reasoning, that one grasps the truth of reality' (Luc Ferry, *ibid.* p. 95).
227. Luc Ferry, *ibid.* p. 96 (original emphases).
228. Luc Ferry, *ibid.* p. 97.
229. Luc Ferry, *ibid.* p. 97.
230. Luc Ferry, *ibid.* p. 97.
231. Luc Ferry introduced Walther Schoenichen (1876–1956) as follows: 'A committed National Socialist himself, holder of the Chair of the Protection of Nature at the University of Berlin, he was writing a series of works until the late 1950s on Germany's mission in the matter, including two essays on the contribution of Hitler's regime: *Naturschutz im dritten Reich* (Berlin, 1934), and *Naturschutz als Völkische und internationale Kulturaufgabe* (Iena, 1942), which no doubt constitutes one of the best commentaries one can read on the significance of Nazi ecology in the eyes of those who were involved in developing it. In it, notably, the legislations are situated within the intellectual history of *German romanticism*' (Luc Ferry, *ibid.* p. 92n (emphasis added).
232. Wilhelm Heinrich Riehl (1823–1897) was a German journalist and novelist focused on German folklore. He is considered of having established cultural anthropology ('Volkskunde') as an academic discipline in Germany.
233. Luc Ferry, *The new ecological order* (The University of Chicago Press, 1995), pp. 98–99.
234. Hans-Peter Breβler, *Ethische Probleme der Mensch-Tier-Beziehung. Eine Untersuchung philosophischer Positionen des 20. Jahrhunderts zum Tierschutz* (Peter Lang, Europäischer Verlag der Wissenschaften, 1997), p. 17.
235. Hans-Peter Breβler, *ibid.* p. 17. Immanuel Kant considered:

But so far as animals are concerned, we have no direct duties. Animals are not self-conscious and are there merely as a means to an end. That end is man. … Our duties towards animals are merely indirect duties towards humanity. Animal nature has analogies to human nature, and by doing our duties to animals in respect of manifestations of human nature, we indirectly do our duty towards humanity (Immanuel Kant, 'We have Only Indirect Duties to Animals,' in Kerry S. Walters and Lisa Portmess (eds.), *Ethical Vegetarianism. From Pythagoras to Peter Singer* (State University of New York Press, Albany, 1999), p. 269.

236. Hans-Peter Breβler, *ibid.* pp. 17–18.
237. Hans-Peter Breβler, *ibid.* p. 18.
238. Hans-Peter Breβler, *ibid.* p. 18. In the scope of the study at hand, it may be interesting to note how Salt invoked 'rationalism' for his claim for vegetarianism:

I advance no exaggerated or fanciful claim for Vegetarianism. It is not, as some have asserted, a 'panacea' for human ill; it is something much more *rational* – an essential part of the modern humanitarian movement, which can make no true progress without it. Vegetarianism is the diet of the future, as flesh-food is the diet of the past (Henry S. Salt, 'The Humanities of Diet,' in Kerry S. Walters and Lisa Portmess (eds.), *Ethical Vegetarianism. From Pythagoras to Peter Singer* (State University of New York Press, Albany, 1999), p. 125 (emphasis added).

239. Hans-Peter Breβler, *Ethische Probleme der Mensch-Tier-Beziehung. Eine Untersuchung philosophischer Positionen des 20. Jahrhunderts zum Tierschutz* (Peter Lang, Europäischer Verlag der Wissenschaften, 1997), p. 18. Schopenhauer's equalisation of animals and humans, basing on his philosophy of the will (*Die Welt als Wille und Vorstellung* (1819), may be reconsidered in light of Luc Ferry's studies on links between the animal liberation movement and totalitarianism. In the same breath, other famous advocates for animal rights and vegetarianism affiliated with totalitarianism could be mentioned; for instance, German composer Richard Wagner (1813–1883) (see Richard Wagner, 'Human Beasts of Prey and Fellow-Suffering,' in Kerry S. Walters and Lisa Portmess (eds.), *Ethical Vegetarianism. From Pythagoras to Peter Singer* (State University of New York Press, Albany, 1999), pp. 89–95; and, of course, vegetarian Adolf Hitler himself (see, for instance, Colin Spencer, *The Heretic's Feast. A History of Vegetarianism* (University Press of New England, Hanover, 1995), pp. 304–309.

240. Eduard Kaeser, *Pop Science. Essays zur Wissenschaftskultur* (Schwabe Verlag, 2009), pp. 153–155. Kaeser perceived genetic engineering as standing in the continuity of the philosophy of dissection, reducing animals and other living organisms to mere 'biofacts' (Eduard Kaeser, *ibid.*, p. 155.
241. Eduard Kaeser, *ibid.* pp. 155–156. However, differences between the two approaches are not merely philosophical: from an epistemological point of view, the second approach, the 'ethos of solidarity', takes account of the fact that any observer is inevitably personally involved in carrying out scientific activities such as observations and experimentations. Hence, Kaeser noted that essentially, scientific observation can never focus on the animal as an object of investigation alone, but inevitably involves the relationship between the animal and the observer (Eduard Kaeser, *ibid.* p. 156, citing behavioural scientist Otto Köhler.
242. Luc Ferry, *The new ecological order* (The University of Chicago Press, 1995), pp. XXI–XXII (original emphases).
243. This remark was necessary to distinguish the attempt of the thesis at hand from the key message of *The new ecological order* of Luc Ferry. Ferry, by showing 'how deep ecology casts aside all the gains of human autonomy since the Enlightenment', put forward 'a bracing caution—against the dangers of environmental claims and, more important, against the threat to democracy contained in the deep ecology doctrine when pushed to its extreme' (Luc Ferry, *The new ecological order* (The University of Chicago Press, 1995), back cover). The arguments of Luc Ferry should be taken seriously. However, reminiscences to Nazi ecology alone seems to be an insufficient argument for discrediting contemporary forms of environmentalism altogether. Or, taking it the other way round, it would similarly not hold water to discredit contemporary expressions of legal Positivism by simply making reference to Carl Schmitt, or making scientific Positivism responsible for every expressions of racism and colonialism based on 'scientific' arguments. Rather, the attempt of Luc Ferry to caution against new forms of totalitarianism has to be understood in the political context of the 1980 s. As Daniel Binswanger noted, a new generation of post-Marxian philosophers especially in France rediscovered liberal principles established by political thinkers such as Alexis de Tocqueville (1805–1859) and Hannah Arendt (1906–1975). In the 1980 s and assembled under the umbrella of the Parisian journal *Le Débat,* Luc Ferry, Alexandre Adler, Alain Finkielkraut, Blandine Kriegel and others embarked on a crusade against totalitarianism and in defence of the liberal constitutional state (Daniel Binswanger, 'Was soll man heute Denken?' In *Das Magazin*, issue 29/2010 (Tamedia AG, 30 July 2010), p. 6).
244. Hans-Peter Breβler, for example, argued that the application of genetic engineering on animals is tantamount to their instrumentalisation and

abasement. On these grounds, Breβler concluded that under a regime of actionable animal rights, genetic engineering of animals would inflict penalties (Hans-Peter Breβler, *Ethische Probleme der Mensch-Tier-Beziehung. Eine Untersuchung philosophischer Positionen des 20. Jahrhunderts zum Tierschutz* (Peter Lang, Europäischer Verlag der Wissenschaften, 1997), pp. 198–199).

245. This is the guiding idea of Pierre-Joseph Proudhon's groundbreaking work *What is Property?* (1840). See Horst Stowasser, *Anarchie! Idee, Geschichte, Perspektiven*. Edition Nautilus (Verlag Lutz Schulenburg, 2007), pp. 221–223. Proudhon himself is often characterised as 'founder' or 'father' of Anarchism (Horst Stowasser, *ibid.*, p. 223).
246. Horst Stowasser, *ibid.* pp. 19–21 and 45–49.
247. Horst Stowasser, *ibid.* pp.187–189.
248. Karl Marx and Friedrich Engels coined the famous phrase that '[i]t is not the consciousness of men that determines their being, but, on the contrary, their social being that determines their consciousness' (see Karl Marx and Friedrich Engels, 'Feuerbach, Gegensatz von materialistischer und idealistischer Anschauung (Einleitung)', in Iring Fetscher (ed.), *Karl Marx, Friedrich Engels, Studienausgabe in 4 Bänden*, vol. I (Fischer, 1982), p. 92. For emphasising the difference between German idealist philosophy and their notion of Materialism, Marx and Engels developed their basic argument as follows [in German]:

Ganz im Gegensatz zur deutschen Philosophie, welche vom Himmel auf die Erde herabsteigt, wird hier [d.h. gemäss materialistischer Anschauung] von der Erde zum Himmel gestiegen. D.h., es wird nicht ausgegangen von dem, was die Menschen sagen, sich einbilden, sich vorstellen, auch nicht von den gesagten, gedachten, eingebildeten, vorgestellten Menschen, um davon aus bei den leibhaftigen Menschen anzukommen; es wird von den wirklich tätigen Menschen ausgegangen und aus ihrem wirklichen Lebensprozeβ auch die Entwicklung der ideologischen Reflexe und Echos dieses Lebensprozesses dargestellt. Auch die Nebelbildungen im Gehirn der Menschen sind notwendige Sublimate ihres materiellen, empirisch konstatierbaren und an materielle Voraussetzungen geknüpften Lebensprozesses. Die Moral, Religion, Metaphysik und sonstige Ideologie und die ihnen entsprechenden Bewuβtseinsformen behalten hiermit nicht länger den Schein der Selbständigkeit. Sie haben keine Geschichte, sie haben keine Entwicklung, sondern die ihre materielle Produktion und ihren materiellen Verkehr entwickelnden Menschen ändern mit dieser ihrer Wirklichkeit auch ihr Denken und die Produkte ihres Denkens. Nicht das Bewuβtsein bestimmt das Leben, sondern das Leben bestimmt das Bewuβtsein. In der ersten Betrachtungsweise geht man von dem Bewuβtsein als dem lebendigen

Individuum aus, in der zweiten, dem wirklichen Leben entsprechenden, von den wirklich lebendigen Individuen selbst und betrachtet das Bewußtsein nur als *ihr* Bewußtsein (Karl Marx and Friedrich Engels, *ibid.*, pp. 91–92; original emphasis).

249. Differences between particular strands of postmodernism on the one hand and Marxism/dialectical Materialism on the other hand are vibrant till this day. For instance, Alex Callinicos observed real paradigm shifts between the two approaches: 'The re-emergence of anti-capitalist discourses and movements therefore marks the breakdown of the hegemony that post-modernism has exerted over avant-garde thinking over much of the past two decades. One sign of this intellectual shift is a decline in the almost obsessive concern with cultural questions that came to dominate the radical academy in the 1990s and a renewed preoccupation with the material' (Alex Callinicos, *An Anti-Capitalist Manifesto* (Polity Press, 2003), p. 11.
250. The term 'alter-globalisation' stems from the French word '*Altermondialisme*' and is used because some exponents of the anti-globalisation movement dismiss the common term 'anti-globalisation'. Noam Chomsky, for example, criticised the term anti-globalisation as follows:

The dominant propaganda systems have appropriated the term "globalization" to refer to the specific version of international economic integration that they favor, which privileges the rights of investors and lenders, those of people being incidental. In accord with this usage, those who favor a different form of international integration, which privileges the rights of human beings, become "anti-globalist." This is simply vulgar propaganda, like the term "anti-Soviet" used by the most disgusting commissars to refer to dissidents. It is not only vulgar, but idiotic. Take the World Social Forum, called "anti-globalization" in the propaganda system—which happens to include the media, the educated classes, etc., with rare exceptions. The WSF is a paradigm example of globalization. It is a gathering of huge numbers of people from all over the world, from just about every corner of life one can think of, apart from the extremely narrow highly privileged elites who meet at the competing World Economic Forum, and are called "pro-globalization" by the propaganda system. (…). (Interview with Noam Chomsky by Snježana Matejčić, June 2005, cited in Webster's Online Dictionary, web access: http://www.websters-online-dictionary.org/definitions/globalization?cx=partner-pub-0939450753529744%3Av0qd01-tdlq&cof=FORID%3A9&ie=UTF-8&q=globalization&sa=Search#922; visited October 24, 2010).

References

Al-Hassani, Salim T S (ed.). "1001 Inventions: Muslim Heritage in Our World". *Foundation of Science, Technology and Civilisation* (2nd edition) 2007.

Anghie, Antony. "Imperialism, Sovereignty and the Making of International Law". *Cambridge University Press*, 2005.

Beck, Ulrich. "Was ist Globalisierung?". Suhrkamp Verlag, 1997.

Belser, Eva Maria. "The White Man's Burden. Arbeit und Menschenrechte in der globalisierten Welt". *Stämpfli Verlag*, 2007.

Bernal, John, Desmond. "The Freedom of Necessity". *Routledge & Kegan Paul*, 1949.

Bilen, Osman. "The Historicity of Understanding and The Problem of Relativism in Gadamer's Philosophical Hermeneutics". *The Council for Research in Values and Philosophy*, 2000.

Binswanger, Daniel. "Was soll man heute Denken?". *Das Magazin/Tamedia*, 30 July 2010.

Binswanger, Hans Christoph. "Geld und Magie. Eine ökonomische Deutung von Goethes Faust". *Murmann Verlag*, 2005 (2nd edition).

Böhnigk, Volker. "Weltversionen. Wissenschaft zwischen Relativismus und Pluralismus." *Passagen Verlag*, 1999.

Brenner, Anastasios. "The French Connection: Conventionalism and the Vienna Circle". Published in Michael Heidelberger, Friedrich Stadler (eds.), *History of Philosophy of Science. New Trends and Perspectives.* Kluwer Academic Publishers, 2002, 277–286.

Breβler, Hans-Peter. "Ethische Probleme der Mensch-Tier-Beziehung. Eine Untersuchung philosophischer Positionen des 20. Jahrhunderts zum Tierschutz". *Peter Lang/Europäischer Verlag der Wissenschaften*, 1997.

Bröcker. Walter. "Dialektik Positivismus Mythologie". *Vittorio Klostermann*, 1958.

Callinicos, Alex. "An Anti-Capitalist Manifesto". *Polity Press*, 2003.

Capra, Fritjof. "The Turning Point". *Ex Libris*, 1984 (1982).

Carnap, Rudolf, Hahn, Hans and Neurath, Otto. "The Scientific Conception of the World: The Vienna Circle", known as the 'Vienna Circle Manifesto' in Otto Neurath's *Empiricism and Sociology*, edited by Neurath, Marie and Cohen, Robert S. *D., Reidel Publishing*, 1973, vol. 1 of the Vienna Circle Collection, 299–318.

Carus, A. W. "The Philosopher without Qualities". Published in Michael Heidelberger and Friedrich Stadler (eds.), *History of Philosophy of Science. New Trends and Perspectives.* Kluwer Academic Publishers, 2002, 369–377.

Cho, Sungjoon. "From Control to Communication: Science, Philosophy and World Trade Law". *Cornell International Law Journal*, forthcoming. Available at SSRN. http://ssrn.com/abstract=1583023 (Accessed December 5, 2010, and May 18, 2017).

Eidlin, Fred. “Poppers ethischer und metaphysischer Kognitivismus (Warum Wörter manchmal wichtig sein können)”. Published in Kurt Salamun (ed.), *Karl R. Popper und die Philosophie des Kritischen Rationalismus. Zum 85. Geburtstag von Karl R. Popper*. Rodopi, 1989, 162.

Falter, Jürgen W. “Der ‚Positivismusstreit' in der amerikanischen Politikwissenschaft: Entstehung, Ablauf und Resultate der sogenannten Behavioralismus – Kontroverse in den Vereinigten Staaten 1945–1975”. *Beiträge zur sozialwissenschaftlichen Forschung*, Westdeutscher Verlag, Band 37, 1982.

Ferry, Luc. “The new ecological order”. Original title: *Le nouvel ordre écologique: L'arbre, l'animal et l'homme*. Bernard Grasset, 1992, translated by Carol Volk. *The University of Chicago Press*, 1995.

Frey, Raymond G. “Rights, Killing, and Suffering. Moral Vegetarianism and Applied Ethics”. *Basil Blackwell Publisher*, 1983.

Fuller, Steve. “Thomas Kuhn. A Philosophical History of Our Times”. *The University of Chicago Press*, 2000.

Fuller, Steve. “Social Epistemology”. *Indiana University Press*, 2nd Edition, 2002, (1st Edition 1998).

Gadamer, Hans-Georg. “Wahrheit und Methode”. *J.C.B. Mohr (Paul Siebeck)*, 3rd edition 1960. Idem: *Truth and Method*, translated by William Glen-Doepel, edited by John Cumming and Garrett Barden, 2nd edition. *Sheed and Ward*, 1979.

Georgescu-Roegen, Nicholas “Analytical Economics. Issues and Problems”. MA: *Harvard University Press*, 1967.

Georgescu-Roegen, Nicholas “Energy and Economic Myths. Institutional and Analytical Economic Essays”. NY: *Pergamon Press*, 1976.

Giddens, Anthony. “Living in a Post-Traditional Society”. Published in Ulrich Beck, Anthony Giddens and Scott Lash, *Reflexive Modernization. Politics, Tradition and Aesthetics in the Modern Social Order*. Polity Press, 1994.

Habermas, Jürgen. “Analytische Wissenschaftstheorie und Dialektik. Ein Nachtrag zur Kontroverse zwischen Popper und Adorno”. Published in Heinz Maus, Friedrich Fürstenberg (eds.), *Der Positivismusstreit in der deutschen Soziologie*. Hermann Luchterhand Verlag, 1969.

Habermas, Jürgen. “Kommunikatives Handeln und detranszendentalisierte Vernunft”. *Reclam*, 2001.

Hawking, Stephen. “A Brief History of Time. From the Big Bang to Black Holes”. *Bantam Books*, 1989.

Hobsbawm, Eric J. “Das imperiale Zeitalter 1875–1914”. Original English title: *The Age of Empire 1875–1914*. Campus Verlag GmbH, 2008.

Hoogvelt, Ankie “Globalization and the Postcolonial World. The New Political Economy of Development”. Palgrave Macmillan, 2nd edition, 2001.

Holton, Gerald. "B.F. Skinner and P.W. Bridgman: The Frustration of a *Wahlverwandtschaft*". Published in Michael Heidelberger, Friedrich Stadler (eds.), *History of Philosophy of Science. New Trends and Perspectives.* Kluwer Academic Publishers, 2002, 335–346.

Howse, Robert. "From Politics to Technocracy—and Back Again: The Fate of the Multilateral Trading Regime". *The American Journal of International Law*, 1 [94–117] 98; vol. 96, 2002. Accessed October 21, 2010. http://www.jstor.org/stable/2686127?origin=JSTOR-pdf.

Howse, Robert. "Democracy, Science, and Free Trade: Risk Regulation on Trial at the World Trade Organization". *Michigan Law Review*, 2329, vol. 98, 2000.

Jacob, Margaret C. "Reflections on Bruno Latour's Version of the Seventeenth Century". Published in Noretta Koertge (ed.), *A House Built on Sand. Exposing Postmodernist Myths About Science.* Oxford University Press, 1998, 240–254.

Jäger, Henrik. "Die anderen Quellen der Aufklärung – Wie die chinesische Tradition in das europäische Denken des 17. und 18. Jahrhunderts eingegangen ist". *Neue Zürcher Zeitung*, October 16, 2010, 65.

Kaeser, Eduard. "Pop Science. Essays zur Wissenschaftskultur". *Schwabe Verlag*, 2009.

Kincaid, Harold. "Philosophical Foundations of the Social Sciences. Analyzing Controversies in Social Research". *Cambridge University Press*, 1996.

Klein, Gabriele. "Bodies in Translation. Tango als kulturelle Übersetzung". Published in Gabriele Klein (ed.), *Tango in Translation. Tanz zwischen Medien, Kulturen, Kunst und Politik. transcript Verlag*, 2009.

Koertge, Noretta. "Scrutinizing Science Studies". Published in Noretta Koertge (ed.), *A House Built on Sand. Exposing Postmodernist Myths about Science.* Oxford University Press, 1998, 3–6.

Kostolany, André. "Die Kunst über Geld nachzudenken". *Econ Ullstein List Verlag GmbH*, 2000.

Lash, Scott. "Expert-Systems or Situated Interpretation? Culture and Institutions in Disorganized Capitalism". Published in Ulrich Beck, Anthony Giddens and Scott Lash, *Reflexive Modernization. Politics, Tradition and Aesthetics in the Modern Social Order.* Polity Press, 1994.

Lenin, Vladimir, Iilyich. "Materialismus und Empiriokritizismus. Kritische Bemerkungen über eine reaktionäre Philosophie". Published in *W. I. Lenin. Sämtliche Werke.* Vol. XIII. Translated into German from the 2nd revised Russian Edition, published in 1909. *Verlag für Literatur und Politik*, 1927. English title: *Materialism and Empiriocriticism: Critical Comments on a Reactionary Philosophy.*

Mahdi, Muhsin. "Approaches to the history of Arabic science". Postface to Roshdi Rashed (ed.), *Encyclopedia of the History of Arabic Science* (vol. 3), *Technology, Alchemy and Life Sciences.* Routledge, 1996, 1026–1044.

Marx, Karl. "Capital. A Critique of Political Economy". Vol. 1, translated by Ben Fowkes. *Penguin Books*, 1990.

Marx, Karl and Engels, Friedrich. "Feuerbach, Gegensatz von materialistischer und idealistischer Anschauung (Einleitung)". Publisehed in Iring Fetscher (ed.), *Karl Marx, Friedrich Engels, Studienausgabe in 4 Bänden*, Vol. I, *Fischer*, 1982, 82–138.

Naess, Arne. "Ecology, Community and Lifestyle. Outline for an Ecosophy". Translated and revised by David Rothenberg. *Cambridge University Press*, 1991.

Phillips, Patrick J. J. "The Challenge of Relativism—Its Nature and Limits". *Continuum International Publishing Group,* 2007.

Popper, Karl R. "Logik der Forschung" (English title: *The Logic of Scientific Discovery).* J.C.B Mohr (Paul Siebeck), 1976, 6th edition and Popper, Karl R. "The Logic of Scientific Discovery". *Hutchinson & Co Publishers*, 2nd English edition, 1968.

Popper, Karl R. "Das Elend des Historizismus". Authorised translation from the 2nd English edition *The Poverty of Historicism.* Routledge & Kegan Paul, 1960, translated by Dr. Leonhard Walentik, *J.C.B. Mohr (Paul Siebeck)* 1965.

Popper, Karl R. "Die Logik der Sozialwissenschaften". Published in Heinz Maus, Friedrich Fürstenberg (eds.), *Der Positivismusstreit in der deutschen Soziologie.* Hermann Luchterhand Verlag, 1969.

Popper, Karl R. "Objective Knowledge. An Evolutionary Approach". *Oxford University Press*, 1973.

Popper, Karl R. "Quantum Theory and the Schism in Physics. From the Postscript to the Logic of Scientific Discovery". Edited by W.W. Bartley, III, *Hutchinson & Co. Publishers*, 1982.

Popper, Karl R. "Realism and the Aim of Science. From the Postscript to the Logic of Scientific Discovery". Edited by W.W. Bartley, III, *Hutchinson & Co. Publishers*, 1983.

Popper, Karl R. "Towards an Evolutionary Theory of Knowledg". Published in Karl R. Popper, *A World of Propensities.* Thoemmes Antiquarian Books, 1990.

Popper, Karl R. "The Myth of the Framework. In defence of science and rationality". Edited by M.A. Notturno. *Routledge*, 1994.

Popper, Karl R. "Reason or Revolution?". Published in *The Myth of the Framework. In defence of science and rationality.* Edited by M.A. Notturno. *Routledge*, 1994.

Popper, Karl R. "The Self, Rationality, and Freedom". Published in *Knowledge and the Body-Mind Problem. In defence of interaction.* Edited by M.A. Notturno. *Routledge, London* 1994.

Popper Karl R., and John C. Eccles. "Das Ich und sein Gehirn". Original English title: *The Self and Its Brain—An Argument for Interactionism*, Springer Verlag 1977, 11th edition, Serie Piper, 1994.

Rahula, Basnagoda. "The Untold Story about Greek Rational Thought: Buddhist and other Indian Rationalist Influences on Sophist Rhetoric". *Ph.D. Dissertation submitted to the Graduate Faculty of Texas Tech University*, December 2000, 350. Accessed April 23, 2010. http://etd.lib.ttu.edu/theses/available/etd-07312008-31295015156333/unrestricted/31295015156333.pdf.

Ramonet, Ignacio. "La pensée unique". *Le Monde diplomatique*, January 1995, 1. Accessed October 24, 2010). http://www.monde-diplomatique.fr/1995/01/RAMONET/1144.

Rashed, Roshdi. "The Celestial Kinematics of Ibn al-Haytham". *Arabic Sciences and Philosophy*, vol. 17, 2007, 7–55, 19. Accessed October 14, 2010. http://journals.cambridge.org/action/displayFulltext?type=1&fid=701204&jid=ASP&volumeId=17&issueId=01&aid=701200&bodyId=&membershipNumber=&societyETOCSession=.

Rawls, John. "Geschichte der politischen Philosophie". English original title: *Lectures on the History of Political Philosophy*. American edition by Samuel Freeman, 2007. Translation by Joachim Schulte. *Suhrkamp*, 2008.

Roco, Mihail C. and Bainbridg, William Sims (eds.). "Converging Technologies for Improving Human Performance. Nanotechnology, Biotechnology, Information Technology and Cognitive Science". Joint report of the National Science Foundation (NSF) and the Department of Commerce. *Kluwer Academic Publishers*, 2003. Accessed December 22, 2010. http://www.wtec.org/ConvergingTechnologies/Report/NBIC_report.pdf.

Samuelson, Paul A. and Nordhaus, William D. "Economics". *Irwin/McGraw-Hill*, 1998, 16th edition.

Sapir, Jacques. "Les trous noirs de la science économique. Essai sur l'impossibilité de penser le temps et l'argent". *Éditions Albin Michel*, 2003.

Schramm, Matthias. "Ibn al-Haythams Weg zur Physik". *Franz Steiner Verlag*, 1963.

Shiva, Vandana. "Earth Democracy. Justice, Sustainability, and Peace". *Zed Books*, 2005.

Shrader-Frechette, Kristin S. "Risk Analysis and Scientific Method. Methodological and Ethical Problems with Evaluating Societal Hazards". *D. Reidel Publishing*, 1985.

Shrader-Frechette, Kristin S. "Risk and Rationality. Philosophical Foundations for Populist Reforms". *University of California Press*, 1991.

Spencer, Colin. "The Heretic's Feast. A History of Vegetarianism". *University Press of New England*, 1995.

Störig, Hans Joachim. "Kleine Weltgeschichte der Philosophie". 2 Volumes. *Fischer*, 1979/1980.

Stowasser, Horst. "Anarchie! Idee, Geschichte, Perspektiven". *Edition Nautilus, Verlag Lutz Schulenburg*, 2007.

Stump, David J. "From the Values of Scientific Philosophy to the Value Neutrality of the Philosophy of Science". Published in Michael Heidelberger, Friedrich

Stadler (eds.), *History of Philosophy of Science. New Trends and Perspective.s* Kluwer Academic Publishers, 2002, 147–158.

Taleb, Nassim Nicholas. "Fooled by Randomness. The Hidden Role of Chance in Life and in the Markets". Penguin Books, 2004, 2nd edition.

Traub, Rainer. "Sturz in den Schatten". *SPIEGEL GESCHICHTE*, issue 5, 2010, 96–99.

Tuana, Nancy. "Coming to Understand. Orgasm and the Epistemology of Ignorance". Published in Robert N. Proctor and Londa Schiebinger (eds.), *Agnotology. The Making and Unmaking of Ignorance.* Stanford University Press, 2008, 108–145.

Uebel, Thomas. "The Poverty of 'Constructivist' History (and Policy Advice)". Published in Michael Heidelberger, Friedrich Stadler (eds.), *History of Philosophy of Science. New Trends and Perspectives.* Kluwer Academic Publishers, 2002, 379–389.

Von Daeniken, Kathi and Schnegg, Brigitte. "Gender as a Horizontal Issue within NCCR Trade Regulation". Handout to the presentation provided at the *Annual Conference 2010 of NCCR Trade Regulation*, June 29, 2010, at the World Trade Institute in Bern.

Wagner, Richard. "Human Beasts of Prey and Fellow-Suffering". Published in Kerry S. Walters and Lisa Portmess (eds.), *Ethical Vegetarianism. From Pythagoras to Peter Singer.* State University of New York Press, 1999, 89–95.

Weiler, Joseph H. H. "The Rule of Lawyers and the Ethos of Diplomats: Reflections on WTO Dispute Settlement". Published in Roger B. Porter, Pierre Sauvé, Arvind Subramanian, and Americo Beviglia Zampetti (eds.), *Efficiency, Equity, and Legitimacy. The Multilateral Trading System at the Millennium.* Brookings Institution Press, 2001, 334–350.

Zarrilli, Simonetta "International trade in GMOs and GM products: National and Multilateral Legal Frameworks". *Policy Issues in International Trade and Commodities Study Series.* 2005, 29. United Nations Conference on Trade and Development (UNCTAD). Accessed August 17, 2010. http://www.unctad.org/en/docs/itcdtab30_en.pdf.

CHAPTER 4

Two Concepts of Risk

There are basically two concepts of risk. One is rooted in the individualistic and rational philosophy of the Enlightenment and early Capitalism. The other stems from anti-modernist movements associated with romanticism and the alienation of man from nature.

1 A Concept for Entrepreneurs

The first notion of *risk* stems from an individualistic concept designed for economic actors. Entrepreneurs, shareholders and speculators required tools for mastering risks and chances of their investments. In economic terms, 'risk' can be understood as a counterpart to 'chance'. 'Risk' indicates the probability whether a certain investment turns out to be a profit or a loss. According to economic theory, risk increases with profits expected. Thus, risk may be understood as the price for profit expectation. An economic notion of risk is expressed, for example, by the *Dictionary of Economics* (2003) defining risk as follows:

> A state in which the number of possible future events exceeds the number of events that will actually occur, and some measure of > probability can be attached to them. This definition distinguishes risk from > uncertainty, in which the probabilities are unknown. A gambler, for example, face risk because he/she could either be very much richer tomorrow or (more likely) slightly poorer, depending on whether a roulette wheel spins the ball into the right hole – and the odds of the roulette wheel are known. ≫Bernoulli's hypothesis; probability.

M. Burkard, *Conflicting Philosophies and International Trade Law*,
Philosophy, Public Policy, and Transnational Law,
https://doi.org/10.1007/978-3-319-61067-2_4

> It is normally assumed that economic agents dislike risk (≫risk aversion) and in the market for financial assets the riskier an asset, the higher the expected return investors will require of it (>expected utility; portfolio theory). (...)[1]

Therefore, the individualistic concept of risk can best be understood as a tool for deciding upon economic activity, in particular investment. Hence, in economics, risk is essentially a management tool and is primarily addressed as a risk management problem. Peter L. Bernstein explained the economic rationale underlying the concept of risk management as follows:

> The essence of risk management lies in maximizing the areas where we have some control over the outcome while minimizing the areas where we have absolutely no control over the outcome and the linkage between effect and cause is hidden from us.[2]

Usually, the origins of risk are related to Humanism, the Renaissance and Enlightenment philosophy. In *Against the Gods* (1998), Peter L. Bernstein, for example, told 'the story of a group of thinkers whose remarkable vision revealed how to put the future at the service of the present'.[3] According to that popular legend, risk was some kind of a 'revolutionary idea' which, out of a sudden enlightenment, transformed Western society: 'Like Prometheus, they defied the gods and probed the darkness in search of the light that converted the future from an enemy into an opportunity'.[4] Popular narratives about risk are relating contemporary economy to Enlightenment philosophy and Rationalism. Thereby, today's economy is presented as the result of rational developments triggered by Enlightenment philosophy and science. Again Bernstein:

> By defining a rational process of risk-taking, these innovators provided the missing ingredient that has propelled science and enterprise into the world of speed, power, instant communication, and sophisticated finance that marks our own age. Their discoveries about the nature of risk, and the art and science of choice, lie at the core of our modern market economy that nations around the world are hastening to join. Given all its problems and pitfalls, the free economy, with choice at its center, has brought humanity unparalleled access to the good things of life.[5]

In light of critical research, however, common narratives about risk have to be questioned. For instance, Pierre-Charles Pradier observed that widespread beliefs about the origins of risk are stemming from two particularly popular legends. In *La notion de risqué en économie* (2006), Pierre-Charles Pradier found that both legends are incongruent with recent research findings.[6] Following Pradier, these two narratives are called the *modernist thesis* and the *nautical novel* respectively.[7] The modernist thesis about the origins of risk can be read as an appendix to the history of capitalism, as written by the historical school and Max Weber in particular. The nautical novel, on the other hand, emerged from works of earlier philologists who themselves might have been influenced by the historical school. Thus, popular legend has it that the concept of risk came along with European seafaring which, in turn, is portrayed as an expression of a novel, enlightened 'spirit of capitalism'.

1.1 The Modernist Thesis

The modernist thesis about the origins of risk stands in the tradition of a certain group of historians perceiving modern times as a specific European phenomenon. According to scholars such as Werner Sombart, Max Weber and Niklas Luhmann, the rise of the risk concept fell into a period in European history distinguished by grand discoveries, religious reformation and the event of capitalism.[8] In *The Protestant Ethic and the Spirit of Capitalism,* Max Weber argued for an affinity between religious reformation and Protestantism, on the one hand, and the development of capitalism, on the other hand.[9]

The modernist thesis of risk can also be illustrated by the approach of Niklas Luhmann. Luhmann observed that at the time when the word 'risk' emerged in the Late Middle Ages in Europe, existing European languages already provided 'words for danger, venture, chance, luck, courage, fear (angst), adventure (aventuyre)'.[10] Therefore, Luhmann assumed 'that a new term comes into use to indicate a problem situation that cannot be expressed precisely enough with the vocabulary available'.[11] Given the fact that the Late Middle Ages (fourteenth–fifteenth century) marked the beginnings of European overseas expansion, religious turmoil and early stages of capitalism, Luhmann connoted 'risk' with a turning point in European history. By doing so, Luhmann carries on the German historiographic tradition of scholars like Werner Sombart, Max Weber and many others. In effect, the modernist conception perceives the spreading of the word 'risk' as 'a consequence (or an aspect) of the development of Capitalism'.[12] And the development of capitalism, in turn, is perceived by the modernist conception as the result of a unique historical coincidence, merging religious, technical and economic elements at a certain point of time and exclusively on European soil.

Pradier (2006, p. 9) pointed out that the modernist thesis about the emergence of risk thus amounts to an 'illustration of the seductive intellectual construction' established by Weber and other adepts of the historical school: the development of commerce, insurance and innovative financial instruments coincided with the emergence of capitalism, both following religious reformation. Pradier noted that therefore, in perspective of the modernist thesis, the proliferation of the word *risk* appeared as a consequence (or as an aspect) of the development of capitalism.

Pradier observed a particular expression of the modernist thesis emphasising sociological rather than religious features. This specification of the modernist thesis, called the *bourgeois legend*,[13] connoted the development of capitalism with the rise of a new social class, namely the bourgeoisie or the middle classes. According to such a reading, that new social class, i.e. the bourgeoisie, developed and applied new economic and political practices unsettling traditional regimes. Pradier observed that followers of the bourgeois legend, such as Robert Pirenne, were of the view that the new merchant class was made out of adventurers without any rootage into the local environment, resembling to masses of vagabonds roaming around the world.[14] From such a perspective, i.e. the notion of a sudden rise of a new social class, the concept of risk was one of the novel management tools developed and applied by the new bourgeoisie for pursuing their economic objectives.

1.2 The Nautical Novel

The nautical novel is based on etymological explanations for the word *risk*. Albeit etymological dictionaries are presenting various hypotheses for explaining origins of the word *risk*, most of them are finally arriving at some nautical connotation.[15] Pradier observed that a popular explanation has it that the word risk stems from the Latin word *resecare*, *reseco*, meaning to clip, cut off, abscise (*réséquer* in French). As an intermediary, the vulgarised Latin word *resecum* is invoked, meaning 'something which cuts', that is, a cliff or a reef. Eventually, the etymological explanation for the word *risk* is presented as 'the condition undergone by merchandise at sea'.[16]

Proponents of the nautical novel further pointed at morphologic proximities between words meaning reef and danger in Castilian, a language stemming from Latin. In Castilian, the *riesgo* can be translated as meaning either reef or danger.[17] Other scholars noted that the word *risque* succeeded the earlier word *rixe*.[18] However, Pradier observed that this shift of meaning took place only in Castile and in Langue d'Oc and did not occur before the end of mediaeval times.[19]

Focusing on etymology rather than on nautical imprints, Pradier noted another trace followed by philologists Arbogast Schmitt and Walther von Wartburg looking for Byzantine roots of the word *risk*. However, Pradier interposed that Byzantine roots of the word *risk* cannot be traced before the thirteenth century when amalgamations with Italian words were already notorious.[20]

Though, at least until recently, most etymological traces of the word 'risk' seemed to disappear in historical nebulae. This finding led Niklas Luhmann to conclude that '[t]he etymology of the word [risk] is unknown'. Nevertheless, Luhmann added the allusion that '[s]ome suspect it to be Arabic in origin'.[21]

In fact, more recent research hypotheses—yet fully to explore—are pointing at Arabic origins of the word *risk*. Once only an anecdote in a supplement to the French *Dictionnaire de la langue française*, the new hypothesis has gained ground among scholars and is now considered the most likely.[22] According to this hypothesis, the word *risk* is derived from the Arabic word *rizq*, which is translated as 'provision, part of the goods which God allocates to every man'.[23]

In an etymological dictionary of words of Arabic origins used in the German language, Nabil Osman provided the following explanation for the word 'risk':

> (…) [arab. rizq: that part of livelihood which is dependent on God's grace or fortune]: venture, peril, (running the) risk of losing.[24]

Osman explained that the word 'risk' was borrowed from the Arabic word *rizq* by Italian commercial language in the middle of the sixteenth century and turned into the Italian words *risico*, and *risco*.[25] Osman noted that the Arabic word *rizq* lives on in the Spanish words *arrisco* and *riesgo*, meaning 'danger', and the Portuguese word *risco*, standing for venture, the Italian words *risico* and *risco*, the French word *risque*, and the Rumanian word *rizic*.[26]

The hypothesis of Arabic origins of the word 'risk' is all the more plausible because there are hundreds of words of Arabic origin in European languages. For the German language alone, Nabil Osman counted and commented around 500 words of Arabic origin. The word 'hazard', for example, is also of Arab origin. Osman explained that the word 'hazard' stems from the Arabic *az-zahr*, meaning dice or gamble.[27]

However, other experts warned that the understanding of the Arabic word *rizq* may have changed over time and may be different from modern concepts of 'risk'. Professor Reinhard Schulze from the Institute for Islamic Studies and Oriental Philology of the University of Bern pointed at the requirement for distinguishing between normative and historical approaches towards the Arabic word *rizq*. With a view on normative interpretations, Schulze observed that the Arabic word *rizq* has 'practically nothing to do' with contemporary concepts of 'risk'.[28] According to Professor Schulze, a theological approach towards the Arabic word *rizq* might be taken into account. Thus, *rizq* could be understood as 'that provided by God' and 'God as the provider' (*razzaq*). In light of Sufi texts on the faith in God, *rizq* could hence be understood as 'that determined by God', meaning 'that which cannot be influenced by man'. In semantic terms, Schulze further noted that the Arabic word *rizq* is usually connoted with something beneficial (in terms of a *beneficium*).[29] Imponderables implied in contemporary risk concepts might thus stem from the initial ignorance of man regarding God's will. Theological reasoning centred around the question whether God would grant beneficence or not. Today, in contrast, economic risk concepts rather focus on the question whether losses may occur or not.

Shifts in the meaning of words are usually reflections of changes on the ground. With a view on the origins of the word 'risk', one has to consider significant changes in northern Italy between the eleventh and the fourteenth century. With respect to risks related to long-distance trade, in particular, forms of risk perception and risk management changed dramatically. In eleventh century Italy, Pradier observed, merchants were, at the same time, combatants accompanying their merchandise in order to protect it against pirates.[30] In fourteenth century Italy, however, modern techniques of risk control, in particular, underwriting schemes and early forms of insurance, replaced armed convoys.[31] Taking into account these changes on the ground, shifts in the meaning of the word 'risk' reflecting these factual changes are plausible. In the eleventh century, the danger of pirate ships appearing on the horizon was perceived rather as a question of fate than as an issue of risk management. However, coming along with the development of financial risk control techniques such as underwriting and insurance, risks became increasingly manageable. Shifts of meaning from the Arabic *rizq* to mediaeval and finally contemporary concepts of risk may well be reflections of such changes on the ground.

A simple but striking argument for Arabic origins of the word 'risk' is provided by general history. Overcoming the *modernist thesis*, contemporary historiography acknowledges the superiority and the power of attraction which emanated from the Arab empire during the Islamic Golden Age (mid-eigth to the mid-thirteenth century).[32] As Emilio Ferrín, professor for Arabic studies in Sevilla, explained, the Arab empire was the dominant culture of its time. According to Ferrín, the *Dar al-Islam*, the 'House of Islam', was comparable to 'the West' of today.[33] With a view on trade, in particular, Ferrín explained that the Mediterranean was 'the highway of the Middle Ages', dominated by Arab seafarers and traders in similar ways as was most of the landmass around it.[34] Hence, Arabic was the predominant business language for long-distance trade and of maritime trade in particular during the Islamic Golden Age. Taking into account that Arabic was the *lingua franca* of maritime trade and the eminent role of risk considerations in long-distance transactions, the hypothesis of Arabic origins of the word 'risk' seems rather plausible.[35]

In any case, Pradier arrived at the conclusion that the use of the world *risk* can be traced back much farther than to the outgoing mediaeval ages. That finding is important because it disproves popular allusions of risk with seafaring and modern capitalism, i.e. the nautical novel and the modernist thesis.[36] Whereas he simply disqualified the nautical novel as an 'amusing story', Pradier urged that the modernist thesis must be disproved.[37] Pradier based his request on the following arguments. First, the merchants were not a distinct class since the eleventh century. Hence, it is quite possible that the term 'risk' was a word used by warriors. Second, the modernist thesis was entirely disproved by evidence that the spirit of capitalism was already very vivid in the Italy of the *trecento*, i.e. the fourteenth century in Italy.[38]

2 Response from the *Risk Society*

Maybe the nautical novel and the modernist thesis are so persuasive because they are able to depict an essential feature of risk, that is, its expansive character. Thus, albeit inappropriate for explaining historical origins of risk, it has to be acknowledged that the nautical novel and the modernist thesis are facilitating an intuitive understanding why the word 'risk' spread rapidly in a certain period of European history. Pradier distinguished two periods of the propagation of the word 'risk'; the historical epoch called 'modern' where uses and meanings of the word 'risk' expanded rapidly, and the contemporary epoch where the word 'risk' got an abstract sense.[39]

Starting with the 'modern' epoch and the seventeenth century, in particular, Pradier observed that the word 'risk' permeated from specific maritime applications[40] into figures of commercial speech and general business language. But the word 'risk' was not yet a common term in the seventeenth century.[41] For the eighteenth century, Pradier noted a 'linguistic evolution' coming along with transformations in society. The seventeenth century was characterised by financial booms and busts such as the famous Dutch tulip bubble, voyages (for example, the voyages ventured by James Cook and Jean-François de La Pérouse), and a general fascination for adventure.[42] It was the seventeenth century in which a 'vocabulary of gambling' was developed: centring on the notion of *adventure*, words like *chance* and *fortune*, on the one hand, and danger and *peril*, on the other hand, became popular for expressing the spirit of the time.[43] During the eighteenth century, however, the use of the word 'risk' started to recede. Between 1750 and 1800, Pradier observer, the frequency of the word 'risk' in literature decrease by half.[44]

Turning to the contemporary epoch which brought along the *Risk Society*, Pradier noted, at first, a linguistic phenomenon. On the one hand, Pradier noted, the word 'risk' is used in the sense of a 'probable danger'. However, in insurance providers' tongue, 'risk' also took the meaning of the probability of that danger to manifest, that is, the mathematical expectation of the liability case.[45] Hence, 'risk' started of becoming confounded with its assessment and with those embodying it, the insured. Insurers began to characterise their clients as 'risks'; speeding motorists as 'bad risks', and cautious motorists as 'good risks'.[46] Indeed, the *Black's Law Dictionary* provided the following explanation of terms used in insurance business:

> … 5. *Insurance*. A person or thing that an insurer considers as hazard; someone or something that might be covered by an insurance policy < she's a poor risk for health insurance > …[47]

Pradier concluded that such transpositions of meanings, of terms and content, subject and object, opened up a wide range of new applications for the term 'risk'.[48] Thus, in the contemporary epoch, risk lost its earlier connotation with entrepreneurial activity or gambling at the stock exchange.[49] In other words, risk evolved into a common term, reflecting the self-conception of the *Risk Society* of today.

In the 1980s, social sciences joined the risk discourse. Social sciences and sociology, in particular, analysed the relationship of societies and risks from a different angle, adding a new perspective to the economic and scientific theories of risk. Ulrich Beck, for example, encapsulated the *zeitgeist* when he established the term 'risk society'. In his groundbreaking work *Risk Society*, first published in 1986, Beck showed that in contemporary societies, conflicts over wealth distribution were increasingly overlaid by conflicts over the allocation of risks.[50]

In *Risk: A Sociological Theory*, first published in 1991, Niklas Luhmann worked out differences between 'risk' and 'danger'. According to Luhmann, *risk* is a mode of action adopted voluntarily in the pursuit of profit; *danger*, on the other hand, denotes the status of people negatively affected by decisions over risks taken by others. Luhmann noted that

> … we will give the concept of risk another form with the help of the distinction of risk and danger. The distinction presupposes (thus differing from other distinctions) that uncertainty exists in relation to future loss. There are then two possibilities. The potential loss is either regarded as a consequence of the decision, that is to say, it is attributed to the decision. We then speak of risk – to be more exact of the risk of decision. Or the possible loss is considered to have been caused externally, that is to say, it is attributed to the environment. In this case, we speak of danger.[51]

Hence, sociologists worked out that imbalances between those deciding over risks and those affected by them are characterising features of *Risk societies*. In contrast to financial risks taken by individuals as entrepreneurs or shareholders in early capitalist societies, environmental risks, in particular, are borne by society as a whole.

Much in line with Luhmann's observations, the *New Shorter Oxford English Dictionary* defined *risk* as follows:

- Danger; (exposure to) the possibility of loss, injury, or other adverse circumstance. (…)
- (Exposure to) the possibility of commercial loss (…) (a) in the case of insured property or goods, (b) as part of economic enterprise and the source of entrepreneurial profit. (…)

- A chance or possibility of danger, commercial loss, or other risk. (…)
- A person considered a liability or danger; a person exposed to risk. (…)[52]

And Webster's *Third New International Dictionary* provides the following definition of *risk*:

- the possibility of loss, injury, disadvantage, or destruction: [contingency, danger, peril, threat] (…)
- the chance of loss or the perils to the subject matter of insurance covered by a contract
- the degree of probability of such loss. (…)[53]

In technical language, risk is typically defined as 'the product of the degree of harm a given event would cause, and its probability of occurrence', providing the following formula[54]:

$$R = P \times C$$

In the formula provided, R stands for risk, P for probability and C for the consequence. Hence, 'the essence of risk consists of the probability of an adverse event and the magnitude of its consequences'.[55]

The notion of risk by the *Risk Society* is concisely expressed by the Codex Alimentarius Commission, defining risk as

> a 'function of the probability of an adverse health effect and the severity of that effect, consequential to a hazard(s) [in food]'.[56]

Whereas risk management is the preserve of economic sciences, risk assessment typically requires the assistance of natural sciences, in particular, the so-called quarantine sciences[57] and environmental sciences.

Risk societies perceive risk from the perspective of possible adverse effects, rather than making a weighing between probable losses and profits. From a citizen's perspective, risks decided by others materialise as societal 'dangers', whereas eventual profits are reaped elsewhere, by anonymous corporations eventually. On these grounds, there is public discomfort with technical approaches trying to balance 'potential gains and losses' in risk evaluation. Technical approaches for 'rationally' assessing gains and losses related to technology applications are typically despised as 'technocratic'.

Expressions of technocratic attempts are, for instance, classifications and categorisations of risk suggested by Mandl and Lathrop:

(i) *risk of multiple fatalities*: probability of exceeding specific numbers of fatalities per year;
(ii) *societal risk*: total expected fatalities per year;
(iii) *group risk*: probability of an individual in a specific exposed group becoming a fatality per year;
(iv) *individual risk*: probability of an exposed individual becoming a fatality per year.[58]

It is hence unsurprising that those who may be affected by 'dangers' are requiring a thorough assessment, i.e. quantification, of risk. Among risk experts, there seems to be widespread consensus that the term risk 'refers to a situation in which it is possible confidently to quantify both the magnitude of and the probabilities for a defined range of outcomes (such as forms or degrees of harm in food safety)'.[59] With respect to 'dangers' occurring in *Risk societies*, public concern is focusing on ways and means to assess and quantify risks. At least in democratic *Risk societies*, citizens are able to make their voices heard in case a danger has been established. But the assessment of risks deriving from the application of modern technologies typically requires similarly sophisticated equipment as for its fabrication; hence citizens are calling for unbiased risk assessment.

In terms of a summary, one can observe at least two meanings of the term 'risk': on the one hand, there is the individualistic notion of risk, particularly in vogue in seventeenth century Europe. The individualistic notion of risk is essentially a tool for expanding the room for manoeuvre for individual entrepreneurs, willing to take risks for anticipated chances. It was that very first meaning of risk which became, in the European context, one of the guiding principles of classical liberalism. Pat O'Malley observed:

> In 19th century liberalism, entrepreneurs were those who had amassed sufficient capital to bear the loss of failure without becoming a burden on others – without subjecting their families to hardship, or the state of maintenance. (…) Notwithstanding more pressing concerns with poverty and pauperism, the state did much to foster this practice of freedom. Innovations such as limited liability encouraged risk-taking by protecting the financial security of capitalist adventurers. Stock exchanges were allowed considerable powers of self-government. … [t]he argument that capitalist risk-taking provided fundamental benefits to society was a trump card that could usually be played to

> forestall intervention. Entrepreneurs were thus a privileged and exceptional class, given special licence and protection in order to engage in the creative uncertainty that effectively was inaccessible to most.[60]

With industrialisation, however, individual ventures of entrepreneurs became socially relevant; large-scale plants, for example for the chemical and synthetic industry, and mass production raised question with regard to labour conditions, human health and the environment. In other words, the individualistic notion of risk was overlaid by a societal notion of risk, expressing feelings of exposure and subjection to extrinsic forces—or Luhmann's 'dangers'. The shift from an individualistic notion of risk to a societal notion of risk was reflected by a transformation of the hegemonic political doctrine of the time, i.e. liberalism. Whereas the individualistic notion of risk was a guiding principle of classical liberalism, a more 'social' notion of risk became a characterising feature of 'social liberalism'. Pat O'Malley explained that problems with sanitation and public hygiene, in particular, led to the insight 'that it was often easier to solve social problems by changing the laws and physical environment in which people lived and worked, than it was to change the people themselves'.[61] On the basis of such findings, liberalism became more open to compulsory policies intervening into previously inviolable private spheres. Or, in the words of Patrick Atiyah: 'Poverty itself was more easily controlled when many of its causes—sickness, unemployment, old age—were directly tackled by the state'.[62] This 'social' form of liberalism combined the classical liberal doctrine with utilitarianism and positivism. O'Malley noted:

> The justification for such intervention, scarcely challenged in the 19th century, was that the compulsions of sanitation were for the good of all. This was a utilitarian 'fact' demonstrable through the objectivity of statistical demonstration and rendered intelligible through scientific knowledge. In turn, the scale and costs of the enterprises meant that, for the most part, only the state could undertake them. Hence, these were rightly a state project. By the middle of the 19th century, this imagery of the social body as an organic whole made visible through statistics, governable in terms of positivistic science, and for which the state took responsibility, was already appearing from *within* the (utilitarian) rationality of classical liberalism. The example also suggests that the discovery of the social was not simply a self-generating quirk of liberalism. Equally it reflected the ascendancy of science and a faith in scientific expertise, in which probability and risk were imbricated. The 'invention' of the social thus binds together liberalism and modernism in an uneasy melange in which issues of freedom and compulsion are never far from the surface.[63]

For these reasons, it is important to bear in mind that actually two notions of risk exist and are used concurrently. The ambiguity of the term 'risk', characterising its contemporary use, is of particular relevance in public risk debates where the two understandings of risk may intermingle, depending on one's personal standpoint. The one perceives a certain venture in light of eventual profits and losses, whereas the other experiences the same venture as an uninfluenceable 'danger' impending in the future without corresponding gains. Whereas an entrepreneurial understanding of risk is a guiding principle of classical liberalism and neo-liberalism, a more social interpretation of risk is a characterising feature of social liberalism. Whether the one or the other perspective is adopted, the understanding of the word 'risk'—as well as its implications—will change.

The antagonistic perspectives of entrepreneurial risk-takers, on the one hand, and risk-averse citizens, on the other hand, can be well described by the model of the *homo aleatorius*, and the *homo prudens*, respectively. *Homo aleatorius*, the risk-taker, John Adams noted, lives according to aphorisms such as 'nothing ventured nothing gained' and 'no risk, no reward'.[64] *Homo prudens*, in contrast, is the zero-risk man. According to Adams, '[h]e personifies prudence, rationality and responsibility'.[65] To attribute rationality solely to prudence, however, is a contested approach. Economic theories and finance, in particular, are relating risk and risk management to rational behaviour. A merger of risk-taking and rationality can be recognised in Walras' model of *homo oeconomicus; homo oeconomicus* always acts 'rational' and rational behaviour is considered tantamount to profit maximisation.[66]

Notes

1. Graham Bannock, Ron Baxter and Evan Davis, "Dictionary of Economics", *Profile Books* (2003): 338.
2. Peter L. Bernstein, "Against the Gods. The Remarkable Story of Risk". *John Wiley & Sons* (1998): 197.
3. Bernstein (1998), p. 1.
4. Bernstein (1998), *ibid.*
5. Bernstein (1998), p. 2.
6. Pierre-Charles Pradier, "La notion de risqué en économie". *Éditions La Découverte* (2006): In particular 8–15.
7. Classification, terminology and the critical approach to popular narratives about the origins of risk are taken from Pradier (2006), pp. 8–15.
8. Pradier (2006), p. 8.

9. Pradier (2006), pp. 8–9. Max Weber developed the thesis of a decisive role of Protestantism, in particular Calvinism, for the formation of Capitalism in two essays first published in 1904/1905 under the title encapsulating his argument as *The Protestant Ethic and the Spirit of Capitalism.*
10. Niklas Luhmann, "Risk: A Sociological Theory". Translated from the German original version by Rhodes Barrett. *Walter de Gruyter* (1993): 10. In footnote no. 25, Luhmann referred to Bruno Kuske who had pointed at the proximity of the German words "Angst" (fear) and "Abenteuer" (adventure) with today's common perceptions of the term "risk".
11. Luhmann 1993, p. 10. In the same sense also Bernstein (1998, p. 8) who noted that "[t]he word 'risk' derives from the early Italian *risicare*, which means 'to dare'. In this sense, risk is a choice rather than a fate. The actions we dare to take, which depend on how free we are to make choices, are what the story of risk is all about. And that story helps define what it means to be a human being".
12. Pradier (2006), p. 9.
13. Pradier mentioned François Fourquet who introduced the term bourgeois legend (*légende bourgeoise* in French) for (dis-)qualifying a historiography pretending that merchant capitalism was a 'foreign body' emerging from feudalism on its own volition (Pradier 2006, p. 10), with reference to Francois Fourquet, "Richesse et puissance: une généalogie de la valeur". *La Découverte*, 1989.
14. Pradier (2006), p. 9; with reference to Robert Pirenne, but without indicating a specific source of information.
15. The "Standard Dictionary of the English Language", for example, explains that the term 'risk' is derived from the French word *risque* and the Italian words *rischio* and *risicare*, meaning to dare. Ultimately, the word risk is traced back to the Greek word *rhiza*, meaning cliff, root (Funk & Wagnalls "Standard Dictionary of the English Language", International Edition, Volume Two, *Funk & Wagnalls*, New York [1969]: 1087). "The Concise Oxford English Dictionary" explains that the origins of the word *risk* are the French words risqué and risquer which, in turn, are stemming from the Italian words *risco*, meaning 'danger', and *rischiare*, meaning 'run into danger' ("Concise Oxford English Dictionary". *Oxford University Press* (2008, 11th Edition, revised): 1241.
16. Pradier (2006), p. 9; with references to Friedrich Christian Diez, "Etymologisches Wörterbuch der Romanischen Sprachen", *Adolph Marens*, Bonn (1853); and Alain Rey, "Dictionnaire historique de la langue française", *Le Robert* (1992).
17. Pradier (2006) p. 9.

18. Pradier, *ibid.* p. 9, with reference to Pierre Guiraud, "Dictionnaire des étymologies obscures", *Payot* (1982, reedited 1994).
19. Pradier, *ibid.* p. 9.
20. Pradier, *ibid.*, pp. 9–10. Before the thirteenth Century, a hapax legomenon, that is a word which only appears once in written records of a particular language, was dated 1156. But its unclear nature and arguable translation impaired the significance of the hapax in question (Pradier, *ibid.*, p. 10).
21. Luhmann (1993), p. 9.
22. Pradier (2006), p. 10. Pradier referred to the "Dictionnaire de la langue française" simply as "the Littré", a common token alluding to its principal author, Émile Littré.
23. Pradier, *ibid.* p. 10. (In French: riszq: "provision, part de biens que Dieu attribue à chaque homme"; translation by the author).
24. Nabil Osman (ed.), "Kleines Lexikon deutscher Wörter arabischer Herkunft", *Verlag C.H. Beck* (2007): 102. The German word 'Geschick' can be translated either in the sense of fate and destiny, or in the sense of dexterity, adroitness, aptitude and skills, or in the sense of fortune and luck. The German words 'Wagnis', 'Gefahr', and 'Verlustgefahr' have been translated by 'venture', 'peril', and the expression "(running the) risk of losing", respectively (translation by the author).
25. Nabil Osman, *ibid.* p. 102.
26. Nabil Osman, *ibid.* p. 102.
27. Nabil Osman, *ibid.* p. 59. After the sack of Baghdad by the Mongols in 1258 and the conquest of Constantinople by the Ottomans in 1453, the Ottoman Empire with the new capital Istanbul took virtually over the leading role from the Arab empire. Thereafter, many words adapted from the Turkish language found their way to Europe. A particular word was *tulip* (from the Persian word *dülbend*, meaning 'turban'). In this respect, Klaus Kreiser recounted the story of Ogier Ghiselain von Busbecq (1520/1521–1592) who visited the Court of Sultan Suleiman I the Magnificent (1494–1566). From his visits to Istanbul in 1555 and 1556–1562, von Busbecq brought the tulip flower to Europe which eventually led to the *tulip mania* or *tulipomania* in the Netherlands (Klaus Kreiser, "Geschichte Istanbuls. Von der Antike bis zur Gegenwart", *Verlag C.H. Beck* [2010]: 57). After the tulip bulb had been adapted in the Dutch climate, the tulipomania enfolded as a speculative bubble in the 1630s.
28. Reinhard Schulze, Institute for Islamic Studies and Oriental Philology of the University of Bern, E-mail of July 22, 2008 (on file with the author).
29. Reinhard Schulze, *ibid.*
30. Pradier (2006), p. 12.
31. Pradier, *ibid.*, p. 13.

32. The term Islamic Golden Age usually describes the rule of the Abbasids, beginning with the shift of the capital of the caliphate from Damascus to Baghdad in 762 to the sack of Baghdad by the Mongols in 1258.
33. Annette Bruhns, "Ein Traum von Atlantis", in *SPIEGEL GESCHICHTE*, issue 5, 2010 [pp. 79–85], p. 81. Whereas the *Dar al-Islam*, the 'House of Islam', referred to the Arab empire as hegemonic power, the 'House of Wisdom' (*Dar al-Hikmah*) was the leading scientific institution of its time in Baghdad. The 'House of Wisdom' attracted the most inventive brains of its time:

"These medieval brains met every day for translation, reading, writing, discourse, dialogue and discussion. The place was a cosmopolitan melting pot and the languages that were spoken and written included Arabic, the lingua franca, Farsi, Hebrew, Syriac, Aramaic, Greek, Latin and Sanskrit, which was used to translate the ancient Indian mathematics manuscripts" (Salim T S Al-Hassani (ed.), "1001 Inventions: Muslim Heritage in Our World", 2nd edition published by Foundation of Science, Technology and Civilisation (FSTC, 2007), pp. 46–49).

34. Bruhns (2010), p. 81.
35. Recent research seems to indicate that already in the 12th century, Italian merchants started to adapt the word *resicum* from the Arab word *rizq* and that the former became rapidly a standard term of the commercial vocabulary in the western Mediterranean (see, for instance, Sylvain Piron, "L'apparition du *resicum* en Méditerranée occidentale, XIIe - XIIIe siècles", in Emmanuelle Collas-Heddeland et al. (eds.), *Pour une Histoire culturelle du risque. Genèse, évolution, actualité du concept dans les sociétés occidentales.* Editions Histoire et Anthropologie (2004): 59–76.
36. Pradier (2006), p. 10. In his own words, Pradier wrote: "Malgré l'incertitude qui les entoure, ces recherches étymologiques conduisent à tenir pour certain que l'usage du mot 'risqué' est de loin antérieur à la fin du Moyen Âge, ce qui contredit la *thèse moderniste*" (Pierre-Charles Pradier, *ibid.*).
37. Pradier, *ibid.* p. 12. In French, Pradier called the nautical novel "une histoire plaisante".
38. Pierre-Charles Pradier, *ibid.* p. 12. Recent research refutes the modernist thesis for many reasons. Emilio Ferrín, for example, came to the conclusion that the city states of al-Andalus in Moorish Spain were, in fact, "precursors of the Renaissance" (Bruhns 2010, p. 84).
39. Pradier, *ibid.* pp. 12–13.
40. Pradier distinguished between the use of the word risk and its etymological and historical origins. The use of the word risk, in fact, seems of having first

appeared on European seashores in the context of maritime trade. However, instead of taking this finding as proof for the nautical novel, Pradier opened the floor for considering fact-based alternatives. A probable alternative seems to suggest an Arabic origin of the word *risk*, which can be supported with various interfaces between European powers, on the one hand, and Arab and Ottoman powers on the other hand. In this regard, points of culmination were the Arab rule in Spain (8th–13th centuries) and Sicily (10th–11th centuries) and the series of crusades (11th–13th centuries) in which European powers were involved with both mercantile and belligerent interests. This amalgamation of commercial and strategic interests was highlighted by Pradier as a source of 'risky' ventures by maritime entrepreneurs (*imprenditori*), chivalric entrepreneurs (*chevaliers*) and belligerent entrepreneurs (*condottiere* and mercenaries) (see Pradier 2006, pp. 12–13). Venice, for example, made profitable use of the crusades both economically and strategically. Enrico Dandolo, the Doge of Venice from 1195 to 1205, seized the opportunity of the 4th crusade (1202–1204)—which he misdirected—for eliminating Venice's major competitor in the east, that was, Byzantium (see, for instance, Kreiser 2010, pp. 39–41. Kreiser observed that famous objects commonly associates with Venice, e.g., the *Tetrarchi*, the *Pilastri Acritani*, and the *Quadriga of San Marco*, are booty from Constantinople (Kreiser, *ibid.*, p. 41). Karam Khella went a step further, arguing that the elimination of Byzantium as a competitor was actually the main strategic objective of Venice's involvement in the crusades (see Karam Khella, "Geschichte der arabischen Völker". *Theorie und Praxis Verlag* (1991, 2nd Edition): 132–140). From a meta-perspective, finally, Ernest Mandel brought "the plundering of Byzantium" in line with, firstly, the colonisation of Baltic and north-eastern territories in Europe (which will again be mentioned below), and secondly, with the origins of merchant capitalism itself. Mandel noted:

"[A]ll historical evidence confirms that the sudden appearance of large amounts of 'capital' (in the form of a stock of precious metals and other treasure) in a society previously confined almost exclusively to natural economy (to the output of goods possessing only use-value) was the result not of 'frugality' and 'thrift' but of large-scale piracy, robbery, violence, theft, enslavement of men and trade in slaves. The history of the origins of West European usury and merchant capital between the tenth and the thirteenth centuries, from the piracy in the Mediterranean through the plundering of Byzantium by the Fourth Crusade to the regular plundering razzias into the Slav territories of Central and Eastern Europe, is very eloquent in this respect" (Ernest Mandel, "Introduction" to Karl Marx, *Capital. A Critique of Political Economy.* Vol. 1, translated by Ben Fowkes. *Penguin Books* [1990]: 62).

41. Pradier (2006), pp. 13–14.
42. Pradier (2006), p. 14.
43. Pradier, *ibid.* pp. 13–14. Pradier used the French term "vocabulaire de l'aléatoire" which the author tries to translate as "vocabulary of gambling".
44. Pradier, *ibid.* pp. 14–15. Looking at this astounding regression, Pradier asked rhetorically whether the "century of science", *i.e.*, the 18th century, was not able to stand the doubt (in French: "Est-ce à dire que le 'siècle de la science' ne supporte pas le doute?"
45. Pradier, *ibid.* p. 15.
46. Pradier, *ibid.* p. 15.
47. Bryan A. Garner (ed.), "Black's Law Dictionary", 9th Edition (Thomson Reuters, 2009), p. 1442.
48. Pradier (2006), p. 15. Pradier denoted the linguistic phenomenon of shifting meanings of words as *metonymy*.
49. Pradier, *ibid.* p. 15.
50. Ulrich Beck, "*Risikogesellschaft. Auf dem Weg in eine andere Moderne*". *Suhrkamp* (1996, 1st edition 1986): 25. In 1999, Beck published the book *World Risk Society* where he transposed the idea of the "*Risk Society*" to the global level. In fact, the question "Who bears the risks and who reaps the profits?" is even more critical at international levels than at national levels were constitutions may balance conflicting interests among winners and losers in risk conflicts.
51. Luhmann (1993), pp. 21–22.
52. Lesley Brown (ed.), "The New Shorter Oxford Dictionary", Vol. 2. *Clarendon Press* (1993): 2609. Notes about etymological sources of *risk* refer to the French word *risque* and the Italian words *risco*, *rischio*, and *rischiare*, meaning "run into danger". Furthermore, for *risk* as a verb, the New Shorter Oxford English Dictionary provides, among others, for the following descriptions: "Venture on; accept the chance of (a thing, doing)" (Lesley Brown et al., *ibid.*).
53. Philip Babcock Gove (ed.), "Webster's Third New International Dictionary of the English Language Unabridged". *Könemann* (1993): 1961.
54. Brian Wynne, "Risk Assessment of Technological Systems—Dimensions of Uncertainty". Published in Brian Wynne (ed.), *Risk Management and Hazardous Waste. Implementation and the Dialectics of Credibility* (Springer, 1987).
55. Steve Rayner, "Learning from the Blind Men and the Elephant, or Seeing Things Whole in Risk Management". Published in Vincent T. Covello, Lester B. Lave, Alan Moghissi, and V.R.R. Uppuluri, *Uncertainty in Risk Assessment, Risk Management and Decision Making.* (Plenum Press, 1987): 208.

56. 'Definitions of Risk Analysis Term Related to Food Safety', at the end of the "Working Principles for Risk Analysis for Application in the Framework of the Codex Alimentarius", Section IV of the *Procedural Manual* of the Codex Alimentarius Commission, 19th edition, 2010, p. 92.
57. The term *quarantine sciences* refers to sciences originally used for establishing risks to human, animal and plant health at border controls, for example toxicology, biochemistry, veterinary sciences and plant sciences. Nowadays, the term *quarantine sciences* commonly refers more generally to sciences applied in food safety inspections and the control of epizootics and plant diseases.
58. Christoph Mandl and John Lathrop, "Comparing Risk Assessments for Liquefied Energy Gas Terminals—Some Results". Pulished in Howard C. Kunreuther and Eryl V. Ley (eds.), *The Risk Analysis Controversy. An Institutional Perspective* (Springer, 1982): 43.
59. Adrian Ely, Andy Stierling, Marion Dreyer, Ortwin Renn, Ellen Vos, and Frank Wendler, "The Need for Change", in Marion Dreyer and Ortwin Renn (eds.) *Food Safety Governance. Integrating Science, Precaution and Public Involvement* (Springer, 2009): 15.
60. Pat O'Malley, "Risk, Uncertainty and Government". *Routledge-Cavendish*, 2006 (1st edition 2004): 33–34 (footnotes omitted).
61. O'Malley, *ibid.*, p. 40, citing Patrick Atiyah, "The Rise and Fall of Freedom of Contract". Clarendon (1979): 628.
62. O'Malley, *ibid.*, p. 40, citing Patrick Atiyah,, "The Rise and Fall of Freedom of Contract". Clarendon (1979): 628.
63. O'Malley (2006), p. 41 (original emphasis, footnotes omitted).
64. John Adams, "Risk". *Routledge*, 2009 (first published in 1995): 16–17. Adams cited William Blake as quoting: 'Prudence is a rich, ugly old maid courted by Incapacity' (John Adams, *ibid.*, p. 17).
65. Adams, *ibid.*, p. 16.
66. The fictitious character of the *homo oeconomicus* was invented by economist Léon Walras (1834–1910) for applying mathematical formulae and models on economic sciences.

References

Bannock, Graham, Baxter, Ron, and Davis, Evan. "Dictionary of Economics". *Profile Books*, 2003.

Beck, Ulrich. "Die Risikogesellschaft. Auf dem Weg in eine andere Moderne". *Suhrkamp Verlag*, 1996 (1st edition 1986).

Beck, Ulrich. "World Risk Society". *Polity Press in association with Blackwell Publishers*, 2005 (first published 1999).

Bernstein, Peter L. "Against the Gods. The Remarkable Story of Risk". *John Wiley & Sons*, 1998.

Bruhns, Annette. "Ein Traum von Atlantis". *SPIEGEL GESCHICHTE,* vol. 5, 2010, 79–85.

Ely, Adrian, Stierling, Andy, Dreyer, Marion, Renn, Ortwin, Vos, Ellen and Wendler, Frank. "The Need for Change". Published in Marion Dreyer and Ortwin Renn (eds.), *Food Safety Governance. Integrating Science, Precaution and Public Involvement.* Springer-Verlag, 2009, 11–27.

Garner Bryan A. (ed.). "Black's Law Dictionary", *Thomson Reuters*, 2009, 9th edition.

Gove, Philip Babcock (ed.). "Webster's Third New International Dictionary of the English Language Unabridged". *Könemann Verlagsgesellschaft*, 1993.

Kreiser, Klaus. "Geschichte Istanbuls. Von der Antike bis zur Gegenwart". *Verlag C.H. Beck*, 2010.

Luhmann, Niklas. "Risk: A Sociological Theory". Translated from the German original version by Rhodes Barrett. *Walter de Gruyter*, 1993.

Mandel, Ernest. "Introduction" to Karl Marx, *Capital. A Critique of Political Economy.* Vol. 1. Translated by Ben Fowkes. *Penguin Books*, 1990, 11–86.

Mandl, Christoph and Lathrop, John. "Comparing Risk Assessments for Liquefied Energy Gas Terminals – Some Results". Published in Howard C. Kunreuther and Eryl V. Ley (eds.), *The Risk Analysis Controversy. An Institutional Perspective. Proceedings of a Summer Study on Decision Processes and Institutional Aspects of Risk held at IIASA, Laxenburg, Austria, 22–26 June, 1981.*Springer-Verlag, 1982.

Osman, Nabil (ed.). "Kleines Lexikon deutscher Wörter arabischer Herkunft". *Verlag C.H. Beck*, 2007.

Pat O'Malley, "Risk, Uncertainty and Government". *Routledge-Cavendish*, 2006 (1st edition 2004).

Piron, Sylvain. "L'apparition du *resicum* en Méditerranée occidentale, XIIe - XIIIe siècles". Published in Emmanuelle Collas-Heddeland *et. al.* (eds.), *Pour une Histoire culturelle du risque. Genèse, évolution, actualité du concept dans les sociétés occidentales.* Editions Histoire et Anthropologie, 2004, 59–76. Accessed October 25, 2010. http://halshs.archives-ouvertes.fr/docs/00/03/76/66/PDF/apparition_du_resicum.pdf.

Pradier, Pierre-Charles. "La notion de risqué en économie". *Éditions La Découverte*, 2006.

Rayner, Steve. "Learning from the Blind Men and the Elephant, or Seeing Things Whole in Risk Management". Published in Vincent T. Covello, Lester B. Lave, Alan Moghissi and V.R.R. Uppuluri (eds.), *Uncertainty in Risk Assessment, Risk Management, and Decision Making.* NY: Plenum Press, 1987, 207–212.

CHAPTER 5

Two Functions of Risk

In the previous chapter, the dual notion of risk, i.e. individualistic and societal, was established. It was shown that the different notions of risk are related to different philosophical approaches, in particular, positivism and relativism. In the following, it will be shown how impacts caused by the two antagonistic notions of risk established above, i.e. entrepreneurial and social notions of risk respectively, can be observed on the ground.

The examples selected for demonstrating the two functions of risk are agricultural food production, one of the oldest fields of economic activity,[1] on the one hand, and food consumption as a basic human necessity, on the other hand.

The function of risk in agriculture is analysed at both ends of production, i.e. at the supply side and at the demand side. Approached from two sides, from the perspective of agricultural entrepreneurs (producers) as well as from the standpoint of food consumers (society), risk shows its Janus face: risk estimates are turning out to be different depending on whether the perspective of agricultural producers or one of food consumers is taken up. In other words, risk estimates are relative, contingent upon the viewpoint of the observer. From the perspective of farmers acting in economically rational ways, limits to risk-taking in output rises are set by economic considerations only, e.g. profitability. From a consumers' perspective, however, there is little reason for risk-taking in food safety issues, leaving aside eventual price incentives. From a consumers' perspective, it seems rational to call for prudence and precaution.

M. Burkard, *Conflicting Philosophies and International Trade Law*, Philosophy, Public Policy, and Transnational Law, https://doi.org/10.1007/978-3-319-61067-2_5

From an economic perspective, the reason for the antagonism between food producers and food consumers are the 'credence' characteristics of food. With respect to food, 'credence' means 'that consumers are unable to determine food safety characteristics themselves, often even after consumption'.[2] In this respect, Lee Ann Jackson and Marion Jansen observed:

> In markets for credence goods, producers cannot be expected to give consumers all the information they require to evaluate the quality or the characteristics of a good, because producer and consumer interests do not coincide. In particular, when deciding on optimal product characteristics, producers will take into account production costs, the probability that low product safety has negative health effects and the cost health damage will generate for producers. Consumers, instead, are interested [in] the probability of health effects and the actual damage those health effects may cause to them. In the case of credence goods, where the origin of eventual health problems is hardy traceable the damage claims producers can be expected to face are likely to be significantly lower than the actual health damage incurred. As a consequence, credence good markets are markets where producers are tempted to take higher risks than consumers would consider desirable.[3]

From the perspective of sociology, the antagonism between food producers and consumers was conceived as the result of the juridification of food handling previously regulated by cultural values. Eva Barlösius explained transitions from culturally framed food traditions to food regulation based on abstract laws by reference to Max Weber's sociology of law.[4] As soon as food production and food processing became issues of conflicting economic interests, Barlösius explained, juridification started to replace traditional norms. Because traditional norms and culture seemed unable to arbitrate between the interests of commercial food producers, on the one hand, and safety-oriented food consumers, on the other hand, food had to be regulated by law. The legitimacy of food safety regulation could no longer be based on cultural values, but had to be based on a new and common denominator; that was, empirical rationality and rational procedures.[5] With a view on the scope of the study at hand, Barlösius' observation that levels of abstraction and generalisation of food regulations are increasing proportionally to increases in market size is of particular relevance. Barlösius' observation means that food safety regulation at regional or international levels, for example, food safety regulation by the European Union or by the Codex Alimentarius Commission, may increase tensions between food traditions based on cultural values and food regulation based on empirical rationality.[6]

1 Liberalisation

In this paragraph, it will be shown that farmers' response to risk is not fundamentally different than the risk response of entrepreneurs in other economic sectors. Responses of farmers towards risks seem to be rather similar across cultures and continents. The behaviour of individual farmers at microeconomic levels is best conceived by applying rational economic theories rather than by relying on the hypothesis of cultural relativism. Remaining differences will be identified as differences with regard to concrete living conditions. In the following, the behaviour of farmers under conditions of risk will be analysed at three stages of agricultural development; these are subsistence farming, diversified farming and finally commercial farming.

1.1 Risk Prevention in Subsistence Farming

In *Economic Development*, Michael Todaro and Stephen Smith provided an analytical framework for looking at farmers' behaviour in situations of risk.[7] Thereby, Todaro and Smith focused, in particular, on farming conditions in developing countries (DCs) and least-developed countries (LDCs).

To begin with, an important statement of Todaro and Smith shall be mentioned. Todaro and Smith noted that the resistance of peasant farmers in DCs and LDCs to innovation in agriculture is often attributed 'as a sign of incompetence or irrationality'.[8] However, Todaro and Smith rebutted that depreciation of peasant farming as 'misguided convictions of some foreigners'.[9] On the contrary, Todaro and Smith pointed at the economic rationale guiding peasant farmers:

> … [G]iven the nature of the peasants' environment, the uncertainties that surround them, the need to meet minimum survival levels of output, and the rigid social institutions into which they are locked, most peasants behave in an economically rational manner when confronted with alternative opportunities.[10]

Along with persisting (neo-)colonial stereotypes, Todaro and Smith identified shortcomings of neoclassical economic approaches as responsible for problems in understanding subsistence farming. Todaro and Smith acknowledged that 'the traditional two-factor neoclassical theory of production' provided '[s]ome insight into the economics of subsistence agriculture'.[11] In particular, Todaro and Smith admitted that the neoclassical theory 'provides an economic rationale for the observed low productivity of traditional agriculture in the form of the law of diminishing marginal productivity'.[12] However, Todaro and Smith observed that the neoclassical theory 'does not satisfactorily explain why small-scale farmers are often resistant to technological innovation in farming techniques or to the introduction of new seeds or different cash crops'.[13] Todaro and Smith summarised the failure of the neoclassical theory to explain the behaviour of peasant farmers as follows:

> According to the standard theory, a rational income or profit-maximizing farm or firm will always choose a method of production that will increase output for a given cost (in this case, the available labor time) or lower costs for a given output level. But the theory is based on the crucial assumption that farmers possess 'perfect knowledge' of all technological input-output relationships as well as current information about prevailing factor and product prices. This is the point at which the theory loses a good deal of its validity when applied to the environment of subsistence agriculture. Furthermore, when access to information is highly imperfect, transaction costs of obtaining this information are usually high. Given price uncertainty, peasant farmers often face price bands (often wide ranges) rather than a single input price. Along with limited access to credit and insurance, such an environment is not conducive to the type of behavior posited by neoclassical theory and goes a long way toward explaining the actual risk-averse behavior of peasant farmers, including their caution in the use of purchased inputs such as fertilizer.[14]

As an alternative to neoclassical theory, Todaro and Smith have developed an approach for the better understanding of small-scale farmers' behaviour in situations of risk. Todaro and Smith established the parameters of their alternative approach towards subsistence farming as follows:

> Subsistence agriculture is thus a highly risky and uncertain venture. It is made even more so by the fact that human lives are at stake. In regions where farms are extremely small and cultivation is dependent on the uncertainties of variable rainfall, average output will be low, and in poor years, the peasant and his family will be exposed to the very real danger of starvation. In such

> circumstances, the main motivating force in the peasant's life may be the maximization not of income but of his family's chances of survival. Accordingly, when risk and uncertainty are high, a small farmer may be very reluctant to shift from a traditional technology and crop pattern that over the years he has come to know and understand to a new one that promises higher yields but may entail greater risks of crop failure. When sheer survival is at stake, it is more important to avoid a bad year (total crop failure) than to maximize the output in better years. Risk-avoiding peasant farmers are likely to prefer a technology of food production that combines a low *mean* per-hectare yield with low *variance* (fluctuations around the average) to alternative technologies and crops that promise a higher mean yield but also present the risk of a greater variance.[15]

Todaro and Smith provided two microeconomic derivations for their findings. Illustrated by a first figure, Todaro and Smith compared two farmers, farmer A and farmer B. Farmer A's productivity is near the minimum consumption requirement (MCR). The MCR may be taken as the minimum necessary for the sheer physical survival of Farmer A and his family, yet some sort of starvation minimum. Any output below the MCR would have drastic consequences. The productivity of farmer B, on the other hand, is near the minimum desired consumption level (MDCL). The MDCL indicates the minimum level of consumption under given conditions, in that case, the production patterns of farmer B. For obvious reasons, farmer A, labouring at the brink of starvation, will try to avoid risk by any means. Farmer B, on the other hand, is producing well above subsistence levels and is, therefore, more disposed to change and innovate. As a result, farmer B may increase productivity even further, whereas farmer A may remain 'in a self-perpetuating poverty trap'.[16]

The second figure provided by Todaro and Smith compared two situations, technique A and technique B, representing different probabilities for crop yields, but also different levels of variance (fluctuations around the average). The two graphs illustrating the comparison show that technique A leads to a lower mean crop yield than technique B. But on the other hand, technique A also comes along with lower levels of variance, in that case fluctuations around the mean yield, than technique B. In such a situation, small-scale farmers with productivities barely higher than subsistence levels would most reasonably opt for technique A, thus paying for a lower level of variance with a lower mean yield. Todaro and Smith concluded: 'Evidence is clear that farmers pay for "self-insurance" of this type with much lower returns'.[17]

As a major cause for disappointing results delivered by programmes aimed at increasing agricultural productivity especially among small-scale farmers in Africa, Todaro and Smith identified the 'failure to provide adequate insurance (both financial credit and physical "buffer" stocks) against the risk of crop shortfalls, whether these risks are real or imagined'.[18] Based on the above findings, Todaro and Smith concluded that peasant farmers' behaviour is based on rational economic principles:

> We may conclude that peasant farmers do act rationally and are responsive to economic incentives and opportunities. Where innovation and change fails to occur, we should not assume that peasants are stupid, irrational, or conservative; instead, we should examine carefully the environment in which the small farmer operates to search for the particular institutional or commercial obstacles that may be blocking or frustrating constructive change. Efforts to minimize risk and remove commercial and institutional obstacles to small-farmer innovation are therefore essential requirements of agricultural and rural development.[19]

In sum, the extension of the neoclassical theory of production by Todaro and Smith provided the following insights[20]:

1. Peasant farmers 'do act rationally and are responsive to economic incentives and opportunities'. Thus, in principle, economic theory applies to peasant farmers in the same way as to other farmers and to economic agents in general.
2. However, the applicability of economic theory in an individual case is contingent upon 'the environment in which the small farmer operates' and 'the particular institutional or commercial obstacles that may be blocking or frustrating constructive change'.[21]
3. Along with the removal of institutional and commercial obstacles, 'efforts to minimize risk' have been identified as additional conditions for constructive change. Risk factors have been identified at three levels:

    (i) at the 'soft' or knowledge level as data gaps and imperfect market information;
    (ii) at the financial level as limited access to credit and insurance facilities; and
    (iii) at the physical level as missing buffer stocks against crop failure.

As soon as a peasant is able to increase production above the minimum consumption requirement (MCR) and to overcome the 'self-perpetuation poverty trap' of producing near subsistence levels, he has the chance of approaching the stages of diversified and specialised farming, respectively.[22]

1.2 *Risk Mitigation in Diversified Farming*

In many cases, peasant farmers are doomed of labouring around the minimum consumption requirement (MCR) level. However, as soon as a peasant farmer manages to approach the higher minimum desirable consumption level (MDCL), he will likely enter the stage of mixed or diversified farming. Todaro and Smith characterised diversified farming as 'a logical intermediate step in the transition from subsistence to specialized production'.[23] Specifically, diversified farming is characterised by the supplementation of staple crop cultivation by new cash crops, such as fruits, vegetables, coffee, tea, pyrethrum and animal husbandry.[24] Looking from a perspective of contemporary agricultural development, Todaro and Smith identified two particular factors which are limiting agricultural output under conditions of subsistence farming, but may be addressed by means of investment and innovation.[25] These limiting factors are labour and land, respectively.[26]

With regard to labour shortages, Todaro and Smith observed: '... [W] here labor is in short supply during peak planting seasons, as in many parts of Africa, simple laborsaving devices (such as small tractors, mechanical seeders, or animal-operated steel plows) can be introduced to free labor for other farm activities'.[27] In cases of land shortages, on the other hand, Todaro and Smith noted:

> ... [T]he use of better seeds, fertilizers, and simple irrigation to increase the yields of staple crops like wheat, maize, and rice can free part of the land for cash crop cultivation while ensuring an adequate supply of the staple food. The farm operator can thus have a *marketable surplus*, which he can sell to raise his family's consumption standards or *invest* in farm improvements. Diversified farming can also minimize the impact of staple crop failure and provide a *security* of income previously unavailable.[28]

In the above phrases, basic elements for agricultural transformation are expressed. By addressing the problem of limited factors of productions, i.e. labour and land, by technical and financial means, overall productivity can be increased. The surplus obtained may then be reinvested, thus setting in motion a perpetual motion machine for profit generation. This beneficial circle is the exact opposite of the self-perpetuating poverty trap observed under conditions of subsistence farming. Besides the two characteristic features of the capability to overcome limiting production factors and the ability for reinvestments, there is a third distinct feature of diversified farming. As mentioned above by Todaro and Smith, diversified farming also provides a security against the risks of crop failure. Addressing the risk of crop failure through diversification is not an invention of diversified farming. Peasant farmers are commonly mitigating risks of crop failure by applying methods of crop rotation. One may call this prototype of agricultural security 'hedging by crop diversification'. Diversified farming, in contrast, enables diversification not only horizontally, across different (staple) crops, but also vertically, by using monetary gains from earlier sales of cash crops as superior forms of security. By combining traditional methods of hedging, i.e. rotation and diversification across staple crops for self-consumption, with new methods of 'financial hedging', i.e. savings, communities of diversified family farms achieved high levels of self-sufficiency and food security.

In diversified farming, all elements characterising modern risk concepts can be observed, yet in an embryonic stage:

(i) technical innovation;
(ii) entrepreneurial motivation for production increase, capital accumulation and reinvestment;
(iii) financial instruments for hedging generated surpluses.

However, diversified farming is not only the 'logical intermediate step in the transition from subsistence to specialized production' in agricultural development at microeconomic levels, but also in the broader historical perspective. From a historical point of view, Mazoyer and Roudart showed that the three characteristic features distinguishing diversified farming from earlier stages of agricultural production appeared concomitantly at a particular period of time in the cold temperate regions of northwestern Europe.[29]

Beginning with technical innovation, Mazoyer and Roudart noted that technical innovations in agricultural production, in particular, the shift from the scratch plough or ard to the mouldboard plough, enabled significant production increases. In combination with the use of the scythe,

the harrow and the roller, the introduction of the mouldboard plough gave rise to a new agricultural production system based on ploughing, draft animals and fallowing. Mazoyer and Roudart observed:

> In the cold temperate regions, this new equipment made it possible to expand the previously limited practices of cultivation and animal rising by using hay, stabling livestock during the dead season, and using manure. The development of these practices gave rise to a new cultivated ecosystem, which from then on included hay meadows and extended arable lands. The latter were better manured, better plowed, and generally cultivated in a triennial rotation. Thus a new agrarian system appeared which, despite the high costs of the necessary equipment, spread widely throughout the cold, temperate regions, where it facilitated a considerable growth in production and agricultural activity. (…) The agricultural revolution of the Middle Ages carried the rural economy in the West to the threshold of modern times.[30]

However, as Mazoyer and Roudart noted, improvements in agricultural infrastructure, in particular, in mouldboard ploughs, scythes, carts and harrows, required investment capital. Investment capital, on the other hand, can only be mobilised if there is a prospect of return of such investment. Where this double condition was met, agricultural production expanded significantly. Mazoyer and Roudart observed:

> … [A] system based on cultivation using the [mouldboard] plow requires large investments in equipment, buildings, livestock, and labor. Such a system can develop only on condition of leading to gains in productivity, which allow a return to these investments and gains in production, which make it possible to feed larger numbers of livestock and people. (…) [T]his double condition … was fulfilled in the cold temperate regions of middle Europe (…).[31]

New technical equipments, in particular, the mouldboard plough, enabled the valorisation of hitherto unprofitable areas. Mazoyer and Roudart noted:

> In the northern half of Europe, the potential of the new system of cultivation was immense. In already populated regions, the transition from the ard [*i.e.* scratch plough] to the [mouldboard] plow made possible the doubling or tripling of production and population. Moreover, use of the plow could also develop in vast areas that had remained until then unexploited because they could not be cultivated under the old ard system. The new areas included

> forests and moors that existed either on permeable and leached soils that were not fertile for cultivation without manure or on soils that were too heavy to be cultivated without the plow.[32]

The clearing of land, usually starting near existing villages and areas already under cultivation, became a more and more systematised operation: '[I]t was a question of moving as quickly as possible to establish hay meadows, pastures, and arable lands that were cleared, stumped, and drained for long-term use, and making *profitable use* of the recently acquired new equipment associated with the animal-drawn plow'.[33]

At this point, the second feature of the risk concept applied on agriculture, i.e. entrepreneurial motivation, comes into play. Entrepreneurial spirit was awakened because the new lands which were formerly inaccessible by the old scratch ard technique and which now became exploitable by new methods of mouldboard ploughing, were, in fact, not unclaimed. Becoming aware of the prospects, various authorities were quick to claim lordship over these new territories. Mazoyer and Roudart commented on these particular sorts of rural entrepreneurs as follows:

> Naturally, this clearing of nearby lands hardly passed unnoticed by the local nobility. They quickly recognized the additional revenues that they could draw from the cleared lands and encouraged such clearing by imposing relatively small taxes on those performing the work. Thus, little by little, the unexploited lands around each village disappeared. (…) [W]hen these new lands were clearly isolated, the new villages were established on a sort of pioneer front that gradually advanced onto new colonized lands. In this way, lords, abbots, and other *entrepreneurs of clearing* were learning methods that they then made the most of in launching larger and more distant colonization enterprises.[34]

However, when it came to the colonisation of distant virgin lands, the local nobility's financial capacity was often not sufficient. Hence, they had to join forces with peers, or interestingly, with bourgeois of the cities. Mazoyer and Roudart described the joint efforts of landed gentry and urban bourgeoisie for colonising distant territories as follows:

> In order to undertake such enterprises [*i.e.* the colonisation of distant virgin lands] successfully, these lords, as powerful as they were, had to seek out partners among those who were able to contribute to the financing and implementation of the necessary work. Thus there developed contracts of

> feudal property between two lords, or between a lord and a religious establishment.[35] (...) All these [colonising] efforts were organized and directed by *entrepreneurs*, who, for the most part, were bourgeois of the cities, or even the youngest sons of noble families, wealthy farmers, or servants who were confided this task by their masters. In exchange for their services and possible advances in money, these *entrepreneurs* received part of the profits from the operation, either in the form of lands to exploit on their own account or in the form of a fraction of the taxes due from the newly settled peasants.[36]

Along with the titleholders, i.e. the gentry, and the bourgeoisie chipping in financial means and entrepreneurial know-how, a third group was obviously needed, namely those doing the effective clearing on the ground. Mazoyer and Roudart provided two examples for illustrating how the labour force required for colonising new lands was recruited. The first example related to the German conquest of northeastern and Baltic territories, the second to the construction of polders in Flanders.

With regard to the first example, the German conquest of northeastern and Baltic territories, Mazoyer and Roudart provided the following account:

> The great plains of northeastern Europe, for example, still largely covered with a mixed forest of broadleaf and conifer trees, were occupied by relatively spares Slavic or Baltic populations who still practiced slash-and-burn agriculture. The colonization of these regions took place after their military conquest and the conqueror's consolidation of power. These preliminary tasks were entrusted by German princes to orders that were both military and religious, such as the order of the Teutonic Knights (*Chevaliers Teutoniques*) who conquered Eastern Prussia and the Baltic countries or the order of the Knights of the Sword (*Chevaliers Porte-Glaive*), who besieged Courland. These expeditions, presented as crusades aimed at evangelizing the pagan populations of the East, frequently ended up by subjugating them or even exterminating and replacing them with German colonists. The latter were attracted by the favorable conditions of settlement promised by the entrepreneurs. In the end, the exploitation of these regions with the powerful means provided by the equipment associated with the new agrarian system based on the [mouldboard] plow led to the formation of a new and vast cereal-growing basin, well served by a network of rivers flowing into the Baltic. Over the centuries, the grain production of this basin was collected by the large merchants of the Hanseatic cities and exported to Scandinavia, England, the Netherlands, etc.[37]

In the case of German colonisation of northeastern Europe and the Baltic, the third group, along with the gentry and bourgeois financiers and entrepreneurs, were German colonists. But who were these colonists? Mazoyer and Roudart portrayed these new settler-colonists in the following way:

> … [T]hese territories also attracted masses of peasants who were fleeing serfdom, abuses of power, lack of land and poverty, all of which were rife in overpopulated regions dominated by the older ard [*i.e.* scratch plough] system of cultivation. During the whole period of the clearings, the powerful had to meet the needs of these peasants and assist them by providing seeds, equipment, and livestock. They also had to allow them a share in the profits of the operation by granting them perpetual title to a rather large tenure through payment of a moderate fixed tax called 'quitrent' (*le cens*). Otherwise, free to come and go, these peasants were going to offer their services on other clearing sites where the conditions offered were more favorable.[38]

The example of the valorisation of coastal marshlands in Flanders shows how not only Members of the gentry and wealthy bourgeois and entrepreneurs, but also Members of the third group, i.e. peasants and commoners joined forces for colonising new lands. Mazoyer and Roudart described the reasons for the draining and the process of building associations as follows:

> The lower valleys of the Rhine, the Yser, and the Aa were overpopulated and frequently submerged by marine encroachments. In the eleventh century, responding to pressures from the local populations and lords, the counts of Flanders, ultimately masters of this "low country", undertook to dry it out. They had large dikes constructed and entrusted the exploitation of the contained lands to the monasteries. At first, the dried-out but still saline marshes were transformed into meadows for sheep, then into meadows for cows, with scattered sheep pens and cowsheds. In the twelfth century, when the lands were sufficiently desalinated, plowing began and cereals were planted. Villages of farmers were then established. In the thirteenth century, the maintenance of the installations and the management of water were taken over by local association of users, the *draining syndicates* (or *wateringues*), which operated under the control of agents of the counts of Flanders. In two centuries, the Netherlands became a prosperous agricultural country (…).[39]

Therefore, it was not by coincidence that the Netherlands became forerunners of what Roudart and Mazoyer called the first agricultural revolution of modern times. Because of land scarcities, agricultural production was intensified by introducing new agrarian systems without using fallowing.[40]

The entrepreneurial attitude which 'modern' farmers began to express in the sixteenth century in the Netherlands may be illustrated in comparison with a contemporary land consolidation project, the Dutch 'Zuiderzee Reclamation Project'. The farmers settling on new lands created behind polders expressed particular motivation. Charles Takes observed:

> As a result of the careful selection, the group of farmers in the new land is, more than anywhere else, composed of people who have a modern outlook on life. Being modern became a norm here. The people in the polders keep an eye open for all kinds of innovations and experiments; they are, in general, more dynamic than the average farmer in the old land.[41]

These examples show that the 'entrepreneurial spirit' did not only materialise in Members of the gentry and the bourgeoisie, but also among the peasantry given that chances were within reach. On these grounds, Mazoyer and Roudart came to the following conclusion:

> Thus, at the periphery of the ancient world in which diverse forms of servitude still existed, a new world began to be formed. This world included independent peasants, whether quitrent farmers, tenant farmers, or sharecroppers, as well as entrepreneurs and wage earners – a modern world, in fact.[42]

A characterising feature of this 'modern world' was the increase in commercial activity, in particular, commodity trade. As a result of production growth, '[peasants sold ¨their increased surplus, the nobility sold a large part of the products from their reserves and from the taxes in kind which they continued to receive (…) and newly cultivated regions exported their surplus'.[43] As a consequence, the business of merchants and traders became increasingly important, and markets and fairs emerged in formerly remote villages, linking them together in a growing commercial network.[44] However, long-distance trade, be it by land or by sea, was always a risk. At this point, it shall be looked at the third criterion of a risk concept applied on agriculture, that is, financial hedging. By looking at the agricultural landscape of the late Middle Ages from a risk perspective, one can observe three particular situations were risk considerations come into play in agricultural production:

The first risk situation appears at the production stage, thus it is called producers' or farmers' risk. However, in contrast of subsistence farmers, the main concern is no longer variance, *i.e.* fluctuations around average yields. Farmers producing for markets are facing a risk which subsistence farmers do not, namely fluctuations around average prices, that is, *volatility*.

In his work *Against the God—The Remarkable Story of Risk (1998)*, Peter L. Bernstein worked out the important link between volatility and farmers' indebtedness:

> The particulars may have changed over time, but the farmer's fundamental need for controlling risk has not. Farmers cannot tolerate volatility, because they are perennially in debt. Their huge investments in land and equipment and in inventories of seed and fertilizer make bank financing unavoidable. Before the farmer sees any money coming his way, he has to pay for his inputs, plant his crop, and then, constantly fearful of flood, drought, and blight, wait months until harvest time. His great uncertainty is what the price will be when he is finally in a position to deliver his crop to the market. If the price he receives is below his cost of production, he might be unable to pay his debts and might lose everything.[45]

However, farmers operating within a market system are usually in the position to hedge themselves against commercial risks. The oldest hedging instrument developed in agriculture is the selling in advance of an expected harvest at an anticipated price. Bernstein described the requirement for contracts for future crop delivery as hedging instruments and their mode of operation as follows:

> The farmer is helpless before the risk of weather and insects, but he can at least escape the uncertainty of what his selling price will be. He can do that by selling his crop when he plants it, promising future delivery to the buyer at a prearranged price. He may miss out on some profit if the price rise, but the *futures contract* will protect him from catastrophe if prices fall. He has passed along the risk of lower prices to someone else.[46]

From frugal origins based on farmers' needs, pre-selling has evolved in the course of time into elaborate financial instruments today known as *futures*, a particular form of derivatives.[47] Bernstein observed that '[s]ophisticated as they may appear in the fancy dress in which we see them today, their role in the management of risk probably originated centuries ago down on the farm'.[48] Continuing his retrospect, Bernstein provided the following overview of the evolution of futures contracts:

> In the twelfth century, sellers at medieval trade fairs signed contracts, called *lettres de faire*, promising future delivery of the items they sold. In the 1600 s, Japanese feudal lords sold their rice for future delivery in a market called *cho-ai-mai* under contracts that protected them from bad weather or warfare. For many years, in markets such as metals, foreign exchange, agricultural products, and, more recently, stocks and bonds, the use of contracts for future delivery has been a common means of protection against the risk of volatile prices. Futures contracts for commodities like wheat, pork bellies, and copper have been trading on the Chicago Board of Trade since 1865.[49]

Thus, one may note that producers' or farmers' risks were hedged by means of *lettres de faire*, i.e. sorts of *futures contracts* designed for advanced sales of expected harvest at anticipated prices, already in the twelfth century.

A second risk situation appears at the trading stage, thus it is called traders' or merchants' risk. In this respect, Mazoyer and Roudart observed:

> The merchant trade was very lucrative, but also very risky. Convoys of merchandise were at the mercy of bandits along the main roads and pirates at sea, of accidents and bad weather, all of which caused numerous losses. To guard against these occurrences, merchants traveled in caravans and financed commercial expeditions with several people in order to *share the risks.*[50]

Thus, along with physical equipment, merchants addressed trade risks by cost-sharing arrangements. Additionally, merchants also 'invested a part of their capital in *less risky businesses*: industrial workshops, mines, mills, property investment, loans against security, but also (...) in large land-clearing enterprises and agricultural and animal breeding estates'.[51] Because alternative investments in 'less risky businesses' are tantamount to classical risk management techniques called *diversification*, one may consider that traders' or merchants' risks were hedged, *inter alia*, by means of investment diversification. However, a more innovative instrument for hedging goods in transit emerged in the thirteenth century, namely the trade bill. As Jacques Le Goff noted, trade bills enabled merchants not only to reduce the risk of transport, but also to mitigate exchange problems and to profit from different exchange rates, eventually.[52]

A third risk situation appears at the stage of wholesale, manufacturing and processing, short entrepreneurial risks. A major risk of entrepreneurs consists in the risk of loosing the means of production, *i.e.* their investment goods such as mills, bakehouses, manufactories, winepresses, etc. These entrepreneurial risks are of particular interest because the way they were addressed was, in fact, groundbreaking. The new agricultural entrepreneurs, regardless whether aristocratic, cleric or bourgeois, directed respective investments to the most profitable ventures.[53] In a paragraph entitled *The Birth of Capitalism*, Mazoyer and Roudart traced the origins of stock companies back to the establishment and operating of mills. According to Mazoyer and Roudart, the new agricultural entrepreneurs, for the purpose of profit maximisation, called on wage labourers:

> They [*i.e.* the agricultural entrepreneurs] employed wage laborers who did not generally contribute to the financing of means of production. This was so for the mills in the Toulouse region (…). These mills gave rise to the formation of the *first known joint stock companies* in the twelfth century. In the following century, these stocks yielded an interest on capital ranging from 19 to 25 percent per year, and there was no longer a single miller among the shareholders. These were already *true capitalist enterprises* in which the search for profit motivated the investment of capital and where the wage laborers did not share in the capital.[54]

The historical arguments established by Mazoyer and Roudart indicate that beginnings of agricultural commercialisation are dating back to the Middle Ages.[55] Such clusters of commercial agriculture coincided with hot spots of early forms of capitalism (proto-capitalism). Modern forms of agricultural production, trade and commerce required, in turn, new forms of risk management. As instruments for risk management were developed, specifically, early forms of futures contracts, commercial bills of exchange, and prequels of stock companies.[56]

Bringing the microeconomic observations of Todaro and Smith together with the historical findings of Mazoyer and Roudart, one may perceive diversified farming as an intermediate step between subsistence and commercial farming in two respects; from a historical perspective and with regard to contemporary agricultural development. On the one hand, diversified farming can be associated with technical innovation, entrepreneurial motivation and sophisticated risk management instruments. On the other hand, the fact remains that in the stage of diversified farming, a solid stock of staple crops is still necessary for satisfying basic food requirements of farming families. In other words, in the stage of diversified farming, certain quotas of land and labour are still absorbed by cultivating staple crops for direct consumption by the producers themselves. These persisting quotas of land and labour, ensuring high degrees of self-sufficiency among farming communities, are capitalised and mobilised in the third stage of agricultural development, that is, commercial or highly specialised agriculture.

1.3 Risk Management in Commercial Farming

From an economic perspective, commercial farming is characterised by the application of purely economic criteria, such as profit maximisation and cost minimisation. Production is increased through the application of petrochemical inputs, such as fertilisers, pesticides and fungicides, hybrid or genetically modified seeds, and the application of hormones for growth promotion purposes. Todaro and Smith summarised the characteristics of commercial farming as follows:

> In specialised farming, the provision of food for the family with some marketable surplus is no longer the basic goal [as was the case in diversified farming]. Instead, pure commercial profit becomes the criterion of success, and maximum per-hectare yields derived from synthetic (irrigation, fertilizer, pesticides, hybrid seeds, etc.) and natural resources become the object of farm activity. Production, in short, is entirely for the market. Economic concepts such as fixed and variable costs, saving, investment and rates of return, optimal factor combinations, maximum production possibilities, market prices, and price supports take on quantitative and qualitative significance. The emphasis in resource utilization is no longer on land, water, and labor as in subsistence and often mixed farming. Instead, capital formation, technological progress, and scientific research and development play major roles in stimulating higher levels of output and productivity.[57]

The most characteristic feature of commercial agriculture is, however, specialisation on a single crop or livestock which is selected according to profitability considerations. The focus on one major crop or animal species is a prerequisite for most efficient applications of machinery and the utilisation of economies of scale. With respect to specialisation, Todaro and Smith observed:

> The common features of all specialized farms, therefore, are their emphasis on the cultivation of one particular crop, their use of capital-intensive and in many cases laborsaving techniques of production, and their reliance on economies of scale to reduce unit costs and maximize profits. In some ways, specialised farming is no different in concept or operation from large industrial enterprises. In fact, some of the largest specialized farming operations in both the developed and especially the less developed nations are owned and managed by large agribusiness multinational corporate enterprises.[58]

In commercial agriculture, not only agricultural production, but also associated risks are considered in purely economic terms. Under conditions of commercial farming, risk has lost to be an existential threat to the farming family but became a mere question of economic success or failure. Therefore, commercial farming, in similar ways as other commercial enterprises, can be characterised as willing to take risks, in principle. Expressions of the risk-seeking attitude of commercial farming can be seen in the willingness to introduce new technologies in agricultural production. In this regard, most prominent was the introduction of synthetic fertilisers and pesticides in the second half or the twentieth century (1st Green Revolution) and the contemporary proliferation of genetically modified seeds (2nd Green Revolution).

A common feature of risks associated with commercial farming is that risks related to production increase, such as pesticides, hormones and genetically modified organisms (GMOs), are taken consciously by agricultural producers. Hence, in contrast to the occurrence of risk factors in the form of undesired weeds and animal diseases, for instance, pesticides, hormones and genetically modified (GM) seeds are used purposefully. The purposeful introduction of risks under conditions of, at least, partial knowledge is an issue which Ulrich Beck referred to as *manufactured uncertainty*. In *World Risk Society (2005)*, Beck noted with regard to the concept of *manufactured uncertainty*:

> So the contemporary concept of risk associated with risk society and manufactured uncertainty refers to a peculiar *synthesis of knowledge and unawareness*. To be precise, two meanings, namely risk assessment based on empirical knowledge (automobile accidents, for instance), on the one hand, and making decisions and acting on risk in indefinite uncertainty, that is, indeterminacy, on the other, are being conflated here. In this sense, the concept of 'manufactured uncertainty' has a double reference. First, more

> and better knowledge, which most people assess in unreservedly positive terms, is becoming the source of new risks. (…) Second, however, the opposite is also true: risks come from and consist of unawareness (non-knowledge).[59]

Turning to genetically modified organism (GMOs) specifically, Beck considered GMOs as examples of *manufactured uncertainties.* Beck observed:

> [The controversy about genetically modified food] is first of all actually a good example of what Anthony Giddens and I are calling *manufactured uncertainties*: nobody, neither the experts nor the layperson, knows what the consequences will be. The victory of science once again imposes on us the burden of making crucial decisions which may affect our very survival without any proper foundations in knowledge. Thus this is a matter not of risk but of uncertainty. There is a pragmatic indication of this. If you ask 'Are genetically modified food industries privately (adequately) insured?' the answer is 'No'. Thus the industries and their experts say 'no risk', but the private insurance businesses say 'too risky, no (cheap) insurance'.[60]

The view of Beck is underscored by Colin Tudge. In his book *So Shall we Reap* (2004), Tudge noted:

> Most alarming of all, though, is that much of the danger of modern food is *caused* by modern practice. It clearly results directly from the modern, obsessive attempt to cut the cost of production; and above all (since labour is generally the most expensive input) to replace traditional husbandry, and the people who practise that husbandry, with machinery and industrial chemistry. Yet the cutting of costs is not intended to produce cheap food, as is often sanctimoniously claimed, but to maximize the margin between the cost of production and the sale price. The same industry that goes to such length to cut costs, dedicates the rest of its energy to 'adding value'. In short, the greatest hazards of modern food are not those of nature, or of bad luck. They follow, as night follows day, from policy.[61]

The economic rationale underlying agricultural production is evident in commercial agriculture. But it was shown that economic theory is, in principle and under the said conditions, applicable to farmers and to agricultural production as a whole. Obviously, though, this finding implies some degree of generalisation and objectivity because it is based on the assumption that the same economic rationale applies to farmers everywhere. What makes the difference, though, is the specific condition under which a particular farmer is producing. Hence, in applying economic theories to agricultural production, the specific environment in which the farmer operates has to be taken into account. In other words, the economic conditions under which a particular farmer operates and the political environment within which agricultural production takes place are *relative*. In contrast, the economic rationale of farmers, following economic theories of production increase, is a *common*, i.e. *general* feature among 'rational' economic actors throughout. Thus, in principle, Walras' model of the *homo oeconomicus* is considered applicable to farming as well, leading to an *agricola oeconomicus*.[62]

Summing up, it was shown that at the microeconomic level, individual farmers do not behave different than other economic subjects facing risks. In other words, farmers' response to risk is not fundamentally different than the risk response of entrepreneurs in other economic sectors. Furthermore, it can be shown that risk responses of farmers are similar across cultures and continents. Hence, the behaviour of individual farmers at microeconomic levels is well conceived by applying general economic theories, rather than by referring to cultural relativism.

2 Regulation

In the previous paragraph, it was shown that agricultural producers, i.e. farmers, are predominantly following an economic rationale. In contrast, the demand side, i.e. consumers, seems to be more complex. In fact, it is the demand side where a multitude of considerations, such as cultural and religious beliefs, ethical values and environmental considerations, have to be taken into account. In this paragraph, consumers' attitude towards food safety risks and the resulting *relativism* in food safety regulation shall be outlined.

As outlined in the previous paragraph, the main issue of farmers is production increase. Consumers' main concern, on the other hand, is the reliability of the purchased food. From an economic point of view, there is no direct incentive for food producers to pursue another objective than profitability, for instance, food safety. It is only the potential negative reaction of consumers which prompts food producers to take into account food safety requirements. In other words, the degree of food safety in a given society depends on the ability of consumers, sometimes together with retailers, to enforce the safety requirements deemed necessary.

Different societies have developed different systems for enforcing food safety requirements. On small village markets where consumers and producers met face to face, food safety was mainly, and at certain places still is, an issue of empirical testing, i.e. physical examination by looking, smelling and testing. At bigger markets, food control needs to be organised. Historically, the task of food safety control was assigned to towns' guilds or other municipal authorities. In industrialised societies, food safety became an issue of scientific analysis and indirect control systems through standardisation requirements. These three phases of food-safety approaches shall be further examined in the following three paragraphs.

2.1 Food Testing on Local Markets

At basic stages of agricultural development, surplus production was, and in many places still is, the exception rather than the rule. Under conditions of basic agricultural production, the bulk of production, mainly consisting of staple crops, is used for the daily consumption needs of the farming family. Occasional surpluses, though, are sold at nearest market places, usually at the local village or at the closest town.[63] Farmers selling their surplus produce on local markets themselves have to deal with respective customers personally. Some authors emphasise the important role personal contact between food producers and food consumers is playing with respect to food safety in particular. In his book *So Shall We Reap* (2004), Colin Tudge noted that it was 'very difficult for traditional growers and processors to cheat people who lived in the same village, or the same street'.[64] In her book '*Not on the Label*' (2004), Felicity Lawrence compared situations where personal producer–consumer contact takes place with the situation without such contact. Her findings, although referring to the beginnings of the industrial revolution and to an urban context, are viable in general. Lawrence observed: 'Whereas before, an unscrupulous butcher or baker might have been restrained by the knowledge that any shortcuts he chose could poison his neighbours and friends, now he could hide in the anonymity of distance and the city'.[65] Additionally, one might add that within social networks, personal experience enables clients to detect food adulteration themselves and to come back to incriminated vendors at any given opportunity.

In *Food Safety and the WTO* (2001), Marsha Echols gave the following account of food testing on local markets:

> People determine whether a food is safe through personal experience with it or through the personal experience of others – a sort of *experiential empiricism*. There is little need for food safety regulation, because foods and food production are linked to daily life. People are familiar with the provenance of what they eat and know which local foods can be harmful and under which circumstances.[66]

2.2 *Corporate Food Control by Municipal Authorities*

The need for food control emerged when food production and food consumption became more and more separated, the former taking place in rural areas, whereas a growing urban population required organised food supply.[67] However, as soon as food supply became an organised business, food adulteration emerged as a problem, too. In ancient and mediaeval times, food adulteration was predominantly an issue of replacing costly ingredients with cheaper ones.[68] Insofar, increasing risks to human health was the unintended side-effect of adulteration, not its primary intent. Accordingly, food regulation usually covered both aspects; i.e. safety aspects and health protection, as well as purity aspects, the prevention of fraud and consumer protection.

As Echols noted, food regulation dates back to ancient times:

> The structure for regulating foods during the traditional farming stage[69] often focuses on consumer protection, economic adulteration and food purity. There is evidence of regulations and enforcement mechanisms dating to ancient times. The Assyrians established weights and measures for grains. As early as 200 BC India punished the economic adulteration of grains and oils. During the same era Chinese officials tried to prevent consumer fraud. Egypt had food labeling rules. The ancient Athenians issued purity standards for beer and wine, wile the Romans instituted a system to control frau and bad produce. Ancient religious and sectoral laws also were directed at food purity such as the pre-Christian era Egyptian, Hebrew and Islamic laws regarding the handling of meat.[70]

Reay Tannahill observed that already the *Codex Hammurabi*, a law code enacted by King Hammurabi of Babylon around 1750 BC, contained prescriptions regarding the quality of, *inter alia*, beer.[71]

In mediaeval towns particularly in Europe, guilds and crafts played important roles in food control. Some tales of food adulteration from mediaeval times are rather pictorial, as well as certain stories of draconian sanctions issued by municipal or other authorities to contain such malpractice. Echols observed:

> Countries in Europe protected the safety and quality of eggs, sausages, cheese, beer, wine and bread, often through guilds. For example, during the middle ages in England, the guild of the spice traders – the Pepperers – obtained a King's Charter as the Grocers' Company, which established a code to protect the quality and integrity of the foods under their authority and a body of inspectors to enforce it.[72]

Other examples were meat inspectors in France called *langueyeurs* because they particularly inspected hog languets in search for ulcers.[73]

Certain staple foods were of outstanding importance. The purity of bread, for instance, was of such concern that it became an issue of royal authorities. Echols told that the 'Assize of Bread of King John in England in 1202 authorized punishments, including eventual pillorying and banishment, for a baker if "any default be found in [his]bread"'.[74]

Interestingly, models of food regulation established in the motherland were sometimes used in colonial territories as well. In the case of bread market regulation in the USA, William Patrick observed:

> In the colonies, local food laws were passed to regulate the weight of loaves of bread baked commercially. These laws, called 'assizes of bread', established a standard weight for loaves that was in relation to the current price of wheat and flour. Essentially, these laws fixed prices by regulating the profit of the middleman and baker, but leaving the price of grain open to fluctuate with the market. In 1646, the Massachusetts Bay Colony ordered every baker to use a distinct mark for his bread and keep the assize of the loaves as had been established by law. Inspectors were chosen and given authority to enter bakeries and weigh bread to assure that the law was being obeyed. Bakers who were found to be cheating the public were required to surrender their goods to the inspector, who would keep a third of the bread for himself – as payment for his time – and give the rest to the poor.[75]

Generally, it was upon local authorities, in conjunction with guilds and crafts, to assure the purity of foods and to protect the health and good faith of consumers in European towns during the Middle Ages. Echols observed:

> In addition to the regulation by the guilds, local authorities also exercised authority over the safety of food sold by butchers, bakers and fish merchants, among others, during the Middle Ages. The responsibility of the local magistrate was to assure the population of a 'bonne et loyale' food supply in sufficient quantity. 'From one end of Christian Europe to another, the basic principles were the same.' Food and beverages sold must be 'worthy of entering the human body,' have a good aroma and flavor, be neither filthy nor smelly, and be without substitute ingredients or additives, which were often used to disguise product defects. The manipulation of food was denounced because, as stated by Berthold de Ratisbonne, the fraud of the shoemaker, the tailor, the blacksmith or the merchant 'affects only property', while that of the butcher who puffs up his old meat to make it look better or of the tavern keeper who adds flavor to his wines or beer that have gone bad 'endangers life', transforming them into murderers and making them lose their soul. The punishments included the destruction of the merchandise, fines and the denial of the right to exercise the profession.[76]

On the ground, however, food control in premodern times was not very different than that by consumers on village markets: using experiential empiricism, e.g. visual impression, observation of weight and volume, smelling and tasting, as well as the vast experience accumulated in respective guilds and crafts, were the main tools for ensuring food safety and the detection of adulteration in pre-scientific times.

With a view on later developments, it is noteworthy that in federal states, food safety regulation was not only assigned to local guilds and crafts and enforced by local authorities, but was also the constitutional prerogative of Member states. With regard to the situation in the USA in the nineteenth century, Pollack and Shaffer noted that '[t]he regulation of food and environmental safety in the US were traditionally matters for state and local governments. They took primary responsibility, for example, for the inspection of slaughterhouses in the nineteenth century'.[77]

In another federal state, Switzerland, food adulteration was of similar concern in the late nineteenth and early twentieth century. Although many Member states had already established food safety regulation within their respective jurisdiction, in 1897 the Swiss amended their federal constitution, allowing federal authorities to introduce food safety regulation at the federal level. Reasons provided for this move were, *inter alia*, the following:[78]

- differences in Member states' food safety regulation;
- differences in the way Member states' regulation defined the fact of food adulteration, and the penalties prescribed, therefore;
- the lack of Member states' competence to enforce controls at the border.

The latter point, the divergence between federal authorities responsible for border control and Member states' authorities mandated with food safety regulation and enforcement, seemed of having been an argument of a particular weight. In fact, Ernst Laur of the Swiss Farmers' Union observed that a large proportion of adulterated merchandise was imported. But because the Swiss Member states were not entitled to conduct control measures at national frontiers, adulterated goods could enter the Swiss market unchecked.[79]

2.3 *Food Safety Legislation at National Levels*

Most authors agree that food adulteration as a mass phenomenon coincided with the beginnings of the Industrial Revolution.[80] For instance, Felicity Lawrence observed that 'the first mass adulterations came with the Industrial Revolution, and as with labour conditions, the historic parallels are instructive'.[81] Lawrence provided the following explanation for this coincidence:

> Feeding cities with their newly urbanized populations required new supply systems. Whereas previously most people would have grown their own food or bought from their immediate neighbours, city dwellers were dependent on much longer chains[82] and soon became ignorant of how their food was made. With no legal obstacles and fierce competition, adulteration became commonplace.[83]

No surprise, though, that 'some of the worst and most blatant examples of adulteration come from early-nineteenth-century Britain, where the industrialization of the world truly began'.[84] In the following, it shall be shown that the Industrial Revolution brought along essential features for large-scale food adulteration.[85] These essential features were, first, the existence of an impoverished segment of the population. This segment, the poor city dwellers, was relying on cheap food supply and thus had to accept adulterated food despite knowing about potential hazards. Second, food providers had been subjected to fierce competition through the liberalisation of previously tightly regulated local markets.[86]

Addressing the abolishing of traditional food regulation, a case study of the bread market in Victorian England may be instructive. Colin Tudge provided the following insights into the liberalisation of the traditional system for regulating bread:

> [F]rom 1266 until 1815 the quality and price of bread and ale in England had been fixed by a system of Assizes (local courts), following royal and later parliamentary edict. Local inspectors watched over foods apart from bread and ale, and whoever drifted from the straight and narrow was punished (not least in the pillory). But the early nineteenth century was the first golden age of free trade. (…) The committee that abolished the Assize of Bread declared: 'Your Committee are distinctly of the opinion that more benefit is likely to result from the effects of a free competition … than can be expected to result from any regulations under which [the bakers] could possibly be placed'. (…) In the days of the Bread Assizes, bakers simply did the job that was statutorily required of them. When free trade ruled, more and more bakers came into the market, and they fought each other like dogs for custom. By 1850, there were 50000 bakers and three-quarters of them were 'undersellers': they sold their bread effectively for less than the cost of production. They could achieve this, as one disaffected employee put the matter, 'only by first defrauding the public, and next getting eighteen hours' work out of the men for twelve hours' wages'.[87]

The example of bread and the appearance of 'undersellers' prepare the ground for asking about the reasons why the bread market failed at the beginning of the nineteenth century in England. Tudge observed that commentators have offered 'totally opposite explanations' for this market failure: on the one hand, there were those blaming 'the newly emerging big companies, like the new brewers, with their near or actual monopolies: for they were so powerful they could call the shots, and get away with whatever they wanted'.[88] Other commentators, on the other hand, pointed out that, in fact, the big companies had the higher standards: '[i]t was the smaller traders who cheated more', because 'small traders, in particular, were forced to cut corners'.[89]

Along with effects resulting from the liberalisation of the bread market through the abolishment of the Assize of Bread, the bread example further shows the increasing role of labour costs in food processing and food adulteration alike. It is therefore not a coincidence that one of the most critical analysts of the Industrial Revolution in England, Karl Marx, also bore witness to the worrying conditions under which bread was manufactured. With regard to adulterations in the baking trade, in particular, Marx observed:

> The incredible adulteration of bread, especially in London, was first revealed by the Committee of the House of Commons 'on the adulteration of articles of food' (1855-6), and by Dr. Hassall's work *Adulterations Detected*. The consequence of these revelations was the Act of 6 August 1860, 'for preventing the adulteration of articles of food and drink', an inoperative law, as it naturally shows the tenderest consideration for every 'freetrader' who decides to turn an honest penny' by buying and selling adulterated commodities. The Committee itself more or less naïvely formulated its conviction that free trade essentially meant trade with adulterated, or as the English ingeniously put it, 'sophisticated' goods. In fact, this kind of 'sophistry' understands better than Protagoras how to make white black, and black white, and better than the Eleatics[90] how to demonstrate before your very eyes that everything real is merely apparent.[91]

Marx had already singled out the dubious role played by 'undersellers' in the baking trade, an observation corroborated by Colin Tudge (see above). Marx noted that there were two branches of bakers involved in the baking trade:

> In London there are two sorts of bakers, the 'full priced', who sell bread at its full value, and the 'undersellers', who sell it at less than its value. The latter class comprises more than three-quarters of the total numbers of bakers (…) The undersellers, almost without exception, sell bread adulterated with alum,[92] soap, pearl-ash, chalk, Derbyshire stone-dust, and other similar agreeable, nourishing and wholesome ingredients. (…) Sir John Gordon stated before the committee of 1855 [*i.e.* the Committee of the House of Commons 'on the adulteration of articles of food'] that 'in consequence of these adulterations, the poor man, who lives on two pounds of bread a day, does not now get one-fourth part of nourishing matter,[93] let alone the deleterious effects on his health'. Tremenheere [H. S Tremenheere was the commissioner appointed to examine 'the grievances complained of by the journeymen bakers'] states … as the reason why a 'very large part of the working class', although well aware of this adulteration, nevertheless accept the alum, stone-dust, etc. as part of their purchase, that it is for them 'a matter of necessity to take from their baker or from the chandler's shop such bread as they choose to supply'. As they are not paid their wages before the end of the week, they in their turn are unable 'to pay for the bread consumed by their families during the week, before the end of the week', and

> Tremenheere adds on the evidence of witnesses, ‘it is notorious that bread composed of those mixtures is made expressly for sale in this manner’. (…)[94]

The example of the baking trade demonstrated some of the conditions abetting food adulteration, such as the existence of impoverished segments of the population, the economic need to save labour costs, and the lack of regulation, or, the lack of implementation of, and compliance to, that regulation. With regard to the latter point, i.e. regulation and control of food safety and food quality, legislative procedures take centre stage. The point is made here that food producers, in this case, the ‘undersellers’, were not willing to adjust their profitable methods of production in ways which are more acceptable to society of their own accord. In other words, the increase of food production methods which are hazardous to human health (or to other values) required restrictions imposed by society.

In economic terms, the requirement for third-party regulation of food markets was addressed as the problem of ‘credence’ goods markets, i.e. markets with information asymmetries. With respect to food, ‘credence’ characteristics mean that consumers are usually unable to evaluate food safety characteristics themselves, in particular, those of processed foods. With respect to the requirement for societal intervention in credence goods markets, Lee Ann Jackson and Marion Jansen noted:

> Regulatory intervention of a third party, typically a government agency, can therefore be justified on efficiency grounds in markets characterized by credence goods characteristics. Government regulatory interventions in these markets aim at providing consumers with the information they need to take appropriate consumption decisions.[95]

Typically, societal response to hazardous commercial activity is triggered by some sort of scandal. Again, the example of the bread market in nineteenth century England can be used as a teaching play for many more food scandals yet to come in history. It was the today well-known sequence of the first round of public inquiries coming to rather reserved recommendations, which, however, induced public outcry which, in turn, was compelling policymakers to adopt sturdier positions vis-à-vis the incriminated economic sector; in that case the baking trade. With his peculiar sardonic words, Marx described the awakening of the public, realising the magnitude of the bread scandal, as follows:

> At all events the Committee [*i.e.*, the Committee of the House of Commons 'on the adulteration of articles of food' (1855-6)] had directed the attention of the public to its 'daily bread', and therefore to the baking trade. At the same time the cry of the London journeymen bakers against their over-work rose in public meetings and petitions to Parliament. The cry was so urgent that Mr H. S. Tremenheere, also a Member of the above-mentioned Commission of 1863, was appointed a Royal Commissioner of Inquiry. His report, together with the evidence given, moved the public not in its heart but in its stomach. Englishmen, with their good command of the Bible, knew well enough that man, unless by elective grace a capitalist, or a landlord, or the holder of a sinecure, is destined to eat his bread in the sweat of his brow, but they did not know that he had to eat daily in his bread a certain quantity of human perspiration mixed with the discharge of abscesses, cobwebs, dead cockroaches and putrid German yeast, not to mention alum, sand and other agreeable mineral ingredients. Without any regard for His Holiness 'Free Trade', the hitherto 'free' baking trade was therefore placed under the supervision of state-appointed inspectors (at the close of the Parliamentary session of 1863), and by the same Act of Parliament work from 9 in the evening to 5 in the morning was forbidden for journeymen bakers under 18. The last clause speaks volumes as to the over-work in this old-fashioned, homely line of business.[96]

The fact that public outcry is required for introducing legislative procedures for the restriction of hazardous business conduct became a common feature in the history of food safety regulation. As mentioned above, countries experience challenges induced by industrialisation at different points in time. A scandal comparable to the public outcry following inquiries of the baking business in England was the public outrage following the publication of Upton Sinclair's novel 'The Jungle' in 1906 in the USA.[97] William Patrick gave the following account of the effects of Sinclair's publication on public opinion:

> The American public was rightfully disgusted after reading Sinclair's graphic but realistic disclosures. In fact, almost overnight, sales of meat and meat products declined by 50 percent. Added pressure was put on Congress to take action. *Even the wounded meat industry recognized that government regulation could mean renewed sales.* In this message to Congress on December 5, 1905, President Theodore Roosevelt strongly urged passage of new food and drug laws.
>
> Finally, on June 30, 1906, Congress passed the first federal Pure Food and Drugs Act, according to which it became a federal crime to mislabel or adulterate foods, drinks, and drugs *intended for interstate commerce.*

> The provisions of the law were to be enforced by the Bureau of Chemistry in the Department of Agriculture. Wiley[98] was appointed by Secretary of Agriculture James Wilson to administer and enforce the landmark legislation – the cornerstone of the future Food and Drug Administration.[99]

Of particular importance for the shaping of public opinion in food quality and food safety matters are women activists. For example, William Patrick highlighted the fact that women's groups were pivotal for the adoption of the US Pure Food and Drugs Act in 1906, and again for the US Federal Food, Drug, and Cosmetic (FDC) Act in 1938. Patrick noted that women activists in the USA 'had been lobbying for a federal food and drug law' during the last quarter of the nineteenth century: 'Although women could not vote at that time, their outraged demands were being increasingly heeded by politicians'.[100]

Food safety, however, requires more than legislation. The maintenance of food safety levels deemed appropriate is a constant task, requiring, *inter alia*, effective compliance and control mechanisms. Effective compliance and control is usually assigned to specific authorities, such as the Food and Drug Administration (FDA) of the US. But the effectiveness of authorities is dependent on various factors which may vary from country to country. Especially in developing countries, scarce resources and impoverished segments of urban dwellers, dependent on cheap food supply in rather similar ways as were their fellow sufferers in Victorian England, may provide fertile grounds for food adulteration.

A case study of the milk industry in Uganda may shed some light on food safety problems in a developing country (DC) in general and problems of compliance and enforcement of regulation in DCs in particular. In her study *Supply Chain and Liberalisation of the Milk Industry in Uganda* (2005), Pamela Mbabazi examined effects of the liberalisation of the milk industry which took place in Uganda in the 1990s. A direct effect of liberalisation was the mushrooming of the informal sector. Mbabazi observed:

> The dramatic increase in the number of informal milk traders is a recent phenomenon prompted by the liberalisation of the milk sector in Uganda. This informal channel sells raw milk and undercuts the formal supply chain by selling it at low prices because they add no value to the milk, in most cases do not pay any taxes and do not bother with quality control. As mentioned before, this informal channel controls about 80 per cent of the market and as

> such the two existing processing factories in Ankole [a south-western area of Uganda] now operate at less than 50 per cent of their installed capacity. [101]

Though, the liberalised milk market in Uganda witnessed a deterioration of quality and safety levels. Mbabazi, listening to different players in the milk sector, noted the following statements:

> Some farmers alleged that some traders add chemicals to the milk while testing it at the village level as many obviously do not mind about the quality of milk sold as long as they get their profits.
>
> Some of the customers interviewed in both Mbarara and Kampala noted that at times the milk tastes rather different and that they often notice that it is adulterated but have no option and end up still buying it because it is all they can afford. According to Mr. Isha, quality control officer, at DDA [Dairy Development Authority], many traders have in the past added hydrogen peroxide, sodium bicarbonate or potassium dichromate (starch) to increase the viscosity. He noted that most milk buyers and vendors add water as well which, in most cases is very dirty, to increase the volumes and profits. He explained that tests carried on some samples by the DDA have found milk to contain residues of other chemicals like formalin, sodium carbonate and boric acid in order to make the milk look fresh appearance for several days after milking, traders illegally introduce these chemicals into the milk to arrest bacterial or viral growth and lower the acidity of milk.[102]

However, food safety is more than an issue of hygiene and scientific assessment. As Eva Barlösius observed, food safety regulation is tensely connoted to cultural values.[103] Observations by Lydia Petránová with regard to milk processing in Bohemia and Moravia in the early twentieth century not only provided insight into food safety issues, but also in cultural aspects and the relationship between food and gender. Petránová reported:

> The war [World War I] situation led not only to the stagnation of industrial dairies, but also to a forced return of traditional methods of milk preparation. All centrifuges in households were sealed by the authorities so that the government could not be cheated on the fat content of expropriated milk. And so the age-old *latka* [an earthenware vessel with an outlet at the bottom, used for separating cream from milk] again took the place of the centrifuge. It appears that the return to primitive equipment and techniques was not simply a necessary evil, but also a means of self-realization. At the beginning

> of the twentieth century ethnologists also recorded a renewal of superstitions, especially in relation to domestic churning. The traditional taboos about the place and time for successful churning, the prohibition on food and borrowing objects outside of the house during churning, laying objects with a great semiotic status under the churn (such as blessed objects, a comb, a man's shirt) and other practices bear traces of apotropic and mimicry magic from the realm of the ancient culture of agrarian societies. Milk processing, which can be considered one of the most archaic activities in the household, retained the use of magical objects the longest.[104]

Thus, an important finding seems to be that economic conditions are not the only factors determining the degree of industrialisation of food production and food safety levels. Rather, Lydia Petránová stated:

It is my opinion that non-economic and psychological factors also played a definite negative role in this process. Their causes can be sought in the following:

1. The strong traditions connected with one of the most archaic activities act as a stabilizing factor and a brake on progress.
2. Traditional processing of milk was almost exclusively in the hands of women, who remained longer than men outside the reach of specialist education. At the same time, in the spirit of their anthropological differences and their mission as the guardian of life, they always favoured the tested, and treated the new with distrust.
3. Consumption again was largely in the hands of women. Consumers from overcrowded worker quarters, as the first or second generation to be living in the city, were susceptible to the myth of 'healthy fresh milk from the country' from distributors and of 'artificial' pasteurized milk from dairies.[105]

Examples provided so far seem to indicate that food safety laws were commonly the result of political processes at respective national levels. Political processes at national levels were typically involving the public, policymakers and affected or interested economic sectors. And food laws resulting from such political processes were, in turn, reflecting prevailing interests at respective national levels. The political as well as the deliberative character of food laws—quite similar to laws in general—is not a new phenomenon. With regard to food laws in British colonies in North America, William Patrick observed:

> The colonies enacted numerous food inspection laws to establish standard weights and measures, including the sizes of casks and barrels used to store and ship foods such as fish, pork, beef, and four. These laws often *reflected the significance of a particular industry* to each colony's economy: Massachusetts had strict laws governing fishing, its foremost industry; New York hat though regulations for the beef industry; and Virginia and Maryland regulated their tobacco industry carefully.[106]

As a conclusion, one may note that food laws essentially were the outcome of political procedures at respective national levels. Accordingly, latent conflicts between consumers and food manufacturers over appropriate levels of food safety protection were resolved by means of political deliberation at respective national levels. And different levels of protection set forth by respective national legislation translated into different border controls and food safety requirements for imported agricultural products.

With regard to underlying philosophical questions, food safety risk regulation at national markets, i.e. at macroeconomic levels, is considered as an example where cultural relativism comes into play. In other words, the regulation of risk is not something absolute, for instance, based on 'objective' science. Rather, risk regulation in modern *Risk societies* is relative, based on the specific needs established through deliberative procedures in a particular society.

The deliberative, yet political character of food safety legislation can be exemplified by different approaches of different political ideologies. In this respect, Pat O'Malley distinguished between classical liberalism and social liberalism. In classical liberalism, O'Malley observed, '[s]ubjects were to be exposed to uncertainties'.[107] Accordingly, O'Malley noted, '[t]he heroic status of the entrepreneur as the creator of social good through risk to his own capital served to protect this class from regulation aimed at protecting consumers from adulterated food and drugs'.[108] In perspective of social liberalism, in contrast, 'science and risk were to tame uncertainty, to magnify its powers and minimise its harms'.[109] Thus, science-based administrative regulation had to be put in place in order to minimise harms resulting from uncertainty.[110]

Notes

1. Mazoyer and Roudart, for example, dated the beginnings of agricultural cultivation, marked by the "change from predation to agriculture", to the Neolithic, that is, between 10,000 and 5000 years before the present. The

evolution from predation to agriculture is known as the "Neolithic Agricultural Revolution" (see Marcel Mazoyer and Laurence Roudart, "A History of World Agriculture. From the Neolithic Age to the Current Crisis." Translated from the French original by James H. Membrez. *Monthly Review Press* (2006): in particular pp. 45–46 and 71–75).

2. Lee Ann Jackson and Marion Jansen, "Risk assessment in the international food safety policy arena. Can the multilateral institutions encourage unbiased outcomes?" (2010) *Food Policy* 35 (2010): 538–547, 539 (footnote omitted).
3. Jackson and Jansen 2010, p. 539.
4. Eva Barlösius, "Soziologie des Essens. Eine sozial- und kulturwissenschaftliche Einführung in die Ernährungsforschung". *Juventa Verlag* (1999): 206.
5. Eva Barlösius, ibid. pp. 205–207.
6. Eva Barlösius, ibid. pp. 205–207. Emphasising international implications of food regulation, a paragraph of Barlösius' analysis shall be provided in full (in German):

Insbesondere politische, ökonomische und technische Neuorientierungen bewirken den Geltungsverlust von Küchentraditionen. Die Schaffung der EU und die Internationalisierung des Lebensmittelhandels sind Beispiele für politische und wirtschaftliche Neuorientierungen, auf die jeweils mit Herausbildung und Weiterentwicklung lebensmittelrechtlicher Regelungen reagiert wird, wie dem Europäischen Lebensmittelrecht und dem Codex Alimentarius, der unter Leitung der FAO und der WHO entwickelt wird und in dem internationale Verfahrensleitsätze zusammengefaßt sind. Die Anpassung lebensmittelrechtlicher Regelungen an das vergrößerte Geltungsgebiet führt zumeist zu einer höheren Abstraktion der Vorschriften, die sich immer weiter von der konkreten Rezeptur entfernen und statt dessen Verfahrensstandards normieren. Insofern drängt die Entwicklung des Lebensmittelrechts in die von Niklas Luhmann identifizierte Richtung einer zunehmenden Formalisierung, bei der die Legitimation immer häufiger durch Verfahren hergestellt wird. (Eva Barlösius, ibid., p. 207)

7. Michael P. Todaro and Stephen C. Smith, "Economic Development." *Addison-Wesley* (2009, 10th Edition), in particular the chapter on "Subsistence Farming: Risk Aversion, Uncertainty, and Survival", pp. 454–460.
8. Todaro and Smith, ibid. p. 454.
9. Todaro and Smith, ibid. p. 454. In fact, such "misguided convictions of some foreigners" are updates of narratives from the colonial epoch. Todaro and Smith observed: "An understanding of the major role that risk and

uncertainty play in the economics of subsistence agriculture would have prevented early and unfortunate characterizations of subsistence or traditional farmers as technologically backward, irrational producers with limited aspirations or just plain 'lazy natives' as in the colonial stereotype" (Todaro and Smith, ibid. p. 457).

10. Todaro and Smith, ibid. p. 454.
11. Todaro and Smith, ibid. p. 454. Todaro and Smith described the two-factor neoclassical theory of production as an approach "in which land (and perhaps capital) is fixed, labor is the only variable input, and profit is maximized" (Todaro and Smith, ibid. p. 454).
12. Todaro and Smith, ibid. p. 454.
13. Todaro and Smith, ibid. p. 454.
14. Todaro and Smith, ibid. pp. 454–455 (emphasis and footnote omitted). As examples for purchased inputs, one may add genetically modified (GM) seeds.
15. Todaro and Smith, ibid. p. 455 (original emphases).
16. Todaro and Smith, ibid. pp. 455–456.
17. Todaro and Smith, ibid. p. 456.
18. Todaro and Smith, ibid. p. 457. The lack of physical buffer stocks was reflected by food riots in several developing and least-developed countries during the food crisis in 2008.
19. Todaro and Smith, ibid. p. 457 (footnote omitted).
20. The purpose of this paragraph is not to give a full account of Todaro's and Smith's considerations of rural transformation and agricultural development. Rather, the paragraph is meant to shed light on the question whether there are general principles and objective criteria governing agricultural activity. It was shown that the general principle underlying farmers' choice is the same which is leading other entrepreneurs, viz. the economic rational of production increase. Nevertheless, a comment on the extension of the neoclassical theory by Todaro and Smith is required. The remark relates to an issue going without saying at the microeconomic level of individual farmers, namely the precondition of an existing and accessible market for farmers' produce. Hurdles for accessing markets are already a problem at local and regional levels of many developing and least-developed countries. For example, problems of transport, such as poor roads, endemic roadblocks, and absent public transport combined with high fuel prices may impair farmer's access to regional markets. Such factual hurdles are, of course, implicitly covered by the reference to institutional and commercial obstacles, as mentioned by Todaro and Smith. In an international context, however, problems of market access are not only factual in nature, but may appear in the form of regulatory hurdles. Therefore, in the context of international trade, it has to be explicitly added

that the responsiveness of agricultural producers to economic incentives is contingent upon a fourth criterion, i.e., market access.

21. Typically, the call for "removing commercial and institutional obstacles" is associated with liberalisation policies. However, there are examples showing that the removal of commercial and institutional obstacles to small-farmers may well translate into a re-regulation of certain sectors. An example of a vulnerable sector further weakened by hastily implemented liberalisation policies is the milk industry in Uganda. Although acknowledging that the liberalisation of the milk sector had led to an initial boom, a study by Pamela Mbabazi showed that the liberalisation policies brought along a range of new problems to Uganda's milk industry. Mbabazi observed that the milk industry in Ankole, an area in south-western Uganda, "has recently faced a lot of challenges including oversupply, low producer prices, lack of markets, quality problems and poor regulations" (Pamela Mbabazi, "Supply Chain and Liberalisation of the Milk Industry in Uganda". *Fountain Publishers* (2005): 108). With view on regulatory requirements, Mbabazi concluded:

> In an increasing globalised world, governments in developing countries, in collaboration with non-state actors need to support fragile and infant enterprises like the dairy industry in Ankole to survive. This calls for among other things, *effective government regulation* of the industry and the implementation of conducive policies that will promote and rejuvenate the sector. A major conclusion from the study therefore, is that liberalisation per se is not conducive for the fragile milk industry in Ankole. Although scholars such as Halit Yanikkaya (2003), have argued that open economies foster industrial development, the experience of the milk industry in Ankole seems to suggest the opposite. Unbridled competition coupled with the lack of regulation has hurt the milk industry. The lack of an effective regulatory mechanism in the era of liberalisation has increasingly led to limited profitability and hampered the growth of the industry. (Pamela Mbabazi, *ibid.*, pp. 108–109, footnote omitted, emphasis added)

22. Evolutionary stages of agricultural production are specified in different manners. From an economic perspective, Todaro and Smith identified "three broad stages in the evolution of agricultural production. The first is the pure, low-productivity, mostly *subsistence-level peasant farm*, still prevalent in Africa. The second stage is what might be called *diversified or mixed family agriculture*, where a small part of the production is grown for consumption and a signification part for sale to the commercial sector, as in much of Asia. The third stage represents the modern farm, exclusively engaged in *high-productivity specialised agriculture* geared to the

commercial market, as in developed countries and often found in the highly urbanized developing countries" (2009, p. 453, footnote omitted, emphases added). From a cultural-historical perspective, Marsha Echols identified four prototypes of agricultural production systems, namely (i) *traditional* farming, (ii) *production* agriculture, (iii) agricultural production applying *novel technologies*, in particular biotechnology, and (iv) *hybrid* systems combining elements of the other stages (Marsha A. Echols, "Food Safety and the WTO. The Interplay of Culture, Science and Technology". *Kluwer Law International* (2001): pp. 29–40, emphases added). From the perspective of agricultural history, Mazoyer and Roudart, in contrast, put forward a concept of *agricultural systems*. Agricultural systems are, for instance, slash-and-burn agricultural systems in forest environments, hydraulic agrarian systems in the Nile valley, the mountain agrarian systems of the Inca Empire, agrarian systems based on fallowing or based on mechanised labour, etc. Furthermore, Mazoyer and Roudart identified epoch-making periods between one agricultural system and another as agricultural revolutions or agricultural crises, e.g. the Neolithic agricultural revolution, the agricultural Revolution of the Middle Ages, the crisis of agricultural systems based on fallowing, the first and the second agricultural revolution of modern times, and the contemporary agrarian crisis. (see Mazoyer and Roudart 2006, in particular pp. 46–52 on the concept of agrarian systems)

23. Todaro and Smith 2009, p. 460.
24. Todaro and Smith, ibid. p. 460.
25. As Todaro and Smith have explained earlier, the neoclassical two-factor theory of production is based on the assumption that land (and perhaps capital) is a fixed parameter, whereas "labour is the only variable input" (Todaro and Smith, ibid. p. 454).
26. In rural reality particularly in least-developed countries, both conditions are likely to apply simultaneously, worsened by the absence of any capital even for the smallest investment, thus lowering peasants' living condition virtually to a "self-perpetuating poverty trap".
27. Todaro and Smith, ibid. p. 460.
28. Todaro and Smith, ibid. p. 460 (emphases added).
29. Mazoyer and Roudart 2006, Chap. 7 on the agricultural revolution of the Middle Ages in northwestern Europe, pp. 259–311.
30. Mazoyer and Roudart, ibid. p. 260.
31. Mazoyer and Roudart, ibid. p. 281. However, agricultural transformation in the Middle Ages happened gradually, thus confirming the microeconomic analysis of Todaro and Smith historically. That gradual rural transformation was depicted by Mazoyer and Roudart in the following way:

One or two scythes, a cart, a plow, a harrow, a roller, and relatively large farm buildings to shelter the hay, litter, and increased numbers of livestock are, essentially, the working capital of the new farmer of the thirteenth century, not counting the small tools, sickles, hoes, and spades that from then on have working parts made of iron. All of that represents, in the end, ten times the value of the equipment, buildings, and livestock of its much smaller homologue of the tenth century, which hardly possessed more than an ard, a packsaddle, small tools, often entirely made of wood, a simple house for the farmer and family, and far fewer animals. It is then quite improbable that a relatively unproductive farm practicing cultivation with an ard could all at once increase its working capital tenfold by acquiring the whole set of means for implementing the new system based on the plow. Even on the largest estates, this costly accumulation of equipment had to be gradual. Among the peasants in villages undergoing transformation, mutual aid operated for a long time between those who owed a plow and those who owed a cart or a harrow. Undoubtedly, it necessarily took several generations for the majority of farms in a region to be outfitted with a nearly complete set of equipment. (Mazoyer and Roudart, ibid. p. 270)

32. Mazoyer and Roudart, ibid. pp. 286–287.
33. Mazoyer and Roudart, ibid. p. 287 (emphasis added).
34. Mazoyer and Roudart, ibid. pp. 287–288 (emphasis added).
35. As an example of a religious establishment particularly active in rural valorisation, Mazoyer and Roudart singled out the Order of Cistercians. In context of improvements in iron and steel processing accompanying the agricultural revolution of the Middle Ages, Mazoyer and Roudart observed that "[t]he network of Cistercian monasteries, a vast empire of agricultural enterprises and iron factories spread across Europe, played an important role in the diffusion of these new processes [i.e. iron and steel processing]" (Mazoyer and Roudart, ibid. p. 295.
36. Mazoyer and Roudart, ibid. p. 288 (emphases added).
37. Mazoyer and Roudart, ibid. pp. 289–290 (original italics).
38. Mazoyer and Roudart, ibid. p. 290 (original italics).
39. Mazoyer and Roudart, ibid. p. 289 (footnote omitted, original italics).
40. Mazoyer and Roudart, ibid., pp. 309 and 313–331, and Reay Tannahill, "Kulturgeschichte des Essens. Von der letzten Eiszeit bis heute". Original title: "Food in History". Translated by Joachim A. Frank, published by Eyre Methuen Ltd., London. *Paul Neff Verlag* (1973): 331. From a development perspective, the Netherlands provide an interesting example for economic development spurred by the expansion and intensification of agricultural production. In fact, in the Dutch Golden Age, rationalism was not only applied in philosophy (Cartesianism), but also in trade (Dutch

East India Company) and in agriculture, leading to the commodification of agricultural products through commodity exchanges. Till today, *Flora Holland*, the flower auction in Aalsmeer, next to Amsterdam-Schiphol, is the biggest flower market of the world [Andres Wysling, "Aalsmeer—Welthandelsplatz für Blumen", in *Neue Zürcher Zeitung* (September 28, 2010): p. 31].

41. Charles A. P. Takes, "New Settlement and Land Consolidation in The Netherlands". Published in Raanan Weitz (ed.), *Rural Development in a Changing World*. The MIT Press (1971): 450. The focus on agricultural innovation extended to tulips which were imported from the Ottoman Empire. The enthusiasm about tulip cultivation finally resulted in the tulip bubble at the Amsterdam Stock exchange in the 1630s, thus providing an early example of relationships between agriculture and speculation. André Kostolany, for instance, noted that tulip bulbs at the Amsterdam Stock exchange were no longer flowers but became mere objects of speculation. And according to Kostolany, basic mechanisms of booms and busts at the stock exchange remained rather unchanged over time (André Kostolany, "Die Kunst über Geld nachzudenken". *Econ Ullstein List Verlag* (2000): 146–149). Similarities can be seen, for instance, between the tulip bubble and the food crisis of 2008. In both cases, financial instruments originally developed for hedging farmers' risks against price volatility, e.g. futures, became sources of new risks in the hand of speculators.
42. Mazoyer and Roudart 2006, p. 290.
43. Mazoyer and Roudart, ibid. p. 297.
44. Mazoyer and Roudart, ibid. p. 297.
45. Peter L. Bernstein, "Against the Gods. The Remarkable Story of Risk". *John Wiley & Sons* (1998): 305–306. The indebtedness of farmers provides an instructive example of the way (financial) risks and profits are allocated in commercial farming systems. In the 1980s, Fritjof Capra observed that the use of petrochemicals, combined with rising energy prices, were pushing farmers into the dept trap. After 1945, at the beginning of the *Green Revolution*, oil was relatively cheap, thus farmers became easily dependent on new petrochemical products such as fertilisers and pesticides. However, as oil prices started to rise, farmers suffered from escalating downstream product prices imposed by petrochemical companies. Therefore, despite rising productivity, debts of farmers increased. And at the end of the production chain, rising energy prices were reflected in increasing percentages of total food costs; in his 1982 book *The Turning Point*, Capra assessed that percentage at 60%, meaning that the oil costs accounted for 60% of total food prices in those days (Fritjof Capra, "Wendezeit. Bausteine für ein neues Weltbild". *Ex Libris* (1984): 284. The scheme for allocating risks and profits known from the Green Revolution

seems to be replayed by the *Biotech Revolution*. For instance, it was reported that suicide rates are massively increasing among Indian farmers cultivating genetically modified cotton varieties. Major reasons for this worrying development have been identified as increasing indebtedness, decreasing earnings and rising dependency on costly irrigation systems, fertilisers and pesticides. Joseph Keve provided the following report on effects of genetically modified 'miracle seeds' in India:

During the three days from 9th to 11th of March 2010, 10 farmers committed suicide in Vidarbha region of Maharashtra, one of the richest states in India. Since 1998, Vidarbha witnessed over 40000 farmer suicides. Indebtedness is the single most reason that drives these people to their deaths. Prices of seeds, chemical fertilizers and pesticides went up by 300 per cent during the last 10 years. Laxman Wankhede of Ijani village in Yavatmal district committed suicide in October 2009. 'For generations we had managed with traditional seeds, home-made organic fertilizers and herbal pest-repellants. Agricultural scientists and agents of seed-fertilizer-pesticide companies advised us and we changed over to the miracle seeds, fertilizers and pesticides. When he couldn't bear the harassment by those who had given him loans, my husband consumed the bottle of the pesticide that he had bought with the last loan' (…)". (Joseph Keve, contribution to the Global Forum on Food Security and Nutrition, Proceedings of Discussion No. 53 on *Livestock Keepers' Rights – An Important Concept for Food Security*? 8 March to 6 April 2010, p. 28; and Joseph Keve, "Selbstmord wegen Baumwolle", in *Die Wochenzeitung*, January 21, 2010, p. 11)

Thus, changes from conventional to genetically modified 'miracle seeds' are mainly motivated by promises for higher economic profits. With view on the example of *Bt brinjal*, an eggplant (Indian: *brinjal*) genetically modified with a gene from the bacillus thuringiensis (Bt), Rina Chandran observed: "Even though the genetically modified seeds for eggplant would be likely to cost three times as much as regular seeds and farmers would need to purchase seeds for every sowing rather than reusing crop seeds, proponents say the extra expenses would be compensated by lower pesticide costs and less devastating crop losses" (Rina Chandran, "India balks at genetically modified crops", *International Herald Tribune*, February 17, 2010, p. 18).

46. Bernstein 1998, p. 306 (emphasis added).
47. Derivatives appear in two forms: as futures they take the form of contracts promising future delivery at prearranged prices, and as options, providing the opportunity of selling to or buying from the counterpart at prearranged prices (see Bernstein, ibid. p. 305).

48. Bernstein, ibid. p. 305.
49. PBernstein, ibid., pp. 306–307 (original emphasis). Bernstein introduced the history of contracts for future delivery in a chapter on derivatives ("The Fantastic System of Side Bets", pp. 304–328) rather at the end, and not at the beginning of his book where the origins of risk were discussed. Bernstein seemed of having followed the popular combination of the modernist thesis with the nautical novel, the latter renewed by a trade component. As an exemplification, the following excerpt of Bernstein's account of the beginnings of risk shall be displayed:

The concept of thrift and abstinence that characterized the Protestant ethic evidenced the growing importance of the future relative to the present. With this opening up of choices and decisions, people gradually recognized that the future offered opportunities as well as danger, that it was open-ended and full of promise. The 1500 and 1600 s were a time of geographical exploration, confrontation with new lands and new societies, and experimentation in art, poetic forms, science, architecture, and mathematics. The new sense of opportunity led to a dramatic acceleration in the growth of trade and commerce, which served as a powerful stimulus to change and exploration. Columbus was not conducting a Caribbean cruise: he was seeking a new trade route to the Indies. The prospect of getting rich is highly motivating, and few people get rich without taking a gamble". (Bernstein, ibid. p. 21)

The difficulty of integrating century-old traditions of financial hedging developed in agriculture into a consistent history of risk confirms the inappropriateness of popular narratives about the origins of risk, in particular the modernist thesis and the nautical novel; as noted by Pradier (see Pradier 2006, in particular pp. 11–12, where Pradier called the nautical novel an amusing story, at best, and noted that the modernist thesis was disproved completely).

50. Mazoyer and Roudart 2006, p. 299 (emphasis added).
51. Mazoyer and Roudart, ibid. p. 299 (emphasis added).
52. Jacques Le Goff, "Marchands et banquiers du Moyen Âge". *Presses Universitaires de France* (2001, 9th Edition): 27–32. Le Goff noted that, along with commercial markets, parallel markets for trade bills emerged which induced heavy speculation already in the fourteenth and fifteenth century (Le Goff, ibid. p. 32).
53. Mazoyer and Roudart 2006, p. 299.
54. Mazoyer and Roudart, ibid. p. 299 (emphasis added).
55. Whether Mazoyer's and Roudart's finding that (Proto-)capitalism emerged from agricultural origins in the Middle Ages might have implications on the history of risk must remain an open question at this point.

56. In today's perspective, the focus is not on specific situations of actors at different positions in the chain of agricultural production, but rather on different perspectives of various actors on the market as a whole. Rolf Kappel, Reinhard Pfeiffer and Jutta Werner distinguished between tree main actors on the food commodity market:

"The first group of actors are hedgers or commercials. Commercials trade commodities physically on cash markets, either as producers, processors, or merchants. They usually offset their positions in cash markets with opposite positions in future markets, the standard procedure of hedging against prices risks. The second group are speculators or non-commercials, which generally trade in short term, based on views about price developments. Their motivation is not to hedge against price risks, but to make a profit from expected price movements on which they bet. It is important to understand that the speculators are necessary counterparts for hedgers, whose positions usually don't cancel each other out. The third group are investors who regard commodities as assets, like equities, bonds, estates, etc. They usually take long positions through commodity index certificates or swaps, which are provided by banks and other financial institutions. Contrary to short-term-oriented speculators investors hold positions in the longer run, but of course they are also speculators (and counterparts of hedgers) as they bet on future price developments. This is the class of actors whose involvement in commodity markets has grown dramatically over the last years and who are suspected by some observers as the main drivers of the price boom". (Rolf Kappel, Reinhard Pfeiffer and Jutta Werner, "What became of the Food Price Crisis in 2008?" Published in *Aussenwirtschaft* 65 (1) *Verlag Rüegger* (2010): 30. But whether or not speculation is to blame for world famine is, in turn, another matter (see, for instance, Benjamin Triebe, "Das Märchen vom bösen Weizen-Zocker—Der spekulative Handel mit Agrar-Futures ist nicht verantwortlich für den Welthunger", in *Neue Zürcher Zeitung*, October 16, 2010, p. 33).

57. Todaro and Smith 2009, p. 461.
58. Todaro and Smith, ibid., pp. 461–462.
59. Ulrich Beck, "World Risk Society". *Polity Press* (1999/2005): 140 (original emphasis). Elsewhere, Beck defined *manufactured uncertainty* as "a mélange of risk, more knowledge, more unawareness and reflexivity, and *therefore* a new type of risk" (Ulrich Beck, ibid. p. 112, original emphasis). It has to be noted that the term manufactur*ed* uncertainty, as used by Beck, shall not be confused with the term manufactur*ing* uncertainty. The term *manufacturing uncertainty* was used by David Michaels for characterising disinformation campaigns, in particular disinformation by the tobacco

industry (see David Michaels, "Manufactured Uncertainty. Contested Science and the Protection of the Public's Health and Environment". Published in Robert N. Proctor and Londa Schiebinger (eds.), *Agnotology. The Making and Unmaking of Ignorance.* Stanford University Press (2008): 91.

60. Beck 1999/2005, p. 105.
61. Colin Tudge, "So Shall we Reap. What's Gone Wrong With the World's Food—and How to Fix It". *Penguin Books* (2004): 150 (original emphasis). Among other things, Tudge invoked hazards caused by continued mass-use of antibiotics (Tudge, *ibid.* p. 151). However, the thesis that factory farming is a source of new hazards did not remain uncontested. At a brown-bag lecture entitled "Animal disease and the global community: the role of sustainable livestock production and other factors", held the World Trade Institute in Bern, Switzerland, September 7, 2009, Manon Schuppers, epidemiologist and consultant at Safe Food Solutions (SAFOSO), explained the two main arguments coming along with industrialised livestock production: On the one hand, increased livestock density was blamed for increasing risks related to epizootic diseases such as avian influenza and swine flu. On the other hand, backyard rearing of chicken and other livestock was also accused of being responsible for the spread and persistence of epizootics (Daniel Goldstein, "Züchtet der Mensch Krankheiten?" Published in *Der Bund*, September 19, 2009, p. 40).
62. The author is aware that this statement is an oversimplification. The statement is used in a systemic way, considering agriculture as an economic system relying on specific production factors, i.e., land, labour and eventually capital. Thus, the 'rational farmer' (*agricola oeconomicus*) is an adaptation of the *homo oeconomicus* in other economic models and similarly abstract. In particular, the author is aware that there are numerous farmers who are voluntarily foregoing production increases despite the opportunity to reap higher profits. Instead, their focus is on the (re-)development of a "holistic production management system which promotes and enhances agroecosystem health, including biodiversity, biological cycles, and soil biological activity"; this is part of the definition of organic agriculture, as provided by the *Guidelines for the Production, Processing, Labelling and Marketing of Organically Produced Foods* of the Codex Alimentarius Commission (GL 32-1999), adopted 1999 and published in *Organically Produced Foods*, 3rd edition (WHO/FAO, 2007), p. 2.
63. Naturally, there is no clear distinction between occasionally occurring surpluses and regular ones. At basic stages of agricultural production, surplus occurrence is, first of all, contingent upon favourable weather conditions and the absence of adverse effects, e.g., plant pests and animal diseases.

64. Tudge 2004, p. 154, referring to John Burnett, "Plenty and Want", *Penguin Books* (1966).
65. Felicity Lawrence, "Not on the Label. What Really Goes into the Food on Your Plate". *Penguin Books* (2004): 201–202.
66. Marsha A. Echols, "*Food Safety and the WTO. The Interplay of Culture, Science and Technology*". *Kluwer Law International* (2001): 30 (emphasis added, footnotes omitted). In a footnote, Echols relied experiential learning to the precautionary principle, noting that "[m]uch empirical evidence is developed over time, such as the experiences in some cultures that teach from experience which foods are safe. This experiential aspect of learning, which leads to eventual comfort, is akin to the reassurance derived through the precautionary principle" (Echols, ibid. p. 30, footnote no. 9.
67. The relationship between urbanisation and food policies was analysed, among others, by Eva Barlösius in her work about the sociology of food. In particular, Barlösius highlighted the relationship between abandoning subsistence farming and market dependency (Barlösius 1999, p. 202).
68. Using the adulteration of pepper with gravel and twigs in fifteenth century England, Felicity Lawrence noted that "[f]ood manufacturers have always cut corners and substituted cheap alternatives for expensive ingredients" (Lawrence 2004, p. 201).
69. As already noted, Marsha Echols, looking from a cultural-historical perspective, differentiated between four prototypes of agricultural production systems, namely (i) traditional farming, (ii) production agriculture, (iii) agricultural production applying novel technologies, in particular biotechnology, and (iv) hybrid systems combining elements of the other stages (Echols 2001, pp. 29–40). In the book at hand, the microeconomic approach developed by Todaro and Smith is followed, discerning between three broad stages of agricultural production, namely (i) subsistence or peasant farming, (ii) diversified or mixed farming, and (iii) specialised or commercial farming (see Todaro and Smith 2009, p. 453). The Todaro/Smith approach is chosen because of its multidimensionality: first, at the microeconomic level, the Todaro/Smith approach helps to explain contemporary problems of agriculture from a development perspective. Second, in historical perspective, the Todaro/Smith approach enables to follow developments of agricultural production systems through historical time periods. Because of its economical background, the Todaro/Smith model reveals structural similarities across different cultures and time periods rather than to focus on such differences. Third, from a methodological point of view, the Todaro/Smith approach enables to relate the three stages of agricultural production, i.e. subsistence, diversified and commercial farming, with the three stages of food safety control, i.e. personal empiricism, municipal control, and science-based food standards.

70. Echols 2001, p. 31 (footnotes omitted).
71. Reay Tannahill, "Kulturgeschichte des Essens. Von der letzten Eiszeit bis heute". *Paul Neff Verlag* (1973): 66. Other sources provide different dates for the *Codex Hammurabi*, ranging 1750–1790 BC.
72. Echols 2001, p. 31 (footnote omitted). The main concern of the Guild of Pepperers was the adulteration of pepper with gravel and twigs, especially, a malpractice they hoped to prevent with the King's Charter acquired in 1429 (see Lawrence 2004, p. 201). Other sources indicate that the Pepperers acquired the King's Charter already in 1428).
73. Tannahill 1973, p. 204.
74. Echols 2001, p. 31 (footnote omitted). The Assizes were a system of local courts established by royal or parliamentary edict and assigned for regulating bread and ale markets in England (see Tudge 2004, p. 154).
75. William Patrick, "The Food and Drug Administration". *Chelsea House Publishers* (1988): 19.
76. Echols 2001, p. 32 (footnotes omitted).
77. Mark A. Pollack, and Gregory C. Shaffer, "When Cooperation Fails. The International Law and Politics of Genetically Modified Foods". *Oxford University Press* (2009): 43. However, local authorities were seemingly overstrained by the task of supervising large-scale food manufacturers. Factory-like slaughterhouses and meatpackers in the United States in particular gave cause for repeated food safety concerns. For example, General Nelson Miles termed the canned meat, provided by a syndicate in Chicago to the US Army for the Spanish-American War of 1898, as "embalmed beef" (Ernst Laur, "Die Bekämpfung der Lebensmittelfälschung in der Schweiz durch ein eidgenössisches Lebensmittelgesetz. Leitfaden für die Referenten und Vertrauensmänner des schweizerischen Bauernverbandes". Swiss Farmers' Union, Brugg (1906): 66, with reference to the newspaper "Der Bund", issue 68, 1899). The deplorably insanitary and unhygienic conditions in meat packing plants especially in Chicago were also highlighted by Upton Sinclair's novel *The Jungle*, published in 1905. The publication of *The Jungle* expedited the enactment of the first federal Pure Food and Drugs Act of the United States which was passed by Congress in 1906 (Patrick 1988, pp. 26–27).
78. The reasons were taken from a manual issued by the Swiss Farmers' Union in 1906 to brief their representatives for the debates preceding the referendum on the federal food law (see Laur 1906, pp. 5–6).
79. Laur, ibid. p. 6.
80. See, for example, the chapter on food adulteration by Tannahill 1973, pp. 349–352.
81. Lawrence 2004, p. 201.

82. The problem of prolonged food chains may occur in two different forms. The common form is the one mentioned above, i.e., urbanisation and international trade separating food producers from food consumers. However, a second and most important aspect with respect to contemporary questions about food safety and food security alike has to be highlighted, that is, the actual extension of food chains particularly in developing countries through increasing costs of transport. Factors such as poor roads (potholes), inexistent public transport and increasing fuel prices are virtually extending food chains because they require the establishment of informal transportation systems. Informal transportation systems, operated by middlemen, are partaking of the proceeds, thus decreasing the earnings of farmers and increasing the retail price for urban consumers. A case study of an informal distribution system is the plantain market in Uganda. In central Uganda, plantain (*musa paradisiaca*) is the traditional staple crop, called *Matooke*. The particularities of the *Matooke* market in Uganda, which is characterised by, *inter alia*, the weightiness of the plantain, the risk of rapid deterioration combined with demanding customers, bad roads and expensive or inaccessible means of transport, provide a favourable environment for the edging in of middlemen. In the particular case of Uganda, typical middlemen have access to means of transport, e.g. a bicycle, a motorcycle, or a pickup truck. However, depending on the remoteness of the area and other factors, several middlemen may step in. Therefore, it might well be that at first, a middlemen with a bicycle gets the *Matooke* from the farmer in the *hinterland* and pushes it to a collecting point at the nearest tarmac road. At collecting points, secondly, the *Matooke* is collected by other middlemen with motorcycles or pickup trucks, carrying the plantain to trading centres on the outskirts of the capital city, Kampala, or directly to certain wholesalers with whom they are collaborating. Unsurprisingly, though, the retail price for *Matooke* is far higher than the prices paid to producing farmers. On the other hand, in Uganda many people can make a living from the *Matooke* business. These observations made by the author with view on the problem of transporting *Matooke* are corroborated by findings from Pamela Mbabazi with regard to transportation problems related to milk. Mbabazi noted that "[t]hree methods of transportation were indicated for transporting/delivering milk from the farm to the collecting centres. These include by pick-up/car, in containers carried on the head and by bicycle" (Mbabazi 2005, p. 88).
83. Lawrence 2004, p. 201. Whereas the above-mentioned developments took place in early nineteenth century Britain, similar developments, and similarly induced by industrialisation, occurred in the United States of America in the second half of the nineteenth century. As William Patrick observed:

Unfortunately, in the United States, the last half of the 19th century saw an increasing amount of domestic goods being manufactured and sold under less than honest and sanitary conditions. This was particularly true for food products such as meat, butter, and milk. There were several reasons for the deterioration of goods. The United States at this time was increasingly becoming an industrial rather than an agrarian society. As more and more people lived congested in towns and cities and were thus unable to grow their own food, the reliance on distant markets for food supplies grew. New railroads and other improvements in transportation facilities, along with packaging and manufacturing advancements, permitted larger amounts of food to be distributed over wider areas. Competition in sales often became intense and tempted some companies to adulterate (make impure) or mislabel their products to increase profits or to stay in business. (Patrick 1988, pp. 2122)

84. Tudge 2004, p. 152. A major driver of urbanisation in England was the enclosure movement, whereby the gentry enclosed lands formerly open for common use. What started in the sixteenth century, accelerated in the eighteenth century, inducing rural–urban migration. Mazoyer and Roudart noted:

This enclosure movement continued even more in the eighteenth century, at the height of the agricultural and industrial revolution, this time with the support of Parliament, the majority of whose Members were landowners. From 1700 to 1845, no less than 4000 acts of enclosure authorizing the lords to divide the commons, consolidate their lands, and enclose them were enacted by Parliament. (…) Thus the majority of the English peasantry disappeared (the *yeomen*), were forced to become agricultural wage laborers, beg, migrate towards the cities, become industrial wage laborers, or emigrate to settler colonies. (Mazoyer and Roudart 2006, p. 340)

85. According to John Burnett, "food adulteration virtually became organized crime" before effective legislation was established (quoted in Colin Tudge 2004, p. 153). Therefore, from a historical perspective, the heyday of food adulteration was the period between the abolition of traditional systems of food regulation, e.g., the Assizes in Britain, and the introduction of effective modern legislation (in Britain in the 1870s). And because different countries entered into that period, i.e., the Industrial Revolution, at different points in time, each case requires an individual analysis relative to respective circumstances.
86. On the other hand, increasing feelings of alienation resulting from vanished rootedness in local contexts were encountered by rising nationalism.

A particular expression of nationalism was the so-called national dish. Conceived as an emotional element for nation building—by glorifying 'own' foods and jeering consumers of 'other' foods as 'Krauts' (for Germans), 'Frogs' (for Frenchmen), etc.—'national dishes' also had a specific economic function, namely to privilege national produce. An example for such 'mental protectionism' is the Swiss national dish, the cheese fondue. Established in the world economic crisis of 1929, the cheese fondue required different cheese varieties from different regions in Switzerland. In fact, the purpose of this particular recipe was to strengthen Swiss cheese producers against foreign competition, particularly against cheese produced in Holland already on an industrial scale (Barlösius 1999, p. 148.

87. Tudge 2004, p. 154.
88. Tudge, ibid. p. 154.
89. Tudge, ibid. p. 154. Tudge draw an analogy between the baking trade in Victorian England and the present-day situation under conditions of globalisation: "Under the present, spreading rules of globalization, farmers worldwide will again be obliged to fight like dogs and undercut each other, just like Victorian England's bakers" (Tudge, ibid. p. 155).
   *The Eleatics were Greek philosophers of the sixth and fifth centuries B.C., who held that Being alone was true, and that everything outside the one fixed Being was merely apparent (original asterisk, original explanation).
90. Karl Marx, "Capital. A Critique of Political Economy", vol. 1, translated by Ben Fowkes. *Penguin Books* (1990): p. 358 (footnotes omitted, original asterisk).
91. Alum (potassium aluminium sulphate) was applied for whitening inferior flour and for bulking it out. An inquiry of 1848 ("A Treatise on the Falsifications of Food") considered that the fraudulent use of alum was common practice (Tudge 2004, p. 152).
92. Colin Tudge noted that some of the added ingredients, albeit not directly hazardous, could nevertheless affect human health. In this respect, Tudge pointed at the example of oatmeal which "was commonly bulked out with barley meal, which is not only cheaper but also less nutritious". Tudge further observed that "[t]he high mortality among the pauper children in Drouitt's institution in 1850 was ascribed to oatmeal tricked out with barley, which reduced their intake of energy and essential fats even further, and gave them diarrhoea for good measure (which in the modern world, particularly in poor countries, often precipitates malnutrition)" (Colin Tudge, *ibid.* p. 152).
93. Marx 1990, p. 278, footnote no. 14.
94. Jackson and Jansen 2010, p. 539.
95. Marx 1990, p. 359 (footnote omitted).

96. The following excerpt from *The Jungle* may put across the public repercussion caused by Sinclair's book:

There was never the least attention paid to what was cut up for the sausage; there would come all the way back from Europe old sausage that had been rejected, and that was moldy and white—it would be doused with borax and glycerine, and dumped into the hoppers, and made over again for home consumption. There would be meat that had tumbled out on the floor in the dirt and sawdust, where the workers had tramped and spit uncounted billions of consumption germs. There would be meat stored in great piles and thousands of rats would race over it. It was too dark in those storage areas for a man to see well, but a man could run his hand over these piles of meat and sweep off handfuls of the dried dung of rats. These rats were nuisances, and the packers would put poisoned bread out for them; they would die, and then rats, bread, and meat would go into the hoppers together. (Patrick 1988, p. 26, citing from Upton Sinclair's The Jungle)

97. Harvey Wiley was the chief chemist of the US Department of Agriculture from 1883 to 1912.
98. Patrick 1988, pp. 26–27 (emphases added). Emphasis was put on the interests of the meat industry and the scope of the first federal Pure Food and Drugs Act of 1906 because it shows the function of food safety regulation as a scheme for consolidating a single market within common national borders. As noted by Colin Tudge with regard to the situation in Victorian England, the big corporations were usually more receptive to stricter food safety legislation than smaller businesses, because national food laws not only imposed restrictions, but also offered new opportunities for companies aiming at operating at the national level and able to comply with higher standards. This observation seems to be particularly applicable to federal states where food safety regulation previously remained a constitutional prerogative of Member states. With regard to the situation in the United States of America, Pollack and Shaffer noted that "[b]y the beginning of the twentieth century, however, the growth of interstate trade in the US meant that, in order to be effective, food safety regulation would also have to reach across state lines. The US Congress responded to this challenge in 1906 and 1907 by using its powers under the Interstate Commerce clause of the Constitution to adopt the first comprehensive federal food safety legislation, namely the Pure Food and Drugs Act and the Federal Meat Inspection Act" (Pollack and Shaffer 2009, p. 43; footnote omitted).
99. Patrick 1988, p. 26.
100. Mbabazi 2005, p. 93.

101. Mbabazi 2005, p. 94 (footnote omitted). In Mbabazi's case study on the milk market in Uganda, one may recognise main features of the distorted bread market in Victorian England. First, there is an impoverished segment of the population which, despite knowing about potential hazards, continues to purchase adulterated products because it is relying on cheap foods. Second, there is fierce competition caused by the liberalisation of previously regulated markets. Whereas in nineteenth century England, it was the 'undersellers' trading in adulterated bread, in today's Uganda, it is the 'informal sector' trading in adulterated milk. However, whereas the nineteenth century England was able to absorb informal labour in the formal sector, by providing jobs in the booming industry in particular, the status of the informal sector in Uganda seems to be rather different. In Uganda, as in many part of Africa, policies implemented pursuant to the Washington Consensus have effected in a virtual deindustrialisation. Many infant industries, such as the textile industry, have collapsed. As a result, the informal sector remains, beside the public sector, an important provider of income and services. Therefore, a crackdown on the informal sector would, most likely, not increase food safety, but endanger entire food distribution systems and food security as a whole.
102. Barlösius 1999, in particular pp. 205–207.
103. Lydia Petránová, "From traditional to industrial milk processing", in Martin R. Schärer and Alexander Fenton (eds.), Food and Material Culture. Proceedings of the Fourth Symposium of the International Commission for Research into European Food History. Tuckwell Press (1998): 276.
104. Petránová, ibid., pp. 284–285. With special regard to women's attitude to pasteurisation, Petránová observed: "The housewife from the country, living in the city for the first or second generation, preferred 'guaranteed fresh country milk' over processed milk from dairies. There was particular distrust of pasteurisation. Pasteurised milk in bottles was considered a 'city fabrication', 'artificial milk', and so on. It is emblematic that the main consumers of processed milk were hospitals, charity institutions and schools. Middle-class urban households usually had regular certified suppliers. At the same time it is typical how grudgingly women accepted the principles of modern milk processing, principles which resulted in relieving unnecessary effort, saved them time and reduced the health risk to the entire family" (Lydia Petránová, ibid., pp. 276–277).
105. Patrick 1988, pp. 19–20 (emphasis added).
106. Pat O'Malley, "Risk, Uncertainty and Government". Routledge-Cavendish (2006, 1st edition 2004): 30.

107. O'Malley, ibid., pp. 33–34. In The Search for Pure Food (1975), Ingeborg Paulus could even provide evidence for "the sense of moral outrage that was generated by efforts to criminalise manufacturers' adulteration of food and drugs—even where this resulted in the poisoning of many consumers" (Pat O'Malley, ibid., p. 34, footnote no. 4).
108. O'Malley, ibid., p. 30.
109. O'Malley, ibid., p. 34, footnote no. 4.

References

Bannock, Graham, Baxter, Ron, and Davis, Evan. "Dictionary of Economics". *Profile Books*, 2003.

Barlösius, Eva. "Soziologie des Essens. Eine sozial- und kulturwissenschaftliche Einführung in die Ernährungsforschung". *Juventa Verlag*, 1999.

Beck, Ulrich. "Die Risikogesellschaft. Auf dem Weg in eine andere Moderne". *Suhrkamp Verlag*, 1996 (1st edition 1986).

Beck, Ulrich. "World Risk Society". *Polity Press in association with Blackwell Publishers*, 2005 (first published 1999).

Bernstein, Peter L. "Against the Gods. The Remarkable Story of Risk". *John Wiley & Sons*, 1998.

Capra, Fritjof. "The Turning Point". *Ex Libris*, 1984 (1982).

Chandran, Rina "India balks at genetically modified crops". *International Herald Tribune*, February 17, 2010, 18.

Echols, Marsha A. "Food Safety and the WTO. The Interplay of Culture, Science and Technology". Kluwer Law International, 2001.

Goldstein, Daniel. "Züchtet der Mensch Krankheiten?". Published in *Der Bund*, September 19, 2009, p. 40. Accessed December 20, 2010.

Jackson, Lee Ann and Jansen, Marion. "Risk assessment in the international food safety policy arena. Can the multilateral institutions encourage unbiased outcomes?". *Food Policy*, 2010, vol. 35, 538–547.

Kappel, Rolf, Pfeiffer, Reinhard and Werner, Jutta. "What became of the Food Price Crisis in 2008?". Verlag Rüegger, 2010, 65(1) *Aussenwirtschaft*, 21–47.

Keve, Joseph. Contribution to the Global Forum on Food Security and Nutrition, Proceedings of Discussion No. 53 on *Livestock Keepers' Rights—An Important Concept for Food Security?* March 8 to April 6, 2010, 28. Accessed December 21, 2010. http://km.fao.org/fileadmin/user_upload/fsn/docs/PROCEEDINGS_Livestock.pdf.

Keve, Joseph. "Selbstmord wegen Baumwolle". *Die Wochenzeitung*, January 21, 2010, 11.

Kostolany, André. "Die Kunst über Geld nachzudenken". *Econ Ullstein List Verlag GmbH*, 2000.

Laur, Ernst. "Die Bekämpfung der Lebensmittelfälschung in der Schweiz durch ein eidgenössisches Lebensmittelgesetz. Leitfaden für die Referenten und Vertrauensmänner des schweizerischen Bauernverbandes". *Swiss Farmers' Union*, 1906.

Lawrence, Felicity. "Not on the Label. What Really Goes into the Food on Your Plate". *Penguin Books*, 2004.

Le Goff, Jacques. "Marchands et banquiers du Moyen Âge". *Presses Universitaires de France*, 2001, 9th edition.

Marx, Karl. "Capital. A Critique of Political Economy". Vol. 1, translated by Ben Fowkes. *Penguin Books*, 1990.

Mazoyer, Marcel and Roudart, Laurence. "A History of World Agriculture. From the Neolithic Age to the Current Crisis". Translated from the French original by James H. Membrez. *Monthly Review Press*, 2006.

Mbabazi, Pamela. "Supply Chain and Liberalisation of the Milk Industry in Uganda". *Fountain Publishers*, 2005.

Michaels, David. "Manufactured Uncertainty. Contested Science and the Protection of the Public's Health and Environment". Published in Robert N. Proctor and Londa Schiebinger (eds.), *Agnotology. The Making and Unmaking of Ignorance*. Stanford University Press, 2008, 90–107.

O'Malley, Pat. "Risk, Uncertainty and Government". *Routledge-Cavendish*, 2006 (1st edition 2004).

Patrick, William. "The Food and Drug Administration". (Know your government —Series). *Chelsea House Publishers*, 1988.

Petránová, Lydia "From traditional to industrial milk processing". Published in Martin R. Schärer and Alexander Fenton (eds.), *Food and Material Culture. Proceedings of the Fourth Symposium of the International Commission for Research into European Food History*. Tuckwell Press, 1998, 268–286.

Pollack, Mark A. and Shaffer, Gregory C. "When Cooperation Fails. The International Law and Politics of Genetically Modified Foods". *Oxford University Press*, 2009.

Takes, Charles A. P. "New Settlement and Land Consolidation in The Netherlands". Published in Raanan Weitz (ed.), *Rural Development in a Changing World*. The MIT Press, 1971.

Tannahill, Reay. "Kulturgeschichte des Essens. Von der letzten Eiszeit bis heute". Original title: *Food in History*. Translated by Joachim A. Frank, published by Eyre Methuen. *Paul Neff Verlag*, 1973.

Todaro, Michael P. and Smith, Stephen C. "Economic Development". *Addison-Wesley*, 2009, 10th edition.

Triebe, Benjamin. "Das Märchen vom bösen Weizen-Zocker—Der spekulative Handel mit Agrar-Futures ist nicht verantwortlich für den Welthunger". *Neue Zürcher Zeitung*, October 16, 2010, 33.

Tudge, Colin. "So Shall we Reap. What's Gone Wrong With the World's Food—and How to Fix It". First published by Allen Lane 2003. Published in Penguin Books with a new afterword. *Penguin Books*, 2004.
Wysling, Andres. "Aalsmeer—Welthandelsplatz für Blumen". *Neue Zürcher Zeitung*, September 28, 2010.

CHAPTER 6

The Battle for Agriculture

Agriculture provides an example *par excellence* for showing how the two opposing worldviews, i.e. positivism and relativism, are approaching the same issue from different perspectives. Based on the two opposing worldviews, two approaches to the agrarian question came in conflict. That conflict was especially intense in the nineteenth century, where the contours of what Mazoyer and Roudart called 'the second agricultural revolutions of modern times' emerged.[1] For bridging the previous chapter on philosophical and epistemological concepts with conflicting approaches towards agriculture in the nineteenth century, the terms used in that conflict shall be reviewed and reutilised in the following.

1 Empirical Versus Rational Agriculture

For geographical reasons, the separation of farmland and emerging cities such as New York was of particular concern in the USA. A major reason for raising criticism of agricultural systems based on the separation of production and consumption were insights made by the then new soil sciences. In short, soil sciences established that the disruption of soil nutrient cycles due to the separation of production and consumption leads to a decline in natural soil fertility. On these grounds, the nineteenth century witnessed rising criticism against an agricultural system benefiting traders to the detriment of farmland and farmers deprived from soil fertility and income. Interestingly, though, the accused 'spoliation system' was coined 'empirical agriculture', i.e. a system 'in which the conditions of the

M. Burkard, *Conflicting Philosophies and International Trade Law*, Philosophy, Public Policy, and Transnational Law,
https://doi.org/10.1007/978-3-319-61067-2_6

reproduction of the soil were violated'.[2] On the other hand, a 'rational agriculture' was conceived, which would 'give back to the fields the conditions of their fertility'.[3]

The term 'empirical agriculture', reminding of logical empiricism and empiriocriticism, was used by Justus von Liebig (1803–1873), a chemist particularly influential in organic chemistry and the development of soil science. Liebig contrasted 'empirical agriculture' with 'rational agriculture'; whereas the former was spurred by increasing separations of farmland and town, i.e. agricultural production and food consumption, the latter focused on the maintenance of soil nutrient cycles. Considering Liebig's critique of 'empirical agriculture', Foster and Magdoff noted:

> In his *Letters on Modern Agriculture* (1859), Liebig argued that the 'empirical agriculture' of the trader gave rise to a 'spoliation system' in which the 'conditions of the reproduction' of the soil were violated. Soil nutrients were 'carried away in produce year after year, rotation after rotation.' Both the open system of exploitation of American farming and the so-called 'high farming' of European agriculture were thus forms of 'robbery.' 'Rational agriculture,' in contrast, would give 'back to the fields the conditions of their fertility'.[4]

Because of his contribution to the development of synthetic fertilisers based on nitrogen, Liebig is nowadays, usually, solely considered the pioneer of soil enhancement by using fertilisers. In his days, however, Liebig campaigned for economic fertiliser use and the recycling of nutritive elements, turning him into a 'precursor of today's ecologists'.[5] Because of its continued, yet increasing relevance, Liebig's fundamental insight shall be further outlined. In this regard, Foster and Magdoff observed:

> In his *Letters on the Subject of the Utilization of the Municipal Sewage Addressed to the Lord Mayor of London* (1865) Liebig argued – based on the condition of the Thames – that the two problems of the pollution of the cities with human and animal excrement and the depletion of the natural fertility of the soil were connected, and that organic recycling that would return nutrients to the soil was indispensable part of a *rational* urban-agricultural system.[6]

From an economic perspective, empirical agriculture was criticised by Henry Charles Carey (1793–1879), a US economist 'who throughout the 1850s laid stress on the fact that long distance trade arising from the separation from town and country was a major factor in the net loss of soil nutrients and the growing crisis in agriculture'.[7] In his *Principles of Social Science* (1858), Carey wrote: '[A]s the whole energies of the country are given to the enlargement of the trader's power, it is no matter of surprise that its people are everywhere seen employed in "robbing the earth of its capital stock"'.[8] Hence, from an economic perspective, the different approaches of 'empirical agriculture' and 'rational agriculture' were mirrored in different outcomes regarding winners and losers: whereas 'empirical agriculture' benefited traders, 'rational agriculture' was meant to maintain soil fertility and thus the intrinsic wealth of farmers.

In the following, the terms 'empirical agriculture' and 'rational agriculture' are used for characterising conflicting approaches towards agriculture. Whereas, the former is relying on the input of synthetic fertilisers for increasing productivity, the latter aims at maintaining soil nutrient cycles. Thus, 'empirical agriculture' stands for agricultural systems where the production and the consumption of food are detached to the benefit of trade. 'Rational agriculture', in contrast, stands for attempts to rejoin agricultural production and food consumption by closing nutrient cycles for the maintenance of soil fertility.

In the following, the differences between the two approaches in agriculture shall be worked out in more detail.

2 Dissenting Objectives

As mentioned above, agriculture provides an example *par excellence* for showing how the two opposing worldviews, i.e. positivism and relativism, approaches the same issue from different perspectives. In the following, these differences are worked out at three levels, namely (1) where objectives are defined, (2) where methods are applied and (3) where restrictions on production and levels of protection are determined. To begin with, the question how respective objectives are defined shall be addressed.

2.1 Growth

It was shown above that, in principle, microeconomic theory can be applied also to farming. In particular, it was shown that the rationale behind farming activities is basically the same economic rationale driving other economic actors: as any other economic actor, farmers aim at maximising production, income and profit. In other words, the 'rational' approach of the *homo oeconomicus* is applied on farmers, resulting in an *agricola oeconomicus.* Applying new technologies, improved seeds and fertilisers, yields are increased. In simple terms, the growth-approach can be summarised by the following formula:

> Improved seeds + nitrogen + water → increased yields[9]

In the textbook *Introduction to Agricultural Economics (2002)*, John Penson et al. explained the economic rationale governing activities of 'rational' farmers as follows:

> Like any business, farms, input manufacturers, food processors, fiber manufacturers, and others involved with the transportation and trade of food and fiber products at the wholesale and retail levels are in the business to make a profit. The same can be said of the nation's farmers and ranchers. Throughout this textbook, we will assume businesses are motivated by the goal of maximising profits. The economic objective helps us to understand the economic decisions businesses make in the short run and the long run. We are not suggesting that these businesses ignore other meaningful objectives, such as personal, social, or environmental objectives. However, businesses' main concerns will always be with economic profits.[10]

The scientific or 'rational' world-conception extends the paramount economic objective from the micro to macro levels and in particular to international trade. Conceiving states in similar manners as the 'rational' *homo oeconomicus*, the economistic approach assumes that economic gains are the sole objective of 'rational' states trading among themselves. In a nutshell, Penson et al. summarised the economic rationale underlying the theory of international trade as follows:

> The basis for trade is differing opportunity costs among nations. To receive gains from trade, nations must specialize in the production of goods for which they are most efficient and exchange those goods with other nations. Through increased specialization and exchange, all nations can benefit from trade, and world economic welfare will be increased.[11]

Core to the perception of international trade in agricultural products is the theory of comparative advantage, first developed by David Ricardo in 1817.[12] Melaku Geboye Desta noted:

> Stated in policy terms, the theory teaches that international trade based on the comparative advantage of countries, and not on the artificial incentives resulting from protective trade barriers (such as quotas or tariffs) or stimulants (such as export subsidies), enhances global welfare in the interest of all trading nations. In line with the laissez faire philosophy of Adam Smith, the theory of comparative advantage makes a compelling case in favour of the least possible level of government intervention on the flow of international trade. As summarized by Nobel Laureate Paul Samuelson, 'there is essentially only one argument for free trade or freer trade, but it is an exceedingly powerful one, namely: Free trade promotes a mutually profitable division of labor, greatly enhances the potential real national product of all nations, and makes possible higher standards of living all over the globe.[13]

Hence, the prospect of 'higher standards of living all over the globe' is the promise underlying attempts for liberalising international trade in agricultural products.

Albeit trade liberalisation in agricultural products remained a particularly thorny issue, the objective of integrating agriculture fully into the world trading system is widely being upheld. Desta observed:

> And the result of all those developments is, at least from the legal perspective, definitively encouraging. A separate *Agreement on Agriculture* has emerged out of it. Although its practical impact might be modest in the short-run, the existence of a detailed set of legal rules governing the sector is hoped to furnish a reasonable degree of certainty, predictability, and rule of law in international relations involving the agricultural sector. The groundwork has now been laid for a rules-governed and operationally effective GATT discipline on agriculture. (…) Negotiations are already underway to push the agricultural reform process further. However, full integration of agriculture into the system still appears to be a long distance away.[14]

The economistic objective of creating a market-oriented agricultural trading system at the international scale was initiated by ministers at the Punta del Este meeting in 1986, launching the Uruguay Round. Considering agriculture, the *Ministerial Declaration on the Uruguay Round* stated:

> The CONTRACTING PARTIES agree that there is an urgent need to bring more discipline and predictability to world agricultural trade by correcting and preventing restrictions and distortions (…).

> Negotiations shall aim to achieve greater liberalization of trade in agriculture and bring all measures affecting import access and export competition under strengthened and more operationally effective GATT rules and disciplines, taking into account the general principles governing the negotiations, by:
>
> (i) improving market access through, inter alia, the reduction of import barriers;
> (ii) …
> (iii) minimizing the adverse effects that sanitary and phytosanitary regulations and barriers can have on trade in agriculture, taking into account the relevant international agreements.[15]

The Agreement on Agriculture (AoA), part and parcel of the Uruguay Round and entered into force in 1995, referred to the Punta del Este Declaration in the preamble as follows:

> Members,
>
> *having decided* to establish a basis for initiating a process of reform of trade in agriculture in line with the objectives of the negotiations as set out in the Punta del Este Declaration;
>
> *Recalling* that their long-term objective as agreed at in the Mid-Term Review of the Uruguay Round 'is to establish a fair and market-oriented agricultural trading system and that a reform process should be initiated through the negotiation of commitments on support and protection and through the establishment of strengthened and more operationally effective GATT rules and disciplines' (…)

A distinct feature characterising 'empirical agriculture,' that is, growth- and market-oriented agriculture, is the application of scientific method at all levels of agricultural production. First and paramount, economic sciences are setting the objective of agricultural production, that is, production increase, return on investment and growth. Second, latest innovations of applied sciences are providing most efficient means for agricultural production, e.g. genetic engineering and nanotechnology. Third, restrictions on agricultural production for protecting consumers are objectively determined, by applying physical sciences and *quarantine sciences*[16] in particular. By focusing on paramount economic objectives, the 'empirical', i.e. the economistic conception of agriculture is essentially *anthropocentric*. The economistic conception of food production is also *short-time* oriented because return on investment is a key objective.

The scientific or 'empirical' approach towards food production could be illustrated by a linear curve upwards, from the lower left corner to the upper right corner of the chart, expressing the one-dimensional economic objective of production increase and growth.

2.2 *Equilibrium*

As mentioned above, 'rational agriculture' implies the maintenance of soil nutrient cycles. Thus, the objective of production is somewhat relativised by the objective of sustenance. The objective of sustenance and requirements for maintaining nutrient circles are leading to a circular understanding of agriculture and a *long-term* perspective. Farming activities are centring on the preservation of equilibrium between input and output, production and recovery in the long run. Preservation of equilibrium requires the circulation rather than the exhaustion of nutrients by recycling of manure and other nutritious components. By acknowledging the dependency on microorganisms, farm animals, plants, water, the sun, yet the whole environment within which it is taking place, 'rational agriculture' or, in contemporary language, sustenance farming is potentially *ecocentric*. Sustenance farming could be depicted by a circular figure rather than by a linear growth curve.

The concept of 'rational agriculture,' i.e. sustenance farming, is intrinsically multidimensional. The objective of production is balanced by the objective of sustenance. The objective of sustenance is achieved by the maintenance of nutrient circles.

In the scope of the study at hand, it has to be emphasised that the basis of relativist calls for sustaining nutrient circles is no less scientific than the economistic foundation of growth-oriented agriculture. Whereas growth-oriented agriculture is based on laws developed by economic sciences, sustenance agriculture is based on principles established by natural sciences, in particular biology and environmental sciences. The basic principles are related to the production and destruction of the biomass. The basic principles determining production and destruction of biomass are called photosynthesis, on the one hand, and respiration, on the other hand. The process of photosynthesis is expressed by the following equation[17]:

Carbon dioxide + water + photons → sugar + oxygen (if chlorophyll is present)

As a formula: $CO_2 + H_2O$ (+light + chlorophyll) → (HCHO) + O_2

Thus, plants living basically on water and carbon dioxide, produce various forms of sugars, which, in turn, are the basis for the formation of many other organic substance, such as nucleic acids, protein and lipids. The organic matter produced by plants forms, directly or indirectly, the diet for animals and humans. Thus, direct or indirect consumption of plants provides animals and humans with organic material and energy. With respect to the latter, energy is produced through a process inverse to that of photosynthesis, namely respiration. Respiration is expressed by the following equation[18]:

Sugar + oxygen → carbon dioxide + water + energy

Or, as a formula: (HCHO) + $O_2 \rightarrow CO_2 + H_2O$ + energy

The two fundamental scientific processes of photosynthesis and respiration are the basis for balanced ecological systems. The tool enabling ecological systems to stay balanced is the process of recycling. Mazoyer and Roudart summarised the principles governing ecological equilibria and recycling as follows:

> When an ecosystem is in equilibrium, i.e., when the quantity of organic matter produced each year by photosynthesis is equal to the quantity of organic matter destroyed by respiration and decomposition of the litter, then the quantities of carbon dioxide, water, nitrogen, and various mineral salts, which are absorbed and stabilized in organic matter, are in principal equal to those released by respiration and decomposition. In the same way, the quantities of oxygen released by photosynthesis are compensated by those used by respiration and decomposition. A stable ecosystem neither 'creates' nor 'loses' anything; it recycles everything.[19]

Political thinkers such as Vandana Shiva applied and extended scientific principles of ecological equilibria to a theory of sustenance economy. By the same token, stable societies are not only defended, but also taken as examples for achieving sustenance in today's context. Vandana Shiva explained:

> Sustainable societies move in a stable state – with, not against, the cycles of life. To be in stable state is not to be motionless; it involves movement and

> progression within an orbit, like an electron around the atom or the moon around the earth. The ecological consciousness of ancient civilizations allowed them to progress in an ecologically stable way. But just as classical physics is incapable of explaining or understanding the motion of the electron, conventional market economics interpret stability as stagnation and not as movement at all. Indigenous cultures of the Amazon, of the Andes, or the Himalayas are examples of living cultures that have been sustainable over millennia and, where not destroyed by the globalized economy, are sustainable even today.[20]

Modern concepts of 'rational agriculture,' i.e. sustenance farming, are going beyond the objective of maintaining nutrient cycles. Contemporary calls for 'rational agriculture' and sustenance farming respectively, emphasise social, cultural and political dimensions of agriculture. In a contemporary understanding, sustenance farming implies that the tasks of defining objectives, of choosing appropriate methods of production and of determining levels of protection are assigned to the people involved and concerned, i.e. farming communities and consumers respectively. It is thus the emphasis of social, cultural, historical and political dimensions which associated the concept of 'rational agriculture' to relativist positions. In contrast to 'empirical agriculture', 'rational agriculture' always implies a balance between several objectives. First and foremost, the objectives of production increase, on the one hand, and the maintenance of nutrient cycles, on the other hand, have to be balanced. Thus, 'rational agriculture' and modern expressions thereof, such as sustenance farming, are intrinsically multidimensional.[21]

Basic principles of 'rational' or sustenance farming are the objective of sustenance and requirements for maintaining nutrient circles. Thus, 'rational' or sustenance agriculture can be depicted by a circular move and a *long-term* perspective. Farming activities are centring on the preservation of equilibria between input and output, production and recovery in the long run. Preservation of the equilibrium requires the circulation rather than the exhaustion of nutrients by recycling of manure and other nutritious components. By acknowledging the dependency on microorganisms, farm animals, plants, water, the sun, yet the whole environment within which it is taking place, sustenance farming is potentially *ecocentric*. Sustenance farming could be depicted by a circular figure rather than by a linear growth curve.

Considering the contrasting objectives of 'empirical', i.e. growth-oriented agriculture on the one hand, and 'rational', i.e. equilibrium-centred agriculture on the other hand, one may see that both are 'based on science': whereas the growth-oriented approach towards agriculture is based on economic sciences, the equilibrium-centred approach is based on natural sciences, in particular biology and soil science. In light of that finding, currently popular descriptions of distinct forms of agricultural systems seem to be unfounded, yet confused. Nowadays, growth- or market-oriented food production, formerly known as 'empirical agriculture', is frequently characterised as 'rational'. On the other hand, sustenance agriculture, formerly known as 'rational agriculture', is regularly called 'non-scientific', 'romantic', or even 'irrational' these days.[22] Nowadays, the term 'rational' is commonly used synonymic for 'efficient' and not for denoting a particular intellectual orientation.[23]

José Lutzenberger considered that the contemporary confusion of terminology mirrors an underlying confusion between science and technology. According to Lutzenberger, technology has gained supremacy over science, virtually taking the latter into the service of technical progress. According to Lutzenberger, the 'empirical development of technologies', mostly patentable products, is aimed at making 'big deals'. Thus, knowledge as the aim of science was replaced by the pursuit of patents and registered trademarks through 'empirical research'.[24]

3 Different Methods

As mentioned above, agriculture provides an example *par excellence* for showing how the two opposing worldviews, i.e. positivism and relativism, approaches the same issue from different perspectives. In the following, these differences are worked out by looking at what sort of methods are applied for achieving the respective objectives.

3.1 Labour

The 'rational' objective of profit maximisation through specialisation and the division of labour was mirrored in agriculture in two major ways. A first specialisation established a specialisation between farmers, establishing farms specialised in the cultivation of a single crop or the production of a single animal product. This specialisation of production was due to the introduction of cheap nitrogen fertilisers, enabling farmers to give up intercropping and specialise in most profitable crops or animal production. John Foster and Fred Madgoff commented:

> With the widespread availability of nitrogen fertilizers, there was no longer a need to rely on legume crops, which convert atmospheric nitrogen into a form that plants can use, to supply non-legumes with sufficient fertility. The legume clover and alfalfa hay crops had previously been fed to ruminant animals such as beef and dairy cows and sheep. Once there was no need to grow those crops to supply nitrogen for non-legume crops (wheat, corn, barley, tomatoes), farms could more easily specialize as either crop or livestock operations.[25]

A second specialisation took place with regard to the human–animal relationship. The rearing of animals was successively detached from farming and concentrated near the emerging large-scale processing plants, thus separating cropland cultivation from animal production. John Foster and Fred Madgoff observed:

> … [C]orporations began to encourage production of animals near the few large processing facilities that they operated. They selected locations that offered certain advantages such as lax environmental laws, negligible threat of union activity, and low wages. The large processors were also increasingly marketing their products under brand names and, to have a uniform and predictable product, needed to control as much of the entire process as possible – either by producing the animals on their own corporate farms or under production contracts where the farmer might not even own the animals and had to follow strict instructions form their corporate employer. Thus animal production became concentrated in certain regions (…).[26]

Specialisation in agricultural production was contingent upon technical innovation. In fact, cornerstones of what Mazoyer and Roudart called 'the second agricultural revolutions of modern times' were a series of technological innovations in applied sciences. In particular, sciences related to agricultural machinery (mechanisation and processing), agricultural chemistry (synthetic fertilisers, pesticides, fungicides and herbicides), agricultural biology (seed selection and animal breeding) and veterinary sciences (vaccines, antibiotics) were mentioned.[27]

One may thus say that modern agriculture is based on a twofold separation: at first, industrialisation separated townspeople from farmland,

and specialisation separated and differentiated animal production from crop production, second.

From an economic point of view, this twofold separation was the basis for establishing divisions of labour and regional and international specialisation of production. The first separation induced by industrialisation, i.e. separation of townspeople from farmland, was the precondition for the vertical division of labour. Upstream, a 'network of extractive industries and industries manufacturing new means of production (fertilizers, treatment products such as pesticides and antibiotics, motors, machines, fuel, and other supplies) takes the place of the old activities that supplied agriculture, be they artisanal (cartwrights, smiths, saddlers, builders) or agricultural (production of draft animals and manure, manufacture of farm implements)'.[28] Downstream, processing industries are supplied with agricultural raw materials. The processing industry consists of food producers, e.g. flour millers, dairy processing industries, sugar refineries, breweries, oil factories, etc. and of non-food producers, such as the textile industry. Most of these industrial manufactures 'were replacing manufactures formerly carried out on farms and in small artisanal units'.[29]

The second separation mentioned, that between animal production and crop production and further differentiations within respective modes of production, was the precondition for implementing horizontal division of labour. Because it refers back to the underlying economic rationale of comparative advantage, the horizontal division of labour is explained by citing Mazoyer and Roudart in full:

> The specialisation of farms and regions has led to the separation and regional grouping of different branches of plant and animal production that formerly were found together at the farm or village level. Specialization has given birth to regional agrarian systems, which contribute, each in their own way, to supplying the same national or international market. These specialised regional systems are complementary, interdependent subsystems, in which the landscape itself conveys the horizontal division of labor characteristics of the new multiregional agricultural and food system that has developed.[30]

One may conclude that market-oriented agriculture follows the basic rules of industrial production, i.e. mechanisation, division of labour and specialisation.

However, the separation between townspeople and farmlands, differentiations within modes of agricultural production and resulting labour divisions and regional and international specialisation caused various concerns, in particular, among early agronomists and contemporary sociologists and environmentalists.

3.2 Resources

Critics of growth-oriented agriculture observed that the tremendous production increases achieved by the 'second agricultural revolution' are contingent upon continued supply with external resources which are mainly exhaustible, in particular oil. Fuel is the premise for mechanisation, whereas the production of fertilisers requires significant energy inputs. With regard to the latter, Mazoyer and Roudart observed that the 'considerable increase in output per hectare of crops in the course of the last few decades results principally from increasing use of fertilizers, even if the improvement from treatments and from the mechanical work of preparing and maintaining cultivated lands also played a role in this increase'.[31] The production of nitrogen fertilisers is particularly energy intensive. Foster and Magdoff, examining energy efficiency in growth-oriented farming, observed that '[o]f all the energy used to produce an acre of corn in the Unites States cornbelt—including fuel, wear and tear on machinery, seeds, and pesticides—nitrogen fertilizer accounts for the largest amount (double the next largest category), approximately 40%'.[32] Considering required fossil energy inputs for intensive agricultural production all in all, some authors concluded that 'the amount of energy invested to produce a desired yield surpasses the energy harvested'.[33] In other words, the tremendous increase in agricultural production achieved by growth-oriented agriculture is virtually fuelled by fuel.

However, also other fossil components indispensable for growth-oriented agricultural production are exhaustible. Particularly critical in this regard is phosphate. Estimates are indicating that stocks of phosphates will be exhausted even before oil reserves.[34]

Based on the recognition of the long-term instability of an agricultural system based on exhaustible resources, contemporary ecologist called for a reorientation towards stable agricultural production methods based on renewable resources. Vandana Shiva noted: 'Contemporary ecology movements represent a renewed attempt to establish that steadiness and stability are not stagnation, and that balance with nature's essential ecological processes is not scientific and technological backwardness, but rather a sophistication toward which the world must strive if planet earth and her children are to survive'.[35] The emphasis on the sophistication of stable and balanced agricultural systems shows the close link between ecological agriculture and traditional knowledge. Susette Biber-Klemm underscored the important role of traditional knowledge not only for local food security, but also 'for humanity and its long-term survival as a whole'. In particular, Biber-Klemm noted that '[s]ophisticated crop rotation systems lead to sustainable and durable production and resource use'.[36]

As an alternative to unstable market-oriented agricultural production relying on exhaustible natural resources, authors such as Vandana Shiva were calling for 'an ecological transition to produce more food using fewer resources'.[37] Drawing from examples provided by traditional agricultural systems, ecological agriculture and organic farming are depicted as models 'based on mixed and rotational cropping, and the production of a diversity of crops'.[38] Attempts for an ecological transition of agricultural production are based on the recognition that polycultures are providing higher yields than monocultures. The reason for this is the land equivalent ratio which can be explained by the following example:

> For example, by planting sorghum and pigeon pea mixtures, one hectare will produce the same yield as 0.94 hectares of sorghum monoculture and 0.68 hectares of pigeon pea monoculture. Thus, one hectare of polyculture produces what 1.62 hectares of monoculture can produce. This is called the land equivalent ratio.[39]

Miguel Altieri explains that the reduction and finally elimination of agrochemical use requires 'major changes in management to assure adequate plant nutrients and to control crop pests'.[40] Benefits from agrobiodiversity can be maximised 'when livestock, crops, animals, and other farm resources are used (including good rotational designs) to optimize production efficiency, nutrient cycling, and crop protection'.[41]

Hence, some characterising features of ecological alternatives to growth-oriented agriculture may be summarised as the maintenance of nutrient cycles, crop rotation and the production of a diversity of crops.

At macro levels, attempts for an ecological transition of agricultural production translate into a call for self-determination at local levels. Cornerstones of agricultural self-determination at local levels are the concepts of food sovereignty and seed sovereignty.[42] In particular, with view on the latter, *i.e.* seed sovereignty, close links between ecological agriculture, functioning local communities and the oral tradition of knowledge has to be emphasised. In this regard, Biber-Klemm observed:

> The use and improvement by farmers of landraces in the production and development of food and agriculture remains essential for many people. In many instances seed production relies on the informal sector, being based on the knowledge about seed selection and storage (often held by women) and the exchange of seeds between farmers and farms.[43]

Miguel Altieri emphasised that attempts for ecological changes in agriculture must not stop at addressing forms of agricultural production, but address the structures of industrialised agriculture, in particular, farm size and land tenure. On these grounds, Altieri criticised some trends in organic farming only changing forms of production, e.g. the substation of synthetic insecticides by biological ones, but not addressing structural requirements, such as land reform.[44]

From a geopolitical viewpoint, John H. Perkins' arguments went even further. Albeit admitting that according to economic theory, free trade will increase welfare among all parties involved, Perkins expressed the following reservations:

> The problem with the free-trade mantra is not that it contains no reasonable ideas but that it directs our attention away from issues shown in this book [i.e. Geopolitics and the Green Revolution] to be of deep and abiding importance. For example, free-trade ideas neglect to inquire into the links among biological productivity (agricultural harvest), economic value, and the acquisition of political power. The physiological necessity for food means that any person not in possession of food can be subjected to enormous coercion as they attempt to trade whatever they have produced for food. This is a relationship that is all but invisible in the ideas justifying free trade as a guide to agricultural policy.[45]

On these grounds, one can conclude that ecological transition of agricultural production does not stop with a change in production processes, such as the preservation of soil nutrient cycles. Instead, today's interdependence of agricultural markets is making it impossible to conceive an ecological transition of agricultural production without flanking policy measures, in particular measures protecting food and seed sovereignty.

In the next chapter, it is shown how the different concepts of agriculture are translating into conflicting scopes of protection.

4 Incongruent Scopes of Protection

As mentioned above, agriculture provides an example *par excellence* for showing how the two opposing worldviews, i.e. positivism and relativism, approaches the same issue from different perspectives. In the following, these differences are worked out by focusing on the question how respective levels of protection are determined, based on different objectives and different underlying rationales. In conclusion, it is argued that it is not as much as different levels of protection, but different scopes of protection characterising conflicting understandings of agriculture, for the main part.

4.1 Anthropocentric

It was shown above that industrialised food production tends to expand unless it is stopped by constraints established by society, in particular, food safety laws. In other words, the economic rationale of growth is spurring increased production unless external limitations are reached. Such limitations may be natural limitations, e.g. the depletion of natural resources, or restrictions implemented by society, e.g. food safety laws. From a positivist point of view, the only restrictions which reasonably can be justified are restrictions based on 'objective' science and scientific risk assessment.[46] It is up to science, in particular, the so-called *quarantine sciences*, to assess whether protective measures are necessary to protect humans, animals or plants. The spirit of the science-based approach for limiting agricultural production is expressed by Article 2.2 of the Agreement on the Application of Sanitary and Phytosanitary Measures (SPS Agreement) which reads as follows:

> Members shall ensure that any sanitary or phytosanitary measure is applied only to the extent necessary to protect human, animal or plant life or health, is based on scientific principles and is not maintained without sufficient scientific evidence (…).

The SPS Agreement further prescribes that scientific assessments have to evaluate 'the potential for adverse effects to human or animal health' and 'the likelihood of entry, establishment or spread of pests or diseases', respectively (Article 4 of Annex A of the SPS Agreement).

The limits for agricultural production are thus determined by requirements of human health at first, and the need for protecting animals and crops from diseases and pests thereafter. However, a further look into the SPS Agreement shows that its approach towards animal and plant safety is, in fact, focused on the protection of investment. The economic perspective of the SPS Agreement can be demonstrated, for instance, by looking at the factors which can be taken into account in assessing the risk to animal and plant life or health. With regard to risks to animal and plant life or health, it is first and foremost economic factors which can be taken into account. Article 5.3 of the SPS Agreement reads:

> In assessing the risk to animal or plant life of health and determining the measure to be applied for achieving the appropriate level of sanitary and phytosanitary protection from such risk, Members shall take into account as relevant *economic* factors: the potential damage in terms of loss of production or sales in the event of the entry, establishment or spread of a pest or disease; the costs of control or eradication in the territory of the importing Member; and the relative cost-effectiveness of alternative approaches to limiting risks (emphasis added).

In other words, animals and plants are protected primarily in light of economic considerations. With regard to animal protection in commercial farming, Mazoyer and Roudart observed:

> However, such carefully selected and richly fed animals represent substantial fixed capital as well as such a significant potential product heavily burdened with costs that losses of animals resulting from diseases or accidents are less and less tolerable. The risks from diseases are much stronger since the animals are concentrated in large numbers in huge buildings. That explains why rigorous sanitary precautions are taken in order to reduce losses and why, despite their high costs, a panoply of preventive treatments (vaccines) and curative treatments (serums, antibiotics), and even surgery in case of necessity (caesarians, settings of fractures), are called upon.[47]

Protection of investments is also the rationale underlying phytosanitary measures. With respect to crop protection, Mazoyer and Roudart noted:

> Annual crops certainly represent less significant fixed capital than animals or perennial plants. However, as a crop develops the expenses of seeds, fertilizers, labor, and fuel accumulate and often end up representing more than half of the expected revenue from the harvest. The margin between this revenue and these costs must then cover a portion of the fixed costs of the

> farm (amortization of the equipment and buildings, etc.). No losses of even an insignificant part of the harvest can be permitted. In order to limit the losses that could result from abundance of weeds, from the proliferation of insects, from infestations of fungus, bacteria, or harmful viruses, large quantities of herbicides, insecticides, and other pesticides have to be used.[48]

Hence, as far as animals and plants are concerned, sanitary and phytosanitary measures (SPS measures) are also investment protection measures. It seems thus justified to conclude that approaches relying on quarantine sciences are standing in the tradition of *anthropocentric* philosophical concepts: the principal objective is the protection of human health. The protection of animals and plants, on the other hand, is contingent upon their respective economic value.

Beside their anthropocentric scope, approaches relying on quarantine sciences for determining appropriate levels of protection are also *universalistic* insofar common validity of science-based levels of protection is presumed.

4.2 Ecocentric

In contrast to anthropocentric concepts for determining appropriate levels of protection (ALOP), alternative approaches for determining ALOP can usually be characterised as utilitarian, ecocentric, or holistic. Utilitarian, ecocentric and holistic approaches have in common an extension of the scope of protection. Whereas anthropocentric concepts for determining ALOP are focused on the well-being of humans (and related protection of investments made in animals and crops), ecocentric approaches, in particular, are extending the scope of protection beyond human well-being. Ecocentric approaches, in particular, are based on the belief that humans in general and farmers, in particular, shall live in symbiosis with animals and plants. Marie-Hélène Léon, for instance, discerned between two notions of the human–nature relationship; the notion of symbiosis applied by agroecologists, and the exploitative approach adopted by agro-industrialists.[49] The latter, Léon observed, are exploiting natural resources till exhaustion. Agroecologists, in contrast, are following the basic principle of attributing value to all things and creatures, regardless whether or not they have been produced by man.[50] Hence, ecocentric approaches can be characterised as assigning intrinsic value to animals and plants, biodiversity and natural resources, as well as to nature as a whole.

Unsurprisingly though, ecocentric proposals for the determination of appropriate levels of protection (ALOP) are in stark contrast to the definition of ALOP established by the SPS Agreement. Mazoyer and Roudart, for instance, based their proposals for the determination of ALOP upon the analysis of principles governing 'empirical', i.e. efficient food production. They identified these principles as profit maximisation and production increase:

> Without curbing their use, fertilizers, pesticides, and animal pharmaceuticals continue to be employed up to their profitability levels, i.e., sometimes well beyond their level of harm. Without strict bans, dangerous but profitable products will be used. Lacking an absolute ban, questionable raw materials will be used by the animal feed industry. The most irreplaceable sites will be cultivated. The rarest species will be destroyed.[51]

In similar ways, Mazoyer and Roudart traced back excesses of modern food production to the economic rationale underlying it, namely regional and international specialisation of production, on the one hand, and resulting competition, on the other hand:

> Where do such outcomes come from if not from the mechanisms of competitive development, mechanisms that turn out to be so effective in pushing the means, methods, and organizations of production to abundance, but can also end up just as effectively carrying them beyond the well-understood bounds of usefulness to excess?[52]

On these grounds, Mazoyer and Roudart found 'little sense in believing that it would be possible without risk to do without prohibitions, rules of production, and draconian controls…'[53] Thus, according to Mazoyer and Roudart, 'draconian controls', not deregulation, are the building blocks for achieving appropriate levels of protection (ALOP) for ecological agriculture.

Ecocentric or holistic concepts for determining appropriate levels of protection (ALOP) are usually coming along with a certain notion of relativism. Alternative concepts of ALOP typically consider that the setting of limits to agricultural production is essentially a task assigned to the people concerned, not to scientists. In a relativist conception, it is up to respective societies, i.e. producers and consumers, to define appropriate levels of protection (ALOP).

From a grass roots perspective, Vandana Shiva considered that food sovereignty and seed sovereignty cannot be (re-)established without political measures. Thus, in contrast to the market-oriented approach, ecological agriculture implies regulation. According to Vandana Shiva, it would be 'an error' to leave 'decisions on the distribution of goods and services and on environmental impact to unregulated and nonaccountable market forces'.[54] However, the regulation required should not be delegated to some centralised power, but should be effected according to people's needs. Calling it *localisation* of power, Vandana Shiva explains how an ecological transition of agriculture is contingent upon political change:

> Localization does not imply autarky or insularity. It involves subjecting the logic of globalization to the test of sustainability, democracy, and justice in each concrete instance of foreign or large-scale investment. (…) Social regulation of the market requires strong community rights and social policies – and this is not the same as individual consumer choice. The contest between the transnational corporations, the force behind globalization, and the citizens and local communities, the force behind localization, spins off into a contest over what kind of state will regulate corporations while recognizing and enhancing freedom for people.[55]

Calling it 'people's protectionism', Vandana Shiva argued for a shift of centralised powers to self-governing structures at the local levels for making decisions with regard to food and seed sovereignty and the environment.[56] Shiva explained that uniform food laws introduced by central governments are running counter to peoples' interests. To this purpose, Shiva presented the example of an Indian food safety law introduced in 1998 banning indigenous mustard oil and other unpacked edible oils. On the other hand, previously existing import restrictions were removed. According to Shiva, the effects of these new safety and packaging regulations and import liberalisation were devastating:

> India has used the coconut, groundnut, linseed, mustard, sunflower, and sesame for edible oil. The main consequence of eliminating import restrictions was the destruction of our oilseed biodiversity and the diversity of our edible oils and food cultures. It is also a destruction of economic democracy and economic freedom to produce oils locally, according to locally available resources, and locally appropriate food culture. Since indigenous oilseeds are high in oil content, they can be processed at the household or community level, with eco-friendly, decentralized, and democratic technologies.[57]

Based on that and other examples, Vandana Shiva concluded that different food systems require different food laws because uniform regulation tends to discriminate small producers and local produce. Shiva observed:

> The response of government to the mustard oil contamination in 1998 was to demand that every *ghani* (oil mill) have a lab, a chemist, and must package its oil. This response was inappropriate for the scale and method of production. One million ghanis were shut down, 20,000 small and tiny oil processors were criminalized by an inappropriate law that opened the flood gates for import of soy oil.[58]

Furthermore, Shiva recognised that '[d]ifferent foods have different safety risks and need different safety laws and different systems of management'.[59] The alternative concept of Vandana Shiva for protecting food and feed sovereignty is inspired by the multilevel food safety regulation of the European Union. In Europe, Shiva found, 'there are different standards for organic, for industrial, and for genetically engineered foods. Organic standards are set by organic movements, while the standards for genetic engineering are set at the European level through the novel food laws. There is, in addition, the movement to protect the cultural diversity of food, through "unique" and "typical" food standards'.[60]

Because modes of production are taken into account, ecocentric approaches for determining ALOP can be characterised as process-based. Because this point refers back to the biotech dispute, it shall be further explained with the help of arguments put forward by Vandana Shiva:

> Different food systems need different levels of management for safety. It is inappropriate to lump together all kinds of food – organic, industrial, GMOs – into one category. How food is processed determines its quality, nutrition, and safety. Home-processed bread is not the same as industrial bread. They are not 'like products' to use WTO terminology. They are different products in terms of their ecological content and public health impact. A factory-raised chicken is not the same as a free-range chicken, both in terms of animal welfare and in terms of food quality and safety. GM corn is not the same as organic corn. The former contains antibiotic resistance markers, viruses used as promoters, and genes for producing toxins. Regulating Bt corn for safety needs different systems than regulating organic corn, just as factory farming needs different regulatory processes than free-range chicken.[61]

On these grounds, Vandana Shiva developed a food safety system for India, applying different regulation at different levels for different risks established by different scientific approaches:

- At local levels, an 'organic processing law' applies 'for local, natural, small-scale food processing' which is governed by local and village communities, residents' associations or local municipalities. Shiva argued that '[c]ommunity control through citizen participation is the real guarantee for safety'.[62] However, community control is not exercised by quarantine sciences, but by traditional knowledge. Shiva declared: 'Our science of food is based on Ayurveda, not the reductionist science that has treated unhealthy food as safe'.[63]
- At national levels, an 'industrial-processing law' to address adulterations and food hazards in industrial foods.
- A 'GM food law' addressing imports, labelling, segregation and traceability of foods deriving from the application of biotechnology. Shiva noted that the 'GM food law' should be 'drafted by the central government, but states and local communities should be free to introduce stricter standards. If regions want to be GMO-free, this should be allowed under the principles of decentralized democracy'.[64]

The multilevel food safety concept suggested by Vandana Shiva runs counter to unified food regulation. India, Shiva explained, 'must craft her laws for her conditions. These laws must be appropriate to the level and content they address. A law for all food systems is a law that privileges large-scale industrial and commercial establishments and discriminates and criminalizes the small, the local, the diverse'.[65]

The concept of Vandana Shiva, by taking into account diverse conditions and by calling for variable regulation, may be characterised as 'relativistic'. Additionally, it has to be noted that Shiva's concept also implies a rejection of the universal applicability of 'reductionist science', referring to Ayurveda as an alternative at local levels.

Considering the global picture, Mazoyer and Roudart found that the 'draconian controls' necessary 'for preventing unsustainable excesses and for assuring ecological agriculture' require implementation and enforcement at the international scale:

> There is then, very little sense in believing that it would be possible without risk to do without prohibitions, rules of production, and draconian controls (…). Moreover, in an open world economy, rules of use, prohibitions,

and codes of good conduct must be shared and strictly applied by the producers of all countries, without which those who respect them will be penalized by the unfair competition of the others. A well planned, ecological agriculture and quality food will exist at this price. It is illusory to pretend that generalized deregulation leads to the best of all possible worlds and that the free market is capable of avoiding disequilibria, the fluctuating actions and reactions of the conjuncture, excesses, waste, poverty, and abandonments, which are in fact the counterpart of the impetuous competitive development of the agricultural revolution itself.[66]

In a nutshell, ecocentric approaches towards agriculture are requiring 'draconian' regulations in particular at the international level, by leaving room for manoeuvre for divergent rules at local levels at the same time. Hence, due to such differentiation, ecological alternatives to anthropocentric approaches for determining appropriate levels of protection (ALOP) can be considered 'relativistic'.

5 GMOs, the Last Frontier

The example of biotech regulation in the USA and in the European Union, respectively, provides an instructive example for showing how allegedly science-based regulation is actually 'political'.

5.1 *Product-Based Regulation in the USA*

Commonly, the regulatory approach of the USA towards GMO regulation is appraised as being 'based on science'. However, it can be observed that the US regulation of biotechnology applications in agriculture was driven by political considerations to a similar extent as in the European Union. The following selected milestones may shed light on the issue:

The first milestone was a conference which took place in 1975 in Asilomar, California. The Asilomar conference brought together leading scientists working in the new field of genetic engineering. As observed by Ulrich Beck in *World Risk Society* (1999), at that time the debate about pros and cons of biotechnology was not only driven, but also more or less confined to scientists working in the field. Following Beck, it was this confinement of the debate to the scientific community and the absence of political and economic pressure which enabled a 'reflexive consensus', as Beck termed it:

> It is indeed very interesting to notice that at first there was a reflexive consensus among the leading scientists in the field about these uncertainties and potential threats. As a result of a conference at Asilomar, California, in 1975, American scientists effectively called a halt to their work. There were fears of a biological weapon more terrible than the atomic bomb and of rogue organisms escaping from the laboratory to infect humans or crops.[67]

In the aftermath of the Asilomar conference, 'it was unclear which way the US would go—whether toward greater precautionary regulation of the technology's use or toward its promotion'.[68] The second milestone consists in the observation that the US Environmental Protection Agency (EPA) was inclined to the former, i.e. to a rather precautionary approach, initially. In their work *When Cooperation Fails*, Mark Pollack and Gregory Shaffer noted:

The EPA in particular supported a 'process-based' approach to regulate GMOs, noting that 'the most appropriate way to distinguish between 'new' and 'naturally occurring' microorganisms is by the methods or processes by which they are produced'. Some EPA officials maintained that the agency held existing authority under the Toxic Substances Control Act to regulate GMOs as 'new' chemical substances. Since the criterion for the EPA authority was based on 'newness,' it was in EPA's interest to find that GM varieties were fundamentally novel based on the genetic-engineering *process*.[69]

The third milestone consisted in the fierce pro-industry stance of the Reagan Administration, entering the White House in January 1981. The Reagan Administration started by setting up a Biotechnology Science Coordinating Committee (BSCC) with the task to reshuffle the institutional and regulatory setup as yet established for addressing biotechnology questions. Therefore, on institutional grounds, the BSCC transferred powers from the Environmental Protection Agency (EPA) to the United States Department of Agriculture (USDA) and the Food and Drug Administration (FDA). The transfer of institutional powers away from the EPA opened the floor for a regulatory change from a process-based to a product-based approach.[70] Pollack and Shaffer summarised the institutional and regulatory changes implemented by the Reagan Administration as follows:

> The result [of institutional and regulatory changes] was a curtailment of EPA's role and an elevation of those of the USDA and FDA. In 1986,

> after public notice and comment, the Office of Science and Technology Policy (OSTP) in the Reagan Administration issued a 'Coordinated Framework for the Regulation of Biotechnology' that continues to shape US biotech regulation today. Crucially, the OSTP concluded that the techniques of biotechnology are not inherently risky and that biotechnology could therefore be adequately regulated by existing federal agencies under existing statutes, obviating the need for new legislation dedicated specifically to regulating GMOs. The Coordinated Framework established a division of responsibilities among the three US regulators, with the FDA serving as the primary regulator for GM foods, the USDA charged with oversight of the planting of GM crops, and the EPA limited to overseeing the environmental and food safety impact of GM crops that have pesticidal characteristics.[71]

In a study entitled *Promotion Versus Precaution: The Evolution of Biotechnology Policy in the United States* (2006), Adam Sheingate pointed at three particular repercussions of the Reagan White House's policy choice in favour of green biotechnology. First, with regard to regulatory policy, the efforts of the Reagan White House refocused the GMO debate away from risks and onto 'commercial opportunities of biotechnology and its importance of a strategic sector for international economic competition'.[72] Second, at administrative levels, the product-based approach implied the assignment of regulatory tasks according to product categories. Sheingate noted that the division of administrative authority 'along product lines enhanced the role of the FDA and USDA in the regulatory process at the expense of EPA'.[73] Third, the reallocation of administrative powers among US agencies 'became to be reflected in the jurisdiction of congressional committees over biotechnology issues. Oversight hearings on the regulation of agricultural biotechnology, for example, fell within the jurisdiction of the House and Senate agriculture committees'.[74]

Additionally, the policy choice of the Reagan Administration in favour of the commercialisation of biotechnology applications in agriculture also changed the rules of the game in policy making. Pollack and Shaffer observed that the institutional and regulatory reshuffle, in fact, weakened biotechnology sceptics in the USA:

> The Reagan Administration was able to move primary regulatory responsibility to the USDA, whose primary constituency is agricultural trade associations, and in the process, shift primary legislative oversight to the agricultural committees of the House and Senate. In the 1990s in the White House, the US Council on Competitiveness would take the lead on biotech

> policy formation. These choices have made it more difficult for GM skeptics to use the existing regulatory and political framework to impede approval of GM crops and foods in the US.[75]

Cornerstone of the US Coordinated Framework was the presupposition 'that the process of biotechnology itself poses no unique risks'.[76] Based on that presumption, an approach focusing on specific products, and not on the process of their making, was established. The established product-based approach led to the conclusion 'that products engineered by biotechnology should therefore be regulated under the same laws as conventionally produced products with similar compositions and intended uses'.[77]

Though, as a preliminary conclusion, it is noted that the US approach towards biotechnology was shaped by decisive policy interventions, steered by the Reagan Administration. The policy intervention resulted in the establishment of a product-based approach, based on the presumption that genetically modified (GM) products are *substantially equivalent*[78] to their conventional counterparts. Thus, the presumption that biotechnology, as a technical process, does not pose unique risks led to the establishment of a product-based approach, basically treating GM crops as equivalent to their conventional counterparts.

Though, it is the product-based approach which essentially discerns the regulatory approach of the USA towards GMOs from the regulation of green biotechnology in the European Union. As Adam Sheingate noted:

> [I]t is the product-based approach of the Coordinated Framework that distinguishes the US regulatory regime from the precautionary, process-based approach to agricultural biotechnology in Europe. The history of the Coordinated Framework reveals that this outcome grew out of a political process, a period of *policy entrepreneurship* sparked by the commercialisation of biotechnology.[79]

The product-based approach relies on empirical testing on a case-by-case basis. It could, therefore, be related to 'empirical' agriculture.

5.2 *Process-Based Regulation in the European Union*

In short, the approach of the European Union (EU) towards biotechnology applications in agriculture was shaped by, first, a climate of public alert due to various food scandals which effected in, second, a decay of public trust in food safety surveillance. In response, third, the European Commission was prompted to adopt a cautious stance towards GMOs.

A first difference between the regulatory approaches towards GM crops adopted by the USA and the European Union, respectively, was the broader environment within which the debate enfolded. Whereas the debate in the USA was initially steered by scientists, culminating in the 1975 Asilomar conference, the setting was rather different in the European Union. Ulrich Beck, it is unequivocal manner, described the broader landscape within which the GMO debate in European countries enfolded as follows:

> In February 1999, the British consumer, still terrified by the BSE crisis, was shocked by headlines proclaiming 'Frankenstein Food' – an approach which reached its climax on the front page of *The Daily Mirror*, a leading British newspaper. It featured a picture of Tony Blair, genetically modified to look like Boris Karloff, complete with green face and neckbolt, under the headline 'The Prime Monster'. This was the mass media's response to Blair's attempt to restore trust by demonstratively eating genetically modified food in public with his daughter.[80]

Indeed, the GMO debate in Europe fell amidst a public already on alert caused by various food scandals, such as the outbreak of bovine spongiform encephalopathy (BSE). The BSE scandal in particular affected the credibility of food safety surveillance systems across the European Union. Pollack and Shaffer observed that the BSE scandal 'generated extraordinary public awareness of food-safety issues and widespread public distrust of regulators and scientific assessments'.[81] The second feature of the GMO debate in Europe, the decay of public trust in established food safety systems, was analysed by Pollock and Shaffer:

> Prior to the admission of the BSE risk, 'the European Commission had relied on the advice of the [EU's] Scientific Veterinary Committee, which was chaired by a British scientist and primarily reflected the thinking of the British Ministry of Agriculture, Fisheries, and Food – advice which subsequently proved flawed'. There was thus considerable scepticism as to the political independence of the committee's 'scientific' advice.[82]

As a consequence, the approach finally adopted by the European Union for regulating GMOs was moulded by political considerations. The resulting cautious approach of the EU for regulating GMOs was reflected in an administrative setup quite different from that adopted by the US. In the USA, regulatory powers had been shifted away from the Environmental Protection Agency (EPA) to the US Department of Agriculture (USDA) and the Food and Drug Administration (FDA). Within the bureaucracy of the European Commission, on the other hand, regulatory powers were gradually transferred from the Directorate-General (DG) for Science, Research and Development (DG XII) to the DG for the Environment. Pollack and Shaffer observed that over time, DG Environment took the lead over DG Science, Research and Development, as well as over DG Agriculture:

> Increasingly, according to observes such as Cantley, DG Environment cut out DG Science, Research and Development from policy influence, 'prefer [ing] to consult its own experts,' and reluctant to accept other experts' advice, especially those wary of the advisability of new legislation. DG Environment knew it lacked allies in DG Science, Research and Development for its desired regulatory role, which DG Science found to be duplicative and without scientific justification.[83]

The DG Environment adopted an approach based on the consideration 'that GM crops needed to be assessed in environmental terms'.[84] The result was an approach focusing on the process by which GM crops were produced, rather than on particularities of the products itself. This process-based approach outlined in a Community Framework for the Regulation of Biotechnology, prepared by the DG Environment and released by the European Commission in 1986. Though, by 1986, the regulatory landscape in the USA and in the European Union, respectively, differed in significant ways. Whereas in the USA, a product-based approach was implemented, the European Commission, following the DG Environment, had adopted a process-based approach. Reasons for this divergency are many.[85] One factor marking an important difference was the fact that biotech industries based in the USA and in European countries deployed different political leverage. Pollock and Shaffer noted:

> As many commentators have noted, the biotech industry was not as well organized in Europe and was unable to mobilize political resources to prevent the enactment of process-based GM regulation that was framed in environmental terms. Thus by 1986, the year of both the US Coordinated

> Framework and the EC Community Framework, Europe and the US had started down different paths.[86]

The product-based approach of the European Commission materialised in two outstanding regulatory frameworks.[87] The first set of rules was incorporated in Directive 90/220 on the Deliberate Release into the Environment of Genetically Modified Organisms. A cornerstone of Directive 90/220 was the implementation of a process-based approach. As Pollock and Shaffer noted: 'In contrast with US agencies, which elected to regulate GM foods only in terms of their final characteristics as *products*, the European Commission elected to apply distinctive regulations to GM foods as a function of the *process* through which they were developed'.[88]

With regard to procedural matters, Directive 90/220 set forth a comprehensive body of rules for the approval of biotech products.[89] The first step for any request for deliberate release of a GMO into the environment was an application to the competent authority of the EU Member state in which the release was meant to take place. Importantly, the application had to include a risk assessment which was then evaluated by the Member state authority according to the criteria set forth in Directive 90/220. In case of rejection of the application, the procedure would end at stage one. In case of approval, however, the application would be forwarded to stage two, which consisted of the European Commission, on the one hand, and the other EU Member states governments, on the other hand. At stage two, again two alternatives existed. If no objections were raised against the application by either governments of other EU Member states or the European Commission, the GMO at issue would be released for marketing throughout the European Union. If, however, governments of other EU Member states or the European Commission would object to the application, the latter would be subject to qualified scrutiny. In case of objections to the application, Directive 90/220 authorised the European Commission to carry out its own risk assessment. After having assessed the GMO at issue, the European Commission had to submit its draft decision whether to admit or to reject the application to a Regulatory Committee composed of representatives of EU Member states. At this third stage of the approval procedure, the EU Member-states representatives, assembled in the Regulatory Committee, had the option of either to approve a draft decision submitted by the European Commission by a qualified majority of votes. Or, in case, the Regulatory Committee disapproved the European Commission's draft decision, the latter had to be forwarded to the Council of the European Union (the Council of Ministers). At this final stage of the approval procedure, two particularities set forth by Directive 90/220 have to be mentioned. First, the Council of the European Union could approve draft decisions of the European Commission by qualified majority, but could reject them only by unanimous vote. Second, in case the Council of the European Union failed to arrive at a decision within a period of 3 months, Article 21 of Directive 90/220 authorised the European Commission to adopt the proposed measures.

Additionally, Article 16 of Directive 90/220 set forth a safeguard clause, upon which the EU Member states could 'provisionally restrict or prohibit' the marketing of biotech products on their respective territory. The condition for triggering the safeguard clause was the provision of new evidence for risks to human health or the environment posed by the GMO at issue.

Summarising the regulatory framework established by Directive 90/220, Pollack and Shaffer identified three particular gateways enabling politicians to influence decisions on the approval of biotech products in the European Union:

> First, it was politicians who enacted a new regulatory framework for the growing and marketing of GM foods and crops. Second, it was the [European] Commission, consisting of political officials designated by Member-states governments, which would make the decision whether to approve individual GM varieties. Third, the [European] Commission's decisions are subject to review by committees of Member-states representatives, and ultimately by national politicians in the Council of Ministers.[90]

The second set of rules was intended to supplement Directive 90/220 by addressing genetically modified (GM) foods. Established in 1997, Regulation 258/97 Concerning Novel Foods and Novel Food Ingredients, so-called Novel Foods Regulation, was also based on a process-based approach. The process-orientation was expressed by the definition of 'novel foods' covering all foods and food ingredients that had 'not hitherto been used for human consumption to a significant degree within the Community'.[91] As Pollock and Shaffer explained, this definition 'included both GM foods as well as foods produced from, but not containing, GMOs (for example, oils processed from GM crops but no longer containing any traces of GM material)'.[92] Thus, the Novel Foods Directive covers not only foods containing GMOs, as well as foods produced by processes involving GMOs, for example genetically modified bacteria.

As did Directive 90/220, Regulation 258/97 also provided a safeguard clause for individual EU Member states in case of the establishment of risks deriving from GMOs.

Together, Directive 90/220 and Regulation 258/97 established a regulatory framework which 'was more complex, more decentralized, and more politicized than the US system'.[93] Pollack and Shaffer explained:

> It was more decentralized because of the key role of Member states to start, oppose, and reject (through the imposition of safeguards) the approval of a GM seed or food. It was more politicized because of the involvement of politicians in the approval process. And it was more complex in that it created more institutional 'veto points', where the approval of new GM varieties or the release and marketing of EU-approved varieties could be blocked.[94]

The process-based approach of the European Union takes into account various factors. It could, therefore, be associated rather with 'rational' than with 'empirical' agriculture.

5.3 *The Political Nature of Regulation*

Following Pollock and Shaffer, the US and the EU regulatory schemes for addressing biotech products may be characterised by the following antipodes (Table 1):

Comparisons between the regulatory systems for biotech products of the USA and the European Union are typically meant to highlight transatlantic differences.[95] Such approaches, however, tend to pass over a significant similarity, that is the fact that both systems are the result of

Table 1 Comparison of US and EU biotech regulations

Characteristics	*Entity*	
	United States	*European Union*
Approval procedure	Administrative	Politicised
Approach	Product-based	Process-based
Doctrine	Substantially equivalence	Precautionary principle
Governance	Centralised	Decentralised
Business-orientation	One-stop shop	Complex
Institutional	Technocratic	Democratic

political decisions in the first place. In the case of the USA, it was shown that it was the Reagan White House pushing for a business-friendly approach in regulating GMOs. In particular, it was the Reagan Administration's Office of Science and Technology Policy (OSTP) issuing the 'Coordinated Framework for the Regulation of Biotechnology' that laid down the substantially equivalence doctrine, considering biotechnology as a mere continuation of traditional plant breeding and thus genetically engineered crops not substantially different than their conventional counterparts. From an institutional perspective, it was the Reagan White House which mandated the Biotechnology Science Coordinating Committee (BSCC) to transfer regulatory powers away from the Environmental Protection Agency (EPA) mainly to the United States Department of Agriculture (USDA) (and to the Food and Drug Administration (FDA) to some extent). Therefore, the establishment of the substantially equivalence doctrine, the downgrading of the EPA, and the implementation of the product-based approach were, first of all, the result of policy choices by the Reagan Administration.

Similar findings have been made with regard to the formation of the regulatory system for addressing GMOs in the European Union. Albeit the resulting system was rather different, the establishment of the EU regulatory system mainly followed political considerations. At his point, it seems sufficient to recall the BSE crisis as setting the scene for a cautious approach to risk regulation in general, and the prevalence of the Directorate-General (DG) for the Environment above the DG for Science, Research and Development (DG XII) within the intra-Commission power struggle. As a result, the DG Environment was, unlike the Environmental Protection Agency (EPA) in the USA, able to root the EU Community Framework for the Regulation of Biotechnology in an environmental angle. As a result of these policy choices, in the European Union, the notion prevailed 'that GM crops needed to be assessed in environmental terms'.[96] The result was a process-based approach subsequently implemented in Directive 90/220 and Regulation 258/97.[97]

The US system, comprising of the substantially equivalence doctrine and a product-based approach, is usually depicted as being based on 'sound' science. In comparison, the EU system, purporting a process-based approach and relying on the precautionary principle, is said to be more politicised. However, both systems have been initially chosen by political and administrative authorities following their respective political agendas. In the USA, it was the Reagan Administration pushing for a business-friendly approach. In the European Union, on the other hand, it was the European Commission and the DG Environment, in particular, pushing for a precautionary approach. In other words, despite US and EU frameworks for regulating GMOs are differing significantly, they are both the result of policy choices in the first place. The Reagan Administration did curtail the Environmental Protection Agency (EPA) on political grounds, in order to foster US biotech companies. And the European Commission adopted a cautious stance in order to stabilise the European food market and to restore the credibility of EU authorities and Community regulation.

The reason why the political rationale underlying the US regulatory framework for GMOs is usually neglected—whereas the political nature of the EU regulations may be overdrawn sometimes—can be seen in the misconception of US agencies as politically neutral and purely technocratic institutions. However, Pollack and Shaffer noted that the relevant US agencies are not operating in a political vacuum:

> US regulation of food safety by specialized [US] agencies is sometimes contrasted with European regulation of GMOs by politicians. It is contended that decision-making by these US agencies is more neutral and technocratic. However, none of the three US agencies (USDA, EPA, or FDA) are technically 'independent agencies' in the sense used in the US political context in which independent agencies refer to agencies that Congress has created to be independent of the executive branch, such as the Federal Reserve Bank, Federal Trade Commission, and Federal Communications Commission. The USDA is a cabinet-level department within the executive; the FDA operates within the US Department of Health and Human Services, and the EPA, although not a 'department', operates under executive branch control. (…)[98] Moreover, all federal agencies, whether 'independent' or not of the executive branch, are subject to various legislative-branch control devices, such as Congress's ability to pass new legislation,[99] to allocate or withhold funds, or to object to key appointments, which limit their autonomy. US regulatory agencies' actions are likewise subject to extensive administrative law requirements under the US Administrative Procedure Act, requiring prior notice and comment of all proposed regulations, backed up by judicial review before the federal courts. Interest groups can use these procedures to constrain agencies' ability to operate, especially when coupled with constraints on these agencies' enforcement budgets.[100]

Marsha Echols worked out relationships between different agricultural prototypes, i.e. systems of agricultural production and regulatory approaches. Echols considered the US positioned in an agricultural prototype characterised by a segregation of food production and culture. In such a technology-driven agricultural system '[f]ood production and culture no longer overlap, since the majority of people have no personal knowledge about the production of what they eat. Farming must confront genetic engineering of seeds and plants, irradiation and technologies that create fortified and functional foods'.[101] Importantly, though, US regulation is seen as a reflection of US agricultural policies and US agribusiness structure:

> The involvement of corporations and large cooperatives in vertically integrated farming and the use of cutting edge production technologies and techniques, coupled with sophisticated marketing, give agribusiness its business slant. U.S. policy exhibits confidence in agribusiness, in the ability of science and scientific methodology to ensure a safe food supply and in new technologies like genetic modification. Its regulatory structure reflects the economic importance of the business of food production and the accompanying technological innovations. There is less direct financial support for farmers domestically, with the assumption that exports will help efficient farmers to survive. Hence the emphasis on market access and fair trade competition'.[102]

The point which is stressed here is that both systems for regulating biotech products in the USA as well as in the European Union are the outcome of policy choices.[103] Albeit the US system is typically characterised as based on 'sound science', whereas the EU system is usually termed to be 'politicised', both systems have been established in line with respective political agendas. The fact that a regulatory system, albeit referring to 'sound science', may well have been established upon political intentions is a finding with the following consequences. First, the finding that regulatory systems invoking 'sound science' are nevertheless able to perform political functions may complicate and intensify frictions between different regulatory systems at the international level. With regard to the *Biotech* dispute between the USA and the European Union in particular, the finding that the application of a science-based approach is not tantamount to political neutrality may call into question the role of impartial arbiter attributed to science by the WTO Agreement on the Application of Sanitary and Phytosanitary Measures (SPS Agreement). The finding that even regulatory systems purportedly based on science may intrinsically be

Table 2 Comparison of US and EU biotech policies

Characteristics	*Entity*	
	United States	*European Union*
Decision-maker	Reagan White House	EU Commission
Policy	Industry-oriented	Consumer and farmer-oriented
Rationale	US dominance of international markets	Legitimacy of EU institutions, stability of the common market

value-laden casts doubt on the role of science in the SPS Agreement in particular.[104] Second, in view of the following general discussion of positivism, it shall be noted that the reference to science does not exclude a political agenda from the outset.

The following table shows how *both* the US *and* the EU regulatory framework for biotech products were established in line with respective political rationales and were implemented through agencies prone to political interferences (Table 2).

The above findings made in context of biotech regulation can be fairly generalised. Similar attempts for instrumentalising science have been observed particularly in trade disputes involving novel technologies for food production. Another telling example in this regard was the 2-year controversy in the Codex Alimentarius Commission about 'Statements of Principle Concerning the Role of Science in the Codex Decision-Making Process and the Extent to which other Factors are taken into Account' (in the following: *Statements of Principle*). Reviewing the dispute over the *Statements of Principle* fought out within the Codex Alimentarius Commission, Josling et al. observed that

> … the United States and [the] European Union sought to propagate decision criteria that favored their domestic agricultural policy regimes. The United States and its allies argued that food safety standards should rest solely on scientific evidence, while Europe and its allies sought to introduce a 'need' criterion, which held that productivity-enhancing food technologies threatened the livelihoods of economically marginal farmers and were not 'needed' in the face of excess global capacity. A compromise resulted in a statement that Codex standards 'shall be based on the principle of sound scientific analysis and evidence', but, where appropriate, Codex will consider 'other legitimate factors' in protection consumer health and promoting fair trade practices …[105]

Different agricultural policies are leading to different regulatory approaches which, in turn, are providing different foundations for the judiciary, both domestically and internationally. In this respect, Elizabeth Fisher showed that different regulatory regimes may lead to different approaches towards risk analysis by panels and the Appellate Body. Particularly referring to the case *EC—Hormones*, Fisher found that the Panel was following US regulatory doctrine, whereas the Appellate Body's approach rather reflected regulatory policies of the EU:

> [T]he Panel's risk assessment/risk management distinction is a product of US regulatory politics, and, in embracing this distinction, the Panel also embraced the RI [*i.e.* rational-instrumental] paradigm that has dominated US risk regulation for the last 20 years. In contrast, the Appellate Body could be understood as reflecting the more deliberative nature of EU regulatory standard-setting.[106]

In terms of a summary of previous paragraphs, two basic approaches towards agriculture have been identified. On the one hand, there is growth —or market-oriented agriculture, formerly also called 'empirical agriculture'. The objective of 'empirical agriculture', namely production increase and profit maximisation, is shaped by economic sciences. The objective is achieved by applying labour-saving, i.e. efficient and innovative technologies such as large-scale mechanisation and automation, genetic engineering and cloning. Limits to market-oriented agricultural production are established in an 'objective' manner, by relying on empirical testing carried out by quarantine sciences. By determining appropriate levels of protection (ALOP), anthropocentric criteria are applied. Because the determination of appropriate levels of protection (ALOP) is based on the same sciences, i.e. quarantine sciences, and anthropocentric criteria are basically the same everywhere, namely health protection and the protection of investments in animals and crops, resulting levels of protection are basically globally valid and can thus be standardised at the international level.

On the other hand, there is equilibrium-centred or sustenance agriculture, formerly also called 'rational agriculture'. The objective of 'rational agriculture', namely the maintenance of soil nutrient cycles and the well-being of rural communities including all animals, plants and natural resources which they are built upon, follows basic principles, as established by natural sciences. The objectives are achieved by applying resource-saving and locally adapted technologies and traditional knowledge. If sustenance agriculture would dominate, no limits to production would be required because production is meant to remain more or less stable. However, considering globalised realities of today, the protection of persisting and new forms of sustenance farming would require 'draconian regulation' in particular at the international level. At local levels, in turn, food safety would be assured by community control based on traditional forms of knowledge such as Ayurveda and empirical testing on respective local markets. Thus, appropriate levels of protection (ALOP) would be determined by the (local) people concerned and contingent upon different modes of production.

Because modes of production shall be taken into account, ecocentric approaches for determining ALOP have been characterised as process-based. Vandana Shiva stressed that '[d]iverse production processes and products need laws and science appropriate to them. Chemical processing needs chemistry labs and chemists, GMOs need genetic ID laws, organic processing needs indigenous science and community control'.[107] Hence, different products would attract different regulation; for local products local rules would apply, whereas for industrial products national and international standards might be appropriate. Finally, genetically modified organisms (GMOs) would be the object of particularly strict regulation, taking into account preferences of local communities. The resulting regulatory landscape would be one of regulatory fragmentation: at the international level, 'draconian controls' would protect persisting and new forms of sustenance farming. However, at national levels and particularly at local levels, scopes and levels of protection would be varying considerably, according to specific requirement of respective communities.

Today, however, the regulatory landscape is dominated by the rules of the World Trade Organisation (WTO). With regard to the determination of appropriate levels of protection (ALOP) in particular, the Agreement on the Application of Sanitary and Phytosanitary Measures (SPS Agreement) takes centre stage. The SPS Agreement basically requires that protective measures are based on a risk assessment, carried out by quarantine sciences. As mentioned above, the scope of the SPS Agreement is anthropocentric, i.e. covering measures to protect human health and related agricultural investments. Because the scope of ecocentric approaches towards the determination of appropriate levels (ALOP) is broader than the scope of anthropocentric approaches, a range of measures based on ecocentric worldviews would, in principle, fall outside the narrow scope of the SPS Agreement. But because of the broad interpretation of the scope of the SPS

Agreement, protective measures based on ecocentric worldviews may nevertheless be considered in light of the disciplines set forth by the SPS Agreement.[108] On this account, measures based on ecocentric worldviews are challenged to qualify for approval by rules and disciplines actually designed according to a different, namely anthropocentric, world-conception. According to SPS rules, the challenge to qualify for 'scientificity' has to be accepted by putting forward a risk assessment pursuant to Article 5 of the SPS Agreement. This is why fundamental controversies translate into 'scientific' disputes.[109] However, the transformation of fundamental controversies into scientific disputes seems inappropriate for addressing the former. In particular, examples of WTO disputes over applications of growth hormones to cattle (*EC—Hormones*) and biotechnology in food production (*EC—Biotech*) are showing that the science-based approach of the SPS Agreement is inappropriate to address fundamental controversies between opposing world-conceptions. Rather than addressing underlying fundamental questions, SPS disputes are fought out by emplacing contradictory 'risk assessments'. Thus, risk disputes became proxies for underlying controversies between conflicting worldviews. However, as Tracey Epps observed, 'the SPS Agreement is not the appropriate venue where health is not a concern and disputes turn on public morals and concerns about socio-economic factors, such as maintaining a traditional rural sector'.[110] In fact, when conflicting world-conceptions are at stake, the science-based approach of the SPS Agreement leaves interested parties no alternative than to bend scientific arguments into the shape of respective political agendas.

Notes

1. Marcel Mazoyer and Laurence Roudart, "A History of World Agriculture. From the Neolithic Age to the Current Crisis". Monthly Review Press (2006): 375 *et seq.*
2. John Bellamy Foster and Fred Magdoff, 'Liebig, Marx, and the Depletion of Soil Fertility: Relevance for Today's Agriculture,' in Fred Magdoff, John Bellamy Foster, and Frederick H. Buttel (eds.), *Hungry for Profit. The Agribusiness Threat to Farmers, Food, and the Environment* (Monthly Review Press, 2000), p. 46.
3. John Bellamy Foster and Fred Magdoff, *ibid.* p. 47 (footnote omitted).
4. John Bellamy Foster and Fred Magdoff, *ibid.,* pp. 46–47, with reference to Justus von Liebig's *Letters on Modern Agriculture.*
5. John Bellamy Foster and Fred Magdoff, *ibid.* p. 47 (footnote omitted).

6. John Bellamy Foster and Fred Magdoff, *ibid.* p. 47 (emphasis added).
7. John Bellamy Foster and Fred Magdoff, *ibid.* p. 46.
8. John Bellamy Foster and Fred Magdoff, *ibid.*, p. 46, with reference to Henry Carey's *Principles of Social Science.*
9. Adapted from John H. Perkins, *Geopolitics and the Green Revolution. Wheat, Genes, and the Cold War* (Oxford University Press, 1997), p. 256.
10. John B. Penson, Oral Capps, and C. Parr Rosson III, *Introduction to Agricultural Economics.* 3rd Edition (Prentice Hall, 2002), p. 137.
11. John B. Penson, Oral Capps, and C. Parr Rosson III, *ibid.* p. 522.
12. The law of comparative advantage, first presented by David Ricardo (1772–1823) in his book *On the Principles of Political Economy and Taxation* published in 1817, essentially purports that even states which are less efficient than others may reap gains from trade by exporting goods where their relative or comparative advantage is greatest and import goods where their relative or comparative advantage is least (John B. Penson, Oral Capps, and C. Parr Rosson III, *ibid.* p. 514).
13. Melaku Geboye Desta, *The Law of International Trade in Agricultural Products. From GATT 1947 to the WTO Agreement on Agriculture* (Kluwer Law International, 2002), p. 2 (footnotes omitted).
14. Melaku Geboye Desta, *ibid.* p. 9 (original italics). However, more nuanced voices can also be heard. Cottier and Oesch, for example, pointed out that trade liberalisation of agricultural products alone is not enough: "Trade liberalisation on its own, and without appropriate flanking policies, merely serves a small number of efficient producer countries but does little or nothing for the subsistence of the millions of farmers in a majority of developing countries. The present tools and instruments available in the WTO will need further development much beyond the reduction of tariffs and subsidies to which the rules of the present Agreement on Agriculture are essentially dedicated to" (Thomas Cottier, Matthias Oesch, *International Trade Regulation. Law and Policy in the WTO, the European Union and Switzerland. Cases, Materials and Comments* (Staempfli Publishers, 2005), p. 714).
15. *Ministerial Declaration on the Uruguay Round, (Punta del Este Declaration)*, cited from John Croome, *Reshaping the World Trading System. A history of the Uruguay Round* (World Trade Organization Publication Services, Geneva 1995), Annex, pp. 382–392, in particular p. 387.
16. As already mentioned, the term *quarantine sciences* refers to sciences originally used for establishing risks to human, animal and plant health at border controls, for example toxicology, biochemistry, veterinary sciences and plant sciences. Nowadays, the term *quarantine sciences* commonly

refers more generally to sciences applied in food safety inspections and the control of epizootics and plant diseases.

17. Relevant information was taken from Marcel Mazoyer and Laurence Roudart, *A History of World Agriculture. From the Neolithic Age to the Current Crisis* (Monthly Review Press, 2006), p. 53.
18. Relevant information was taken from Marcel Mazoyer and Laurence Roudart, *A History of World Agriculture. From the Neolithic Age to the Current Crisis* (Monthly Review Press, 2006), p. 54.
19. Marcel Mazoyer and Laurence Roudart, *ibid.* p. 54.
20. Vandana Shiva, *Earth Democracy. Justice, Sustainability, and Peace* (Zed Books, 2005), p. 51.
21. The term 'multifunctionality' is only expressing one particular notion of agriculture in a relativist framework. The functionalism implied in the word 'multifunctionality' shows that the approach of multifunctionality conceives agriculture as performing certain functions in the service of man. This instrumental or anthropocentric view on agriculture differs from ecocentric approaches ascribing intrinsic values to nature, for example the *deep ecology* approach.
22. It shall not be denied that, in fact, segments of the 'rational,' i.e. organic farming movement are inclined to metaphysics. In this respect, one could mention biodynamic agriculture based on the anthroposophical world-conception of Rudolf Steiner (1861–1925), for instance. On the other hand, however, growth-orientation may be far from a 'rational' concept either. Economist Hans Christoph Binswanger, for instance, interpreted modern finance as a contemporary version of the legendary quest for the philosopher's stone. But instead of transforming materials into gold, monetary capital transforms natural resources into more money, thus transcending time and mortality in eternal growth (Hans Christoph Binswanger, *Geld und Magie. Eine ökonomische Deutung von Goethes Faust* (Murmann Verlag, 2005), in particular pp. 120–122. In the real world, however, marvellous capital expansion rather resembles to deception than to magic. Looking at the recent US subprime mortage crisis, for instance, the *TIME* magazine reported:

"As a trader, what you needed was to take a market in which bonds were thinly traded and *magically* fill it with more-tradeable highly rated AAA material. By the *magic* of CDOs [i.e. collateralised debt obligations] you could do just that. CDOs are often created out of the lowest-rated, seldom-traded portions of other bond offerings. And by the mid-2000s most of those bonds were backed by home loans to borrowers with poor credit ratings – toxic waste, in the parlance. Subprime-mortage bonds went into the CDO blender BBB and came out AAA. All of a sudden, traders were making big money" (Stephen Gandel, 'The Case Against Goldman Sachs', in *TIME*, May 3, 2010, p. 24 (emphasis added).

23. In German, there is a distinction between *rational*, meaning 'rational' in the philosophical or epistemological sense, and *rationell*, meaning economically efficient. In fact, one may observe that the term 'rational' has not only lost its role for denoting a particular intellectual orientation, but has reversed its meaning. Today, the term 'rational' usually comes along with an implicit pretence of an 'objective' or 'neutral' stance, thus virtually an intellectual non-position. In the WTO context, the term 'rational' is often used for characterising positions in line with the paramount economic rationale of trade liberalisation and market expansion. In particular, scientific positions in line with the economic rationale are usually those taken up by short-term oriented quarantine sciences and applied sciences. On the other hand, scientific positions which are not corresponding with paramount economic objectives are denounced as being 'non-scientific' or even 'irrational.' Hence, upon closer examination, contemporary uses of the term 'rational' seem to be far from 'objective' or 'neutral'; rather, the word 'rational' carries along economic value judgements. It is precisely the preponderance of an economic rationale which is in the centre of the relativist critique. Relativists do not question risk analysis as a method, but the (mis-)use of risk as an economic paradigm. A critique of the usurpation of risk as an economic paradigm points at the ideology inherent to the economistic risk concept. As shown above, the risk paradigm presumes economic growth as the paramount objective of human activity. In this sense, relativist approaches in risk theory can be understood as a response to objectivist and positivist approaches presuming a 'given' objective to risk and risk analysis, namely expansion of 'rational' activity and economic growth. Because alternative approaches beyond the economistic risk paradigm are criticising the implicit objective of the latter, that is, economic expansion, they are sometimes called 'radical' or 'fundamentalist.' However, from a naïve perspective, one might question the meaning of 'radical.' Is an approach focusing on genuine human values, i.e. common and sustained survival, really 'radical'? Or is the term 'radical' more suitable for characterising allegedly 'objective' and 'rational' approaches presuming that all humans are just one-dimensional *homines oeconomici?*
24. José Lutzenberger, Die selbstmörderische Sinnlosigkeit der modernen Landwirtschaft, in Jerry Mander, Edward Goldsmith (eds.), *Schwarzbuch Globalisierung. Eine fatale Entwicklung mit vielen Verlierern und wenigen Gewinnern* (Riemann Verlag, 2002), pp. 344–345.
25. John Bellamy Foster and Fred Magdoff, 'Liebig, Marx, and the Depletion of Soil Fertility: Relevance for Today's Agriculture,' in Fred Magdoff,

John Bellamy Foster, and Frederick H. Buttel (eds.), *Hungry for Profit. The Agribusiness Threat to Farmers, Food, and the Environment* (Monthly Review Press, 2000), p. 52. In similar ways, also mineral elements are recycled. Mazoyer and Roudart even spoke of a 'balance sheet' with regard to the (re-)cycling of minerals:

"All things considered, over the course of a given period, the fluctuations in the inflow and outflow of minerals in the soil solution are equilibrated according to a sort of balance sheet. On one side are the additions of minerals from several sources (solubility of the parent rock, fixation of atmospheric nitrogen, decomposition of the humus and organic manure, additions of chemical fertilizers) to which it is necessary to add the stock of preexisting minerals. On the other side are the losses of minerals during the period under consideration (drainage, denitrification, recrystallization, removal of minerals through harvests of plant and animal products, and, if need be, the gathering up of animal excrement) and the residual mineral stock" (Marcel Mazoyer and Laurence Roudart, *A History of World Agriculture. From the Neolithic Age to the Current Crisis* (Monthly Review Press, 2006), p. 59).

26. John Bellamy Foster and Fred Magdoff, *ibid.* pp. 52–53.
27. Marcel Mazoyer and Laurence Roudart, *A History of World Agriculture. From the Neolithic Age to the Current Crisis* (Monthly Review Press, 2006), in particular pp. 375–391. With view on recent developments, such as applications of biotechnology (seed modification and animal cloning), nanotechnology and computer sciences in food production, one could speak of a 'third agricultural revolution'. In a report on the integration of nanotechnology, biotechnology, information technology and cognitive science (NBIC), entitled *Converging Technologies for Improving Human Performance*, prospects for 'empirical' agriculture were envisioned as follows:

"Farmers have long appreciated the advantages of science and technology; the convergence of nanotechnology, biotechnology, and information technology could significantly improve their effectiveness. For example, nanoscale genetics may help preserve and control food production. In expensive nano-enabled biosensors could monitor the health and nutrition of cattle, transmitting the data into the farmer's personal computer that advises him about the care the animals need. In the same way, sensors distributed across farmland could advise the farmer about the need for water and fertilizer, thus avoiding wastage and achieving the most profitable acreage crop yield (National Research Council 1997). Bio-nano convergence can provide new ways of actually applying the treatment to the crops, increasing the efficiency of fertilizers and pesticides" (Mihail C. Roco and William Sims Bainbridg (eds.), *Converging Technologies for Improving Human Performance. Nanotechnology, Biotechnology, Information Technology and Cognitive Science.* Joint report of the National Science Foundation (NSF) and the Department of Commerce (Kluwer, 2003), p. 20). For more detail, see Norman Scott and Hongda Chen, *Nanoscale Science and Engineering for Agriculture and Food Systems.* A Report submitted to Cooperative State Research, Education and Extension Service, based on a National Planning Workshop held from November 18–19, 2002, in Washington, DC. (USDA, 2003), in particular pp. 8–11.

28. Marcel Mazoyer and Laurence Roudart, *A History of World Agriculture. From the Neolithic Age to the Current Crisis* (Monthly Review Press, 2006), p. 396. Of increasing importance in this respect are the livestock feed industries.
29. Marcel Mazoyer and Laurence Roudart, *ibid.* p. 396. For example, Mazoyer and Roudart mentioned the manufacturing of salted meats, butter, canned foods, beers, etc., a tendency extending to winemaking, candy, baking, and ready-made meals recently (Marcel Mazoyer and Laurence Roudart, *ibid.*).
30. Marcel Mazoyer and Laurence Roudart, *ibid.* p. 396.
31. Marcel Mazoyer and Laurence Roudart, *ibid.* p. 386.
32. John Bellamy Foster and Fred Magdoff, 'Liebig, Marx, and the Depletion of Soil Fertility: Relevance for Today's Agriculture,' in Fred Magdoff, John Bellamy Foster, and Frederick H. Buttel (eds.), *Hungry for Profit. The Agribusiness Threat to Farmers, Food, and the Environment* (Monthly Review Press, 2000), p, 54.
33. See, for instance, Miguel A. Altieri, 'Ecological Impacts of Industrial Agriculture and the Possibilities for Truly Sustainable Farming,' in Fred Magdoff, John Bellamy Foster, and Frederick H. Buttel (eds.), *Hungry for Profit. The Agribusiness Threat to Farmers, Food, and the Environment* (Monthly Review Press, 2000), 81. Similar conclusions were reached by Ladan Sobhani and Simon Retallack in their study on the role of agriculture in climate change (see Ladan Sobhani and Simon Retallack, Der Weg in die 'Klimakatastrophe,' in Jerry Mander, Edward Goldsmith (eds.), *Schwarzbuch Globalisierung. Eine fatale Entwicklung mit vielen Verlierern und wenigen Gewinnern* (Riemann Verlag, 2002), p. 371. Vandana Shiva provided a productivity analysis showing that "a polyculture system can produce 100 units of food from 5 units of inputs, whereas an industrial system requires 300 units of input to produce the same 100 units. The 295 units of wasted inputs could have provided 5900 units of food" (Vandana Shiva, *Earth Democracy. Justice, Sustainability, and Peace* (Zed Books,

2005), pp. 104–105). Based on findings from productivity analyses, Shiva countered the argument that industrial agriculture is the only way for feeding a growing world population:

"Industrial agriculture as been promoted, financed, and subsidized in spite of the high cost to the environment. The argument used is that these ecological costs are a necessary part of increasing productivity. However, the productivity of industrial agriculture is actually negative. More resources are used as inputs than are produced as outputs. Usually productivity is increased by the implementation of labor displacing machinery and chemicals. However, labor is not the scarce input. Land and water are. If, instead of focusing on labor costs, we take energy, natural resources, and external inputs into account, then industrial agriculture does not have higher productivity than ecological alternatives. Over the last 50 years, the shift from internal input to high external input agriculture has resulted in a 66-fold decrease in productivity. (...) [S]ince resources, not labor, are the limiting actor in food production, it is resource productivity, which is the relevant measure. What is needed is more efficient resource use so that the same resources can feed more people. A 66-fold decrease of food producing capacity in the context of resources use is not an efficient strategy for using limited land, water, and biodiversity to feed the world" (Vandana Shiva, *ibid.,* pp. 104–105).

34. On this note, see, for instance, José Lutzenberger, Die selbstmörderische Sinnlosigkeit der modernen Landwirtschaft, in Jerry Mander, Edward Goldsmith (eds.), *Schwarzbuch Globalisierung. Eine fatale Entwicklung mit vielen Verlierern und wenigen Gewinnern* (Riemann Verlag, 2002), pp. 335–336.
35. Vandana Shiva, *Earth Democracy. Justice, Sustainability, and Peace* (Zed Books, 2005), pp. 51–52.
36. Susette Biber-Klemm and Danuta Szymura Berglas, 'Problems and Goals,' in Susette Biber-Klemm and Thomas Cottier (eds.), *Rights to Plant Genetic Resources and Traditional Knowledge. Basic Issues and Perspectives* (World Trade Institute/CABI, 2006), p. 22.
37. Vandana Shiva, *Earth Democracy. Justice, Sustainability, and Peace* (Zed Books Ltd., London 2005), p. 104.
38. Vandana Shiva, *ibid.* p. 105.
39. Vandana Shiva, *ibid.* p. 105. Shiva extended her analysis to farm income, noting that "[s]mall farms in West Bengal growing 55 different crops gave incomes of 227,312 rupees per acre; a farm with 14 crops gave 94,596 rupees while a monoculture farm brought in only 32,098 rupees per acre" (Vandana Shiva, *ibid.*).

40. Miguel A. Altieri, 'Ecological Impacts of Industrial Agriculture and the Possibilities for Truly Sustainable Farming,' in Fred Magdoff, John Bellamy Foster, and Frederick H. Buttel (eds.), *Hungry for Profit. The Agribusiness Threat to Farmers, Food, and the Environment* (Monthly Review Press, 2000), p. 87.
41. Miguel A. Altieri, *ibid.*
42. Vandana Shiva, *Earth Democracy. Justice, Sustainability, and Peace* (Zed Books, 2005), p. 152. Shiva presented the terms *Bija swaraj* for seed sovereignty and *Anna swaraj* for food sovereignty.
43. Susette Biber-Klemm and Danuta Szymura Berglas, 'Problems and Goals,' in Susette Biber-Klemm and Thomas Cottier (eds.), *Rights to Plant Genetic Resources and Traditional Knowledge. Basic Issues and Perspectives* (World Trade Institute/CABI, 2006), p. 22.
44. Miguel A. Altieri, 'Ecological Impacts of Industrial Agriculture and the Possibilities for Truly Sustainable Farming,' in Fred Magdoff, John Bellamy Foster, and Frederick H. Buttel (eds.), *Hungry for Profit. The Agribusiness Threat to Farmers, Food, and the Environment* (Monthly Review Press, 2000), pp. 88–89.
45. John H. Perkins, *Geopolitics and the Green Revolution. Wheat, Genes, and the Cold War* (Oxford University Press, 1997), pp. 266–267. In the scope of the study at hand, Perkins' observations regarding countries adopting policies for achieving food self-sufficiency are particularly interesting. With reference to case studies considering India, Mexico and the United Kingdom, Perkins noted that countries adopting policies for food self-sufficiency "may continue to do so in the future, despite the ideological assertion that free trade is a better way to go" (John H. Perkins, *ibid.*, p. 267). It may be added that in the wake of the food crisis of 2008, more countries might follow the path towards food self-sufficiency.
46. However, remnants of food restrictions based on cultural or religious considerations may still persist here and there, for example restrictions with regard to alcohol or porcine products.
47. Marcel Mazoyer and Laurence Roudart, *A History of World Agriculture. From the Neolithic Age to the Current Crisis* (Monthly Review Press, 2006), p. 391.
48. Marcel Mazoyer and Laurence Roudart, *ibid.* p. 391.
49. Marie-Hélène Léon, *Grippe Aviaire, ESB… Le Délire Sanitaire. Plaidoyer pour une civilisation de la vie* (L'Harmattan, Paris 2007), p. 90.
50. Marie-Hélène Léon, *ibid.* p. 90. In French, the paragraph describing the model of agro-ecology reads as follows: "Pour se placer dans cette perspective idéal-typique, il convient d'adopter un postulat de base, celui d'accorder de la valeur aux objets, aux êtres, aux éléments, non créés par

l'humanité, sur lesquels elle n'a pas eu d'influence directe quant à leur genèse" (Marie-Hélène Léon, *ibid.*).

51. Marcel Mazoyer and Laurence Roudart, *A History of World Agriculture. From the Neolithic Age to the Current Crisis* (Monthly Review Press, 2006), p. 440.
52. Marcel Mazoyer and Laurence Roudart, *ibid.*
53. Marcel Mazoyer and Laurence Roudart, *ibid.*
54. Vandana Shiva, *Earth Democracy. Justice, Sustainability, and Peace* (Zed Books, 2005), p. 89.
55. Vandana Shiva, *ibid.*
56. Vandana Shiva, *ibid.* p. 90.
57. Vandana Shiva, *ibid.* pp. 153–154.
58. Vandana Shiva, *ibid.* p. 158.
59. Vandana Shiva, *ibid.* p. 156.
60. Vandana Shiva, *ibid.* pp. 156–157.
61. Vandana Shiva, *ibid.* p. 158.
62. Vandana Shiva, *ibid.* p. 157.
63. Vandana Shiva, *ibid.*
64. Vandana Shiva, *ibid.*
65. Vandana Shiva, *ibid.*
66. Marcel Mazoyer and Laurence Roudart, *A History of World Agriculture. From the Neolithic Age to the Current Crisis* (Monthly Review Press, 2006), p. 440.
67. Ulrich Beck, *World Risk Society* (Polity Press, 2005), p. 106. It is interesting to note that the "reflexive consensus" among scientists in the 1970/80ies extended to biological weaponry, an issue commonly excluded from the current GMO debate framed by safety and trade concerns.
68. Mark A. Pollack, and Gregory C. Shaffer, *When Cooperation Fails. The International Law and Politics of Genetically Modified Foods* (Oxford University Press, 2009), p. 45 (footnote omitted).
69. Mark A. Pollack, and Gregory C. Shaffer, *ibid.* p. 45 (original emphasis, footnote omitted).
70. Mark A. Pollack, and Gregory C. Shaffer, *ibid.* p. 46.
71. Mark A. Pollack, and Gregory C. Shaffer, *ibid.* p. 46 (footnotes omitted).
72. Adam D. Sheingate 'Promotion Versus Precaution: The Evolution of Biotechnology Policy in the United States' (2006), 36 *British Journal of Political Science*, 253.
73. Adam D. Sheingate *ibid.*
74. Adam D. Sheingate *ibid.*
75. Mark A. Pollack, and Gregory C. Shaffer, *When Cooperation Fails. The International Law and Politics of Genetically Modified Foods* (Oxford University Press, 2009), p. 47 (footnotes omitted).

76. Mark A. Pollack, and Gregory C. Shaffer, *ibid.* p. 46, citing from the 2004 report of the Pew Initiative on Food and Biotechnology.
77. Mark A. Pollack, and Gregory C. Shaffer, *ibid.* p. 46, citing from the 2004 report of the Pew Initiative on Food and Biotechnology.
78. For a critique of the substantial equivalence—doctrine see, *inter alia*, Alexia Herwig, 'Transnational Governance Regimes for Foods Derived from Bio-Technology and their Legitimacy', in Christian Joerges, Inger-Johanne Sand, and Gunther Teubner (eds.), *Transnational Governance and Constitutionalism* (Hart Publishing, 2004), [pp. 199–222], in particular pp. 221–222. In terms of a conclusion, Herwig found that the application of substantial equivalence to GMO risk assessments "camouflages the normative issues underlying the risk regulation of GMOs in a way that is hardly consistent with the concept of deliberative legitimacy" (Alexia Herwig, *ibid.*, p. 222).
79. Adam D. Sheingate 'Promotion Versus Precaution: The Evolution of Biotechnology Policy in the United States' (2006), 36 *British Journal of Political Science*, 252 (emphasis added).
80. Ulrich Beck, *World Risk Society* (Polity Press, 2005), pp. 106–107.
81. Mark A. Pollack, and Gregory C. Shaffer, *When Cooperation Fails. The International Law and Politics of Genetically Modified Foods* (Oxford University Press, 2009), p. 64.
82. Mark A. Pollack, and Gregory C. Shaffer, *ibid.* p. 64 (footnote omitted). In Britain, the management of the BSE crisis amounted to a PR fiasco for the authorities involved. Pollack and Shaffer observed:

"Within Britain itself, UK scientists continued to reassure the public regarding the lack of BSE risk with information that was soon contradicted. The British Minister of Agriculture even had himself photographed with his four-year old daughter eating hamburgers to demonstrate that British beef was 'perfectly safe' when it turned out that the risk was real and other children died from it" (Mark A. Pollack, and Gregory C. Shaffer, *ibid.* p. 64, footnote omitted).

83. Mark A. Pollack, and Gregory C. Shaffer, *ibid.* p. 60. Thomas Bernauer observed that the DG Environment "opened an important door for environmental and consumer group influence on the European Union's regulatory policy" (Thomas Bernauer, *Genes, Trade, and Regulation. The Seeds of Conflict in Food Biotechnology* (Princeton University Press, 2003), p. 79).
84. Mark A. Pollack, and Gregory C. Shaffer, *ibid.* p. 59.

85. One factor particularly stressed by Pollack and Shaffer consisted of the fact that the US legal system, in contrast to European legal systems, relies on tort liability and class actions. Pollack and Shaffer observed:

"The US legal system imposes *tort liability* on producers whose products cause harm, which can lead to substantial damage awards. The US legal system couples these liability rules with procedures that facilitate the bringing of lawsuits. 'Class action' procedures initiated by entrepreneurial attorneys and individual claims financed on a 'contingency fee' basis, facilitate the ability of parties with less income to bring legal claims. These liability rules and legal procedures create market incentives for sellers of GM products in the US to take precautions. (…) European legal systems, in contrast, generally neither provide for significant tort damage awards, nor for analogous procedures that facilitate individual and class action law suits. It is thus not surprising that European regulators take a more stringent regulatory approach on account of their greater responsibility for any potential harm that could occur" (Mark A. Pollack, and Gregory C. Shaffer, *ibid.* p. 53, original emphasis).

Whereas Pollock and Shaffer emphasised differences between common law and civil law systems, they rejected simplistic characterisations of "either the US or the EU as the more risk-averse beyond the context of agricultural biotechnology" (Mark A. Pollack, and Gregory C. Shaffer, *ibid.* p. 42). In terms of a summary of various reasons for different approaches in the US and the EU for regulating green biotechnology, Pollack and Shaffer concluded: "We believe that the best explanation for these enduring differences [between the US and Europe] is that US and European interest groups have pursued their interests within existing institutional and cultural contexts that, together with contingent events, provided opportunities as well as constraints, to define issues and frame perceptions of GM foods in different ways" (Mark A. Pollack, and Gregory C. Shaffer, *ibid.* p. 76).

86. Mark A. Pollack, and Gregory C. Shaffer, *ibid.* p. 60 (footnote omitted).
87. In the following, the focus is on Directive 90/220 on the deliberate release of GMOs and on Regulation 258/97 on GMO foods, thus letting aside Directive 90/219 on the contained use of GMOs.
88. Mark A. Pollack, and Gregory C. Shaffer, *When Cooperation Fails. The International Law and Politics of Genetically Modified Foods* (Oxford University Press, 2009), p. 60 (original emphases).
89. The summary of the rules of procedure governing the approval of biotech products under Directive 90/220 are mainly taken from Mark A. Pollack, and Gregory C. Shaffer, *ibid.* pp. 60–62.
90. Mark A. Pollack, and Gregory C. Shaffer, *ibid.* p. 62.
91. Mark A. Pollack, and Gregory C. Shaffer, *ibid.* p. 63.

92. Mark A. Pollack, and Gregory C. Shaffer, *ibid.* p. 63 (footnote omitted).
93. Mark A. Pollack, and Gregory C. Shaffer, *ibid.* p. 63.
94. Mark A. Pollack, and Gregory C. Shaffer, *ibid.* p. 63. Pollock and Shafer were eager to add that they did "not use the term 'politicized' in a derogatory way". Indeed, Pollock and Shaffer accounted for views considering "that the European approach is more 'democratic', as opposed to a US technocratic approach". Hence, the major focus of Pollock and Shaffer was to demonstrate that, "from an institutional perspective, the regulation of GM foods and crops in Europe has been channelled through a political process more than a purely administrative one" (Mark A. Pollack, and Gregory C. Shaffer, *ibid.* pp. 63–64).
95. Joost Pauwelyn, for instance, introduced the terms "European Absolutism' and 'American Voluntarism' for approaching the phenomenon (see Joost Pauwelyn, *Optimal Protection of International Law. Navigating between European Absolutism and American Voluntarism* (Cambridge University Press, 2008), in particular pp. 16–25).
96. Mark A. Pollack, and Gregory C. Shaffer, *ibid.* p. 59.
97. Recently, however, the EU Commission seems of changing its approach towards GMOs. In particular, the competence for GMOs shifted from the rather GM-sceptical Environmental Commissioner Stavros Dimas to the Commissioner for Health & Consumers, John Dalli (Steffi Ober, 'Dalli, Dalli—Die neue EU-Kommission setzt auf Gentechnik', in *umwelt aktuell*, Mai 2010, p. 15. The new regulatory framework of the EU concerning GMOs basically consists of three main legal texts: (1) Directive 2001/18/EC on the deliberate release of GMOs into the environment (replacing Directive 90/220/EEC), (2) Regulation 1829/2003/EC on GM food and feed (replacing Regulation 258/97), and (3) Regulation 1830/3003/EC on traceability and labelling of GMOs and food and feed produced thereof.
98. Providing examples of political inference, Pollack and Shaffer observed that "[t]he executive branch is periodically accused of using these agencies for political purposes, as when a senior USDA economist came under fire 'for suggesting that the Bush administration could maximize votes in key dairy states by keeping milk prices high through the election', or when EPA political appointees are accused of suppressing scientific studies showing global warming trends, arsenic levels in water, or particulate concentrations in air" (Mark A. Pollack, and Gregory C. Shaffer, *When Cooperation Fails. The International Law and Politics of Genetically Modified Foods* (Oxford University Press, 2009), p. 52, footnotes omitted).
99. Examples of political inference by the legislative branch are the Delaney Clause and the debate about saccharin. The Delaney Clause was an amendment introduced in 1958 to the Food, Drugs and Cosmetic Act

which forbade any food additive found to induce cancer during laboratory and/or animal testing. Because the amendment did not rely on threshold levels but ruled out carcinogens even at minuscule levels, the Delaney Clause "was opposed even by the FDA and many scientists" (William Patrick, *The Food and Drug Administration* (Chelsea House Publishers, 1988), pp. 38–39). In 1972, the USDA intended to ban saccharin because of alleged carcinogenicity, but US Congress passed special legislation for keeping saccharin on the market (National Research Council, *Risk Assessment in the Federal Government: Managing the Process* (National Academy Press, 1983), p. 14).

100. Mark A. Pollack, and Gregory C. Shaffer, *When Cooperation Fails. The International Law and Politics of Genetically Modified Foods* (Oxford University Press, 2009), pp. 51–52 (original footnotes omitted).
101. Marsha A. Echols, *Food Safety and the WTO. The Interplay of Culture, Science and Technology* (Kluwer Law International, 2001), p. 37.
102. Marsha A. Echols, *ibid.* p. 37. Thomas Bernauer emphasised the predominant role played by the agribusiness in shaping US regulatory policy (see Thomas Bernauer, *Genes, Trade, and Regulation. The Seeds of Conflict in Food Biotechnology* (Princeton University Press, 2003), p. 94–100.
103. This conclusion is, of course, not limited to the US and the EU. Turkey, for instance, is challenged by its position between the GMO-critical EU and the GMO-friendly US. In this respect, Zeynep Kivilcim observed that

"… [T]he decision on the adoption of agrobiotechnology was not motivated by the needs of Turkish farmers or oriented to the concerns of consumers. The administrative authorities were constrained by pressure from multinational agrobiotechnology companies.

The regulatory work on agrobiotechnology in Turkey and the position of Turkish delegations during the negotiations for international treaties on biosafety are closely followed by American authorities. Interviews with Turkish officials reveal that the US Department of Agriculture and the American Embassy organize briefings or sometimes visits to the USA for concerned Turkish ministerial officials and Members of parliament in order to communicate the benefits of the use of modern biotechnology in agriculture. (…) This pressure is real and effective. However, the Turkish government has also to fulfil its legal obligations under the Cartagena Protocol on Biosafety. Furthermore, EU membership is a political priority and the EU Member countries are the main importers of Turkey's agricultural products. Hence, the adoption of the community legal framework in the field of agriculture is a constant strain on the Turkish authorities" (Zeynep Kivilcim, 'The Legal Framework for Agrobiotechnology in Turkey: The Challenges to the Implementation of the Precautionary Principle,' in Karapinar, Baris, Adaman,

Fikret, and Ozertan Gokhan (eds.), *Rethinking Structural Reform in Turkish Agriculture: Beyond the World Bank's Strategy* (Nova Science Publishers, 2010), [pp. 265–280], p. 277.

104. In this respect, Marsha Echols noted that "[t]he United States and its principal consumer organizations had been leaders in the campaign for the science-based *SPS Agreement*" (Marsha A. Echols, *Food Safety and the WTO. The Interplay of Culture, Science and Technology* (Kluwer Law International, 2001), p. 37, footnote no. 59).
105. Tim Josling, Donna Roberts and David Orden, *Food Regulation and Trade. Toward a Safe and Open Global System* (Institute for International Economics, 2004), footnote no. 8, pp. 43–44. Josling et al. added that "[s]ubsequent efforts by Codex to translate these principles into more specific guidance have achieved some progress, but fundamental differences in approaches to risk management are still evident ..." (Tim Josling et al., *ibid.*).
106. Elizabeth Fisher, 'Beyond the Science/Democracy Dichotomy: The World Trade organisation Sanitary and Phytosanitary Agreement and Administrative Constitutionalism', in Christian Joerges and Ernst-Ulrich Petersmann (eds.), *Constitutionalism, Multilevel Trade Governance and Social Regulation* (Hart Publishing, 2006), [pp. 327–349], p. 345 (footnotes omitted).
107. Vandana Shiva, *Earth Democracy. Justice, Sustainability, and Peace* (Zed Books, 2005), p. 158.
108. In particular, the scope of the SPS Agreement was significantly broadened by the panel in *EC—Biotech* considering that GMOs are covered by the SPS Agreement and by establishing strict requirements for the applicability of the Cartagena Protocol in trade disputes. With respect to the broad interpretation of the scope of the SPS Agreement by case law, Lukasz Gruszczynski noted that,

"[a]s a consequence of the broad interpretation of the conditions pertaining to its applicability, the Agreement appears to cover different regulatory measures, some of them exceeding traditional SPS risks. In particular, indirect risks as well as some environmental risks, which are reducible to animal and plant life and health and which result from the entry, establishment and spread of pests, proved to constitute an SPS risk" (Lukasz Gruszczynski, Regulating Health and Environmental Risks under WTO Law. A Critical Analysis of the SPS Agreement (Oxford University Press, 2010), p. 71).

109. It is not denied that most WTO disputes are motivated by more tangible interests than philosophical world-conceptions. The aim of the study at

hand is, however, to demonstrate that by focusing on tangible interests only, underlying causes of WTO disputes can hardly be understood, yet settled.

110. Tracey Epps, International Trade and Health Protection. A Critical Assessment of the WTO's SPS Agreement (Edward Elgar, 2008), p. 305.

References

Altieri, Miguel A. "Ecological Impacts of Industrial Agriculture and the Possibilities for Truly Sustainable Farming". Published in Fred Magdoff, John Bellamy Foster and Frederick H. Buttel (eds.), *Hungry for Profit. The Agribusiness Threat to Farmers, Food, and the Environment.* NY: Monthly Review Press, 2000, 77–92.

Beck, Ulrich. "World Risk Society". *Polity Press in association with Blackwell Publishers*, 2005 (first published 1999).

Bernauer, Thomas "Genes, Trade, and Regulation. The Seeds of Conflict in Food Biotechnology". *Princeton University Press*, 2003.

Biber-Klemm, Susette, and Berglas, Danuta Szymura. "Problems and Goals". Published in Susette Biber-Klemm and Thomas Cottier (eds.), *Rights to Plant Genetic Resources and Traditional Knowledge. Basic Issues and Perspective.* World Trade Institute and CABI, 2006, 3–55.

Binswanger, Hans Christoph. "Geld und Magie. Eine ökonomische Deutung von Goethes Faust". *Murmann Verlag*, 2005 (2nd edition).

Cottier, Thomas, and Oesch, Matthias. "International Trade Regulation. Law and Policy in the WTO, the European Union and Switzerland. Cases, Materials and Comments". *Staempfli Publishers*, 2005.

Desta, Melaku Geboye. "The Law of International Trade in Agricultural Products. From GATT 1947 to the WTO Agreement on Agriculture". *Kluwer Law International*, 2002.

Croome, John. "Reshaping the World Trading System. A history of the Uruguay Round". *World Trade Organization Publication Services*, 1995.

Echols, Marsha A. "Food Safety and the WTO. The Interplay of Culture, Science and Technology". Kluwer Law International, 2001.

Epps, Tracey. "International Trade and Health Protection. A Critical Assessment of the WTO's SPS Agreement". Edward Elgar, 2008.

Fisher, Elizabeth. "Beyond the Science/Democracy Dichotomy: The World Trade Organisation Sanitary and Phytosanitary Agreement and Administrative Constitutionalism". Published in Christian Joerges and Ernst-Ulrich Petersmann (eds.), *Constitutionalism, Multilevel Trade Governance and Social Regulation.* Hart Publishing, 2006, 327–349.

Foster, John Bellamy and Magdoff, Fred. "Liebig, Marx, and the Depletion of Soil Fertility: Relevance for Today's Agriculture". Published in Fred Magdoff, John Bellamy Foster and Frederick H. Buttel (eds.), *Hungry for Profit. The Agribusiness Threat to Farmers, Food, and the Environment.* Monthly Review Press, New York 2000, 43–60.

Gandel, Stephen. "The Case Against Goldman Sachs". *TIME*, May 3, 2010, 24.

Josling, Tim, Roberts, Donna, Orden, David. "Food Regulation and Trade. Toward a Safe and Open Global System". *Institute for International Economics*, 2004.

Kivilcim, Zeynep. "The Legal Framework for Agrobiotechnology in Turkey: The Challenges to the Implementation of the Precautionary Principle". Published in Baris Karapinar, Fikret Adaman, and Gokhan Ozertan (eds.), *Rethinking Structural Reform in Turkish Agriculture: Beyond the World Bank's Strategy.* Nova Science Publishers, 2010, 265–280.

Léon, Marie-Hélène. "Grippe Aviaire, ESB... Le Délire Sanitaire. Plaidoyer pour une civilisation de la vie". *L'Harmattan*, 2007.

Lutzenberger, José. "Die selbstmörderische Sinnlosigkeit der modernen Landwirtschaft". Published in Jerry Mander and Edward Goldsmith (eds.), *Schwarzbuch Globalisierung. Eine fatale Entwicklung mit vielen Verlierern und wenigen Gewinnern.* Original title: *The Case against the Global Economy.* Earthscan Publications, 2001. German translation by Helmut Dierlamm and Ursel Schäfer. *Riemann Verlag*, 2002, 327–354.

Mazoyer, Marcel and Roudart, Laurence. "A History of World Agriculture. From the Neolithic Age to the Current Crisis". Translated from the French original by James H. Membrez. *Monthly Review Press*, 2006.

National Research Council. "Risk Assessment in the Federal Government: Managing the Process". *National Academy Press*, 1983.

Ober, Steffi. "Dalli, Dalli – Die neue EU-Kommission setzt auf Gentechnik". *umwelt aktuell*, Mai 2010, 15. Accessed December 19, 2010. http://www.eu-koordination.de/PDF/ua2010-05.pdf.

Patrick, William. "The Food and Drug Administration". (Know your government – Series). *Chelsea House Publishers*, 1988.

Pauwelyn, Joost. "Optimal Protection of International Law. Navigation between European Absolutism and American Voluntarism". *Cambridge University Press*, 2008.

Penson, John B., Capps, Oral and Rosson, C. Parr. "Introduction to Agricultural Economics". *Prentice Hall*, 2002, 3rd edition.

Perkins, John H. "Geopolitics and the Green Revolution. Wheat, Genes, and the Cold War". *Oxford University Press*, 1997.

Pollack, Mark A. and Shaffer, Gregory C. "When Cooperation Fails. The International Law and Politics of Genetically Modified Foods". *Oxford University Press*, 2009.

Roco, Mihail C. and Bainbridg, William Sims (eds.). "Converging Technologies for Improving Human Performance. Nanotechnology, Biotechnology, Information Technology and Cognitive Science". Joint report of the National Science Foundation (NSF) and the Department of Commerce. *Kluwer Academic Publishers*, 2003. Accessed December 22, 2010. http://www.wtec.org/ConvergingTechnologies/Report/NBIC_report.pdf.

Scott, Norman and Chen, Hongda. "Nanoscale Science and Engineering for Agriculture and Food Systems". A Report submitted to Cooperative State Research, Education and Extension Service, based on a National Planning Workshop held from November 18–19, 2002, in Washington, DC. *USDA*, 2003. Accessed December 22, 2010. http://www.nseafs.cornell.edu/web.roadmap.pdf.

Shiva, Vandana. "Earth Democracy. Justice, Sustainability, and Peace". *Zed Books*, 2005.

Sobhani, Ladan and Retallack, Simon. "Der Weg in die 'Klimakatastrophe'". Published in Jerry Mander and Edward Goldsmith, (eds.), *Schwarzbuch Globalisierung. Eine fatale Entwicklung mit vielen Verlierern und wenigen Gewinnern*. Original title: *The Case against the Global Economy*. Earthscan Publications, 2001 German translation by Helmut Dierlamm and Ursel Schäfer. *Riemann Verlag*, 2002, 365–385.

PART II

The Science-Based Approach of the SPS Agreement in Particular

In Part II, the science-based approach of the SPS Agreement will be examined. The science-based approach of the SPS Agreement is considered as a particular application of the doctrine of separating facts and values in risk assessment. The science-based approach of the SPS Agreement is perceived as an expression of the positivist belief that science is 'objective' and 'value-neutral', and therefore, an appropriate arbiter in trade disputes. Analysing the jurisdiction of panels and the Appellate Body in selected SPS cases, it is shown that panels have tried to establish a rather positivist interpretation of 'science' and 'risk assessment'. The Appellate Body, on the other hand, has tried to find some middle ground between a positivist and a relativist interpretation of SPS provisions. In terms of a conclusion, it is shown that the application of the science-based approach has led to a resurfacing of problems known from epistemology.

CHAPTER 7

A Promise for Objectivity

1 Freer Trade in Agricultural Products

In historical perspective, the Agreement on the Application of Sanitary and Phytosanitary Measures (SPS Agreement) may be understood as a flanking element in the negotiations about the role of agriculture in the world trading system. In this respect, agriculture has always been a special issue in trade negotiations. Thomas Cottier and Matthias Oesch observed:

> For cultural, political and other non-economic reasons, the farming sector of some industrialised counties has long failed to adapt its structure to the shift in the supply-demand relationship. Agricultural production in many countries, in particular Western Europe, largely remained in the hands of small family businesses. They tend to be less efficient, more labour-intensive and more fraught with risk than the large scale production methods and corporate structures prevalent in other economic sectors. Often, nature and topography impose hardships and exert limitations on structural adjustment towards larger scale operations. Moreover, farmers' political influence in most countries reflects longstanding traditions in society and has remained disproportionately high compared to their demographic and economic share.[1]

Although the GATT 1947 attempted to initiate trade liberalisation also in the field of agriculture, respective disciplines remained tenuous. Both big players, the European Economic Community (EEC) as well as the United States (US), pursued protectionist agricultural policies. The EEC established its heavily subsidised Common Agricultural Policy (CAP), and the

M. Burkard, *Conflicting Philosophies and International Trade Law*,
Philosophy, Public Policy, and Transnational Law,
https://doi.org/10.1007/978-3-319-61067-2_7

US obtained a waiver virtually exempting US agricultural policies from GATT disciplines. Furthermore, the possibility to veto the establishment of panels, to inhibit the adoption of reports and to obstruct implementation, left agricultural policies under the GATT 1947 system weak.[2]

The WTO Agreement on Agriculture (AoA), negotiated during the Uruguay Round, explicitly addresses agriculture as an issue of multilateral trade regulation. In essence, the AoA subdued agriculture under the same regulatory principles as other goods. This change of agriculture from a national prerogative to an issue of multilateral trade regulation is also referred to as 'commodification' of agriculture and its products. The main legal tool for achieving the objective of commodification was the requirement to convert quantitative restrictions into bound tariffs, a process called 'tariffication'.[3] Although states still have some room for manoeuvre within their respective tariff bands, the AoA significantly restricted the capacity of states to protect their agricultural markets. National stakeholders in agriculture found themselves virtually locked into a system whereby higher levels of protection for respective agricultural markets than those agreed on during the Uruguay Round had faded away. In this situation, the only safeguard for reintroducing protection for national agricultural markets are trade restrictions justified on sanitary or phytosanitary grounds.

However, in order to avoid a shifting of quantitative restrictions in particular to protectionist measures disguised as sanitary and phytosanitary measures, the SPS Agreement was established in conjunction with the AoA. In this regard, Lukasz Gruszczynski noted that '[t]here was a compelling fear among the negotiators that liberalization of international trade in the agricultural sector, which was an important item of the Uruguay Round, could be undermined by the increased recourse of the countries to SPS measures'.[4]

The paramount objective of the SPS Agreement is to discern sanitary and phytosanitary measures (SPS measures) necessary for the protection of life and health of humans, animals and plants, on the one hand, from protectionist measures disguised as SPS measures, on the other hand. In other words, '[T]he SPS Agreement was considered necessary to avoid the replacement of the pre-WTO agricultural protectionism with new protectionist measures, particularly health and sanitary requirements'.[5]

The palpable fear of negotiators was that the specific objective of the Uruguay Round, namely to integrate agricultural products under the general GATT/WTO regime of tariff reductions and subsidy cutbacks by way of establishing the Agreement on Agriculture (AoA), could be jeopardised. As John Croome noted:

> Imported agricultural products, like domestic produce, must be safe and free from diseases and pests. Moreover, its is accepted that countries should play safe: if there is real doubt whether imports might bring – for instance – a cattle disease or a plant pest into a country or region free from that disease or pest, then those imports may be banned. However, just because sanitary and phytosanitary measures are applied everywhere, and public fears about food safety, in particular, are easily aroused, they are open to misuse as barrier against competition from imports. With the Uruguay Round expected to reduce tariffs and subsidies affecting agricultural trade, there was a danger that countries would be tempted to make increased used of SPS measures as an alternative form of protection.[6]

More specifically, with view on particular GATT disputes, there were also misgivings that governments could give into pressure by consumer groups against technically modified foods, such as hormone-treated meat and genetically modified organisms (GMOs). In this respect, John Croome observed:

> There was also concern, reinforced by some specific disputes brought to GATT that, in response to consumer of other pressures, governments might introduce SPS measures to ban imports produced with the use of particular techniques or ingredients about which fears had, *without scientific justification*, been aroused.[7]

In a nutshell, the SPS Agreement may be perceived as a safeguard for the promise contained in the Agreement on Agriculture, that is, to improve market access for agricultural products. The relationship between liberalisation of trade in agriculture and the SPS Agreement was summarised by ministers at the Punta del Este meeting in 1986, launching the Uruguay Round. Considering agriculture, the *Ministerial Declaration on the Uruguay Round* stated:

> The CONTRACTING PARTIES agree that there is an urgent need to bring more discipline and predictability to world agricultural trade by correcting and preventing restrictions and distortions (…).
>
> Negotiations shall aim to achieve greater liberalization of trade in agriculture and bring all measures affecting import access and export competition under

> strengthened and more operationally effective GATT rules and disciplines, taking into account the general principles governing the negotiations, by:
>
> (i) improving market access through, inter alia, the reduction of import barriers;
> (ii) ...
> (iii) minimizing the adverse effects that sanitary and phytosanitary regulations and barriers can have on trade in agriculture, taking into account the relevant international agreements.[8]

Marsha Echols summarised the promise for more objective regulation of international food trade, as implied in the SPS Agreement, as follows:

> The Agreement on the Application of Sanitary and Phytosanitary Measures (...) resolves the culture/commerce conflict in favor of commercial manufacturers, business consumers and many ordinary purchasers by protecting tariff concessions, particularly those made in the Agreement on Agriculture. This balance benefits consumers and businesses alike, according to economists from David Ricardo through Paul Samuelson and others. Consequently, import bans, health-related product standards, quarantine, testing and other requirements based only on local perceptions of what is safe to eat are unacceptable. The balance in favor of commerce was hailed at the signing of the General Agreement on Tariffs and Trade (...) and the 1995 Agreement Establishing the World Trade Organization (...) by trade experts and others, including many developing countries that had faced sanitary restrictions on their exports of fish, peanuts and other products.[9]

2 Deference to Science

The tool for achieving the objective of restricting food safety as a pretext for disguised protectionism was the deference to science. The SPS Agreement 'makes scientific principles and analysis the only valid basis for a permanent food safety measure, thereby limiting the ability of a government to place its citizens' cultural or religious beliefs about food above international commerce'.[10] The requirement for scientific justification turns the SPS Agreement into a preservative for tariff concessions, 'particularly those made in the Agreement on Agriculture'.[11]

By invoking scientific principles for preserving tariff concessions, the SPS Agreement was characterised as being 'a legal turning point'.[12] Marsha Echols noted:

> Its science-based rules displace centuries of food traditions and national attitudes toward food and food safety. The extent of this legal incursion into the cultural, psychological and sociological arena continues to evolve, as governments struggle in various *fora* to test and define the remaining sovereignty, as well as the nature and scope of the required underpinnings for food safety measures.[13]

The science-based approach, together with the requirement to base SPS measures on international standards (Article 3.1 of the SPS Agreement) shifted regulatory powers to international standard setting organisations. In particular to the Codex Alimentarius Commission, the World Organisation for Animal Health (OIE),[14] and the framework of the International Plant Protection Convention (IPPC). Because standards developed by these international bodies are presumed to be scientifically justified (Article 3.1 of the SPS Agreement), it is rather difficult for national governments to introduce or maintain higher levels of protection (Article 3.3 of the SPS Agreement).

The SPS Agreement marks a shift from the rule-based approach of the two-pronged test of GATT Article XX to a science-based approach. Instead of asking whether an SPS measure is 'necessary', the first question under the SPS Agreement is whether the SPS measures are scientifically justified. Only if this first question is answered in the affirmative, a second set of questions asks whether the measure at issue is consistent with general GATT/WTO rules and principles (consistency, trade-restrictiveness, etc.).

A prerequisite for scientific justification is that an SPS measure is 'based on' a risk assessment. The SPS Agreement provides for two distinguished types of risk assessments, one considering pests and diseases, and the other focusing on food safety in the narrow sense. Additionally, the SPS Agreement provides for simplified risk assessment procedures in cases where scientific evidence is insufficient (Article 5.7 of the SPS Agreement).

The first type of risk assessment is addressing risks from animal diseases and plant pests. This first type of risk assessment is defined by the first clause of Annex A(4) of the SPS Agreement as follows:

> Risk assessment – The evaluation of the likelihood of entry, establishment or spread of a pest or disease within the territory of an importing Member (...) (emphasis added).

The Appellate Body in the case *EC—Hormones* clarified that 'likelihood' has to be understood as 'probability', i.e. 'a higher degree or a threshold of potentiality or possibility'.[15]

The Panel in the case *Australia—Salmon* found that a 'risk assessment' in the sense of the first definition of Annex A(4) of the SPS Agreement

> (...) not only has to state that there is a *possibility* of the disease of concern being introduced into Australia when imports of the salmon products further examined would be allowed, but also needs to provide some evaluation or estimation of the likelihood or probability, expressed either qualitatively or quantitatively, of these diseases thus being introduced and of the associated biological and economic consequences then occurring. In our view, the SPS Agreement does not require that such evaluation needs to be done quantitatively. Moreover, we consider that this requirement on *how* a risk assessment should *evaluate* risk does not at all imply that a risk assessment in accordance with Article 5.1 needs to demonstrate a certain magnitude or threshold *level* or *degree* of risk (expressed either quantitatively or qualitatively).[16]

The Appellate Body in the case *Australia—Salmon* agreed with the Panel that a risk assessment does not require a quantitative evaluation of the probability of adverse effects occurring and that the 'likelihood may be expressed either quantitatively or qualitatively'.[17] Furthermore and in line with the Panel, the Appellate Body confirmed its statement expressed in the case *EC—Hormones* 'that there is no requirement for a risk assessment to establish a certain magnitude or threshold level of degree of risk'.[18]

The second type of risk assessment is addressing food (and feed) safety risks in the narrow sense, i.e. so-called food-borne risks. This second type of risk assessment is defined by the second clause of Annex A(4) of the SPS Agreement as follows:

> Risk assessment – (...) the evaluation of the *potential* for adverse effects on human or animal health arising from the presence of additives, contaminants, toxins or disease-causing organisms in food, beverages or feedstuffs (emphasis added).

The Appellate Body in the case *EC—Hormones* explained that 'the ordinary meaning of "potential" relates to "possibility" and is different from the ordinary meaning of "probability"'.[19]

However, beside the differences outlined in Annex A(4) of the SPS Agreement, both types of risk assessments are following the same principles of the SPS Agreement. These are, essentially, the requirements outlined in Article 5 of the SPS Agreement for proper 'risk assessments'. Article 5 of the SPS Agreement, in turn, is based upon basic rights and obligations (Article 2 of the SPS Agreement). At the heart of the basic rules and obligations is paragraph 2 of Article 2 of the SPS Agreement, requiring, inter alia, 'that any sanitary or phytosanitary measure … is based on scientific principles and is not maintained without sufficient scientific evidence…'

Additionally, the SPS Agreement offers a presumption of justification for measures which 'conform to' international standards.[20] Literally, the SPS Agreement provides that SPS measures 'which conform to international standards, guidelines or recommendations shall be deemed to be necessary to protect human, animal or plant life or health, and presumed to be consistent with the relevant provisions of this Agreement and the GATT 1994' (Article 3.2 of the SPS Agreement).[21] In consequence, risk assessments are most critical in cases where governments intend to establish SPS measures resulting in higher levels of sanitary protection than would be achieved by measures based on the relevant international standard. For such cases, i.e. where governments are intending to establish higher levels of sanitary protection, the SPS Agreement requires, in essence, a scientific justification (Article 3.3 of the SPS Agreement).[22]

In the end, reliance on scientific principles and scientific justification is the underlying rationale of the SPS Agreement. Whether governments are basing SPS measures on international standards, or are opting for higher levels of protection: either way, 'science' is chosen to determine whether an SPS measures is justified or not. In the first instance, international standards are presumed to be scientifically sound, and for higher levels of protection, scientific justification is required. Or, as Marsha Echols puts it:

> The SPS Agreement obligates governments to rely on scientific evidence in the development of a sanitary measure and makes scientifically confirmed risk the only acceptable justification for a permanent SPS measure. A risk assessment is integral to these requirements. Scientific principles and science, as opposed to tradition, are assumed to provide certainty and objectivity.[23]

At first view, the text of the SPS Agreement seems to be quite clear. Any SPS measures must be 'based on' a risk assessment and on scientific evidence and not maintained without scientific justification. However, a closer look reveals some inherent ambiguities. For example, the text of the SPS Agreement did not express whether risk assessments must assess risks quantitatively or whether qualitative risk assessments are sufficient. And what does 'based on science' really mean? What is the notion of science implied in the SPS Agreement? Because the negotiators of the SPS Agreement wisely refrained from defining basic terms such as science and risk, it was upon panels and the Appellate Body to do so. However, by approaching fundamental questions related to science and risk, panels and the Appellate Body were challenged by allegedly banned epistemological ambiguities.

3 Resurfacing Swamplands

First, the SPS Agreement does not define the term 'science' directly.[24] However, from the wording of paragraph 1 of Annex A of the SPS Agreement, which circumscribes sanitary and phytosanitary (SPS) measures and the hazards against which the SPS measures shall protect, one can draw some conclusions with regard to the scientific disciplines potentially involved in examining these hazards.

Paragraph 1 of Annex A of the SPS Agreement specifies the following hazards:

(a) '(...) pests, diseases, disease-carrying organisms or disease-causing organisms';
(b) '(...) additives, contaminants, toxins or disease-causing organisms in foods, beverages or feedstuffs';
(c) '(...) diseases carried by animals, plants or products thereof, or from the entry, establishment or spread of pests',
(d) '(...) other damage ... from pests'.

Basically, paragraph 1 of Annex A of the SPS Agreement refers to animal diseases, plant pests and food additives and food-borne hazards, which can be summarised as 'quarantine hazards'. Considering the scientific disciplines able for ascertaining such hazards, one has to refer to physical sciences in the field, e.g. chemistry, biochemistry, biology, molecular and microbiology, plant physiology, veterinary medicine, food sciences, etc.

Henceforth, the range of physical sciences able for ascertaining quarantine hazards, as addressed by the SPS Agreement, is referred to as the *numerus clausus* of 'quarantine sciences'.[25]

Therefore, referring to the wording of the Appellate Body in *EC—Hormones*,[26] the hazards mentioned in paragraph 1 of Annex A of the SPS Agreement seem to be 'matters (…) susceptible of quantitative analysis by the (…) the physical sciences'.

The Panel, on the one hand, revealed its perception of 'science' by contrasting the '*scientific* examination of data and factual studies' in a risk assessment procedure with the '*policy* exercise involving social value judgements made by political bodies' in the process of risk management.[27] The Panel described the risk management phase as involving 'non-scientific considerations, such as social value judgements'.[28]

The contrasting of the scientific realm of risk assessment with the non-scientific policy space of risk management indicates that the Panel discerned 'science' from 'policy' and 'scientific examinations of data and factual studies' from 'non-scientific social value judgements'.

Based on its differentiation between scientific risk assessment and policy-driven risk management, the Panel considered that reports of political bodies 'which *evaluate* the scientific and other reports submitted to them, are not part of the *risk assessment* process, but of the *risk management* process (…)'.[29] Hence, the Panel did not recognise several reports of the European Parliament[30] and of the EC Economic and Social Committee[31] as 'risk assessments'.

On the other hand, the reasoning of the Appellate Body seemed of having emanated from a broader view of 'science' compared to that of the Panel. In this respect, the following statement of the Appellate Body with regard to the Panel's observations on risk assessment shall be recalled: '… [T]o the extent that the Panel purports to exclude from the scope of a risk assessment in the sense of Article 5.1 all matters not susceptible of quantitative analysis by the empirical or experimental laboratory methods commonly associated with the physical sciences, we believe that the Panel is in error'.[32] The Appellate Body continued to explain that '[s]ome of the kinds of factors listed in Article 5.2 such as "relevant processes and production methods" and "relevant inspection, sampling and testing methods" are not necessarily or wholly susceptible of investigation according to laboratory methods of, for example, biochemistry or pharmacology'.[33] Then, the Appellate Body stressed 'that the risk that is to be evaluated in a risk assessment under Article 5.1 is not only risk ascertainable in a science laboratory operating under strictly controlled conditions, but risk in human societies as they actually exist (…)'.[34]

It is this broader notion of science which might have contributed, among other reasons, to the Appellate Body's rejection of the Panel's concept of separating 'scientific' risk assessment from policy-driven risk management. In line with its broader perception of science, the Appellate Body concluded that the Panel's exclusion of general control problems, e.g. problems of abuse of veterinary drugs, from the scope of application of Article 5.1 and 5.2 of the SPS Agreement, amounted to 'a fundamental legal error'.[35] Hence, from the perspective of the Appellate Body, the Panel's exclusion of problems related to the deficient administration of veterinary drugs from the scope of risk assessment in the sense of Article 5 of the SPS Agreement and their transferral to the risk management phase would effect in 'a more restrictive interpretation of "risk assessment" than is justified by the actual terms of Article 5.2, Article 8 and Annex C of the *SPS Agreement*'.[36]

From the diverging statements of the Panel, on the one hand, and the Appellate Body, on the other hand, one can conclude that the latter adopted a more inclusive approach towards the notion of science than the former. According to the Appellate Body, not only quantitative analysis provided by physical sciences should be considered in risk assessment, but also evaluation methods able to ascertain 'risk in human societies as the actually exist'.[37]

Similarly to the term 'science', the term 'risk' can also not be found in the SPS Agreement as such. The SPS Agreement only contains the term 'risk assessment'.[38]

The Panel in *EC—Hormones* gathered its notion of risk from interpreting the term 'risk assessment'. The Panel considered that the procedure of risk assessment contains the following two elements: (i) *identification* of the *adverse effects* on human health, and (ii) *evaluation* of 'the *potential* or probability of occurrence of these effects'.[39]

From this interpretation of the term risk assessment by the Panel, one can conclude that it understands risk as 'the potential *or* probability of occurrence of adverse effects'.

The Appellate Body in *EC—Hormones* noted that 'the Panel's use of "probability" as an alternative term for "potential" creates a significant concern'.[40] The Appellate Body pointed at differences of the ordinary meanings of the two words. The Appellate Body observed that '[T]he ordinary meaning of "potential" relates to "possibility" and is different from the ordinary meaning of "probability"'. The Appellate Body found that the ordinary meaning of 'potential' is 'that which is possible as opposed to actual: a possibility', whereas 'probability' refers to 'degrees of likelihood: the appearance of truth, or likelihood of being realized ... a thing judged likely to be true, to exist, or to happen'.[41] From these ordinary meanings of words, the Appellate Body inferred that '[P]robability implies a higher degree or a threshold of potentiality or possibility. It thus appears that here the Panel introduces a *quantitative dimension* to the notion of risk'.[42]

With regard to the quantification of risk, Elizabeth Fisher observed that 'there is a close relationship between how risk-problems are characterised and what is understood to be a legitimate role for public administration in addressing them'.[43] Unsurprisingly, though, different perceptions of risk in the case *EC—Hormones* by the Panel and the Appellate Body respectively led to different outcomes.

The Appellate Body's review of the appropriate notion of risk was prompted by a particular statement of a scientific expert and its interpretation by the Panel. The Appellate Body noted down the Panel's reflections as follows:

> In this respect, we note Dr. Lucier's statement that, according to his tentative estimates, between zero and one person in a million who eat 500 grams of meat, treated with oestrogens for growth promotion purposes in accordance with good practice, per day over their lifetimes, get cancer (...). This 0–1 in a million risk is caused by the total amount of oestrogens in treated meat (the amount of endogenous oestrogens being highly variable and, according to Dr. Lucier, already being carcinogenic), not by the small fraction thereof which is added for growth promotion purposes and which is relevant for the purposes of this dispute. Moreover, this estimate only represents a statistical range of 0 to 1 in a million, not a scientifically identified risk.[44]

The Appellate Body observed that the European Communities 'protest [ed] vigorously' against the Panel's interpretation.[45] The European Communities asserted that 'by doing so, the Panel is in effect requiring a Member carrying out a risk assessment to quantify the potential for adverse effects on human health'.[46] The Appellate Body reasoned as follows:

> It is not clear in what sense the Panel uses the term "scientifically identified risk". The Panel also frequently uses the term "identifiable risk", and does not define this term either. The Panel might arguably have used the terms

> "scientifically identified risk" and "identifiable risk" simply to refer to an ascertainable risk: if a risk is not ascertainable, how does a Member ever know or demonstrate that it exists? In one part of its Reports, the Panel opposes a requirement of an "identifiable risk" to the uncertainty that theoretically always remains since science can *never* provide *absolute* certainty that a given substance will not *ever* have adverse health effects. We agree with the Panel that this theoretical uncertainty is not the kind of risk which, under Article 5.1, is to be assessed. In another part of its Reports, however, the Panel appeared to be using the term "scientifically identified risk" to prescribe implicitly that a certain *magnitude* or threshold level of risk be demonstrated in a risk assessment if an SPS measure based thereon is to be regarded as consistent with Article 5.1. To the extent that the Panel purported to require a risk assessment to establish a minimum magnitude of risk, we must note that imposition of such a quantitative requirement finds no basis in the *SPS Agreement*.[47]

Interestingly, though, the conflict over whether the concept of risk implies 'quantitative requirements' persisted over 10 years, reappearing in the *Continued Suspension* case. In this case, the European Communities specifically claimed that 'the Panel erred in requiring the quantification of the risks arising from the consumption of meat containing residues of oestradiol-17β'.[48] In particular, the European Communities argued that a specific question of the Panel to scientific experts could be understood as a quantitative requirement. The Panel has posed the following question to the scientific experts:

> The Panel specifically asked the experts whether the [European Communities] Opinions identified the potential for adverse effects on human health, including the carcinogenic or genotoxic potential, of the residues of oestradiol-17β found in meat derived from cattle to which this hormone had been administered for growth promotion purposes in accordance with good veterinary practice and to what extent the Opinions evaluated the *potential occurrence* of these adverse effects.[49]

The European Communities argued that if the phrase *potential occurrence* is understood as a quantitative requirement, i.e. 'to specify in quantitative terms "to what extent [it] evaluated the potential occurrence of these adverse effects," it would lead to an error in law'.[50] The European Communities asserted that, by referring to "potential occurrence" of adverse effects when asking questions to the experts, the Panel incorrectly 'imposed a quantitative method of risk assessment on the European Communities borrowed from Codex Alimentarius and JECFA'.[51]

The Appellate Body began its examination of the European Communities' claim by recalling its findings on the issue of quantifying risk in *EC—Hormones.* In particular with view on its earlier finding 'that imposition of such a quantitative requirement finds no basis in the *SPS Agreement*',[52] the Appellate Body in the *Continued Suspension* case added the following:

> Although the definition of a risk assessment does not require WTO Members to establish a minimum magnitude of risk, it is nevertheless difficult to understand the concept of risk as being devoid of any indication of potentiality. A risk assessment is intended to identify adverse effects and evaluate the possibility that such adverse effects might arise. This distinguishes an ascertainable risk from theoretical uncertainty. However, the assessment of risk need not be expressed in numerical terms or as a minimum quantification of the level of risk.[53]

With specific regard to the *potential occurrence* of adverse effects on human health of residues found in meat treated with the hormone oestradiol-17β, the Appellate Body noted:

> As the European Communities acknowledges, "a quantitative dimension may not be immediately evident from the ordinary meaning of the words 'potential occurrence'". The terms "potential occurrence of adverse effects" can be understood as referring to the possibility that the adverse effects might occur, without necessarily requiring that this be expressed in numerical terms. This would be consistent with the definition of "risk assessment" in paragraph 4 of Annex A of the *SPS Agreement*, as interpreted by the Appellate Body. Moreover, it would be consistent with the Appellate Body's view that "theoretical uncertainty" is not the kind of risk to be assessed under Article 5.1, but rather the risk to be assessed must be an "ascertainable" risk. In this sense, we agree with Canada that "to examine the 'potential' for adverse effects is to ask whether those adverse effects could ever occur".[54]

In its attempt to define an 'ascertainable risk' somewhere between a 'quantitative notion of risk' and 'theoretical uncertainty', the Appellate Body in *Continued Suspension* noted that the Panel was aware of the difference. The Appellate Body observed:

> Other statements by the Panel confirm that it did not require that the possibility of the risks arising be expressed in numerical terms. For example, the Panel took note of the Appellate Body's finding that a risk assessment can take into account "matters not susceptible of quantitative analysis by the empirical or experimental laboratory methods commonly associated with the physical sciences." The Panel also stated that "it must determine whether the European Communities evaluated the *possibility* that the identified adverse effects came into being, originated, or resulted from the presence of residues of oestradiol-17β in meat or meat products as a result of the cattle being treated with the hormone for growth promotion purposes".[55]

Finally, the Appellate Body turned to the additional argument of the European Communities that the Panel's use of the term 'magnitude' was evidence for its misinterpretation of risk and risk assessment. The European Communities had pointed out the following paragraph where the Panel in *US—Continued Suspension* had used the term 'magnitude':

> Indeed, whether a Member considers that its population should be exposed or not to a particular risk, or at what level, is not relevant to determining whether a risk exists and what its magnitude is. *A fortiori*, it should have no effect on whether there is sufficient evidence of the existence and magnitude of this risk.
>
> A risk-averse Member may be inclined to take a protective position when considering the measure to be adopted. However, the determination of whether scientific evidence is sufficient to assess the existence and ***magnitude*** of a risk must be disconnected from the intended level of protection. (emphasis added)[56]

In response to the European Communities' claim, the Appellate Body in *US—Continued Suspension* firstly observed that the Panel made its statements in the context of its examination whether the provisional ban of the other five hormones was consistent or not. In that respect, the Appellate Body noted that the Panel's statement at issue 'was not made in the context of the Panel's examination of the European Communities' import ban on meat from cattle treated with oestradiol-17β'.[57]

Then, the Appellate Body reiterated that risk assessment implies a notion of potentiality:

> However, we recall that a "risk assessment" involves an indication of potentiality, even though this need not be expressed in numerical terms or as

> a minimum quantification of the level of risk. In this sense, the Panel's reference to "magnitude" is in our view not sufficient to establish that the Panel incorrectly interpreted Article 5.1 and paragraph 4 of Annex A as requiring a quantitative risk assessment.[58]

Therefore, the Appellate Body considered that 'the Panel's reference to "potential occurrence" of adverse health effects could be read consistently with the definition of a risk assessment in paragraph 4 of Annex A of the *SPS Agreement*, as interpreted by the Appellate Body.[59] In consequence, the Appellate Body dismissed the claim of the European Communities 'that the Panel incorrectly interpreted Article 5.1 and paragraph 4 of Annex A of the *SPS Agreement* as requiring quantification of risk'.[60]

In the case *Continued Suspension*, the European Communities seemed of having overstated the Appellate Body's line of argument in *EC—Hormones*. The Appellate Body in *EC—Hormones* was, in fact, concerned about the Panel's equation of potentiality with probability and rejected a quantitative notion of risk. On the other hand, the Appellate Body drew a line of demarcation between risk and uncertainty already in the *Hormones* case, by posing the following rhetorical question: 'The Panel might arguably have used the terms "scientifically identified risk" and "identifiable risk" simply to refer to an ascertainable risk: if a risk is not ascertainable, how does a Member ever know or demonstrate that it exists?'[61]

Therefore, the European Communities' implication in the *Continued Suspension* case that the rejection of a quantitative requirement in risk assessment amounts to a concept of risk 'devoid of any indication of potentiality' went too far. The Appellate Body, considering the European Communities' claim that the Panel's requirement to evaluate the *potential occurrence* of adverse health effects is tantamount to a quantitative specification of the risk at issue, clarified as follows: 'Although the definition of a risk assessment does not require WTO Members to establish a minimum magnitude of risk, it is nevertheless difficult to understand the concept of risk as being devoid of any indication of potentiality'.[62] Further working out the contours of 'risk' vis-à-vis 'uncertainty', the Appellate Body continued: 'A risk assessment is intended to identify adverse effects and evaluate the possibility that such adverse effects might arise. This distinguishes an ascertainable risk from theoretical uncertainty'.[63] From the line of argument developed by the Appellate Body in *EC—Hormones* and *Continued Suspension*, one can draw the conclusion that risks requiring assessment under Article 5 of the *SPS Agreement* are *ascertainable risks.*

Ascertainability, in turn, was discerned by the Appellate Body from quantification or numerical specification, on the one hand, and from theoretical uncertainty, on the other hand. In other words, risk assessment does not need to provide quantification in numerical terms, but require the establishment of *some indication of potentiality* different from theoretical uncertainty. The Appellate Body found it 'difficult to understand the concept of risk as being devoid of any indication of potentiality'.[64] Though, one may assume that the concept of risk, as developed by the Appellate Body, should be understood as being located somewhere within the wide range between quantifiability, on the one hand, and uncertainty on the other hand, yet necessarily coming along with *some indication of potentiality* and ascertainability.

By looking deeper at different interpretations of panels and the Appellate Body of the same basic terms such as science and risk, one may perceive how allegedly banned ambiguities were resurfacing. However, instead of legal ambiguities, as may have been the case under the previous GATT Article XX approach, the new ambiguities were rather epistemological in nature. Hence, the promise for objectivity implied in the science-based approach of the SPS Agreement came along with epistemological questions surrounding the very notion of science. Thus, instead of being an objective arbiter in trade dispute, 'science' turned out to be a new challenge for the WTO DSB. In fact, panels and the Appellate Body were challenged by the relative nature of science. That relative nature of science was once depicted by Karl Popper as 'bold theoretical structures above swamplands':

> The empirical basis of objective science has thus nothing 'absolute' about it. Science does not rest upon solid bedrock. The bold structure of its theories rises, as it were, above a swamp. It is like a building erected on piles. The piles are driven down from above into the swamp, but not down to any natural or 'given' base; and if we stop driving the piles deeper, it is not because we have reached firm ground. We simply stop when we are satisfied that the piles are firm enough to carry the structure, at least for the time being.[65]

Notes

1. Thomas Cottier, Matthias Oesch, *International Trade Regulation. Law and Policy in the WTO, the European Union and Switzerland. Cases, Materials and Comments* (Staempfli Publishers, 2005), p. 712.

2. Thomas Cottier, Matthias Oesch, *ibid.* p. 713. Nevertheless, the GATT 1947 was not without any effect on agriculture. Attempts by GATT 1947 panels to address agricultural policies particularly influenced European attitudes towards international trade rules for agriculture. In this respect, Cottier and Oesch observed: 'However, it is wrong to say that the GATT 1947 essentially excluded agriculture. A considerable number of GATT 1947 panels dealt with agricultural policies, and the EC oftentimes was on the receiving end—an experience which largely shaped the reserved European attitudes towards GATT law and in particular towards its direct effect' (Thomas Cottier, Matthias Oesch, *ibid.*).
3. Thomas Cottier, Matthias Oesch, *ibid.* p. 714.
4. Lukasz Gruszczynski, *Regulating Health and Environmental Risks under WTO Law. A Critical Analysis of the SPS Agreement* (Oxford University Press, 2010), p. 36.
5. Marsha A. Echols, *Food Safety and the WTO. The Interplay of Culture, Science and Technology* (Kluwer Law International, 2001), pp. 3–4.
6. John Croome, *Reshaping the World Trading System. A history of the Uruguay Round* (World Trade Organization Publication Services, 1995), pp. 235–236.
7. John Croome, *ibid.* p. 236 (emphasis added).
8. *Ministerial Declaration on the Uruguay Round, (Punta del Este Declaration)*, cited from John Croome, *Reshaping the World Trading System. A history of the Uruguay Round* (World Trade Organization Publication Services, 1995), Annex, pp. 382–392, in particular p. 387.
9. Echols, 2001, p. 2 (footnotes omitted).
10. Echols 2001, p. 4.
11. Marsha A. Echols, *ibid.*, p. 2.
12. Marsha A. Echols, *ibid.*, p. 3. Stefan Zleptnig considered that the SPS Agreement reflects 'a considerable shift' in international trade regulation, yet 'a new regulatory philosophy' (Stefan Zleptnig, *Non-Economic Objectives in WTO Law. Justification Provisions of GATT, GATS, SPS and TBT Agreements* (Martinus Nijhoff Publishers, 2010), p. 335).
13. Echols 2001, p. 3.
14. The acronym OIE stands for the French term *Office Internationale des Epizooties.* International standard setting also covers controversial issues. For instance, the Codex Alimentarius Commission established an 'Ad hoc Intergovernmental Task Force on Foods Derived from Biotechnology (TFFDBT)' in 1999. An outcome of the work of the TFFDBT was the adoption of 'Principles for the Risk Analysis of Foods Derived from Modern Biotechnology' by the Codex Alimentarius Commission in 2003 (see CAC/GL 44-2003, amended in 2008).
15. *EC—Hormones*, Appellate Body Report, para. 184.

16. *Australia—Salmon*, Panel Report, para. 8.80 (original emphases); with reference to the Appellate Body Report on *EC—Hormones*, para. 186 (-footnote 273).
17. *Australia—Salmon*, Appellate Body Report, para. 124; with reference to paragraph 8.80 of the Panel's Report in *Australia – Salmon*. By confirming the Panel's notion that the evaluation of the probability 'may be expressed either quantitatively or qualitatively', the Appellate Body coevally rejected the dissenting opinion of one of the experts advising the Panel, namely Burmaster, who had argued that a 'risk assessment' must be quantitative (see footnote no. 286 in paragraph 8.83 of the Panel's Report in *Australia —Salmon*).
18. *Australia—Salmon*, Appellate Body Report, para. 124; with reference to paragraph 186 of the Appellate Body's report in *EC—Hormones* (footnote no. 76).
19. *EC—Hormones*, Appellate Body Report, para. 184.
20. International standards form part of the cluster of public standards (see Sufian Jusoh, 'Standards and their Impacts on the Horticulture Trade,' in Baris Karapinar, Fikret Adaman, and Gokhan Ozertan (eds.), *Rethinking Structural Reform in Turkish Agriculture: Beyond the World Bank's Strategy* (Nova Science Publishers, 2010), pp. 356–357.
21. The SPS Agreement explicitly recognises the Codex Alimentarius Commission, the World Organisation for Animal Health (OIE), and the framework of the International Plant Protection Convention (IPPC) as 'relevant international organisations' (preamble, Article 3.4 and Annex A (3) of the SPS Agreement).
22. Marsha Echols called the way the SPS Agreement seeks to implement harmonisation of SPS measures as a 'carrot and stick approach':

The [SPS] Agreement uses a carrot and stick approach to encourage countries to harmonize their sanitary measures around the Codex standards. The carrot is the presumption that accompanies measures conforming to international standards. They are 'deemed' to be necessary and 'presumed' to be consistent with the Agreement and the GATT 1994. When a Member has reason to believe that a sanitary measure not based on the international standard is constraining or has the potential to constrain its exports, it may request from and must be given an explanation by the importing Member. In addition, the notification procedures of Annex B to the Agreement are triggered by the failure of a government to adopt 'substantially the same' content as the international standard, if its 'regulation' might have a significant effect on trade (Marsha A. Echols, *Food Safety and the WTO. The Interplay of Culture, Science and Technology* (Kluwer Law International, 2001), p. 99, footnotes omitted).

23. Marsha A. Echols, *ibid.* p 44. In the context of the case *EC—Biotech*, Oren Perez commented that 'the Panel's submissive approach to science asks from science something it cannot deliver: complete determinacy' (Oren Perez, 'Anomalies at the precautionary kingdom: reflections on the GMO Panel's decision' (2007) 6(2) *World Trade Review*, 278–279).
24. Marsha Echols observed that the language of the SPS Agreement uses the term 'scientific' rather than 'science' and found that the former term 'refers not only to laboratory science but also to an approach or reasoning process that yields sound conclusions. Instead of the focus on (laboratory) "science", the focus should be on objective decision making that considers all factors and views' (Marsha A. Echols, *Food Safety and the WTO. The Interplay of Culture, Science and Technology* (Kluwer Law International, 2001), p. 153).
25. It is referred to 'quarantine hazards' for making reference to animal diseases, plant pests and food-borne hazards, and to 'quarantine sciences' for referring to the physical sciences used for ascertaining these quarantine hazards.
26. *EC—Hormones,* Appellate Body Report, para. 187.
27. *EC—Hormones,* Panel Report, para. 8.94 (emphases added).
28. *EC—Hormones,* Panel Report, para. 8.97.
29. *EC—Hormones,* Panel Report, para. 8.109 (emphases by the Panel).
30. The Nielsen Report of 1981, the first and second Collins Report of 1985 and 1989 respectively, and the Pimenta Report of 1989.
31. Opinions of the EC Economic and Social Committee of 1981 and 1984.
32. *EC—Hormones,* Appellate Body Report, para. 187.
33. *EC—Hormones,* Appellate Body Report, para. 187.
34. *EC—Hormones,* Appellate Body Report, para. 187.
35. *EC—Hormones,* Appellate Body Report, para. 206.
36. *EC—Hormones,* Appellate Body Report, para. 206.
37. However, from this statement of the Appellate Body, it remained open what kind of scientific disciplines might come into effective consideration. The reason for this particular *caveat* lies in paragraph 1 of Annex A of the SPS Agreement. The hazards mentioned in paragraph 1 of Annex A of the SPS Agreement are of a rather narrow range, not exceeding the scope of physical sciences and quarantine sciences, respectively. Hence, one could argue that the concept of the Appellate Body, considered by some as more inclusive and susceptive for non-scientific concerns, might be constrained by the narrow definition of science implied in paragraph 1 of Annex A of the SPS Agreement. Insofar, it will be interesting to see how the concept of the Appellate Body, commended by some as being broader as that of the Panel, will further materialise.
38. Echols (2001, p. 82).

39. *EC—Hormones,* Panel Report, para. 8.98 (emphases by the Panel).
40. *EC—Hormones,* Appellate Body Report, para. 184.
41. *EC—Hormones,* Appellate Body Report, para. 184; with reference in footnote no. 164 to L. Brown (ed.), *The New Shorter Oxford English Dictionary on Historical Principles,* Vol. 2 (Clarendon Press, 1993).
42. *EC—Hormones,* Appellate Body Report, para. 184 (emphasis added). Therefore, by rejecting the Panel's equation of potentiality and probability, the Appellate Body also rejected the Panel's attempt for introducing a quantitative requirement into risk assessment.
43. Elizabeth Fisher, 'Beyond the Science/Democracy Dichotomy: The World Trade organisation Sanitary and Phytosanitary Agreement and Administrative Constitutionalism', in Christian Joerges and Ernst-Ulrich Petersmann (eds.), *Constitutionalism, Multilevel Trade Governance and Social Regulation* (Hart Publishing, 2006), [pp. 327–349], p. 343. Fisher also confirmed that the Panel in *EC—Hormones* 'was clearly influenced by quantitative understandings of risk while the Appellate Body was not' (Elizabeth Fisher, *ibid.*).
44. *EC—Hormones,* Appellate Body Report, para. 185 and footnote no. 166 with reference to the Panel Report in *EC—Hormones,* para. 8.124, footnote no. 331.
45. *EC—Hormones,* Appellate Body Report, para. 185.
46. *EC—Hormones,* Appellate Body Report, para. 185.
47. *EC—Hormones,* Appellate Body Report, para. 186 (emphases by the Appellate Body, footnotes omitted).
48. *US—Continued Suspension*, Appellate Body Report, para. 566.
49. *US—Continued Suspension,* Appellate Body Report, para. 570 (emphasis added), with reference to the Panel Report in the same *US—Continued Suspension* case, para. 7.521 (*ibid.,* footnote no. 1177).
50. *US—Continued Suspension,* Appellate Body Report, para. 571, with reference to the European Communities' appellant's submission, para, 344 (original emphasis, (*ibid.,* footnote no. 1178).
51. *US—Continued Suspension,* Appellate Body Report, para. 566 (footnotes omitted).
52. *EC—Hormones,* Appellate Body Report, para. 186.
53. *US—Continued Suspension,* Appellate Body Report, para. 569. The Appellate Body added that it was 'also mindful that the risk assessment at issue in this case concerns the *potential* for adverse effects under the second sentence of paragraph 4 of Annex A and not an evaluation of likelihood under the first sentence of paragraph 4' (*ibid.,* original emphasis).
54. *US —Continued Suspension,* Appellate Body Report, para. 572 (original underlining, footnotes omitted).

55. *US—Continued Suspension,* Appellate Body Report, para. 573 (emphasis added by the Appellate Body, footnotes omitted).
56. *US—Continued Suspension,* Appellate Body Report, para. 574, with reference to the Panel Report in the same *US—Continued Suspension* case, paras. 7.611 and 7.612 (emphases by the Appellate Body, footnote omitted).
57. *US—Continued Suspension,* Appellate Body Report, para. 574.
58. *US—Continued Suspension,* Appellate Body Report, para. 574.
59. *US—Continued Suspension,* Appellate Body Report, para. 575.
60. *US—Continued Suspension,* Appellate Body Report, para. 575.
61. *EC—Hormones,* Appellate Body Report, para. 186.
62. *US—Continued Suspension,* Appellate Body Report, para. 569. The Appellate Body added that it was 'also mindful that the risk assessment at issue in this case concerns the *potential* for adverse effects under the second sentence of paragraph 4 of Annex A and not an evaluation of likelihood under the first sentence of paragraph 4' (*ibid.,* original emphasis).
63. *US—Continued Suspension,* Appellate Body Report, para. 569.
64. *US—Continued Suspension,* Appellate Body Report, para. 569.
65. Karl R. Popper, *The Logic of Scientific Discovery,* 2nd English edition (Hutchinson & Co Publishers, 1968), p. 111, footnote omitted.

References

Cottier, Thomas, and Oesch, Matthias. "International Trade Regulation. Law and Policy in the WTO, the European Union and Switzerland. Cases, Materials and Comments". *Staempfli Publishers,* 2005.

Croome, John. "Reshaping the World Trading System. A history of the Uruguay Round". *World Trade Organization Publication Services,* 1995.

Echols, Marsha A. "Food Safety and the WTO. The Interplay of Culture, Science and Technology". Kluwer Law International, 2001.

Fisher, Elizabeth. "Beyond the Science/Democracy Dichotomy: The World Trade Organisation Sanitary and Phytosanitary Agreement and Administrative Constitutionalism". Published in Christian Joerges and Ernst-Ulrich Petersmann (eds.), *Constitutionalism, Multilevel Trade Governance and Social Regulation.* Hart Publishing, 2006, 327–349.

Gruszczynski, Lukasz. "Regulating Health and Environmental Risks under WTO Law. A Critical Analysis of the SPS Agreement". *Oxford University Press,* 2010.

Jusoh, Sufian. "Standards and their Impacts on the Horticulture Trade". Published in Baris Karapinar, Fikret Adaman, and Gokhan Ozertan (eds.), *Rethinking Structural Reform in Turkish Agriculture: Beyond the World Bank's Strategy.* Nova Science Publishers, 2010, 355–369.

Popper, Karl R. "Logik der Forschung" (English title: *The Logic of Scientific Discovery)*. J.C.B Mohr (Paul Siebeck), 1976, 6th edition and Popper, Karl R. "The Logic of Scientific Discovery". *Hutchinson & Co Publishers*, 2nd English edition, 1968.

Zleptnig, Stefan. "Non-Economic Objectives in WTO Law. Justification Provisions of GATT, GATS, SPS and TBT Agreements". *Martinus Nijhoff Publishers*, 2010.

WTO Cases

EC—Hormones: EC—Measures Concerning Meat and Meat Products.

- Panel Report WT/DS26/R/USA, WT/DS48/R/CAN, final report circulated August 18, 1997.
- Appellate Body Report WT/DS26/AB/R/USA, WT/DS48/AB/R/CAN, adopted February 13, 1998.

Australia—Salmon: Australia—Measures Affecting Importation of Salmon.

- Panel Report WT/DS18/R, final report circulated June 12, 1998.
- Appellate Body Report WT/DS18/AB/R, adopted November 6, 1998.

United States—Continued Suspension: United States/Canada—Continued Suspension of Obligations in the EC—Hormones Dispute.

- Panel Reports, WT/DS320/R, WT/DS321/R, final reports circulated March 31, 2008.
- Appellate Body Reports, WT/DS320/AB/R, WT/DS321/AB/R, adopted November 14, 2008.

CHAPTER 8

The Panel's Positivist Position

The first prominent WTO dispute decided under the SPS Agreement, the case *EC—Hormones*, was fundamental for the interpretation of the concept of 'risk assessment'. Therefore, in the following, the underlying conceptual dichotomy between approaches of the Panel and the Appellate Body towards 'risk assessment' in the *Hormones* case shall be examined in more detail. The starting point for this examination is the notion that the different approaches of the Panel and the Appellate Body in *EC—Hormones* towards 'risk assessment' is the result of fundamentally different underlying concepts.

The Panel in *EC—Hormones*, when interpreting Article 5 of the SPS Agreement, was obviously inspired by the concept of risk analysis. As mentioned above, the concept of risk analysis was developed and applied, most notably, by the Codex Alimentarius Commission. Hence, no wonder that the Panel explicitly referred to a 'Report of the Joint FAO/WHO Expert Consultation on the Application of Risk Analysis to Food Standards Issues'.[1] An essential feature of the concept of risk analysis is the separation of risk assessment and risk management. Obviously, the Panel also took over this element of the concept of risk analysis when interpreting Article 5 of the SPS Agreement and emphasising two separate aspects contained therein, i.e. 'risk assessment' on the one hand, and 'risk management' on the other hand.

The Appellate Body, on the other hand, adhered to a textual interpretation of Article 5 of the SPS Agreement where, indeed, the term 'risk management' cannot be found. However, refusing a notion of risk

M. Burkard, *Conflicting Philosophies and International Trade Law*,
Philosophy, Public Policy, and Transnational Law,
https://doi.org/10.1007/978-3-319-61067-2_8

management left the Appellate Body challenged by so-called non-scientific factors such as compliance and control problems. The Appellate Body was thus constrained to encompass non-scientific factors into the process of 'risk assessment'.

In the following, statements issued by the Panel in the case *EC—Hormones* shall be analysed in more detail.

1 A Probabilistic Notion of Risk

As shown initially, there are various notions of risk. Introduced by the SPS Agreement, it was upon panels and the Appellate Body to clarify the risk concept in the context of international trade regulation. In this respect, a telling example for showing different approaches of panels and the Appellate Body towards the notion of risk is the question about 'zero risk'. In SPS case law, it was contested whether 'zero risk' is a scientific question or a policy issue, i.e. a question of risk management. From a scientific perspective, there is no such thing as 'zero risk'. From a policy perspective, however, 'zero risk' as a risk management measure is conceivable, for example by implementing an import ban on the hazardous items at issue.

The Panel in the case *EC—Hormones* dealt with the concept of 'zero risk' from a scientific perspective. In particular, the Panel in the *Hormones* case examined the relationship between the notion of risk and statistical significance. In this respect, the Panel questioned scientific experts advising the Panel, in particular, Dr. Lucier. Considering that some of the remarks of Dr. Lucier were 'closely related' to the 'concept of zero risk', the Panel observed: 'Dr. Lucier responded that, to his knowledge, there was no piece of scientific evidence to indicate that any of the six hormones in question had unequivocally caused adverse effects in humans when administered and used properly. However, there was some information available which raised concern for a slight effect on the incidence of human disease'.[2] In this respect, the Panel noted a statement of Dr. Lucier saying that, 'according to his tentative estimates, between zero and one person in a million who eat 500 grams of meat, treated with oestrogens for growth promotion purposes in accordance with good practices, per day over their lifetimes, get cancer'.[3] The Panel reasoned that '[T]his 0–1 in a million risk is caused by the *total* amount of oestrogens in treated meat (the amount of endogenous oestrogens being highly variable and, according to Dr. Lucier, already being carcinogenic), not by the small fraction thereof which is added for growth promotion purposes and which is relevant for the purposes of this dispute'.[4] Considering that 'this estimate only represents a statistical range of 0–1 in a million', the Panel concluded that the risk expressed by this estimate is not sufficient for becoming recognised as 'a scientifically identified risk'.[5]

The European Communities (EC), on the other hand, seemed to perceive 'zero risk' not primarily as an issue of statistical and probability calculations, but as a concept for setting the appropriate level of protection at a 'zero residue' level.[6] The EC argued that 'none of the studies it referred to as part of a risk assessment proves beyond doubt or concludes in an unqualified manner that the presence of residues of the hormones in dispute in meat or meat present *no risk whatsoever*'.[7] In particular, the EC referred to the conclusions of the 1988 JECFA Report which stated 'that residues arising from the hormones at issue used as growth promoters are only *unlikely* to pose a hazard to human health and to the basic premise of JECFA recommendations which aim at establishing standards which correspond to a *no appreciable* or *no significant* risk increase due to the exposure to the substances in question and not to a *zero* risk increase'.[8] The Panel reasoned that 'this residual risk, albeit minute and not appreciable, constitutes the risk (derived from a *risk assessment*) on which the EC ban is based in accordance with Article 5.1, arguing that, according to EC *risk management*, risk other than zero is not acceptable'.[9]

The Panel, however, adhered to the notion of an 'identifiable risk' and found that '[T]he scientific conclusion reflected in the EC measures in dispute is thus that the use of the hormones in dispute for growth promotion purposes, *even in accordance with good practise*, poses an identifiable risk to human health'.[10] The Panel further noted that, according to the experts advising it, 'any use of the hormone in dispute will always leave some residue level, albeit a very small one, the administration of these hormones in accordance with good practice will also leave some residue and thus not achieve the EC "zero residue" level of protection'.[11]

In a general observation, the Panel noted that, 'according to scientists advising the Panel, science can never provide a certainty, i.e. exclude once and for all that a specific substance can ever have adverse health effects'.[12]

With regard to the identifiability of the risks invoked by the EC in particular, the Panel noted that these specific risks were 'not identifiable and that, therefore, these risks can a priori not be *assessed* by scientists (as required in Article 5.1)'.[13]'In this sense', the Panel continued, 'these potential risks, which are present for any substance (also for substances or uses of substances allowed in the EC), are only the consequence of *science not being capable of assuring that no risks will ever arise* from a substance'.[14]

The Panel finally noted that even by a total ban the EC could not achieve the objective of 'zero risk':

> We finally note that the EC objective of 'zero risk' cannot be achieved in practice; not even under the EC ban itself since the European Communities cannot guarantee that there is a *zero probability* that illegal use of the hormones at issue will occur. Moreover, this 'zero risk' objective cannot (…) in any case be achieved for the three natural hormones in dispute since the European Communities allows the ingestion of these same hormones occurring endogenously in meat and other foods as well as the use of these hormones for therapeutic or zootechnical purposes.[15]

To conclude, the Panel in the case *EC—Hormones* perceived 'zero risk' not as part of the determination of the appropriate level of protection, i.e. as part of risk management, but as a scientific concept related to statistical significance and probability calculation. In this regard, the Panel observed that in the scientific realm, 'zero risk' does not exist and hence, rejected the concept of 'zero risk' as a scientific concept.

In the *Salmon* case, the Panel started its considerations of the concept of 'zero risk' by defining risk as 'a possibility of an adverse effect occurring'. Deriving from this notion of risk, the Panel observed the following:

> In this respect, we consider that a risk assessment, on which to base an import prohibition in accordance with Article 5.1, cannot be premised on the concept of 'zero risk'. Otherwise, all import prohibitions would be based on a risk assessment, since there is a risk (i.e., a *possibility* of an adverse event occurring), however remote, associated with most (if not all) imports.[16]

With regard to the case at hand, the Panel cited the following statement from the first submission of Australia: 'Australia does not have a no risk policy with respect to imports of salmon products—imports of heat-treated salmon are permitted. Stopping the import of a particular product does not mean that there is a no risk policy, only that the risk is too high and that the product cannot be treated to reduce the risk to an acceptable level'.[17] The Panel further cited the following statement of the Australian government: 'The Government accepts the strongly expressed view of the Quarantine Review Committee that a policy of "no risk" would be impossible to implement. Such a policy would mean for example a ban on most products'.[18]

In sum, the Panel in *Australia—Salmon* followed the approach of the Panel in *EC—Hormones* observing that in the scientific realm, 'zero risk' does not exist. Hence, the concept of 'zero risk' was rejected again as unscientific.

2 Separating Science and Policy

Paragraph 4 of Annex A of the SPS Agreement contains two types of risk assessments. The risk assessment applied in the case *EC—Hormones* is the second type described in paragraph 4 of Annex A of the SPS Agreement. This second type of risk assessment is defined as 'the evaluation of the potential for adverse effects on human or animal health arising from the presence of additives, contaminants, toxins or disease-causing organisms in food, beverages or feedstuff.'

From this definition, the Panel considered that a risk assessment should '(i) *identify* the *adverse effects* on human health (if any) arsing from the presence of the hormones at issue when used as growth promoters *in meat or meat products*, and (ii) if any such adverse effects exist, *evaluate* the *potential* or probability of occurrence of these effects'.[19]

With regard to Article 5 of the SPS Agreement, the Panel in *EC—Hormones* recognised 'two separate aspects of a Member's decision to enact or maintain a sanitary measure'.[20]

The *first aspect*, the Panel observed, 'relates to the exercise of assessing the risks to human, animal or plant life or health against which a sanitary measure is intended to protect'.[21] This exercise, the Panel noted, 'is referred to in the SPS Agreement as *risk assessment*'.[22] With respect to food safety, in particular, the Panel found that 'the potential adverse effects (if any) related to a specific substance are established together with the probability of occurrence of any such effects'.[23]

The Panel considered that the obligation of Article 5.1 SPS to base sanitary measures on a risk assessment may be viewed 'as a specific application of the basic obligations contained in Article 2.2 of the SPS Agreement (…)'.[24] The Panel further noted that Articles 5.1 to 5.3 SPS are summing up factors which need to be taken into account in making risk assessments.[25]

With respect to Article 5.1 SPS, the Panel noted that '[N]one of the parties suggest that there are "risk assessment techniques developed by the relevant international organizations" (…) which have to be taken into account in a risk assessment for the hormones at issue'.[26] Nevertheless, the Panel made reference to the 'Report of the Joint FAO/WHO Expert Consultation on the Application of Risk Analysis to Food Standards Issues' drafted on request of Codex in March 1995. According to this report, risk assessment is defined as follows:

> The scientific evaluation of known or potential adverse health effects resulting from human exposure to foodborne hazards. The process consists of the following steps: (i) hazard identification, (ii) hazard characterization, (iii) exposure assessment, and (iv) risk characterization. The definition includes quantitative risk assessment, which emphasizes reliance on numerical expressions of risk, and also qualitative expressions of risk, as well as an indication of the attendant uncertainties (p. 6).[27]

Subsequently, the Panel noted a revised version of this definition which was adopted by the Committee on General Principles of the Codex Alimentarius Commission at its 12th session in November 1996, defining risk assessment as follows:

> A scientifically based process consisting of the following steps: (i) hazard identification, (ii) hazard characterization, (iii) exposure assessment, and (iv) risk characterization.[28]

Turning to Article 5.2 SPS, the Panel observed that only three of the factors listed in this paragraph were relevant for a risk assessment of the risks at issue, in particular, available scientific evidence, relevant processes and production methods; and relevant inspection, sampling and testing methods.

The Panel noted in particular 'that none of the parties has argued that factors not listed in Article 5.2, such as consumer preference, can be taken into account in a risk assessment in accordance with Article 5'.[29]

Coming to Article 5.3, the Panel considered that the economic factors listed in this paragraph are relevant in cases related to animal or plant life or health. Because the scope of the Hormones case was limited to issues of human life or health, Article 5.3 SPS was not applicable.

In a concluding remark on the notion of risk assessment, the Panel noted 'that the parties agree that, for the purposes of the EC measures in dispute, a risk assessment in accordance with Article 5 is a *scientific* process aimed at establishing the *scientific* basis for the sanitary measure a Member intends to take'.[30]

Turning to the '*second aspect* of a Member's decision to enact or maintain a sanitary measure', the Panel considered that this second aspect 'relates, *inter alia*, to the determination and application of the *appropriate level of sanitary protection* by that Member against the risks to human, animal or plant life or health which have been assessed in accordance with Articles 5.1 to 5.3'.[31] The Panel noted that this second aspect 'is commonly referred to by the parties to this dispute as an essential part of *risk management*'.[32] According to the Panel, risk management or the determination of the appropriate level of protection consists in deciding 'the extent to which (…) the potential adverse effects related to a specific substance which have been identified in the risk assessment' can be accepted.[33]

Commonly, risk management consists of regulatory activities and the setting of standards. In the SPS Agreement, the term risk management itself is not mentioned in any provision. However, the Panel in the case *EC —Hormones* perceived that the determination of the appropriate level of sanitary or phytosanitary protection (ALOP), as prescribed in Articles 5.4 to 5.6 of the SPS Agreement, is an expression of risk management.[34]

The Panel considered that '[A]rticles 5.4 to 5.6 are particularly relevant to the risk management decision'.[35] In detail, the Panel said that Article 5.4 SPS 'establishes the objective of minimizing negative trade effects in the determination by a Member of its appropriate level of protection'.[36] Article 5.5 SPS 'aims at achieving consistency in the application of the concept of appropriate level of protection'.[37] Article 5.6 SPS, at last, 'provides that the sanitary measure which is finally adopted shall not be more trade-restrictive than required to achieve the appropriate level of protection (…)'.[38]

In the same way, as it did previously with Article 5.1 SPS (see above), the Panel also considered that Articles 5.4 to 5.6 may be viewed 'as specific applications of the basic obligations provided for in Article 2.2 (…) and Article 2.3 (…)'.[39]

Summing up, the Panel perceived the 'risk management' phase as involving 'non-scientific considerations, such as social value judgements'.[40]

With view on the case at hand, the Panel applied the separation of the two aspects of risk assessment, on the one hand, and risk management, on the other hand, by considering, *inter alia*, 'that the non-scientific reports and opinions of the European Parliament and the EC Economic and Social Committee, which evaluate the scientific and other reports submitted to them, are not part of the risk assessment process, but of the risk management process (…)'.[41]

The Panel further elaborated on its perception of risk management when examining risks related to the control or, in other words, the abuse of the hormones at issue. Here, the Panel distinguished between the 'relevant inspection, sampling and testing methods' referred to in Article 5.2 SPS, on the one hand, and general problems of control, e.g. enforcing the observance of good veterinary practice, on the other hand.[42] Whereas the Panel considered the former as being 'specific to a particular substance in a particular food', the latter were considered of being related 'to the economic or social incidence' of a substance and its particular use, e.g. incentives for defiance from good veterinary practices.[43] These economic or social incidences, identified by the Panel as 'non-scientific factors', should 'not be taken into account in risk assessment but in *risk management*'.[44]

Beside the attribution of non-scientific factors to risk management, the Panel emphasised the role of social value judgements in determining the appropriate level of protection:

> We recall that there is a distinction between *risk assessment* which is a *scientific* examination and *risk management* which involves social value judgements. Once the risks have been assessed, i.e., once the risks and their probability of occurrence identified, a Member will need to decide, on the basis of its own value judgement, whether it can accept these risks. In so doing a Member sets its 'appropriate level of sanitary protection'. The determination and application of the appropriate level of protection by a Member is part of risk management.[45]

Based on the separation of risk assessment and risk management, the Panel in the *Hormones* case assigned factors non-accessible by the physical sciences to the risk management phase. In particular, the Panel differentiated between 'risks arising from difficulties of inspecting, sampling or testing which are specific to a particular substance in a particular food'.[46] Such specific risks were considered by the Panel as being covered by Article 5.2 of the SPS Agreement, addressing, *inter alia*, 'the relevant inspection, sampling and testing methods', and thus being part of the risk assessment procedure. In contrast, the Panel was of the view that general control problems, e.g. problems of abuse of veterinary drugs and to ensure compliance with good veterinary practice, 'do not seem to be specific to the substance at issue but to the economic or social incidence related to a substance or its particular use (such as economic incentives for abuse)'.[47]

These general control problems, the Panel found, have to be taken into account in risk management, not in risk assessment.

By transferring non-scientific factors to the risk management phase, the Panel in the case *EC—Hormones* was obviously inspired by the Codex Alimentarius Commission. In 1995, the Codex Alimentarius Commission adopted the *Statements of Principle concerning the Role of Science in the Codex Decision-Making Process and the Extent to which other Factors are Taken into Account* (in the following: *Statements of Principle*). In 2001, the *Statements of Principle* were amended with additional criteria for the consideration of such 'other', i.e. non-scientific factors. Together, the *Statements of Principle* of 1995 and the amendment of 2001 aimed at balancing requirements for 'sound science' with the need for considering 'other factors' in risk assessment.

With respect to the importance of 'sound scientific principles' for the assessment of food safety risks, paragraph 1 of the *Statements of Principle* laid down the following:

> 1. The food standards, guidelines and other recommendations of Codex Alimentarius shall be based on the principle of sound scientific analysis and evidence, involving a thorough review of all relevant information, in order that the standards assure the quality and safety of the food supply.[48]

On the other hand, with respect to the consideration of non-scientific factors, the amendment by the decision of the 24th session of the Codex Alimentarius Commission in 2001 to the *Statements of Principle concerning the Role of Science in the Codex Decision-Making Process and the Extent to which other Factors are Taken into Account* established, *inter alia*, the following *Criteria for the Consideration of the Other Factors Referred to in the Second Statement of Principle*:

- when health and safety matters are concerned, the *Statements of Principle Concerning the Role of Science* and the *Statements of Principle Relating to the Role of Food Safety Risk Assessment* should be followed;
- other legitimate factors relevant for health protection and fair trade practices may be identified in the risk management process, and risk managers should indicate how these factors affect the selection of risk management options and the development of standards, guidelines and related texts;

- consideration of other factors should not affect the scientific basis of risk analysis; in this process, the *separation between risk assessment and risk management* should be respected, in order to ensure the scientific integrity of the risk assessment; (…).[49]

Together, the two Statements of Principle, i.e. the *Statements of Principle Concerning the Role of Science in the Codex Decision-Making Process and the Extent to which other Factors are Taken into Account*, including the *Criteria for the Consideration of the Other Factors Referred to in the Second Statement of Principle*, and the *Statements of Principle Relating to the Role of Food Safety Risk Assessment*, are winnowing factors assessable by natural sciences and science-based risk assessment, on the one hand, from 'other legitimate factors', on the other hand. And these other legitimate, but non-scientific factors are given over to the risk management process. Hence, the separation of risk assessment and risk management is not only essential for 'ensuring scientific integrity, avoiding confusion over the functions of risk assessors and risk managers and for reducing conflicts of interest', as laid down in paragraph 9 of the *Working Principles for Risk Analysis*,[50] but is also functional for an appropriate consideration of non-scientific factors. In this respect, Catherine Button noted: 'While still not a model of clarity, the *Criteria* document clearly suggests that 'other factors' belong to risk management and should, as far as possible, not be allowed to interfere with the scientific integrity of risk assessment'.[51]

To summarise, Codex distinguishes between factors assessable by natural sciences and science-based risk assessment, on the one hand, from 'other legitimate factors', on the other hand.

According to the concept of risk analysis applied by Codex, these other legitimate, but non-scientific factors have to be considered in the risk management process. And that concept of risk analysis was subsequently adopted by the Panel in the case *EC—Hormones.*

Hence, the doctrine of risk analysis, as applied by the Codex Alimentarius Commission and the Panel in the *Hormones* case, assumes that

(a) the separation of risk assessment and risk management ensures scientific integrity, fosters clear repartition of respective functions of risk assessors and risk managers and reduces conflicts of interest, and
(b) scientific and non-scientific factors can be discerned, thereby assigning the latter to the risk management stage.

Thus, it can be concluded that the Panel in the *Hormones* case, by adopting the scientific approach of the Codex Alimentarius Commission, implicitly also adopted the presumption that facts and values, science and policy can—and should—be separated.

3 Universality of Scientific Standards

An essential presumption of the science-based approach is the belief that levels of protection based on scientific principles are basically universal. An expression of the belief in the universal applicability of health standards based on scientific principles is the objective of harmonisation, expressed in Article 3 of the SPS Agreement. In the following, it shall be shown how panels have tried to reinforce the harmonisation objective, as expressed in Article 3 of the SPS Agreement, in rather positivistic attempts. Article 3.1 of the SPS Agreement reads as follows:

> To harmonize sanitary and phytosanitary measures on as wide a basis as possible, Members shall base their sanitary or phytosanitary measures on international standards, guidelines or recommendations, where they exist, except as otherwise provided for in this Agreement, and in particular in paragraph 3.

The Panel in the case *EC—Hormones* observed that the SPS Agreement 'does not explicitly define the words *based on* as used in Article 3.1'.[52] However, the Panel perceived that Article 3.2 SPS 'equates measures *based on* international standards with measures which *conform to* such standards'.[53] In contrast, the Panel noted that Article 3.3 SPS 'applies more specifically to measures "which result in a *higher level* of sanitary ... protection than would be achieved by measures based on the relevant international standards" or measures "which result in a *level* of sanitary ... protection *different* from that which would be achieved by measures based on international standards"'.[54] From the equation of the terms 'based on' and 'conform to' in Articles 3.1 and 3.2 and the contrast to higher levels of protection according to Article 3.3, the Panel basically recognised two levels of protection reflected in Article 3 SPS. At the first and basic level, there are sanitary measures which 'reflect the same level of sanitary protection as the *standard*'.[55] At the second and higher level, there are sanitary measures implying *higher levels* of protection than provided by the applicable international standard.[56]

The promotion of 'the use of international standards, guidelines and recommendations' was considered by the Panel, referring to the corresponding recognition in the sixth paragraph of the preamble, as '[o]ne purpose of the SPS Agreement'.[57] In line with this consideration, the Panel reasoned that, for this purpose, 'Article 3.1 imposes an obligation on all Members to base their sanitary measures on international standards except as otherwise provided for in the SPS Agreement, and in particular in Article 3.3 thereof'.[58] As a consequence of considering Article 3.1 of the SPS Agreement as an obligation on all WTO Members, the Panel conceived Article 3.3 of the SPS Agreement as 'an *exception* to the general obligation contained in Article 3.1'.[59]

Notes

1. *EC—Hormones*, Panel Report, para. 8.103. In footnote no. 302, the Panel referred to a revised version of this report. In the meantime, the work on risk analysis was integrated in the Procedural Manual of the Codex Alimentarius Commission. See: "Working Principles for Risk Analysis" in Section IV of the Procedural Manual, 19th edition, 2010, pp. 86–91.
2. *EC—Hormones*, Panel Report, para. 8.124, footnote no. 331, referencing to a statement by Dr. Lucier (at para. 6.95) answering to a Panel's question.
3. *EC—Hormones*, Panel Report, para. 8.124, footnote no. 331, with reference to the transcripts of the joint meeting with experts of 18 February 1997 (paras. 742 and 819).
4. *EC—Hormones*, Panel Report, para. 8.124, footnote no. 331 (emphasis by the Panel).
5. *EC—Hormones*, Panel Report, para. 8.124, footnote no. 331.
6. *EC—Hormones*, Panel Report, para. 8.136.
7. *EC—Hormones*, Panel Report, para. 8.149 (emphasis by the Panel).
8. *EC—Hormones*, Panel Report, para. 8.149 (emphases by the Panel).
9. *EC—Hormones*, Panel Report, para. 8.149 (emphases by the Panel, footnote omitted).
10. *EC—Hormones*, Panel Report, para. 8.136 (emphasis by the Panel).
11. *EC—Hormones*, Panel Report, para. 8.136, footnote no. 350.
12. *EC—Hormones*, Panel Report, para. 8.152. The Panel further noted that the EC had not invoked Article 5.7 of the SPS Agreement which 'explicitly deals with situations where there is *scientific uncertainty* regarding risks related to a substance (...)' (footnote no. 366, emphasis added).
13. *EC—Hormones*, Panel Report, para. 8.153 (emphasis by the Panel).
14. *EC—Hormones*, Panel Report, para. 8.153 (emphasis added).

15. *EC—Hormones*, Panel Report, para. 8.154 (emphasis added, footnote omitted).
16. *Australia—Salmon,* Panel Report, para. 8.81 (emphasis by the Panel, footnote no. 274 mentioned hereafter).
17. *Australia—Salmon*, Panel Report, para. 8.81, footnote no. 274, citing from Australia, First Submission, para. 19.
18. *Australia—Salmon,* Panel Report, para. 8.81, footnote no. 274, citing from Australia, Rebuttals, para. 16.
19. *EC—Hormones*, Panel Report, para. 8.98 (original emphases). In the subsequent case *United States—Continued Suspension*, the Panel took into account the Appellate Body's critique of the Panel's equation of potentiality and probability in the first Hormones dispute. The Appellate Body had found that 'the Panel's use of "probability" as an alternative term for "potential" creates a significant concern. The ordinary meaning of "potential" relates to "possibility" and is different from the ordinary meaning of "probability". "Probability" implies a higher degree or a threshold of potentiality or possibility' (*EC—Hormones*, Report of the Appellate Body, para. 184). In the case *Australia—Salmon*, the Appellate Body further worked out the difference between a risk assessment according to Annex A(4) first and second sentence, respectively: The Appellate Body found that the two types of risk assessment are 'substantially different'. Specifically, the Appellate Body noted that '[...] the first type of risk assessment demands an evaluation of the likelihood of entry, establishment or spread of a disease, and of the associated potential biological and economic consequences', whereas the second type of risk assessment '[...] requires only the evaluation of the potential for adverse effects on human or animal health'. And, with view on the Panel's equation of potentiality with probability in the first Hormones dispute, the Appellate Body concluded: 'In view of the very different language used in paragraph 4 of Annex A for the two types of risk assessment, we do not believe that it is correct to diminish the substantial differences between these two types of risk assessments ...' (*Australia—Salmon*, Appellate Body Report, para. 123, footnote no. 69). Therefore, the Panel in *United States—Continued Suspension* considered 'that it is necessary to clarify what constitutes a risk assessment as defined in Annex A(4), second sentence. The Panel considers that Annex A(4) requires a Member to (a) identify the additives, contaminants, toxins or disease-causing organisms in food, beverages or feedstuffs at issue (if any); (b) identify any possible adverse effect on human or animal health; and (c) evaluate the *potential* for that adverse effect to arise from the presence of the identified additives, contaminants, toxins or disease-causing organisms in food, beverages or feedstuffs' (*United States—Continued Suspension,* Panel Report, para. 7.507, emphasis added).

20. *EC—Hormones*, Panel Report, para. 8.91 (underlining added).
21. *EC—Hormones*, Panel Report, para. 8.92.
22. *EC—Hormones*, Panel Report, para. 8.92 (original emphasis); with reference to Article 5 and Annex A of the SPS Agreement in footnote no. 292.
23. *EC—Hormones*, Panel Report, para. 8.92; with reference to paragraph 4 of Annex A of the SPS Agreement in footnote no. 293.
24. *EC—Hormones*, Panel Report, para. 8.93.
25. *EC—Hormones*, Panel Report, para. 8.93 (footnote no. 294 omitted).
26. *EC—Hormones*, Panel Report, para. 8.103 (footnote no. 300 omitted).
27. *EC—Hormones*, Panel Report, para. 8.103.
28. *EC—Hormones*, Panel Report, para. 8.103. The footnote no. 302 refers to the Codex Alimentarius Commission's document CX/GP96/3.
29. *EC—Hormones*, Panel Report, para. 8.105.
30. *EC—Hormones*, Panel Report, para. 8.107 (emphases by the Panel, footnote no. 304 omitted).
31. *EC—Hormones*, Panel Report, para. 8.95 (emphases by the Panel).
32. *EC—Hormones*, Panel Report, para. 8.95 (emphasis by the Panel).
33. *EC—Hormones*, Panel Report, para. 8.95.
34. *EC—Hormones*, Panel Report, para. 8.96.
35. *EC—Hormones*, Report of the Panel, para. 8.96.
36. *EC—Hormones*, Panel Report, para. 8.96 (original emphasis).
37. *EC—Hormones*, Panel Report, para. 8.96 (original emphasis).
38. *EC—Hormones*, Panel Report, para. 8.96 (original emphasis).
39. *EC—Hormones*, Panel Report, para. 8.96.
40. *EC—Hormones*, Panel Report, para. 8.97 (original emphasis).
41. *EC—Hormones*, Panel Report, para. 8.109 (original emphases).
42. *EC—Hormones*, Panel Report, para. 8.146.
43. *EC—Hormones*, Panel Report, para. 8.146.
44. *EC—Hormones*, Panel Report, para. 8.146 (original emphasis). The Panel, however, added that 'even if these factors could be taken into account in a *risk assessment*, we note that the European Communities had not provided convincing evidence that the control (or the prevention of abuse) of the hormones in dispute is more difficult than the control of other veterinary drugs the use of which it allows'. On these grounds, the Panel concluded that 'banning the use of a substance does not necessarily offer better protection of human health than other means of regulating its use' (*EC—Hormones*, *ibid.*).
45. *EC—Hormones*, Panel Report, para. 8.160 (emphases by the Panel).
46. *EC—Hormones*, Panel Report, para. 8.146.
47. *EC—Hormones*, Panel Report, para. 8.146.
48. Paragraph 1 of the *Statements of Principle concerning the Role of Science in the Codex Decision-Making Process and the Extent to which other Factors are*

Taken into Account, adopted by Decision of the 21st Session of the Codex Alimentarius Commission in 1995, in the Appendix on General Decisions of the Commission, at the end of the *Procedural Manual*, p. 180.

49. Decision of the 24th Session of the Codex Alimentarius Commission of 2001 amending the *Statements of Principle concerning the Role of Science in the Codex Decision-Making Process and the Extent to which other Factors are Taken into Account*, in the Appendix on General Decisions of the Commission, at the end of the *Procedural Manual*, pp. 180–181 (emphasis added).
50. *Working Principles for Risk Analysis for Application in the Framework of the Codex Alimentarius*, in Section IV of the *Procedural Manual*, p. 87.
51. Catherine Button, *The Power to Protect. Trade, Health, and Uncertainty in the WTO* (Hart Publishing, 2004), p. 106.
52. *EC—Hormones*, Panel Report, para. 8.72 (italics by the Panel).
53. *EC—Hormones*, Panel Report, para. 8.72 (italics by the Panel).
54. *EC—Hormones*, Panel Report, para. 8.72 (italics by the Panel).
55. *EC—Hormones*, Panel Report, para. 8.73 (original emphasis, footnote omitted).
56. *EC—Hormones*, Panel Report, para. 8.72 (emphasis added).
57. *EC—Hormones*, Panel Report, para. 8.86.
58. *EC—Hormones*, Report of the Panel, para. 8.86.
59. *EC—Hormones*, Panel Report, para. 8.86 (emphasis by the Panel).

Reference

Button, Catherine. "The Power to Protect. Trade, Health, and Uncertainty in the WTO". *Hart Publishing*, 2004.

WTO Cases

EC – Hormones: EC – Measures Concerning Meat and Meat Products.

- Panel Report WT/DS26/R/USA, WT/DS48/R/CAN, final report circulated August 18, 1997;
- Appellate Body Report WT/DS26/AB/R/USA, WT/DS48/AB/R/CAN, adopted February 13, 1998.

Australia – Salmon: Australia – Measures Affecting Importation of Salmon.

- Panel Report WT/DS18/R, final report circulated June 12, 1998;
- Appellate Body Report WT/DS18/AB/R, adopted November 6, 1998.

United States – Continued Suspension: United States/Canada – Continued Suspension of Obligations in the EC – Hormones Dispute.
- Panel Reports, WT/DS320/R, WT/DS321/R, final reports circulated March 31, 2008;
- Appellate Body Reports, WT/DS320/AB/R, WT/DS321/AB/R, adopted November 14, 2008.

CHAPTER 9

The Appellate Body's Quest for Middle Ground

In the following, it shall be shown that the Appellate Body, by rejecting the Panel's differentiation between risk assessment and risk management, also rebutted a notion of risk characterised as quantitative, *i.e.* probabilistic.

In the form of a preliminary consideration, the Appellate Body addressed 'the Panel's efforts to distinguish between "risk assessment" and "risk management"'.[1] In this respect, the Appellate Body 'stress[ed] … that Article 5 and Annex A of the SPS Agreement speak of "risk assessment" only and that the term "risk management" is not be found either in Article 5 or in any other provision of the *SPS Agreement*'.[2] Hence, the Appellate Body found that the Panel's distinction between risk assessment and risk management has no textual basis. The Appellate Body further observed that the Panel 'apparently' employed the distinction between risk assessment and risk management for achieving or supporting 'what appears to be a *restrictive* notion of risk assessment'.[3]

1 Risk in Human Societies

Turning to risk assessment, the Appellate Body started by recalling the Panel's interpretation of that term:

> We note in this connection that the Panel states that, for purposes of the EC measures in dispute, a risk assessment required by Article 5.1 is 'a *scientific* process aimed at establishing the *scientific* basis for the sanitary measure a Member intends to take'. To the extent that the Panel intended to refer to a

M. Burkard, *Conflicting Philosophies and International Trade Law*,
Philosophy, Public Policy, and Transnational Law,
https://doi.org/10.1007/978-3-319-61067-2_9

> process characterized by systematic, disciplined and objective enquiry and analysis, that is, a mode of studying and sorting out facts and opinions, the Panel's statement is unexceptionable. However, to the extent that the Panel purports to exclude from the scope of a risk assessment in the sense of Article 5.1 all matters not susceptible of quantitative analysis by the empirical or experimental laboratory methods commonly associated with the physical sciences, we believe that the Panel is in error. Some of the kinds of factors listed in Article 5.2 such as 'relevant processes and production methods' and 'relevant inspection, sampling and testing methods' are not necessarily or wholly susceptible of investigation according to laboratory methods of, for example, biochemistry or pharmacology. Furthermore, there is nothing to indicate that the listing of factors that may be taken into account in a risk assessment of Article 5.2 was intended to be a closed list. It is essential to bear in mind that the risk that is to be evaluated in a risk assessment under Article 5.1 is not only risk ascertainable in a science laboratory operating under strictly controlled conditions, but also risk in human societies as they actually exist, in other words, the actual potential for adverse effects on human health in the real world where people live and work and die.[4]

As mentioned above, the distinction made by the Appellate Body between a 'quantitative' notion of risk, on the one hand, and an understanding of risk as the 'actual potential for adverse effects ... in the real world', on the other hand, was a prerequisite for subsuming non-scientific factors under the term risk assessment.

The particular question how to address issues of control, *i.e.* the prevention of abuse of the hormones in dispute, was raised by the European Communities (EC) in the broader context of claims arguing that the Panel had failed to carry out its duty under Article 11 of the DSB, namely 'to make ... an objective assessment of the facts of the case'.

With regard to the issue of control and the prevention of abuse in particular, the Appellate Body noted the claim of the EC that 'the Panel failed to take into account the evidence submitted by the European Communities and ignored statements made by some of its own experts'.[5] Analysing the claim, the Appellate Body observed, in fact, that the Panel had neglected evidence concerning the issue of control on the basis of considering 'that the risks related to the general problem of control should not be taken into account in risk assessment...'[6]

The Appellate Body rejected the a priori exclusion of general control problems by the Panel on the ground that these problems should be addressed in the risk management phase. The Appellate Body reiterated that 'the concept of 'risk management' is not mentioned in any provision of the *SPS Agreement* and, as such, cannot be used to sustain a more restrictive interpretation of 'risk assessment' than is justified by the actual terms of Article 5.2, Article 8 and Annex C of the *SPS Agreement*'.[7]

Based upon its rejection of a distinction between risk assessment and risk management, the Appellate Body in *EC—Hormones* also rejected the Panel's exclusion of control problems from the scope of risk assessment. The Appellate Body began its considerations by recalling the text of Article 5.2 of the *SPS Agreement* as follows:

> In the assessment of risks, Members shall take into account available scientific evidence; relevant processes and production methods; relevant inspection, sampling and testing methods; prevalence of specific diseases or pests; existence of pest- or disease-free areas; relevant ecological and environmental conditions; and quarantine or other treatment.[8]

Considering Article 5.2 of the SPS Agreement as a whole, the Appellate Body observed that 'scientific evidence' is only one element to be looked at in risk assessment. In particular, the Appellate Body noted that not all elements mentioned in Article 5.2 of the SPS Agreement are ascertainable by physical sciences:

> Some of the kinds of factors listed in Article 5.2 such as "relevant processes and production methods" and "relevant inspection, sampling and testing methods" are not necessarily or wholly susceptible of investigation according to laboratory methods of, for example, biochemistry or pharmacology. Furthermore, there is nothing to indicate that the listing of factors that may be taken into account in a risk assessment of Article 5.2 was intended to be a closed list.[9]

The Appellate Body in *EC—Hormones* then turned to the question how the particular issue of misuse or abuse of hormones for beef production has to be considered. The Appellate Body noted:

> [T]he scientific studies referred to by the European Communities, in respect of the five hormones involved here, concluded that their use for growth promotion purposes is "safe", if the hormones are administered in accordance with the requirements of good veterinary practice. Where the condition of observance of good veterinary practice (which is much the same condition attached to the standards, guidelines and recommendations of

> Codex with respect to the use of the five hormones for growth promotion) is *not* followed, the logical inference is that the use of such hormones for growth promotion purposes may or may not be "safe". The *SPS Agreement* requires assessment of the potential for adverse effects on human health arising from the presence of contaminants and toxins in food. We consider that the object and purpose of the *SPS Agreement* justify the examination and evaluation of all such risks for human health whatever their precise and immediate origin may be. We do not mean to suggest that risks arising from potential abuse in the administration of controlled substances and from control problems need to be, or should be, evaluated by risk assessors in each and every case. When and if risks of these types do in fact arise, risk assessors may examine and evaluate them. Clearly, the necessity or propriety of examination and evaluation of such risks would have to be addressed on a case-by-case basis. What, in our view, is a fundamental legal error is to exclude, on an a priori basis, any such risks from the scope of application of Articles 5.1 and 5.2. We disagree with the Panel's suggestion that exclusion of risks resulting from the combination of potential abuse and difficulties of control is justified by distinguishing between "risk assessment" and "risk management". As earlier noted, the concept of "risk management" is not mentioned in any provision of the *SPS Agreement* and, as such, cannot be used to sustain a more restrictive interpretation of "risk assessment" than is justified by the actual terms of Article 5.2, Article 8 and Annex C of the *SPS Agreement*.[10]

Mirroring the renewed controversy over risk assessment and risk management, the Panel and the Appellate Body in the case *US—Continued Suspension* also disagreed over the appropriate approach towards non-scientific factors.

Starting point for renewed clashes between conflicting concepts of the Panel and the Appellate Body in the *US—Continued Suspension* case was the claim of the European Communities that the Panel's approach failed to address problems on the ground properly. In particular, the European Communities asserted that the renewed distinction between risk assessment and risk management made by the Panel 'improperly excluded the evidence concerning misuse or abuse and difficulties of control in the administration of hormones to cattle for growth promotion'.[11]

In particular, the European Communities stressed that 'the Panel's discussion of the potential misuse and abuse in the administration of hormones is in the wrong place, to the extent that this is an aspect of risk assessment, in the sense of Article 5.1–5.3 of the *SPS Agreement*, that is applicable across all identified potential risks and for all six hormones'.[12]

The Panel in the *Continued Suspension* case, however, only agreed in the minor point and disagreed in the main point:

> The Panel agrees with the European Communities that the question of misuse and abuse in the administration of hormones may apply to all six hormones at issue and is an element that can be taken into account in risk assessment, as set forth in Article 5.2 of the *SPS Agreement* and confirmed by the Appellate Body in *EC – Hormones*. However, the Panel did not deem it necessary to address this question in the section regarding the conformity with Article 5.1 of the definitive ban on oestradiol-17β, to the extent that the question whether misuse or abuse exists in the administration of hormones did not have an impact on the issues addressed by the Panel under Article 5.1. Indeed, the question of misuse or abuse in the administration of hormones is relevant to the extent that it can lead to higher concentrations of hormone residues in meat and meat products than would occur if good veterinary practices were applied. As stated by the 1999 Opinion, it is an aspect of exposure assessment. In this case, the Panel found that the European Communities had not evaluated specifically the possibility that the adverse effect that it had identified in its risk assessment come into being, originate, or result from the consumption of meat or meat products which contain veterinary residues of oestradiol-17β as a result of the cattle being treated with this hormone for growth promotion purposes. Therefore, whether the concentrations of hormone residues in meat and meat products could be higher as a result of misuse or abuse did not have to be addressed. The Panel does not deem it necessary to move this section to another part of its findings.[13]

On these grounds, 'the Panel decided to delete the section regarding misuse or abuse in the administration of hormones from its final report (…)'.[14]

The Appellate Body in the *Continued Suspension* case conducted a thorough examination of the Panel's arguments with regard to misuse and abuse of hormones for growth promotion purposes. The Appellate Body started by noting that the Panel seemed of having acknowledged that risks of misuse and abuse of hormones are 'an element that can be taken into account in risk assessment, as set forth in Article 5.2 of the *SPS Agreement* and confirmed by the Appellate Body in *EC—Hormones*'.[15] However, the Appellate Body observed that despite that initial acknowledgment, the Panel finally declined to consider problems of abuse and misuse of hormones under Article 5.1 of the SPS Agreement. The Appellate Body noted in particular:

> Although the Panel does not seem to reject a priori the relevance of the potential risks of misuse or abuse, it then states that it was not necessary to address this question in its analysis, to the extent that it did not have an impact on the issue addressed by the Panel under Article 5.1.[16]

The Appellate Body, however, noticed that 'some of the scientific experts consulted by the Panel indicated that risks arising from residues of oestradiol-17β in bovine meat are likely to increase where good veterinary practices in the administration of this hormone are *not* followed'.[17] In particular, the Appellate Body observed:

> Indeed, these experts agreed that their conclusions in relation to the risks posed by oestradiol-17β were predicated on good veterinary practices being followed. Accordingly, the abuse or misuse in the administration of oestradiol-17β has a bearing on the particular risks being assessed by the European Communities. The Panel's conclusion was thus premature because the Panel could not have decided whether the European Communities failed to evaluate specifically the possible adverse effects of residues of oestradiol-17β in meat before considering the evidence on abuse or misuse. The Panel's summary dismissal of the relevance of the evidence on misuse or abuse at the interim review stage gives the appearance of being an ex post rationalization of an earlier decision to exclude such risks from consideration.[18]

The Appellate Body further observed that risk assessments put forward by the European Communities did, in fact, address the issue of misuse or abuse of hormones for beef production. An expert committee convened under EC legislation, the Scientific Committee on Veterinary Measures relating to Public Health (SCVPH), published its opinion on the issue in a report entitled 'Assessment of Potential Risks to Human Health from Hormones Residue in Bovine Meat and Meat Products' on 30 April 1999 (hereafter: the 1999 SCVPH Opinion). The Appellate Body observed that the 1999 SCVPH Opinion particularly addressed the problem of misuse or abuse of so-called hormone implants. In its 1999 Opinion, the SCVPH 'noted that misplaced implants and black market drugs comprise the risk that extremely high levels of residues of hormones remain in edible tissues of animals. In addition, it has to be noted that the contemporaneous use of growth promoting hormones and veterinary therapeutics drugs increases the prevalence of undesirable r[e]sidues in edible tissues of bovines'.[19]

Turning to risk assessments published by the SCVPH in 2002 (hereafter: the 2002 SCVPH Opinion), the Appellate Body learnt that excessive use, misuse or abuse of a particular growth promoter, namely melengestrol acetate (MGA), could result in the violation of tolerance levels established by regulatory authorities. Specifically with regard to MGA, the SCVPH concluded that '[MGA] applied in concentrations exceeding the licensed doses by a factor of 3 would result in a violation of the tolerance levels as proposed by US-FDA'.[20] And with respect to the particular technique of hormone implants, the SCVPH noted that '[m]odel calculations indicated that, depending on the actual implanted total dose, processing of such injection sites can contaminate tons of (minced) meat or meat products with hormone concentrations violating the ADI/MRL levels as proposed by JECFA and other regulatory bodies'.[21]

Again looking at the 2002 SCVPH Opinion, the Appellate Body also found that scientific experiments simulating the disregard of good veterinary practices had been carried out. In the 2002 Opinion, the SCVPH concluded that '(…) these experiments clearly identify a risk for excessive exposure of consumers to residues from misplaced or off-label used implants and incorrect dose regimes. In these cases, levels of oestradiol and its metabolites in muscle, fat, liver and kidney from hormone treated cattle may be twofold up to several hundred folds higher as compared to untreated meat. The level of increase depends on the treatment regime and the actual hormone levels in the implants used'.[22]

Having examined risk assessments put forward by the European Communities, the Appellate Body turned to testimonies of scientific experts for shedding additional light on the question whether misuse or abuse of hormones for beef production increases risks to human health. In particular, the Appellate Body took a look at testimonies of Dr. Guttenplan and Dr. De Brabander. On the question whether the safety of hormone application in beef production is contingent upon observance of good veterinary practices, Dr. Guttenplan answered that adverse effects are 'unlikely if good veterinary practices are followed'. However, Dr. Guttenplan added that, '[i]f good veterinary practices are not followed, the potential for adverse effects may be significant'.[23] The Appellate Body observed that Dr. De Brabander responded in a similar manner, stating that '[i]mproper administration of implants or misplaced implants create potential hazards to human health'.[24] The Appellate Body further noted the opinion of Dr. De Brabander on the effect of misuse or abuse of hormones for beef production on the applicability of Codex standards. In particular, the Appellate Body pointed at the view of Dr. De Brabander that evidence 'regarding misuse or abuse of the hormones at issue in the United States and Canada calls indeed into question the potential applicability of Codex standards with regard to imports of meat from cattle treated with hormones from the United States and Canada'.[25]

From its examination, the Appellate Body draw the conclusion that the Panel dismissed to address the problem of misuse or abuse of hormones in its analysis under Article 5.1 of the *SPS Agreement*, despite evidence provided by the 1999 and 2002 Opinions, i.e. the European Communities' risk assessments, and testimonies by scientific experts. Specifically, the Appellate Body considered the Panel's formal argument that evidence on misuse or abuse of hormones relates to the exposure assessment stage of risk assessment is, on its own, unconvincing:

> The Panel summarily dismissed the relevance of the evidence on misuse or abuse stating that it relates to exposure assessment and adding that it is not necessary to address it given the finding that the European Communities had not evaluated *specifically* the possibility that the adverse effects arise from the consumption of meat from cattle treated with oestradiol-17β for growth-promotion purposes. We recognize that the 1999 Opinion examines the risks of misuse or abuse under the heading "Exposure considerations upon misuse". After discussing the evidence on misuse and abuse, the 2002 Opinion states that 'these data have to be considered in any quantitative exposure assessment exercise.' This, however, cannot justify the Panel's failure to address the evidence on misuse or abuse. The European Communities made it clear that the risks of abuse or misuse were a relevant consideration in its risk assessment. This is confirmed in the 1999 and 2002 Opinions. At least two of the scientific experts consulted by the Panel recognized that the misuse or abuse in the administration of the hormones could give rise to adverse effects. The Panel had a duty to engage with this evidence and with the discussion of this evidence in the SCVPH Opinions. By summarily dismissing the evidence on the misuse or abuse in the administration of the hormones and the consequent conclusions in the SCVPH Opinions in the manner that it did, the Panel incorrectly applied Article 5.1 and the definition of 'risk assessment' in Annex A of the *SPS Agreement*, as interpreted by the Appellate Body.[26]

Accordingly, the Appellate Body in the *Continued Suspension* case arrived at the conclusion 'that the Panel erred in its interpretation and application of Article 5.1 of the SPS Agreement in relation to risks of misuse and abuse in the administration of hormones to cattle for growth-promotion purposes'.[27]

Summarising findings of Panels and the Appellate Body on the issue of non-scientific factors, in a nutshell, one can see the following:

The Panel in *EC—Hormones* was of the view that general problems of compliance and control should be taken into account in risk management. This view was consistent with the doctrine of risk analysis, as applied by Codex.

The Appellate Body's broad concept of risk assessment also covering non-scientific factors runs contrary to the doctrine of risk analysis deferring non-scientific factors to the risk management phase. The Appellate Body's concept rejects the notion of risk management. From an analytical point of view, one might question whether and how the Appellate Body's broad concept of risk assessment, extending to non-scientific factors, *e.g.* general problems of control and compliance, may logically fit into the science-based approach of the SPS Agreement in general.

Having refused the notion of risk management, the Appellate Body in *EC—Hormones* remained challenged by non-scientific factors, for example, compliance and control problems. The Appellate Body was thus constrained to encompass non-scientific factors into the process of risk assessment.

If non-scientific factors are to be included in a risk assessment, then, inevitably, the notion of 'risk' is affected. On these grounds, the Appellate Body in E*C—Hormones* and subsequent WTO legal practice had to adopt a 'qualitative' notion of risk. A qualitative notion of risk, *i.e.* a notion extending over 'risk in human societies as they actually exist' implies, in turn, a broader notion of 'science' able of assessing such risk. However, it was shown that a broader notion of science may pose questions with regard to the rather narrow definition of science implied in paragraph 1 of Annex A of the SPS Agreement. Insofar, it has to be seen whether the concept of the Appellate Body, commended by some of being broader than that of the Panel, may be able to really materialise under existing SPS provisions.

The Panel in the case *US—Continued Suspension* apparently aimed at returning to a formal separation of risk assessment and risk management in ways similar to the attempt of the Panel in *EC—Hormones*. The Appellate

Body in the *Continued Suspension* case, however, insisted that questions about misuse and abuse of hormones must be dealt with under the scope of Article 5.1 of the SPS Agreement.

The overarching conflict over the 'correct' interpretation of risk assessment did not end by the Appellate Body's ruling in *EC—Hormones*. Ten years later, in the subsequent case *United States—Continued Suspension of Obligations in the EC—Hormones Dispute* (hereafter: *US—Continued Suspension*),[28] the Appellate Body felt prompted to recall its earlier findings and to upbraid an apostatising Panel.

What prompted the Appellate Body for doing so were claims by the European Communities that the Panel in the *Continued Suspension* case had adopted 'an extremely narrow and consequently erroneous interpretation of Article 5.1 and failed to take into account that risk assessment and risk management partly overlap in the *SPS Agreement*'.[29] According to the European Communities' assertions, 'the Panel's restrictive interpretation of risk assessment led it to wrongfully exclude from the scope of its analysis under Article 5.1 evidence concerning misuse or abuse and difficulties of control in the administration of hormones to cattle for growth promotion'.[30]

The Appellate Body in *US—Continued Suspension* started its examination 'by reviewing the Panel's understanding of the Appellate Body's interpretation of Article 5.1 in *EC—Hormones* and particularly its discussion of the relevance of risk management factors of the purposes of a risk assessment within the meaning of Annex A and Article 5.1 of the *SPS Agreement*'.[31] The Appellate Body gave the following account of the Panel's understanding of the Appellate Body's ruling in *EC—Hormones*:

> Although the Appellate Body [in *EC – Hormones*] disapproved of the original panel's distinction between 'risk assessment' and 'risk management because it had no textual basis in the Agreement, this Panel [*i.e.*, the Panel in *US—Continued Suspension*] can find no statement by the Appellate Body confirming that what the European Communities describes as risk management is included within the definition of a risk assessment as set forth in Annex A (4) of the SPS Agreement. In fact, the Appellate Body stressed that Article 5 and Annex A speak of *risk assessment* only and that the term *risk management* is not to be found either in Article 5 or in any other provision of the *SPS Agreement*.
>
> The Panel agrees with the Appellate Body that its role as a treaty interpreter is to 'read and interpret the words actually used by the agreement under

> examination, and not words which the interpreter may feel should have been used.' The Panel takes note of the Appellate Body's finding that a risk assessment can take into account 'matters not susceptible of quantitative analysis by the empirical or experimental laboratory methods commonly associated with the physical sciences.' However, the Panel finds that neither that finding nor the text of the Agreement includes within the definition of a risk assessment the concept put forward by the European Communities as 'risk management'.[32]

The Appellate Body observed that the Panel, on these grounds, went on asking the experts whether the SCVPH Opinions, that is, the EC risk assessment, 'identified the potential for adverse effects on human health of residues of oestradiol-17β in the meat of cattle treated with this hormone when applied in accordance with good veterinary practice.'[33]

The Appellate Body further observed that at the interim review stage, the European Communities objected that the Panel 'misinterpret[ed]' what the Appellate Body had said in *EC—Hormones.*[34] As a response to the European Communities' objection, the Appellate Body noted the following response of the Panel:

> The Appellate Body [in *EC – Hormones*] disapproved of the panel's use in the original *EC—Hormones* dispute of the distinction between 'risk assessment and 'risk management because it hat no textual basis. However, this did not mean that the Appellate Body endorsed an interpretation of Article 5.1 or Annex A(4) of the SPS Agreement that included a risk management stage. In fact, it emphatically stated that the term 'risk management' is not to be found in Article 5 of any other provision of the *SPS Agreement.* The Panel, therefore, finds no basis for the European Communities' assertion that the Appellate Body 'confirmed that a risk assessment within the meaning of Article 5.1 includes a risk management stage which is the responsibility of the regulator to carry out and not the scientific bodies'.[35]

In an additional footnote, the Appellate Body in *US—Continued Suspension* further noted the following arguments put forward by the preceding Panel:

> Nowhere in the texts of Article 5.1 and Annex A(4) does the Panel find support for the European Communities' contention that a risk assessment within the meaning of the SPS Agreement includes 'weighing policy alternatives in light of the results of risk assessment and, if required, selecting and

implementing appropriate control options, including regulatory measures.' What the European Communities seems to be describing is how a government chooses an appropriate SPS measure based on a risk assessment. The Panel does not find that this is contemplated by the texts of Article 5.1 and Annex A(4) of the *SPS Agreement.*[36]

In similar perspective, the Appellate Body in *US—Continued Suspension* observed that the preceding Panel 'did not address evidence on misuse or abuse in the administration of the hormones in its analysis under Article 5.7 of the *SPS Agreement*'.[37] In particular, the Appellate Body noted the following reasoning of the Panel with regard to the applicability of Article 5.7 of the *SPS Agreement.* According to the Panel in *US—Continued Suspension*:

> … Article 5.7 is applicable when relevant scientific evidence is not sufficient to undertake a risk assessment in conformity with Article 5.1. Whether instances of misuse or abuse in the administration of hormones exist or not is not as such a scientific issue likely to make a risk assessment within the meaning of Article 5.1 and Annex A(4) of the SPS Agreement impossible.[38]

Concluding on the reasoning of the Panel on the issue of misuse or abuse of hormones and related control problems, the Appellate Body in *US—Continued Suspension* found it 'difficult to reconcile the Panel's understanding of *EC—Hormones* with what the Appellate Body held in that report'.[39]

The Appellate Body in *US—Continued Suspension* recalled that in the case *EC—Hormones*, the Appellate Body 'rejected the rigid distinction drawn by the panel between "risk assessment" and "risk management"', explaining:

> We must stress, in this connection, that Article 5 and Annex A of the SPS Agreement speak of 'risk assessment' only and that the term 'risk management' is not to be found either in Article 5 of in any other provision of the *SPS Agreement.* Thus, the Panel's distinction, which it apparently employs to achieve or support what appears to be a restrictive notion of risk assessment, has no textual basis.[40]

Furthermore, the Appellate Body in *US—Continued Suspension* reiterated the view of the Appellate Body in *EC—Hormones* that 'the concept of "risk management" is not mentioned in any provision of the *SPS Agreement* and, as such, cannot be used to sustain a more *restrictive* interpretation of "risk assessment" than is justified by the actual terms of Article 5.2, Article 8 and Annex C of the *SPS Agreement*'.[41]

As a consequence of its line of reasoning, the Appellate Body in *US—Continued Suspension* arrived at the following conclusion:

> Therefore, in our view, the Panel's interpretation of 'risk assessment' resulted in the same 'restrictive notion of risk assessment' that the Appellate Body found to be erroneous in *EC – Hormones.* The Panel sought in this case to rewrite the Appellate Body Report in *EC – Hormones* and to re-establish the rigid distinction between 'risk assessment' and 'risk management' that the Appellate Body had rejected in that case.[42]

Consequences of opposing views on the concept of risk assessment were, among others, diverging perspectives on the problem of misuse and abuse of hormones for beef production and related control problems. Such problems on the ground are commonly addressed under the heading of 'non-scientific factors' or 'other legitimate factors'.

2 Relativism in Standard-Setting

In the *Hormones* case, the Appellate Body found 'that the Panel has misconceived the relationship between Articles 3.1, 3.2 and 3.3 [of the SPS Agreement]'.[43] The Appellate Body identified the 'general rule—exception' relationship introduced by the Panel with regard to Article 3.1 of the SPS Agreement (the general rule) and Article 3.3 of the SPS Agreement (the exception) as a main cause for the established misconception.[44]

More in detail, the Appellate Body observed 'three legal interpretations' made by the Panel 'en route' of developing the 'general rule—exception' relationship.[45] The first interpretative point related to the equation of 'based on' in Article 3.1 with 'conform to' in Article 3.2 of the SPS Agreement. The second interpretative point related to the 'misconceived' relationship between Articles 3.1, 3.2 and 3.3 of the SPS Agreement. The third interpretative point pertained to the requirements of Article 3.3 of the SPS Agreement. Between these three interpretative points suggested by the Panel, the Appellate Body perceived some sort of 'intertwined' relation.[46]

The Appellate Body 'read the Panel's interpretation that Article 3.2. "equates" measures "based on" international standards with measures which "conform to" such standards, as signifying that "based on" and "conform to" are identical in meaning'.[47] Hence, the Appellate Body understood that '[T]he Panel is thus saying that, henceforth, SPS measures of Members *must* "conform to" Codes standards, guidelines and recommendations'.[48]

However, the Appellate Body disapproved the interpretation of the Panel (1) on textual grounds, *i.e.* because of the ordinary meaning of the terms, (2) because of systematic reasons, namely the respective placing, use and function of the terms 'based on' and 'conform to' in the system of the three paragraphs of Article 3 of the SPS Agreement, (3) and because of the object and purpose of Article 3 of the SPS Agreement in general.

First, applying a grammatical interpretation, the Appellate Body observed that the ordinary meanings of 'based on', on the one hand, and 'conform to', on the other hand, are different. Something is commonly considered to be 'based on' another thing, the Appellate Body noted, 'when the former "stands" or is "founded" or "built" upon or "is supported by" the latter'.[49]

On the other hand, the Appellate Body noted, 'much more is required before one thing may be regarded as "conform[ing] to" another: the former must "comply with, yield or show compliance" with the latter'.[50] Quite different from the ordinary meaning of 'based on', the reference of 'conform to' the Appellate Body found, 'is to "correspondence in form or manner", to "compliance with" or "acquiescence", to "follow[ing] in form or nature"'.[51]

Perceiving the term 'based on' broader and more open than the term 'conform to', the Appellate Body concluded that, on the one hand, a measure 'conforming to' a standard is naturally also 'based on' that standard. On the other hand and in contrast, a measure 'based on' a standard might not qualify for being considered as 'conforming to' that standard, 'as where only some, not all, of the elements of the standard are incorporated into the measure'.[52]

Second, with respect to the systematic in which the terms 'based on' and 'conform to' were used, the Appellate Body observed that the terms were used in different articles, in different contexts' and even in differing paragraphs of the same article. From this finding, the Appellate Body concluded 'that the choice and use of different words in different places in the SPS Agreement are deliberate (...)'.[53]

Third and finally, the Appellate Body took into consideration the object and purpose of Article 3 of the SPS Agreement. In this respect, the Appellate Body noted that the purpose of Article 3 of the SPS Agreement, as indicated in its title and its first paragraph, is '[t]o harmonize sanitary and phytosanitary measures on as wide a basis as possible ...'. In addition, the Appellate Body referred to the preamble of the SPS Agreement which, *inter alia*, states that WTO Members '[d]esir[e] to *further the use of harmonized [SPS]sanitary and phytosanitary measures between Members* on the basis of international standards, guidelines and recommendations developed by the relevant international organizations ...'.[54] Furthermore, the Appellate Body noted that Article 12 of the SPS Agreement established a Committee on SPS measures with the task of, *inter alia*, 'furtherance of its objectives, in particular with respect to harmonization' (Article 12.1 of the SPS Agreement) and to 'encourage the use of international standards, guidelines or recommendations by all Members' (Article 12.2 of the SPS Agreement). Predicating on these findings, the Appellate Body was of the view 'that harmonization of SPS measures of Members on the basis of international standards is projected in the Agreement, as a *goal*, yet to be realized *in the future*'.[55] On the other hand, the Appellate Body perceived the approach of the Panel of equating 'based on' with 'conform to' as requiring WTO Members to harmonise their SPS measures '*in the here and now*'.[56] The approach of the Panel, the Appellate Body noted, would, in effect, 'vest such international standards, guidelines and recommendations (which are by the terms of the Codex *recommendatory* in form and nature) with *obligatory* force and effect', transforming them into 'binding *norms*'.[57] At this point, the Appellate Body invoked the interpretative principle of *in dubio mitius* which instructs treaty interpreters to opt for the interpretation the least onerous if the meaning of a term is ambiguous. In light of the principle of *in dubio mitius*, the Appellate Body rejected the assumption of the Panel 'that sovereign states intended to impose upon themselves the more onerous, rather than the less burdensome, obligation by mandating *conformity* or *compliance with*' international standards, guidelines and recommendations.[58] Hence, the Appellate Body concluded that for sustaining 'such an assumption and to warrant such a far-reaching interpretation, treaty language far more specific and compelling than that found in Article 3 of the *SPS Agreement* would be necessary'.[59]

Thus, the Appellate Body rejected the Panel's notion that the term 'based on' in Article 3.1 can be equated to the term 'conform to' in Article 3.2 of the SPS Agreement.

Having rejected the Panel's perception of a 'general rule—exception' relationship in Article 3 of the SPS Agreement, the Appellate Body embarked on its own examination of the relationship between Articles 3.2, 3.2 and 3.3 of the SPS Agreement.

The Appellate Body started its examination by recalling that, generally speaking, Article 3 of the SPS Agreement covers situations 'where a relevant international standard, guideline or recommendation exists'.[60]

Turning to Article 3 of the SPS Agreement in detail, the Appellate Body observed that the three paragraphs of that Article offer three distinct approaches for WTO Members establishing their respective SPS measures.

First, a WTO Member may choose to adhere to international standards, guidelines or recommendations without reservation. In this case, the WTO Member may opt for the approach offered by the second paragraph of Article 3 of the SPS Agreement. With regard to Article 3.2 of the SPS Agreement, the Appellate Body noted that an SPS measure that 'conforms to' an international standard virtually 'would embody the international standard completely and, for practical purposes, converts it into a municipal standard'.[61] An SPS measure 'conforming to' international standards 'enjoys the benefit of a presumption (albeit a rebuttable one) that it is consistent with the relevant provisions of the SPS Agreement and of the GATT 1994'.[62]

Second, a WTO Member may choose to adopt some, but not all elements of an international standard, guideline or recommendation. In this case, the WTO Member may opt for the approach offered by the first paragraph of Article 3 of the SPS Agreement. With respect to Article 3.1 of the SPS Agreement, the Appellate Body observed that an SPS measure 'based on' an existing international standard 'may adopt some, not necessarily all, of the elements of the international standard'.[63] The consequences of deciding to 'base' an SPS measure 'on' international standards is twofold. A WTO Member 'basing' its SPS measure 'on' an existing international standard does, on the one hand, 'not benefit from the presumption of consistency set up in Article 3.2' of the SPS Agreement.[64] On the other hand, this WTO Member is 'not penalized by exemption of a complaining Member from the normal burden of showing a *prima facie* case of inconsistency with Article 3.1 or any other relevant article of the SPS Agreement or of the GATT 1994'.[65]

Third, a WTO Member may choose to adopt SPS measures resulting in levels of protection different than those implicit in the respective international standards, guidelines or recommendations. With view on Article 3.3

of the SPS Agreement, the Appellate Body explicitly noted that the WTO Member's appropriate level of protection resulting from SPS measures not 'based on' international standards 'may be higher than that implied in the international standard'.[66] The right of WTO Members to determine their respective appropriate levels of protection was considered by the Appellate Body as 'an important right'. At this point, the Appellate Body recalled the sixth preambular paragraph of the SPS Agreement which reads as follows:

> Members,
>
> (...) Desiring to further the use of harmonized sanitary and phytosanitary measures between Members, on the basis of international standards, guidelines and recommendations, developed by the relevant international organizations, including the Codex Alimentarius Commission, the International Office of Epizootics, and the relevant international and regional organizations operating under the framework of the International Plant Protection Convention, without requiring Members to change their appropriate level of protection of human, animal or plant life or health.[67]

On these grounds, the Appellate Body concluded:

> [T]his right of a Member to establish its own level sanitary protection under Article 3.3 of the *SPS Agreement* is an autonomous right and *not* an 'exception' from a 'general obligation' under Article 3.1.[68]

Briefly worded, the Appellate Body rejected the Panel's notion of a 'general rule- exception' relationship between Articles 3.1 and 3.2 of the SPS Agreement, on the one hand, and Article 3.3 of the SPS Agreement, on the other hand. Instead, the Appellate Body stated that the right of a WTO Member to establish its own level of protection is an *autonomous right* and not an exception.

Considering the case *Australia—Salmon*, the Appellate Body initially recalled that the Panel had erroneously considered the heat-treatment requirement as the SPS measure in question, whereas, in fact, it was the import prohibition which has to be analysed.[69] The Appellate Body, however, agreed with the Panel that Article 5.6 and the footnote to this provision require a three-pronged test for examining the 'trade-restrictiveness' of an SPS measure.[70]

Coming to the essential second element of the three-pronged test of Article 5.6 of the SPS Agreement and its footnote, the Appellate Body disagreed with the Panel basically on grounds concerning the question how the appropriate level of protection should actually be determined. In this respect, the Appellate Body observed that the Panel's approach for examining whether Article 5.6 is violated was 'based on the Panel's premise that "the *level of* protection implied or reflected in a sanitary *measure* or regime imposed by a WTO Member can be presumed to be at least as high as the level of protection considered to be *appropriate* by that Member"'.[71]

In contrast to the Panel, the Appellate Body was of the view that Australia had, in fact, determined its appropriate level of protection, putting it at 'high' or 'very conservative' levels, though not at a 'zero-risk' level.[72] However, in situations where a WTO Member had actually determined its appropriate level of protection, the Appellate Body perceived the substitution of the level of protection expressed by that Member with own reasoning of Panels or the Appellate Body as a breach of competence.[73] Or, in the Appellate Body's own words:

> The determination of the appropriate level of protection … is a *prerogative* of the Member concerned and not of a Panel or of the Appellate Body.[74]

Then, the Appellate Body went in for an outline of general remarks on the relationship between the determination of the appropriate level of protection (ALOP), on the one hand, and measures for sanitary or phytosanitary protection, on the other hand. In the following, the reasoning of the Appellate Body on the determination of the appropriate level of protection (ALOP) shall be comprehensively displayed.

The Appellate Body commenced its reflections with the following fundamental statement:

> The 'appropriate level of protection' established by a Member and the 'SPS measure' have to be clearly distinguished. They are not one and the same thing. The first is an *objective*, the second is an *instrument* chosen to attain or implement that objective.[75]

From the provisions of the SPS Agreement, the Appellate Body 'deduced … that the determination by a Member of the "appropriate level of protection" logically precedes the establishment or decision on maintenance of an "SPS measure"'.[76] In particular, the Appellate Body pointed at the following provisions of the SPS Agreement clarifying the chronology of

(1) the determination of the appropriate level of protection, and (2) the subsequent establishment of the SPS measure:

Article 3.3 of the SPS Agreement, which reads, in part, as follows:

> Members may introduce or maintain sanitary or phytosanitary measures which result in a higher level of sanitary or phytosanitary protection than would be achieved by measures based on the relevant international standards … *as a consequence* of the level of sanitary or phytosanitary protection a Member determines to be appropriate …[77]

Article 5 of the SPS Agreement on the *Assessment of Risk and Determination of the Appropriate Level of Sanitary or Phytosanitary Protection* stipulates in its third paragraph, *inter alia*:

> In assessing the risk to animal or plant life or health and *determining* the measure *to be applied for achieving* the appropriate level of sanitary or phytosanitary protection from such risk …[78]

Paragraph 4 of Article 5 of the SPS Agreement addresses, in particular, the determination of the appropriate level of protection, stating that:

> Members should, *when determining* the appropriate level of sanitary or phytosanitary protection, take into account the objective of minimizing negative trade effects.[79]

Finally, Article 5.6 of the SPS Agreement indicates a sequencing, whereby the level of protection is determined at first, followed by the subsequent implementation of the SPS measure:

> … *when establishing or maintaining* sanitary or phytosanitary measures to achieve the appropriate level of sanitary or phytosanitary protection, Members shall ensure that such measures are not more trade-restrictive than required to achieve their appropriate level of sanitary or phytosanitary protection … [80]

With respect to Article 5.6 of the SPS Agreement, the Appellate Body concluded:

> The words of Article 5.6, in particular the terms '*when establishing or maintaining* sanitary … protection', demonstrate that the determination of

> the level of protection is an element in the decision-making process which logically *precedes* and is *separate* from the establishment or maintenance of the SPS measure". It is the appropriate level of protection which determines the SPS measure to be introduced or maintained, not the SPS measure introduced or maintained which determines the appropriate level of protection. To imply the appropriate level of protection from the existing SPS measure would be to assume that the measure always achieves the appropriate level of protection determined by the Member. That clearly cannot be the case.[81]

Having established that the Panel's implication from the SPS measure to the appropriate level of protection is wrong, the Appellate Body went on with general remarks on whether the SPS Agreement imposes an obligation on WTO Members to effectively determine their respective 'appropriate levels of protection (ALOP)'. In this regard, the Appellate Body concurred with the Panel that the SPS Agreement 'does not contain an explicit provision which obliges WTO Members to determine the appropriate level of protection'.[82] However, and in contrast to the Panel, the Appellate Body perceived that an obligation to determine the appropriate level of protection is 'implicit in several provisions of the SPS Agreement, in particular, in paragraph 3 of Annex B, Article 4.1, Article 5.4 and Article 5.6 of the SPS Agreement'.[83] This implicit obligation to determine the appropriate level of protection is, according to the Appellate Body, not an obligation to determine the appropriate level of protection 'in quantitative terms'.[84] On the other hand, the Appellate Body emphasised in general terms that '[t]his does not mean, however, that an importing Member is free to determine its level of protection with such vagueness or equivocation that the application of the relevant provisions of the SPS Agreement, such as Article 5.6, becomes impossible'.[85] Paving the way for Panels to establish the appropriate level of protection of WTO Members failing to do so themselves, the Appellate Body declared it as 'obviously wrong' to interpret the SPS Agreement 'in a way that would render nugatory entire articles or paragraphs … of this Agreement and allow Members to escape from their obligations under this Agreement'.[86] As a consequence, the Appellate Body believed 'that in cases where a Member does not determine its appropriate level of protection, or does so with insufficient precision, the appropriate level of protection may be established by Panels on the basis of the level of protection reflected in the SPS measure actually applied'.[87] Otherwise, the Appellate Body recalled its general remarks, 'a Member's failure to comply with the implicit obligations to determine its appropriate level of protection—with sufficient precision—would allow it to escape from its obligations under this Agreement and, in particular, its obligations under Articles 55 and 5.6'.[88]

However, in the case *Australia—Salmon*, things were different. Refocusing on the case at hand, the Appellate Body found that 'Australia determined its appropriate level of protection, and did so with sufficient precision to apply Article 5.6 (…)'.[89] In the *Salmon* case, the two problems were that (1) the Panel substituted Australia's determination of its appropriate level of protection with the assumption that this level is reflected in the SPS measures actually applied and (2) that the Panel erroneously took the heat-treatment requirement as the SPS measure at issue, whilst it was the import prohibition which should have been taken under consideration. The first problem was a legal question addressed and clarified by the Appellate Body (see above).

The second problem, however, was a factual issue which would have required the Appellate Body 'to examine whether any of the possible *alternative SPS measures* […] [*i.e.*, the five alternative quarantine policy options mentioned in Australia's evaluation Report from 1996] would achieve Australia's appropriate level of protection'.[90] Such an examination would presuppose that the Appellate Body would 'know what level of protection could be achieved by each of these alternative SPS measures'.[91] In this respect, however, the Appellate Body recalled the factual findings of the Panel indicating that Australia's evaluation report, *i.e.* Australia's 1996 Final Report, 'does not substantively *evaluate* the relative risks associated with these different options [i.e., the five quarantine policy options mentioned in the 1996 Final Report] …'[92] Hence, the Appellate Body was facing a situation within which it was 'impossible to verify in an objective manner on the basis of the 1996 Final Report, whether any of the alternative policy options discussed in this report would achieve Australia's appropriate level of protection (…)'.[93]

Summarising interpretations of the appropriate level of protection (ALOP) in the case *Australia—Salmon*, one may observe that the Panel perceived the concept of the determination of the appropriate level of protection (ALOP) as a reflection of, and thus implied in, the SPS measure at issue. The Appellate Body disagreed. In contrast, the Appellate Body clearly separated and recognised (1) the determination of the appropriate level of protection (ALOP) as a *policy objective* from (2) the subsequent implementation of an SPS measure as an *instrument* for achieving the policy objective. Hence, one may conclude that the Appellate Body in the *Salmon* case acknowledge the role of policy in the process of determining appropriate levels of protection (ALOP).

3 Panels and the Appellate Body Between Epistemological Antipodes

Comparing the different approaches of Panels and the Appellate Body, respectively, one may note that the former follows the concept of risk analysis more closely, whereas the latter follows a textual interpretation of the SPS Agreement. The rather objectivist approach of Panels is correct in following the concept of risk analysis, but exceeds text and presumable intention of WTO Members, as the Appellate Body recalled. The contextualist interpretation of the Appellate Body, on the other hand, is according to the text and presumably according to the intention of WTO Members. But by refuting a notion of risk management, the Appellate Body's approach runs in conflict with the concept of risk analysis.

Opposing interpretations of risk and risk assessment by Panels and the Appellate Body, respectively, are conveying the impression of a 'hither and thither'. However, considering that at the heart of the controversy are lying different philosophical approaches and epistemological concepts, then the flip-flopping interpretation may be better conceived as an oscillation between two opposing poles, namely positivism and relativism: whereas Panels adopted a rather positivist approach, the Appellate Body, on the other hand, tried to find some middle way between positivist and relativist risk conceptions.[94]

Sungjoon Cho perceived the *Hormones* dispute as a 'conflict of paradigms' in the Kuhnian sense. From a paradigmatic perspective, the Panel's findings represented 'mainstream science':

> First of all, it may be useful to capture this interpretive fissure as a conflict of "paradigms" in the Kuhnian sense. Here, two paradigms clashed over the safety of hormones in food. One paradigm, which the U.S. and the panel adopted, focuses on the *level* of hormone residue in the human body regardless of its pathway or metabolites. Under this paradigm, there is no significant regulatory difference between naturally-occurring hormones in foods (such as hormones in milk or broccoli) and artificially-injected hormones (such as hormones in cattle). This paradigm represents the mainstream view or the "normal science," according to Kuhn, which is

> incorporated in the international standards (the Codex standards). Therefore, the panel ruled that the EC violated the WTO norms (the SPS Agreement) by treating like situations (naturally-occurring hormones and artificially-injected hormones) in an unlike manner (no regulatory intervention v. a total ban).[95]

In contrast, the ruling of the Appellate Body reflected an alternative paradigm, coming along as a more inclusive, rather non-technical approach:

> The AB de facto substituted its own version of science for the conventional version of science when it identified a "fundamental difference" between these two situations. The AB observed that any attempt to compare them would lead to "absurdity." The AB replaced *techne*, which is represented by the laboratory science, with *phronesis*, which is based on common sense-based science befitting the "real world where people live and work and die." Under this interpretation, the EC did not violate Article 5.5 of the SPS Agreement since these two situations were not comparable in the first place.[96]

On the basis of the concept of administrative constitutionalism, Elizabeth Fisher provided a convincing explanation for diverging concepts of risk contrived by Panels and the Appellate Body respectively. Starting point of Fisher's analysis is the distinction between two paradigms in administrative constitutionalism: on the one hand, there is the rational-instrumental paradigm of administrative constitutionalism, and on the other hand there is the deliberative-constitutive understanding of administrative constitutionalism (see Chap. 2 above). Interestingly, Fisher related diverging concepts of risk contrived by Panels and the Appellate Body to these different paradigms of administrative constitutionalism. With regard to the Panel's approach in the case *EC—Hormones* in particular, Fisher observed:

> For the Panel, the task of a member's regulatory body in setting a standard was to apply the facts to a normative prescription by using an analytical methodology, and its decision is a perfect example of defining risk assessment in RI [i.e. rational-instrumental] terms. Standard-setting was largely characterised as a compartmentalised process in which the standard-setter identified the facts and then applied those facts to a pre-ordained normative prescription. As this was the case, the process of assessing the EU's compliance wit the SPS Agreement was understood as requiring the scrutiny of the analytical methodology of the risk assessment and the methodological

> rigour of the scientific basis. (...) Risk assessment was not complicated by scientific uncertainty or socio-economic complexity.[97]

In contrast, the approach of the Appellate Body towards risk assessment was characterised by Fisher as more inclusive, complex and differentiated:

> Implicit in the Appellate Body's approach is an appreciation of the complexities in assessing risk and the problems of scientific uncertainty. The Appellate Body was not being 'scientific' or 'anti-scientific' but was instead requiring the assessment of risk to be on a broader basis than understanding risk assessment as an *analytical straitjacket* would allow. In other words, the Appellate Body was conceptualising standard-setting and risk assessment more as reasoning processes than as fact-finding processes. (...) The Appellate Body's approach can be treated as being underpinned by a DC [i.e. deliberative-constitutive] approach. Standard-setting was understood to be a complex enterprise not easily kept within the boundaries of stringent risk-assessment methodologies. Instead, the Appellate Body assessed the compatibility of the EU's measures with the Agreement by determining whether the EU had carried out a coherent process of reasoning.[98]

As the reason, underlying different approaches towards risk and risk assessment by the Panel and the Appellate Body in *EC—Hormones*, Fisher identified different opinions about the very purpose of the SPS Agreement. For the Panel, the SPS Agreement was an instrument for the harmonisation of SPS measures following international standards. For the Appellate Body, in contrast, the objective of the SPS Agreement was the identification and invalidation of protectionist measures camouflaged as SPS measures. According to Fisher, the difference of approach of the Panel and the Appellate Body towards risk assessment in *EC—Hormones*

> ... can be understood as a product of the fact that the Panel and the Appellate Body understood the SPS Agreement as serving different purposes. The Panel largely characterised the Agreement as being a means for reducing regulatory heterogeneity. As this was the case, the Agreement was understood to require the harmonisation of standards on the basis of international standards. The imposition of an RI [i.e. rational-instrumental] approach would seem to provide a greater guarantee of this occurring, because it would appear to give a lesser role for discretion by placing the same analytical burden on decision-makers. In contrast, the Appellate Body understood the Agreement as being far more about ensuring that bogus SPS measures were invalidated. As this was the case, it was not so much concerned with ensuring

> that standards were consistent, as concerned that they were 'genuine' SPS measures. The DC [i.e. deliberative-constitutive] approach is entirely consistent with this, and the complexity of risk as recognised by this paradigm is a major reason why different Members may legitimately have different measures.[99]

Drawing on this considerations, one may characterise the Panel's approach rather as offensive, whereas the Appellate Body's approach seems to be rather defensive; whereas the Appellate Body seems to content itself to the purpose of detecting disguised protectionism, the Panel's approach seems to go further, following some kind of rather offensive market-opening agenda. Such an interpretation is supported by scholars emphasising economic implications of different interpretative approaches. Sungjoon Cho, for instance, pointed at distributive effects coming along with different interpretative paradigms:

> For example, the European paradigm against the hormone-treated beef tends to protect European cattle growers who mainly produce hormone-less beef from the influx of American hormone-treated beef. Therefore, it is in the vital interest of the American farmers to shift the European paradigm in a way which may permit their products to circulate in the European market.[100]

Catherine Button suggested a more pragmatic explanation for the fact that Panels and the Appellate Body put forward different risk assessment concepts. Button considered that the intention of the Appellate Body for refusing to discern between risk assessment and risk management 'does not appear to have been to reject the general scheme of risk regulation (…) or to suggest that risk assessment may be overtly policy-driven at the expense of scientific risk assessment'.[101] As Button remarked, the intention of the Appellate Body was rather to indicate 'that risk assessment can and should extend beyond the laboratory, into evaluating "risk in human society as they *actually exist*"'.[102] Notably, Button pointed at another intention which may have motivated the Appellate Body to avoid the risk assessment —risk management distinction. Button considered that in case the traditional distinction between risk assessment and risk management would be transposed into the SPS Agreement, 'it could be argued that, absent reference to risk management, risk management decisions not explicitly mentioned in the Agreement are beyond the WTO's jurisdiction'. Accordingly, Button observed that the Appellate Body's refusal 'to confine references to risk assessment in the SPS Agreement to the activities which fall within risk assessment in regulatory practice, the Appellate Body has opened up the possibility of reviewing a wider range of risk management decisions'.[103]

In a nutshell, the conflicting approaches to risk assessment by Panels and the Appellate Body, respectively, effected in the following established unresolved issues:

First, there was confusion how to address non-scientific factors: should non-scientific factors be considered in a stage separated from risk assessment, namely in the risk management stage, as suggested by the objectivist approach of the Panel? Or should non-scientific factors be considered in a comprehensive attempt covering both risk assessment and risk management aspects, as prescribed by the rather constructivist approach of the Appellate Body?

Sue Davis, for instance, noted a gap between theory and practice with regard to the recognition of 'other legitimate factors' under the SPS Agreement. On the one hand, Davis noted that 'other legitimate factors' have been recognised by EU food safety regulation, as well as by the Codex Alimentarius Commission. Davis noted:

> The role of 'other legitimate factors' has been recognized in EU legislation including the General Food Law Regulation and the GM food and feed regulations. They are also explicitly referred to in the Codex Working Principles for Risk Analysis for Food Safety for Application by Governments (Codex Alimentarius Commission 2007). In a UK context, the Food Standards Agency has responsibility for protecting the health of consumers, but also for protecting other consumer interests in relation to food (UK Food Standards Act 1999), although this responsibility has remained poorly defined.[104]

On the other hand, however, Davis observed a gap specifically between regulatory announcing and scientific risk assessment. Notably, Davis stressed that 'it remains unclear how much weight will be given to these "other legitimate factors" in practice, particularly if they are at odds with the scientific risk assessment'.[105]

With respect to the problem of non-scientific factors, Catherine Button noted:

> When it comes to the role of social and cultural factors, the waters are even muddier. The Appellate Body refused to draw a firm distinction between risk

> assessment and risk management under the SPS Agreement. This decision exacerbated the confusion already surrounding the question of whether such factors have a legitimate role in risk assessment, and continues to undermine the emerging international consensus on this question – the Codex Alimentarius Commission adopted a statement identifying reference to 'other legitimate factors' as part of the risk management process.[106]

Second, different approaches by Panels and the Appellate Body towards risk and risk assessment led to diverging view on the determination of appropriate levels of protection (ALOP): is the determination of higher levels of protection an exception, as suggested by the positivist Panel approach? Or is the determination of ALOP in any case a 'sovereign right', as ruled by the Appellate Body?

With regard to the provisions of the SPS Agreement addressing the determination of appropriate levels of protection (ALOP) vis-à-vis the paramount objective of harmonisation, Catherine Button established a lack of clarity:

> At a broader level, there seems to be a lack of real clarity on the nature of the system that the SPS Agreement's harmonisation provisions envisage. There is no indication of how the world trading system is to move beyond the disharmony of a formal obligation to 'base' measures on international standards coupled with an autonomous right to enact higher standards to full harmonisation. This lack of clarity and vision contributes to the tension between international supervision and national regulatory power. A far-reaching examination of the harmonisation question is in order. Such an examination should address the broader question of where decision-making power over health standards should be located – with Members, with international bodies or with WTO adjudicators?[107]

For Lukasz Gruszczynski, Article 3 'is probably on of the most obscure provisions in the whole SPS Agreement'.[108] Gruszczynski explained that obscurity with an initial disagreement among the drafters of the Agreement, 'with one group of countries supporting the establishment of strict harmonization disciplines and others seeking guarantees for rather unrestrained national regulatory freedom in the area of SPS risk'.[109] Gruszczynski further confirmed the notion that the Panel particularly in the case *EC—Hormones* followed the objective of establishing 'strict harmonisation disciplines', whereas the Appellate Body, by applying the principle of *in dubio mitius*, left some room for 'national regulatory freedom':

> If on considers this lack of precision [of Article 3 of the SPS Agreement], the approach taken by the Appellate Body appears to be fully understandable. In accordance with the principle of *in dubio mitius*, and in the absence of the proof to the contrary, one may rationally assume that WTO Members impose on themselves less burdensome obligations rather than more onerous. Consequently, Article 3.1 and 3.3 apply to different situations with Article 3.2 operating as some kind of reward for complying with international standards. Conceptualizing Article 3.1 and 3.3 as a rule and an exception would strengthen the harmonization objective of the SPS Agreement, without a clear indication of such an intent in the text of the relevant provision, and would further constrain the ability of WTO Members to set their own levels of protection ...[110]

Third, there was vagueness surrounding the issue of 'zero risk': should attempts to achieve 'zero-risk' be refuted on the ground that they are scientifically impossible, as suggested by the rather objectivist Panel? Or should attempt for achieving 'zero-risk' be allowed as viable policy options, as decided by the rather constructivist Appellate Body?

Fourth and finally, there was uncertainty on how to consider provisional measures and issues of precaution: are provisional measures some sort of extended inference bridges in risk assessments, as seemed to be the finding of Panels and the Appellate Body alike? Or shall precaution be addressed as a risk management measure in its own right, as suggested by certain constructivist risk theorists based on uncertainty considerations? What shall be the role of the precautionary principle in WTO law in general?

Notes

1. *EC—Hormones*, Appellate Body Report, para. 181.
2. *EC—Hormones*, Appellate Body Report, para. 181.
3. *EC—Hormones*, Appellate Body Report, para. 181 (emphasis added).
4. *EC—Hormones*, Appellate Body Report, para. 187 (original emphases, footnotes omitted).
5. *EC—Hormones*, Appellate Body Report, para. 143 (footnotes omitted).
6. *EC—Hormones*, Appellate Body Report, para. 143.
7. *EC—Hormones*, Appellate Body Report, para. 206.
8. Article 5.2 of the *SPS Agreement*, as cited by the Appellate Body in *EC—Hormones*, para. 187.
9. *EC—Hormones*, Appellate Body Report, para. 187.
10. *EC—Hormones*, Appellate Body Report, para. 206 (emphasis by the Appellate Body, footnotes omitted).

11. *US—Continued Suspension*, Appellate Body Report, para. 543 and footnote 1133, with reference to the European Communities' appellant's submission, para. 325. At the oral hearing, the Appellate Body observed the European Communities' emphasis on problems on the ground, noting that "the European Communities confirmed that its appeal focuses on misuse and abuse in the administration of hormones only, and that it is not claiming that the Panel erroneously excluded other factors on the basis of its general distinction between 'risk assessment' and 'risk management'." (*ibid.*, footnote 1133).
12. *US—Continued Suspension*, Panel Report, para 6.164.
13. *US—Continued Suspension*, Panel Report, para 6.164 (footnotes omitted).
14. *US—Continued Suspension*, Panel Report, para 6.166.
15. *US—Continued Suspension*, Appellate Body Report, para. 547.
16. *US—Continued Suspension*, Appellate Body Report, para. 547.
17. *US—Continued Suspension*, Appellate Body Report, para. 547 (emphasis added).
18. *US—Continued Suspension*, Appellate Body Report, para. 547.
19. *US—Continued Suspension*, Appellate Body Report, para. 548, with reference to the 1999 SCVPH Opinion, p. 32 (*ibid.*, footnote 1140).
20. *US—Continued Suspension*, Appellate Body Report, para. 549, with reference to the 2002 SCVPH Opinion, p. 11 (*ibid.*, footnote 1141).
21. *US—Continued Suspension*, Appellate Body Report, para. 549, with reference to the 2002 SCVPH Opinion, p. 11 (*ibid.*, footnote 1141).
22. *US—Continued Suspension*, Appellate Body Report, para. 549, with reference to the 2002 SCVPH Opinion, pp. 11 and 12 (*ibid.*, footnote 1142).
23. *US—Continued Suspension*, Appellate Body Report, para. 550 (footnote omitted).
24. *US—Continued Suspension*, Appellate Body Report, para. 550 (footnote omitted).
25. *US—Continued Suspension*, Appellate Body Report, para. 551 (footnote omitted).
26. *US—Continued Suspension*, Appellate Body Report, para. 553 (footnotes omitted, emphasis on *specifically* by the Appellate Body).
27. *US—Continued Suspension*, Appellate Body Report, para. 555.
28. In the *US—Continued Suspension* case, the EC complained about continued suspensions of obligations by the United States and Canada. Because of substantial overlaps, the same panellists were selected for examining both complaints and for issuing reports in both cases (United States: DS320, Canada: DS321).

29. *US—Continued Suspension*, Appellate Body Report, para. 537 and footnote no. 1125 with reference to the European Communities' appellant's submission, para. 308.
30. *US—Continued Suspension*, Appellate Body Report, para. 537.
31. *US—Continued Suspension*, Appellate Body Report, para. 538.
32. *US—Continued Suspension*, Appellate Body Report, para. 538; citing from the Panel Report in *US—Continued Suspension*, paras. 7.519 and 7.520; and from the Panel Report in *Canada—Continued Suspension*, paras. 7.491 and 7.492 (footnotes omitted).
33. *US—Continued Suspension*, Appellate Body Report, para. 539.
34. *US—Continued Suspension*, Appellate Body Report, para. 540; with reference to the Panel Report in *US—Continued Suspension*, para. 6.97; and to the Panel Report in *Canada—Continued Suspension*, para. 6.89.
35. *US—Continued Suspension*, Appellate Body Report, para. 540; with reference to the Panel Report in *US—Continued Suspension*, para. 6.99; and to the Panel Report in *Canada—Continued Suspension*, para. 6.91 (footnote omitted).
36. *US—Continued Suspension*, Appellate Body Report, para. 540, footnote no. 1129; with references to the Panel Report in *US—Continued Suspension*, para. 6.102; and to the Panel Report in *Canada—Continued Suspension*, para. 6.94.
37. *US—Continued Suspension*, Appellate Body Report, para. 540, footnote no. 1129.
38. *US—Continued Suspension*, Appellate Body Report, para. 540, footnote no. 1129; with references to the Panel Report in *US—Continued Suspension*, para. 7.603; and to the Panel Report in *Canada—Continued Suspension*, para. 7.578.
39. *US—Continued Suspension*, Appellate Body Report, para. 541.
40. *US—Continued Suspension*, Appellate Body Report, para. 541; with reference to the Report of the Appellate Body in *EC—Hormones*, para. 181.
41. *US—Continued Suspension*, Appellate Body Report, para. 541, with reference to the Report of the Appellate Body in *EC—Hormones*, para. 206 (emphasis on *restrictive* by the Appellate Body). With respect to Article 5.2, Article 8 and Annex C in particular, the Appellate Body in *US —Continued Suspension* pointed at its earlier observation that the text of Article 5.2 ("relevant processes and production methods; relevant inspection, sampling and testing methods"), Article 8 and Annex C ("control, inspection and approval procedures") "is amply sufficient to authorize the taking into account of risks arising from failure to comply with the requirements of good veterinary practice in the administration of hormones for growth promotion purposes, as well as risks arising from difficulties of control, inspection and enforcement of the requirements of good

veterinary practice"(*US—Continued Suspension*, Appellate Body Report, para. 541, footnote no. 1131; with reference to the Report of the Appellate Body in *EC—Hormones*, para. 205).

42. *US—Continued Suspension*, Appellate Body Report, para. 542 (footnote omitted, underlining added).
43. *EC—Hormones,* Appellate Body Report, para. 104.
44. *EC—Hormones,* Appellate Body Report, paras. 104 and 158.
45. *EC—Hormones,* Appellate Body Report, para. 159.
46. *EC—Hormones,* Appellate Body Report, para. 1159.
47. *EC—Hormones,* Appellate Body Report, para. 162.
48. *EC—Hormones,* Appellate Body Report, para. 162 (emphasis by the Appellate Body).
49. *EC—Hormones,* Appellate Body Report, para. 163; with reference to *The New Shorter Oxford English Dictionary on Historical Principles.*
50. *EC—Hormones,* Appellate Body Report, para. 163.
51. *EC—Hormones,* Appellate Body Report, para. 163; with reference to *The New Shorter Oxford English Dictionary on Historical Principles.*
52. *EC—Hormones,* Appellate Body Report, para. 163.
53. *EC—Hormones,* Appellate Body Report, para. 164.
54. *EC—Hormones,* Appellate Body Report, para. 165 (emphasis by the Appellate Body).
55. *EC—Hormones,* Appellate Body Report, para. 165 (emphases by the Appellate Body).
56. *EC—Hormones,* Appellate Body Report, para. 165 (emphases by the Appellate Body).
57. *EC—Hormones,* Appellate Body Report, para. 165 (emphases by the Appellate Body, footnote omitted).
58. *EC—Hormones,* Appellate Body Report, para. 165 (emphases by the Appellate Body); with reference to the principle of *in dubio mitius* in footnote no. 154.
59. *EC—Hormones,* Appellate Body Report, para. 165.
60. *EC—Hormones,* Appellate Body Report, para. 169.
61. *EC—Hormones,* Appellate Body Report, para. 170.
62. *EC—Hormones,* Appellate Body Report, para. 170.
63. *EC—Hormones,* Appellate Body Report, para. 171.
64. *EC—Hormones,* Appellate Body Report, para. 171.
65. *EC—Hormones,* Appellate Body Report, para. 171.
66. *EC—Hormones,* Appellate Body Report, para. 172.
67. *EC—Hormones,* Appellate Body Report, para. 172 (underlining by the Appellate Body).
68. *EC—Hormones,* Appellate Body Report, para. 172 (emphasis by the Appellate Body).

69. *Australia—Salmon,* Appellate Body Report, para. 191.
70. *Australia—Salmon,* Appellate Body Report, para. 194.
71. *Australia—Salmon,* Appellate Body Report, para. 196 (original emphases).
72. *Australia—Salmon,* Appellate Body Report, para. 197, with reference to paragraph 8.107 of the Panel's Report in *Australia—Salmon*).
73. *Australia—Salmon,* Appellate Body Report, para. 199. The Panel had reached the conclusion that it had to complement Australia's inchoate determination of its appropriate level of protection by interpreting Article 11 of the DSU in the following way:

Our examination under Article 5.6 is not aimed at a de novo review of what sanitary measure Australia should have chosen to achieve its appropriate level of protection. On the other hand, we cannot completely defer this decision to Australia and thus not give effect to Article 5.6. Our mandate under Article 11 of the DSU requires us to 'make an objective assessment of the matter before [us], including an objective assessment of the facts of the case' (Panel Report on *Australia—Salmon,* para. 8.172, with reference to the Appellate Body Report on *EC—Hormones,* paras. 110–119, in particular para. 117).

74. *Australia—Salmon,* Appellate Body Report, para. 199 (emphasis by the Appellate Body).
75. *Australia—Salmon,* Appellate Body Report, para. 200 (emphasis by the Appellate Body). In an additional footnote (no. 160), the Appellate Body noted "[t]hat the level of protection and the SPS measure applied have to be clearly distinguished results already from our Report in *European Communities—Hormones* ... para. 214".
76. *Australia—Salmon,* Report of the Appellate Body, para. 201.
77. *Australia—Salmon,* Appellate Body Report, para. 202 (emphasis by the Appellate Body).
78. *Australia—Salmon,* Appellate Body Report, para. 202 (emphasis by the Appellate Body).
79. *Australia—Salmon,* Appellate Body Report, para. 202 (emphasis by the Appellate Body).
80. *Australia—Salmon,* Appellate Body Report, para. 203 (emphasis by the Appellate Body).
81. *Australia—Salmon,* Appellate Body Report, para. 203 (emphases by the Appellate Body).
82. *Australia—Salmon,* Appellate Body Report, para. 205. Similar considerations of the Panel are expressed in paragraph 8.107 of the Panel's Report on *Australia—Salmon*).

83. *Australia—Salmon*, Appellate Body Report, para. 205 (footnote no. 161 omitted). In footnote no. 162, the Appellate Body additionally referred to Articles 5.8 and 12.4 of the SPS Agreement.
84. *Australia—Salmon,* Appellate Body Report, para. 206.
85. *Australia—Salmon,* Appellate Body Report, para. 206.
86. *Australia—Salmon,* Appellate Body Report, para. 206.
87. *Australia—Salmon,* Appellate Body Report, para. 207.
88. *Australia—Salmon,* Appellate Body Report, para. 207.
89. *Australia—Salmon,* Appellate Body Report, para. 207.
90. *Australia—Salmon,* Appellate Body Report, para. 208 (emphases by the Appellate Body).
91. *Australia—Salmon,* Appellate Body Report, para. 208.
92. *Australia—Salmon,* Appellate Body Report, para. 209, with reference to paragraph 8.90 of the Panel's Report on *Australia—Salmon* (emphasis already in the Panel's version, brackets added by the Appellate Body).
93. *Australia—Salmon,* Appellate Body Report, para. 210. This problem was accentuated by the fact that the Panel had examined the alternative quarantine options "only in comparison to the erroneous yardstick of the level of protection implied from the heat-treatment requirement" (paragraph 211 of the Appellate Body's Report on *Australia—Salmon*).
94. It shall be noted that there are other views expressing more conciliatory rather than antithetic understandings of the diverging interpretations put forward by panels and the Appellate Body respectively. Lukasz Gruszczynski, for instance, perceived "the approach of the Appellate Body not as a general rejection of the concept of risk management within the SPS Agreement, but rather as a dismissal of restrictive, and in fact incorrect, formulation of risk assessment" (Lukasz Gruszczynski, *Regulating Health and Environmental Risks under WTO Law. A Critical Analysis of the SPS Agreement* (Oxford University Press, 2010), p. 223). On such grounds, but without textual basis, Gruszczynski suggested the recognition of risk management within the existing SPS Agreement, arguing that such a move would not alter rights and obligations of WTO Members, but "helps to conceptualize SPS disciplines in a clear and more consistent manner" (Lukasz Gruszczynski, *ibid.*, p. 225). The view underpinning the underlying thesis of the book at hand locates both panels and the Appellate Body between the antipodes positivism and relativism. However, whereas panels particularly in early SPS cases are considered of having adopted a rather positivist approach, the Appellate Body seems of having struggled for some middle position from the outset. Because the science-based approach of the SPS Agreement restricts the potential discretion of legal interpreters significantly, the Appellate Body could barely have gone farther to the left end of the spectrum, *i.e.* to the relativist end, but had to confine itself to the

quest for some middle course. Joanne Scott commented on such inbuilt constraints of the SPS Agreement as follows:

> Though the AB speaks soft words of Member State autonomy, qualitative modes of risk assessment, and deference to minority opinion, the science-based obligations have a hard edge. They constitute numerous benchmarks according to which legality will be assessed (…) All in all soft words should not be allowed to obscure the searching nature of the risk assessment inquiry (Joanne Scott, *The WTO Agreement on Sanitary and Phytosanitary Measures* (Oxford University Press, 2007), pp. 137–138).

On these grounds, the Appellate Body's approach is not perceived as being relativist, but as seeking some kind of middle position between the positivist and the relativist end of the spectrum.

95. Sungjoon Cho, 'From Control to Communication: Science, Philosophy and World Trade Law' (2010) Cornell International Law Journal, forthcoming (original emphasis, footnotes omitted). Available at SSRN: http://ssrn.com/abstract=1583023 (visited December 5, 2010).
96. Sungjoon Cho, *ibid.* (original italics, footnotes omitted).
97. Elizabeth Fisher, 'Beyond the Science/Democracy Dichotomy: The World Trade organisation Sanitary and Phytosanitary Agreement and Administrative Constitutionalism', in Christian Joerges and Ernst-Ulrich Petersmann (eds.), *Constitutionalism, Multilevel Trade Governance and Social Regulation* (Hart Publishing, 2006), [pp. 327–349] 341–342 (footnotes omitted).
98. Elizabeth Fisher, *ibid.* p. 343 (footnote omitted, emphasis added).
99. Elizabeth Fisher, *ibid.* p. 344 (footnotes omitted).
100. Sungjoon Cho, 'From Control to Communication: Science, Philosophy and World Trade Law' (2010) Cornell International Law Journal, forthcoming (footnote omitted). Available at SSRN: http://ssrn.com/abstract=1583023 (visited December 5, 2010).
101. Catherine Button, *The Power to Protect. Trade, Health, and Uncertainty in the WTO* (Hart Publishing, 2004), p. 101. In this respect, however, Button observed that other authors, namely Crawford-Brown, Pauwelyn and Smith, as well as Trebilcock and Soloway, voiced concerns that the Appellate Body's "elision of risk assessment and risk management allows more scope for policy decisions to creep into risk assessment processes" (*ibid.*, footnote no. 42).
102. Catherine Button, *ibid.*, p. 101, with reference to the report of the Appellate Body in *EC—Hormones*, para. 187 (emphasis added by Button).
103. Catherine Button, *ibid.*, p. 102.
104. Sue Davis, 'A Consumers' Association's Perspective on the Governance Framework,' in Marion Dreyer and Ortwin Renn (eds.) *Food Safety*

Governance. Integrating Science, Precaution and Public Involvement (Springer-Verlag, 2009), p. 224.

105. Sue Davis, 'A Consumers' Association's Perspective on the Governance Framework,' in Marion Dreyer and Ortwin Renn (eds.) *Food Safety Governance. Integrating Science, Precaution and Public Involvement* (Springer-Verlag, 2009), p. 224.
106. Catherine Button, *The Power to Protect. Trade, Health, and Uncertainty in the WTO* (Hart Publishing, 2004), p. 231. Button anticipated negative consequences of the Appellate Body's handling of non-scientific factors by arguing that, "[i]f other factors are considered as part of risk assessment, it will lose its claim to be as free from politics and policy as is practicable. If this happens, even the ideal of scientific risk assessment will have been sacrificed and, as a consequence, the value of scientifically-based methods of risk regulation will be called into question" (Catherine Button, *ibid.*, p. 107).
107. Catherine Button, *ibid.*, pp. 63–64 (footnote omitted).
108. Lukasz Gruszczynski, *Regulating Health and Environmental Risks under WTO Law. A Critical Analysis of the SPS Agreement* (Oxford University Press, 2010), p. 104.
109. Lukasz Gruszczynski, *ibid.*, pp. 104–105.
110. Lukasz Gruszczynski, *ibid.*, p. 105 (footnote omitted).

References

Button, Catherine. "The Power to Protect. Trade, Health, and Uncertainty in the WTO". *Hart Publishing*, 2004.

Cho, Sungjoon. "From Control to Communication: Science, Philosophy and World Trade Law". *Cornell International Law Journal*, forthcoming. Available at SSRN. Accessed December 5, 2010. http://ssrn.com/abstract=1583023.

Davis, Sue. "A Consumers' Association's Perspective on the Governance Framework". Published in Marion Dreyer and Ortwin Renn (eds.), *Food Safety Governance. Integrating Science, Precaution and Public Involvement.* Springer-Verlag, 2009, 223–231.

Fisher, Elizabeth. "Beyond the Science/Democracy Dichotomy: The World Trade Organisation Sanitary and Phytosanitary Agreement and Administrative Constitutionalism". Published in Christian Joerges and Ernst-Ulrich Petersmann (eds.), *Constitutionalism, Multilevel Trade Governance and Social Regulation.* Hart Publishing, 2006, 327–349.

Gruszczynski, Lukasz. "Regulating Health and Environmental Risks under WTO Law. A Critical Analysis of the SPS Agreement". *Oxford University Press*, 2010.

Scott, Joanne. "The WTO Agreement on Sanitary and Phytosanitary Measures". *Oxford University Press*, 2007.

WTO Cases

EC—Hormones: EC—Measures Concerning Meat and Meat Products.
—Panel Report WT/DS26/R/USA, WT/DS48/R/CAN, final report circulated August 18, 1997;
—Appellate Body Report WT/DS26/AB/R/USA, WT/DS48/AB/R/CAN, adopted February 13, 1998.
Australia—Salmon: Australia—Measures Affecting Importation of Salmon.
—Panel Report WT/DS18/R, final report circulated June 12, 1998;
—Appellate Body Report WT/DS18/AB/R, adopted November 6, 1998.
United States—Continued Suspension: United States/Canada—Continued Suspension of Obligations in the EC—Hormones Dispute.
—Panel Reports, WT/DS320/R, WT/DS321/R, final reports circulated March 31, 2008;
—Appellate Body Reports, WT/DS320/AB/R, WT/DS321/AB/R, adopted November 14, 2008.

PART III

Future Prospects for Regulation

In part II, it was shown that panels have tried to establish a rather positivist interpretation of 'science' and 'risk assessment'. The Appellate Body, on the other hand, has tried to find some middle ground between a positivist and a relativist interpretation of SPS provisions. However, it was pointed at new legal questions deriving from the middle position taken up by the Appellate Body. Essentially, the SPS jurisprudence did not achieve of resolving transatlantic trade conflicts for good, especially not those over hormones and GMOs. Despite deference to science and scientific principles, trade disputes continue. The key question why trade disputes are ongoing despite the SPS measures at issue are—or should be—'based on science' is addressed in the following part three on future prospects for regulation.

From a theoretical perspective, the fact that disputes about the appropriateness of certain levels of protection continue to occur at the international level despite a 'science-based approach' applied can be interpreted in two ways:

First, it may be the case that scientific rigour, albeit defining appropriate levels of protection to a large extent, has not (yet) become the sole and determining yardstick in every case. Particularly in politicised issues, such as hormones and GMOs, levels of protection seem to be determined by political means, at the end of the day. Thus, from an objectivist perspective, the main problem seems to be that risk assessments at national levels are 'contaminated' by national policy considerations.

A second, more profound interpretation of the fact that disputes over sanitary and phytosanitary protection persist at international levels may question the objectivity of science itself. Whereas the first alternative presumes that science is objective in principle, the second alternative considers that science—and scientists—are intrinsically embedded in, and a part of, the society within which they operate. The first approach, in consequence, must advocate for a separation of scientific and political procedures and assign primacy to the former. Because of its belief in the ability of science to establish the facts of the matter in a definite, *i.e.* 'positive' way, the first approach is called *positivist* or *objectivist.* The second approach, on the other hand, conceives science as part and parcel of respective societies and performing before the background of a specific historical, cultural and economic context. Because the societal matrix upon which a specific scientific apparatus is operating is considered unique and distinguished from others, the outcome of respective scientific endeavours is thus relative to that particular society it is operating in. Therefore, the latter approach is termed *relativist, contextualist* or *constructivist.*

Looking from an epistemological footing, two alternative attempts are conceivable in principle: the first alternative aims at accomplishing the objectivist attempt of the science-based approach of the SPS Agreement. This is the positivist proposal of pursuing and further enforcing the harmonisation of SPS standards at the global scale. The second alternative attempts to achieve a return to a more sovereignty-oriented approach, as was the case under the previous GATT Article XX regime. This is the rather contextualist, constructivist or relativist proposal for an abandonment of harmonisation as a main objective of the SPS Agreement. Instead of science, deliberation and negotiation at international levels shall address fundamental cultural, philosophical and political conflicts underlying trade disputes. However, following such a contextualist approach implies that panels and the Appellate Body must continue to rely upon consistency examinations—similar to the previous GATT Article XX considerations—for examining whether an SPS measures is justified or not. Hence, the contextualist approach may attenuate the promise for considerable openings of agricultural markets implied in the science-based approach of the SPS Agreement.

The two alternative proposals for reforming the SPS Agreement are discussed in the following chapters.

CHAPTER 10

The Positivist Solution

From a positivist perspective in the proper sense of the word, the jurisdiction of the Appellate Body may be seen as a misconception of the science-based approach of the SPS Agreement. Positivists may claim that the Appellate Body did not interpret the science-based approach of the SPS Agreement 'positivistic' enough: despite of relying on science and scientific evidence, as expressed by international standards, the Appellate Body recognised the determination of appropriate levels of protection (ALOP) as a sovereign right of WTO Members (and not as an exemption, as found by the Panel), thus counterbalancing the objective of worldwide harmonisation of SPS measures (Article 3.1 of the SPS Agreement). Therefore, and with view on the cases of hormones and GMOs, objectivists would claim that the promise of market opening for agricultural products was jeopardised by the rather contextualist approach of the Appellate Body.

Positivists may criticise the softening of the harmonisation objective in Article 3 of the SPS Agreement by the Appellate Body in *EC—Hormones*. From a positivist perspective, the objective of harmonising SPS measures should rather become compulsory. Considering the fact that 'science' has been established as 'objective yardstick' by the SPS Agreement, positivists question whether there is room for manoeuvre for national governments to decide upon health protection and safety issues. Essentially, positivists may argue that science is universal and has therefore little to do with politics and national boundaries.[1]

M. Burkard, *Conflicting Philosophies and International Trade Law*,
Philosophy, Public Policy, and Transnational Law,
https://doi.org/10.1007/978-3-319-61067-2_10

John Jackson, for instance, wondered whether calls for 'zero risk' can be contained as long as there are remnants of national sovereignty in risk evaluation. Jackson noted:

> An interesting 'sovereignty' aspect of the SPS Agreement is the language related to 'risk' when products can cause certain health dangers, such as taken up in the WTO *Beef Hormones* case (evaluating the risk of artificial growth hormones causing cancer) and the *Asbestos* case (relating to GATT Article III national treatment, and implicating but not deciding about the TBT Agreement). The SPS Agreement contains tortured negotiated language trying to reconcile international goals of liberalizing trade and thus requiring scientific evidence of potential harm (to avoid barriers that are really due to protectionist motives), while still giving each Member the 'sovereign' right to determine the level of risk which should be tolerated in its society. Since science often declares that there is no such thing as totally risk-free circumstances, to allow a society to determine that only risk-free products can be imported is to deliver a blow to trade liberalization. This is clearly one of the most interesting (and perplexing) issues in the perpetual tug-of-war between national and international authority and the question of which government level will have the authority to make the determination of acceptable science and some minimal threshold of the risk requirement.[2]

John Jackson summarised challenges caused by internationalised health and safety issues as follows:

> (...) the subject of health clearly demands attention at an international level, for several reasons. First, as recognised at least a century and half ago, various health issues transgress national borders, and by at least 1920 it was recognised that increased world trade created added dangers of transmittal of communicable diseases. Much more recently the scourge of HIV-AIDS, and the scare caused by the possible SARS (severe acute respiratory syndrome) epidemic, as well as the current potential disaster of avian influenza demonstrated poignantly the importance of the WHO (World Health Organization) and actually led that organization to begin work on revising its International Health Regulations (IHRs) to better accommodate international activity.[3]

Considering the global nature of contemporary health and safety risks such as avian influenza, swine flu and the issue of GMOs, positivists tend to argue that responses to such risks should also be global. In particular, positivists question why risk assessment and risk management should remain in respective national domains. Insofar, national sovereignty in risk assessment and risk management seems to duplicate endeavours of international organisations such as WHO, the Codex Alimentarius Commission, IPPC and OIE. Therefore, a positivist solution to identified problems with risk assessment and risk management in the context of the SPS Agreement might consist in a clear attribution of the whole process of risk analysis, i.e. risk assessment and risk management, to international organisations.[4] That path is already sketched out in Articles 3.1. and 3.2 of the SPS Agreement, reading as follows:

Article 3

Harmonisation

1. To harmonise sanitary and phytosanitary measures on as wide a basis as possible, Members shall base their sanitary or phytosanitary measures on international standards, guidelines or recommendations, where they exist, except as otherwise provided for in this Agreement, and in particular in paragraph 3.
2. Sanitary or phytosanitary measures which conform to international standards, guidelines or recommendations shall be deemed to be necessary to protect human, animal or plant life or health, and presumed to be consistent with the relevant provisions of this Agreement and of GATT 1994.
3. Members may introduce or maintain sanitary or phytosanitary measures which result in a higher level of sanitary or phytosanitary protection than would be achieved by measures based on the relevant international standards, guidelines or recommendations, if there is a scientific justification, or as a consequence of the level of sanitary or phytosanitary protection a Member determines to be appropriate in accordance with the relevant provisions of paragraphs 1 through 8 of Article 5.[5] Notwithstanding the above, all measures which result in a level of sanitary or phytosanitary protection different from that which would be achieved by measures based on international standards, guidelines or recommendations shall not be inconsistent with any other provision of this Agreement.

However, the objective of harmonisation, as expressed in Articles 3.1 and 3.2 of the SPS Agreement, is relativised by the permission granted to WTO members to opt for higher levels of protection (Article 3.3 of the SPS Agreement). Therefore, a positivist solution to the problem of risk controversies in SPS disputes would consist in declaring conformity of SPS measures to international standards mandatory and abrogating Article 3.3 of the SPS Agreement. Hence, Article 3 of the SPS Agreement, after a positivist revision, would read as follows:

> Article 3
>
> Harmonisation
>
> 1. To harmonise sanitary and phytosanitary measures on as wide a basis as possible, Members shall base their sanitary or phytosanitary measures on international standards, guidelines or recommendations, where they exist, except as otherwise provided for in this Agreement, and in particular in paragraph 3.
> 2. Sanitary or phytosanitary measures which conform to international standards, guidelines or recommendations shall be deemed to be necessary to protect human, animal or plant life or health, and presumed to be consistent with the relevant provisions of this Agreement and of GATT 1994.
> 3. [*Deleted*].

In effect, the positivist proposal would address problems established in SPS case law by internationalising risk management: national governments would no longer be able to exercise discretion in determining levels of protection deemed appropriate, but would have to align respective SPS measures to international standards.

Substantive harmonisation of SPS measures at the global scale would mark the final triumph of what Marsha Echols called the new paradigm of food as commerce. From this perspective, the SPS Agreement, applying principles of the physical sciences, provides the basis for the application of principles of the economic sciences in international food trade, in particular, David Ricardo's law of comparative advantage. In other words, the positivist attempt for substantive harmonisation of SPS measures would fulfil the promise for objective regulation of international food trade implied in the science-based approach of the SPS Agreement. Marsha Echols once encapsulated the positivist dream of an objective regulatory framework for international food trade as follows:

> The Uruguay Round's agricultural negotiators, in their effort to prevent such use of food safety standards, rejected the deeply held historical, cultural and

religious justifications. To limit the use of protectionist food safety measures, the Agreement [on the Application of Sanitary and Phytosanitary Measures] makes scientific principles and analysis the only valid basis for a permanent food safety measure, thereby limiting the ability of a government to place it's citizens' cultural or religious beliefs about food above international commerce. Food safety is cast neutrally in the perceived certainty of chemistry, biology and applied economics.[6]

Notes

1. The absurdity of a national connotation of science was best demonstrated by attempts of German scientists to develop "German Physics" ("Deutsche Physik") or "German Mathematics" ("Deutsche Mathematik)" during the "Third Reich" in Nazi Germany. For example, the "aether theory" ("Äther-Theorie") of the physician Philipp Lenards, or the "Intuitionism" (Intuitionismus") of the mathematician Ludwig Bieberbach not even gained acceptance within the streamlined German scientific community after 1933 and disappeared together with national socialist rule in 1945 (see Steffen Richter, 'Die 'Deutsche Physik'', in Herbert Mehrtens and Steffen Richter (eds.), *Naturwissenschaft, Technik und NS-Ideologie. Beiträge zur Wissenschaftsgeschichte des Dritten Reiches* (suhrkamp taschenbuch, 1980), pp. 116–141; and Helmut Lindner, ''Deutsche' und 'gegentypische' Mathematik. Zur Begründung einer 'arteignen Mathematik' im 'Dritten Reich' durch Ludwig Bieberbach', in Herbert Mehrtens and Steffen Richter (eds.), *Naturwissenschaft, Technik und NS-Ideologie. Beiträge zur Wissenschaftsgeschichte des Dritten Reiches* (suhrkamp, 1980), pp. 88–115.
2. John H. Jackson, *Sovereignty, the WTO and Changing Fundamentals of International Law* (Cambridge University Press, 2006), p. 247; with reference to the Appellate Body Reports concerning the cases *EC – Hormones,* para. 124, and *Australia—Salmon*, para. 125.
3. John H. Jackson, ibid. p. 245 (footnotes omitted).
4. However, it has to be recalled that international standards are not developed according to scientific principles only. In this respect, Lee Ann Jackson and Marion Jansen emphasised:

"Codex standards are the outcome of multilateral negotiations based upon risk assessment. It is important to communicate this fact to the public and thus signal that scientific evidence is only one of the determinants of Codex international food safety standards, albeit a very prominent one" (Lee Ann Jackson and Marion Jansen, 'Risk assessment in the international food safety policy arena. Can the multilateral institutions encourage unbiased outcomes?' (2010) 35 *Food Policy* [538–547] 546).

5. Footnote no. 2 to this paragraph explains the following: "For the purposes of paragraph 3 of Article 3, there is a scientific justification if, on the basis of an examination and evaluation of available scientific information in conformity with the relevant provisions of this Agreement, a Member determines that the relevant international standards, guidelines or recommendations are not sufficient to achieve its appropriate level of sanitary or phytosanitary protection."
6. Marsha A. Echols, *Food Safety and the WTO. The Interplay of Culture, Science and Technology* (Kluwer Law International, 2001), p. 4 (footnotes omitted).

References

Echols, Marsha A. "Food Safety and the WTO. The Interplay of Culture, Science and Technology". Kluwer Law International, 2001.

Jackson, John H. "Sovereignty, the WTO and Changing Fundamentals of International Law", *Cambridge University Press*, 2006.

Jackson, Lee Ann and Jansen, Marion. "Risk assessment in the international food safety policy arena. Can the multilateral institutions encourage unbiased outcomes?". *Food Policy*, 2010, vol. 35, 538–547.

Lindner, Helmut. "'Deutsche' und 'gegentypische' Mathematik. Zur Begründung einer 'arteignen Mathematik' im 'Dritten Reich' durch Ludwig Bieberbach". Published in Herbert Mehrtens and Steffen Richter (eds.), *Naturwissenschaft, Technik und NS-Ideologie. Beiträge zur Wissenschaftsgeschichte des Dritten Reiches.* Suhrkamp, 1980, 88–115.

Richter, Steffen. "Die 'Deutsche Physik'". Published in Herbert Mehrtens and Steffen Richter (eds.), *Naturwissenschaft, Technik und NS-Ideologie. Beiträge zur Wissenschaftsgeschichte des Dritten Reiches. Suhrkamp*, 1980, 116–141.

CHAPTER 11

The Relativist Response

From the perspective of relativists and subjectivists, SPS cases are proving that science is not objective and that the science-based approach does not work. Relativists and subjectivists would particularly point at the *Hormones* and the *Biotech* cases where scientific experts rallied in opposing camps, contradicting each other.

Hence, in view of subjectivists, the main problem is the expectation elicited by the SPS Agreement that science and scientific risk assessments are appropriate yardsticks for assessing risks and for evaluating the legitimacy of SPS measures.

Beside the problem of diverging scientific views and scientific uncertainty, subjectivists focus on the inappropriateness of science to address non-scientific factors, for example, control issues or legitimate ethical concerns.

In this respect, relativists and subjectivists note that the Appellate Body interpreted the term risk assessment in the SPS Agreement in a context-sensitive and holistic way, thus rejecting the Panel's objectivistic approach in the two *Hormones* cases.

In addition, relativists and subjectivists observe that the Appellate Body rejected the Panel's view that the right to opt for higher levels of protection is an exception. Hence, if the determination of higher levels of protection is considered a sovereign right, then the objective of global harmonisation of SPS measures should be abandoned. By criticising objectivistic attempts of panels, relativists might thus agree with the approach of the Appellate Body to a large extent. For relativists, contextualists/constructivists, the

M. Burkard, *Conflicting Philosophies and International Trade Law*,
Philosophy, Public Policy, and Transnational Law,
https://doi.org/10.1007/978-3-319-61067-2_11

objectivistic approach of certain panels went too far. In contrast, relativists tend to suggest that the sovereign right of WTO Members to determine the level of protection deemed appropriate should be made explicit, to the detriment of the objective of harmonisation.

On these grounds, relativists and subjectivists hold that the prospect for future regulation lies in a revision of the SPS Agreement in line with relativist arguments. The focus of a relativists' attempt to revise the SPS Agreement would be to abandon science and scientific risk assessments as principal arbiter for evaluating SPS risks. The recognition that science is not objective and risks are social constructs forbids the assignment of a particular role to science above other considerations, in particular, legal reason. Ultimately, subjectivist would advocate for a reassignment of SPS measures under the GATT Article XX jurisprudence, or under a similar, law-driven regime.

Paragraph 2 of Article 2 of the SPS Agreement contains the fundamental prescription that any sanitary or phytosanitary measures must be 'based on scientific principles' and can only be maintained with 'sufficient scientific evidence'.

The full text of Article 2 of the SPS Agreement reads as follows:

Article 2

Basic Rights and Obligations

1. Members have the right to take sanitary and phytosanitary measures necessary for the protection of human, animal or plant life or health, provided that such measures are not inconsistent with the provisions of this Agreement.
2. Members shall ensure that any sanitary or phytosanitary measure is applied only to the extent necessary to protect human, animal or plant life or health, is based on scientific principles and is not maintained without sufficient scientific evidence, except as provided for in paragraph 7 of Article 5.
3. Members shall ensure that their sanitary and phytosanitary measures do not arbitrarily or unjustifiably discriminate between Members where identical or similar conditions prevail, including between their own territory and that of other Members. Sanitary and phytosanitary measures shall not be applied in a manner which would constitute a disguised restriction on international trade.
4. Sanitary or phytosanitary measures which conform to the relevant provisions of this Agreement shall be presumed to be in accordance

> with the obligations of the Members under the provisions of GATT 1994 which relate to the use of sanitary or phytosanitary measures, in particular, the provisions of Article XX(b).

Paragraph 2 of Article 2 expresses the basic principle of the science-based approach of the SPS Agreement. Together with Article 5.1, with which Article 2.2 should 'constantly be read together',[1] are forming the backbone of an objectivist interpretation of the SPS Agreement. A relativist attempt for reforming the SPS Agreement would aim to cancel the second and the last clause of paragraph 2 of Article 2 of the SPS Agreement, at least:

Article 2

Basic Rights and Obligations

1. [Original text]
2. Members shall ensure that any sanitary or phytosanitary measure is applied only to the extent necessary to protect human, animal or plant life or health [*2nd and 3rd clause cancelled*].
3. [Original text]
4. [Original text]

Article 3 of the SPS Agreement projects the objective of harmonising sanitary and phytosanitary measures of WTO Members in line with international standards (the full text of paragraphs 1–3 of Article 3 of the SPS Agreement was displayed in the previous paragraph). The harmonisation objective is laid down in paragraph 1 of Article 3. The harmonisation objective is further amplified by the presumption in paragraph 2 that national SPS measures conforming to international standards are consistent with relevant provisions of the SPS Agreement and of GATT 1994. Paragraph 3 of Article 3 finally makes the option for higher levels of protection that those provided by international standards contingent upon scientific justification. In sum, paragraphs 1–3 of Article 3 of the SPS Agreement are limiting national sovereignty considerably.

From a relativist point of view, one would emphasise the inappropriateness of harmonisation as paramount objective. Whereas relativists might agree that harmonisation can be used as a tool for trade facilitation, they would reject harmonisation as final purpose. Relativists, taking differences of perception as a starting point, would partake in the idea that international standards could serve as guidelines for risk policies, at best. But constructivists would refute the idea that international standards are becoming quasi-mandatory, as happened through the SPS Agreement. Therefore, from a constructivistic perspective, harmonisation as a tool for trade facilitation is subordinate to the right of people to determine the level of protection they consider appropriate.[2] Robert Howse, for instance, suggested an alternative to harmonisation:

> Where there is a concern that domestic regulations may constitute protectionist cheating on negotiated trade concessions, an alternative to harmonization may well be to enhance confidence in the ability to distinguish legitimate domestic regulations from protectionist cheating. Requiring that regulations be defensible in a *rational, deliberative public process* of justification may well enhance such confidence, while at the very same time serving, not frustrating, democracy.[3]

At first, subjectivist would suggest a wording consistent with the sixth clause of the preamble. Second, subjectivists would turn down the privilege for SPS measures conforming to international standards, as contained in paragraph 2 of Article 3. Third, constructivist would reformulate paragraph 3 of Article 3 as a truly 'sovereign right' of Members, hence abrogating the requirement for scientific justification. From a relativists' point of view, paragraphs 1–3 of Article 3 of the SPS Agreement should be rephrased as follows:

Article 3

Harmonisation

1. [*Members shall further the use of harmonised sanitary and phytosanitary measures, on the basis of international standards, guidelines and recommendations developed by the relevant international organisations, including the Codex Alimentarius Commission, the International Office of Epizootics, and the relevant international and regional organisations operating within the framework of the International Plant Protection Convention, without requiring Members to change their appropriate level of protection of human, animal or plant life or health.*]
2. [*Deletion*]
3. Members may introduce or maintain sanitary or phytosanitary measures which result in a higher level of sanitary or phytosanitary protection than would be achieved by measures based on the relevant international standards, guidelines or recommendations [*rest deleted*].

> Notwithstanding the above, all measures which result in a level of sanitary or phytosanitary protection different from that which would be achieved by measures based on international standards, guidelines or recommendations shall not be inconsistent with any other provision of this Agreement.

In sum, relativist proposals are aiming to nullify the science-based approach of the SPS Agreement, as well as the harmonisation objective implied. Ultimately, relativist attempts may strive for a return to some kind of GATT Article XX jurisprudence, or to a similar regime based on human judgement rather than science. Its relativism is expressed by the notion that food is intrinsically different from other products:

> Food is culture and, in other ways, is different from most other subjects of trade. Cars, legal services and patents are neither physical necessities nor ingested so as to become a physical building block for each human being. Seattle also sent the message that global is not always good in the minds of the vocal public. The potential global impact of genetic modifications on the food supply is a target for those who oppose the current economics/science focus of what we eat.[4]

Notes

1. *EC—Hormones*, Appellate Body Report, para. 180.
2. The question how broad the term "concerned people" has to be understood is at the heart of the debate about global sustainability. Whereas traditional concepts were focusing on consumers and importing countries, both of implicit Western origin, new approaches are pointing at vital interests of producers, in particular small-scale agricultural producers in developing countries (see, for instance, Elisabeth Bürgi, 'Trade Law and Responsible Investment,' 2nd chapter of the study of Elisabeth Bürgi, Katja Gehne and Simone Heri on *Legal Instruments to foster responsible Investment in Agriculture: A human Rights, Agricultural Trade and Investment Law Perspective*, commissioned by the International Land Coalition in cooperation with the NCCR Trade Regulation, World Trade Institute (Draft, forthcoming), pp. 2–3.
3. Robert Howse, 'Democracy, Science, and Free Trade: Risk Regulation on Trial at the World Trade Organization' (June 2000) 98 *Michigan Law Review*, 2329 et seq. (emphasis added).
4. Marsha A. Echols, *Food Safety and the WTO. The Interplay of Culture, Science and Technology* (Kluwer Law International, 2001), p. 6.

References

Bürgi, Elisabeth. Trade Law and Responsible Investment. Published in Elisabeth Bürgi, Katja Gehne and Simone Heri, *Legal Instruments to foster responsible Investment in Agriculture: A human Rights, Agricultural Trade and Investment Law Perspective.* Commissioned by the International Land Coalition in cooperation with the NCCR Trade Regulation, World Trade Institute (draft, forthcoming).

Echols, Marsha A. Food Safety and the WTO. The Interplay of Culture, Science and Technology. Kluwer Law International, 2001.

Howse, Robert. Democracy, Science, and Free Trade: Regulation on Trial at the World Trade Organization. *Michigan Law Review*, 2329, vol. 98, 2000.

WTO Cases

EC—Hormones: EC—Measures Concerning Meat and Meat Products.

Panel Report WT/DS26/R/USA, WT/DS48/R/CAN, final report circulated August 18, 1997.

Appellate Body Report WT/DS26/AB/R/USA, WT/DS48/AB/R/CAN, adopted February 13, 1998.

CHAPTER 12

A Critical Approach

Either proposal sketched out in the previous chapters, i.e. the positivist attempt as well as the relativist response, seem untenable. Reasons for this finding are as follows.

The relativist struggle against the science-based approach and the objective of harmonisation particularly expressed by Articles 2 and 3 of the SPS Agreement is leading to legal uncertainty. If any WTO Member is free to introduce levels of protection at random and no objective yardstick is provided for detecting protectionist intent, international trade would be unpredictable. In fact, following the relativist suggestion would expose international trade to the arbitrariness of conflicting national interests. Under such arbitrariness and lawlessness, weaker and less influential states would suffer in particular. For exemplifying the issue, a case study is provided showing how a rational, science-based approach might eventually strengthen positions of DCs and LDCs in particular. The case study tells about EU import bans of Nile perch from Lake Victoria.[1] Andrew Mold provided the following story:

> East African fish exporters have been adversely affected by frequent bans in the EU markets. Between 1994 and 1999, a total of four bans were imposed on fish exports from the three countries over SPS standards. (…) In 1997, for instance, the EU responded to a cholera outbreak in East Africa by imposing a ban on fish imports from any country in the region, without first investigating the potential dangers involved. Following the intervention of the WHO, which pointed out that fish were an unlikely means of transmitting cholera, the ban was rescinded.

M. Burkard, *Conflicting Philosophies and International Trade Law*,
Philosophy, Public Policy, and Transnational Law,
https://doi.org/10.1007/978-3-319-61067-2_12

> Because of the ban, capacity utilization at fish processing plants fell to barely 50 per cent and, in the case of the United Republic of Tanzania, the workforce in the fish processing plants was reduced by about 40 per cent. The issue of frequent bans by the EU has caused severe adverse social and economic effects for the three countries, leading to unemployment, depressed prices and the loss of export earnings, losses which Uganda and the United Republic of Tanzania can least afford. With regard to public health concerns, in particular cholera outbreaks, which triggered some of the bans, the WHO Director-General stressed "the almost non-existent risk to countries importing food from cholera-affected countries".
>
> Another ban was imposed on 16 January 1998 by the European Commission on the importation of fresh, frozen and processed fishery products from the United Republic of Tanzania, Kenya, Uganda and Mozambique, again on grounds of concern for public health. Nevertheless, it was reported that over 2000 tests and inspections by the European Commission of the United Republic of Tanzania's fish processing establishments before 6 January 1998 had failed to produce positive tests of any of the alleged bacteria. Moreover, the EU notification, G/SPS/N/EEC/4, circulated on 4 March 1998, conceded that no international standard, guideline, or recommendation existed on the subject (although there are specific recommendations by both WHO and FAO). In its complaints to the WTO regarding the ban, the United Republic of Tanzania questioned its consistency with Articles 2.2 and 5.7 of the SPS Agreement. Recommendations by Codex and the International Commission on Microbiological Specifications for Food (ICMSF) did not consider import prohibition as an appropriate response to the alleged public health concern.[2]

The case study on the EU import bans of Nile perch is all the more telling when compared with the reaction of Japan in face of the very same questions. Japan, similarly known for high food safety standards, adopted a much more reasonable approach. In fact, a World Bank report found that the key problem of Japanese importers was not sanitary or quality issues, but the name and the origin of the fish:

> Japanese importers do not have any problems with regard to sanitary conditions and the quality of the products. The key problem is the naming of the fish, which had to be changed after the adjustment of the Japanese labeling regulation. Retailers experienced this marketing problem for the fist time in 2002. Japanese consumers are not familiar with this fish that used to be called and labeled in Japan shiro-suzuki ("white sea-bass"). The English name "Nile Perch" and the origin (Africa) does not appeal to them. (…)[3]

> Most of the Japanese buyers have longstanding business relations with the suppliers of Nile Perch from Kenya, Tanzania, and Uganda. The Japanese buyers have confidence in the suppliers, because the latter work according to HACCP standards and the EU hygiene directive (91/493/EEC). The suppliers have their own laboratories and always present inspection data of the export lots to the buyers. (...) Because Nile Perch is consumed after cooking, the regulations of the Food Sanitation Law do not require a sampling inspection on imports, but only an examination of the documents. However, since Nile Perch is a product from the tropics, all importers carry out private inspections for general bacteria count, Coliform organisms, Vibrio Parahaemolyticus, Salmonella, and Staphylococcus, on every import. (...) Toward the end of 1998, an item appeared on the internet that a pesticide that paralyzes fish was being used in Uganda. The EU set a temporary import ban on Uganda that was lifted in the first half of 1999. The Japanese importers acted quickly to carry out private inspections on every import of Ugandan Nile Perch to check for this pesticide. All inspections found that no such pesticide was present. Also, the Ugandan authorities issued certificates that there is no residue of such pesticide. The unease was resolved without any big damage to the demand, and Japan did not set an import ban.[4]

The case study of EU import bans on Nile perch from Lake Victoria shows that irrational fears may prevail over rational scientific assessment particularly in cases concerning toxins such as pesticides and potentially contagious diseases such as cholera, avian influenza, etc. In this case, significantly, scientific rationality was upheld by international organisations such as the WHO and the ICMSF, whereas EU authorities, facing public excitement and cautious retailers, took political rather than science-based decisions.[5]

Looking into the future, other potential controversies with the potential for eruption into open trade disputes are already glowing. Issues coming along with climate change such as the 'food miles' controversy seem particularly sensitive with regard to a blurring between legitimate concern and protectionist impulse. The food miles controversy began with British retailers, e.g. Tesco and Marks & Spencer,[6] applying plane symbols[7] to air-freighted products, in particular, fresh produce from Kenya and various agricultural products from New Zealand. Whereas the trade minister of New Zealand, Phil Goff, accepted the plane symbols as 'legitimate information for consumers', he argued that the food miles concept is too narrow for addressing sustainability issues. Phil Goff noted that by considering the 'ecological footprint' in total, it is shown that lamb meat from New Zealand requires only 25% of the energy input needed for British lamb products even if transportation is taken into account. Kenya's High Commissioner in Britain, Joseph Muchemi, initiated a 'Grown under the Sun' campaign, highlighting that despite air-freighting, carbon emissions for producing, packaging and transportation of horticultural products are still favourable for Kenyan products grown under the African sun instead of being produced in energy-intensive greenhouses in the UK. Scientists from the UK have joined the debate, questioning the scientific basis of the carbon prints approach, thus conflicting with various British NGOs, the National Farmers Union (the UK) and its 'buy local' campaign.[8]

In light of such examples, the relativist suggestion resembles the opening of the Pandora's box: it virtually derails any rule-based trading system. Might replace rules, and arbitrariness replaces the discursive settlement of disputes. In the end, epistemological pluralism results in a plurality of rules without recognised scientific method and no accepted standards. The spirit underlying the relativist proposal was best depicted by Shrader-Frechette, noting:

> At the left end of the spectrum, the pluralist end, are epistemological anarchist Paul Feyerabend and others who believe that there is no scientific method, that 'anything goes', and that 'no system of [scientific] rules and standards is ever safe'.[9]

The positivist attempt, however, seems untenable as well.

The positivist solution to declare conformity of SPS measures to international standards mandatory and to abrogate Article 3.3 of the SPS Agreement nullifies the room for manoeuvre for national sovereigns in risk analysis procedures. In particular, mandatory alignment to international standards renders the latter virtually unquestionable. Under a positivist regime of risk governance, WTO Members would no longer dare to deviate from international standards. By the same token, there would be no incentive for carrying out risk assessments suggesting different levels of protection than those established international standards. Hence, the positivist attempt would practically monopolise scientific knowledge in the field of action of international standard setting organisations. Standards issued by international organisations, in particular, the Codex Alimentarius Commission, IPPC and OIE would come along with the aura of scientific verity. Yet, international SPS standards bestowed with paramount scientific authority would come along with a notion of absolute sanctity.

However, as noted by Karl Popper, absolute and irrefutable scientific verdicts impede scientific debate and monopolise 'scientific truth'. In this respect, Popper emphasised that '[t]he empirical basis of objective science has thus nothing 'absolute' about it'.[10] Popper further approached the epistemological conundrum contained in the two opposites *objective—relative* and *subjective—absolute.*[11] Citing Hermann Weyl, Popper explained:

> … this pair of opposites, *subjective – absolute* and *objective – relative* seems to me to contain one of the most profound epistemological truths which can be gathered from the study of nature. Whoever wants the absolute must get subjectivity – ego-centricity – into the bargain, and whoever longs for objectivity cannot avoid the problem of relativism.' And before this we find, 'What is immediately experienced is *subjective and absolute* …; the objective world, on the other hand, which natural science seeks to precipitate in pure crystalline form … is relative.[12]

And with reference to Robert Reininger, Popper observed that 'although the absolute is indeed experienced, and for that reason can be intuitively felt, it yet refuses to be expressed in words'.[13]

The first opposite, *objective—relative*, is the characterising feature of the critical scientific method. As explained by Popper, scientific knowledge is never absolute, but relative; it must be accessible to others and their critique. This is what neopositivists of the Vienna Circle once called *intersubjectivity*.

In a nutshell, such a model of scientific stimulation can best be described in the allegoric language put forward by Karl Popper in *The Logic of Scientific Discovery* in his metaphor of bold theoretical structures erected above swamplands, representing scientific endeavour. In pursue of this metaphor, Malachi Hacohen noted:

> Where they can, scientists should endeavor to construct as solid a building as the moving sands under them would allow. Of course, the structure cannot hold indefinitely. Eventually, it will collapse, nay, scientists will demolish it when they find they can build a better one. But the uncertainty of the structure did not inhibit the growth of knowledge. If decisions on whether, where, and how to build were not always possible, and the solidity of the different structures controversial – indeed even the condition of the moving

> sands may not be a consensus – criticism of existing and proposed structures was always possible. Openness to criticism helped eliminate error. Conventions set the rules of debate, and traditions set its terms, but they, too, were subject to change.[14]

Thus, surprisingly, critical scientific method is intrinsically dialectical. From a procedural point of view, the critical scientific method resembles legal systems based on the principle of adversary proceedings.[15]

The other opposite, *subjective—absolute*, is the characterising feature of *arithmomorphic* concepts. It is recalled that Nicholas Georgescu-Roegen introduced the term *arithmomorphic* concept to betoken scientific concepts expressing reality in real numbers. Georgescu-Roegen worked out the antinomy between arithmomorphic concepts and dialectical concepts of science; between concepts based on the idea that reality is scientifically ascertainable and reducible to one single number, on the one hand, and concepts emphasising the continuous flow of things requiring iterative approaches for grasping reality. The positivistic critique of dialectical concepts is encapsulated in the sentence of 'the muddled waters of Hegelian dialectics'.[16]

By pointing at its arithmomorphic and anti-dialectic position, Georgescu-Roegen revealed an essential feature of positivism, namely its belief in the final truth. In this respect, Georgescu-Roegen observed, the position of positivism resembles that of the Catholic Church: from a positivistic point of view, dialectic concepts of science 'are antagonistic to science: knowledge proper exists only to the extent to which it is expressed in *arithmomorphic* concepts. The position recalls that of the Catholic Church: holy thought can be expressed only in Latin'.[17]

Hence, surprisingly again, the positivistic approach towards scientific truth, as suggested by the positivist proposal at hand, is intrinsically arithmomorphic and anti-dialectical. From a procedural point of view, the positivistic method resembles to legal systems based on the principle of accusatorial or interrogative proceedings.[18]

The scientific method proposed by Popper is fundamentally different from the binary approach towards 'the truth' applied by arithmomorphic concepts. In fact, the scientific method is characterised by the opposite *objective—relative*. With reference to Karl R. Popper, a critical scientific method can be characterised as

> a method of trial and the elimination of errors, of proposing theories and submitting them to the severest tests we can design. If, because of some

> limiting assumptions, only a finite number of competing theories are regarded as possible, this method may leas us to single out *the* true theory by eliminating all its competitors. Normally – that is to say in all cases in which the number of possible theories is infinite – this method cannot ascertain which of the theories is true; nor can any other method. It remains *applicable*, though inconclusive.[19]

Popper also pointed at the fact that it is not upon scientists to be 'objective' in the first instance. Rather, it is the result, the findings of scientific research, which must be able to withstand critical inquiry. Popper noted:

> It should be obvious that the objectivity and the rationality of progress in science is not due to the personal objectivity and rationality of the scientist. Great science and great scientists, like great poets, are often inspired by non-rational intuitions. So are great mathematicians. As Poincaré and Hadamard have pointed out, a mathematical proof may be discovered by unconscious trials, guided by an inspiration of a decidedly aesthetic character, rather than by rational thought. This is true, and important. But obviously, it does not make the result, the mathematical proof, irrational. In any case, a proposed proof must be able to stand up to critical discussion: to its examination by competing mathematicians.[20]

The very difference between a critical scientific method, on the one hand, and the positivistic concept is contained in the opposites *objective—relative* and *subjective—absolute*. Whereas the scientific method is inherently self-critical and conscious about its own inconclusiveness, thus following the opposite *objective—relative*, the positivist concept is founded upon the belief that an absolute, genuine scientific 'truth' can be found some day. In the context of a broader discussion of belief versus (critical) knowledge, Popper observed:

> I used to take price in the fact that I am not a belief philosopher: I am primarily interested in ideas, in theories, and I find it comparatively unimportant whether or not anybody 'believes' in them. And I suspect that the interest of philosophers in belief results from that mistaken philosophy which I call 'inductivism'. They are theorists of knowledge, and starting from subjective experience they fail to distinguish between objective and subjective knowledge. This leads them to believe in belief as the genus of which knowledge is a species ('justification' or perhaps a 'criterion of truth' such as clarity and distinctness, or vivacity, or 'sufficient reason', providing the specific difference).[21]

As Popper explained, the critical approach is inevitably broader than mere collections of 'true' facts, attempts which Popper disqualified as 'subjective knowledge' or 'inductivism'. At the heart of critical knowledge, Popper explained, stands the criterion of falsifiability, or refutability:

> This criterion of demarcation between empirical and non-empirical theories I have also called the criterion of falsifiability or the criterion of refutability. It does not imply that irrefutable theories are false. Nor does it imply that they are meaningless. But it does imply that, as long as we cannot describe what a possible refutation of a certain theory would be like, that theory may be regarded as lying outside the field of empirical science.[22]

The argument of Popper in favour of a critical method in science is based on his finding that 'there is no such thing as induction'.[23] Based on his refutation of induction, Popper went on reasoning that inductive 'inference to theories, from singular statements which are 'verified by experience (whatever that may mean), is logically inadmissible'.[24] On these grounds, Popper concluded:

> Theories are, therefore, *never* empirically verifiable. If we wish to avoid the positivist's mistake of eliminating, by our criterion of demarcation, the theoretical systems of natural science, then we must choose a criterion which allows us to admit to the domain of empirical science even statements which cannot be verified.[25]

That criterion is *falsifiability*. According to Popper, it is the criterion of whether a theory can be falsified rendering that theory 'scientific'. Succinctly, Popper explained the criterion of falsifiability and, by the same token, delivered a critique on the positivist dogma as follows:

> ... I shall certainly admit a system as empirical or scientific only if it is capable of being tested by experience. These considerations suggest that not the *verifiability* but the *falsifiability* of a system is to be taken as criterion of demarcation. In other words: I shall not require of a scientific system that it shall be capable of being singled out, once and for all, in a positive sense; but I shall require that its logical form shall be such that it can be singled out, by means of empirical tests, in a negative sense: *it must be possible for an empirical scientific system to be refuted by experience.*[26]

From a sociological point of view, Ulrich Beck analysed effects of the application of the critical method on society. In effect, the critical method does not only stimulate scientific discussion, but may translate into broader discourse in the 'risk society'. For this phenomenon, Ulrich Beck introduced the terms 'self-critical society' and 'discursivity.' Beck noted:

> In other words, risk society is by tendency also a self-critical society. Insurance experts (involuntarily) contradict safety engineers. While the latter diagnose zero risk, the former decide: uninsurable. Experts are undercut or deposed by opposing experts. Politicians encounter the resistance of citizens' groups, and industrial management encounters morally and politically motivated organized consumer boycotts. Administrations are criticized by self-help groups. Ultimately, even polluter sectors (for instance, the chemical industry in the case of sea pollution) must count upon resistance from affected sectors (in this case the fishing industry and the sectors living from seashore tourism). The latter can be called into question by the former, monitored and perhaps even corrected.[27]

With respect to biotechnology, in particular, Beck emphasised the need for scientists to be able to express doubts and uncertainties freely:

> [S]cientists must above all reflect, respect and confess their ignorance. It is up to them to make their uncertainties clear, whatever the professional, financial and political implications are. They should feel free to express their doubts in the broader public. There have been far too many attempts to evade this responsibility. This, of course, would not bring risk conflict to an end, but lead to a new one in which the relationship between science, the economy and democracy must be readjusted.[28]

The observation of Ulrich Beck that critical science and adversarial discourse may stimulate self-reflexivity at national levels leads to the reasoned expectation that similar stimulating effects might also occur in the broader, international context. In particular, it is argued that scientific dissent, expressed openly at international fora, *e.g.* those provided by the WTO dispute settlement body (DSB) for instance, may also stimulate critical discourse at respective national levels of parties involved in the dispute. Contrariwise, scientific dissent at national levels may translate into critical debate at international bodies, such as the Codex Alimentarius Commission. Alexia Herwig, for instance, explicitly applied criteria of self-reflexivity and meta-scientific contextualisation to transnational risk governance:

> Only a continuous questioning of scientific findings and an exploration of its contingency on power or interest and underlying normative understandings can help validate science. In other words, in order to be of use in the legitimate regulation of risk, science has to be anchored in communicative spheres with regard to normative issues outside its own system of reference.[29]

On such grounds, it is considered that the positivist approach is inappropriate for epistemological reasons. Sharing the emphasis on philosophical foundations of conflicting positions in international trade, the following conclusion of Sungjoon Cho shall be cited:

> Philosophical discussions on hermeneutics have important ramifications on the current debate on international trade and risk science. At present, there is little shared understanding among WTO Members on the very meaning of science or scientific justification as to the health risks of various food additives or other food modification technologies. Given this situation, any impulsive legal-regulatory attempt in the international level to impose a specific paradigm of science in a specific trade dispute is likely to invite more disputes, rather than resolving them. In this regard, the theory of philosophical hermeneutics tends to offer some practical suggestions.[30]

Therefore, it is abstained from suggesting an 'impulsive legal-regulatory attempt in the international level to impose a specific paradigm of science', i.e. to further increase the positivist notion of risk and science already existing in the current SPS Agreement. By the same token, however, also relativist attempts for unlimited regulatory discretion are refuted. In fact, positivist and relativist attempts are considered to represent the two extremes of the same epistemological spectrum: on the one end, the *subjective* end, there are relativist proposals for unlimited regulatory discretion of national sovereigns. At the other end of the spectrum, the *absolute* end, there are positivist attempts for establishing international regulatory frameworks based on allegedly 'objective' and 'sound' science. In contrast, a proposal shall be developed based on the epistemological opposite *objective—relative*. The proposed approach is inherently critical and based on contradictory procedures.[31] The critical approach, as suggested, shall stimulate scientific self-reflexivity and competition. A critical approach is considered preferable to a positivistic system enforcing ultimate 'scientific truth' by means of quasi-mandatory international standards, and preferable to a relativistic approach suggesting an 'anything goes' attitude in risk regulation.

1 Multilayered Risk Governance

It was shown how various attempts tried to find ways for discerning legitimate from illegitimate SPS measures. Many of these attempts focused on separating factual considerations from political judgement, i.e. risk assessment from risk management. It was also shown that the SPS Agreement tried to achieve a distinction between SPS measures motivated by legitimate health concerns and illegitimate protectionist intent by referring to scientific principles. However, discussions reviewed above showed that the real objective for separating risk assessment and risk management, namely to ensure scientific integrity, was sometimes overshadowed by philosophical and political arguments.

The critical approach, as developed in the following, aims at refocusing on the core question of applied risk analysis: how can we ensure scientific integrity?

In the current setting provided by the SPS Agreement, risk issues are addressed at various governance levels. Typically, risks are assessed at national levels, or in the case of the EU, at regional levels. On the other hand, national risk managers have to take into account standards developed by international organisations such as Codex, IPPC and OIE. In this light, one may conceive that actually, risk analysis procedures are taking place in a multilayered setting, ranging from national to international dimensions.

The critical approach developed in the study at hand aims at addressing the multilayered character of contemporary risk analysis. The approach outlined hereafter is informed, in particular, by a proposal suggested by Thomas Cottier. Before the background of a risk landscape encompassing several layers of governance, Cottier suggested a vertical separation of risk assessment and risk management. With regard to risk assessment and risk management of GMOs, Cottier noted:

> The book [i.e. *When Cooperation Fails*] also encourages studying the topic in terms of multi-level governance and as a matter of allocating appropriate powers to appropriate levels. It is not a matter of uniformly addressing biotechnology in international law, but of identifying those elements that

need regulation on this level in order to avoid unjustified barriers to access and trade.[32]

Multilevel or multilayered governance can be characterised as 'a graduated concept of constitutionalism which puts more emphasis on process and interaction than on strict conceptual boundaries and momentous events of constitution making, focusing on how the constitutional functions can be secured, considering the different levels of governance as forming part of an overall constitutional system'.[33] In other words, the focus of the theory of multilevel governance is on governmental functions as they are effectively executed instead of centring on formal constitutional texts which were written mainly before regional and international layers of governance have emerged.

In so doing, the theory of multilayered governance aims to allocate powers, tasks and obligations to the various layers of governance according to respective functions and in rational ways. This focus on governmental functions[34] is taken as a model and employed for reallocating risk analysis procedures.

The core idea of the theory of multilayered governance, i.e. its focus on function but not on form, meets Codex' 'functional separation' of risk management and risk assessment. As outlined previously, the approach of Codex to 'functionally separate' risk management and risk assessment basically consists in a separation of the two distinct functions of risk managers, on the one hand, and risk assessors, on the other hand. Codex achieves a separation of risk management and risk assessment by assigning their respective functions to different organisational structures. Essentially, the function of managing risks in the framework of Codex is assigned to respective Codex Committees and finally to the Commission of the Codex Alimentarius (CAC). On the other hand, the function of assessing risks is assigned to Committees and meetings of individual experts selected and assembled by the Food and Agriculture Organization of the United Nations (FAO) and the World Health Organisation (WHO). In particular, these scientific expert bodies are the Joint FAO/WHO Expert Committee on Food Additives (JECFA), the Joint FAO/WHO Meetings on Pesticide Residues (JMPR.), and the Joint Meetings on Microbiological Risk Assessment (JEMRA). Whereas the Codex Committees and the Commission of the Codex Alimentarius are driven by initiatives of representatives of Member Countries, the scientific experts assembled in JECFA, JMPR and JEMRA are working under the auspices of international organisations, namely the Food and Agriculture Organization of the United Nations (FAO) and the WHO. In other words, the function of managing risks at the international level is assigned to Codex bodies driven by Member country interests, whereas the function of scientifically assessing risks is sourced out into the realm of international organisations. Simplified, international risk management, i.e. negotiating international standards, guidelines and recommendations, is a function carried out by delegates of Member countries, whereas risk assessment, i.e. the scientific evaluation of risks, is sourced out to specialised expert bodies beyond the reach of Codex Members.

The theory of multilayered governance seems particularly well suited for addressing transboundary health and safety concerns. GMOs, SARS, avian influenza and swine flu are examples of global threats which can only be addressed by regional and international organisations transcending national sovereignty. John Jackson summarised challenges caused by internationalised health and safety issues as follows:

> (…) the subject of health clearly demands attention at an international level, for several reasons. First, as recognised at least a century and half ago, various health issues transgress national borders, and by at least 1920 it was recognised that increased world trade created added dangers of transmittal of communicable diseases. Much more recently the scourge of HIV-AIDS, and the scare caused by the possible SARS (severe acute respiratory syndrome) epidemic, as well as the current potential disaster of avian influenza demonstrated poignantly the importance of the WHO (World Health Organization) and actually led that organization to begin work on revising its International Health Regulations (IHRs) to better accommodate international activity.[35]

With respect to transboundary challenges to health and safety, the theory of multilayered governance, sometimes also called post-Westphalian or post-Weberian approaches, provides an appropriate response. The theory of multilevel governance basically considers that 'the erosion of territorially-bound sovereignty—due to the weakening of state borders as well as to the increasing supra-nationalization of policy areas crucial for the effectiveness and 'output-oriented' legitimation of welfare states in face of structural deficit of 'input-oriented' legitimation—defines a new challenging conditions for post-Westphalian nation states: the *blurring the external differentiation* calls for an *increasing internal differentiation* as a condition for policy effectiveness and legitimacy'.[36]

In fact, legitimacy and scientific integrity are challenged by various sources of interferences. Examples are directives from superior administrative units, as was the case in *Australia—Salmon*, lobbying or other sorts of political or economic interventions. Challenged by such cases, the theory of multilevel governance suggests to assign risk assessment to levels beyond the reach of stakeholders involved in risk analysis procedures at respective national levels. In other words, because an outsourcing of risk assessment within national governmental structures does not ensure unbiased outcomes, the theory of multilevel governance suggests an assignment of risk assessment to other levels of governance beyond national reach. In this respect, one might think about regional or international levels. In fact, a survey on SPS cases shows that only risk evaluations carried out at the regional or at the international level were accepted as 'proper risk assessments' in the sense of Article 5.1 of the SPS Agreement by Panels and the Appellate Body (*EC—Hormones*, *EC—Biotech*). On the other hand, in none of the prominent SPS cases was a risk evaluation carried out at the national level accepted as a 'proper risk assessment' (*Australia—Salmon*, *Japan—Agricultural Products*).

In the case *EC—Hormones*, risk assessments were carried out by various scientific committees at the regional[37] and at the international[38] level, in particular, JECFA. The regional and international risk assessments were subsequently accepted as 'proper risk assessments' by the Panel and by the Appellate Body. All these risk evaluations carried out at the regional or at the international level came to the conclusion that the hormones in question are 'safe' if administered according to good agricultural practices.[39] On the other hand, risk evaluation reports put forward by the European Communities for justifying their import ban on hormone-treated meat were not accepted as proper risk assessments in the sense of Article 5.1 of the SPS Agreement by the Panel and the Appellate Body.

In the case *Australia—Salmon*, the alleged risks for the Australian Atlantic salmon were assessed at national levels, i.e. by Australia, a procedure which was not accepted by the panel and the Appellate Body as a proper risk assessment in the sense of Article 5.1 SPS. In this case, the Panel observed a 'rather substantial change in conclusions' between a risk evaluation report issued in May 1995 by Australia's Quarantine and Inspection Service (AQIS) approving the importation of salmon under certain conditions, and a later report published in May 1996 by Australia's Department of Primary Industries and Fisheries recommending an uphold of the import prohibition.[40] Although Australia claimed that the reversal was based on new scientific data and considerations, the experts advising the Panel all declined that new scientific evidence had been originated with regard to the questions at issue.[41] Therefore, the Panel considered that 'the decisive reason for reversing the 1995 Draft Report's conclusions—that the salmon products further examined should be allowed into Australia under specific conditions—might well have been inspired by domestic pressures to protect the *Australia—Salmon* industry against import competition'.[42] In this respect, the Panel also pointed at a statement made by Canada arguing that Tasmanian salmon producers 'lobbied furiously' against the report issued in May 1995 by AQIS and 'even hired a lobby firm ... to reverse the conclusion…'.[43] Obviously, thought, the Australian risk assessment[44] was influenced by the Department of Primary Industries and Fisheries so as to justify the intended measure, i.e. to ban the importation of salmon.[45]

In the case *Japan—Agricultural Products II*, the risk of the introduction of the codling moth into Japan was assessed at the national level, i.e. by Japanese authorities in a '1996 Pest Risk Assessment of Codling Moth', a procedure which was not accepted by the Appellate Body as a proper risk assessment in the sense of Article 5.1 SPS. Therefore, both the Panel and the Appellate Body found that the measure to address the alleged risks, i.e. the varietal testing requirement, was adopted without a 'proper risk assessment' on which it should have been based.

In the case *EC—Biotech*, the Panel only accepted the risk evaluations conducted at the regional level, i.e. by the leading competent authority[46] and by the EC scientific committees[47] as 'proper risk assessments'. In contrast, the Panel refused to accept the various documents produced at national levels, i.e. by individual EC Member States,[48] as 'proper risk assessments'.

The survey reveals that the inconsistencies between the outcome of the risk assessment and the risk management measures, which were supposed to be based upon the outcome of the risk assessment, were most striking in the cases *EC—Hormones* and *EC—Biotech* where the risk assessment was undertaken at a different level (regional or international) from the risk management (national and regional level, respectively).

In the *Biotech* case, the discrepancies between the risk assessments undertaken by the leading competent authority, i.e. the authority of the EC Member States to which the product applications were originally submitted, and the EC scientific committees and the reasons given by the EC Member States to justify their individual safeguard measures were apparent. Against the findings of the proper risk assessments undertaken by the leading competent authority and the EC scientific committees that there was 'no evidence' that the biotech products in question presented any greater risk for human health or the environment than its conventional counterparts, some EC Member States went on banning certain biotech products.

In the *Biotech* case, the panel examined and rebutted a wide range of documents put forward by the EC Member States for justifying their respective safeguard measures as either not constituting proper risk assessments or as not being 'based on' a proper risk assessment pursuant to Annex A(4) and Article 5.1 of the SPS Agreement.[49] The reasons for this verdict of the Panel varied for each document. For example, the Panel noted that

- documents put forward by Austria[50] to justify its safeguard measure against the importation of T25 maize lacked of 'evaluation of likelihood' of gene flows from GMOs[51];
- documents put forward by France for justifying its safeguard measure against the importation of MS1/RF1 oilseed rape did 'not 'evaluate' the likelihood of the risks of establishment, entry or spread of a pest (*in casu*, hybrid plants)...'[52];
- a document put forward by Germany[53] for justifying its safeguard measure against the importation of Bt-176 maize 'asserts that there is a potential for adverse effects on human or animal health" from the presents of antibiotic resistance marker genes (ARMG), but the study "does not determine likelihoods'[54];
- some documents put forward by Greece[55] for justifying its safeguard measure against the importation of Topas oilseed rape addressed herbicide tolerant GM crops (GMHT crops) 'in general rather than focusing specifically on the Topas oilseed rape, and none of these studies evaluates the likelihood of adverse effects from the entry, establishment or spread of GMHT crops according to the SPS measures which might be taken by Greece to reduce any potential risks'[56];
- a document put forward by Italy[57] for justifying its safeguard measure against the importation of T25 maize, MON810 maize, MON809 maize and Bt-11 maize 'constitutes, not a complete, self-contained, scientific evaluation of the potential for adverse effects on human or

animal health due to toxicity and the development of antibiotic resistance, but only part of such an evaluation'[58];

- a document put forward by Luxembourg for justifying its safeguard measure against the importation of Bt-176 maize 'calls for, but does not itself provide, further evaluation of the mechanism of gene transfer which might lead to the development of antibiotic resistance and of the risk of development of insects resistant to Bt toxin'[59];

On the other hand, the Panel recognised risk assessments carried out at the EC Community level as complying with the requirements of Annex A (4) and Article 5.1 of the SPS Agreement. In this respect, the Panel observed 'that the assessments carried out by the lead CA[60] and by the EC scientific committees[61] constitute "risk assessments" within the meaning of Annex A(4) and Article 5.1 of the *SPS Agreement*'.[62] In contrast to the EC Member States evaluations rebutted by the Panel for not constituting proper risks assessments, the Panel admitted that the evaluations carried out at the EC Community level 'evaluated the likelihood of potential adverse effects on human health and/or the environment, as well as the associated potential consequences, according to the proposed use of the specific biotech product under consideration'.[63]

In cases where risk assessments were carried out entirely at national levels, these risk assessments were not accepted as proper risk assessments in the sense of Article 5.1 of the SPS Agreement (*Australia—Salmon, Japan—Agricultural Products II*). On the other hand, it can be observed that Panels and the Appellate Body accepted risk evaluations carried out at regional and international levels (*EC—Hormones, EC—Biotech*). However, in these cases, proper risk assessments carried out at regional and international levels drew different conclusions than reports and studies put forward by the respective respondents for justifying their respective SPS measures in the WTO disputes in question (*EC—Hormones, EC—Biotech*).

Considering the cases *EC—Hormones* and *EC—Biotech*, it was shown that reports and studies put forward by respondents for justifying their respective SPS measures in the WTO disputes at issue were objected by other, scientifically more 'objective' risk assessments carried out at regional and international levels. Such findings challenge the scientific integrity of risk assessments carried out at respective national levels. In the same way, questions arise with regard to the clarity about respective functions of risk assessors and risk managers and potential conflicts of interest among national authorities. Hence, the concept of the Appellate Body to merge risk assessment and risk management into one operation, i.e. the 'SPS risk assessment', may educe the sort of problems the doctrine of risk analysis tries to avoid by establishing a 'function separation' of risk assessment and risk management. Or, as Codex put: 'There should be a functional separation of risk assessment and risk management, in order to ensure the scientific integrity of the risk assessment, to avoid confusion over the functions to be performed by risk assessors and risk managers and to reduce any conflict of interest'.[64] However, corruption of scientific integrity, confusion over the role of risk assessors and risk managers, and conflicts of interests could be observed in several SPS cases. In the case *Australia—Salmon*, scientific integrity was corrupted by the Australian Department of Primary Industries and Energy reversing the scientific findings of its Quarantine and Inspection Service for protectionist motives.[65] Confusion over the functions of risk assessors and risk managers became apparent in the *EC—Hormones* case.[66] Conflicts of interests were found by the Appellate Body in the *Continued Suspension* cases, considering that institutional affiliations of scientific experts with JECFA 'compromised the adjudicative independence and impartiality of the Panel'.[67]

On the basis of the theory of multilevel governance, it is suggested to engage in a clear vertical separation of powers and functions. Hereby, risk assessment would be assigned to those international bodies already concerned with the elaboration of international standards in the relevant fields, i.e. Codex, OIE and IPPC. For making the system operational, the task of providing risk assessments in individual cases could be assigned to bodies already established by Codex, OIE and IPPC, in particular, the respective scientific expert committees and working groups. For instance, in the Codex system, the most prominent scientific expert committees are the Joint FAO/WHO Expert Committee on Food Additives (JECFA), the Joint FAO/WHO Expert Meetings on Pesticide Residues (JMPR), and the Joint FAO/WHO Expert Meetings on Microbiological Risk Assessment (JEMRA). Expert committees and working groups of scientific experts convening under the auspices of the three mentioned international organisations, i.e. Codex, OIE and IPPC, could be used as nuclei for establishing international networks for risk assessments on the basis of specific mandates by individual WTO Members wishing to introduce an SPS measure. Such an international risk assessment network open for all interested countries would be of particular value for developing and least developed countries currently prevented from fully participating in SPS procedures owing to limited scientific resources.

A vertical separation of risk assessment and risk management would resolve one of the major problems of the current SPS Agreement, that is, the question where and how to address non-scientific factors. As explained above, it remains unclear up to now in which stage of the risk analysis process non-scientific factors should be addressed: should non-scientific factors be considered in the risk management stage and separated from scientific risk assessment, as suggested by the rather objectivist approach of the panel? Or should non-scientific factors be considered in a comprehensive attempt covering both risk assessment and risk management aspects, as prescribed by the rather constructivist approach of the Appellate Body?

With respect to the problem of non-scientific factors, the solution offered by the proposal suggested here follows the objectivist attempt of the panels in the *EC—Hormones* and *Continued Suspension* cases. By vertically separating scientific questions from risk management issues, it is clear that non-scientific factors belong to the risk management phase which shall be dealt with at respective national levels. The assignment of non-scientific questions to risk management corresponds with the majority opinion in the risk analysis circle. The Codex Alimentarius Commission, for instance, issued 'Statements of Principle Concerning the Role of Science in the Codex Decision-Making Process and the Extent to which other Factors are taken into Account' (in the following: *Statements of Principle*) which were adopted in 1995. The second principle of the *Statements of Principle* made it clear that Codex, in principle, takes into account non-scientific factors:

> 2. When elaborating and deciding upon food standards Codex Alimentarius will have regard, where appropriate, to other legitimate factors relevant for the health protection of consumers and for the promotion of fair practices in food trade.[68]

However, this 'rather obscure provision', as Button[69] called it, kept silent how and to what extent 'other legitimate factors' have to be taken into account by Codex. Therefore, Codex' *Statements of Principle* were subsequently clarified by 'Criteria for the consideration of the Other Factors Referred to in the Second Statement of Principle', adopted in 2001. The amendment clarified that

> other legitimate factors for health protection and fair trade practices may be identified in the risk management process, and risk managers should indicate

> how these factors affect the selection of risk management options and the development of standards, guidelines and related texts.[70]

By the same token, the 2001 amendment reconfirmed that 'consideration of other factors should not affect the scientific basis of risk analysis; in this process, the separation between risk assessment and risk management should be respected, in order to ensure the scientific integrity of the risk assessment'.[71] From this wording, it is clear that 'other legitimate factors' have to be considered in the risk management phase. Obviously, though, the *Statements of Principle* were drafted with view on today's organisation of Codex, that is, with Codex committees such as CCFA and the CCCF acting as risk managers and scientific committees and expert meetings such as JECFA, JEMRA and JMPR functioning as risk assessors. However, there is nothing that speaks against the application of rules developed for separating risk assessment and risk management in standard setting procedures at the international level to individual SPS risk assessments. Whereas risk assessors would basically remain the same, i.e. international expert bodies, risk managers would be authorities from WTO Members intending to establish an SPS measure. Hence, the coverage of the relevant 'Criteria for the consideration of the Other Factors Referred to in the Second Statement of Principle' could be expanded as follows:

> Other legitimate factors for health protection and fair trade practices may be identified in the risk management process, and risk managers should indicate how these factors affect the selection of risk management options and the development of standards, guidelines and related texts [*and SPS measures*].

By establishing a clear institutional separation between risk assessment and risk management, the proposal at hand may also help to clarify problems surrounding precaution. Actually, it would be an issue for discussion between risk assessors and risk managers how and to what extent considerations of precaution may be factored into a concrete risk assessment policy at issue. The requirement for discussion issues of precaution openly and thoroughly in the process of establishing a risk assessment policy may clarify whether there is enough scientific foundation for justifying a provisional measure in the sense of Article 5.7 of the SPS Agreement or not. That line of argument follows, in fact, the current Codex policy with regard to precaution. Paragraph 11 of the 'Working Principles for Risk Analysis for

Application in the Framework of the Codex Alimentarius' points at the threshold of 'sufficient scientific evidence' for further proceedings:

> Precaution is an inherent element of risk analysis. Many sources of uncertainty exist in the process of risk assessment and risk management of food related hazards to human health. The degree of uncertainty and variability in the available scientific information should be explicitly considered in the risk analysis. Where there is sufficient scientific evidence to allow Codex to proceed to elaborate a standard or related text, the assumptions used for the risk assessment and the risk management options selected should reflect the degree of uncertainty and the characteristics of the hazard.[72]

Albeit in a vertical setting where risk assessors would operation at the international level and risk managers at respective national levels, the questions would remain rather similar. In cases where there is 'sufficient scientific evidence', risk managers at respective national levels might proceed to introduce provisional SPS measures according to Article 5.7 of the SPS Agreement. If, however, risk assessors are unable to provide 'sufficient scientific evidence' even for justifying a provisional measure, it would remain upon respective national risk managers to decide whether or not to introduce SPS measures solely on the basis of the precautionary principle.

The focus of a reform of the SPS Agreement in line with the above considerations is, at first view, on Article 5. In its current form, Article 5 of the SPS Agreement implies that risk assessments are carried out at respective national levels. Paragraph 1 of Article 5 of the SPS Agreement, entitled *Assessment of Risk and Determination of the Appropriate Level of Sanitary or Phytosanitary Protection,* reads as follows:

> 1. Members shall ensure that their sanitary or phytosanitary measures are based on an assessment, as appropriate to the circumstances, of the risks to human, animal or plant life or health, taking into account risk assessment techniques developed by the relevant international organizations.

Cornerstone of a reform of the SPS Agreement following the above considerations would be a reformulated paragraph 1 of Article 5 of the SPS Agreement. The following wording may serve as starting point for such a discussion[73]:

Article 5 (new)

Risk Assessment

> 1. Members shall ensure that their sanitary or phytosanitary measures are based on an [*international*] assessment, as appropriate to the circumstances, of the risks to human, animal or plant life or health [*determined by respective international organisations and accredited specialised scientific research institutions*].

2 The Criterion of Falsifiability

A vertical separation of risk assessment from risk management would most likely free the former from the grip of respective national authorities. Thus, by assigning risk assessment to organisations operating at the international level, i.e. Codex, IPPC and OIE, the danger of political interferences would most likely decrease. Hence, the internationalisation of risk assessment, as suggested by a reformulated Article 5.1 of the SPS Agreement, seems to be appropriate for addressing the predominant fear of disguised protectionism. The attempt for reformulating Article 5.1 of the SPS Agreement, however, seems inappropriate to ensure scientific integrity vis-à-vis corporate influence. Whereas political influence of national governments over risk assessors operating at the international level is likely to decrease, similar positive effects are not expected with regard to potential influence exerted by corporate interests. For shedding light on the issue, the example of the tobacco industry's influence on WHO is presented.

In 1999, the then Director General of the WHO, Gro Harlem Brundtland, appointed a committee of experts to investigate efforts of the tobacco industry to undermine WHO's tobacco prevention policies and related research. The committee of experts was chaired by Thomas Zeltner, the then director of the Swiss Federal Office of Public Health (FOPH).[74] The report of the committee of experts, entitled *Tobacco Company Strategies to Undermine Tobacco Control Activities at the World Health Organization* was released in August 2000. For illustration, some excerpts from that report shall be displayed without further comment[75]:

> Evidence from tobacco industry documents reveals that tobacco companies have operated for many years with the deliberate purpose of subverting the efforts of the World Health Organization (WHO) to control tobacco use.

> The attempted subversion has been elaborate, well financed, sophisticated, and usually invisible.
>
> That top executives of tobacco companies sat together to design and set in motion elaborate strategies to subvert a public health organization is unacceptable and must be condemned.
>
> … the documents show that tobacco companies sought to divert attention from the public health issues, to reduce budgets for the scientific and policy activities carried out by WHO, to pit other UN agencies against WHO, to convince developing countries that WHO's tobacco control program was a "First World" agenda carried out at the expense of the developing world, to distort the results of important scientific studies on tobacco, and to discredit WHO as an institution.
>
> …the documents show that tobacco companies hid behind a variety of ostensibly independent quasi-academic, public policy, and business organizations whose tobacco industry funding was not disclosed. The documents also show that tobacco company strategies to undermine WHO relied heavily on international and scientific experts with hidden financial ties to the industry.

A telling example of a 'scientific expert' with 'hidden financial ties to the industry' was Professor of Medicine Ragnar Rylander who for years was on the payroll of the tobacco industry and disseminated research findings on the innoxiousness of smoking.[76]

'Hidden financial ties to the industry' were again established when expert advice to the WHO with regard to the pandemic flu A/H1N1 was investigated. For example, it was established that an expert involved in the elaboration of guidelines for the application of antiviral drugs received money from GlaxoSmithKline and Roche, the manufacturers of the antiviral drugs 'Relenza' and 'Tamiflu', respectively.[77]

Alexia Herwig pointed at structural aspects of industry's interference with international scientific bodies, in particular at the problem of inadequate funding:

> The tobacco industry was able to hire a former Executive and Technical Secretary of JMPR as a consultant, who was the approached by the WHO to act as temporary adviser to the JMPR without disclosing his source of funding. There was also evidence suggesting some scientists evaluating milk hormones in 1997 in the JECFA were sponsored by industry. While the real impact of 'hired' scientists on the final evaluation is hard to assess,

> the possibility of capture cannot be ruled out. Although the WHO has a roster of experts, financial constraints have forced scientific committees to rely on outside experts. The FAO and the WHO meet the attendance costs of experts, but do not pay honoraria, thus giving experts an incentive to accept industry contributions.[78]

A major problem of scientific risk assessment is the fact that risk assessors are usually not establishing scientific data themselves but are relying on publicly available research data. Considering the generation—or fabrication —of scientific data, the example of the Tobacco Industry Research Council (TIRC) shall be provided. Robert Proctor observed that the tobacco industry applied various strategies for 'disestablishing facts'. One of these disestablishing strategies of the tobacco industry was

> ...to fund research that would *seem* to be addressing tobacco and health, while really doing nothing of the sort. The chief instrument for this was the Tobacco Industry Research Council (TIRC), established in 1954, with great fanfare in full-page ads published in 448 of the national's leading newspapers. The TIRC (later renamed the Council for Tobacco Research) eventually funded hundreds of millions of dollars of research, very little of which had anything to do with smoking. Little of it ever addressed the question supposedly in doubt: whether and to what extent cigarettes are bad for your health. The political value of research of this kind (mostly basic biochemistry) was the *fact of its being funded* – which allowed the industry to say it was "studying the problem." Industry researchers knew from the beginning what they were supposed to find (and not find): per instructions from the Tobacco Institute, the TIRC was supposed to manifest confidence that "we do not now know what causes lung cancer or any other kind of cancer." Press releases and publications from the industry beat this drum pretty hard. In lawyerly fashion, health implications were thought of as "charges" to be refuted rather than as topics to be honestly investigated.[79]

Indeed, the question of the financing of scientific research is at the heart of the risk assessment problem. Lee Ann Jackson and Marion Jansen, analysing the issue thoroughly, described the state of play as follows:

> If relevant scientific evidence was provided by independent scientists whose empirical work is driven by a pure interest in making science progress, chances would be high that the party providing the largest amount of evidence is indeed defending the paradigm that will ultimately be proven to be 'correct', in the sense that it supports standards that impede the sale of unsafe

> products while they allow for the global circulation of safe products. But in practice private sector players with commercial interests in one or the other outcome of the empirical evidence race have an important role in the generation of relevant scientific evidence and there is reason to believe that this creates a bias in the persuasion game.[80]

At this point, it is essential to remind that scientific expert bodies such as JECFA, JEMRA and JMPR working in the field of food safety, i.e. with committees of the Codex Alimentarius Commission, are not generating scientific data themselves, nor do they commission scientific work by third parties. Rather, scientific expert bodies working in the field of food safety, i.e. JECFA, JEMRA and JMPR, are relying on existing scientific data generated by third-party sources.[81] By issuing a 'call for information', scientific expert bodies working on food safety, e.g. JECFA, are collecting research data and studies on the substances at issue from all available sources preceding their respective meetings. In this respect, the role of unpublished data is of interest. There is no mechanism to ensure that unpublished data are coming to the eyes of risk assessors, regardless whether they are operating at national or at the international level.[82] Manufacturers, for example, are only 'expected to submit all relevant published and unpublished data'.[83] But also providers of scientific data operating in the public domain, such as governments, NGOs, research institutes and universities, are just invited, but not obligated to submit relevant scientific data.[84] Considering this state of play, Lee Ann Jackson and Marion Jansen concluded:

> JECFA risk assessment only relies on studies carried out by external laboratories. The scientific evidence used by JECFA, i.e. Codex, is therefore only as neutral as the evidence generated by external laboratory, i.e. through R&D generated with private sector or national public sector funding.[85]

As long as scientific expert bodies operating at the international level are supplied by research data provided by various different sources, in particular, private sector funded as well as public sector funded research data, a critical assessment of such data, by comparison, seems possible. In reality, however, provision of scientific data is contingent upon respective financial, technological and institutional resources. The problem of insufficient scientific data from developing countries is widely acknowledged.[86] A rather new phenomenon, at least in the European context, is the incremental permeability of boundaries between public and private funding sources for scientific research. The underlying rationale for blurring boundaries between public and private research funding are 'innovation policies' reducing the role of science to a promoter of economic growth. In this respect, Helga Nowotny introduced the term 'propertization' of scientific data and scientific knowledge in general.[87] Nowotny noted: 'Once science could claim to have several, perhaps contradictory functions. Today, its overriding function is to initiate, sustain, and be the main driving force behind innovation'.[88]

As Nowotny indicated, impacts of innovation policies fostering cooperation models between the private sector and public research institutions, e.g. public-private partnerships, joint ventures, third-party funds, technology transfer, spin-off companies, etc. are far reaching. At this point, the single aspect of data control through corporate influence shall be further discussed. As an example, it is pointed at a cooperation agreement between the then Novartis Agro Discovery Institute (Nadi, today Syngenta) and the University of Berkeley of 1998. For five million US-Dollars per year, Novartis got the option to buy all licences of the Faculty of Biology of the University of Berkeley. Additionally, the corporation was entitled to delegate two of the five Members of the board deciding over the distribution of research funds. Finally, university employees could get access to additional Novartis funds provided that they agreed to seek for the company's approval before publishing research data.[89] Whereas such direct control of scientific data might be exceptional, indirect influencing of research data is on the increase. Typically coming along as private donations or sponsoring, indirect influencing of public research institutions does not aim at influencing concrete research data, but the research agenda. In this respect, Marcel Hänggi put in figuratively, saying that it would be rather unlikely that companies such as Syngenta or Novartis would ever sponsor professorships for mediaeval studies and glaciology: 'Sponsoring influences the agenda of research', Marcel Hänggi observed.[90]

Considering this state of play, two approaches seem conceivable. An ambitious approach might propose to equip international scientific bodies with the resources necessary to probe and compile scientific data themselves. Albeit enticing at first glance, the ambitious proposal is discarded in the following. The dismissal, however, is not motivated by the enormous political, financial and organisational challenges the ambitious proposal would bring about. At first, the reluctance is based on epistemological demur. Depicting international organisations equipped with proper research infrastructure such as laboratories with permanently employed scientific staff and commissioned to execute risk assessments for WTO Members on a mandatory basis, one may easily see the emergence of a powerful scientific superstructure. In addition, one has to bear in mind that the same international organisations would continue to function as reference points for the setting of international standards. Recalling Article 3.2 of the SPS Agreement and the presumption of GATT/WTO compatibility of SPS measures conforming to international standards, one may well perceive the joint effect of mandatory assignments or risk assessments to international organisations and the legal bias towards levels of protection set by the very same international organisations.

In this respect, considerations of the Appellate Body in the *Continued Suspension* case shall be recalled. In this case, the Appellate Body agreed to the European Communities' argument that the panel infringed due process requirements by consulting with JECFA experts. In particular, the Appellate Body considered

> ... that there was an objective basis to conclude that the institutional affiliation with JECFA of Drs. Boisseau and Boobis, and their participation in JECFA's evaluations of the six hormones at issue, was likely to affect or give rise to justifiable doubts as to their independence or impartiality given that the evaluations conducted by JECFA lie at the heart of the controversy between the parties. The appointment and consultations with Drs. Boisseau and Boobis compromised the adjudicative independence and impartiality of the Panel. Therefore, we find that the Panel infringed the European Communities' due process rights as a result of the Panel having consulted with Drs. Boisseau and Boobis as scientific experts.[91]

That statement of the Appellate Body refers to the fact that risk assessment experts are rare and often active in various fora, for example, in research institutions at national levels and in expert committees at the international level. Quite similar to the *Continued Suspension* case, it is unlikely to assume that scientific experts active in the standard-setting process of international organisations would easily revise preceding findings when commissioned by an individual WTO Member to conduct a particular risk assessment later one. If scientific resources and excellent scientific personnel, in particular, would be available in abundance, the ambitious approach might be further explored. But considering the 'human factor' leading to some kind of subjective bias in favour of scientific data in whose finding one was personally involved, scepticism seems advisable. In addition to that inherent bias towards existing levels of protection defined by international standards, the legal bias of Article 3.2 has to be taken into account. In the current setting of the existing SPS Agreement, the option for higher levels of protection is disqualified by the presumption contained in Article 3.2 of the SPS Agreement privileging SPS measures 'conform to' international standards. Hence, without a simultaneous reform of Article 3.2 of the SPS Agreement, the inherent bias towards predefined levels of protection, as explained above, would continue to be reinforced by the legal presumption of Article 3.2 of the SPS Agreement.

Finally, with respect to standard-setting processes conducted by international organisations, that is, risk management at the international level, one has to take into account additional structural imbalances. Taken the Codex Alimentarius Commission, for example, one has to note that close links to industry are one of its characterising features. With regard to Codex-industry links, Thorsten Hüller and Matthias Leonhard Maier observed:

> For one thing, close links with industry have deep roots in Codex history; in early years, the practice was even for Member delegations to be directly sponsored by industry. For another, consumer organisations themselves acknowledge that 'the food industry employs the best scientists', which is clearly an important asset in the science-centred Codex process – notwithstanding the emphasis that is constantly put upon the distinction between (scientific) risk assessment and (political) risk management. Last but not least, there are also close personal ties between the food industry and public officials in this field, so that, in some cases, industry organisations with observer status at the Codex also employ former governmental officials and even former delegates to Codex meetings.[92]

Structural biases are particularly well reflected in imbalances regarding organisations accompanying national delegations at meetings of international standard setting organisations. Taking Codex, for example, the following observations have been made:

> [A]mong the 156 NGOs currently in observer status at the Codex, more than 100 can clearly be categorised as representing the interests of food producers (agriculture and industry) or traders. The remainder mainly comprise scientific and professional organisations, while only 10 organisations represent consumer, health or environmental interests. If we look more

> specifically at the NGOs which actually attend CAC meetings, the pattern is similar. The bias is, in fact, even stronger if we take into account the size of delegations. Only one consumer organisation sent more than one person to the 2005 session of the CAC, while the same was true of about half the industry organisations, seven of which had three or more people on their teams and thus more than most national delegations.[93]

Taken together, the scientific upgrading of international organisations with physical equipment and the legal bias towards levels of protection (pre) defined by standards set by the same international organisations would render the latter virtually untouchable. Therefore, a rather similar conclusion is put forward as was the case with regard to the positivist proposal. Regarding attempts for enforced harmonisation of international standards, the conclusion was drawn that such positivist proposals would practically monopolise scientific knowledge in the field of action of international standard-setting organisations such as the Codex Alimentarius Commission, the IPPC and the OIE. Assigning international organisations with both scientific (risk assessment) and regulatory (standard-setting) powers resembles to the council of scientific experts forming the supreme intellectual institution in Comte's positivist conception of the world.

For these reasons, the ambitious approach for equipping international organisations with physical research facilities as a solution to the problem of private corporate influence and for achieving 'scientific neutrality' is finally considered inappropriate. Albeit in favour for additional research facilities at the disposal of international organisations in general, the ambitious approach is not considered a panacea for achieving the specific goal in question, i.e. to effectively contain corporate interference. Given the manifold and complex ways of corporate influence, only an approach taking into account findings from epistemology seems to be effective in the long run. However, albeit moderate in terms of physical resources, an approach based on epistemology may turn out to be demanding in other, more fundamental respects.

Following Popperian epistemology, scientific knowledge should centre on the opposite *objective—relative*. In this sense, paradoxically, objectivity is achievable only for the price of some sort of relativity: an argument is 'true' only as long as nobody puts forward a better argument refuting the former. In this regard, the Appellate Body's emphasise on minority or dissenting scientific opinions is of particular importance. In *EC—Hormones*, the Appellate Body stated:

> The "scientific basis" of SPS measures cannot be confined to the formalized conclusions of committees called upon to review or analyze the risks a substance may pose. Those conclusions are just one of the elements to be taken into account. The "available scientific evidence", referred to in Article 5.2, includes both generally held or majority scientific views as well as minority, or dissenting, scientific opinion (often first expressed by individual scientists).[94]

The importance of minority or dissenting scientific opinion becomes all the more manifest if considered not only with view on individual cases, but in a systemic perspective. Assuming a positivist setting, submissions of minority or dissenting scientific opinions in SPS disputes would be rather unlikely. The new monopoly to carry out risk assessments for WTO Members, combined with the de facto power of standards issued by the same international organisations would basically impede WTO Members to introduce minority or dissenting scientific arguments in SPS disputes. Therefore, an alternative, yet truly critical, approach is outlined in the following, aiming at making the epistemological opposite *objective—relative* work at the international level.

Cornerstone of the critical approach is the focus on scientific integrity. First and rather classical, reliable science is seen as an effective tool for detecting protectionist motives underpinning the establishment or maintenance of SPS measures. Second and more innovative, scientific integrity is seen as an essential prerequisite for the disclosure of biases in scientific arguments in favour of commercial interests and implicit market-opening agendas.

As discussed above, scientific integrity may be imperilled both by political as well as by economic forces. As a shelter against political influence, i.e. protectionist intent, it was suggested to assign scientific risk assessment procedures to international organisations. Internationalisation of risk assessment procedures is considered the objective element of the critical approach. Internationalisation alone, however, was found insufficient to shield scientific risk assessment from corporate influence. Furthermore, also a positivist solution to the problem of private sector influence, i.e. the establishment of scientific superpowers at the international level, was considered inappropriate for containing corporate interference. Therefore, a relative element is required, allowing and even fostering a permanent scrutiny of scientific knowledge in the WTO context. Hence, a critical approach is contingent upon mobilisation and open discourse of all available sources of scientific knowledge. On these grounds, firstly, WTO Members should not be obliged to rely on risk assessments conducted by international organisations. However, there should be a strong incentive for relying on such international risk assessments. Second, the presumption of GATT/WTO compatibility for SPS measures which conform to international standards, as implied in Article 3.2 of the SPS Agreement, is perceived as an obstacle to the competition of scientific arguments on equal terms. In fact, Article 3.2 of the SPS Agreement, as it stands today, is an impediment to free choice of different levels of protection deemed appropriate by respective WTO Members. Thus, in epistemological perspective, incentives are provided for scientific conformity, not for scientific competition. Taking together, the critical approach put forward in the following consists of combining the internationalisation of risks assessment with the presumption of GATT/WTO compatibility, as currently provided by Article 3.2 of the SPS Agreement. Thereby, risk assessments carried out by international organisations shall be privileged by the presumption of GATT/WTO compatibility. Following the critical approach proposed here, a reformulated Article 3.2 of the SPS Agreement would thus read as follows:

> 2. Sanitary or phytosanitary measures [*based on risk assessments carried out by international organisations*] shall be deemed to be necessary to protect human, animal or plant life or health, and presumed to be consistent with the relevant provisions of this Agreement and of GATT 1994.

Other provisions of the SPS Agreement, in particular Articles 3.1, 3.3 and 5, would remain unchanged.

A reform of Article 3.2 of the SPS Agreement in line with the critical approach suggested would basically provide two results.

First, a reformulated Article 3.2 of the SPS Agreement would lead to the harmonisation of risk assessment procedures. The presumption of GATT/WTO compatibility, as expressed by a reformulated Article 3.2 of the SPS Agreement, would be a strong incentive for WTO Members to commission international organisations with the task of carrying out their respective risk assessments. The internationalisation of risk assessment procedures would not only guarantee state-of-the-art risk assessments, but also release the latter from political influence exerted by individual WTO Members. Procedural harmonisation forms the objective element of the critical approach.

The second element of the critical approach consists of an opening up of policy space for national risk managers. That purpose shall be achieved by a gradual model, offering a range of policy options to risk managers. In most common cases, WTO Members may contentedly agree to levels of protection provided by international standards. This is the case foreseen in Article 3.1 of the SPS Agreement which shall remain unchanged. A difference to the status quo, however, would be that compliance with international standards would become truly voluntary again. As already mentioned, the abrogation of the presumption of GATT/WTO compatibility for SPS measures conforming to international standards in Article 3.2 of the SPS Agreement would restore the voluntary character of international standards.[95] In effect, risk managers of WTO Members would be disburdened from that legal presumption and free to opt for higher levels of protection (Article 3.3 of the SPS Agreement). However, because risk assessment shall be carried out by international organisations, risk managers could not introduce SPS measures arbitrarily and deliver scientific justification in addition, that is, only on request in the event of a dispute. Rather, national risk managers would be requested to put forward risk assessment policies on behalf of international risk assessors, eventually resulting in higher levels of protection. The critical approach, suggesting an increased used of risk assessment policies as a joint exercise of international risk assessors and risk managers operating at respective national levels, corresponds with the proposal made by Lee Ann Jackson and Marion Jansen. In their lucid paper on the question whether risk assessment in the international food safety policy arena may provide unbiased outcomes, Lee Ann Jackson and Marion Jansen argued for more policy options in risk analysis procedures. In particular, Jackson and Jansen suggested that risk assessors should analyse a range of policy options and that risk managers should choose from a whole, 'menu of policy options'. Enlarging the range of policy options evaluated by risk assessors, Jackson and Jansen argued, 'would provide policy makers with a more complete assessment of the risk implications of the policy basket at their disposal'[96]:

> Codex standards are the outcome of multilateral negotiations based upon risk assessment. It is important to communicate this fact to the public and thus signal that scientific evidence is only one of the determinants of Codex international food safety standards, albeit a very prominent one. The possible trade-offs between economic and political interests on the one hand and public health interests on the other hand, could become more tangible if the

> outcome of Codex risk assessment was a '*menu of policy options*'. Existing Codex procedures already allow for this and we encourage the increased use of this practice. We also propose that risk assessors play a more important role in defining the range of policy options to be analysed. One advantage of the suggested set-up could be that countries deviating from the internationally agreed standards may choose one of the other options analysed by the Codex risk assessors.[97]

Importance and functioning of risk assessment policies can be demonstrated by looking at the example of aflatoxins. Concerning aflatoxins as a trade issue, a major question centred on whether the European Communities could introduce higher levels of protection than recommended by JECFA and how such stricter EU standards could be scientifically justified. Whereas JECFA recommended limit values for total aflatoxin at 15 ppb (parts per billion), the EC introduced limit values for total aflatoxin at 4 ppb. Looking at the EC standards, JECFA considered that a hypothetical downward adjustment of the standard for aflatoxin from 20 parts per billion (ppb) to 10 ppb would reduce the cancer risk by only approximately two cancer cases annually per 1 billion people. Albeit the risk effects might be considered rather small, a cause-and-effect relationship was nevertheless scientifically ascertained. Applying suggestions for enlarging policy space for risk managers to the aflatoxin example, risk assessment policies issued by risk managers may commission risk assessors to elaborate 'menus' of available policy options, ranging from JECFA's standards down to 'zero risk'.

The idea of enlarging the scope of policy options at the disposal of risk managers is at the heart of the proposal based on the epistemological opposite *objective—relative;* in fact, it is the centrepiece of its relativistic component. However, as already indicated, the provision of a full 'menu of policy options' requires to abandon the preference of SPS measures conforming to international standards, expressed by Article 3.2 of the existing SPS Agreement. Otherwise, the bias towards SPS measures conforming to international standards, as established by the presumption of GATT/WTO conformity in Article 3.2 of the SPS Agreement, would nullify attempts for enlarging the policy space for national risk managers. In fact, by providing more policy space for national risk managers, the critical approach aims at neutralising inherent biases of the current SPS Agreement. As Lee Ann Jackson and Marion Jansen observed, a major bias of the SPS Agreement stems from the fact that the SPS Agreement deals with 'credence' goods.

As explained above (see Chap. 5 above), the term 'credence' indicates an information bias concerning certain product characteristics. This is obviously the case with regard to food safety characteristics where producers have an information advantage over consumers. At the international level, however, the information bias of food producers translates into a bias in favour of export interests built into the SPS framework. The main reason for this state of play is the fact that food products are credence goods. Implications of a globalised market for food products, i.e. credence goods, were explained by Lee Ann Jackson and Marion Jansen as follows:

> We have argued that in the case of food additives or products that are often characterized by credence good characteristics, exporting firms can be expected to take a more lenient stance towards food safety than consumers, while importing firms can be expected to take a more stringent stance towards food safety than consumers. We have also argued that in a globalized world, exporting firms can expect very large profits from introducing new products and that it is therefore in their commercial interest to provide scientific evidence that supports product standards they consider appropriate. For importers, instead, it is rather less likely to be profitable to generate scientific evidence in support of stringent standards. Increasing the role of scientific evidence for the setting of international food safety standards or the ruling of international trade disputes may thus lead to an inherent bias in favour of export interests in the absence of appropriate checks and balances.[98]

As a means for checking and balancing scientific data provided by interested private sector players, it was suggested to equip international organisations with the means necessary to generate scientific data themselves. However, and leaving the question of funding aside, one has to question whether to furnish international organisations with scientific hardware alone might be able to solve the problem of ensuring scientific integrity at the international level. As the example of corporate infiltration of WHO's work on tobacco prevention showed, corporate interest always finds ways for influencing scientific enterprise. And if out of the current international safety organisation Codex, IPPC and OIE a scientific superstructure would emerge, agency capture by corporate interests would become an even bigger threat. As outlined above, scientific superstructures assigned to carry out mandatory risk assessments for individual WTO Members as well as to set general safety standards would virtually monopolise scientific knowledge. Obviously, such a scientific 'Supreme Court' would attract corporate interest even more. A critical approach, in contrast, aims at ensuring scientific integrity by encouraging scientific critique. For stimulating scientific critique, it is suggested to abrogate the presumption of GATT/WTO compatibility expressed by the current Article 3.2 of the SPS Agreement and to facilitate the development of alternative risk assessment policies and the establishment of levels of protection deviating from international standards. From the perspective of epistemology, the encouragement to come up with alternative levels of protection provides a systemic safeguard against 'uniform thinking' (*pensée unique*) in risk assessment. Because new levels of protection of individual WTO Members deviating from those provided by international standards inevitably question the latter, there will be a constant scientific discourse about the appropriateness of certain levels of protection. The relative element of the critical approach, namely the enlargement of policy space for national risk managers, thus ensures critical scientific discourse and, in the long run, scientific objectivity.

However, there might be cases were the above suggestions are not sufficient to ensure independent and unbiased risk assessment. In this respect, one might think of cases where national risk managers suspect risk assessors of international organisations to be biased considering their previous involvement in standard setting procedures. Such was the case in the *Continued Suspension* dispute where the Appellate Body held

> … that there was an objective basis to conclude that the institutional affiliation with JECFA of Drs. Boisseau and Boobis, and their participation in JECFA's evaluations of the six hormones at issue, was likely to affect or give rise to justifiable doubts as to their independence or impartiality given that the evaluations conducted by JECFA lie at the heart of the controversy between the parties.[99]

Personal biases of risk assessors towards conclusions previously achieved in standard setting procedures may be particularly crucial in cases where there are majority and minority scientific opinions. Imagine that a majority scientific view is expressed by a certain international standard, a WTO Member relying on minority scientific opinion may reasonably commission other risk assessors than those involved in the setting of the international standards at issue. One might further think of situations where national risk managers distrust procedures conducted in the realm of international organisations on political grounds, e.g. because the international organisation in question may be biased towards Westerners, whereas the risk managers were from a non-Western country. Finally, one might think about constellations where risk managers suspect international risk assessors of ideological or personal biases, for example, of being industry-friendly, or anti-business, and the like.

For such rather extreme cases, an ultimate safeguard is proposed. In case a certain WTO Member refuses to rely on a risk assessment carried out by an international organisation, that WTO Member shall be free to do so. Instead, the concerned WTO Member may rely on a risk assessment conducted by its own risk assessors and by its own means. This is actually the reason for suggesting that Article 5 of the SPS Agreement shall remain unchanged. However, unlike today, there would be a strong disincentive for WTO Members to rely on risk assessments conducted at respective national levels. Considering the suggested presumption of GATT/WTO compatibility of SPS measures based on international risk assessments, expressed by a reformulated Article 3.2 of the SPS Agreement, reliance on a national risk assessment would become rather unattractive. But, in terms of *ultima ratio*, WTO Members shall have the possibility to rely on the safeguard of basing their SPS measures on a national risk assessment provided, of course, that all other obligations of the SPS Agreement, in particular, the requirement for scientific justification, are met.

Reforming the SPS Agreement in line with the proposal suggested here would resolve another major problem, namely the question how to determine appropriate levels of protection (ALOP). As shown earlier, the SPS Agreement in its current form led to confusion how to consider ALOP: is the determination of higher levels of protection an exception, as suggested by the positivist panel approach? Or is the determination of ALOP in any case a 'sovereign right', as ruled by the Appellate Body? In similar respect, it was unclear whether 'zero risk' might be an option either in risk assessment or in risk management: should attempt to achieve 'zero-risk' be refuted on the ground that they are scientifically impossible, as suggested by the rather objectivist panel? Or should attempts for achieving 'zero-risk' be allowed as viable policy options, as decided by the rather constructivist Appellate Body? Or is 'zero risk', logically seen, unattainable anyway?

The proposal for a critical approach towards SPS risk analysis suggests a graduation and fine-tuning of levels of protection. The graduation suggested shall replace the rather coarse differentiation between privileged SPS measures conforming to international standards, on the one hand, and other SPS measures. Instead, the proposal suggests an extension of the privilege of GATT/WTO compatibility to all SPS measures which are based on a risk assessment carried out by an international organisation. The proposal aims at encouraging state-of-the-art risk assessments, thereby fostering scientific integrity vis-à-vis political interferences. An expanded coverage of GATT/WTO compatibility would extend to SPS measures achieving higher levels of protection, given that the corresponding risk assessments have been conducted by international organisations. Hence, a differentiation would no longer be made between SPS measures conforming to international standards, on the one hand, and other SPS measures. Instead, a differentiation would exist between SPS measures based on risk assessments carried out by international organisations, on the one hand, and SPS measures based on risk assessments conducted at respective national levels, on the other hand. Therefore, the reform proposal put forward by the critical approach can be summarised as a shift from the objective of substantive harmonisation of SPS measures to the objective of a procedural harmonisation of SPS measures. The strong incentive for WTO Members to commission international organisations with the task to carry out risk assessments shall ensure state-of-the-art risk assessments and scientific integrity. This is the objective element of the proposal, preventing a relativistic 'anything goes' in SPS trade regulation. The enlargement of policy space for national risk managers, on the other hand, represents the relative element of the critical approach. Taken together, the objective and the relative element of the proposed critical approach shall encourage critical scientific discourse, thereby auto-correcting inherent biases in international risk regulation in the long run. In effect, to follow the critical approach suggested here would imply an expansion of the very objective of the SPS Agreement. The objective of the SPS Agreement would no longer be only to guard over fair competition in agricultural trade. A reformed SPS Agreement, in conjunction with associated international organisations such as Codex, OIE and IPPC, shall assume the additional role of a guardian for open competition of scientific opinions at the international level.

3 Outlook

Albeit the critical approach seems to be far more modest than farther-reaching relativist or positivist proposals, its implementation implies changes in various respects. Institutionally, the rather ephemeral structure of scientific expert bodies convening at the international level might turn out to be insufficient. For example, scientific expert bodies such as JECFA,

JEMRA and JMPR are only convening for specific meetings, hence on part-time basis. Increasing workload, however, may require more permanent structures. For example, one could think of a paramount scientific committee, jointly established by WHO and FAO, organising scientific advice at the international level. It has to be noted that proposals for reforming the scientific apparatus at the international level are under consideration anyway. For instance, the *Report of the Evaluation of the Codex Alimentarius and other FAO and WHO Food Standards Work* recommended

> ...that FAO and WHO establish a scientific committee of eminent scientists to provide to Codex and the two Organizations, over-arching scientific advice, including on emerging challenges and to provide guidance and quality control to JECFA, JEMRA, JMPR and ad hoc committees. A joint FAO/WHO Secretary to the Scientific Committee and Coordinator for Risk Assessment and Food Safety and Health Scientific Advice should be appointed and housed in WHO. The secretariats to the existing JECFA, JEMRA and JMPR should continue as at present. (…)[100]

Workload increase is mainly due to the link the SPS Agreement established between international trade rules and previously voluntary standards of international organisations, in particular, Codex, IPPC and OIE. Therefore, it seems that requirements for institutional reform of international organisations such as Codex, IPPC and OIE for accommodating new tasks and responsibilities are established either way.

However, political and economic implications coming along with the suggested critical approach seem to be much more sensitive.

By many of its critics, as well as by some of its supporters, the SPS Agreement was perceived as an instrument for increased market opening. In fact, the SPS Agreement shows certain features indicating a bias towards a market opening agenda. Yet, the science-based approach of the SPS Agreement is a powerful tool excelling the objective of containing protectionism. The requirement for scientific justification does not only focus on protectionist measures, but also implies a normative judgement whether an SPS measures is necessary or not. In this respect, Catherine Button noted that the aim of the SPS Agreement is 'broader than to eliminate sham health measures':

> By impugning SPS measures without a proper scientific basis, the SPS Agreement not only identifies instances of protectionism parading as health

> protection, it also identifies instances in which markets are *unnecessarily* closed by scientifically unsupported health measures. The SPS Agreement seeks to eliminate a whole set of trade barriers that do not result from protectionism per se, but may exist simply because of domestic regulatory resource limitations, or because consumer fears gave rise to demands for regulation. By seeking to limit health barriers to trade on a scientific basis, the SPS Agreement has a distinct (if limited) market-opening agenda.[101]

The market-opening agenda of the SPS Agreement, as an effect of the requirement for scientific justification, is accentuated by data and information asymmetries on the globalised market for 'credence' goods. As Lee Ann Jackson and Marion Jansen explained, producers of novel foods, in particular, have an information advantage with regard to the 'credence' characteristics of their respective products. Accordingly, transnational corporations are major producers of scientific data and are able, to a certain extent, to control the publication and non-publication of scientific data. Such data and information asymmetries on globalised food markets may thus lead, as Jackson and Jansen noted, 'to an inherent bias in favour of export interests in the absence of appropriate checks and balances'.[102]

However, considering the SPS Agreement as an instrument for trade promotion is not the only approach possible. In the alternative, one might perceive the SPS Agreement in the role of arbitrator between conflicting producer and consumer interests at the global level, hence between food exporting and food importing countries. Such an alternative approach would build upon the requirement for appropriate checks and balances to address inherent biases of the SPS Agreement in favour of export interests. The critical approach aims at implementing checks and balances into the SPS framework. In particular, the proposed reformulated Article 3.2 of the SPS Agreement shall encourage expressions of diverging scientific opinions in the WTO context. Thus, a rebalance of inherent biases in the SPS architecture shall not be achieved by authoritative scientific verdicts, but by recognising that scientific 'truth' is transient and therefore only achievable at the price of scientific pluralism. Recognition of scientific pluralism, however, might effect in a wider range of safety regulations permissible under renewed SPS rules. Obviously though, critics may point at potential economic losses such as higher transaction costs due to increased complexity in multilateral safety regulation. The potential occurrence of such economic losses, albeit difficult to estimate hypothetically, is not denied. Nevertheless, it is argued that potential economic disadvantages must be weighed against expected advantages. Several advantages are expected to come along with the implementation of the critical approach. First and broadly, a general relaxation of the SPS framework is expected. Currently, for instance, many issues with the potential for erupting into real trade disputes are relocated to international organisations such as the Codex Alimentarius Commission, the IPPC and the OIE. Such proxy wars may cause significant delays in the standard setting process of the said international organisations. An interesting case is the example of Aflatoxin M_1 in milk where it took Codex a decade to come up with a standard:

> The Committee on Food Additives and Contaminants (CCFAC) started work on elaborating a maximum level for Aflatoxin M1 in milk in 1990. At its session in 1991, CCFAC was informed that the International Dairy Federation (IDF) had proposed a guideline maximum level of 0.05ìg/kg in bulk milk. At its 1992 session, CCFAC agreed to forward a proposed draft maximum level of 0.05ìg/kg for Aflatoxin M_1 in liquid milk to the Codex Commission for acceptance at Step 5 despite statements by several countries that a level of 0.5ìg/kg was sufficient for consumer health protection. (…)
>
> JECFA reported that the difference in theoretical additional risk of liver cancer between the two levels was negligible. A number of delegations cited this determination in supporting a draft maximum level of 0.5ìg/kg. However, the EU stressed that 0.5ìg/kg was higher than the current level and would not be acceptable to EU consumers in view of health concerns. Some delegations noted that the level of 0.05ìg/kg seemed not to be achievable in some regions of the world. They also stated that a reduction in the maximum level might entail a significant reduction in the availability of milk in developing countries and would, therefore, have nutritional implications. (…)[103]

There is a general impression that trade disputes spilling over into rather 'technical' international organisations such as Codex, IPPC and OIE have led to a 'politicization' of the latter.[104] With respect to food safety controversies in particular, Josling et al. observed that

> … because of the heightened legal status of its standards under the SPS agreement and its wide coverage in the area of food standards, the work of the Codex bodies has become especially sensitive. As a result, the prevailing judgment is that of the three standard-setting institutions referenced in the SPS agreement, the SPS agreement has politicized decision making within Codex more than in the other standards organisations.[105]

The 'politicization' of organisations commissioned to develop international standards 'based on science' is reflected by a tendency to decision-making by vote rather than by consensus. With respect to food safety issues, in particular, Josling et al. noted the following cases of majority rule and dissent:

> (1) the two-year debate over the 1995 Codex 'Statements of Principle', (2) the 1995 vote on Codex beef hormone standards, (3) the 1997 vote on Codex mineral water standards, and (4) the failure of Codex to adopt JECFA's recommended standard for recombinant bovine somatotropin (rbST), a synthetically produced version of a naturally occurring hormone intended to increase milk production.[106]

However, the new role assigned to international standard setting organisations by the SPS Agreement not only leads to a politicization of science, but also to a scientification of the political debate. For instance, the Codex evaluation report identified the discussion of scientific questions by risk managers as the main reason for prolonged standard setting exercises. Explicitly, the report noted that '[o]ne result of CCFAC not receiving draft standards from JECFA is that CCFAC spends a lot of time discussing risk assessment issues that rightly belong in JECFA and this slows down decision making'.[107] The intrusion of scientific discussion into the realm of risk management is interpreted as a consequence of the science-based approach implemented in the SPS Agreement. Because henceforth no arguments other than scientific ones are heard, risk managers, i.e. government representatives, were virtually compelled to invoke 'science' for justifying their respective messages. Paradoxically, though, the science-based approach of the SPS Agreement did not achieve to separate risk assessment and risk management once and for all, but induced, in fact, a mutual permeability between the two. Without any dash of irony, one may thus state that the positivist attempt for enforcing impermeable barriers between facts and values and between science and politics has effectively caused some sort of osmosis between the two.

In rather similar ways, the dispute settlement system of the WTO gets blocked by prolonged disputes. Most prominent, there are the *Hormones* case and the subsequent *Continued Suspension* case. As argued by many observers, also the *Biotech* case may see a next episode.

It is now argued that increased persistence of trade disputes and their spillover effects into international organisations, thereby delaying the setting of international standards, has to be taken into account. Seen in this way, pending trade disputes and frustrated standard settings at the international level should be accounted for as welfare costs similar to those allegedly caused by differing regulation.[108]

Following the critical approach suggested here, persistent WTO disputes, particularly those concerning novel foods with 'credence' characteristics, e.g. hormone-treated meat and GMOs, are perceived as consequences of a too narrow range of policy options available under the current SPS Agreement. Therefore, it is proposed to widen the range of available policy options, but without opening the Pandora's box unleashing a relativist 'anything goes'. A wider range of available policy options and scientific pluralism would ease tensions in the SPS framework in general.

In particular, implementing the critical approach would lead to a reassortment of respective roles of science and law in international risk assessment. The science-based approach of the SPS Agreement and in particular certain of its interpreters, such as the panels in the *Hormones* and in the *Continued Suspension* cases, assigned the role of arbitrator in trade disputes to 'science'. Attempts for choosing 'science' for impartial arbiter in trade disputes are standing in the positivist tradition. The assignment of the role of impartial arbiter to 'science' makes only sense under the presumption that 'science' is able to produce ultimate and objective 'truth'. Following Popperian epistemology, the critical approach rejects the presumption of an objective and ultimate scientific 'truth'. Rather, the critical approach suggested here emphasises the requirement to respect possibilities and limitations of both, science and law. From such a critical viewpoint, scientific controversies should be fought out with scientific arguments, whereas political conflicts should be addressed with political negotiations, deliberation and legal proceedings. Starting with the question what science can and what science cannot, it is referred to Catherine Button. In short, Button explained that science and scientific justification is not tantamount to the legitimacy of an SPS measure. Button put it that

> … [S]cientific justification is not a litmus test for protectionism. In other words, the existence or non-existence of a scientific justification is not determinative of protectionism. Some measures without a scientific basis will be protectionist and others will not. Conversely, some regulations motivated by protectionist impulses may nevertheless be scientifically justifiable.[109]

On the other hand, the requirement for scientific justification enables to discern whether an SPS measure at issue is necessary or unnecessary to protect human, animal or plant life and health: 'By impugning SPS measures without a proper scientific basis, the SPS Agreement not only identifies instances of protectionism parading as health protection, it also identifies instances in which markets are *unnecessarily* closed by scientifically unsupported health measures'.[110] However, even in case an SPS measures is considered necessary to protection human, animal or plant life and health, the determination of the appropriate level of protection will still require additional, extra-scientific argumentation. To make it short, the critical approach considers science to be an indispensable tool for (a) weighing arguments whether an SPS measure may be necessary, and (b) for balancing whether the envisaged level of protection may be appropriate. Thus, scientific justification is an indispensable feature qualifying SPS measures for further examination. Figuratively speaking, science is perceived as some sort of *watershed*, discerning between SPS measures coming along without any scientific foundations, thus rebuttable from the outset, and SPS measures qualifying for further proceedings. It is from this perspective that the term 'scientific justification' reveals its true meaning: it shall justify an SPS measure, i.e. a political decision. Hence, in the SPS context, 'science' never stands alone; it is always carried along with a political objective. That is the reason why 'science' in the SPS context should be addressed as a necessary, yet alone insufficient component of a political objective or legal claim. Scientific justification is a necessary part bolstering the principal argument, that is, the SPS measure, but not the principal issue itself.

In rather similar ways as the watershed image, Catherine Button referred to science as an organising principle:

> [S]cience's promise of value-neutrality has, in some respects, turned out to be illusory. Perhaps science never really promised to be entirely value-free; when international trade negotiators chose science as the benchmark of legitimate health regulation, they probably imputed to science a greater degree of value-neutrality and a greater degree of certainty than science would have claimed for itself. Time, and the experience of decisions being made under the SPS Agreement, have shown that science is not entirely value-free and that uncertainty is a feature of scientific risk assessment, not anathema to it. While this dose of reality does mean that science can no longer be regarded as

> an *uncomplicated* and *uncontroversial* means by which to determine when trade must give way to health, its value as an organising principle survives.[111]

On the other hand, however, the critical approach disagrees with any positivist attempts to assign science the role of impartial arbitrator in trade disputes. This role, it is argued, belongs to law. Only law, for instance, is able to decide whether a scientifically justifiable SPS measure may be nevertheless motivated by protectionist intent. This counts all the more for decisions on the appropriateness of levels of protection. Only law is able to decide whether the choice for a level of protection higher than that provided by the relevant international standard seems to be motivated by protectionist intent or not. Emphasising the need for broadening the narrow focus on scientific questions to other, non-scientific issues, Catherine Button found:

> When WTO panels review health measures under the SPS Agreement, they are not only dealing with underlying scientific questions, such as whether the particular substance is harmful, but also with hybrid questions which draw in other kinds of expertise that are relevant to the questions such as whether the least trade-restrictive measures has been employed. As Howe observes, the expertise that WTO panels need is situated at the intersection of science and regulation. (…) These non-scientific factors are particularly important in determining the level of protection and the regulatory means for achieving that level …[112]

In effect, the critical approach focuses on genuine functions of science and law, respectively. The role of science is understood as inherently mercurial, driven by contradictory theories and debatable empirical findings. Hereby, science assumes distinct functions. One the one hand, science is an ally of economic progress. On the other hand, science can be applied to draw limits to economic endeavours considered too risky by society.

The role of law, in turn, shall be defined by reference to the critical scientific method. At the interface between science and law at the international level, the following questions emerge: Who shall review and eventually falsify scientific evidence at the international level? In particular, who shall be the arbitrator between diverging scientific views expressed in trade disputes before the WTO DSB? According to the positivistic proposal, scientific controversies are decided authoritatively and at the highest, i.e. international level by assumingly impartial scientific or technical organisations and experts. The 'scientific truth' thereby established may be absolute for the moment, but comes at the price of subjectivity, i.e. the subjective viewpoint of the very few deciding in that particular moment and in those particular expert committees. A critical approach, in contrast, relies on practical falsification through contradictory procedures. A critical approach may provide only relative scientific certainty, but keeps the door open for critical review, thus fostering progressive scientific knowledge. Whereas the positivistic approach pays for absolute 'scientific truth' with subjectivity, the critical method only achieves relative certainty, but obtains what Popper called 'objective knowledge'.

In his book *Social Epistemology (1988/2002)*, Steve Fuller addressed the problem of scientific authority and critical review. Summarising arguments made by proponents of an 'open society', such as Karl R. Popper in *The Open Society and Its Enemies* (1945) and Randall Albury in *The Politics of Objectivity* (1983), Steve Fuller noted:

> Thus, if objective knowledge can be produced under the 'open society,' that fact would seem to legitimate the pursuit of liberal democracy in society at large. (…) Without necessarily compromising the objectivity of the research, this move toward politicization would force scientist to argue for their positions in a forum larger than the strictly professional ones to which they have grown accustomed. To ensure that this increase in democracy is a truly critical exercise, and not simply an exercise in informed consent, not only must the public cross-examine the scientists, but the scientists must also cross-examine each other in order to demystify one another's rhetoric.[113]

From a sociological point of view, Ulrich Beck argued for some sort of forum on which opposing scientific views could be exchanged in open transparency. Beck started by discerning between two notions of science; classical laboratory science, on the one hand, and public discursivity, on the other hand. Beck recognised that both types of science have respective shortcomings. Beck observed that laboratory science 'is systematically more or less blind to the consequences which accompany and threaten its successes'.[114] Public discussion, on the other hand, is 'media-dependent, manipulable, sometimes hysterical and in any case devoid of a laboratory', hence dependent on research carried out in the public domain (universities).[115] Basing on these considerations, Beck argued for some kind of 'forum' on which opposing views could be played off. Beck noted:

> In both cases, we are concerned with a completely different type of knowledge: on the one hand, specialised, complex, dependent on methodology, and, on the other, oriented towards fundamentals and fundamental errors (for instance in the setting of maximal acceptable levels, which cannot be corrected in an individual case). The goal ought to be to *play* the narrow-mindedness of laboratory science *off* against the narrow-mindedness of everyday consciousness and the mass media and vice versa (in Popper's sense). For that, one requires stages or *forums*, perhaps a kind of 'Upper House' or 'Technology Court' that would guarantee the division of powers between technology development and technology implementation.[116]

Beck's 'Upper House' or 'Technology Court' is apparently not to be confused with ideas such as the positivist proposal to establish an international scientific authority or earlier suggestions for the creation of a 'Science Court'.[117] Quite the contrary, Beck suggested a forum where 'the narrow-mindedness of laboratory science' could be played off against 'the narrow-mindedness of everyday consciousness and the mass media and vice versa (in Popper's sense)'.

Rather than by the 'Science Court', Beck's suggestion for a 'Technology Court' seems of having been inspired by Shrader-Frechette's proposal for a 'technology tribunal'. Stemming from her analysis that risk assessment inevitably implies controversies over values, Shrader-Frechette developed an adversarial approach to risk assessment. Shrader-Frechette explained her proposal for 'adversary proceedings carried out in democratic, rather than elitist, fashion',[118] as follows:

> Pursuing the insight that several current methods of risk assessment have failed because analysts ignored the value components in their work, I believe that any fruitful method of risk analysis must explicitly address controversies over values. One of the best ways to do this is to pursue an *adversary method* of assessment, a method premised on the fact that desirable risk analyses are likely to be a product of rational interaction and compromise among those who disagree about how to evaluate a given risk.[119]

Shrader-Frechette called her model for public participation in an adversary setting 'the technology tribunal'.[120] The technology tribunal operates at three distinct stages. In the first stage, a tribunal is established, 'composed of scientists and citizens, to identify the significant questions of science, technology, and policy associated with the controversial issue in question'.[121] At the second stage, 'a panel of impartial scientists *and* laymen' is presiding over 'an adversary proceeding'.[122] In detail, the adversary proceeding is meant to unfold as follows:

> During this [adversary] proceeding, *advocates* debate the technical and policy questions that are in dispute. In addition to presenting their own cases, the debaters are able to cross-examine opponents and to criticize their arguments.[123]

At the third stage, finally, the panel of judges, i.e. 'impartial scientists and laymen', releases its decision 'as to the scientific *and* policy factors relevant to the disputed questions'.[124] Obviously with view on a domestic policy environment, Shrader-Frechette continued that the decision of the panel shall made public, 'and is designed to provide the basis for reaching political decisions through the democratic process'.[125]

Arguably, Popper, Beck and Shrader-Frechette have conceived that such fora for democratic risk discourses were assigned at respective domestic levels.

However, it is argued that the idea of democratic risk discourse at the international level, in particular before the WTO DSB, is even more necessary than at respective national levels.

In situations of scientific dissent in the wake of a trade dispute, opposing governments will try their respective best for providing scientific arguments in favour of their respective positions. The positions of opposing governments, in turn, are influenced by domestic pressure groups. Thus, finally, it is domestic policy shaping respective positions in trade disputes. Therefore, even if one assumes that particular segments of the scientific community are serving corporate interests, governments may be constrained to turn to alternative scientific experts due to public pressure. In other words, in cases where pressure from civil society at domestic levels is overwhelming, it may outweigh corporate influence in scientific research and scientific risk assessment. An example of research activity induced by civic resilience was the protest of segments of civil society in European Countries against the introduction of genetically modified organisms. Switzerland is a telling example in this regard. In 2005, the Swiss people accepted a moratorium on the use of genetically modified organisms (GMOs) for agricultural purposes. In response, the government launched the National Research Programme (NRP 59) on 'Benefits and Risks of the Deliberate Release of Genetically Modified Plants'. For the first 5 years, 2005–2010, the NRP 59 was funded with 12 million Swiss Francs.[126] Expecting the final report of the NRP 59 in the year 2013, the government extended the moratorium accordingly.[127]

Considering these arguments, the establishment and strengthening of adversarial litigation procedures and contradictory dispute settlement systems at the international level are the order of the day. In this perspective, the current WTO dispute settlement system corresponds already rather well with the principle of adversarial procedures. With respect to scientific knowledge, adversarial disputes over sanitary and phytosanitary (SPS) issues are of particular value. The fact that SPS disputes are usually reflecting underlying scientific controversies, and *vice versa*, adversarial procedures should be (re-)considered as veritable sources of knowledge. From this perspective, WTO panels and the Appellate Body are rapprochements of what Shrader-Frechette depicted as 'panels of impartial scientists and laymen'. The floor provided by panels and the Appellate Body is considered as being a promising intermediate stage for organised 'play-offs' between 'laboratory science' and 'public discursivity' at the international level. In particular in highly contested SPS disputes, such as the *Hormones* and the *Biotech* cases, the trend towards transparent and adversarial risk discourse at the international level is well underway.

Considering the requirement for adversarial procedural principles outlined above, the WTO dispute settlement system seems already well suited for accommodating scientific controversies at the international level. In this respect, a successive improvement of the handling of epistemological problems by panels and the Appellate Body can be observed. Lukasz Gruszczynski, for instance, established significant advancements of the capacity of panels and the Appellate Body to address complex issues of risk. In particular, Gruszczynski observed remarkable ameliorations between earlier SPS jurisprudence and the Appellate Body's approach in the *Continued Suspension* case:

> [A] part of the earlier jurisprudence subscribed to a simplified and incorrect conception of science and an overly technical view of risk assessment. Many concepts, such as insufficiency of scientific evidence or risk assessment, were defined in purely scientific terms without proper regard of their socio-cultural dimension. (…) Imposing a *monolithic and imperialist vision of science* on all WTO Members obviously cannot correctly account for all those elements and will generate questions as to the appropriateness of such a supervision system.

> The majority of the above concerns were, however, properly addressed by the Appellate Body in its recent *US/Canada – Continued Suspension* report. (…) For instance, insufficiency of scientific evidence was recognized as a relational category which may depend on normative values, such as the level of protection or the attitude of risk assessors. This recognition permitted the Appellate Body to acknowledge that insufficiency is a multidimensional concept that is determined not only by scientific developments but may also result from differences in the appreciation of available scientific information.[128]

Therefore, the current system, leading to controversial risk assessments, should be upheld in principle. On any account, the current system should not be replaced by a 'monolithic and imperialist' scientific body at the international level absorbing critical or dissenting scientific considerations. Rather, one might think of revising the *Understanding of Rules and Procedures Governing the Settlement of Disputes* of the WTO in a way that in future SPS disputes, voices of civil societies are better heard, not less. In the medium term, ways should be explored for enabling public participation also in cases of scientific controversies at the international level, in particular in SPS disputes.[129]

In fact, at the international level and in particular in trade disputes, the democratic element, i.e. citizens' participation, is still wanting. This point requires attention because at the international level, decisions of the WTO DSB are marking the end of democratic processes at respective national levels; this stands in contrast to Shrader-Frechette's model of a technology tribunal which is meant to prepare the ground for subsequent democratic processes enfolding at national levels. Transposing the adversary model of the technology tribunal at the international level, the ideal case would even consist of two democratic processes at respective domestic levels, leading to controversial results and conflicting trade policies. As examples, the transatlantic controversies over hormone-treated meat and biotechnology applications in agriculture and food production are invoked. In these cases, democratic processes, on both sides of the Atlantic, fuelled by respective domestic interest groups, have led to conflicting regulatory regimes and contradictory approaches to risks related to hormones and genetically modified organisms (GMOs) respectively. As foreseen by Shrader-Frechette's model of the technology tribunal, the controversial approaches clashed at the international level, in the court rooms of WTO panels and the Appellate Body. However, panels and the Appellate Body themselves are not representatives of what Shrader-Frechette called 'laymen'. Rather, the term 'laymen', as used by Shrader-Frechette, is somewhat misleading in the WTO context. In WTO panels and the Appellate Body, the term 'laymen' refers to the capacity of panellists of being not scientific experts, but predominantly trade lawyers. Taking the technology tribunal as a model, the DSB of the WTO should be reformed in order to enable participation of laypersons in the literal sense of the word, i.e. civil society representatives from respective parties involved in the dispute as panellists or associate judges with voting rights.[130] In terms of an innovative proposal, one might think about assigning scientific questions to a 'scientific jury' of laypersons standing by the side of panels and the Appellate Body. In particular, when scientific questions relevant for public health, animal welfare, development or the environment are at stake, it might be appropriate to disburden the DSB from resolving politically sensitive scientific questions by solitary decision. Marsha Echols, for example, postulated that '[c]onsumers should be permitted to comment on the existence and seriousness of a possible hazard, to present research and otherwise to help define the hazard'.[131] In particular, when socio-economic considerations are at stake, it seems to make sense to complement the dispute settlement bodies with some sort of democratic component reflecting the range of different perspectives and interests involved. According to certain critics, the ability of the DSB to address complex scientific questions is limited.[132] On the other hand, the capability and suitability of deliberative models for deciding upon controversial scientific problems has been confirmed by recent research. Various studies, *e. g.* by Joanne Scott and Elisabeth Ehrensperger, have shown the suitability and applicability of deliberative models to transnational structures such as the SPS Committee[133] and the United Nations Commission on Human Rights (UNCHR).[134] Current examples for the validity of deliberative approaches under various cultural contexts are practices of 'deliberative democracy' applied in the Chinese coastal district of Zeguo, steered by Stanford Professor James S. Fishkin and his team. According to a TIME magazine report, the process enfolds as follows:

> Each year, 175 people are scientifically selected to reflect the general population. They are polled once on the major decisions they'll be facing. Then they are given a briefing on those issues, prepared by experts with *conflicting views*. Then they meet in small groups and come up with questions for the experts – issues they want further clarified. Then they meet together in plenary session to listen to the expert's response and have a more general

> discussion. The process of small meetings and plenary is repeated once more. A final poll is taken, and the budget priorities of the assembly are made known and adopted by the local government. It takes three days to do this. The process has grown over five years, from a deliberation over public works (new sewage-treatment plants were favored over road-building) to the whole budget shebang. By most accounts it has succeeded brilliantly, even though the participants are not very sophisticated: 60% are farmers.[135]

According to Prof. James Fishkin, an essential condition for the success of 'deliberative democracy' is that people are given real power. In this respect, James Fishkin observed:

> If people think their voice actually matters, they'll do the hard work, really study their briefing books, ask the experts smart questions and then make tough decisions. *When they hear the experts disagreeing, they're forced to think for themselves.* About 70% change their minds in the process. (...) If you give people real choices and real consequences, they will make real decisions.[136]

For these reasons, it is suggested to establish, based on Article 13 of the SPS Agreement a 'scientific jury'. The 'scientific jury' shall be composed of true laypersons and decide upon scientific questions for the attention of the DSB. Following the model of 'deliberative democracy', the 'scientific jury' shall be organised independently from the DSB, preferably under the auspices of an independent research programme. Following findings of Prof. Fishkin, it shall be guaranteed that the 'scientific jury' has a real say on scientific matters in SPS disputes, if necessary by amending respective rules of procedure.

More inclusive procedures before the DSB would also help to tackle another epistemologically sensitive problem, that is, how to consider minority scientific opinions. In this regard, Lukasz Gruszczynski observed that 'the SPS case law has failed to establish clear criteria which could be used in the assessment of the credibility of minority scientific opinions'.[137] With view on proceedings in the *Biotech* case in particular, Gruszczynski observed that '[t]he panel ignored the minority opinions and decided a number of issues on the basis of what may be labelled as the best science approach'.[138] Furthermore, with regard to the *Continued Suspension* case, Gruszczynski noted that 'the structure of the fact-finding process (eg the formulation of questions to experts) and the arbitral choices between conflicting and contradictory opinions led to the practical exclusion of minority scientific views'.[139] As a major obstacle for the consideration of minority scientific opinions in SPS disputes, the requirement for specificity was identified by Gruszczynski:

> One of the immanent features of minority scientific opinions is their lower level of conclusiveness and limited empirical basis (…). Sometimes they establish little more than the theoretical possibility of risk rather than a concrete causal relationship between a risk agent and an adverse effect. This is a place where a panel should be particularly careful. Rejecting such scientific minority opinions only because they do not meet a specificity requirement may indeed interfere with the right of WTO Members to establish their ALOP. This problem is particularly important if a particular area of scientific research is new (eg genetic manipulations).[140]

Putting more weight on inclusive procedures before the DSB would also increase transparency with regard to criteria applied for assessing the credibility of scientific opinions.

Emphasising contradictory procedures for epistemological reasons does not mean to neglect polycentric and participatory (as opposed to court-centric and hierarchical)[141] procedures already in place in the SPS context. Emphasising the important role of the SPS Committee (Article 12 of the SPS Agreement), Joanne Scott noted:

> [T]he activities of the committee may be tentatively cited as adding credence to constructivist accounts which place emphasis upon the value of argumentation and persuasion, and upon the possibility of deliberative learning. (…) The committee provides a framework for the inculcation of trust between Members. It seems also to induce a heightened sense of empathy with the situation of others, with this contribution to shifts in policy preferences which are not readily explicable in the language of self-interest.[142]

The importance of the SPS Committee as an alternative venue for the deliberative handling of conflicts over different risk paradigms was underlined by Sungjoon Cho, who noted:

> Notably, an increasing number of SPS disputes have recently been resolved under the SPS Committee. Nearly thirty percent of "specific trade concerns" reported to the SPS Committee were addressed by discussions and consultations under the Committee process. Although those specific trade concerns handled in the SPS Committee may or may not involve controversies related directly to

> different paradigms of risk science, this extra-judicial peer review mechanism still offers an operable avenue for regulatory dialogue over risk science.[143]

Alas, it has to be stressed that also the SPS Committee is driven by executive branches of respective WTO Members. As Joanne Scott noted, representatives of WTO Members are usually either 'diplomats attached to UN or WTO missions in Geneva, or specialists drawn from national ministries in SPS covered fields'.[144] Scott further observed that these government representatives may be accompanied by alternates and advisers and that '[i]t is not unknown (but seemingly not common) for Members to introduce persons connected to private undertakings—for example producer associations—as part of their delegation'.[145] Considering the manifold biases inherent in the SPS framework in favour of corporate interests, as explained at various occasions in the paper at hand, it is suggested to amend the rules of procedure of the SPS Committee. Such an amendment shall aim to achieve better balanced national delegations. In particular, there should be a requirement for national delegations for equal representation of potentially conflicting interest groups, *i.e.* industry representatives on the one hand, and delegates from consumer, environmental and animal rights NGOs on the other hand.

However, the problem of proindustry biases of national delegations accredited to international bodies is not unique to the SPS Committee. Similar concerns have been raised with regard to Codex bodies. A striking example was the overrepresentation of corporate representatives in the Codex Committee on Pesticide Residues (CCPR):

> Looking, for example, at the Codex Committee on Pesticide Residues (CCPR) – establishing maximum residue limits (MRLs) for pesticides in food – industry presence is striking. Lisa Lefferts of Consumer International reported: 'The Global Crop Protection Federation delegation, which represents the pesticide industry, included 30 Members at the 1998 meeting. Three of the four Members of the Swiss delegation represent industry (Novartis and Nestec/Nestlé). Mingled into other delegations are representatives from Dow, Monsanto, and a multitude of multinational companies, from Avcare to Zeneca'.[146]

On such grounds, amending the rules of procedure of the SPS Committee only seems insufficient. Rather, it is suggested to align all international bodies relevant for SPS risk assessment with requirements for better-balanced representation of interests. Therefore, the proposal for amending or establishing rules of procedure for national delegations to international bodies extents, in particular, to the Codex Alimentarius Commission, the World Organisation for Animal Health (OIE), and the Framework of the International Plant Protection Convention (IPPC).

Taken together, the suggestions put forward in this paper are differing from both positivist and relativist proposals. On the one hand, the critical approach recognises science as an indispensable source of knowledge. On the other hand, however, the critical approach means to relinquish the ideal of objective, yet 'pure' science. Rather, the critical approach is based on epistemological foundations, in particular, the critical scientific method and the epistemological opposite *objective—relative*. Thus, implementing the critical approach means to re-contextualise science, exposing it to permanent criticism by peers and society at large. In this regard, the proposal at hand comes close to considerations put forward by Alexia Herwig, observing the following:

> The contextualisation of science depends, in large measure, on the public availability of the scientific studies, and the clear articulation of its underlying assumptions and normative choices. For instance, how risk assessment is methodologically defined introduces variations in scientific findings as a result of the selection of the population group that is exposed; or of the appropriate factor by which to extrapolate from animal studies to humans; or of the selection of the relevant exposure level (common are lowest-observable-effect and no-observable-effect). The decision whether or not to set a standard for a vulnerable population group results in the redistribution of risk, especially if the substance or technology brings benefits for other less susceptible population groups.[147]

Turning to the practical implementation of the critical approach, the WTO DSB is considered an appropriate forum 'larger than the strictly professional ones' for the cross-examination of scientists at the international level. By doing so, controversial scientific positions put forward by conflicting parties would be openly scrutinised and discussed. Decisions taken by the WTO DSB, assisted by the 'scientific jury', will, in turn, cause repercussions at domestic levels of the parties involved. Thus, a critical discourse spanning from national levels to the international level and back again will constantly query established scientific paradigms. In the end, scientific disputes fought out before the

WTO DSB might become the nucleus at the international level for more 'open societies' among WTO Members.

Whereas the positivistic proposal implies an instrumentalisation of science in the service of a market-opening agenda, the role of science is conceived differently here, namely from an epistemological point of view. From an epistemological point of view, the role of science is to provide scientific insights for increased knowledge to the service of all. With respect to risk assessment, in particular, science has to provide insights into short- and long-term risks based on scientific criteria, not based on economic preferences. On these grounds, the 'populist reforms' advocated by Shrader-Frechette in 1991 are not primarily the task of governments and risk managers. The democratisation of science, as postulated by Shrader-Frechette and others, is first and foremost the task of science itself. As long as science is not willing to reflect on its role in society and to share its respective findings with the public, that public is not able to hear its arguments. Or, to build upon the imagery of Max Ernst (1891–1976) and his meaningful painting entitled 'When Reason Sleeps, the Sirens Sing', the association is evoked that, as long as reason keeps sleeping, the public is prone to the singing of neo-romantic sirens.

Notes

1. Nile perch (*Lates niloticus*) is a freshwater fish widespread in African waters. Lake Victoria, located in East Africa, is the second largest freshwater lake on earth and is shared by Kenya, Tanzania and Uganda.
2. Andrew Mold, *Non-Tariff Barriers—Their Prevalence and Relevance for African Countries.* African Trade Policy Centre (ATPC), Work in Progress No. 25, October 2005, p. 13.
3. Theo H. Jonker, Hiroshi Ito, Hiroji Fujishima, *Food Safety and Quality Standards in Japan. Compliance of Suppliers from Developing Countries* (The World Bank, 2004), p. 32.
4. Theo H. Jonker, Hiroshi Ito, Hiroji Fujishima, ibid. pp. 36–37.
5. It has to be noted, however, that rules and regulations based on science and rational argument alone are no guarantee for fair practice. In the case study on Nile perch, for instance, politics prevailed over rational arguments at the end of the day. Andrew Mold observed:

"Yet despite all this evidence in favour of the affected countries, none felt in a position to be able to use the WTO's Dispute Settlement Mechanism against the EU. Commenting on the limited possibilities of taking legal action in this case, an anonymous WTO delegate from one of the countries implicated stated that 'the WTO formally objected to this notion [that the fish were infected with cholera] because there was no scientific proof that our fish was infected. Yet we could not afford to go through the dispute settlement process with the EC for various reasons. We eventually settled the matter bilaterally with the EC after suffering huge losses of fish exports. Really, the power of enforcement of the rulings coming out of the dispute settlement system is based on your capacity to retaliate against a country that has bent the rules. As a small country, however, the impact of retaliating against a big country is virtually nil, though some developing [countries] have been able to do this with some amount of success' " (Andrew Mold, *Non-Tariff Barriers —Their Prevalence and Relevance for African Countries.* African Trade Policy Centre (ATPC), Work in Progress No. 25, October 2005, p. 13).

6. Albeit an initiative of private retailers so far, the food and carbon miles debate has the potential of becoming a WTO issue. A former British minister has already expressed the idea of a new tax on agricultural imports depending on the number of miles the product was transported. Similar initiatives for declaring application of plane symbols on air-freighted products mandatory are foreseeable. The view that private standards are being promoted by retailers and various NGOs in the name of pretended consumer interests, but in fact bolster the less altruistic interests of the promoters, was also expressed by Robert Falkner from the Center for European Studies at Harvard University in a workshop on 'Government Regulation, Identity Preservation and Private Standards—GM-products in the Food Chain', held at the World Trade Institute in Berne, Switzerland, May 4th and 5th, 2007.
7. The plane symbol would probably fall under the TBT Agreement. Because a risk of some sort must be ascertainable both under the SPS Agreement as well as under the TBT Agreement, basic questions about scientific evidence seem to be comparable anyway.
8. See, for instance, Catherine Riungu, 'UK farming lobby seeks ban on airfreighted organic imports', in *The East African*, June 18, 2007; Catherine Riungu, 'Strong shilling hurting us, say Kenya flower farmers', in *The East African*, July 23, 2007; and Rudolf Hermann, 'Neuseeländische Kiwis unter Klima-Sünder-Verdacht. „Foodmiles"-Debatte bereitet Kopfschmerzen in Wellington', in *Neue Zürcher Zeitung*, August 3, 2007. See also *The Economist*, lead story on 'Good food? Why ethical shopping harms the world', December 9, 2006.
9. Kristin S. Shrader-Frechette, *Risk and Rationality. Philosophical Foundations for Populist Reforms* (University of California Press, 1991), p. 7 (footnote omitted). From a legal and economic point of view, regulatory spillover effects were addressed as gaps between 'jurisdiction' and

'impact' or as 'external accountability gap'. Precisely with regard to the profound socio-economic impact of EU safety regulations on the Lake Victoria area, Joanne Scott noted:

"In the context of a globalizing market for agricultural products, a familiar gap has emerged between 'jurisdiction' and 'impact'. Political fragmentation co-exists with deep market integration. It may be the EU which regulates, but the EU's trading partners also pay an economic price, and undergo far-reaching societal transformations in a bid to secure compliance. It is this disjuncture between regulatory jurisdiction and regulatory impact which is said by some to constitute one of the most pressing normative problems of our time, particularly when it comes to the actions of powerful states. It is said to generate an 'external accountability gap', or an absence of 'accountability to people outside of the acting entity, whose lives are affected by it' (Joanne Scott, *The WTO Agreement on Sanitary and Phytosanitary Measures* (Oxford University Press, 2007), pp. 43–44, footnotes omitted).

10. Karl R. Popper, *The Logic of Scientific Discovery*, 2nd English edition, (Hutchinson & Co Publishers, 1968), p. 111.
11. In fact, Popper referred to, and cited from, the works of Hermann Weyl, Max Born, Immanuel Kant and Robert Reininger.
12. Karl R. Popper, *The Logic of Scientific Discovery*, 2nd English edition, (Hutchinson & Co Publishers, 1968), p. 111, footnote no. 4; citing Hermann Weyl (German edition) *Philosophie der Mathematik und Naturwissenschaft* (1927), p. 83; (English edition) *Philosophy of Mathematics and Natural Science* (Princeton, 1949), p. 116).
13. Karl R. Popper, *The Logic of Scientific Discovery*, 2nd English edition, (Hutchinson & Co Publishers, 1968), p. 111, footnote no. 4; citing Robert Reininger, *Das Psycho-Physische Problem* (1916), p. 29. The fact that the opposite *absolute—subjective* cannot be captured in words was put in the following poetic verse (in German): *Spricht* die Seele, so spricht, ach! schon die *Seele* nicht mehr"; (in English): "If the souls *speaks* then alas it is no longer the *soul* that speaks" (Karl R. Popper, ibid., original emphasis). The reference to the soul and the psyche recalls the tremor of the rational idea of man caused by psychoanalytical sciences, in particular by Sigmund Freud (1856–1939). In contrast to Romanticism, psychoanalysis questioned rational conceptions of man on scientific grounds. Inspired by new psychoanalytical science, for instance Sigmund Freud's work *Die Traumdeutung* (1899; in English: *The Interpretation of Dreams*), artist Max Ernst (1891–1976) expressed the tension between reason and psyche by a telling painting entitled *When Reason Sleeps, the Sirens Sing* (1960; in German: *Wenn die Vernunft schläft, singen die Sirenen)*. For the influence

of psychoanalytical science on arts see, for example, Ulrich Bischoff, *Max Ernst 1891–1976. Jenseits der Malerei* (TASCHEN, 2005), pp. 14–15.

14. Malachi Hacohen, 'Critical Rationalism, Logical Positivism, and the Poststructuralist Conundrum: Reconsidering the Neurath-Popper Debate', in Michael Heidelberger, Friedrich Stadler (eds.), *History of Philosophy of Science. New Trends and Perspectives* (Kluwer Academic Publishers, 2002), p. 319 (footnote omitted). However, Hacohen also pointed at some critical points of Popper's concept of scientific criticism, noting that "Popper may have been over-confident about methodology's capacity to guide critical debate and produce a consensus" (Malachi Hacohen, ibid.). In particular, Hacohen called attention to the following problem:

"As Popper discarded foundationism, intersubjective criticism became objectivity's new grounds. Criticism and testing operated by consensus and convention. How did intersubjective criticism really work? It was not clear that access was available to the whole public, certainly not equal access. Once ideas entered the public sphere, who won? Did the logic (or methodology) of science really set the rules of discussion? Without a sociology of science, public criticism remained a regulative ideal at best. Moreover, Paul Feyerabend and Thomas Kuhn charged that Popper could not account for most 'correct' historical decisions in favor of better theories. If the key to scientific progress was the psychology, sociology, and routine of scientific communities, not criticism and testing, then Popper's efforts to erect a rational edifice of science and explain the growth of knowledge as a rational process was problematic" (Malachi Hacohen, ibid. p. 320).However, with respect of social conditions of rational deliberative processes, Hacohen noted that some of the students of Popper had started to research on social conditions amenable for open criticism and rational discourse. Hacohen considered such inquiries, focusing on societal requirements for rational deliberation as most promising:

"We may discover that a particular polity is optimal for Popperian science, and it may require *democratization* of all spheres of life—state and economy, academy and laboratory. Such inquiry need not undermine Popper's belief in learning from error; indeed, such belief is a prerequisite. Our ability to learn from error is the issue dividing Popper from both positivists and poststructuralists. Popper was as instructive in refusing 'poststructuralism' as he was in reshaping the legacy of the Viennese late enlightenment" (Malachi Hacohen, ibid. p. 320, emphasis added).

15. A fundamental difference between common law and civil law systems is the way trials are conducted. Whereas in common law systems the adversary method is applied, civil law systems are applying accusatorial (in criminal law cases) and interrogative (in civil law cases) methods. The difference between the two systems lies in the roles assumed by judges and lawyer in respective trial proceedings. With view on adversary systems, Sharon Byrd observed:

"In England and the United States it is the parties themselves, through their legal representatives, who present their conflicting views of the facts of the case. Each is permitted to portray the story behind the dispute as he or she sees it, with the jury left to determine the 'real' facts of the case and to apply the law as the judge has instructed to those facts when reaching its verdict. The common law judge acts more as a referee over the courtroom debate, determining what the lawyers may and may not present as evidence to the jury and generally keeping order throughout the legal process" (B. Sharon Byrd, *Introduction to Anglo-American Law & Language*, 2nd edition/ *Einführung in die anglo-amerikanische Rechtssprache*, 2. Auflage (Verlag C. H. Beck, 2001), p. 78. Rules of adversary procedures are also characterised as systems based on *procedural justice*, defining justice "as the result of the process" (B. Sharon Byrd, ibid., p. 79).

16. Nicholas Georgescu-Roegen, *Analytical Economics. Issues and Problems* (Harvard University Press, 1967, Massachusetts), pp. 21–35. Dialectical concepts, on the other hand, may be traced back to the sentence of Herakleitos considering that "one cannot step twice into the same river".
17. Nicholas Georgescu-Roegen, *Analytical Economics. Issues and Problems* (Harvard University Press, 1967, Massachusetts), p. 27, italics added. Georgescu-Roegen's comparison between positivism and the Catholic Church is revealing in two respects: first, it explains that both ideologies are sharing a faith in absolute truth; second, it shows that the Catholic Church and positivism are sharing the belief that inquisitorial procedures are appropriate for the search for truth.
18. In civil law systems, accusatorial (in criminal law cases) and interrogative (in civil law cases) methods are applied. With view on the role of the judge in civil law systems, Sharon Byrd observed:

"In continental European nations, the judge plays the more active role in questioning of witnesses and taking of evidence. (…) Perhaps, one reason why this system dominates in continental Europe is because it is the judge who is the factfinder at trial. Consequently, *it is he who must be convinced of the truth of certain facts* before being able to apply the law to those facts in reaching his judgement" (B. Sharon Byrd, *Introduction to Anglo-American Law & Language*, 2nd edition/*Einführung in die anglo-amerikanische Rechtssprache*, 2. Auflage (Verlag C.H. Beck, 2001), p. 78, emphasis added. Rules of accusatorial and interrogative procedures are also characterised as systems based on *substantive justice*, defining justice "as *the ability of a highly trained expert, in the person of the judge, to find the truth* and *establish justice in some higher sense of the word*" (B. Sharon Byrd, ibid., p. 79, emphasis added).

19. Karl R. Popper, *Objective Knowledge. An Evolutionary Approach* (Oxford University Press, 1973), p. 16 (original emphases). In this context, Popper introduced the famous allegory of Einstein and the amoeba:

„The main difference between Einstein and an amoeba (...) is that Einstein *consciously seeks for error elimination.* He tries to kill his theories: he is *consciously critical* of his theories which, for this reason, he tries to *formulate* sharply rather than vaguely. But the amoeba cannot be critical *vis-à-vis* its expectations or hypotheses; it cannot be critical because it cannot *face* its hypotheses: they are part of it. (Only objective knowledge is criticizable: subjective knowledge becomes criticizable only when it becomes objective. And it becomes objective when we *say* what we think; and even more so when we *write* it down, or *print* it.)" (Karl R. Popper, ibid. pp. 24–25, original emphases).

20. Karl R. Popper, *The Myth of the Framework. In defence of science and rationality.* Edited by M.A. Notturno (Routledge, 1994), p. 13 (footnotes omitted).
21. Karl R. Popper, *Objective Knowledge. An Evolutionary Approach* (Oxford University Press, London, 1973), p. 25, footnote omitted. Popper concluded: "This is why (...) I do not believe in belief" (ibid.).
22. Karl R. Popper, *The Myth of the Framework. In defence of science and rationality.* Edited by M.A. Notturno (Routledge, 1994), p. 88. It has to be noted that Popper's criterion of falsifiability or refutability has to be discerned from the principle of verification, as usually applied in scientific theory and advocated by logical positivists in particular. With view on the latter, Stump observed that "Logical Positivists, and especially Alfred Ayer, championed the principle of verification as the tool for removing metaphysical nonsense from philosophy and leaving a scientific core" (see David J, Stump, ‚From the Values of Scientific Philosophy to the Value Neutrality of the Philosophy of Science', in Michael Heidelberger, Friedrich Stadler (eds.), *History of Philosophy of Science. New Trends and Perspectives* (Kluwer Academic Publishers, 2002), pp. 153–154). On the

other hand, attention should be paid to the fact that Popper's concept of *critical rationalism* is counter to positivism in the same way as it takes up position against relativism:

"For I want to say a few words against the widespread doctrine of sociological relativism, often unconsciously held, especially by sociologists who study the ways of scientists and who think that they thereby study science and scientific knowledge. Many of these sociologists do not believe in objective truth, but think of truth as a sociological concept. Even a former scientist such as the late Michael Polanyi thought that truth was what the experts *believe* to be true—or, at least, the great majority of the experts. But in all sciences, the experts are sometimes mistaken. Whenever there is a breakthrough, a really important new discovery, this means that the experts have been proven wrong, and that the facts, the objective facts, were different from what the experts expected them to be. (...)
I guess, indeed, that it is the suppressed sense of our own fallibility that is responsible for our despicable tendency to form cliques and to go along with whatever seems to be fashionable: that makes so many of us howl with the wolves. Alls this is human weakness, which means it ought not to exist. But it does exist, of course; it is even to be found among some scientists. And as it exists, we ought to combat it; first in ourselves, and then, perhaps, in others. For I hold that science *ought* to strive for objective truth, for truth that depends only on the facts; on truth that is above human authority and above arbitration, and certainly above scientific fashions. Some sociologists fail to understand that this objectivity is a possibility towards which science (and therefore scientists) should aim. Yet science *has* aimed at truth for at least 2500 years." (Karl R. Popper, 'Towards an Evolutionary Theory of Knowledge', in Karl R. Popper, *A World of Propensities* (Thoemmes Antiquarian Books, 1990), pp. 33–34 (original emphasis).

23. Karl R. Popper, *The Logic of Scientific Discovery*, 2nd English edition, (Hutchinson & Co Publishers, 1968), p. 40. As a reminder: Popper called "an inference 'inductive' if it passes from *singular statements* (sometimes also called 'particular' statements), such as accounts of the results of observations or experiments, to *universal statements*, such as hypotheses or theories" (Karl R. Popper, ibid., p. 27).
24. Karl R. Popper, ibid. p. 40.
25. Karl R. Popper, ibid. p. 40 (original emphasis, footnote omitted).
26. Karl R. Popper, ibid., pp. 40–41 (original emphases, footnote omitted).
27. Ulrich Beck, 'The Reinvention of Politics: Towards a Theory of Reflexive Modernization', in Ulrich Beck, Anthony Giddens and Scott Lash,

Reflexive Modernization. Politics, Tradition and Aesthetics in the Modern Social Order. Polity Press, 1994), p. 11.

28. Ulrich Beck, *World Risk Society* (Polity Press, 1999/2005), p. 107.
29. Alexia Herwig, 'Transnational Governance Regimes for Foods Derived from Bio-Technology and their Legitimacy', in Christian Joerges, Inger-Johanne Sand, and Gunther Teubner (eds.), *Transnational Governance and Constitutionalism* (Hart Publishing, 2004), [pp. 199–222], p. 221.
30. Sungjoon Cho, 'From Control to Communication: Science, Philosophy and World Trade Law' (2010). Cornell International Law Journal, forthcoming. Available at SSRN: http://ssrn.com/abstract=1583023 (visited December 5, 2010).
31. With its focus on procedural aspects, the critical approach suggested here shows similarities with Shrader-Frechette's *scientific proceduralism*, defined as "a 'middle position' on the methodological spectrum of views about how to guarantee the rationality of risk evaluation" (Kristin S. Shrader-Frechette, *Risk and Rationality. Philosophical Foundations for Populist Reforms* (University of California Press, 1991), p. 8).
32. Thomas Cottier, review of Mark A. Pollack's and Gregory C. Shaffer's, *When Cooperation Fails. The International Law and Politics of Genetically Modified Foods* (Oxford University Press, 2009), in 9(2) *World Trade Review* (2010), p. 394. Earlier, but without addressing multilayered governance, Cottier argued for "a clear distinction between risk assessment based on scientific evidence and risk management" (see Thomas Cottier, 'Risk Management experience in WTO dispute settlement', in David Robertson and Aynsley Kellow, *Globalization and the Environment. Risk Assessment and the WTO* (Edward Elgar, 2001), p. 57).
33. Thomas Cottier and Maya Hertig, 'The Prospects of 21st Century Constitutionalism', in Georg Kohler and Urs Marti (eds.), *Konturen der neuen Welt(un)ordnung* (De Gruyter, 2003), pp. 161–162. However, with respect to various calls for democratising international organisations and supra-national entities, it has to bear in mind that the focus on function may come at the price of a degradation of democratic legitimacy. Guy Peters and Jon Pierre, for example, used the term "Faustian bargain" for describing the dilemma with the multi-level governance approach. Peters and Pierre observed that multi-level governance "needs to be critically assessed in order to facilitate a debate regarding its outcomes. Clearly, there is much in multi-level governance suggesting that it has a high problem-solving capacity and that it is likely to generate efficient outcomes. That said, multi-level governance also has features, which, call its democratic nature into question" (Guy Peters and Jon Pierre, 'Multi-level Governance and Democracy: A Faustian Bargain?' in Ian Bache and

Matthew Flinders (eds.), *Multi-level Governance* (Oxford University Press, 2004), p. 88).

34. According to Gerald Allan Cohen, functional approaches are trying to explain a cause by their consequence: "To establish that a social practice *A* exists in order to do *B*, we must establish a law that relates *A*'s disposition to do *B* with *A*'s existence. In short, we must show that it is a law that when *A* would be useful (or serve its function), *A* comes to exist." Thus, functional approaches are relying on "consequence law" (Harold Kincaid, *Philosophical Foundations of the Social Sciences. Analyzing Controversies in Social Research* (Cambridge University Press, 1996), p. 109, with reference to Gerald A. Cohen, *Karl Marx's Theory of History: A Defence* (Princeton University Press, 1978).
35. John H. Jackson, *Sovereignty, the WTO and Changing Fundamentals of International Law* (Cambridge University Press, 2006), p. 245 (footnotes omitted).
36. Enrico Gualini, *Multi-level Governance and Institutional Change. The Europeanization of Regional Policy in Italy* (Ashgate Publishing, 2004), p. 44 (original emphasis, footnote omitted).
37. The Lamming Report, the EC Scientific Conference.
38. The OIE Symposium, the International Agency for Research on Cancer (IARC) Monographs, the 1988 and 1989 JECFA Reports.
39. *EC—Hormones*, Panel Report, para. 8.124.
40. *Australia—Salmon*, Panel Report, para. 8.154. The risk evaluation report issued by Australia's Quarantine and Inspection Service (AQIS) in May 1995 was entitled "Draft Import Risk Analysis—Disease risks associated with the importation of uncooked, wild, ocean-caught salmon product from the USA and Canada". Hence, the Panel called it the "1995 Draft Report". Because the report published in May 1996 by Australia's Department of Primary Industries and Fisheries was the final version of Australia's Import Risk Analysis, the Panel called it the "1996 Final Report".
41. *Australia—Salmon*, Panel Report, para. 8.154. In footnote no. 424, the Panel cited one of the scientific experts, Rogers, stating that the 1996 Final Report "seems to consider the scientific advice but then reaches a political decision, following public consultation".
42. *Australia—Salmon*, Panel Report, para. 8.154. This finding of the Panel was uphold by the Appellate Body in its Report on *Australia—Salmon*, para. 173.
43. *Australia—Salmon*, Panel Report, para. 8.154, footnote 425.
44. The 1996 Final Report.
45. The Panel observed that "the decisive reason for reversing the 1995 Draft Report's conclusion—that the salmon products further examined should

be allowed into Australia under specific conditions—might well have been inspired by domestic pressures to protect the *Australia—Salmon* industry against import competition" *(Australia—Salmon*, Panel Report, para 8.154; finding upheld by the Appellate Body Report, paras. 170, 173). The 1995 Draft Report was written by the Australian Quarantine and Inspection Service (AQIS), whereas the 1996 Final Report was published by the Department of Primary Industries and Fisheries *(Australia—Salmon*, Panel Report, paras. 2.28, 2.30).

46. That is, the competent authority (CA) of the EC Member State to which the product applications were originally submitted.
47. EC Scientific Committee on Plants (SCP), EC Scientific Committee on Food (SCF), EC Scientific Committee for Pesticides (SCPE), EC Scientific Committee on Animal Nutrition (SCAN).
48. The Reasons Documents, the Hoppichler Study, the Hilbeck study, the BEC reports, etc.
49. Oren Perez, '*Anomalies at the precautionary kingdom: reflections on the GMO Panel's decision*' (2007), 6(2) *World Trade Review*, 271.
50. *E.g.* the "Hoppichler study".
51. *EC—Biotech*, Panel Reports, para. 7.3046.
52. *EC—Biotech*, Panel Reports, para. 7.3116.
53. *E.g.* a study from the Öko-Institut e.V. on the „Therapeutical relevance of antibiotics in connection with the use of antibiotic resistance genes in transgenic plants".
54. *EC—Biotech*, Panel Reports, para. 7.3151.
55. Several reports resulting from the Farm Scale Evaluations (FSEs) conducted in the United Kingdom.
56. *EC—Biotech*, Panel Reports, para. 7.3170.
57. The opinion by the Italian Superior Institute of Health of July 2000.
58. *EC—Biotech*, Panel Reports, para. 7.3188.
59. *EC—Biotech*, Panel Reports, para. 7.3205.
60. The competent authority of the EC Member State where the GMO at issue is to be placed on the market for the first time.
61. In the case *EC—Biotech*, the EC Scientific Committee on Food (SCF) and the EC Scientific Committee on Plants (SCP) were involved in risk assessment.
62. *EC—Biotech*, Panel Reports, para. 7.3027, footnotes added.
63. *EC—Biotech*, Panel Reports, para. 7.3027, footnote omitted. The EC scientific committees found that the biotech products in question did not present any risk. See, *inter alia*, Oren Perez, '*Anomalies at the precautionary kingdom: reflections on the GMO Panel's decision*' (2007), 6(2) *World Trade Review*, 265–280.

64. Paragraph 9 of the '*Working Principles for Risk Analysis* for Application in the Framework of the Codex Alimentarius', Section IV of the *Procedural Manual* of the Codex Alimentarius Commission, 19th edition, 2010, p. 87.
65. *Australia—Salmon*, Panel Report, para 8.154; finding upheld by the Appellate Body, Appellate Body Report, paras. 170, 173.
66. *EC—Hormones*, Appellate Body Report, para. 206.
67. *US/Canada—Continued Suspension*, Appellate Body Reports, paras. 456–482, in particular para. 481; reversing Panel's findings in *US—Continued Suspension*, paras. 6.22, 6.62–6.63 and 7.85/*Canada—Continued Suspension*, paras. 6.21, 6.57–6.58 and 7.83.
68. Codex Alimentarius Commission, 'Statements of Principle Concerning the Role of Science in the Codex Decision-Making Process and the Extent to which other Factors are taken into Account', in the *Procedural Manual*, 19th edition (Secretariat of the Joint FAO/WHO Food Standards Programme, 2010), p. 180.
69. Catherine Button, *The Power to Protect. Trade, Health, and Uncertainty in the WTO* (Hart Publishing, 2004), p. 106.
70. Codex Alimentarius Commission, 'Statements of Principle Concerning the Role of Science in the Codex Decision-Making Process and the Extent to which other Factors are taken into Account', in the *Procedural Manual*, 19th edition (Secretariat of the Joint FAO/WHO Food Standards Programme, 2010), p. 180.
71. Codex Alimentarius Commission, 'Statements of Principle Concerning the Role of Science in the Codex Decision-Making Process and the Extent to which other Factors are taken into Account', in the *Procedural Manual*, 19th edition (Secretariat of the Joint FAO/WHO Food Standards Programme, 2010), p. 180.
72. Working Principles for Risk Analysis for Application in the Framework of the Codex Alimentarius, in Section IV of the *Procedural Manual* of the Codex Alimentarius Commission, 19th edition (Secretariat of the Joint FAO/WHO Food Standards Programme, 2010), p. 87.
73. At a workshop entitled *Food Safety Risk Assessment at the International Level: Do Existing Mechanisms Ensure Unbiased Outcomes?* held at the World Trade Institute in Bern, Switzerland, October 3, 2007, distinguished experts had been invited to discuss risk assessment problems from different angles. The proposed wording is a synthesis of reform proposals developed by hosts and workshop participants. A special thank goes to Philippe Verger, head of the research unit Met@risk of the National Institute for Agricultural Research (INRA) in Paris, for his valuable and dedicated contributions, and to Susan Plattner, scientific editor of the World Trade Institute, for revising the draft of article 5.1.

74. The other experts involved were Dr David Kessler, Dean, Yale School of Medicine, USA; Dr Anke Martiny, Executive Director of Transparency International, Germany; and Dr Fazel Randera, Inspector General of Intelligence, South Africa.
75. All quotes are taken from the report of Thomas Zeltner et. al., *Tobacco Company Strategies to Undermine Tobacco Control Activities at the World Health Organization. Report of the Committee of Experts on Tobacco Industry Documents* (World Health Organisation, July 2000), p. iii.
76. Eduard Kaeser, *Pop Science. Essays zur Wissenschaftskultur* (Schwabe Verlag Basel, 2009), pp. 40–41. The report of the inquiry commission of the University of Geneva of September 6, 2004 about the hidden activities of Professor Ragnar Rylander in the service of the tobacco industry, in particular of Philip Morris, can be accessed following this link: http://www.unige.ch/rectorat/pdf/Rylander.pdf (accessed May 18, 2017).
77. The main report establishing conflicts of interests at WHO was jointly drafted by Deborah Cohen, editor of the British Medical Journal (BMJ), and Philip Carter, a journalist working with the Bureau of Investigative Journalism in London; see: Deborah Cohen and Philip Carter, 'Conflicts of Interest. WHO and the pandemic flu 'conspiracies',' in British Medical Journal (BMJ), June 3 2010. The report was commented, among others, by Alan Niederer, 'Neue Kritik an der WHO,' in *Neue Zürcher Zeitung* no. 127, June 5, 2010, p. 26.
78. Alexia Herwig, 'Transnational Governance Regimes for Foods Derived from Bio-Technology and their Legitimacy', in Christian Joerges, Inger-Johanne Sand, and Gunther Teubner (eds.), *Transnational Governance and Constitutionalism* (Hart Publishing, 2004), [pp. 199–222], p. 220 (footnotes omitted).
79. Robert N. Proctor, 'Agnotology. A Missing Term to Describe the Cultural Production of Ignorance (and Its Study),' in Robert N. Proctor and Londa Schiebinger (eds.), *Agnotology. The Making and Unmaking of Ignorance* (Stanford University Press, 2008), p. 14 (original emphasis, footnote omitted).
80. Lee Ann Jackson and Marion Jansen, 'Risk assessment in the international food safety policy arena. Can the multilateral institutions encourage unbiased outcomes?' (2010) 35 *Food Policy* [538–547] 540.
81. It is important to note that the observed dependency on third-party data applies to food safety issues, first of all. The time-honoured World Organisation for Animal Health (OIE) for instance, runs a network of collaborating centres and reference laboratories all over the world. Founded already in 1924 in Paris and operating outside UN structures, OIE issues international standards in the forms of the International Animal Health Code and the International Aquatic Animal Health Code

respectively (See, for instance, Tim Josling, Donna Roberts and David Orden, *Food Regulation and Trade. Toward a Safe and Open Global System* (Institute for International Economics, 2004), p. 42; and the OIE website: http://www.oie.int/ (accessed May 18, 2017).

82. The problem of no access to company data is also of concern in the field of drug testing. For example, the British Medical Journal (BMJ) revealed that risk assessments for the drug oseltamivir (*Tamiflu*) have been based on questionable scientific data. According to the BMJ editorial, the Tamiflu case shows that the whole system of drug control is not working because scientific evidence "remains shrouded in secrecy":

"The current system isn't working. Worse than that, it gives a false sense of security. The system's failures have left a legacy of drug evaluations for which, in the absence of better information, we must assume the same levels of confusion and uncertainty as for oseltamivir. The drug industry directly or indirectly undertakes the majority of all drug evaluations, so most of the evidence used to support drug policy and treatment remains shrouded in secrecy. In only a minority of cases will the data have been subject to full independent analysis and interpretation. In many if not most cases, the only people who have seen the entire dataset are company employees" (Fiona Godlee, Mike Clarke, 'Why don't we have all the evidence on oseltamivir?' in *British Medical Journal*, December 8, 2009).

83. Lee Ann Jackson and Marion Jansen, 'Risk assessment in the international food safety policy arena. Can the multilateral institutions encourage unbiased outcomes?' (2010) 35 *Food Policy* [538–547] 542.
84. Lee Ann Jackson and Marion Jansen, ibid.
85. Lee Ann Jackson and Marion Jansen, ibid. 543.
86. See, for instance, Lee Ann Jackson and Marion Jansen, 'Risk assessment in the international food safety policy arena. Can the multilateral institutions encourage unbiased outcomes?' (2010) 35 *Food Policy* [538–547] 543.
87. Helga Nowotny, 'The Changing Nature of Public Science', in Helga Nowotny et al., The Public Nature of Science under Assault. Politics, Markets, Science and the Law (Springer Verlag, 2005) [1–28] 1.
88. Helga Nowotny, ibid. 12.
89. The example was taken from Marcel Hänggi, 'Unterwegs zu McScience?' in *Die Wochenzeitung*, Nr. 50, December 15, 2005, pp. 6–7.
90. Marcel Hänggi, ibid. The following example may confirm Hänggi's observations. In November 2010, it was announced that the company Syngenta sponsors a professorship for 'sustainable agroecosystems' within in the new centre of competence 'World Food System' of the Swiss Federal Institute of Technology in Zurich (ETHZ). See 'ETH Zürich und

Syngenta lancieren neue Professur', in *ETH Life*, published November 11, 2010, web access: http://www.ethlife.ethz.ch/archive_articles/101111_Syngenta_MM (visited November 21, 2010, and May 18, 2017). Another example of agenda-setting through sponsoring was the donation of 25 million Swiss Francs by food giant Nestlé to the Brain Mind Institute of the Swiss Federal Institute of Technology in Lausanne (EPFL), as announced in November 2006 (see Marcel Hänggi, 'Liaisons dangereuses', in *Die Wochenzeitung*, December 7, 2006).

91. *US/Canada—Continued Suspension*, Appellate Body Reports, para. 481; reversing Panel's findings in *US—Continued Suspension*, paras. 6.22, 6.62–6.63 and 7.85/*Canada—Continued Suspension*, paras. 6.21, 6.57–6.58 and 7.83.
92. Thorsten Hüller and Matthias Leonhard Maier, 'Fixing the Codex? Global Food-Safety Governance Under Review', in Christian Joerges and Ernst-Ulrich Petersmann (eds.), *Constitutionalism, Multilevel Trade Governance and Social Regulation* (Hart Publishing, 2006), [pp. 268–299], pp. 279–280 (footnotes omitted).
93. Thorsten Hüller and Matthias Leonhard Maier, ibid., p. 279 (footnotes omitted).
94. *EC—Hormones*, Appellate Body Report, para. 27.
95. Before the coming into force of the SPS Agreement and its presumption of GATT/WTO compatibility of SPS measures conforming to international standards, the latter were conceived as voluntary standards. Marsha Echols considered that the SPS Agreement, with its harmonisation provisions, "elevates the Codex Alimentarius Commission from an obscure role to one of potentially immense importance in international food trade. Codex was selected as the principal relevant international organization because of its technical and scientific expertise and because the 'clear overarching purpose of the work of the Commission is international harmonization of standards'…" (Marsha A. Echols, *Food Safety and the WTO. The Interplay of Culture, Science and Technology* (Kluwer Law International, 2001), p. 100).
96. Lee Ann Jackson and Marion Jansen, 'Risk assessment in the international food safety policy arena. Can the multilateral institutions encourage unbiased outcomes?' (2010) 35 *Food Policy* [538–547] 542.
97. Lee Ann Jackson and Marion Jansen, ibid. 546.
98. Lee Ann Jackson and Marion Jansen, ibid.
99. Appellate Body Reports in *US/Canada—Continued Suspension*, para. 481; reversing Panel's findings in *US—Continued Suspension*, paras. 6.22, 6.62–6.63 and 7.85/*Canada—Continued Suspension*, paras. 6.21, 6.57–6.58 and 7.83.

100. W. Bruce Traill, Rachel Bedouin, Katharine Gourlie, Jerri Husch, Alicia Lustre (eds.), *Report of the Evaluation of the Codex Alimentarius and other FAO and WHO Food Standards Work* (FAO/WHO, November 15, 2002), Executive Summary, finding no. 23.
101. Catherine Button, *The Power to Protect. Trade, Health, and Uncertainty in the WTO* (Hart Publishing, 2004), p. 45 (original emphasis, footnote omitted).
102. Lee Ann Jackson and Marion Jansen, 'Risk assessment in the international food safety policy arena. Can the multilateral institutions encourage unbiased outcomes?' (2010) 35 *Food Policy* [538–547] 546.
103. W. Bruce Traill, Rachel Bedouin, Katharine Gourlie, Jerri Husch, Alicia Lustre (eds.), *Report of the Evaluation of the Codex Alimentarius and other FAO and WHO Food Standards Work* (FAO/WHO, November 15, 2002), para. 184, box 3: Maximum Level for Aflatoxin M_1 in Milk. A standard prescribing a maximum level of 0.5ìg/kg was finally adopted in 2001.
104. From such findings, however, one should not deduce an increase in the number of trade disputes without further consideration. For instance, at a workshop entitled *Food Safety Risk Assessment at the International Level: Can Multilateral Institutions Encourage Unbiased Outcomes?* held at the World Trade Institute in Bern, Switzerland, on May 18, 2009, no direct causality between the entry into force of the SPS Agreement and the number of formal requests tabled at relevant international bodies, e.g. Codex, the SPS Committee and the WTO DSB, was established.
105. Tim Josling, Donna Roberts and David Orden, *Food Regulation and Trade. Toward a Safe and Open Global System* (Institute for International Economics, 2004), p. 43.
106. Tim Josling, Donna Roberts and David Orden, ibid.
107. W. Bruce Traill, Rachel Bedouin, Katharine Gourlie, Jerri Husch, Alicia Lustre (eds.), *Report of the Evaluation of the Codex Alimentarius and other FAO and WHO Food Standards Work* (FAO/WHO, November 15, 2002), para. 184.
108. It has to be noted that economic benefits allegedly arising from the harmonisation of standards are controversial. Josling et al., for example, observed:

"However, the normative basis for harmonization is not overwhelming, and there is little evidence to indicate that international standards in foods have succeeded notably in opening up trade. Therefore, it must be concluded that international standards have improved the functioning of food markets, but more by improving the quality of regulation, which mostly benefits consumers, than by reducing transactions costs of exporting to specific countries, which delivers more benefits to exporters" (Tim Josling, Donna Roberts and David Orden, *Food Regulation and Trade. Toward a Safe and Open Global System* (Institute for International Economics, 2004), p. 204).

109. Catherine Button, *The Power to Protect. Trade, Health, and Uncertainty in the WTO* (Hart Publishing, 2004), p. 45.
110. Catherine Button, ibid. p. 45 (original emphasis).
111. Catherine Button, ibid. p. 229 (original emphases).
112. Catherine Button, ibid. pp. 54–55 (footnote omitted).
113. Steve Fuller, *Social Epistemology*. 2nd Edition (Indiana University Press, 2002), p. 286. In *The Open Society and Its Enemies* (1945), Karl R. Popper stressed on the mutual interdependency of critical (scientific) discourse and open i.e. democratic societies. Nassim Nicholas Taleb summarised Popper's considerations as follows:

"Popper believed that any idea of Utopia is necessarily closed owing to the fact that it chokes its own refutations. The simple notion of a good model for society that cannot be left open for falsification is totalitarian" (Nassim Nicholas Taleb, *Fooled by Randomness. The Hidden Role of Chance in Life and in the Markets*. 2nd Edition (Penguin Books, 2004), pp. 128–129).

114. Ulrich Beck, 'The Reinvention of Politics: Towards a Theory of Reflexive Modernization', in Ulrich Beck, Anthony Giddens and Scott Lash, *Reflexive Modernization. Politics, Tradition and Aesthetics in the Modern Social Order*. Polity Press, 1994), p. 30.
115. Ulrich Beck, ibid. pp. 30–31.
116. Ulrich Beck, ibid. p. 31 (emphases added).
117. The idea of establishing a 'Science Court' was considered by the Carter Administration in 1978, following suggestions of Arthur Kantrowitz (Kristin S. Shrader-Frechette, *Risk Analysis and Scientific Method. Methodological and Ethical Problems with Evaluating Societal Hazards* (D. Reidel Publishing Company, Dordrecht/Holland, 1985), p. 207). In contrast to her proposal for a 'technology tribunal', Shrader-Frechette worked out two characteristic features of the (positivist) attempt for establishing a 'Science Court.' First, the panel of the 'Science Court' was meant of being composed of scientists only, without involving laypersons. Second, the 'Science Court' was meant to consider scientific facts only and setting aside any policy questions or value issues (Kristin S. Shrader-Frechette, ibid.). Kantrowitz himself condensed the idea of the Science Court as follows: "The purpose of the science court begins with the separation of facts from values and is an attempt to deal with the myth of the unprejudiced expert" (Roxanne S. Khamsi, 'Courting the Facts.

Arthur Kantrowitz and the History of the Science Court,' in *Dartmouth Undergraduate Journal of Science* (DUJS, 2000). However, despite his aim 'to deal with the myth of the unprejudiced expert,' Kantrowitz assigned the role of final judge to scientists themselves. In this respect, Khamsi observed that, according to Kantrowitz' model, "[t]rained scientists would act as judges—although, to avoid bias, they would not be experts in the disputed issue. After hearing both sides present their evidence, including techniques and results, the panel of judges would render a decision" (Khamsi, ibid.). Hence, Kantrowitz' model for a 'Science Court' conflates both the premise and the aim of positivism: based on the assumption that consent can be reached over facts if the latter are separated from values, positivism aims at establishing final 'scientific truths'.

118. Kristin S. Shrader-Frechette, *Risk Analysis and Scientific Method. Methodological and Ethical Problems with Evaluating Societal Hazards* (D. Reidel Publishing, 1985), p. 208.
119. Kristin S. Shrader-Frechette, ibid. p. 205 (emphasis added).
120. Kristin S. Shrader-Frechette, ibid. p. 206.
121. Kristin S. Shrader-Frechette, ibid., pp. 206–207.
122. Kristin S. Shrader-Frechette, ibid. p. 207 (emphasis added).
123. Kristin S. Shrader-Frechette, ibid. p. 207 (emphasis added).
124. Kristin S. Shrader-Frechette, ibid. p. 207 (emphasis added).
125. Kristin S. Shrader-Frechette, ibid. p. 207. Shrader-Frechette added the reservation that the panel's decision shall be made public unless national security is at stake (Kristin S. Shrader-Frechette, ibid.).
126. See the website of the Swiss National Research Programme (NRP 59) on 'Benefits and Risks of the Deliberate Release of Genetically Modified Plants' athttp://www.nfp59.ch/e_portrait_details.cfm (accessed August 15, 2010, and May 18, 2017).
127. In 2013, the government presented a draft legal text for regulating GMOs. Because of broad opposition, government and parliament protracted the moratorium once more until 2021. See press release of the Swiss government of 18th December 2015: https://www.admin.ch/gov/de/start/dokumentation/medienmitteilungen.msg-id-60062.html (accessed May 18, 2017). With view o the *US—Animals* case, some experts came to the conclusion that "Switzerland would need to demonstrate that it had (i) made best efforts to remedy the insufficiencies in the relevant scientific evidence and (ii) reviewed the meauser accordingly within a reasonable period of time as recalled in *US—Animals*" (Michael Hahn et. al., "The Jurisprudence of the World Trade Organization in 2015", published in *Swiss Review of International and European Law*, 26 (2016), no. 2, p. 357.

128. Lukasz Gruszczynski, *Regulating Health and Environmental Risks under WTO Law. A Critical Analysis of the SPS Agreement* (Oxford University Press, 2010), pp. 272–273 (emphasis added).
129. Issues of transparency and public participation are also issues in Codex and related scientific expert bodies. The experts evaluating the Codex, for instance, came to the following conclusion: "We believe that consumers and other interest groups could be more actively involved in discussions by experts on risk assessment procedures and protocols and in expert advice on risk management and communication" (W. Bruce Traill, Rachel Bedouin, Katharine Gourlie, Jerri Husch, Alicia Lustre (eds.), *Report of the Evaluation of the Codex Alimentarius and other FAO and WHO Food Standards Work* (FAO/WHO, November 15, 2002), para. 193).
130. In this respect, the proposal suggested here goes further than that of other authors arguing that public participation is first and foremost a domestic problem. The latter position is represented, for instance, by Tracey Epps, *International Trade and Health Protection. A Critical Assessment of the WTO's SPS Agreement* (Edward Elgar, 2008), p. 301.
131. Marsha A. Echols, *Food Safety and the WTO. The Interplay of Culture, Science and Technology* (Kluwer Law International, 2001), p. 154.
132. With view on the earlier SPS jurisprudence in particular, Lukasz Gruszczynski, for instance, held that "[t]he WTO dispute settlement bodies seem to be poorly equipped to make complex scientific determinations as they simply lack relevant expertise" (Lukasz Gruszczynski, *Regulating Health and Environmental Risks under WTO Law. A Critical Analysis of the SPS Agreement* (Oxford University Press, 2010), p. 272). However, with view on recent jurisprudence, in particular the *Continued Suspension* case, Gruszczynski relativised his statement, recognising "that the deficiencies and failures of the case law ... should not be seen as a criticism of the whole system but rather as an appeal for specific adjustments" (Lukasz Gruszczynski, ibid., p. 273).
133. Joanne Scott, *The WTO Agreement on Sanitary and Phytosanitary Measures* (Oxford University Press, 2007), pp. 41–75.
134. Elisabeth, Ehrensperger, *Die Allgemeine Erklärung der Menschenrechte als Modellfall der Deliberation. Theorie, Dokumente, Analyse* (Nomos Verlagsgesellschaft, 2006).
135. Joe Klein, 'Tough Issues. What if we gave people real choices and real consequences and let them make decisions?' in *TIME*, September 13, 2010, p. 17 (emphasis added).
136. Joe Klein, ibid.; (emphasis added).
137. Lukasz Gruszczynski, *Regulating Health and Environmental Risks under WTO Law. A Critical Analysis of the SPS Agreement* (Oxford University Press, 2010), p. 137.

138. Lukasz Gruszczynski, ibid., footnote omitted)
139. Lukasz Gruszczynski, ibid., footnote omitted).
140. Lukasz Gruszczynski, ibid., p. 139.
141. Joanne Scott applied these terms for emphasising the role of the SPS committee vis-à-vis to the WTO dispute settlement system (see Joanne Scott, *The WTO Agreement on Sanitary and Phytosanitary Measures* (Oxford University Press, 2007), pp. 74–75.
142. Joanne Scott, ibid. p. 75 (footnote omitted). It is before the background of that peculiar atmosphere of deliberative rapprochement in the SPS Committee that an alternative account of the Nile perch dispute shall be told. At first, the reason provided above for the inaction of East African countries against scientifically unfounded EU safety measures was one of might: according to an anonymous WTO delegate, retaliatory power of small East African countries against the big EU is virtually nil. In the context of the work of the SPS Committee, however, Joan Scott provided an alternative explanation for the forgoing of formal WTO dispute settlement procedures:

"The issue [i.e. EU safeguard measures relating to the importation of, *inter alia*, fish] was raised by Tanzania in the committee, which gained the support of the observer representative of the World Health Organization (WHO). The WHO representative observed that cholera was not only a problem in these four countries, and that at least 50 countries around the world were affected by regular outbreaks. He pointed to the 'almost non-existing risk to countries importing food from cholera-affected countries', and expressed the view that the European measure was not necessary. He drew attention to the WHO guidance on the topic and to the finding that '[a]lthough there is a theoretical risk of Cholera transmission associated with some food commodities moving in international trade, this has rarely proved significant and authorities should seek means of dealing with it other than by applying an embargo on importation'. The WHO also assisted in ongoing bilateral consultations between the countries concerned. Though the EC objected that WHO involvement was not appropriate, it removed the measure following consultations and reassurances that the necessary guarantees to protect health were in place" (Joanne Scott, ibid. p. 53, footnotes omitted).

Examples such as the EU safeguard measures against East African fresh produce importation were the reason for Joanne Scott stressing the importance of the SPS Committee's capacity for deliberative conflict resolution and preventive peer review of SPS measures. In the case of EU safeguard measures against East African imports, these measures were reviewed against the benchmark of WHO standards in the SPS Committee. Scott described the peer review function of the SPS Committee as follows:

"(…) WHO guidelines were called in aid of this proposition [i.e. to impugn the EU measures], representing default standards, departure from which was seen as requiring justification. It is evident that the standards according to which peer review [by the SPS Committee] proceeds are open-ended in the extreme. The standards are elaborated in dispute settlement, but the cases tend to be fact-heavy and law-light, and concomitantly thin in the statements of precedential value which they offer. Against this backdrop, the role of the committee is not only passive in relation to these standards. It too constitutes a forum for their elaboration, operating as a *contextualizing regime* whereby the standards are elaborated in the course of consideration of specific problems. In the course of their repeated interactions, Members arrive at settled (though not necessarily authoritative, from the point of view of the dispute settlement bodies) understandings of the meaning of the agreement in context" (Joanne Scott, ibid. pp. 53–54, footnotes omitted, emphasis added).

143. Sungjoon Cho, 'From Control to Communication: Science, Philosophy and World Trade Law' (2010). Cornell International Law Journal, forthcoming. Available at SSRN: http://ssrn.com/abstract=1583023 (visited December 5, 2010; footnote omitted).
144. Joanne Scott, *The WTO Agreement on Sanitary and Phytosanitary Measures* (Oxford University Press, 2007), p. 49.
145. Joanne Scott, ibid., footnote no. 22.
146. Helena Paul and Ricarda Seinbrecher, *Hungry Corporations. Transnational Biotech Companies Colonise the Food Chain* (Zed Books, 2003), p. 153; with footnote no. 22 referencing to Lisa Lefferts, 'Changing the Rules of the Codex Club', 43 *Pesticides News* (March 1999) 6.
147. Alexia Herwig, 'Transnational Governance Regimes for Foods Derived from Bio-Technology and their Legitimacy', in Christian Joerges, Inger-Johanne Sand, and Gunther Teubner (eds.), *Transnational Governance and Constitutionalism* (Hart Publishing, 2004), [pp. 199–222], pp. 220–221.

References

Beck, Ulrich. "The Reinvention of Politics: Towards a Theory of Reflexive Modernization". Published in Ulrich Beck, Anthony Giddens and Scott Lash, *Reflexive Modernization. Politics, Tradition and Aesthetics in the Modern Social Order*. Polity Press, 1994.

Beck, Ulrich. "World Risk Society". *Polity Press in association with Blackwell Publishers*, 2005 (first published 1999).

Bischoff, Ulrich. "Max Ernst 1891-1976. Jenseits der Malerei". *TASCHEN*, 2005.

Button, Catherine. "The Power to Protect. Trade, Health, and Uncertainty in the WTO". *Hart Publishing*, 2004.

Byrd, B. Sharon. "Introduction to Anglo-American Law & Language". *Verlag C. H. Beck*, 2001 (2nd edition).

Cho, Sungjoon. "From Control to Communication: Science, Philosophy and World Trade Law". *Cornell International Law Journal*, forthcoming. Available at SSRN. http://ssrn.com/abstract=1583023 (Accessed December 5, 2010, and May 18, 2017).

Cohen, Deborah and Carter, Philip. "Conflicts of Interest. WHO and the pandemic flu 'conspiracies'". *British Medical Journal (BMJ)*, June 3 2010. http://www.bmj.com/cgi/content/full/340/jun03_4/c2912 (accessed August 15, 2010, and May 18, 2017).

Cottier, Thomas. Review of Mark A. Pollack and Gregory C. Shaffer's, *When Cooperation Fails. The International Law and Politics of Genetically Modified Foods.* Oxford University Press, 2009. *World Trade Review*, 2010, vol. 9, no. 2, 391–395.

Cottier, Thomas. "Risk Management experience in WTO dispute settlement". Published in David Robertson and Aynsley Kellow, *Globalization and the Environment. Risk Assessment and the WTO.* Edward Elgar, 2001, 41–62.

Cottier, Thomas, and Hertig, Maya. "The Prospects of 21st Century Constitutionalism". Published in Georg Kohler and Urs Marti (eds.), *Konturen der neuen Welt(un)ordnung.* De Gruyter, 2003.

Echols, Marsha A. "Food Safety and the WTO. The Interplay of Culture, Science and Technology". Kluwer Law International, 2001.

Ehrensperger, Elisabeth. "Die Allgemeine Erklärung der Menschenrechte als Modellfall der Deliberation. Theorie, Dokumente, Analyse". Nomos Verlagsgesellschaft, 2006.

Epps, Tracey."International Trade and Health Protection. A Critical Assessment of the WTO's SPS Agreement". Edward Elgar, 2008.

Fuller, Steve. "Social Epistemology". *Indiana University Press*, 2nd Edition, 2002, (1st Edition 1998).

Georgescu-Roegen, Nicholas "Analytical Economics. Issues and Problems". MA: *Harvard University Press*, 1967.

Godlee, Fiona, Clarke, Mike. "Why don't we have all the evidence on oseltamivir?". *British Medical Journal*, December 8, 2009. http://www.bmj.com/content/339/bmj.b5351.full (Accessed December 22, 2010, and May 18, 2017).

Gualini, Enrico. "Multi-level Governance and Institutional Change. The Europeanization of Regional Policy in Italy". *Ashgate Publishing*, 2004.

Hacohen, Malachi. "Critical Rationalism, Logical Positivism, and the Poststructuralist Conundrum: Reconsidering the Neurath-Popper Debate". Published in Michael Heidelberger, Friedrich Stadler (eds.), *History of Philosophy of Science. New Trends and Perspectives*. Kluwer Academic Publishers, 2002, 307–324.

Hahn, Michael, *et. al.,* "The Jurisprudence of the World Trade Organization in 2015". Published in *Swiss Review of International and European Law*, 26 (2016), no. 2, 357.

Hänggi, Marcel. "Unterwegs zu McScience?". *Die Wochenzeitung*, December 15, 2005, 6–7. Accessed November 21, 2010. http://www.woz.ch/files/wirtsch_u_wissensch.doc.

Hänggi, Marcel. "Liaisons dangereuses". *Die Wochenzeitung*, December 7, 2006. Accessed November 21, 2010. http://www.woz.ch/dossier/nestle/14197.html.

Hermann, Rudolf. "Neuseeländische Kiwis unter Klima-Sünder-Verdacht. "Foodmiles"-Debatte bereitet Kopfschmerzen in Wellington". *Neue Zürcher Zeitung*, August 3, 2007.

Herwig, Alexia. "Transnational Governance Regimes for Foods Derived from Bio-Technology and their Legitimacy". Published in Christian Joerges, Inger-Johanne Sand, Gunther Teubner (eds.), *Transnational Governance and Constitutionalism*. Hart Publishing, 2004, 199–222.

Hüller, Thorsten and Maier, Matthias Leonhard. "Fixing the Codex? Global Food-Safety Governance Under Review". Published in Christian Joerges and Ernst-Ulrich Petersmann (eds.), *Constitutionalism, Multilevel Trade Governance and Social Regulation*. Hart Publishing, 2006, 268–299.

Jackson, John H. "Sovereignty, the WTO and Changing Fundamentals of International Law", *Cambridge University Press*, 2006.

Jackson, Lee Ann and Jansen, Marion. "Risk assessment in the international food safety policy arena. Can the multilateral institutions encourage unbiased outcomes.

Jonker, Theo H., Ito, Hiroshi and Fujishima, Hiroji. "Food Safety and Quality Standards in Japan. Compliance of Suppliers from Developing Countries". *The World Bank*, 2004, 36–37. Accessed October 30, 2010.http://vle.worldbank.org/bnpp/files/TF051844REGIONALGLOBALJapanCountrySurveyF.pdf.

Josling, Tim, Roberts, Donna, Orden, David. "Food Regulation and Trade. Toward a Safe and Open Global System". *Institute for International Economics*, 2004.

Kaeser, Eduard. "Pop Science. Essays zur Wissenschaftskultur". *Schwabe Verlag*, 2009.

Khamsi, Roxanne S. "Courting the Facts. Arthur Kantrowitz and the History of the Science Court". *Dartmouth Undergraduate Journal of Science*. DUJS online, 2000. http://dujs.dartmouth.edu/wp-content/uploads/2008/04/04-science-history.pdf (Accessed October 19, 2010, and May 18, 2017).

Kincaid, Harold. "Philosophical Foundations of the Social Sciences. Analyzing Controversies in Social Research". *Cambridge University Press*, 1996.

Klein, Joe. "Tough Issues. What if we gave people real choices and real consequences and let them make decisions?'". *TIME*, September 13, 2010.

Gruszczynski, Lukasz. "Regulating Health and Environmental Risks under WTO Law. A Critical Analysis of the SPS Agreement". *Oxford University Press*, 2010.

Mold, Andrew. "Non-Tariff Barriers – Their Prevalence and Relevance for African Countries". *African Trade Policy Centre (ATPC)*, Work in Progress No. 25, October 2005. Accessed October 30, 2010.

http://www.uneca.org/atpc/Work%20in%20progress/25.pdf.

Niederer, Alan. "Neue Kritik an der WHO". *Neue Zürcher Zeitung*, June 5, 2010, 26.

Nowotny, Helga: "The Changing Nature of Public Science". Published in Helga Nowotny, Dominique Pestre, Eberhard Schmidt-Assmann, Helmuth Schulze-Fielitz, Hans-Heinrich Trute, *The Public Nature of Science under Assault. Politics, Markets, Science and the Law*.Springer Verlag, 2005, 1–28.

Paul, Helena and Seinbrecher, Ricarda. "Hungry Corporations. Transnational Biotech Companies Colonise the Food Chain". *Zed Books*, 2003.

Perez, Oren. 2007. Anomalies at the precautionary kingdom: reflections on the GMO Panel's decision. *World Trade Review* 6 (2): 265–280.

Peters, Guy, and Pierre, Jon. "Multi-level Governance and Democracy: A Faustian Bargain?" Published in Ian Bache and Matthew Flinders (eds.), *Multi-level Governance*. Oxford University Press, 2004.

Popper, Karl R. "Logik der Forschung" (English title: *The Logic of Scientific Discovery)*. J.C.B Mohr (Paul Siebeck), 1976, 6th edition and Popper, Karl R. "The Logic of Scientific Discovery". *Hutchinson & Co Publishers*, 2nd English edition, 1968.

Popper, Karl R. "Objective Knowledge. An Evolutionary Approach". *Oxford University Press*, 1973.

Popper, Karl R. "Towards an Evolutionary Theory of Knowledg". Published in Karl R. Popper, *A World of Propensities*. Thoemmes Antiquarian Books, 1990.

Popper, Karl R. "The Myth of the Framework. In defence of science and rationality". Edited by M.A. Notturno. *Routledge*, 1994.

Proctor, Robert N. "Agnotology. A Missing Term to Describe the Cultural Production of Ignorance (and Its Study)". Published in Robert N. Proctor and Londa Schiebinger (eds.), *Agnotology. The Making and Unmaking of Ignorance*. Stanford University Press, 2008, 1–33.

Riungu, Catherine. "UK farming lobby seeks ban on airfreighted organic imports". *The East African*, June 18, 2007.

Riungu, Catherine. 'Strong shilling hurting us, say Kenya flower farmer". *The East African*, July 23, 2007.

Scott, Joanne. "The WTO Agreement on Sanitary and Phytosanitary Measures". *Oxford University Press*, 2007.

Shrader-Frechette, Kristin S. "Risk and Rationality. Philosophical Foundations for Populist Reforms". *University of California Press*, 1991.

Shrader-Frechette, Kristin S. "Risk Analysis and Scientific Method. Methodological and Ethical Problems with Evaluating Societal Hazards". *D. Reidel Publishing*, 1985.

Stump, David J. "From the Values of Scientific Philosophy to the Value Neutrality of the Philosophy of Science". Published in Michael Heidelberger, Friedrich Stadler (eds.), *History of Philosophy of Science. New Trends and Perspective.s* Kluwer Academic Publishers, 2002, 147–158.

Taleb, Nassim Nicholas. "Fooled by Randomness. The Hidden Role of Chance in Life and in the Markets". Penguin Books, 2004, 2nd edition.

Traill, W. Bruce, Bedouin, Rachel, Gourlie, Katharine, Husch, Jerri, Lustre, Alicia (eds.). "Report of the Evaluation of the Codex Alimentarius and other FAO and WHO Food Standards Work". *FAO/WHO*, November 15, 2002. http://www.fao.org/docrep/meeting/005/y7871e/y7871e00.htm#E11E13 (Accessed November 24, 2010, and May 18, 2017).

Zeltner, Thomas, *et. al.* "Tobacco Company Strategies to Undermine Tobacco Control Activities at the World Health Organization". *Report of the Committee of Experts on Tobacco Industry Documents.* World Health Organisation, July 2000. Accessed October 28, 2010. http://www.who.int/tobacco/media/en/who_inquiry.pdf.

WTO Cases

EC – HormonesEC – Hormones: EC – Measures Concerning Meat and Meat Products.

—Panel Report WT/DS26/R/USA, WT/DS48/R/CAN, final report circulated August 18, 1997;

—Appellate Body Report WT/DS26/AB/R/USA, WT/DS48/AB/R/CAN, adopted February 13, 1998.

Australia – Salmon: Australia – Measures Affecting Importation of Salmon.

—Panel Report WT/DS18/R, final report circulated June 12, 1998;

—Appellate Body Report WT/DS18/AB/R, adopted November 6, 1998.

United States – Continued Suspension: United States/Canada – Continued Suspension of Obligations in the EC – HormonesEC – Hormones Dispute.

—Panel Reports, WT/DS320/R, WT/DS321/R, final reports circulated March 31, 2008;

—Appellate Body Reports, WT/DS320/AB/R, WT/DS321/AB/R, adopted November 14, 2008.

EC – Biotech: European Communities – Measures Affecting the Approval and Marketing of Biotech Products.

—Reports of the Panel, WT/DS291, 292, 293/R, adopted November 21, 2006.

US – Animals: United States – Measures Affecting the Importation of Animals, Meat and other Animal Products.

—Report of the Panel, WT/DS447/R (2015).

Annex: Synopsis of Reform Proposals

In the following synopsis, proposals for reforming the SPS Agreement, as discussed above, are outlined in a contrasting manner.[1]

Positivist Proposal	Critical Approach	Relativist Proposal
Preamble		
Original Text		
Members, *Reaffirming* that no Member should be prevented from adopting or enforcing measures necessary to protect human, animal or plant life or health, subject to the requirement that these measures are not applied in a manner which would constitute a means of arbitrary or unjustifiable discrimination between Members where the same conditions prevail or a disguised restriction on international trade; *Desiring* to improve the human health, animal health and phytosanitary situation in all Members; *Noting* that sanitary and phytosanitary measures are often applied on the basis of bilateral agreements or protocols; *Desiring* the establishment of a multilateral framework of rules and disciplines to guide the development, adoption and enforcement of sanitary and phytosanitary measures in order to minimize their negative effects on trade; *Recognizing* the important contribution that international standards, guidelines and recommendations can make in this regard; *Desiring* to further the use of harmonized sanitary and phytosanitary measures between Members, on the basis of international standards, guidelines and recommendations developed by the relevant international organizations, including the Codex Alimentarius Commission, the International Office of Epizootics, and the relevant international and		

(continued)

M. Burkard, *Conflicting Philosophies and International Trade Law*,
Philosophy, Public Policy, and Transnational Law,
https://doi.org/10.1007/978-3-319-61067-2

(continued)

regional organizations operating within the framework of the International Plant Protection Convention, without requiring Members to change their appropriate level of protection of human, animal or plant life or health;

Recognizing that developing country Members may encounter special difficulties in complying with the sanitary or phytosanitary measures of importing Members, and as a consequence in access to markets, and also in the formulation and application of sanitary or phytosanitary measures in their own territories, and desiring to assist them in their endeavours in this regard;

Desiring therefore to elaborate rules for the application of the provisions of GATT 1994 which relate to the use of sanitary or phytosanitary measures, in particular the provisions of Article XX(b)[2];

Hereby agree as follows:

Comment

In the preamble, the paramount role of science for the application of the SPS Agreement is not mentioned

From an objectivist point of view, that omission could be considered as a desideratum to be addressed in a revision of the SPS Agreement

From a critical perspective, science is perceived as necessary, but not sufficient component of risk assessment. Hence, an explicit reference to science would be no priority

Subjectivists, on the other hand, would insist on the current wording. Subjectivists can also agree with the current phrasing of the harmonisation objective, because its open wording allows a reading whereby recognition of international standards takes place on a voluntary basis

Article 1

General Provisions

Original Text–no comments

Article 2

Basic Rights and Obligations

Original Text

1. Members have the right to take sanitary and phytosanitary measures necessary for the protection of human, animal or plant life or health, provided that such measures are not inconsistent with the provisions of this Agreement

2. Members shall ensure that any sanitary or phytosanitary measure is applied only to the extent necessary to protect human, animal or plant life or health, is based on scientific principles and is not maintained without sufficient scientific evidence, except as provided for in paragraph 7 of Article 5

3. Members shall ensure that their sanitary and phytosanitary measures do not arbitrarily or unjustifiably discriminate between Members where identical or similar conditions prevail, including between their own territory and that of other Members. Sanitary and

(continued)

(continued)

phytosanitary measures shall not be applied in a manner which would constitute a disguised restriction on international trade
4. Sanitary or phytosanitary measures which conform to the relevant provisions of this Agreement shall be presumed to be in accordance with the obligations of the Members under the provisions of GATT 1994 which relate to the use of sanitary or phytosanitary measures, in particular the provisions of Article XX(b)

Comment

Paragraph 2 of Article 2 expresses the basic principle of the science-based approach of the SPS Agreement. In the same way, Article 2 and Article 5, which should "constantly be read together",[3] are forming the backbone of an objectivist interpretation of the SPS Agreement. Furthermore, the first clause of paragraph 2 of Article 2 limits the application of SPS measures to the narrow scope of sanitary and phytosanitary objectives, thus excluding other objectives such as ethical concerns

Positivists insist on the current wording of Article 2	From a critical viewpoint, the important *watershed* function of science in risk assessment, discerning between scientifically justifiable SPS measures and initially rebuttable ones, is acknowledged. Hence, there is no requirement for a rephrasing of Article 2	A subjectivist attempt for reforming the SPS Agreement would primarily focus on the cancellation of the second and the last clause of paragraph 2 of Article 2 of the SPS Agreement, at least
Positivist Proposal	Critical Approach	Relativist Proposal
Article 2.2		
2. [Original Text]	2. [Original Text]	2. Members shall ensure that any sanitary or phytosanitary measure is applied only to the extent necessary to protect human, animal or plant life or health [*2nd and 3rd clause deleted*]

Article 3

Harmonization

Original Text

1. To harmonize sanitary and phytosanitary measures on as wide a basis as possible, Members shall base their sanitary or phytosanitary measures on international standards, guidelines or recommendations, where they exist, except as otherwise provided for in this Agreement, and in particular in paragraph 3
2. Sanitary or phytosanitary measures which conform to international standards, guidelines or recommendations shall be deemed to be necessary to protect human, animal or plant life

(continued)

(continued)

or health, and presumed to be consistent with the relevant provisions of this Agreement and of GATT 1994

3. Members may introduce or maintain sanitary or phytosanitary measures which result in a higher level of sanitary or phytosanitary protection than would be achieved by measures based on the relevant international standards, guidelines or recommendations, if there is a scientific justification, or as a consequence of the level of sanitary or phytosanitary protection a Member determines to be appropriate in accordance with the relevant provisions of paragraphs 1 through 8 of Article 5.[4] Notwithstanding the above, all measures which result in a level of sanitary or phytosanitary protection different from that which would be achieved by measures based on international standards, guidelines or recommendations shall not be inconsistent with any other provision of this Agreement

4. Members shall play a full part, within the limits of their resources, in the relevant international organizations and their subsidiary bodies, in particular the Codex Alimentarius Commission, the International Office of Epizootics, and the international and regional organizations operating within the framework of the International Plant Protection Convention, to promote within these organizations the development and periodic review of standards, guidelines and recommendations with respect to all aspects of sanitary and phytosanitary measures

5. The Committee on Sanitary and Phytosanitary Measures provided for in paragraphs 1 and 4 of Article 12 (referred to in this Agreement as the "Committee") shall develop a procedure to monitor the process of international harmonization and coordinate efforts in this regard with the relevant international organizations

Comment

From a positivist perspective, there is no room for higher levels of protection than those provided by 'universal' science, expressed by international standards. Hence, objectivists aim at abrogating Article 3.3 of the current SPS Agreement	The reform proposal put forward by the critical approach implies a shift from the objective of substantive harmonisation of SPS measures to the objective of a procedural harmonisation of SPS measures. The first and objective element of the critical proposal consists of a strong incentive for WTO Members to commission international organisations with the task to carry out risk assessments shall ensure state-of-the art risk assessments and scientific integrity. Thereby, a relativistic 'anything goes'	From a constructivistic point of view, the undesirability of enforced harmonisation is emphasised. An enforcement of harmonisation is implied in the presumption of GATT/WTO compatibility of SPS measures which 'conform to' international standards. Whereas constructivists might agree that harmonisation can be a useful tool for trade facilitation, they reject harmonisation as exclusive and paramount objective enforced to the detriment

(continued)

(continued)

	in SPS trade regulation shall be prevented. The second and relativist element of the critical proposal consists of enlarging the policy space of national risk managers. Taken together, the objective and the relative element of the proposed critical approach shall encourage critical scientific discourse at the international level, following the epistemological opposite *objective–relative*	of other legitimate purposes. Constructivists, taking differences of perception as a 'sovereign right', refute the idea that international standards are becoming quasi-mandatory, as happened through the SPS Agreement. Therefore, first, subjectivists might suggest a wording consistent with the sixth clause of the preamble. Second, subjectivists would turn down the privilege for SPS measures conforming to international standards, as contained in paragraph 2 of Article 3. Third, constructivists would reformulate paragraph 3 of Article 3 as a truly "sovereign right" of Members, hence abrogating the requirement for scientific justification
Positivist Proposal Article 3.1	Critical Approach	Relativist Proposal
1. [Original Text]	1. [Original Text]	1. [*Members shall further the use of harmonized sanitary and phytosanitary measures, on the basis of international standards, guidelines and recommendations developed by the relevant international organizations, including the Codex Alimentarius Commission, the International Office of*

(continued)

(continued)

		Epizootics, and the relevant international and regional organizations operating within the framework of the International Plant Protection Convention, without requiring Members to change their appropriate level of protection of human, animal or plant life or health]
Article 3.2 Positivist Proposal 2. [Original Text]	Critical Approach 2. Sanitary or phytosanitary measures [*based on risk assessments carried out by international organisations*] shall be deemed to be necessary to protect human, animal or plant life or health, and presumed to be consistent with the relevant provisions of this Agreement and of GATT 1994	Relativist Proposal 2. [*Deletion*]
Article 3.3 3. [*Deletion*]	3. [Original Text]	3. Members may introduce or maintain sanitary or phytosanitary measures which result in a higher level of sanitary or phytosanitary protection than would be achieved by measures based on the relevant international standards, guidelines or recommendations [*rest deleted*]. Notwithstanding the above, all measures which result in a level of sanitary or phytosanitary protection different from that which would be

(continued)

(continued)

	achieved by measures based on international standards, guidelines or recommendations shall not be inconsistent with any other provision of this Agreement

[1]Positivist positions were sometimes also characterised as objectivist. For relativist positions, the terms subjectivist, contextualist and constructivist are used for expressing similar, albeit not identical meanings
[2]In this Agreement, reference to Article XX(b) includes also the chapeau of that Article
[3]*EC—Hormones,* Appellate Body Report, para. 180
[4]Footnote no. 2 to this paragraph reads as follows: "For the purposes of paragraph 3 of Article 3, there is a scientific justification if, on the basis of an examination and evaluation of available scientific information in conformity with the relevant provisions of this Agreement, a Member determines that the relevant international standards, guidelines or recommendations are not sufficient to achieve its appropriate level of sanitary or phytosanitary protection"

Index

M. Burkard, *Conflicting Philosophies and International Trade Law*, Philosophy, Public Policy, and Transnational Law,
https://doi.org/10.1007/978-3-319-61067-2

CPSIA information can be obtained
at www.ICGtesting.com
Printed in the USA
BVHW01*0429210118
505874BV00006B/21/P

9 783319 610665